DEVELOPING **MATHEMATICS**

Photocopiable teaching resources for mathematics

NUMBER FACTS AND CALCULATIONS

Ages 8–9

Hilary Koll and Steve Mills

A & C Black • London

Contents

Knowing and using number facts

Use knowledge of addition and subtraction facts and place value to derive sums and differences of pairs of multiples of 10, 100 or 1000

Identify the doubles of two-digit numbers; use to calculate doubles of multiples of 10 and 100 and derive the corresponding halves

Derive and recall multiplication facts up to 10 × 10, the corresponding division facts and multiples of numbers to 10 up to the tenth multiple

Use knowledge of rounding, number operations and inverses to estimate and check calculations; identify pairs of fractions that total 1

Calculating

Add or subtract mentally pairs of two-digit whole numbers; refine and use efficient written methods to add and subtract two- and three-digit whole numbers and £.p

Multiply and divide numbers to 1000 by 10 and then 100 (whole-number answers), understanding the effect; relate to scaling up or down

Develop and use written methods to record, support and explain multiplication and division of two-digit numbers by a one-digit number, including division with remainders

Find fractions of numbers, quantities or shapes

Use a calculator to carry out one- and two-step calculations involving all four operations; recognise negative numbers in the display, correct mistaken entries and interpret the display correctly in the context of money

Published 2008 by A & C Black Publishers Limited
38 Soho Square, London W1D 3HB
www.acblack.com

ISBN 978-0-7136-8451-3

Copyright text © Hilary Koll and Steve Mills 2008
Copyright illustrations © Andy Robb 2008
Copyright cover illustration © Jan McCafferty 2008
Editors: Lynne Williamson and Marie Lister
Designed by Billin Design Solutions Ltd

The authors and publishers would like to thank Catherine Yemm and Judith Wells for their advice in producing this series of books.

A CIP catalogue record for this book is available from the British Library.

Printed and bound in Great Britain by Halstan Printing Group, Amersham, Buckinghamshire.

A & C Black uses paper produced with elemental chlorine-free pulp, harvested from managed sustainable forests.

Introduction

100% New Developing Mathematics: Number Facts and Calculations is a series of seven photocopiable activity books for children aged 4 to 11, designed to be used during the daily maths lesson. The books focus on the skills and concepts for Knowing and Using Number Facts and Calculating as outlined in the Primary National Strategy *Primary Framework for literacy and mathematics*. The activities are intended to be used in the time allocated to pupil activities. They aim to reinforce the knowledge and develop the skills and understanding explored during the main part of the lesson, and to provide practice and consolidation of the learning objectives contained in the Framework document.

Number Facts and Calculations

The strand 'Knowing and Using Number Facts' of the *Primary Framework for mathematics* is concerned with helping pupils to begin to learn number facts and to use them when solving problems and calculating. This strand includes addition and subtraction facts, doubling and halving, counting forwards and backwards in equal-sized steps, multiplication (times tables) and division facts, knowledge of multiples and factors, squares, roots and primes, and involves building of number operations and their relationships with each other. Also included in this strand of the curriculum is work on using approximations to estimate the size of an answer to a calculation and checking that the answer is appropriate.

The strand 'Calculating', also addressed in this book, covers the four main operations and includes mental and written methods, together with calculations involving fractions, decimals and percentages. Broadly speaking, these two strands address topic areas that were described under the 'Calculations' strand title of the former National Numeracy Strategy *Framework for teaching mathematics*. For further information, the Primary National Strategy Guidance Paper on Calculation is a useful document recommending an approach to calculation to be used for each of the four operations. This can be found at www.standards.dfes.gov.uk/primaryframework/Papers/mathematics/.

Number Facts and Calculations Ages 8–9 supports the teaching of mathematics by providing a series of activities to develop essential skills in learning simple number facts and beginning to appreciate ideas of addition, subtraction, multiplication and division. The following objectives are covered:

- use knowledge of addition and subtraction facts and place value to derive sums and differences of pairs of multiples of 10, 100 or 1000;
- identify the doubles of two-digit numbers; use to calculate doubles of multiples of 10 and 100 and derive the corresponding halves;
- derive and recall multiplication facts up to 10 × 10, the corresponding division facts and multiples of numbers to 10 up to the tenth multiple;
- use knowledge of rounding, number operations and inverses to estimate and check calculations;
- identify pairs of fractions that total 1;
- add or subtract mentally pairs of two-digit whole numbers, e.g. 47 + 58, 91 − 35;
- refine and use efficient written methods to add and subtract two- and three-digit whole numbers and £.p;
- multiply and divide numbers to 1000 by 10 and then 100 (whole-number answers), understanding the effect; relate to scaling up or down;
- develop and use written methods to record, support and explain multiplication and division of two-digit numbers by a one-digit number, including division with remainders, e.g. 15 × 9, 98 ÷ 6;
- find fractions of numbers, quantities or shapes, e.g. $\frac{1}{5}$ of 30 plums, $\frac{3}{8}$ of a 6 by 4 rectangle;
- use a calculator to carry out one- and two-step calculations involving all four operations; recognise negative numbers in the display, correct mistaken entries and interpret the display correctly in the context of money.

Extension

Many of the activity sheets end with a challenge (**Now try this!**), which reinforces and extends children's learning, and provides the teacher with an opportunity for assessment. These might include harder questions, with  numbers from a higher range, than those in the main part of the activity sheet. Some extension activities are open-ended questions and provide an opportunity for children to think mathematically for themselves. Occasionally the extension activity will require additional paper or that the children write on the reverse of the sheet itself. Many of the activities encourage children to generate their own questions or puzzles for a partner to solve.

NOW TRY THIS!

Organisation

Very little equipment is needed, but it will be useful to have available: calculators, coloured pencils, counters, dice, cubes, coins, scissors, glue, squared paper, number lines, number grids and number tracks.

Where possible, children's work should be supported by ICT equipment, such as number lines and number tracks on interactive whiteboards, or computer software for comparing and ordering numbers. It is also vital that children's experiences are introduced in real-life contexts and through practical activities. The teachers' notes at the foot of each page and the more detailed notes on pages 6 to 11 suggest ways in which this can be done effectively.

To help teachers select appropriate learning experiences for the children, the activities are grouped into sections within the book. However, the activities are not expected to be used in this order unless stated otherwise. The sheets are intended to support, rather than direct, the teacher's planning.

Some activities can be made easier or more challenging by masking or substituting numbers. You may wish to re-use pages by copying them onto card and laminating them.

Accompanying CD

The enclosed CD-ROM contains all of the activity sheets from the book and a program that allows you to edit them for printing or saving. This means that modifications can be made to further differentiate the activities to suit individual pupils' needs. See page 12 for further details.

Teachers' notes

Brief notes are provided at the foot of each page, giving ideas and suggestions for maximising the effectiveness of the activity sheets. These can be masked before copying.

Further explanations of the activities can be found on pages 6 to 11, together with examples of questions that you can ask. Solutions to activities can be found on pages 63 and 64.

Whole-class warm-up activities

The tools provided in A & C Black's *Maths Skills and Practice* CD-ROMs can be used as introductory activities for use with the whole class. In *Maths Skills and Practice* CD-ROM 4, the following activities and games could be used to introduce or reinforce 'Number Facts and Calculations' objectives:

- *Stomper 2*
- *Hot teddies*
- *Balls of fire*
- *Table tennis 2*
- *Ghost house*
- *Basket ball*
- *Place value 2*
- *Snowboarder 2*
- *What problem?*
- *Crane game*
- *Granny crunch 2*

The following activities provide some practical ideas that can be used to introduce or reinforce the main teaching part of the lesson, or provide an interesting basis for discussion.

Chains

Say a number, such as 'three thousand, five hundred and thirty-two', which the children write down. Now say a series of instructions, asking the children to write the outcome each time. For example, say, 'Add ten', 'Subtract one thousand', 'Add three hundred'. After several instructions ask, 'What's your number now?' If the children have kept a record, then it is easy to see where they went wrong if they make an error.

Fraction choices

Write a number on each of four pieces of paper, e.g. 4, 3, 6 and 8. Pin these around the room, one on each wall. Call out a question, e.g. 'What is one-fifth of twenty?' The children point to the piece of paper showing the number 4. Other questions could include: 'What is one-half of sixteen, one-third of nine, two-thirds of nine, one-fifth of forty, three-quarters of four?'

Question cards

Make sets of flash cards with a question on one side and the answer on the other. For example, one set might focus on the multiplication facts for the seven times table. Children can work in pairs, with all the questions face up on the table. Each child takes a turn to point to a card and give an answer to the question. If correct, they keep the card. It can quickly be seen which questions children are unsure of, as these will be left until last. An alternative game is for each child to point to a card for their partner to answer.

Bags of fun

Draw two bags on the board with numbers inside.

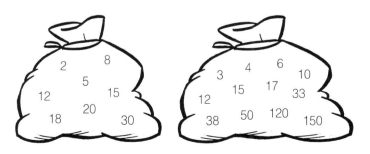

Ask children to choose two numbers from the first bag and to use them in any type of calculation to make any number in the second bag, e.g. 20 + 30 = 50, 8 × 15 = 120.

Notes on the activities

Knowing and using number facts

Use knowledge of addition and subtraction facts and place value to derive sums and differences of pairs of multiples of 10, 100 or 1000

Provide oral questions at every opportunity to encourage the children to practise recalling the number facts and to support their written work. Put questions into a wide range of settings and contexts, ensuring that real-life and classroom contexts are maximised, for example 'There are 150 children in school, 80 of whom are juniors. How many children are infants?' Use the full range of addition and subtraction vocabulary, including: *and, add, altogether, total, sum, plus, take, minus, subtract, take away, difference* etc.

Darting about (page 13)

This activity encourages the children to use and draw upon a range of the number facts that it is recommended they should have memorised by this age. Children will require good recall of these facts to be able to add and subtract multiples of 10, 100 or 1000. You could use this activity whenever you feel children need to practise using different number bonds and tables.

Sets of numbers such as 2, 3, 6 and 2, 5, 6, produce more than ten possible numbers between 1 and 20 and the numbers 1, 2, 6 and 1, 3, 6 produce 12 solutions, for example:

1, 3, 6

6 ÷ 3 − 1 = 1	6 + 3 + 1 = 10	6 − 3 − 1 = 2
6 × 1 − 3 = 3	6 + 1 − 3 = 4	
6 + 3 − 1 = 8		
6 × 1 + 3 = 9	3 − 1 × 6 = 12	6 − 1 × 3 = 15
6 × 3 − 1 = 17	6 × 3 × 1 = 18	6 × 3 + 1 = 19

The least useful throws of the dice include 1, 1, 1 and 5, 5, 5 etc. Collect a class list of possible solutions for different sets of throws.

SUGGESTED QUESTIONS:

• Can you subtract here instead of adding?
• How many different ways can we find altogether?

Difference walls (page 14)

At the start of the lesson build up lists of numbers with given differences to encourage the children to spot patterns in the digits of the numbers, for example:

Difference of 20	Difference of 70
20 → 40	20 → 90
30 → 50	30 → 100
40 → 60	40 → 110
50 → 70	50 → 120
60 → 80	60 → 130 etc.

Do this for other differences and encourage the children to describe patterns they notice in the numbers.

SUGGESTED QUESTIONS:

• What will the tens digit of the number be if it is 60 more than 130?
• What is the difference between 170 and 230?

Cheese triangles (page 15)

Encourage the children to use their knowledge of additions of single-digit numbers to help them answer these multiples of 10 questions, for example 7 + 4 + [   ] = 18 is related to 70 + 40 + [   ] = 180.

SUGGESTED QUESTIONS:

• How quickly did you answer these?
• How did you work this out?

Square dance (page 16)

This activity encourages the children to develop using and applying strategies to solve these problems, including perseverance and trial and improvement strategies. A further tactic which could be recommended is for the children to find the total of all the cards (3600) and subtract this from the total number multiplied by 4 (for example 1200 × 4). The number that this produces (4800 − 3600 = 1200) tells you the total of the four corner numbers. In other words this can help you to find the four numbers at the corners of the square first.

The children should also be encouraged to work with these numbers as single-digit numbers, such as 3 + 8 rather than 30 + 80, to enable them to work more quickly and then to adjust the answers at the end.

SUGGESTED QUESTIONS:

• What number facts did you use to help you work out that those numbers total 1400?
• How could you arrange four of these numbers so that there is always a difference of 200 between them?

Water slide (page 17)

Remind the children to watch out for whether the question is an addition or a subtraction. Children could work with a partner and take it in turns to use a stopwatch to time each other to see how long they take and whether they can do it quicker on a second occasion.

SUGGESTED QUESTIONS:

• What is 400 + 700? How do you know?
• Which fact did you use to help you?

Sitting ducks (page 18)

The children should be encouraged to work with these numbers as single-digit numbers, for example 3 thousand + 8 thousand rather than 3000 + 8000, to enable them to work more quickly and then to adjust the answers at the end. In the extension activity, the children have to find ways to land on five multiples of 1000, for example 3000 + 8000 + 4000 + 5000 + 7000. Children could then find which have the largest and smallest totals.

SUGGESTED QUESTION:

• Can you make a puzzle like this where the route has different answers with the answer 13 000?

Identify the doubles of two-digit numbers; use to calculate doubles of multiples of 10 and 100 and derive the corresponding halves

Children will be familiar with the doubles of numbers to 20, and their corresponding halves. Continue to practise these and extend this first to doubles of multiples of 10 and then to doubles of two-digit numbers. Discuss the strategies that children can use to derive these from facts that they know already. Also encourage children to appreciate that any even number is the double of another number as it is even and a multiple of 2, for example 82 is the double of 41.

Double or halve (page 19)

This sheet can be used for a range of doubling and halving purposes and could be available in the classroom for children to use as and when they feel necessary. Partitioning can be done in a variety of ways, including three-digit numbers, for example:

136 → 120 + 16
        60 + 8 → 68

SUGGESTED QUESTIONS:

• What is double 76? Half 132?
• How could you partition the number to help you?

Double trouble (page 20)

This activity can help children to begin to appreciate that when doubling larger numbers, such as between 75 and 100, the number can be thought of as 50 + a number, for example 76 = 50 + 26 and therefore they can double the number quickly and effectively: double 50 = 100 and double 26 is 52, thus double 76 = 152.

SUGGESTED QUESTION:

• Have you checked your answers?

At the sales (page 21)

Discuss different ways in which each number could be partitioned to halve it, for example 134 could be partitioned into 130 + 4, 100 + 34, 120 + 14, 120 + 10 + 4 etc. Encourage the children to say which way they find easiest to halve the number.

SUGGESTED QUESTIONS:

• How did you halve this number?
• Could you partition the number in a different way?
• Which way do you find easier?

Double bugs (page 22)

Double bugs make a useful classroom display and encourage the children to see the link between doubling multiples of 1, 10 and 100.

SUGGESTED QUESTION:

• Have you checked your answers?

Half bugs (page 23)

Half bugs can be displayed in the classroom to encourage the children to see the link between halving multiples of 1, 10 and 100.

SUGGESTED QUESTION:

• How could you check your answers?

Derive and recall multiplication facts up to 10 × 10, the corresponding division facts and multiples of numbers to 10 up to the tenth multiple

Children should learn tables by heart in order to perform multiplications and related divisions. Encourage them to recognise patterns in the digits of the answers to help them to check and to use inverses to find related division and multiplication facts, for example for 4 × 7 = 28, the related facts 7 × 4 = 28, 28 ÷ 7 = 4 and 28 ÷ 4 = 7 can be determined.

Provide oral questions in a variety of contexts and using a wide range of vocabulary, for example 'What are seven sixes? Multiply seven by six. What is the product of seven and six? Seven times six is…? How many is seven groups of six?' etc.

Sleepover dreamtime (page 24)

This activity encourages the children to recall facts from the ×7 and 7× tables. Revise the multiples at the start of the lesson and encourage the children to describe patterns, for example odd × 7 = odd   even × 7 = even etc.

SUGGESTED QUESTION:

• What helps you to remember this fact?

Spot the dice (page 25)

At the start of the lesson, say the 8× table as a class. Discuss patterns in the answers in the table and ways to remember them. For the extension activity, the children can play the game in pairs. They will require two dice per pair.

SUGGESTED QUESTIONS:

• What times-table could you use to help you work out facts in the 8 times-table if you can't remember them?
• Which 8 times-table facts do you find easiest or hardest to remember?

Fingers of fun (page 26)

Learning the ×9 or 9× tables can be introduced quite early, as this method of finding the answers using their fingers provides lots of confidence for children who find memorising facts difficult. Gradually, over time, the children require less use of their fingers to find the answers.

SUGGESTED QUESTIONS:

• What is 6 × 9?
• What will the tens digit be?
• How do you know?
• Does this work for all facts in the ×9 table?

7

Animal antics (page 27)

Ask the children to work in pairs, and provide each pair with timers or stopwatches to use to time each other tackling each block.

SUGGESTED QUESTIONS:

- Which times-tables facts do you find easiest or hardest to remember? What could you do to help you to remember them or work them out?

Tables and division testing cards (pages 28 and 29)

These testing activities can be photocopied onto thin card and laminated to provide more permanent classroom resources. If laminated, the children could write answers on paper or on the cards themselves in temporary marker pen. Encourage the children to mark their own so that they have an opportunity to see which facts they have made errors with.

SUGGESTED QUESTIONS:

- Have you checked this answer?
- How could you use the multiplication fact $3 \times 6 = 18$ to help you with this division question?

Movin' on (page 30)

This sheet encourages quick recall. As an extra extension activity, the children can make up their own tracks.

SUGGESTED QUESTIONS:

- Which multiplication fact did you use to help you work out that division? How could you check that your answer is correct?

Stick 'em up (page 31)

For this activity the children need to derive quickly, or recall, division facts for the more difficult times-tables facts, for example 6×7 and 7×8. It might be useful for some children to have access to the 6, 7, 8 and 9 times-tables for them to refer to.

SUGGESTED QUESTION:

- How could you use facts in the 2 times-table or the 4 times-table to help you to divide by 8, if you can't remember facts in the 8 times-table?

Connections (page 32)

Write 12 on the board and ask what numbers are factors of 12, for example '12 is a multiple of 3', '12 is a multiple of 4'.

SUGGESTED QUESTIONS:

- Which times-tables have the answer 36?
  So 36 is a multiple of which numbers?

World tour (page 33)

This activity encourages the children to quickly determine which numbers a number is a multiple of, for example recalling that 72 is a multiple of 8 and of 9. Display the multiplication tables to 10×10 on the classroom wall for the children to refer to. Each pair will require a dice, a counter and one activity sheet.

SUGGESTED QUESTION:

- Which other number could you have crossed off?

Use knowledge of rounding, number operations and inverses to estimate and check calculations; identify pairs of fractions that total 1

Encourage children to develop the habit of checking their answers every time they calculate.

Although the children do not need to be able to add and subtract fractions, it is useful for them to know fraction pairs that total 1, as this crops up in everyday situations.

Part and parcel (page 34)

Before copying this page for higher-attaining children, you could delete the lines to the blank parcels.

SUGGESTED QUESTIONS:

- How do you know that $\frac{9}{20}$ and $\frac{11}{20}$ total 1?
- How did you work out the fractions that should be on the blank parcels?

Andy, Sandy and Mandy (page 35)

At the start of the lesson revise rounding numbers to the nearest ten and making suitable estimates.

SUGGESTED QUESTION:

- What is 67 to the nearest ten?

Computer glitch (page 36)

Any written or informal methods of calculation are suitable for checking these calculations. Discuss inverses and ensure that the children appreciate that they should take the final answer and apply the inverse calculation to it in order to check the calculation.

SUGGESTED QUESTIONS:

- What is the inverse of subtraction?
- How did you know that half of 184 is not 72?

Calculating

Add or subtract mentally pairs of two-digit whole numbers; refine and use efficient written methods to add and subtract two- and three-digit whole numbers and £.p

For mental addition and subtraction the use of number lines and grids provides a visual support for this work. Children should be encouraged to use their own supporting jottings and diagrams as they develop their own mental strategies.

As children begin to work towards written methods such approaches need to be maintained and refined.

The banker's game and Save and spend cards (pages 37 and 38)

It is important that the children understand how a balance sheet works, where amounts earned are added to the existing balance or amounts spent are subtracted from the balance. Emphasise that each new transaction should be recorded on a new line of the balance sheet.

SUGGESTED QUESTIONS:

- What method did you use to add £37? Would you use a similar method to add £39? What other method could you use?

Trampoline (page 39)

Encourage the children to use estimation and known number facts, to aim to make numbers that will total the numbers on the trampoline. Children aged eight and nine should be confident in adding numbers in a vertical column arrangement.

SUGGESTED PROMPT/QUESTION:

- Show me how you completed that addition.
- How could you check your answer?

Animal additions (page 40)

The children could be asked to find the totals of other three-letter words, for example: *bed, row, toy, buy, old, toe, die, mix, hit, pen, cup, ice, ham, zoo.*

SUGGESTED PROMPT:

- Explain to me how you worked out the total of these three numbers.

Curious cube (page 41)

At the start of the lesson, discuss the strategy of looking at the units digits of the two numbers to be added and seeing which will add to make a multiple of 10, for example numbers ending with the units digits 3 and 7, 4 and 6, etc.

SUGGESTED PROMPT:

- Explain how you worked out the answer.

Supermarket stacks (page 42)

This activity encourages the children to add adjacent numbers and to write the total.

SUGGESTED QUESTIONS/PROMPT:

- How could you work out this answer on paper?
- How could you set it out in columns?
- Show me what you would do.

Captain Dynamic (page 43)

These questions involve subtracting a two-digit number from a three-digit number. The children could use a written column method of subtracting involving partitioning or they could use more informal methods, as appropriate.

SUGGESTED QUESTIONS/PROMPT:

- How could you work out this answer on paper?
- How could you set it out in columns?
- Show me what you would do.

Crack the codes (page 44)

At the start of the lesson, practise partitioning three-digit numbers in different ways, for example:

$$645 \rightarrow 600 + 40 + 5 \rightarrow 600 + 30 + 15$$
$$\rightarrow 500 + 140 + 5 \rightarrow 500 + 130 + 15$$

This type of partitioning is drawn upon when using the most common written method of subtraction, known as decomposition.

SUGGESTED PROMPT/QUESTION:

- Show me how you completed that subtraction.
- How could you check your answer?

Tallest man ever (page 45)

As a further extension, the children could research and compare the heights of other famous people.

SUGGESTED PROMPT:

- Explain to me how you worked out the difference between these two numbers.

Multiply and divide numbers to 1000 by 10 and then 100 (whole-number answers), understanding the effect; relate to scaling up or down

As children develop an understanding of ideas of place value, they can begin to appreciate the effect of multiplying and dividing numbers by 10 and 100. Encourage them to describe the process as moving digits rather than focusing on the removal or addition of zeros, as this can hamper their later understanding of multiplying and dividing decimals in this way.

As children develop an understanding of the four operations and their relationships with each other, it is vital that they appreciate their inverse nature, for example knowing that division is the inverse of multiplication. As they develop an awareness of this they should begin to see that for every multiplication or division fact there are three related facts that are implied, for example:

$$20 \div 5 = 4 \quad 20 \div 4 = 5 \quad 4 \times 5 = 20 \quad 5 \times 4 = 20$$

Under the microscope (page 46)

At the start of the lesson, practise counting up in tens and ask the children to say the answer for any given one-digit number multiplied by 10. Then extend to any two-digit number multiplied by 10.

SUGGESTED PROMPT/QUESTION:

- Describe what happens to a number when it is multiplied by 10.
- What happens to the digits of the number?

Tidying up (page 47)

Ask the children to explain what happens when numbers are multiplied or divided by 10 or 100. Highlight explanations that involve digits moving rather than zeros being added to or removed from the ends of numbers.

SUGGESTED PROMPT/QUESTIONS:

- Describe what happens to a number when it is multiplied by 100/10/divided by 10/100.
- What happens to the digits of the number?
- What has happened to change this number into this number?

Dicing with dinosaurs (page 48)

Discuss with the children the commutative and associative laws of multiplication (without using these terms), i.e. that multiplication can be done in any order, grouping numbers in any way, and the answer will be the same, for example $3 \times 5 \times 4$ can be worked out by multiplying the 5 and the 4 together first to make 3×20, which is perhaps an easier calculation than 15×4.

More confident children could use a 1–10 dice.

SUGGESTED QUESTIONS:

- What method did you use to multiply those numbers together?
- How do you decide what method to use to multiply a two-digit number by a one-digit number?

Set totals: 1 and 2 (pages 49–50)

This activity requires the children to arrange the cards in each set in different ways so that the total of the answers is as large as possible. It can help to develop Using and Applying strategies, such as trial and improvement, and perseverance.

SUGGESTED QUESTIONS:

- How did you work out this answer? Did you use partitioning?

Detective Dog (page 51)

These kinds of puzzle can be written onto large sheets of paper and displayed on the classroom wall as a puzzle board. The numbers themselves could be changed each day to provide a new challenge and the children could try to find the solutions in spare moments during the school day.

SUGGESTED QUESTION:

- How did you work out this answer?

Beautiful brooches (page 52)

Encourage the children first to work out all the multiplications and then to use the key to find the related letters.

If the children complete the extension activity suggested in the Teachers' note, they should find that 18 cm of wire is wasted.

SUGGESTED QUESTIONS:

- What multiplication fact helped you to work out the answer?
- How could you check your answers?

Develop and use written methods to record, support and explain multiplication and division of two-digit numbers by a one-digit number, including division with remainders

Appropriate informal and written methods of multiplication and division for this age are outlined in the Primary National Strategy Guidance Paper on Calculation – a useful document recommending an approach to calculation.

This can be found at: www.standards.dfes.gov.uk/primaryframework/mathematics/Papers/

Crazy calculations (page 53)

At the start of the lesson, ask children to tell you different methods that they know for working out the answer to a calculation such as, 53×7. Write these on the board and discuss which children consider to be most efficient.

SUGGESTED PROMPT:

- Explain to me how you worked out the product of these two numbers.

Magic ingredients (page 54)

For this activity, the children could use partitioning to help them multiply two-digit numbers by a one-digit number. Discuss early ideas of distributivity (without using this term); that is, that a number to be multiplied can be partitioned and each part multiplied separately before they are recombined.

SUGGESTED QUESTIONS:

- Why did you choose that method to multiply those numbers?
- How could you check that you have completed that calculation correctly?

Life's a lottery (page 55)

This activity encourages the children to begin to appreciate the nature of remainders and to recall quickly which numbers are multiples of others.

SUGGESTED QUESTIONS:

- What multiplication fact helped you to work out the answer?
- How could you check your answers?

Find fractions of numbers, quantities or shapes

It is important that children develop an understanding of the relationship between division and finding fractions of numbers. Here, children are required to find fractions of numbers and quantities. These can be solved by first finding the unit fraction of the number by dividing by the denominator. For example for $\frac{3}{4}$ of 16, find $\frac{1}{4}$ first by dividing by 4 and then multiply by 3 to find $\frac{3}{4}$ of the number.

Loads-a-money! (page 56)

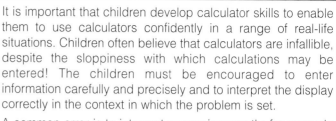

Children who find this activity difficult could exchange the coins of greater value for 1p coins, for example thirty-two 1p coins for 32p, and use grouping or sharing to find the unit fraction. When finding fractions that are not unit fractions, they could then use the numerator of the fraction to find the number of groups that they need and count, add or multiply to work out the required amount of money.

SUGGESTED PROMPT/QUESTIONS:

- Explain to me how you worked out the fractions of these numbers.
- Did you divide first? By which number? Why?

A spoonful of medicine (page 57)

At the start of the lesson, ask the children a variety of times-table facts out of order, for example 6 × 4 = ?, 48 ÷ 8 = ? Check the children understand that to find a fraction of a number, they can divide to find a unit fraction and then multiply to find the number of parts specified.

SUGGESTED PROMPT/QUESTIONS:

- Explain to me how you worked out the fractions of these numbers.
- Did you divide first? By which number? Why?

Drink up! (page 58)

Ask the children to explain how they find fractions of two-digit numbers. Then ask them to discuss with a partner how they would find fractions of the three-digit numbers. Will they use similar methods or different methods?

SUGGESTED PROMPT/QUESTIONS:

- Explain to me how you worked out the fractions of these numbers.
- Did you divide first? By which number? Why?

Spelling fractions (page 59)

Check that the children remember how to find fractions of numbers. Explain that some of the squares will not be coloured in each letter.

SUGGESTED QUESTIONS/PROMPT:

- How did you know that $\frac{2}{3}$ of 12 is 8?
- Colour $\frac{1}{10}$ of the letter N yellow. How many squares will be yellow?

Use a calculator to carry out one- and two-step calculations involving all four operations; recognise negative numbers in the display, correct mistaken entries and interpret the display correctly in the context of money

It is important that children develop calculator skills to enable them to use calculators confidently in a range of real-life situations. Children often believe that calculators are infallible, despite the sloppiness with which calculations may be entered! The children must be encouraged to enter information carefully and precisely and to interpret the display correctly in the context in which the problem is set.

A common error is to interpret money incorrectly, for example thinking that 6.2 means £6 and 2 pence, rather than £6 and 20 pence.

Children should always be encouraged to get an approximate answer to a calculation before using the calculator and to use this to check whether their answer is a sensible one.

Sponsored spell (page 60)

The children should work in pairs to discuss the situations and to decide upon the most appropriate calculation to enter into the calculator to find the answer. Check how the children enter amounts given as pence only – they should be keyed in as decimal numbers less than 1. Always encourage estimating and checking.

During the plenary, discuss how the children solved the problems, and demonstrate different ways of finding the answers.

SUGGESTED QUESTIONS:

- How did you answer this question?
- What did you key into the calculator?
- Did anyone else try it a different way?
- Do you think that is a sensible answer?

Spend, spend, spend! (page 61)

During the plenary, discuss how the children solved the problems, and demonstrate different ways of finding the answers.

SUGGESTED QUESTIONS:

- How did you answer this question?
- What did you key into the calculator?
- Did anyone else try it a different way?
- Do you think that is a sensible answer?

Splish! Splash! Splosh! (page 62)

Revise inverses at the start of the lesson and discuss how calculations can be solved quickly by performing a different calculation. Missing number questions are often answered incorrectly in calculator tests as children see the operation shown and always want to press this key on their calculator. Often they use an ineffectual trial and error approach which can take an endless amount of time.

SUGGESTED QUESTIONS:

- How did you answer this question?
- What did you key into the calculator?

Using the CD-ROM

The PC CD-ROM included with this book contains an easy-to-use software program that allows you to print out pages from the book, to view them (e.g. on an interactive whiteboard) or to customise the activities to suit the needs of your pupils.

Getting started

It's easy to run the software. Simply insert the CD-ROM into your CD drive and the disk should autorun and launch the interface in your web browser.

If the disk does not autorun, open 'My Computer' and select the CD drive, then open the file 'start.html'.

Please note: this CD-ROM is designed for use on a PC. It will also run on most Apple Macintosh computers in Safari however, due to the differences between Mac and PC fonts, you may experience some unavoidable variations in the typography and page layouts of the activity sheets.

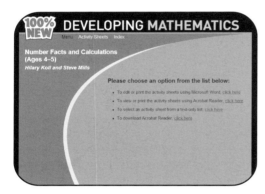

The Menu screen

Four options are available to you from the main menu screen.

The first option takes you to the Activity Sheets screen, where you can choose an activity sheet to edit or print out using Microsoft Word.

(If you do not have the Microsoft Office suite, you might like to consider using OpenOffice instead. This is a multi-platform and multi-lingual office suite, and an 'open-source' project. It is compatible with all other major office suites, and the product is free to download, use and distribute. The homepage for OpenOffice on the Internet is: www.openoffice.org.)

The second option on the main menu screen opens a PDF file of the entire book using Adobe Reader (see below). This format is ideal for printing out copies of the activity sheets or for displaying them, for example on an interactive whiteboard.

The third option allows you to choose a page to edit from a text-only list of the activity sheets, as an alternative to the graphical interface on the Activity Sheets screen.

Adobe Reader is free to download and to use. If it is not already installed on your computer, the fourth link takes you to the download page on the Adobe website.

You can also navigate directly to any of the three screens at any time by using the tabs at the top.

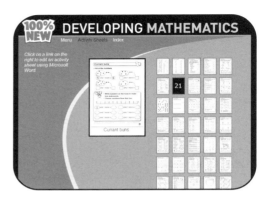

The Activity Sheets screen

This screen shows thumbnails of all the activity sheets in the book. Rolling the mouse over a thumbnail highlights the page number and also brings up a preview image of the page.

Click on the thumbnail to open a version of the page in Microsoft Word (or an equivalent software program, see above.) The full range of editing tools are available to you here to customise the page to suit the needs of your particular pupils. You can print out copies of the page or save a copy of your edited version onto your computer.

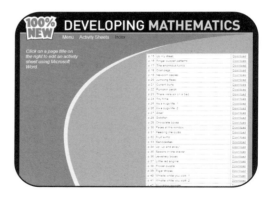

The Index screen

This is a text-only version of the Activity Sheets screen described above. Choose an activity sheet and click on the 'download' link to open a version of the page in Microsoft Word to edit or print out.

Technical support

If you have any questions regarding the *100% New Developing Literacy* or *Developing Mathematics* software, please email us at the address below. We will get back to you as quickly as possible.

educationalsales@acblack.com

Darting about

☆ Roll three dice and write the numbers here. ☐ ☐ ☐

☆ You can add, subtract, multiply or divide the three numbers, using each number only once to make an answer on the dartboard.

☆ Cover it with a counter.

☆ Using the same three numbers, how many counters can you place? ☐

- **Roll the dice again.** ☐ ☐ ☐

- **How many counters can you place?** ☐

NOW TRY THIS!

- **Which four numbers could be rolled so that every number on the dartboard could be made?** ☐ ☐ ☐ ☐

Teachers' note This investigative activity encourages children to draw upon their mental skills and to use addition, subtraction, multiplication and division. For the extension activity, ask the children to record all the different ways that the numbers to 20 and the answer 50 could be made, using four dice. See page 6 for more information.

100% New Developing Mathematics
Number Facts and Calculations:
Ages 8–9
© A & C BLACK

13

Difference walls

- **Colour touching pairs with the difference shown. Number pairs can touch vertically or horizontally but not diagonally. Each wall will show a letter that spells a word.**

1. **Difference of 20**

120	90	110
100	30	80
160	90	150
140	20	180
170	150	130

You need different-coloured pencils.

2. **Difference of 30**

180	260	390
210	190	360
240	120	330
400	280	320
370	340	290

3. **Difference of 40**

880	920	720
530	590	670
490	450	630
360	720	590
400	440	240

4. **Difference of 50**

280	330	540
420	290	490
370	410	510
440	500	460
390	650	600

5. **Difference of 60**

440	520	590
400	510	530
330	590	470
570	640	620
500	550	560

6. **Difference of 70**

540	470	500
330	500	340
260	320	410
190	380	480
650	580	420

- **What word do the letters spell?** _____

NOW TRY THIS!

- **Draw your own wall on squared paper.**
- **Colour it to show a different letter of the alphabet. Then write numbers into the coloured squares that have a difference of 80.**

Teachers' note Ensure the children check all sets of adjacent numbers as a number may match with two numbers, for example for difference of 20, 150 matches with 170 and 130. The children should colour in the touching pairs in different colours. That way it will be obvious which adjacent numbers do not have the difference given.

100% New Developing Mathematic Number Facts and Calculations: Ages 8–9 © A & C BLACK

Cheese triangles

The three angles in each triangle total 180°.

- Add the two given angles and subtract your answer from 180° to find the missing angle.

1. 70° 70° 40°

2. 60° 80°

3. 90° 50°

4. 60° 70°

5. 50° 60°

6. 60° 90°

7. 80° 70°

Teachers' note This activity involves children adding two multiples of 10 and then subtracting the answer from 180. Encourage them to use their knowledge of number facts for single-digit numbers and to see the relationships between those and multiples of 10, e.g. 8 + 7 = 15 so 80 + 70 = 150. Children who complete the extension activity could make up two more puzzles of their own.

100% New Developing Mathematics
Number Facts and Calculations:
Ages 8–9
© A & C BLACK

Square dance

☆ Cut out the cards at the bottom of the page. Arrange them in a square so that each side has the total shown.

☆ Write in the boxes to record your answers.

Each side adds up to 1200

Each side adds up to 1300

Each side adds up to 1400

Each side adds up to 1500

| 100 | 200 | 300 | 400 | 500 | 600 | 700 | 800 |

Teachers' note As an extension activity, ask the children to arrange the cards in a line where the differences between adjacent numbers are always 300 or 400. As a further extension activity, invite children to see which of the following are possible: to arrange the cards in a line where the differences between adjacent numbers are always: a) 100 or 200, b) 200 or 300, c) 400 or 500 etc.

100% New Developing Mathematic
Number Facts and Calculations:
Ages 8–9
© A & C BLACK

Water slide

- **Start at the top and write the answers as you go.**
- **Try to reach the finish as quickly as you can.**

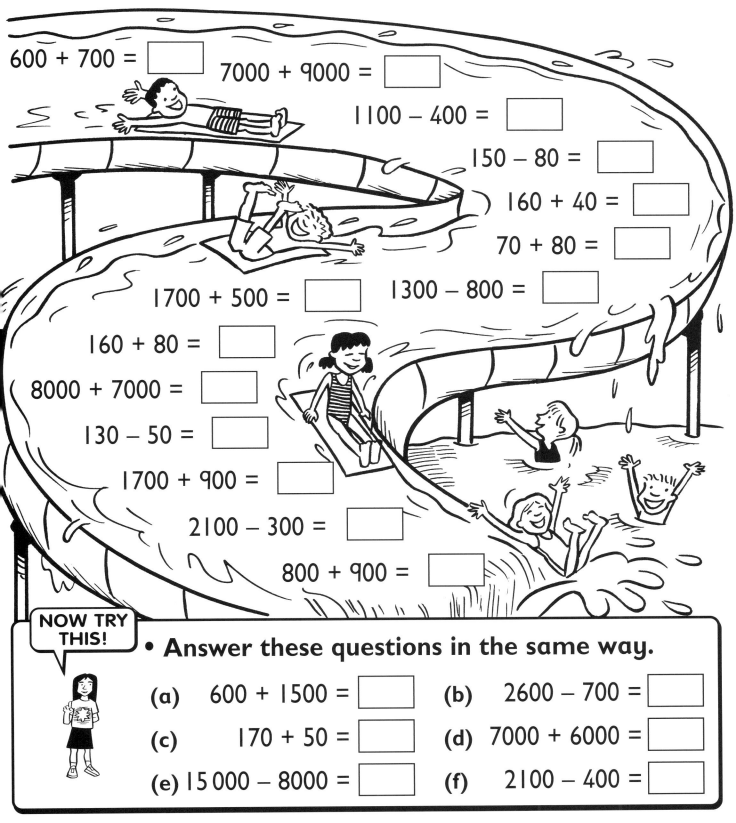

$600 + 700 =$ ☐

$7000 + 9000 =$ ☐

$1100 - 400 =$ ☐

$150 - 80 =$ ☐

$160 + 40 =$ ☐

$70 + 80 =$ ☐

$1700 + 500 =$ ☐

$1300 - 800 =$ ☐

$160 + 80 =$ ☐

$8000 + 7000 =$ ☐

$130 - 50 =$ ☐

$1700 + 900 =$ ☐

$2100 - 300 =$ ☐

$800 + 900 =$ ☐

NOW TRY THIS!

- **Answer these questions in the same way.**

(a) $600 + 1500 =$ ☐ (b) $2600 - 700 =$ ☐

(c) $170 + 50 =$ ☐ (d) $7000 + 6000 =$ ☐

(e) $15\,000 - 8000 =$ ☐ (f) $2100 - 400 =$ ☐

Teachers' note Encourage the children to see the link between the addition and subtraction facts for totals to 20 and the facts of multiples of 10, 100 and 1000, for example 6 + 7 = 13 so 600 + 700 = 1300. Discuss that subtraction and addition are inverses and encourage the children to use addition facts they know to help them quickly derive subtraction facts and vice versa.

100% New Developing Mathematics
Number Facts and Calculations:
Ages 8–9
© A & C BLACK

Sitting ducks

There are six ways of moving from 'start' to 'finish' where you land on three multiples of 1000.

- **Find all six routes.**
  Add the numbers
  you land on to find
  the total for
  each route.

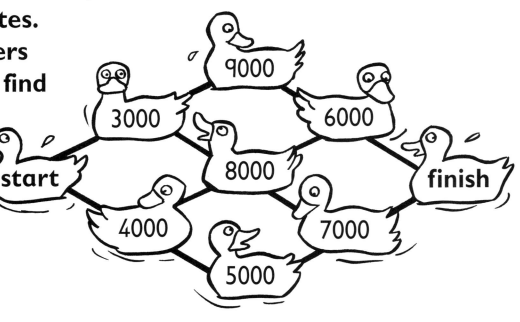

$3000 + 9000 + 6000 = 18\,000$

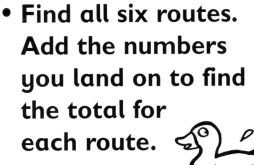

NOW TRY THIS!

- **Find three ways of moving from 'start' to 'finish' where you land on** five **multiples of 1000. Find the total for each route.**

Teachers' note Encourage the children to be systematic when finding different possible routes. Ask further questions about the totals such as, 'Which three-multiple route has the highest total?' 'Which five-multiple route has the lowest total?' 'Can you find a route that has a total of 42 000?'

100% New Developing Mathematic
Number Facts and Calculations:
Ages 8–9
© A & C BLACK

Double or halve

- **Use this sheet to help you double or halve two-digit numbers.**

1.
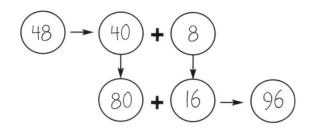

2.
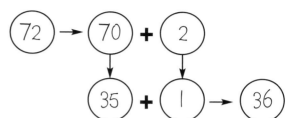

3.
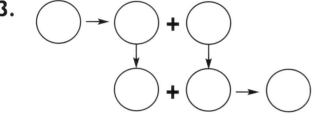

4.

5.
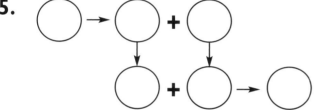

6.
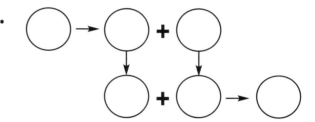

7.

8.

9.
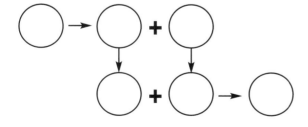

10.
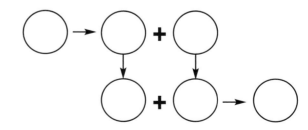

11.
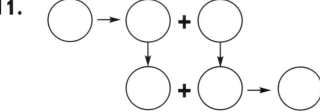

12.
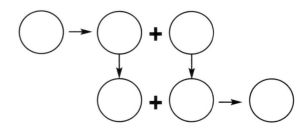

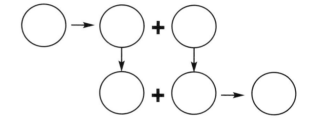
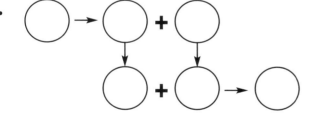
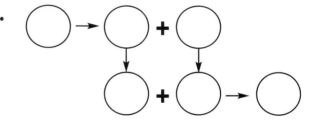

Teachers' note This sheet can be used to introduce the children to partitioning before doubling and halving each part separately. It can be given to children in conjunction with any of the following doubling or halving sheets.

100% New Developing Mathematics
Number Facts and Calculations:
Ages 8–9
© A & C BLACK

Double trouble

1. Double all the numbers | between 26 and 50 |. Write the original number in the correct section of the grid.

51	52 26	53	54	55	56	57	58	59	60
61	62	63	64	65	66	67	68	69	70
71	72	73	74	75	76	77	78	79	80
81	82	83	84	85	86	87	88	89	90
91	92	93	94	95	96	97	98	99	100

2. Double all the numbers | between 76 and 100 |. Write the original number in the correct section of the grid.

151	152 76	153	154	155	156	157	158	159	160
161	162	163	164	165	166	167	168	169	170
171	172	173	174	175	176	177	178	179	180
181	182	183	184	185	186	187	188	189	190
191	192	193	194	195	196	197	198	199	200

NOW TRY THIS!

- **Talk to a partner about patterns you notice in both grids.**

Teachers' note Encourage the children to choose a number, double it and find the answer rather than to choose a number from the grid and halve it, as this will enable them to begin to see connections between numbers between 26 and 50 and those between 76 and 100.

100% New Developing Mathematic
Number Facts and Calculations:
Ages 8–9
© A & C BLACK

At the sales

Everything in the sale is half price!
* **Write the new prices on the labels.**

1. Was £124 — £ 62

2. Was £148 — £

3. Was £158 — £

4. Was £134 — £

5. Was £178 — £

6. Was £152 — £

7. Was £192 — £

8. Was £188 — £

NOW TRY THIS!

These prices have already been halved.
* **What were the original prices?**

£64 £   £76 £   £88 £   £92 £

Teachers' note Children can be given the 'Double or halve' sheet on page 19 to help them to partition the numbers being halved.

100% New Developing Mathematics
Number Facts and Calculations:
Ages 8–9
© A & C BLACK

Double bugs

• **Double the numbers on the first bug and write them on the second bug.**

1. 42 420 4200
84 840 8400

2. 24 240 2400

3. 36 360 3600

4. 48 480 4800

5. 54 540 5400

6. 62 620 6200

7. 53 530 5300

8. 39 390 3900

9. 71 710 7100

10. 69 690 6900

11. 87 870 8700

12. 96 960 9600

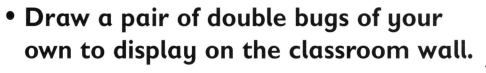

NOW TRY THIS!

• **Draw a pair of double bugs of your own to display on the classroom wall.**

Teachers' note This activity draws the children's attention to the relationships between doubling two-digit numbers and multiples of 10 and 100. The 'Double or halve' sheet on page 19 could be given to the children to help them partition the two-digit number first.

100% New Developing Mathematic Number Facts and Calculations: Ages 8–9
© A & C BLACK

Half bugs

- **Halve the numbers on the second bug and write them on the first bug.**

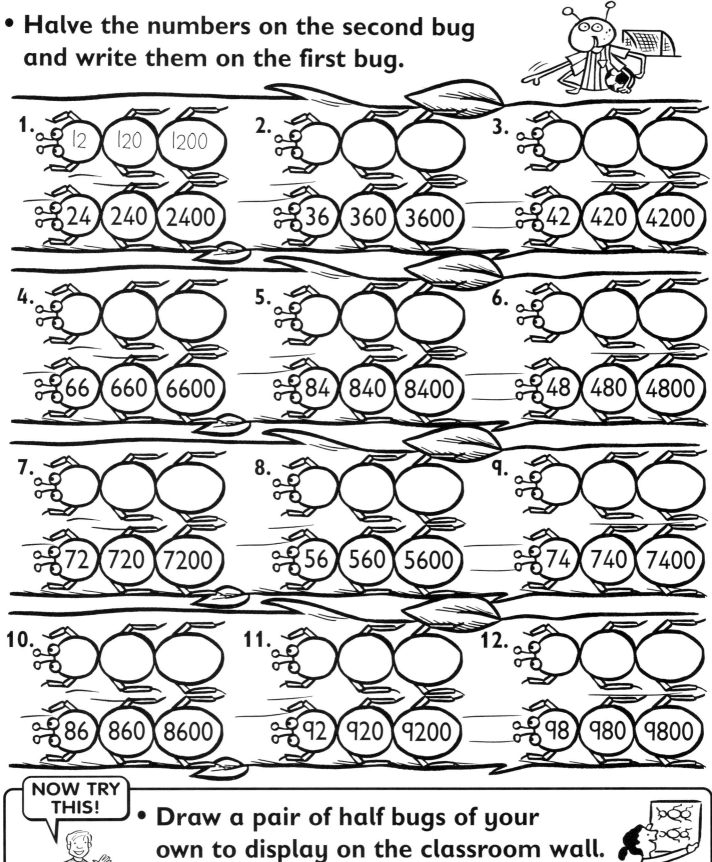

1. 12 120 1200
   24 240 2400

2.
   36 360 3600

3.
   42 420 4200

4.
   66 660 6600

5.
   84 840 8400

6.
   48 480 4800

7.
   72 720 7200

8.
   56 560 5600

9.
   74 740 7400

10.
    86 860 8600

11.
    92 920 9200

12.
    98 980 9800

NOW TRY THIS!

- **Draw a pair of half bugs of your own to display on the classroom wall.**

Teachers' note This activity draws the children's attention to the relationships between halving numbers and multiples of 10 and 100. The 'Double or halve' sheet on page 19 could be given to the children to help them partition the two-digit number first.

100% New Developing Mathematics
Number Facts and Calculations:
Ages 8–9
© A & C BLACK

Sleepover dreamtime

• **Play this game with a partner.**

☆ Cover each number on the bedspread with a counter.

☆ Place the cube anywhere on the pillow trail.

☆ Take turns to roll the dice and move the cube on.

☆ Answer the question. Lift a counter and see if the answer is beneath. If it is, keep the counter. If not, replace it.

☆ The winner is the player with the most counters at the end.

7	49	14	28
35	21	56	63
70	0	42	28
49	42	63	56
14	35	21	0

7×5 4×7 8×7 7×3 7×7 7×2 10×7

3×7 1×7

7×7 5×7

9×7 7×6

0×7 7×4 7×8 6×7 2×7 7×0 7×9

Teachers' note This activity can be given to the children as a homework activity to familiarise them with the multiples of 7 and to help them practise learning the 7 times-table. As each question is landed on, children should say the answer aloud and then select a counter to look beneath.

100% New Developing Mathematic Number Facts and Calculations: Ages 8–9
© A & C BLACK

Spot the dice

In a game, each spot on a dice is worth $\boxed{8}$ points.

- **Write how many points are scored for each pair of dice.**

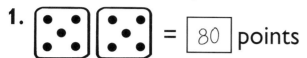

1. = $\boxed{80}$ points

2. = $\boxed{}$ points

3. = $\boxed{}$ points

4. = $\boxed{}$ points

5. = $\boxed{}$ points

6. = $\boxed{}$ points

7. = $\boxed{}$ points

8. = $\boxed{}$ points

9. = $\boxed{}$ points

10. = $\boxed{}$ points

11. = $\boxed{}$ points

12. = $\boxed{}$ points

 **NOW TRY THIS!**

- **Play the game with a partner.**
  - ☆ Take turns to roll two dice. Score $\boxed{8}$ points for each spot.
  - ☆ Roll four times each. Record your points here.

Player 1

Player 2

Total = _____

Total = _____

Teachers' note This sheet can be used to practise other tables facts than the 8 times-table. Change the number 8 to any number to 10 before copying. (Also change the answer to question 1.) For the extension activity, the children could be given a calculator to check their total. The player with the most points is the winner.

100% New Developing Mathematics
Number Facts and Calculations:
Ages 8–9
© A & C BLACK

Fingers of fun

☆ Hold your palms towards you. For **3 × 9** hold down your **third** finger from the left.

☆ **The fingers to the left of the bent finger are each worth 10.**

☆ **The fingers to the right of the bent finger are each worth 1.**

☆ For **4 × 9** or **9 × 4** hold down your **fourth** finger and so on.
   It works for all the 9 times-table!

• **Cut out the cards. Write the answers on the back of each card and test yourself to see how quickly you can learn the facts.**

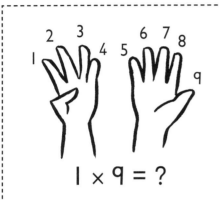

1 × 9 = ?

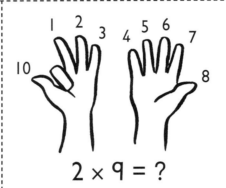

2 × 9 = ?

3 × 9 = ?

4 × 9 = ?

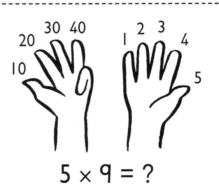

5 × 9 = ?

6 × 9 = ?

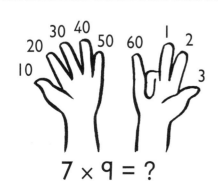

7 × 9 = ?

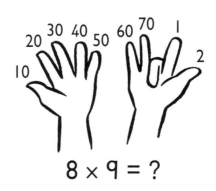

8 × 9 = ?

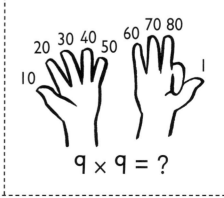

9 × 9 = ?

Teachers' note Show the children how to hold their hands to make each of the facts and include 10 × 9 = 90, which works by holding down the 10th finger (i.e. the right-hand thumb) leaving 9 fingers held up to the left of it, making 90.

100% New Developing Mathematic
Number Facts and Calculations:
Ages 8–9
© A & C BLACK

Animal antics

- **Time yourself to see how quickly you can answer the tables questions in each block.**

$9 \times 4 =$

$4 \times 5 =$

$7 \times 3 =$

$3 \times 8 =$

$9 \times 10 =$

$4 \times 6 =$

$5 \times 9 =$

$6 \times 6 =$

$7 \times 8 =$

$9 \times 7 =$

$7 \times 7 =$

$8 \times 8 =$

Time _____

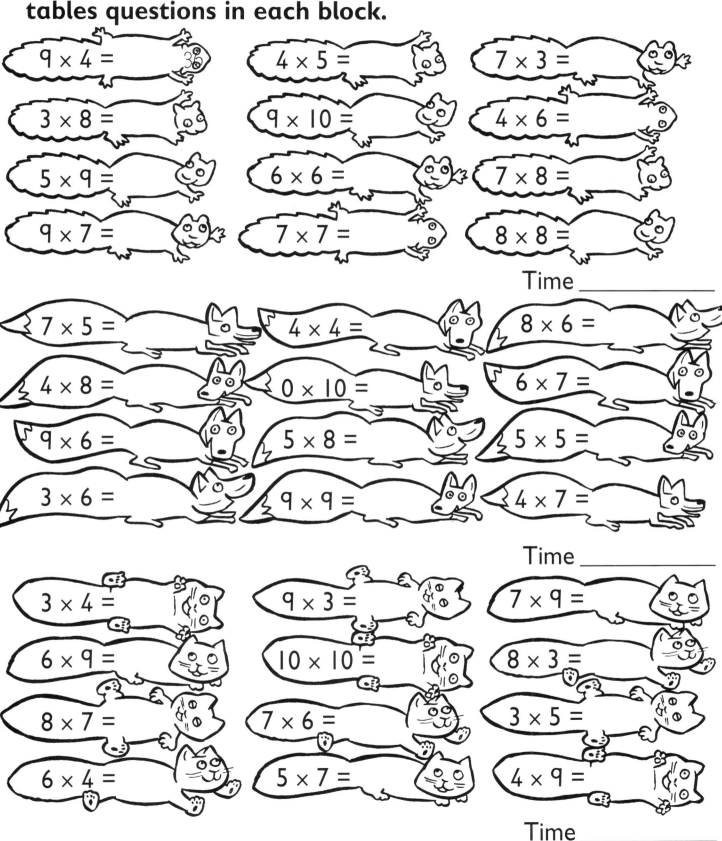

$7 \times 5 =$

$4 \times 4 =$

$8 \times 6 =$

$4 \times 8 =$

$0 \times 10 =$

$6 \times 7 =$

$9 \times 6 =$

$5 \times 8 =$

$5 \times 5 =$

$3 \times 6 =$

$9 \times 9 =$

$4 \times 7 =$

Time _____

$3 \times 4 =$

$9 \times 3 =$

$7 \times 9 =$

$6 \times 9 =$

$10 \times 10 =$

$8 \times 3 =$

$8 \times 7 =$

$7 \times 6 =$

$3 \times 5 =$

$6 \times 4 =$

$5 \times 7 =$

$4 \times 9 =$

Time _____

Teachers' note Edit this page on the CD-ROM or mask and alter the numbers before photocopying in order to provide more variety or differentiation. The most difficult tables facts up to 10 × 10 are included in each of these tests. As an extension activity, the children could colour the facts that they find hardest and which they need to revise further.

100% New Developing Mathematics
Number Facts and Calculations:
Ages 8–9
© A & C BLACK

Tables testing cards

- **Cut out Tests A, B, C and D and write the answers.**
- **Then cut out strips A, B, C and D to check whether your answers are correct.**

Test A	Test B	Test C	Test D	A	B	C	D
3 × 5 =	9 × 9 =	4 × 4 =	2 × 7 =	15	81	16	14
6 × 4 =	5 × 7 =	3 × 8 =	6 × 6 =	24	35	24	36
9 × 2 =	8 × 8 =	6 × 5 =	3 × 0 =	18	64	30	0
7 × 3 =	6 × 10 =	2 × 4 =	8 × 5 =	21	60	8	40
5 × 5 =	8 × 2 =	6 × 3 =	7 × 7 =	25	16	18	49
6 × 9 =	2 × 2 =	10 × 4 =	9 × 8 =	54	4	40	72
4 × 3 =	6 × 7 =	3 × 3 =	9 × 5 =	12	42	9	45
3 × 2 =	9 × 4 =	4 × 8 =	7 × 8 =	6	36	32	56
5 × 4 =	10 × 3 =	2 × 6 =	8 × 10 =	20	30	12	80
0 × 10 =	5 × 2 =	4 × 7 =	9 × 7 =	0	10	28	63
4 × 4 =	3 × 9 =	8 × 6 =	9 × 9 =	16	27	48	81
8 × 3 =	7 × 2 =	5 × 3 =	7 × 5 =	24	14	15	35
5 × 6 =	6 × 6 =	4 × 6 =	8 × 8 =	30	36	24	64
4 × 2 =	0 × 6 =	2 × 9 =	10 × 5 =	8	0	18	50
3 × 6 =	5 × 8 =	3 × 7 =	2 × 8 =	18	40	21	16
4 × 10 =	7 × 7 =	5 × 5 =	2 × 2 =	40	49	25	4
3 × 3 =	9 × 8 =	9 × 6 =	7 × 6 =	9	72	54	42
8 × 4 =	5 × 9 =	3 × 4 =	4 × 9 =	32	45	12	36
6 × 2 =	8 × 7 =	2 × 3 =	2 × 10 =	12	56	6	20
7 × 4 =	10 × 8 =	4 × 5 =	2 × 5 =	28	80	20	10
6 × 8 =	7 × 9 =	8 × 0 =	9 × 3 =	48	63	0	27

Division testing cards

- **Cut out Tests A, B, C and D and write the answers.**
- **Then cut out strips A, B, C and D to check whether your answers are correct.**

Test A	Test B	Test C	Test D	A	B	C	D
$15 \div 5 =$	$81 \div 9 =$	$16 \div 4 =$	$14 \div 7 =$	3	9	4	2
$24 \div 4 =$	$35 \div 7 =$	$24 \div 8 =$	$36 \div 6 =$	6	5	3	6
$18 \div 2 =$	$64 \div 8 =$	$30 \div 5 =$	$0 \div 3 =$	9	8	6	0
$21 \div 3 =$	$60 \div 10 =$	$8 \div 4 =$	$40 \div 5 =$	7	6	2	8
$25 \div 5 =$	$16 \div 2 =$	$18 \div 3 =$	$49 \div 7 =$	5	8	6	7
$54 \div 9 =$	$4 \div 2 =$	$40 \div 4 =$	$72 \div 8 =$	6	2	10	9
$12 \div 3 =$	$42 \div 7 =$	$9 \div 3 =$	$45 \div 5 =$	4	6	3	9
$6 \div 2 =$	$36 \div 4 =$	$32 \div 8 =$	$56 \div 8 =$	3	9	4	7
$20 \div 4 =$	$30 \div 3 =$	$12 \div 6 =$	$80 \div 10 =$	5	10	2	8
$0 \div 10 =$	$10 \div 2 =$	$28 \div 7 =$	$63 \div 7 =$	0	5	4	9
$16 \div 4 =$	$27 \div 9 =$	$48 \div 6 =$	$81 \div 9 =$	4	3	8	9
$24 \div 3 =$	$14 \div 2 =$	$15 \div 3 =$	$35 \div 5 =$	8	7	5	7
$30 \div 6 =$	$36 \div 6 =$	$24 \div 6 =$	$64 \div 8 =$	5	6	4	8
$8 \div 2 =$	$0 \div 6 =$	$18 \div 9 =$	$50 \div 5 =$	4	0	2	10
$18 \div 6 =$	$40 \div 8 =$	$21 \div 7 =$	$16 \div 8 =$	3	5	3	2
$40 \div 10 =$	$49 \div 7 =$	$25 \div 5 =$	$4 \div 2 =$	4	7	5	2
$9 \div 3 =$	$72 \div 8 =$	$54 \div 6 =$	$42 \div 6 =$	3	9	9	7
$32 \div 4 =$	$45 \div 9 =$	$12 \div 4 =$	$36 \div 9 =$	8	5	3	4
$12 \div 2 =$	$56 \div 7 =$	$6 \div 3 =$	$20 \div 10 =$	6	8	2	2
$28 \div 4 =$	$80 \div 8 =$	$20 \div 5 =$	$10 \div 5 =$	7	10	4	2
$48 \div 8 =$	$63 \div 9 =$	$0 \div 8 =$	$27 \div 3 =$	6	7	0	9

Teachers' note These cards can be cut out and used as testing cards for all the division facts for the times-tables up to 10 × 10. The answer strips can be given to the children to help them check their own answers. Encourage the children to note, each time they try a test, which questions and answers they got wrong or could not work out, and to learn them.

100% New Developing Mathematics
Number Facts and Calculations:
Ages 8–9
© A & C BLACK

29

Movin' on

☆ Pick a starting position: 1, 2, 3 or 4. Answer the question.

☆ Move on the same number of places as the answer.

☆ Answer the question you land on and move on. Keep going until you reach the end.

☆ Do you escape or do you get eaten by a crocodile?

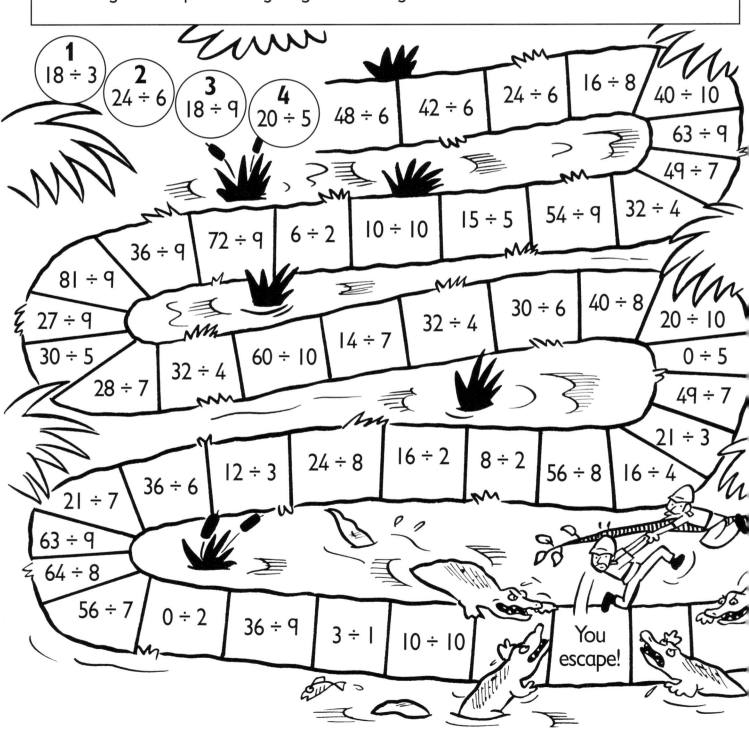

Teachers' note Encourage the children to make the link between multiplication facts and division facts. It might be useful for the tables facts to be displayed on the classroom wall for children to refer to. As an extension activity, ask the children on which number they have to start to escape.

100% New Developing Mathematic
Number Facts and Calculations:
Ages 8–9
© A & C BLACK

Stick 'em up

The children always put the same number of stickers on each page of their books.
• How many stickers are on each page?

1. 54 stickers 6 pages  9

2. 49 stickers 7 pages  ▢

3. 64 stickers 8 pages  ▢

4. 63 stickers 9 pages  ▢

5. 56 stickers 7 pages  ▢

6. 72 stickers 9 pages  ▢

7. 56 stickers 8 pages  ▢

8. 72 stickers 8 pages  ▢

9. 63 stickers 7 pages  ▢

NOW TRY THIS!

• **Use the answers above to help with these.**

(a) ▢ × 8 = 72   (b) 9 × ▢ = 63   (c) 7 × 8 = ▢

(d) ▢ × ▢ = 81   (e) 9 × ▢ = 54   (f) 6 × ▢ = 48

Teachers' note Ensure the children realise that, because of the commutative law, if they know one multiplication fact, for example 7 × 8 = 56, they also know that 8 × 7 = 56. An understanding of this effectively halves the number of facts a child has to learn.

100% New Developing Mathematics
Number Facts and Calculations:
Ages 8–9
© A & C BLACK

31

Connections

Each arrow means is a multiple of .
So 6 →3 means 6 is a multiple of 3.

- **Notice that the arrow goes from the** larger **to the** smaller **number.**
- **Put the numbers shown in the box into the correct circles so that all the arrows are true.**

1.

| 3 | 5 | 10 | 30 |

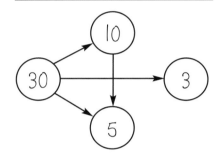

2.

| 3 | 4 | 8 | 24 |

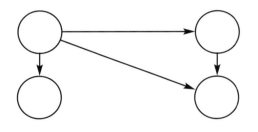

3.

| 3 | 4 | 6 | 9 | 36 |

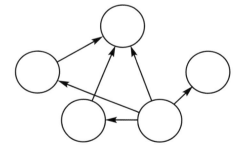

4.

| 3 | 6 | 7 | 21 | 42 |

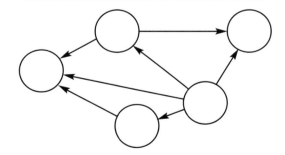

5.

| 6 | 7 | 8 | 14 | 48 | 56 |

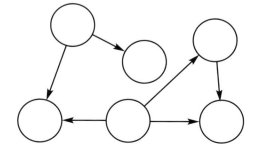

6.

| 2 | 4 | 8 | 16 | 32 |

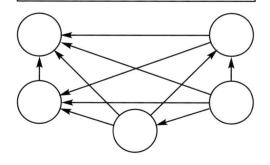

Teachers' note Once the children master what is expected here they can construct their own diagrams and identify which numbers are multiples of which. Similar diagrams can be drawn using the rule 'is a factor of' to encourage the children to identify which numbers are factors of others. As an extension activity, children could make diagrams of their own for a partner to solve.

100% New Developing Mathemati
Number Facts and Calculations:
Ages 8–9
© A & C BLACK

World tour

Around the globe are multiples of numbers up to 10.

• **Play with a partner. You need one small counter and a dice.**

☆ Start in any position around the globe.

☆ Take turns to roll the dice and move the counter forward.

☆ The number you land on may be a multiple of more than one number but you can only cross off one of those numbers from your list.

☆ The winner is the first player to cross off all their numbers.

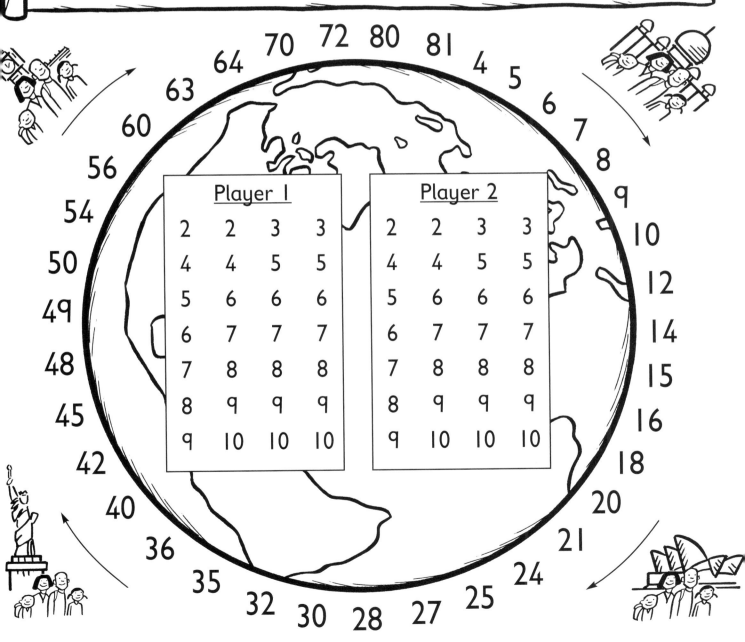

Player 1					Player 2			
2	2	3	3		2	2	3	3
4	4	5	5		4	4	5	5
5	6	6	6		5	6	6	6
6	7	7	7		6	7	7	7
7	8	8	8		7	8	8	8
8	9	9	9		8	9	9	9
9	10	10	10		9	10	10	10

Numbers around the globe: 70 72 80 81 4 5 6 7 8 9 10 12 14 15 16 18 20 21 24 25 27 28 30 32 35 36 40 42 45 48 49 50 54 56 60 63 64

Teachers' note Children could be introduced to the term 'factor' if appropriate. Display the list of multiplication tables up to 10 × 10 for this activity and demonstrate how to use these to find a multiple of the number landed on. As an extension activity, ask the children which of the numbers around the globe is a multiple of 2, 3, 4, 5, 6 and 10.

**100% New Developing Mathematics
Number Facts and Calculations:
Ages 8–9
© A & C BLACK**

33

Part and parcel

- Join pairs of parcels whose fractions total 1.
- Write any missing fractions.

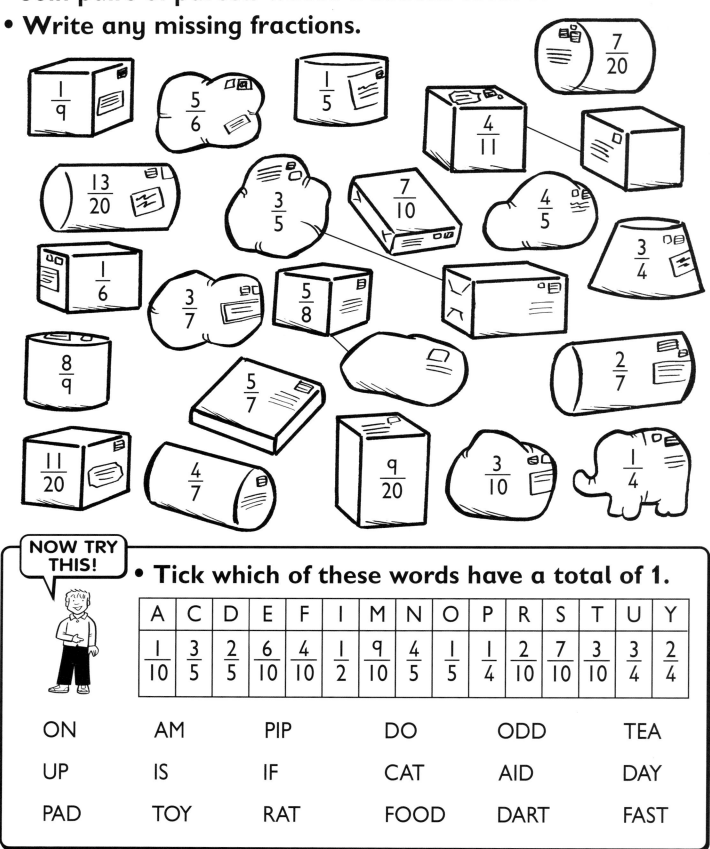

Teachers' note For the extension activity, encourage the children to use the key to find the value of each letter and see whether the fractions add to make 1. Some rely on a simple understanding of equivalence, for example knowing that $\frac{2}{5}$ is equivalent to $\frac{4}{10}$.

100% New Developing Mathematic
Number Facts and Calculations:
Ages 8–9
© A & C BLACK

Andy, Sandy and Mandy

Andy, Sandy and Mandy are
taking part in a maths quiz.
• Tick who says the best approximation.

1. | 34 + 47 |  60    70    80

2. | 67 − 48 |  10    20    30

3. | 127 + 52 |  160    170    180

4. | 171 − 28 |  130    140    150

5. | 173 + 249 |  410    420    430

6. | 64 × 5 |  300    350    400

NOW TRY THIS!

• **Estimate the answers to these questions.**

(a) 268 − 43 ☐   (b) 53 × 8 ☐   (c) 94 ÷ 9 ☐

Teachers' note When estimating the size of an answer encourage the children to round the numbers appropriately or to use their knowledge of tables and number facts to find a fact close to the one in the question.

**100% New Developing Mathematics
Number Facts and Calculations:
Ages 8–9
© A & C BLACK**

35

Computer glitch

A computer keeps making mistakes.
- Check which are wrong using inverses.

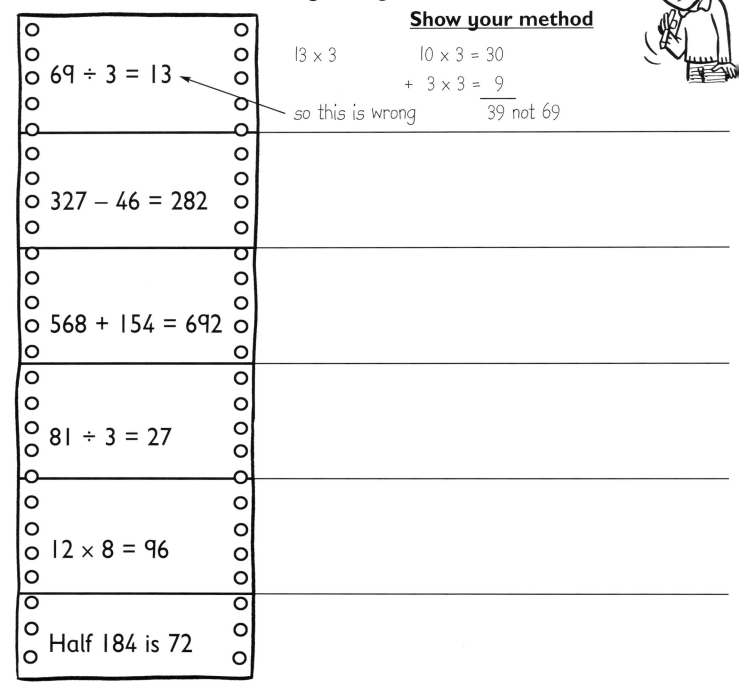

Show your method

13×3 $10 \times 3 = 30$
so this is wrong $+ \ 3 \times 3 = \underline{\ 9}$
                          39 not 69

$69 \div 3 = 13$

$327 - 46 = 282$

$568 + 154 = 692$

$81 \div 3 = 27$

$12 \times 8 = 96$

Half 184 is 72

NOW TRY THIS!

- Talk to a partner about how you checked each one.

Teachers' note At the start of the lesson discuss the meaning of the word 'inverse' and determine which operations are inverse to which. Demonstrate how calculations can be checked using the answer and the inverse calculation, for example to check 354 − 32 = 322 we can add 322 and 32 to see if the answer is 354.

100% New Developing Mathematic◆
Number Facts and Calculations:
Ages 8–9
© A & C BLACK

The banker's game

• ## Play this game with a partner.

You need
I 'Banker's game' sheet each and the 'Save and spend cards'.

☆ Each player starts with £50 in the bank.

☆ Spread the cards face down on the table.

☆ Take turns to pick a card and fill in your banking sheet to show how much you have now.

☆ The winner is the player with the most money when all the cards have been used.

Save (add to your balance)	Spend (subtract from your balance)	Balance
////////	////////	£50

Teachers' note Use this sheet in conjunction with the cards on page 38. Ensure that the children understand how a balance sheet works and demonstrate how it is filled in. The children can play in pairs or small groups and require a recording sheet each.

100% New Developing Mathematics
Number Facts and Calculations:
Ages 8–9
© A & C BLACK

Save and spend cards

Cut out the cards and use them with 'The banker's game'.

It's your birthday! Add £27	Buy a pizza Subtract £9	Clean your dad's car Add £15	Take dog to the vet Subtract £28
Pocket-money day! Add £12	Buy an ice cream Subtract £2	Help your gran Add £13	Buy a DVD Subtract £17
Do a paper round Add £25	Break your mum's vase Subtract £32	Win a prize! Add £37	Take cat to the vet Subtract £16
Pocket-money day! Add £12	Buy a book Subtract £7	The bank pays you interest Add £5	Buy presents for the family Subtract £29
Help your mum Add £17	Lose your purse Subtract £16	Do some babysitting Add £19	Buy a CD Subtract £14

Teachers' note This sheet should be used in conjunction with page 37.

100% New Developing Mathematic
Number Facts and Calculations:
Ages 8–9
© A & C BLACK

Trampoline

☆ Colour a number from each row to make a three-digit number and a two-digit number. Find the total using a written method.

☆ Score a point if your answer matches one of the numbers on the trampoline.

☆ Continue until all the numbers are coloured. How many points did you score?

Record on a separate piece of paper.

three-digit number

700	200	400	■	100	900	500	600
30	20	■	10	80	90	50	30
1	6	9	7	2	■	5	8

+

two-digit number

40	80	20	90	70	60	■	50
■	5	4	6	7	9	3	2

$$\begin{array}{r} 8\,6\,3 \\ +\ \ 3\,8 \\ \hline 9\,0\,1 \end{array}$$

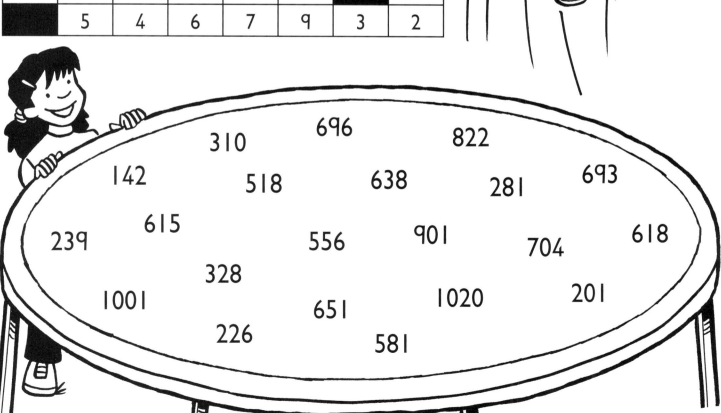

310   696   822
142   518   638   281   693
615   239   556   901   704   618
328
1001   651   1020   201
226   581

Teachers' note Discuss appropriate strategies for finding sums of pairs of two- and three-digit numbers, for example using informal approaches such as drawing number lines, using partitioning to help in the calculation, or using a more traditional column method. Encourage the children to check their answers using subtraction.

100% New Developing Mathematics
Number Facts and Calculations:
Ages 8–9
© A & C BLACK

39

Animal additions

a	b	c	d	e	f	g	h	i	j	k	l	m
28	214	351	531	67	672	833	777	89	369	473	794	335

n	o	p	q	r	s	t	u	v	w	x	y	z
646	64	951	506	748	357	729	26	631	542	914	54	467

- **Find the letters in the key and add the numbers to find the value of each animal.**

(a) `1428` dog

(b) cat

(c) ant

(d) yak

(e) ape

(f) bat

(g) emu

(h) fox

(i) hen

(j) jay

(k) owl

(l) rat

NOW TRY THIS!

- **Write some words with** [four] **letters and find their values.**

Teachers' note For the extension activity, encourage the children to choose different four-letter words. Alternatively, they could find the value of the letters in their own name. Discuss appropriate written methods that could be used to add the numbers, for example using the traditional column method of addition.

40

100% New Developing Mathematic Number Facts and Calculations: Ages 8–9
© A & C BLACK

Curious cube

☆ Choose pairs of three-digit numbers from the curious cube that will have a total that is a multiple of 10 .

☆ Numbers can be taken from any face, reading across or down.

Curiouser and curiouser!

187 + 973

$$\begin{array}{r} 187 \\ + 973 \\ \hline 1160 \end{array}$$

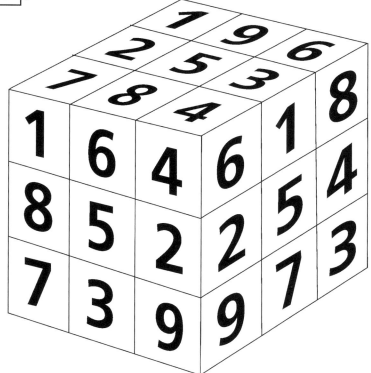

☆ Find ways to make these totals.

(a) 360 $$\begin{array}{r} 196 \\ + 164 \\ \hline 360 \end{array}$$	(b) 380	(c) 410	(d) 440
(e) 450	(f) 830	(g) 840	(h) 970
(i) 1000	(j) 1030	(k) 1470	(l) 1810

Teachers' note The children can use any appropriate method of written addition, such as using the traditional column method without partitioning. Provide scrap paper for the children's jottings.

100% New Developing Mathematics
Number Facts and Calculations:
Ages 8–9
© A & C BLACK

Supermarket stacks

The number on each tin is the total of the numbers on the two tins supporting it.

- Fill in the missing numbers.

298

124 174 158 167

128 185 109 136 131

NOW TRY THIS!

- **Ring the tin which shows the wrong total and write the correct total.**

1459

616 853

287 329 524

Teachers' note The children could use any appropriate method for these additions, including partitioning, drawing number lines, or using written methods leading towards the traditional column method of addition. Encourage children tackling the extension activity to explain which methods they used to check the totals.

100% New Developing Mathematic
Number Facts and Calculations:
Ages 8–9
© A & C BLACK

Captain Dynamic

Captain Dynamic uses subtraction to choose an eight-digit code to keep his superhero identity safe! He thinks of 573 – 86 = 487, so his code is ⬚5⬚7⬚3⬚8⬚6⬚4⬚8⬚7⬚

'Night, Mum.

SUPERHERO

SUPER COMBINATION LOCK

- Use subtraction to find the last three digits of each code. Show your workings.

(a) (4)(3)(9)(7)(4)( )( )( )

(b) (8)(4)(5)(9)(2)( )( )( )

(c) ( )(6)(5)(3)(6)(7)( )( )

(d) ( )(9)(1)(2)(5)(9)( )( )

(e) ( )(8)(0)(7)(7)(5)( )( )

(f) ( )(6)(1)(7)(7)(5)( )( )

NOW TRY THIS!

- Make up two more codes using subtraction.

Teachers' note Encourage the children to use an appropriate written method of subtraction to find each answer, such as using a vertical column method involving partitioning or drawing a number line.

**100% New Developing Mathematics
Number Facts and Calculations:
Ages 8–9**
© A & C BLACK

Crack the codes

- **Answer each question to find which code opens each safe.**

Safe letter	A	B	C	D	E	F	G	H
Code number								

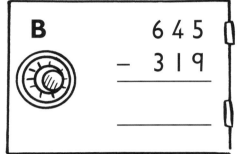

A
```
  7 1 1
- 2 5 7
-------
```

B
```
  6 4 5
- 3 1 9
-------
```

C
```
  4 4 5
- 1 7 7
-------
```

D
```
  6 3 4
- 4 2 8
-------
```

E
```
  5 5 2
- 3 7 3
-------
```

F
```
  8 1 3
- 6 8 4
-------
```

G
```
  7 0 4
- 2 7 6
-------
```

H
```
  9 2 1
- 6 7 2
-------
```

CODES

1. **428**
2. **129**
3. **268**
4. **179**
5. **326**
6. **454**
7. **249**
8. **154**
9. **206**

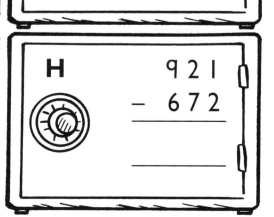

Teachers' note Demonstrate suitable written methods of subtraction that the children could use to answer these questions. Encourage the children to estimate first and then check their answers using a written method of addition. As an extension, ask the children to make up their own 'safe' puzzle for a partner to solve.

**100% New Developing Mathematics
Number Facts and Calculations:
Ages 8–9**
© A & C BLACK

Tallest man ever

The tallest man that ever lived, Robert Wadlow, was ⟨272 cm⟩ tall!

- **Use a written method to find the difference between his height and the heights of these people.**

1.

Zeng Jinlian
(tallest woman ever)
248 cm

_____ cm

2.

Roald
Dahl
198 cm

_____ cm

3.

Elvis
Presley
183 cm

_____ cm

4.

Queen
Victoria
152 cm

_____ cm

5.

Joan
of Arc
149 cm

_____ cm

NOW TRY THIS!

- **Work in a group of three or four.**
- **Measure your heights and fill in the table.**

Name	Height (cm)	Difference between 272 cm and this height

Teachers' note Encourage the children to use an appropriate written method, such as a vertical column method involving partitioning or the more traditional decomposition method. Provide a separate piece of paper for their workings. The children will require a tape-measure, metre sticks or height measurer for the extension activity.

**100% New Developing Mathematics
Number Facts and Calculations:
Ages 8–9**
© A & C BLACK

Under the microscope

When this super microscope is set to $\boxed{\times\ 10}$, each length appears **10 times longer**.

- **Write how long each bug appears if its original length is:**

1. 5 mm

 _____ mm

2. 7 mm

 _____ mm

3. 11 mm

 _____ mm

4. 14 mm

 _____ mm

5. 19 mm

 _____ mm

6. 23 mm

 _____ mm

7. 27 mm

 _____ mm

8. 31 mm

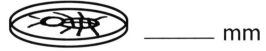 _____ mm

---

NOW TRY THIS!

- **When this super-duper microscope is set to $\boxed{\times\ 100}$, each length appears 100 times longer.**
- **Write how long each bug appears if its original length is:**

(a) 6 mm

 _____ mm

(b) 10 mm

 _____ mm

(c) 14 mm

 _____ mm

(d) 17 mm

 _____ mm

---

Teachers' note Encourage the children to appreciate the movement of the digits rather than focusing on 'putting a zero on the end', as this will cause them difficulties when multiplying decimals in the future, for example 3·5 × 10 = 35, not 3·50.

**100% New Developing Mathematic
Number Facts and Calculations:
Ages 8–9
© A & C BLACK**

Tidying up

• **Write each slip of paper onto the correct bin to show how the number has been changed.**

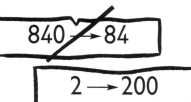 840 → 84

23 → 230

67 → 6700

2 → 200

170 → 17

11 → 110

4100 → 41

58 → 5800

5000 → 50

600 → 6

34 → 3400

70 → 700

300 → 3000

400 → 40

84 → 8400

60 → 6000

9700 → 97

768 → 7680

9800 → 980

57 → 570

500 → 50

x 10	x 100	÷ 10	÷ 100
		840 → 84	

NOW TRY THIS!

• **Write two more true facts on each bin.**

Teachers' note The children should cross off the slip of paper as they write it onto a bin. Encourage them to appreciate the movement of the digits rather than focusing on 'putting a zero on the end or removing it', as this will cause them difficulties when multiplying and dividing decimals in the future, for example 3·5 × 10 = 35, not 3·50.

**100% New Developing Mathematics
Number Facts and Calculations:
Ages 8–9
© A & C BLACK**

Dicing with dinosaurs

• Play this game with a partner.

☆ Take turns to roll the dice three times.

☆ Multiply the numbers together.
If the answer is **even** score **1 point**.
If it is **odd** score **0 points**.

You need
a copy of this sheet each and a dice.

Dice numbers	Answer to multiplication	Odd or even?	Points scored
2 × 5 × 3 =	30	even	1
☐ × ☐ × ☐ =			
☐ × ☐ × ☐ =			
☐ × ☐ × ☐ =			
☐ × ☐ × ☐ =			
☐ × ☐ × ☐ =			
☐ × ☐ × ☐ =			
☐ × ☐ × ☐ =			
☐ × ☐ × ☐ =			
☐ × ☐ × ☐ =			
☐ × ☐ × ☐ =			
		Total	

The highest total wins the game.

NOW TRY THIS!

• **Play again, but this time take the answer to the multiplication and divide it by 2.**
• **Is it easier or harder to score points?**

Teachers' note Multiplying three numbers provides practice of recalling multiplication facts and also of using informal mental or written methods for multiplying larger numbers. Ensure that the children appreciate the commutative and associative nature of multiplication (see page 10).

100% New Developing Mathemat
Number Facts and Calculations:
Ages 8–9
© A & C BLACK

Set totals: 1

• You need Set totals: 2 for this activity.

☆ Cut out the cards from set 1 and arrange them to make five division questions, each with a whole-number answer.

☆ Add the answers to find the 'set total'.

☆ Arrange the cards in different ways to find different 'set totals'.

☆ Repeat for other sets of cards.

What is the highest total you can make?

Set _____

Questions	Answers
Set total	

Set _____

Questions	Answers
Set total	

Set _____

Questions	Answers
Set total	

Set _____

Questions	Answers
Set total	

Set _____

Questions	Answers
Set total	

Set _____

Questions	Answers
Set total	

Set _____

Questions	Answers
Set total	

Set _____

Questions	Answers
Set total	

Set _____

Questions	Answers
Set total	

Teachers' note The children will need several copies of this sheet and a copy of page 50, 'Set totals: 2' for this activity. Encourage the children to record clearly which set of cards is being used and to try to find the largest possible set total.

100% New Developing Mathematics
Number Facts and Calculations:
Ages 8–9
© A & C BLACK

Set totals: 2

- **Cut out one set of cards at a time.**
- **Use them with Set totals: 1.**

Set 4

45	42	36	60	100
÷ 3	÷ 4	÷ 5	÷ 6	÷ 9

Set 3

20	54	30	63	70
÷ 3	÷ 4	÷ 5	÷ 6	÷ 7

Set 2

72	48	35	63	80
÷ 8	÷ 7	÷ 5	÷ 6	÷ 9

Set 1

16	12	48	18	24
÷ 2	÷ 4	÷ 8	÷ 6	÷ 3

Teachers' note This sheet should be used in conjunction with page 49, 'Set totals: 1'. Ensure that only one set of cards is used at a time and that the sets are not mixed up.

100% New Developing Mathematic
Number Facts and Calculations:
Ages 8–9
© A & C BLACK

Detective Dog

- **Cut out the cards.**

Work with a partner.

- **Read each clue and together help Detective Dog solve the division puzzle.**

1. The number is between 40 and 50.

When it is divided by 5 there is a remainder of 3.

When it is divided by 7 there is a remainder of 6.

The number is

2. The number is between 30 and 40.

When it is divided by 3 there is a remainder of 1.

When it is divided by 4 there is a remainder of 1.

The number is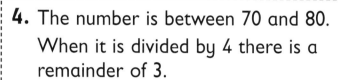

3. The number is between 60 and 70.

When it is divided by 6 there is a remainder of 1.

When it is divided by 4 there is a remainder of 3.

The number is

4. The number is between 70 and 80.

When it is divided by 4 there is a remainder of 3.

When it is divided by 5 there is a remainder of 0.

The number is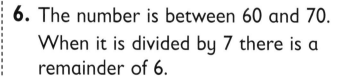

5. The number is between 70 and 80.

When it is divided by 7 there is a remainder of 2.

When it is divided by 6 there is a remainder of 1.

The number is

6. The number is between 60 and 70.

When it is divided by 7 there is a remainder of 6.

When it is divided by 8 there is a remainder of 5.

The number is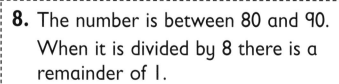

7. The number is between 80 and 90.

When it is divided by 9 there is a remainder of 5.

When it is divided by 4 there is a remainder of 2.

The number is

8. The number is between 80 and 90.

When it is divided by 8 there is a remainder of 1.

When it is divided by 7 there is a remainder of 5.

The number is

Teachers' note Cutting out the cards will help the children to focus on one puzzle at a time. Some children will benefit from having a number line and multiplication tables to refer to. As an extension, ask the children to make up some puzzles of their own for another pair to solve.

100% New Developing Mathematics
Number Facts and Calculations:
Ages 8–9
© A & C BLACK

Beautiful brooches

A jeweller cuts a length of wire into equal-sized pieces to make a brooch. The more pieces of wire that a brooch contains, the more expensive it is.

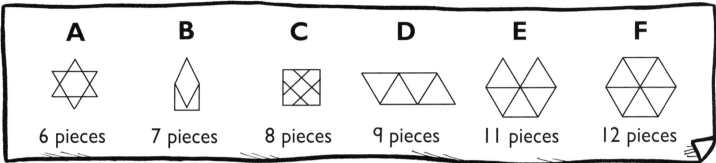

A	B	C	D	E	F
6 pieces	7 pieces	8 pieces	9 pieces	11 pieces	12 pieces

1. He uses a wire **57 cm** long. What is the most expensive brooch he can make, if the wire is cut into:

(a) 6 cm pieces?	**(b)** 7 cm pieces?	**(c)** 9 cm pieces?
57 ÷ 6 = 9 r3 9 pieces [D]		

2. He uses a wire **74 cm** long. What is the most expensive brooch he can make, if the wire is cut into:

(a) 6 cm pieces?	**(b)** 8 cm pieces?	**(c)** 9 cm pieces?

3. He uses a wire **65 cm** long. What is the most expensive brooch he can make, if the wire is cut into:

(a) 7 cm pieces?	**(b)** 8 cm pieces?	**(c)** 9 cm pieces?

Teachers' note Encourage the children to use an appropriate practical, informal or written method of division. As an extension, ask the children to use their answers to work out how much wire was wasted altogether.

100% New Developing Mathematic
Number Facts and Calculations:
Ages 8–9
© A & C BLACK

Crazy calculations

☆ Cut out the cards.

☆ Pick an input card, for example $\boxed{58}$, and an operation card, for example $\boxed{\times 3}$.

☆ Work out the answer to the multiplication. Show your workings on a separate piece of paper.

☆ Try to find the six pairs of cards which will give these output numbers.

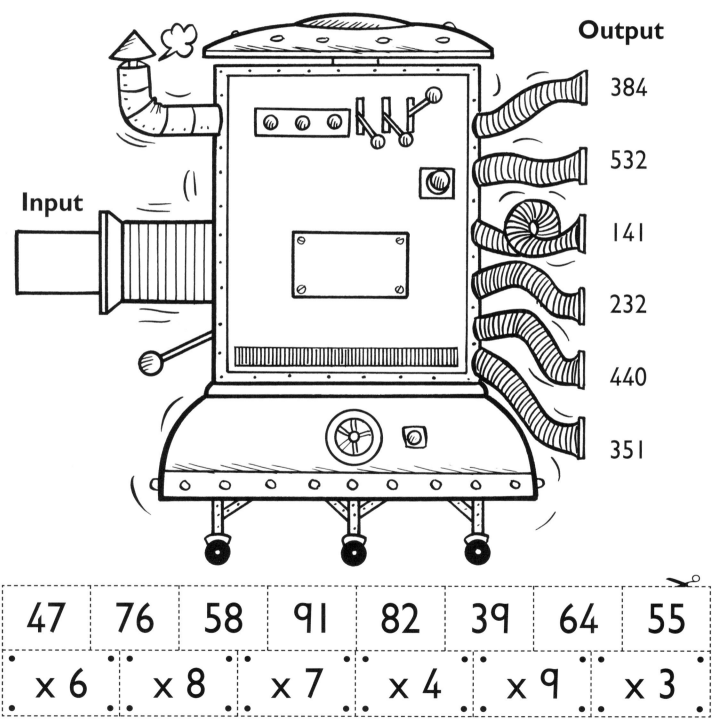

Input

Output

384

532

141

232

440

351

47	76	58	91	82	39	64	55
× 6	× 8	× 7	× 4	× 9	× 3		

Teachers' note The children can use any appropriate method of multiplication, such as using the grid method based on partitioning each two-digit number and multiplying each part separately.

100% New Developing Mathematics
Number Facts and Calculations:
Ages 8–9
© A & C BLACK

Magic ingredients

Griselda is recording the boxed ingredients in her cupboard. She counts the boxes.

- Use multiplication to work out how many of each ingredient she has.

4 boxes of warts

48 warts

7 boxes of slugs

36 slugs

6 boxes of hairballs

24 hairballs

8 boxes of maggots

64 maggots

9 boxes of eyeballs

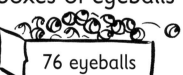

76 eyeballs

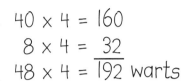

$40 \times 4 = 160$
$8 \times 4 = 32$
$48 \times 4 = 192$ warts

NOW TRY THIS!

- Use a calculator to work out how many ingredients there are altogether. _____

Teachers' note Encourage the children to use an appropriate method of multiplication, such as partitioning in the way shown or using a grid method of multiplication.

100% New Developing Mathematic
Number Facts and Calculations:
Ages 8–9
© A & C BLACK

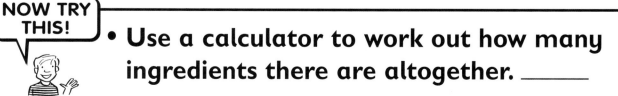

Life's a lottery

• **Divide each of the winning balls by the bonus ball.**

1. 49 84 67 72 96 6 bonus

8 r1 ___ ___ ___ ___ ___

2. 56 74 37 80 47 7 bonus

___ ___ ___ ___ ___ ___

3. 65 84 52 58 98 9 bonus

___ ___ ___ ___ ___ ___

4. 85 42 54 64 95 8 bonus

___ ___ ___ ___ ___ ___

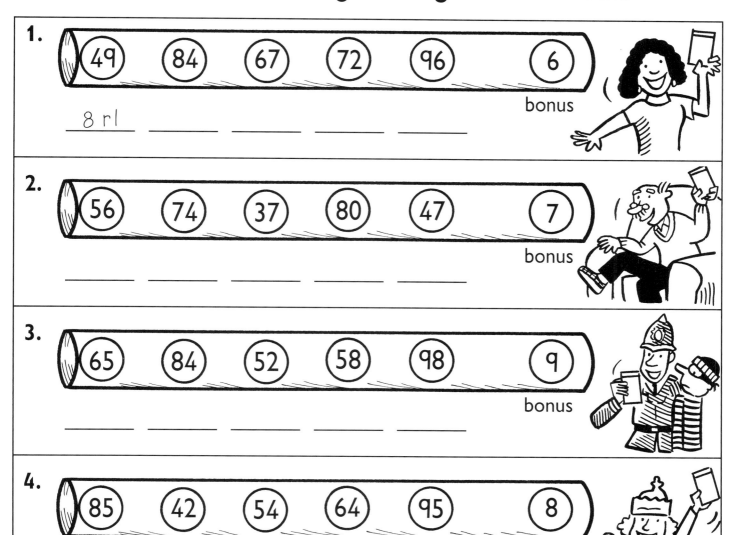

NOW TRY THIS!

• **Write what the bonus ball must be. Then divide by the bonus ball.**

44 84 67 72 98 ◯ bonus

14 r2 ___ ___ ___ ___ ___

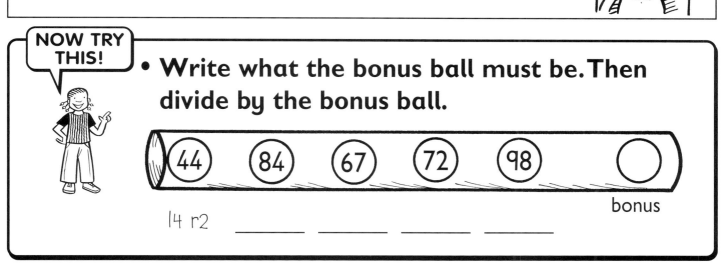

Teachers' note The children could be asked to give the remainder as a fraction, for example 8 and $\frac{1}{6}$, rather than 8 r1.

100% New Developing Mathematics
Number Facts and Calculations:
Ages 8–9
© A & C BLACK

Loads-a-money!

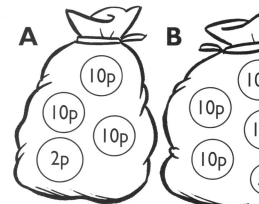
A

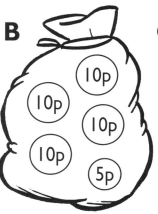
B

C

D **E**

• Find:

1. $\frac{1}{4}$ of A = ___8___ p

2. $\frac{1}{6}$ of C = _____ p

3. $\frac{1}{5}$ of B = _____ p

4. $\frac{1}{3}$ of D = _____ p

5. $\frac{3}{4}$ of A = _____ p

6. $\frac{2}{5}$ of B = _____ p

7. $\frac{4}{5}$ of C = _____ p

8. $\frac{2}{3}$ of D = _____ p

9. $\frac{5}{6}$ of E = _____ p

10. $\frac{3}{8}$ of A = _____ p

11. $\frac{4}{9}$ of D = _____ p

12. $\frac{3}{10}$ of E = _____ p

13. $\frac{3}{20}$ of C = _____ p

14. $\frac{7}{15}$ of B = _____ p

NOW TRY THIS!

• **Work out how much there is in bag F, if:** $\frac{5}{8}$ of F = 15

F

_____ p

Teachers' note At the start of the lesson, demonstrate how a fraction of a quantity can be found by dividing by the denominator (to find the unit fraction) and then multiplying by the numerator, for example $\frac{4}{5}$ of 30 can be found by dividing 30 by 5 to find one-fifth (6), and then multiplying by 4 to find four-fifths, giving the answer 6 × 4 = 24.

100% New Developing Mathematic **Number Facts and Calculations:** **Ages 8–9** © A & C BLACK

A spoonful of medicine

A child's dose of medicine is a fraction of an adult's dose.

• **For each question work out a child's dose.**

1. $\frac{1}{4}$ of 20 ml = 5 ml

2. $\frac{1}{5}$ of 15 ml = ___ ml

3. $\frac{3}{4}$ of 24 ml = ___ ml

4. $\frac{2}{7}$ of 21 ml = ___ ml

5. $\frac{1}{3}$ of 24 ml = ___ ml

6. $\frac{3}{8}$ of 16 ml = ___ ml

7. $\frac{5}{9}$ of 18 ml = ___ ml

8. $\frac{5}{6}$ of 30 ml = ___ ml

9. $\frac{4}{5}$ of 25 ml = ___ ml

10. $\frac{5}{7}$ of 21 ml = ___ ml

11. $\frac{7}{10}$ of 30 ml = ___ ml

12. $\frac{7}{9}$ of 27 ml = ___ ml

13. $\frac{7}{8}$ of 32 ml = ___ ml

NOW TRY THIS!

• **Fill in the adult's dose below.**

$$\frac{6}{7} \text{ of } \underline{\hspace{2cm}} \text{ ml} = 24 \text{ ml}$$

Teachers' note The extension activity requires the children to realise that 24 ml is $\frac{6}{7}$ of the adult dose, and then they need to find one-sixth of 24 and multiply by 7 to give 28.

**100% New Developing Mathematics
Number Facts and Calculations:
Ages 8–9**
© A & C BLACK

Drink up!

• **Answer the questions below about these drinks.**

Drink A	Drink B	Drink C	Drink D	Drink E
			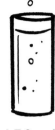	
400 ml	200 ml	450 ml	150 ml	50 ml

1. $\frac{1}{4}$ of A = _____ ml

2. $\frac{1}{5}$ of C = _____ ml

3. $\frac{1}{5}$ of E = _____ ml

4. $\frac{1}{3}$ of D = _____ ml

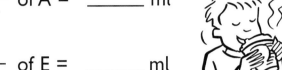

5. $\frac{3}{4}$ of A = _____ ml

6. $\frac{2}{5}$ of B = _____ ml

7. $\frac{4}{5}$ of E = _____ ml

8. $\frac{2}{3}$ of D = _____ ml

9. $\frac{2}{9}$ of C = _____ ml

10. $\frac{3}{8}$ of A = _____ ml

11. $\frac{3}{5}$ of D = _____ ml

12. $\frac{7}{10}$ of B = _____ ml

13. $\frac{3}{25}$ of E = _____ ml

14. $\frac{9}{20}$ of A = _____ ml

NOW TRY THIS!

• **Find $\frac{7}{25}$ of each drink.**

A	B	C	D	E
_____ ml	_____ ml	_____ ml	_____ ml	_____ ml

Teachers' note At the start of the lesson, demonstrate how a fraction of a quantity can be found by dividing by the denominator (to find the unit fraction) and then multiplying by the numerator, for example $\frac{4}{5}$ of 30 can be found by dividing 30 by 5 to find one-fifth (6), and then multiplying by 4 to find four-fifths, giving the answer 6 × 4 = 24.

100% New Developing Mathematic **Number Facts and Calculations:** **Ages 8–9** © A & C BLACK

Spelling fractions

You need different-coloured pencils.

- **Count the number of squares in each letter.**
- **Colour the fractions of each letter shown.**

1.

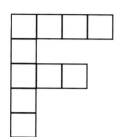

$\frac{2}{5}$ red $\frac{3}{10}$ yellow

2.

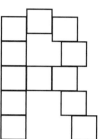

$\frac{1}{6}$ red $\frac{3}{4}$ blue

3.

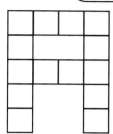

$\frac{1}{7}$ blue $\frac{1}{2}$ green

4.

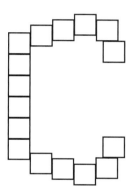

$\frac{3}{4}$ blue $\frac{1}{8}$ green

5.

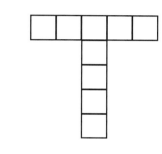

$\frac{2}{3}$ red $\frac{1}{9}$ blue

6.

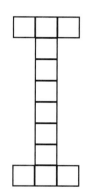

$\frac{1}{12}$ red $\frac{2}{3}$ yellow

7.

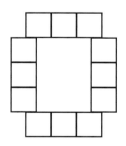

$\frac{1}{12}$ blue $\frac{5}{6}$ green

8.

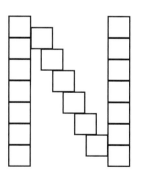

$\frac{3}{4}$ red $\frac{3}{20}$ blue

9.

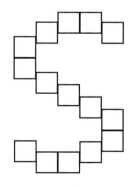

$\frac{3}{5}$ red $\frac{1}{3}$ yellow

NOW TRY THIS!

- **Alongside each letter, write what fraction is uncoloured.**

Teachers' note At the start of the lesson, demonstrate how to count the number of squares in each letter and then divide this number by the denominator (if this is a unit fraction). For the other fractions, multiply by the numerator, for example $\frac{4}{5}$ of 15 can be found by dividing 15 by 5 to find one-fifth (3), and then multiplying by 4 to find four-fifths, giving the answer $3 \times 4 = 12$.

100% New Developing Mathematics
Number Facts and Calculations:
Ages 8–9
© A & C BLACK

59

Sponsored spell

• **Use a calculator to help you answer these questions.**

Work with a partner.

---

1. Ryan is sponsored 17p for each word. He spells 24 words correctly.

How much money does he raise?

---

2. Baljit raises £17.25 and Claire raises £15.35.

How much money do they raise altogether?

---

3. Three children raise exactly the same amount. Together they raise £53.67.

How much money does each child raise?

---

4. Four children raise these amounts:

£14.76   £25.64
£21.17   £9.34

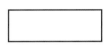

How much less than £100 do they raise altogether?

---

5. Amber raises £19.84. Afterwards, her Dad gives her an extra 87p.

How much money does she raise in total?

---

6. Kieran wants to raise £50. He is sponsored 75p for each word.

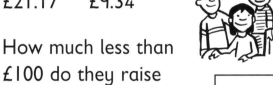

What is the **fewest** number of words he must spell correctly?

---

7. Chloe spells 19 words correctly at £1.13 per word. Jay spells 26 words correctly at 94p per word.

Who raises more money, Chloe or Jay?

---

8. Sam is sponsored 19p for each word. He spells 24 words correctly. He is also given an extra £3.50.

How much money does he raise in total?

Teachers' note Encourage the children to discuss how each question can be solved. Draw attention to the importance of putting two digits after the decimal point for amounts such as 7.2 ⟶ £7.20, and of not mixing up amounts in pounds and in pence. As an extension, ask the children to make up some sponsored spell puzzles of their own for another pair to solve.

100% New Developing Mathematic **Number Facts and Calculations:** **Ages 8–9** © A & C BLACK

Spend, spend, spend!

- **Work with a partner.**
- **Use a calculator to help you answer the questions.**

| Any DVD £17.27 | Memory cards £23.50 | Pack of 4 batteries £5.40 | Any CD £13.85 |

SPECIAL OFFERS

---

1. Abdou bought one DVD, two CDs and four packs of batteries. How much did he spend?

£ _____

2. Leanne bought eight CDs. How much did they cost?

£ _____

---

3. Luca spent £83.10 on CDs. How many did he buy?

£ _____

4. Six of which item costs £103.62?

_____

---

5. How many CDs can Ella buy for £100?

_____

6. How much change from £150 would Dan get if he bought four DVDs and two packs of batteries?

£ _____

---

7. Five CDs cost more than four DVDs. How much more?

£ _____

8. Kayla bought two items. She spent £31.12. What did she buy?

_____

NOW TRY THIS!

- **Make up some more puzzles for another pair to solve.**

Teachers' note Provide children with calculators and encourage them to discuss their strategies for solving the problems. Encourage estimating and checking.

100% New Developing Mathematics
Number Facts and Calculations:
Ages 8–9
© A & C BLACK

Splish! Splash! Splosh!

Jess the dog has shaken water all over Connor's calculations.

- Use a calculator to help you fill in the missing numbers.

1. $358 + 375 =$

2. $57 \div 3 =$

3. $48 \times 9 =$

4. $312 - 253 =$

5. $466 + = 578$

6. $52 \div = 13$

7. $37 \times = 592$

8. $466 - = 375$

9. $ + 46 = 824$

10. $ \div 7 = 32$

11. $ \times 3 = 87$

12. $ - 467 = 238$

NOW TRY THIS!

- Check each answer using the calculator.

Teachers' note Demonstrate how missing numbers can be found using the same operation or its inverse. Point out which number is the largest in each calculation, as this can help the children to decide which operation to use: for addition and multiplication, the answer is the largest; for division and subtraction, the first number in the question is the largest.

100% New Developing Mathemati
Number Facts and Calculations:
Ages 8–9
© A & C BLACK

Answers

p 14
CUBOID

p 15
1. 70° **2.** 40° **3.** 40° **4.** 50° **5.** 70° **6.** 30° **7.** 30°

Now try this!
120°

p 16
Possible answers include:

1200

600	500	100
400		800
200	700	300

1300

100	400	800
700		300
500	600	200

1400

800	500	100
200		600
400	300	700

1500

800	400	300
100		500
600	200	700

Now try this! (in Teacher's note)
Possible answers include:
100, 400, 800, 500, 200, 600, 300, 700
100, 500, 800, 400, 700, 300, 600, 200

p 17
1300   16 000   700   70   200   150   500   2200   240   15 000
80   2600   1800   1700

Now try this!
(a) 2100   **(b)** 1900   **(c)** 220   **(d)** 13 000   **(e)** 7000   **(f)** 1700

p 18
3000 + 9000 + 6000 = 18 000	3000 + 8000 + 6000 = 17 000
4000 + 8000 + 6000 = 18 000	4000 + 8000 + 7000 = 19 000
4000 + 5000 + 7000 = 16 000	3000 + 8000 + 7000 = 18 000

Now try this!
Any three of:
3000   9000   6000   8000   7000 = 33 000
3000   8000   4000   5000   7000 = 27 000
4000   8000   3000   9000   6000 = 30 000
4000   5000   7000   8000   6000 = 30 000

p 20
Now try this!
Each number written in the first grid is 50 less than the corresponding number in the second grid.

p 21
1. £62   **2.** £74   **3.** £79   **4.** £67
5. £89   **6.** £76   **7.** £96   **8.** £94

Now try this!
£128   £152   £176   £184

p 22
Each bug should have a multiple of 1, 10 and 100 beginning with the following digits:
1. 84   **2.** 48   **3.** 72   **4.** 96   **5.** 108   **6.** 124
7. 106   **8.** 78   **9.** 142   **10.** 138   **11.** 174   **12.** 192

p 23
Each bug should have a multiple of 1, 10 and 100 beginning with the following digits:
1. 12   **2.** 18   **3.** 21   **4.** 33   **5.** 42   **6.** 24
7. 36   **8.** 28   **9.** 37   **10.** 43   **11.** 46   **12.** 49

p 25
1. 80   **2.** 40   **3.** 24   **4.** 64   **5.** 80   **6.** 32
7. 48   **8.** 64   **9.** 56   **10.** 88   **11.** 72   **12.** 96

p 27
36	20	21	35	16	48	12	27	63
24	90	24	32	0	42	54	100	24
45	36	56	54	40	25	56	42	15
63	49	64	18	81	28	24	35	36

p 30
Only children beginning in position 4 escape to safety from the crocodiles.

p 31
1. 9   **2.** 7   **3.** 8   **4.** 7   **5.** 8   **6.** 8   **7.** 7   **8.** 9   **9.** 9

Now try this!
(a) 9   **(b)** 7   **(c)** 56   **(d)** 9 × 9   **(e)** 6   **(f)** 8

p 32

p 34
Children should have joined the following fractions with a line:

$\frac{1}{9}$ and $\frac{8}{9}$ $\frac{5}{6}$ and $\frac{1}{6}$

$\frac{1}{5}$ and $\frac{4}{5}$ $\frac{2}{7}$ and $\frac{5}{7}$

$\frac{13}{20}$ and $\frac{7}{20}$ $\frac{9}{20}$ and $\frac{11}{20}$

$\frac{1}{4}$ and $\frac{3}{4}$ $\frac{4}{7}$ and $\frac{3}{7}$

$\frac{7}{10}$ and $\frac{3}{10}$ $\frac{5}{8}$ and $\frac{3}{8}$

$\frac{3}{5}$ and $\frac{2}{5}$ $\frac{4}{11}$ and $\frac{7}{11}$

Now try this!
The following words do not total 1:
DO   IS   IF   PAD   RAT   FOOD   FAST

p 35
1. 80   **2.** 20   **3.** 180   **4.** 140   **5.** 420   **6.** 300

Now try this!
(a) 230   **(b)** 400   **(c)** 10

p 36
Wrong   Wrong   Correct   Correct   Wrong

p 40
(a) 1428   **(b)** 1108   **(c)** 1403   **(d)** 555
(e) 1046   **(f)** 971   **(g)** 428   **(h)** 1650
(i) 1490   **(j)** 451   **(k)** 1400   **(l)** 1505

p 41
(a) 196 + 164 = 360 **(b)** 127 + 253 = 380 **(c)** 157 + 253 = 410
(d) 187 + 253 = 440 **(e)** 196 + 254 = 450 **(f)** 634 + 196 = 830
(g) 653 + 187 = 840 **(h)** 127 + 843 = 970 **(i)** 157 + 843 = 1000
(j) 843 + 187 = 1030 **(k)** 618 + 852 = 1470 **(l)** 958 + 852 = 1810

p 42
```
              1287
         630       657
      298     322     325
```
```
             2197
        1146      1051
     607     539      512
  313     294     245     267
```
Now try this!
1459 should be ringed – the correct answer is 1469.

p 43
(a) 365 **(b)** 753
(c) 586 **(d)** 853
(e) 732 **(f)** 542

p 44

A	B	C	D	E	F	G	H
6	5	3	9	4	2	1	7

p 45
1. 24 cm **2.** 74 cm **3.** 89 cm **4.** 120 cm **5.** 123 cm

p 46
1. 50 mm **2.** 70 mm **3.** 110 mm **4.** 140 mm
5. 190 mm **6.** 230 mm **7.** 270 mm **8.** 310 mm

Now try this!
(a) 600 mm **(b)** 1000 mm **(c)** 1400 mm **(d)** 1700 mm

p 47
× 10		× 100	
23 ➤ 230		67 ➤ 6700	
11 ➤ 110		2 ➤ 200	
70 ➤ 700		58 ➤ 5800	
300 ➤ 3000		34 ➤ 3400	
768 ➤ 7680		84 ➤ 8400	
57 ➤ 570		60 ➤ 6000	

÷ 10		÷ 100	
840 ➤ 84		4100 ➤ 41	
170 ➤ 17		5000 ➤ 50	
400 ➤ 40		600 ➤ 6	
9800 ➤ 980		9700 ➤ 97	
500 ➤ 50			

p 51
1. 48 **2.** 37 **3.** 67 **4.** 75
5. 79 **6.** 69 **7.** 86 **8.** 89

p 52
1. (a) D **(b)** C **(c)** A
2. (a) F **(b)** D **(c)** C
3. (a) D **(b)** C **(c)** B

p 53
64 × 6 = 384 76 × 7 = 532 47 × 3 = 141
58 × 4 = 232 55 × 8 = 440 39 × 9 = 351

p 54
192 warts   252 slugs   144 hairballs
512 maggots   684 eyeballs

Now try this!
1784

p 55
1. 8 r1   14   11 r1   12   16
2. 8   10 r4   5 r2   11 r3   6 r5
3. 7 r2   9 r3   5 r7   6 r4   10 r8
4. 10 r5   5 r2   6 r6   8   11 r7

Now try this!
14 r1   28   22 r1   24   32 r2

p 56
1. 8 **2.** 10 **3.** 9 **4.** 9 **5.** 24 **6.** 18 **7.** 48
8. 18 **9.** 100 **10.** 12 **11.** 12 **12.** 36 **13.** 9 **14.** 21

Now try this!
24p

p 57
1. 5 ml **2.** 3 ml **3.** 18 ml **4.** 6 ml **5.** 8 ml **6.** 6 ml **7.** 10 ml
8. 25 ml **9.** 20 ml **10.** 15 ml **11.** 21 ml **12.** 21 ml **13.** 28 ml

Now try this!
28 ml

p 58
1. 100 ml **2.** 90 ml **3.** 10 ml **4.** 50 ml **5.** 300 ml **6.** 80 ml
7. 40 ml **8.** 100 ml **9.** 100 ml **10.** 150 ml **11.** 90 ml **12.** 140 ml
13. 6 ml **14.** 180 ml

Now try this!
A 112 ml **B** 56 ml **C** 126 ml **D** 42 ml **E** 14 ml

p 59
1. 4 red, 3 yellow **2.** 2 red, 9 blue **3.** 2 blue, 7 green
4. 12 blue, 2 green **5.** 6 red, 1 blue **6.** 1 red, 8 yellow
7. 1 blue, 10 green **8.** 15 red, 3 blue **9.** 9 red, 5 yellow

Now try this!
1. $\frac{3}{10}$ **2.** $\frac{1}{12}$ **3.** $\frac{5}{14}$
4. $\frac{1}{8}$ or equivalent fraction **5.** $\frac{2}{9}$
6. $\frac{3}{4}$ or equivalent fraction **7.** $\frac{1}{12}$
8. $\frac{1}{10}$ or equivalent fraction **9.** $\frac{1}{15}$

p 60
1. £4.08 **2.** £32.60 **3.** £17.89 **4.** £29.09
5. £20.71 **6.** 67 **7.** Jay **8.** £8.06

p 61
1. £66.57 **2.** £110.80 **3.** 6 **4.** DVD
5. 7 **6.** £70.12 **7.** £0.17 **8.** a DVD and a CD

p 62
1. 733 **2.** 19 **3.** 432 **4.** 59 **5.** 112 **6.** 4
7. 16 **8.** 91 **9.** 778 **10.** 224 **11.** 29 **12.** 705

LEAVING CERTIFICATE

HISTORY AND APPRECIATION OF

ART

Tara Fahey
Siobhán Geoghegan-Treacy

FOLENS

Editor: Susan McKeever

Design and layout: Liz White Designs

Copyright and picture research: Priscilla O'Connor, Liz White

Illustrations: William Donohoe

© 2011 Tara Fahey; Siobhán Geoghegan-Treacy

ISBN: 978-1-84741-100-6

Folens Publishers,
Hibernian Industrial Estate,
Greenhills Road,
Tallaght,
Dublin 24

Acknowledgements

I would sincerely like to thank my wonderful husband Declan – the best husband in the world, my beautiful children Robert and Isabella, my mother, father, brother Pat and sisters Maura, Catríona and most especially Mairéad and Therese. Aunty Cissy, Mairead, Sister Phil and uncle Sean. My mother-in-law Mabel, sister-in-law Tina and brother-in-law Damien and all the great team at Folens especially Susan McKeever, Liz White, Ciara McNee and Margaret Burns, my friend and co-author Tara and all my family, friends and colleagues at St Brigid's V.E.C. Loughrea, Co. Galway and Marian College, Ballsbridge Dublin 4. Thanks also to John O'Connor, who asked me to write this book.

Siobhán Geoghegan-Treacy

I would like to say a big thank you to everyone at Folens for their hard work and dedication and to Siobhan for a fun working partnership. Heartfelt thanks also to my wonderful family, John, Gretta, Tracy, Wayne and sister-in-law Suzanne for their encouragement and support. I thank my fantastic friends and colleagues in Marian College and also the students who unknowingly provided a lot of inspiration!

Tara Fahey

Contents

Introduction

Leaving Certificate History and Appreciation of Art provides students and teachers with a clearly written and richly illustrated guide to the Leaving Certificate History of Art course. The History and Appreciation of Art syllabus is divided into six units. All aspects of the syllabus required for are covered in detail to provide both the teacher and the student with all the resources they will need within one book.

Unit 1: Early Irish Art

Unit 2: Romanesque and Gothic Art and Architecture

Unit 3: European Art during the Renaissance c. 1400–c. 1520

Unit 4: The Age of Revolution: French Painting 1780–1880

Unit 5: Modernism

Unit 6: Art Appreciation

This book aims to facilitate both Higher and Ordinary Level students in senior cycle.

The language in the text is clear and appropriate for mixed-ability classes, while the information is presented in an accessible and learner-friendly way.

- ❧ **Dictionary** boxes are used to explain difficult words or art terms.

- ❧ **Biography** boxes give further information on significant or influential people of the time.

- ❧ **Did you know?** boxes develop the students' understanding of the historical and political backgrounds of the artists featured. This extra information is necessary to Higher Level students, as they need to be able to demonstrate their knowledge of the cultural and historical factors involved in art in their essay-style answers.

The styles, techniques and lives of the artists and architects featured are examined and explained clearly to give the reader an insight into the role they played in society and the inspiration for their work. This will also help students relate to art history in a personal way, and they can use the skills and techniques they learn to enhance their own work.

High-quality **colour photographs** are used throughout to represent fully every example of artwork and architecture discussed in the text. Full-page photographs are dedicated to the larger, more complicated or significant works, giving students a better insight into their context, scale and impact. To illustrate further more complex works, **detailed diagrams** are provided.

At the end of each section within each chapter, a selection of **essay-style revision questions** tests the students' knowledge of every aspect of the information they have learned as well as their analytical skills.

unit 1

Early Irish Art

Introduction

The first examples of Irish art date back to 4000 B.C., when people carved abstract decorations into stone in passage graves. From this point on, arts and crafts developed and flourished, and the craftsmen's techniques became more complex and intricate. This can be seen in the objects from the Bronze Age. Outside influences from Europe also added to the knowledge and craftsmanship of the Irish metal and stoneworker, particularly the Celtic influence during the Iron Age. With the arrival of Christianity came what is now known as Ireland's 'Golden Age.' During this age, artists created elaborate metalwork such as the Tara Brooch (see pp. 28–31), exquisitely illuminated manuscripts such as the Book of Kells (see pp. 37–43) and masterful stonework such as the high crosses (see pp. 44–51).

Abstract Art in Prehistory

During the Stone Age patterns and designs incised into stone were geometric and abstract in form, consisting of basic shapes such as triangles, circles and diamonds. We do not know what these designs symbolised, but it is almost certain that they served some ceremonial purpose.

The Stone Age

The Stone Age is so-called because during this time stone was the most valuable material to people. They used it to make tools for cutting and digging and weapons for hunting.

People first came to Ireland around 7000 B.C., during the Middle Stone Age. The first people living in Ireland were nomadic, which means that they did not settle in one place. They travelled around hunting animals and gathering wild food. Later, in the New Stone Age period, people became more settled. They began to farm and cultivate the land for food, and to build permanent dwellings in which to live, and graves in which to bury their dead. Some of these structures still remain in the form of the passage graves.

> ### Did you know?
> The Stone Age is divided into three periods. The Paleolithic (Old Stone Age) lasted from c. 1.8 million years ago to 10000 B.C.; the Mesolithic (Middle Stone Age) from c. 10000 B.C. to 4000 B.C.; and the Neolithic (New Stone Age) from c. 4000 to 2400 B.C. Paleo comes from the Greek *Palaios* which means 'old;' lithic comes from the Greek *lithos*, meaning stone. *Meso* means 'middle' and *neos* means 'new.'

Stone-Age Burial Tombs

The people of the Stone Age built three types of tombs for their dead:

- Dolmens (three large standing stones supporting a large, flat rock).
- Court cairns (a mound, with an oval-shaped entrance courtyard framed by stones).
- Passage graves (a mound with a long underground passage and circular burial chamber).

Passage graves were the largest of the burial tombs and were probably used as a resting place for important members of the community.

The graves may also have had a ceremonial function – carved bowls which were possibly used for rituals have been found near some of the graves. Three significant passage graves can be seen in the Boyne area in Co. Meath:

1 Newgrange
2 Dowth
3 Knowth

▶ *Poulnabrone dolmen, The Burren, Co. Clare*

Stone Carving

This is the earliest form of art in Ireland still in evidence today. The designs in stone visible in the passage graves of Newgrange and Knowth are abstract and geometric in design, the symbols and patterns possibly serving a magical purpose in Stone-Age civilisations. They were also probably used simply to decorate and ornament important structures. The designs which occur most commonly include spiral and concentric circles, chevrons, lozenge shapes, triangles, as well as shield motifs.

Techniques

It is believed that Stone-Age people carved decoration on tombs, kerbstones and stone pillars using claw-edged chisels made of quartz or flint. They used an incised line, cut into the stone as a guideline for the designs, or to create designs in their own right. A number of techniques were used to pattern these stones:

- **Plain picking:** This was the most common method of ornamentation. It involved picking out narrow, broad or medium sized grooves in the surface of the rock. If the line was quite wide, the edges would then be sanded down to create a smooth texture.
- **False relief:** This technique consisted of chiselling away the areas which surrounded the design to leave it standing out in 'relief' from the stone.
- **Pick dressing:** The glacial patina (a fine layer formed by ice) was removed from stones to leave them smooth.

STONE-AGE DESIGN

There were distinctive symbols and patterns which repeatedly appeared in the stone carving of Stone-Age monuments and tombs. Astronomers and archaeologists have studied these for centuries and formed theories about the meanings of these symbols. Some of them are outlined below, but it is important to remember that these are simply interpretations and are not known to be an exact explanation.

Dots: These are the simplest of designs, consisting of a single indentation. A dot is often interpreted as a star.

Crossed lines: This shows two lines intersecting at right angles. They are thought to symbolise the directions of the sun: east, west, north and south.

Circles: These were very popular designs during the Stone Age. It is thought that circles could signify either stars or days.

Concentric circles: These feature circles within circles. There is a theory that these could represent a number of days; for example three circles would mean three days.

Lozenge: This is a four-sided diamond shape. Lozenges are considered to mean a day and a night.

Concentric lozenges: Diamond shapes fitting within each other are interpreted as a number of days and nights.

Triangle: This three-sided shape usually forms a pattern and could be used to represent one item.

Arc: A semicircular curved line is considered to represent half a day.

Concentric arcs: A series of arcs fitting within each other, these could symbolise a series of half days.

Chevrons: These zig-zag lines are thought to symbolise a series of events or items.

Single spiral: This is the simplest spiral design, consisting of a line curved inwards to form a spiral. The shape is thought to symbolise the sun.

Double spiral: In this symbol, both ends of the line are curved into two spiral shapes. These could represent the spring and autumn equinoxes, when day and night are of equal length.

Triskele: This symbol is made up of three spirals thought to symbolise the land, the sea and the sky.

Oval: This rounded oblong shape is often thought to represent a constellation of stars.

Concentric ovals: Oblong shapes fitting within each other are considered to represent a number of star constellations.

NEWGRANGE

The passage grave at Newgrange is situated beside the River Boyne in Co. Meath and was built around 3300–2900 B.C. The construction of the tomb is very complicated and would have been the creation of a large workforce and required sophisticated knowledge both of structural techniques and astronomy. Over the burial chamber a roof box is situated precisely to allow the light of the sun to enter the room on the winter solstice (21 December). This tells us that the builders of the tomb were considerably advanced to align the roof of the grave with the horizon of the dawn on this particular day. It also points to the significance of the sun in the rituals of these people.

▼ *Newgrange, Co. Meath*

Materials

The passage grave is not simply made up of local stones. The granite was mined in the Mourne Mountains in Co. Down and it is thought that the quartz was transported from a mine in the Wicklow Mountains.

Structure

- **The mound:** This measures 85 m in diameter, and is 6 m high in the centre.
- **The kerbstones:** Surrounding the outer surface of the passage grave are 97 kerbstones (horizontally positioned oblong stones), some of which are decorated.
- **Quartz stone:** The wall above the kerbstones is made of white quartz.
- **Standing stones:** A ring of large standing stones circles the tomb from a distance of 15 m. There are only 12 stones at present, but it is believed that there were originally 35 in total.
- **The passage:** This is 19 m long. Along each side of the narrow passage is a row of standing stones, 22 on the left and 21 on the right.
- **The burial chamber:** The chamber is 5 m long and has three burial alcoves. In each part of the chamber are basin stones which were possibly used to hold the ashes of the dead.

Entrance Stone

The entrance stone at Newgrange is the most beautiful and complex example of Stone-Age abstract design in stone carving.

- The entrance stone is a long, oblong-shaped boulder which is 1.3 m high and 3.2 m long.
- The stone itself is green gritstone, which is a type of rock deposited by **glaciation**.

dic·tion·ar·y

Glaciation is the term used for the formation of large ice sheets during an era of extreme cold climate and also refers to their movement and recession through time.

- The sculptors of the entrance stone used the entire surface of the boulder to create a spectacular flowing design. With great skill, they worked the irregularities in the stone into the patterns to achieve this effect.

- The strongly marked patterns are created in a large scale, the largest spiral being 60 cm wide. After the design was completed the entire surface was pick dressed to expose the colour of the stone.

- Most of the design on the front of the entrance stone consists of spiral shapes, divided by a vertical line running down the centre.

- On the left of the line are three spiral shapes rotating clockwise and anticlockwise. To the left of these are three double-banded lozenges surrounded by wavy arcs.

- To the right of the central line are two clockwise spiral shapes, with a double-banded lozenge placed beside them. Above the two spirals are rows of concentric arcs, which are repeated below.

Lintel Stone

The lintel stone (a horizontal stone placed over an opening) over the door is also decorated, this time carved with more geometrical designs. Two incised rows of chevrons ornament the top with a row of lozenge shapes underneath. These were created by picking away the surface of the stone surrounding the shapes, known as a false-relief technique.

Roof Stone

The roof stone in the right recess in Newgrange shows a number of designs mostly spiral in shape, with concentric circles, chevrons and lozenges.

Did you know?

Newgrange is older than even the Great Pyramid at Giza, Egypt.

Standing Stone

Inside the main chamber, a three-pronged spiral is engraved into a large standing stone.

▲ Newgrange entrance stone

▲ Roof box and lintel stone at Newgrange

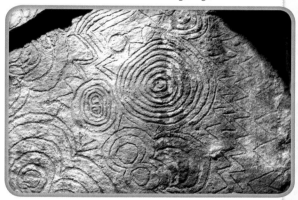

▲ Roof stone at Newgrange

▼ Standing stone at Newgrange

KNOWTH AND DOWTH

The passage graves at Knowth and Dowth are built in a similar style to Newgrange and served the same purpose. However, their construction differs in one major way: both of these tombs have two passages, running from entrances on opposite sides of the mounds.

- In Knowth the western passage measures 34 m in length and the eastern passage is 40 m long. It ends in a **cruciform** chamber similar to that at Newgrange.

- The mound in Dowth is approximately the same size as Knowth but has shorter passages and lower roofs.

- The northern passage at Dowth is 14 m long, ending in a cruciform chamber with a 3 m-high corbelled roof. Corbelling involves protruding pieces of stone to support weight.

- The southern passage at Dowth is 3.5 m long, ending in a single chamber with one recess.

> **dic·tion·ar·y**
>
> **Cruciform** means shaped like a cross.

- There are many different Stone-Age symbols and designs to be found ornamenting the passage graves, including spirals, chevrons, arcs and **rectilinear** patterns.

- Opposite the entrance to the burial chamber in Dowth south are two large orthostats (large standing stones). One of these is particularly interesting as the design incised into the rock consists of flowing lines and shapes, possibly representing a pagan god.

- Another stone of interest is the large stone in the left of the chamber, which has a large incised pattern running over its surface. The stone is almost fully pick-dressed to give it an added texture and pattern.

WHO WERE THE TOMBS FOR?

What kind of people were Newgrange, and its satellite tombs, Knowth and Dowth, built for? Over the years theories have evolved from Irish mythology and folklore about their possible function in history. Some state that these were the burial tombs of the High Kings of Tara; others propose that they were the dwelling places of the Tuatha de Danann – a race of kings who, according to legend, were descended from gods (see p. 74).

> **dic·tion·ar·y**
>
> A **rectilinear** pattern is formed with straight lines placed at right angles.

◀ Stone carvings, Knowth, Co. Meath

Abstract Art in Prehistory Revision Questions

1 Give an account of stone carving in Stone-Age Ireland by discussing the techniques, symbols and designs used.

2 Describe the entrance stone at Newgrange in terms of its size, its decoration and the techniques used to create it.

3 Give a detailed description of the stone-carved decoration found at Newgrange and Knowth.

The Bronze Age

The Bronze Age is a term applied to the time when people began to mix copper and tin to make bronze. Copper had been in use before, but mixing it with tin made it much stronger and therefore more useful and durable. In Ireland, the Bronze Age happened between about 1800 and 500 B.C.

Before this, there was a lot of movement of people throughout Europe. Groups of people arrived in Ireland, bringing with them new cultures, skills and customs. It is thought that these people belonged to four distinct groups which can be worked out by their burial customs.

> **Did you know?**
> The **Early Bronze Age** lasted from c. 1800 B.C. to 1500 B.C.;
> the **Middle Bronze Age** lasted from 1500 B.C. to 1200 B.C.;
> the **Late Bronze Age** lasted from 1200 B.C. to 500 B.C.

- **The Beaker People** were the most dominant of these groups. They came from eastern Europe and settled in two locations in Ireland: the Boyne area in Co. Meath, and along the west coasts of Cork, Clare and Galway. They buried their dead in wedge-shaped tombs, and introduced the bronze axe to Irish culture. They were named after the drinking vessels resembling beakers found in their burial sites.

- **The Food Vessel People** were related to the Beaker culture. Their burial customs involved single graves and cremation (burning their dead). Ceramic food vessels were placed beside their bodies in their graves.

- **The Bowl Food Vessel People** buried the bodies of their dead in a crouched position with a clay bowl beside them.

- **The Urn People** were the latest people to arrive in Ireland during the Early Bronze Age. They were skilled metalworkers and leatherworkers and buried the cremated remains of their dead under upturned clay bowls (like upside-down urns).

These peoples' knowledge of metal brought about huge changes in Ireland. A vast amount of metal tools, weapons and ornaments were created during this era, using new casting techniques, which involved pouring molten metal into shaped moulds made of stone or sand.

Materials and Mining

The immigrant peoples found a plentiful supply of mineral ore with which to work in many Irish locations.

> dic·tion·ar·y
>
> **Mineral ore** means a rock deposit containing valuable minerals.

◀ *Disused lead mines at Glendalough, Co. Wicklow*

Copper

Found at:
- Avoca, Co. Wicklow
- Ballycummisk, Co. Cork
- Mount Gabriel, Co. Cork
- River Roughty, Co. Kerry

Zinc

Found at:
- Glendalough, Co. Wicklow

Lead

Found at:
- River Roughty, Co. Kerry
- Clonmines, Co. Wexford
- Glendalough, Co. Wicklow

Silver

Found at:
- Clonmines, Co. Wexford

Gold

Found at:
- Co. Wicklow

Extracting Ore from Rock

Bronze-Age miners used a series of steps to retrieve the mineral ore from the rock.

1 They lit a fire to expand the substance of the rock.

2 They then threw cold water over the rock. The quick cooling of the rock caused it to shatter.

3 Stone implements were employed to break down the pieces of rock further.

4 The small fragments of rock and mineral ore were then **smelted** down to free the metal.

The most valuable of the objects created were ornaments, which became increasingly more ornate and beautiful as the Bronze Age civilisations progressed in expertise.

dic·tion·ar·y

To **smelt** is to melt mineral ore over heat to extract pure metal, such as gold, iron, or lead, from the rock.

Lunulae

The lunula is the piece of jewellery most commonly associated with the Irish Bronze Age. The name 'lunula' comes from the word 'lunar', which relates to the moon. These necklaces are so-called because they look like a crescent moon. More than 80 lunulae have been found in Ireland. They can be divided into three different types: classical, unaccomplished and provincial.

1 **Classical** lunulae were the most symmetrically decorated and expertly crafted.

2 **Unaccomplished** lunulae show a lesser degree in expertise and are usually thinner, using less gold than the classical style.

3 **Provincial** lunulae are thicker than the other two styles and have more variety in incised decoration.

GOLD LUNULA		
Date	Early Bronze Age, c. 2000 B.C.	
Found	Rossmore Park, Drumbanagher, Co. Monaghan	
Form	Thin, crescent-shaped sheet of gold, slightly thicker at the edges.	
Function	The lunula would have been worn as a necklace on special occasions and was a symbol of the wearer's rank and authority.	

◆ A sheet of gold was hammered flat and then cut into the crescent moon shape. The terminals (ends) of the lunula were twisted. The decoration on these necklaces was usually applied by incision, engraving the details with a fine pointed stylus (pen-like object).

◆ The decoration on the lunula is geometric in design, and is confined mostly to the edges and the terminals.

- The terminals are divided into panels of decoration by double rows of lines with small incised triangular ornaments within them. Large cross-hatched triangles surround these bands.
- Parallel lines run along the interior and exterior edges of the lunula, with a pattern of small triangles etched around them.

Dress Fasteners

The dress fastener, also known as a fibula, originated in northern Europe and was developed in Ireland during the Bronze Age. It was used as a double button which could be inserted into slits in a cloak to hold the edges together.

GOLD DRESS FASTENER	
Date	Late Bronze Age, 900–700 B.C.
Found	Clones, Co. Monaghan in 1820
Form	The handle of the dress fastener is attached to the terminals, which are conical in shape. They are often large and heavy, weighing up to 1,300 grams.
Function	These dress fasteners are thought to be based on a Scandinavian design. The terminals are thought to have been inserted by the wearer into large buttonholes on a cloak or robe. They would have been a sign of power and wealth.

- The terminals and the handle of the dress fastener are hollow. They were fashioned from hammered sheets of gold, and soldered (fused using molten metal) together. The decoration was applied by incision and *repoussé* methods.

- The edges of the terminals are decorated with raised rows of lines, hammered out from the back. The *repoussé* technique can also be seen in the incised concentric circle patterns where a raised bump forms the centre of the circles.

- More incised decoration is situated at the join of the terminals and the unadorned handle. This consists of rows of parallel lines with a border of hatched zigzags.

▲ *Gold dress fastener*

dic·tion·ar·y

Repoussé means the design on the metal is hammered or punched out from the reverse side.

Torcs

Torcs are necklaces formed by twisting lengths of gold. This twisting technique was also used to create bracelets and earrings.

TWO GOLD TORCS	
Date	Middle Bronze Age, c. 1200
Found	Rath of the Synods, Tara, Co. Meath in 1810
Function	Bronze-Age people wore Torcs around the neck as a form of ceremonial decoration.

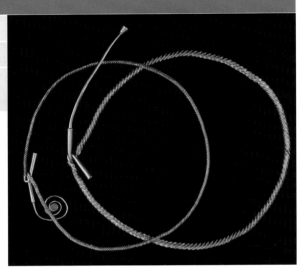

▲ *Two gold torcs*

- These torcs were created by evenly twisting a square bar of gold. Before the bars were twisted they were beaten by a hammer to produce raised edges.
- Apart from the expertly twisted gold, the terminals of the torcs are extended to form clasps. One of these takes the form of a spiral.

Gorgets

The gorget, also known as a collar, is a crescent-shaped necklace with a decorated disc on each end. It is an original Irish invention and dates back to the eighth century B.C.

GLENISHEEN GOLD GORGET	
Date	Late Bronze Age, 800–700 B.C.
Found	Gleninsheen, Co. Clare in 1932
Form	The gold gorget is constructed from five parts; the crescent shape in the middle attached to two double discs at each end. The ends of the crescent are pushed through a slot in the lower disc and stitched together. A slightly larger disc was then placed over the lower disc and the edges are curled over to cover it.
Function	The gold collars are thought to have been worn as a symbol of high rank on ceremonial occasions. They would originally have been fastened around the neck by a cord which was linked to the ends of the collar.

- The Gleninsheen gorget is an outstanding example of early Irish craftsmanship, bringing together many decorative motifs typical of the Bronze-Age era. These include concentric circles, rope patterns, and raised bosses (knobs), both round and conical.
- There are 11 concentric circles placed around the main large concentric circles on the discs.

- Six moulded rope patterns decorate the collar itself.
- In the centre of the two discs are conical bosses.
- Round bosses can be seen around the edges of the discs and the collar. A smaller pattern of round bosses encircle the central concentric circles in the discs.

Decorative Techniques

- A number of techniques were used to create the decoration of the gorget, including *repoussé* and incision.
- Some of the decoration was applied to the gorget by hammering the designs out from the reverse side of the sheet of gold; such as the rope moulding found on the crescent of the collar, and the raised bosses on the discs. This is the *repoussé* technique.
- The concentric circles found on the discs were created by etching into the gold with a fine sharp tool. This is the incision technique.

▲ *Glenisheen gold gorget*

Lock Rings

Lock rings were created during the Late Bronze Age and were designed to hold and secure hair. It is thought that these were an Irish invention as most of these artefacts were discovered in Ireland.

GORTEENREAGH GOLD LOCK RINGS	
Date	Late Bronze Age, 800–700 B.C.
Found	In a field at Gorteenreagh, Co. Clare in 1948
Function	These ornaments are thought to be hair decorations. The wearer would slide a lock of hair into the circular opening in the middle via the slot. The hair was then held in place by the bosses protruding from the tube running through the centre.

- The Gorteenreagh lock rings were discovered along with a hoard of other artefacts, including a gold collar and two gold bracelets. The lock rings are considered to be the largest and finest of their type in Ireland.

- A lock ring is made up of two conical shapes, bound together by a band of gold. A tube runs through the middle of the cones.

- The lock rings, when viewed at close range, are spectacularly decorated. Fine gold wire, tightly bound and soldered into position, adorns the exterior of the rings.

The Bronze Age Revision Questions

1   Describe the origins of metalworking in the Bronze Age, with reference to the people involved, the sources of the metal and the quarrying methods used.

2   Give an account of three gold objects created in Ireland during the Bronze Age under the headings: a) form, b) function, c) decoration, d) techniques used.

The Iron Age

Iron began to replace bronze as the principal metal used in the production of tools and weapons in Ireland during what is now known as the Iron Age. These techniques originated with the Celts between 1000 B.C. and 700 B.C. in the Middle East and spread across Europe and Britain during the sixth and seventh centuries B.C. The spread of the Celts' culture throughout Europe was largely due to their skill in ironworking, as iron was a stronger and more hard-wearing metal than bronze. Ironworking in Ireland is thought to have begun around 350 B.C.

NOTE: Understanding and discussing Iron-Age artefacts from Ireland can be complicated. Unlike Bronze-Age artefacts, which can simply be referred to as belonging to the Early, Middle or Late Bronze Age, many terms are used to describe and date Iron-Age objects. To simplify, all of the objects of this period can be called Iron-Age artefacts; they may also be called Celtic as the techniques and decoration originated with the Celts. This Celtic style is also known as the *La Tène* style and the Irish *La Tène* style is called the *Waldalgesheim* style. So, any of the following terms can be used to describe artefacts of this era:

- Iron Age
- Celtic
- *La Tène*
- *Waldalgesheim*

Iron-Age Structures

Before we discuss the types of artefacts produced during the Iron Age, it is worth setting the scene with some information on the structures that were in place at the same time. The most common form of buildings were forts. The term 'fort' generally indicates some sort of defensive structure but it is thought that this was not necessarily the reason for the existence of these buildings. There were three types of fort created during the Iron Age:

- ring forts
- hill forts
- promontory forts.

Ring Forts

These forts consist of a bank made of earth surrounding a circular space. In Ireland they are often known by other names such as rath, dun, or cathair. In the east of Ireland the banks were chiefly made of earth, whereas in the west where stone was more plentiful, stone walls were used to circle the fort. A ring fort was a communal dwelling place, housing a number of small **wattle and daub** huts.

dic·tion·ar·y

Wattle and daub is a building material used for making walls. It involves wattles (interwoven branches or sticks) being covered with daub (a mixture of clays, mud, dung, and straw), and left to harden.

The domestic animals that were free to roam outside the fort during the day would have been brought inside the banks at night. It is likely that the walls or banks of the fort were used to defend the people and animals from wolves and wild animals rather than invaders.

Hill Forts

Hill forts are less plentiful in Ireland and, as the name suggests, are found on top of hills. The banks of these forts include the entire summit of the hill and are generally much larger than the ring forts in construction. The functions of these forts are unclear to this day. In some cases cairns (see p. 2) are found inside the walls of these forts, leading some scholars to believe that they were used to hold pagan ceremonies.

Promontory Forts

Promontory forts are found in two locations – on the edges of cliffs and high on a spur of a mountain. The cliff-top forts were often built on a narrow peninsula, ensuring that walls were only needed to defend against invaders from land.

Dun Aengus

Dun Aengus is an example of a promontory fort. It towers 100 m above sea level on the Atlantic coast on Inishmore Island, Co. Galway. It is thought that it housed a settlement spanning over 1,000 years so many alterations would have taken place during this time.

- Dun Aengus is made up of three concentric stone walls surrounding the edge of the cliff.
- The innermost wall is the highest, standing at 6 m tall and 4 m thick. This wall surrounds the area, approximately 100 m by 130 m, known as the citadel, which is higher than the surrounding land. This is where people lived in huts made from wattle and daub.
- The stone buttresses supporting the inner wall are thought to have been added during the nineteenth century to preserve the structure.
- The second wall probably enclosed livestock and the places where craftsmen worked. The discovery of bronze artefacts and weapons has led scholars to believe that some forms of metallurgy were practised on the site. There is no natural access to water, so the inhabitants of the settlement may have collected rainwater to use and drink.
- The third and longest wall is thought to have been added at a later date than the other two. As the settlement grew, more space was needed to allow the domestic animals to roam more freely.
- Outside the fort walls thousands of large jagged pieces of limestone, known as ***chevaux-de-frise***, rise from the ground as a further defence against attackers.

dic·tion·ar·y

Chevaux-de-frise is a French term meaning Frisian horses. It dates back to the Frisian tribe from northwest Europe, who defended their land using pointed obstacles to protect themselves against the onslaught of cavalry.

◀ *Aerial view of Dun Aengus, Inishmore, Co. Galway*

Celtic Art

For hundreds of years, a warlike, artistic people called the Celts dominated northwestern Europe. They were originally concentrated around the Rhineland area bordering on France. This was an area of great wealth and importance in Europe at the time. The term *La Tène* describes the style of ornament and culture of the Celts, and comes from a place called La Tène, beside Lake Neuchatel in Switzerland, where a large collection of treasures was discovered.

The Spread of Celtic Culture

The Celtic people were influenced by classical Greek and eastern art forms and derived many of their symbols from these cultures. Celtic art grew and developed, culminating in the *Waldalgesheim* style, the form which was brought to Ireland.

dic·tion·ar·y

Waldalgesheim style

The Early Iron-Age style (c. 480–350 B.C.) began in Europe, particularly in areas of Germany and France, and was believed to have been influenced by ancient Greek and eastern designs. The *Waldalgesheim* style, named after an area in Germany where a hoard of artefacts was discovered, began c. 350 B.C. The style used classical motifs such as the acanthus leaf and the honeysuckle (left) combined with animal and human forms in a free-flowing linear style. Although this style died out in Europe around 290 B.C., it continued to grow and develop in Ireland until c. 150 B.C.

The Celts in Ireland

It is not exactly certain when the Celts arrived in Ireland, but the earliest Iron-Age artefacts found date between 350 and 150 B.C. These were two gold collars discovered in Ardnaglug, Co. Roscommon. It is thought that the Celts settled in the northern part of the country as most of the Iron-Age ritual sites and promontory forts are found there. The *Waldalgesheim* style, brought to Ireland by the Celts, dominated Irish decoration and continued to flourish and develop after it vanished from Europe.

Characteristics of the *La Tène* Style

The *La Tène* style is very different from the previous art styles which were popular in Ireland. Instead of geometric shapes and designs, the Celtic style was much more organic and free-flowing, characterised by foliage and vegetable motifs and symbols which originated from classical eastern and Greek cultures. Highly decorative patterns emerged in the form of **curvilinear** shapes

dic·tion·ar·y

Curvilinear means to be created from, and to be characterised by, curved lines.

portraying tendrils, honeysuckle, lotus flowers, leaves and palms, combined with lyres, (classical stringed instruments) trumpet shapes, scrolls and stylised human, animal or bird heads. Celts used iron for functional objects and weaponry; bronze for ornamental objects and gold for particularly important or significant jewellery or objects.

BROIGHTER HOARD

Date	Early Iron Age, 100–200 B.C.	Found	Beside Lough Foyle, Broighter, Co. Derry. They were discovered at the end of the nineteenth century by a farmer ploughing a field. Important finds of Iron-Age artefacts are often around the shores of lakes as it was a Celtic custom to throw objects such as weapons, jewellery or decorative items into a lake as an offering.

▼ *Broighter Hoard, National Museum – Decorative Arts and History, Dublin*

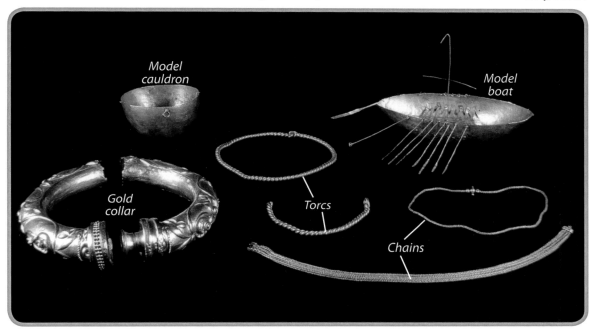

The Broighter Hoard is the most important discovery dating from the Iron Age. It consists of two gold chains, two gold twisted torcs, a decorated gold collar, a gold miniature boat, and a golden bowl.

Broighter Collar

The collar is constructed from two sheets of gold curved to form a convex tube and soldered together. The terminals of the collar have fastening devices known as a mortice and a tenon. The collar would have been worn only on very important ceremonial occasions.

- Intricate, curvilinear, raised patterns of the lotus-bud motif adorn the convex gold ring of the collar. In between these decorations, the surface of the ring itself is filled with criss-crossing concentric circles, continuing the organic, free-flowing style of ornament.

- Between each end of the tube and the terminals is a raised single row of bosses and further raised decoration in the form of trumpets and lentoid (lens-shaped) and circular bosses.

- On the terminals themselves recesses were created to allow a triple row of gold bosses to be inserted. One of these is missing from one of the terminals. On the face of the tenon terminal a raised circular sunburst ornament is featured, surrounding the locking device.

- The raised decoration on the gold tube was created by a technique called 'chasing'. This involved placing the gold sheet over a moulded surface and beating it into shape. This was a more sophisticated and exact way of producing relief decoration than the earlier *repoussé* method. The gold sheets were then heated to form the tube and soldered. The concentric circles were applied by incision using a compass for greater precision.

Gold Model Boat

The boat is based on a typical Celtic wooden sea ship. It features miniature versions of oars, steering oar, rowlocks, mast and seats. The model boat was most likely created as a ceremonial offering to the sea-god Manannán Mac Lir.

- The form of the boat was produced by curving and soldering beaten sheets of gold. The seats were made out of strips of gold, riveted (securely fastened) to the sides of the ship.
- Holes punctured on the upper rim of the boat allow gold wire loops to run through them, holding the oars in place.

Gold Model Cauldron

This small bowl is made from sheets of beaten gold and is shaped in the form of a hanging cauldron.

- Two rings were originally positioned at opposite ends of the bowl to allow the cauldron to be suspended.
- The Broighter cauldron was used as a ritual or ceremonial offering. Large Iron-Age bronze or iron cauldrons were most commonly used for feeding large groups of people on ritual occasions. It could also suggest the idea of a magic cauldron, which was a common idea in European culture and mythology.

Gold Chains

These two necklaces are made by a technique known as loop-in-loop, one consisting of three single-strand loops, and the other of a more complicated multi-loop design. The origin of this technique lies in the Middle East which then spread to Mediterranean cultures. The clasps of the necklaces derive from classical artefacts. These have a decorative function as necklaces, although their presence along with the other items in the hoard suggest they also have a ritual significance.

Gold Torcs

These are twisted bar torcs, similar to those dating to the Bronze Age, but with developments influenced by European styles. There is twisted wire running along the grooves of the torcs and the terminals of the necklaces are fashioned using the hook-in-loop style. This involves a hook twisted on one end, fashioned to fit through a loop on the other to secure the necklace. Twisted-bar torcs were used as ceremonial necklaces.

THE TUROE STONE	
Date	Early Iron Age, c. 50 B.C.
Found	Turoe, Co. Galway
Function	The function of the Turoe Stone, known as a standing stone, is unclear, but it is thought to be a ceremonial site.

This stone is one of many pillar standing stones found in Ireland, dating from this period. It is a huge, heavy granite stone, which suggests that it is native to the area as it would have been extremely difficult to transport.

▼ *The Turoe Stone, Co. Galway*

▼ *Diagram of designs on the Turoe Stone*

- To produce the standing stone, the stone was smoothed first, and then the decoration was applied by carving into the granite. Metal hammers and chisels would have been used to recreate patterns found in metalwork of the era. The background was cut out to expose the patterns and shapes in low relief.

- There are four distinct sides to the Turoe Stone in terms of decoration. Organic tendril shapes mingled with trumpet curves ornament most of the surface. A triskele (three connected curvilinear trumpet shapes) is found on one side. Along the base of the decoration runs a step pattern deriving from the Celtic interest in Greek classicism.

PETRIE CROWN

Date	Early Iron Age, 200–300 B.C.
Found	Unrecorded
Function	The bronze Petrie Crown is generally thought to be an ornate horned headdress, worn for ceremonial occasions, such as fertility and **renewal rituals**.

dic·tion·ar·y

Renewal rituals took place before spring to ensure the successful growth of crops and entailed offerings of grain and even animal sacrifice.

The Petrie Crown, which did not survive intact, was named after the nineteenth-century collector George Petrie who owned it for a number of years.

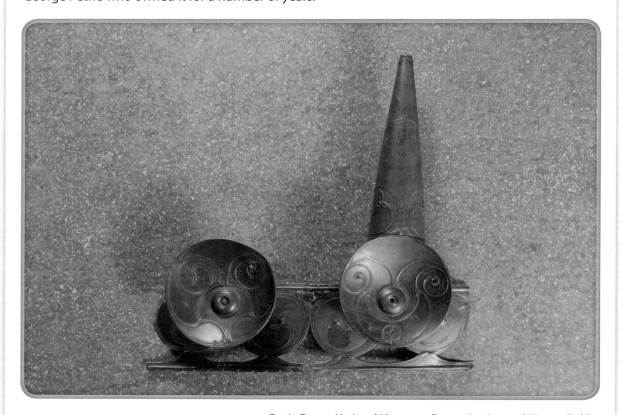

▲ *Petrie Crown, National Museum – Decorative Arts and History, Dublin*

- The surviving sections of the crown consist of two dish-shaped discs (also known as roundels) attached to a band, with a cone rising from behind one of the discs.

- The horn was created by folding a sheet of bronze into the shape of a cone, and then attaching the edges with rivets to a sheet of copper placed underneath.

- It is thought that there was originally another conical shape attached to the second roundel, and that the bronze components were stitched to either a leather or cloth base. This is suggested by the tiny holes cut into the band.

- There is 'wheel-in-circle' decoration to be seen on the bronze band of the crown. Trumpet curves and spirals originating from the centre of the discs decorate the roundels. These terminate in lentoid bosses and stylised bird heads.

- Raised bosses protrude from the centre of the discs, beaten out with the *repoussé* technique. One of the bosses features a red enamel stud. It is thought that the bird heads and the centre of the other boss were, at one time, filled with red enamel also.

- There is more spiral, curvilinear decoration to be seen on the cone ending in two elaborate bird heads. The designs and patterns were applied using a cut-away method of carving. This involved cutting into the surface of an object and removing parts to create a pattern or design.

The Iron Age Revision Questions

1 Explain the origins of the *La Tène* style and discuss the type of decoration to be found on two Iron-Age objects.

2 Give a detailed description of the Broighter Hoard, and discuss the functions of each object within the hoard.

3 Compare and contrast the metalwork and stone carving in Ireland during the Iron Age, by discussing the decoration and the techniques used on both the Turoe Stone and the Petrie Crown.

Christianity in Ireland

Ireland was not always a Christian country. Most people believe that Saint Patrick brought Christianity to Ireland around 432, but before that people were pagans. They believed in, and prayed to, many gods.

With the arrival of Christianity came Roman techniques of design and writing, which were to influence the great art produced in this era. Ireland's conversion to Christianity happened gradually, so paganism survived side by side with it for a time. You can see evidence of this in the stonework created at the time, particularly the pillars.

biography

SAINT PATRICK (c. 390–460) was born in Britain. At the age of 16 he was captured as a slave and brought to Ireland, where he worked as a shepherd. He escaped back to Britain but later returned to Ireland as a missionary, preaching about Jesus Christ. He is Ireland's patron saint, celebrated every year on his death date, 17 March.

The Development of Monasteries

The first Christian religious building appeared in the fifth century and the trend spread quickly across Ireland in the sixth and seventh centuries. These buildings were made of wood and are not in evidence today. Religious sites followed no particular pattern in their layout, although most are believed to include a graveyard, church, and circular 'beehive' huts where the clergy lived. These were surrounded by a circular wall, outside of which communities were established, farming the land and producing craftwork and metalwork.

dic·tion·ar·y

Anglo-Normans were the descendants of the Normans who ruled England following the conquest by William of Normandy in 1066. They came to Ireland in 1169, bringing with them the feudal system.

Religious Orders

In 1169 Ireland was invaded by the **Anglo-Normans**, who brought with them new developments in architecture. After the invasion, great western European religious orders began to arrive, setting up communities all over the country. The most significant of these were the Cistercians, the Franciscans, the Dominicans and the Augustinians, who began to build churches and monasteries on a much larger scale than any previously built in Ireland. Other orders such as the Carmelites and the Benedictines also created monasteries but in lesser numbers.

Layout of monasteries

The monastic sites consisted of a cloister (a sheltered passageway), usually square or rectangular in shape, with open arcaded sides (with arches supported by columns). Around this were situated the church, round tower, dwellings, refectory (dining hall) and kitchen, surrounded by walls for protection.

Churches

The first stone churches were very small, and consisted of only one room. The size varied between 6 and 9 m tall and 4 and 6 m wide. They were constructed with large stones to create thick walls. There was no mortar used so the stones had to fit exactly together to form strong durable walls with a small narrow window in the eastern wall to catch the morning sun. The roofs were also made of stone and were steeply pitched (sloped). The doorways were small, with flat slabs on top.

The Gallurus Oratory (a room or a building meant for prayer) in the Dingle Peninsula, Co. Kerry, is a fine example of a curved, boat-shaped church. The entire building measures 7 m long and 5 m wide, with thick walls 1 m deep.

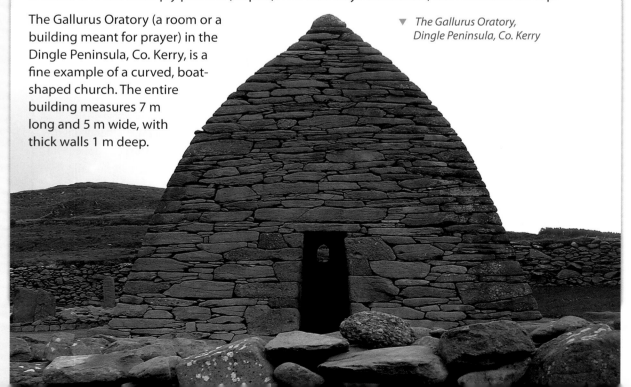

▼ *The Gallurus Oratory, Dingle Peninsula, Co. Kerry*

Round Towers

Round towers are the most distinctive of the early Irish stone buildings built between the end of the ninth and the twelfth centuries. They are very tall, slim buildings, reaching heights between 25 and 30 m high, with tapering (coming to a point) conical roofs. They are all situated close to and sometimes attached to a church or monastery.

Function

The original name for the round tower was *cloigteach*, which translates directly as 'bell house.' In the days when the monasteries were occupied, a bell would have been rung high in the tower to call the monks to prayer. It was also a good viewing point for potential enemies, where a watchman could see for miles. The tower would also have been used as a store for valuables and as a hiding place for the monks themselves in times of attack. The doorway was set high in the wall of the tower, allowing access by ladder only. The monks could enter by use of a rope ladder, which they could then drag inside to prevent attackers from getting inside.

▲ *Round tower at Clonmacnoise, Co. Offaly*

Examples of round towers can be found at Clonmacnoise, Co. Offaly, the Rock of Cashel, Co. Tipperary and at Dysart O' Dea in Co. Clare.

The Function of Early Christian Art

There were a vast number of religious items created with wonderful craftsmanship to celebrate the glory of God in Mass (the ceremony of the Eucharist) and to spread Christianity in the missions abroad. The chalices (cups) and patens (plates) created in the early Christian period are among the finest artistic achievements in Ireland's history.

- Chalices, made of silver or gold, were used to distribute the wine ('blood' of Christ) among the congregation. They also held water, which symbolised purity as demonstrated in baptism rites.

- Patens, also made of silver or gold, were used to give out the Eucharistic bread (the 'body' of Christ, also called communion). At Easter and Christmas ceremonies, the bread was broken into 65 pieces and laid in the paten in the form of a wheeled cross. This custom stems from the Spanish Mozarabic liturgy (system of worship) where each piece of bread represented moments in the life of Jesus.

- Books of the Gospels were also produced. The simplest of these were set on the altar for the everyday readings in the liturgy of the Mass. More complex and ornamental books, such as the Book of Kells, (see pp. 37–43) were used for more ceremonial occasions in the religious calendar.

- A number of carved crosses in wood and metal were created. These were used for processions and were displayed for worship. Some carved crosses housed the relics (parts of a saint's body or pieces of their clothing) of saints or fragments of the True Cross (said to be the cross on which Christ was crucified). They were brought abroad on foreign missions to help with conversion to Christianity.

- Carved stone crosses gave parishes a focus point for religion and served to inspire the rural communities by their images.

- Portable shrines were created to house relics and were often used for missionary purposes.

STONE CARVING

Stone carving is the earliest form of art found in Ireland and was used extensively during the Christian era. Each type of stone brings a different challenge to the sculptor. The two types of stone most commonly used by artists in Ireland were igneous and sedimentary.

Granite

1 **Igneous stone** is formed when liquid magma from the Earth's crust cools and hardens. Granite is an igneous stone. It is very hard, and made up of quartz crystal and feldspar, which contains silica. It is one of the most difficult stones to carve as it cannot be easily cut into. It must be pounded, chipping away crystals to achieve the acquired result. It is not a suitable stone for carving fine details.

2 **Sedimentary stone** is formed in low-lying areas. Rocks which were eroded (worn away) by the sea and weather fall into these areas where they accumulate and compress together. Sedimentary stone can also be created under the sea as a result of plant and animal forms being pressed into the ocean bed. Sandstone is a medium-hard stone constructed from sedimentary sand, silica and calcium carbonate. It can be carved quite easily as large chunks can be chipped off with a single stroke. Limestone is a sedimentary stone created under the sea. It is made up of calcite or calcium carbonate. It is quite soft and even easier to carve than sandstone, allowing smaller details and textures to be cut into the surface.

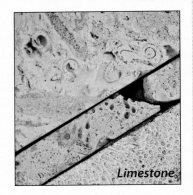

Limestone

Ogham Stones

Developed in Ireland, ogham was a written language derived from the Latin alphabet. It was used between the third and sixth centuries, and was read vertically, from bottom to top. Stone boulders or pillars were incised with this writing to serve as territorial markers, memorials, or indicators of burial sites for wealthy or significant members of the community. It is thought that any Christian imagery which appeared on these pillars was applied at a later date, after the arrival of Christianity.

▲ *Carved stone pillar, Aglish, Co. Kerry*

AGLISH PILLAR	
Date	Fifth to sixth century
Found	In the grounds of a church at Aglish, Dingle Peninsula, Co. Kerry.
Function	It is thought that this stone was erected to commemorate the memory of a Christian. The ogham inscription has been damaged but what remains has been translated to suggest that this is the case.

dic·tion·ar·y

The **Maltese Cross** is a symbol of Christian warriors known as the Knights of Malta. The link with the Mediterranean island of Malta was forged when they arrived there in 1530.

The Aglish pillar consists of a narrow slab of stone.

❧ There is ogham writing carved into the sides of the pillar.

❧ A **Maltese cross** within a circle is carved in relief on the top of the front face of the pillar.

❧ Two **swastikas** are in evidence below the cross, symbolising the Resurrection.

dic·tion·ar·y

A **swastika** is an ancient religious symbol in the shape of a Greek cross, with the ends of the arms bent at right angles. It was later used as the emblem of Nazi Germany (1933–45).

CARVED STONE PILLAR	
Date	Sixth century
Found	Mullamast, Co. Kildare. The pillar was discovered during the demolition of a castle on the hill of Mullamast. It had been re-used as a door lintel in the castle.
Function	It is considered that the stone had been used as a territorial marker for the kings of Leinster, the Uí Dúnlainge family.

▲ *Carved stone pillar, Mullamast, Co. Kildare*

Not every carved stone during the Christian era served a Christian purpose – some, like this irregularly shaped limestone boulder, were created simply to act as territorial markers.

- The decoration on the boulder consists of spiral designs. Some have been cut into the surface, while in other places the background has been chiselled away to reveal the relief design.

- There is no evidence of Christian symbolism on the pillar – the designs are similar to those used in Iron-Age metalwork of the previous era (see pp. 14–19).

Christianity in Ireland Revision Questions

1 Describe the impact of the arrival of Christianity in Ireland, including in your answer the nature of the buildings constructed during this era.

2 Discuss stone carving in the Early Christian period, with reference to form, function and decoration.

Christian Metalwork

During the Christian era, metalwork reached new heights of accomplishment. Craftworkers produced some of the finest pieces of ornamental jewellery and religious artefacts found in Ireland.

Reliquaries

Reliquaries, or vessels to hold relics, were the earliest examples of Christian metalwork in Ireland. While some contained the bodies of saints or holy people such as **Saint Brigid** and the bishops, others housed relics associated with these people, such as staffs, ecclesiastical books or bells. Those containing body parts were more richly adorned with jewels and stone and metalwork carving; however, none has survived fully through the ages. Smaller reliquaries were often portable, allowing them to be easily carried around. They were used on formal and ceremonial occasions, such as the signing of treaties. Another common use of reliquaries was for the collection of church dues from the religious congregation.

biography

As a child, **SAINT BRIGID** (c. 451–525) was inspired by the preaching of Saint Patrick. She became a nun, and founded a monastery for monks and nuns in Kildare. Her symbol is a cross made of rushes, which legend says she wove in order to convert a dying man to Christianity. Her feast day is 1 February.

TWO TOMB-SHAPED SHRINES

Date	Eighth to ninth century
Found	The shrines were discovered in Lough Erne, Tully, Co. Fermanagh by a fisherman.
Function	These were portable shrines, with hinges enabling them to be attached to a strip of cloth to be worn about the neck. Experts believe that the smallest shrine carried relics of continental saints and was placed inside the larger reliquary.

The reliquaries, made of bronze, are based on the form of **late antique** sarcophagi (burial tombs). They are both rectangular-shaped boxes, complete with a gabled roof with hinges on one side for opening the lid.

➠ The larger shrine is the more ornamented of the pair, with a strip of **chip-carved** gold running along the top of the shrine, and a gold inlaid roundel featuring an enamelled stud in the centre.

dic·tion·ar·y

Late antiquity is a term used to describe the era between classical times and the middle ages which took place from the third century B.C to the fourteenth century A.D.

Chip-carving was a method used to carve gold in high relief, creating deep furrows in the metal.

◄ *Two tomb-shaped shrines, National Museum – Decorative Arts and History, Dublin*

Chalices

The chalice was used in Mass in early Ireland as it is today, to hold the water and wine. The congregation received both bread and wine during the ceremony, taking turns to drink from the chalice and receiving communion from a paten. Before Mass, the priest poured water into the chalice, and brought it in a procession into the church. There, he unveiled it in two stages during the ceremony.

ARDAGH CHALICE

Date	Eighth century
Found	Reerasta, Co. Limerick. The chalice was part of a hoard which was discovered under a slab in Reerasta Rath (fort).
Function	The chalice was used in the celebration of Mass. Because of its spectacular craftsmanship it was probably used only on special ceremonial occasions.

▲ *Ardagh Chalice, National Museum – Decorative Arts and History, Dublin*

The chalice is made of silver, with panels of gold **filigree**, gilded (covered with gold) bronze on the stem, and enamel, copper and glass studs. A large crystal is set into the underside of the base. The wide silver bowl of the chalice is joined to the conical base by a sturdy bronze stem. A circular foot ring around the base helps to balance the chalice. The handles are attached to the upper rim of the bowl. The chalice is held together with the aid of a bronze pin through the stem, which is now covered with gold cast ornament.

- A band of gold filigree runs under the rim of the chalice. Some of the panels in the band feature intricately intertwined animal forms. Red enamel and blue glass ***cloisonné*** studs set in silver grilles separate the panels of filigree.

- The handles of the chalice are made of silver with panels of gold filigree and coloured glass. Underneath each handle two large *cloisonné* studs are set into the bowl.

- Underneath the band of filigree, in the centre of each side of the chalice are roundels of decoration. Four studs embellish the border of each roundel with a ***cloisonné*** enamel stud placed in the centre. Panels of gold filigree fill the spaces formed by the arched cross.

dic·tion·ar·y

Filigree is delicate ornamental work usually involving twisted threads of gold, silver or bronze.

dic·tion·ar·y

In the *cloisonné* technique, the artist forms a design by soldering slim strips of metal onto an object, then fills in the compartments formed with different coloured enamels.

- The stem of the chalice is made of gilded bronze, which was created by a technique in which a thin layer of gold was pressed over the bronze decoration.

- The names of the apostles, apart from Judas, appear below the panel of gold filigree, delicately and geometrically incised into the silver. Surrounding the names and the roundel in the centre is a background of incised dots.

- Techniques involved in crafting the chalice include engraving, **enamelling**, *cloisonné* casting, gold filigree and gilding.

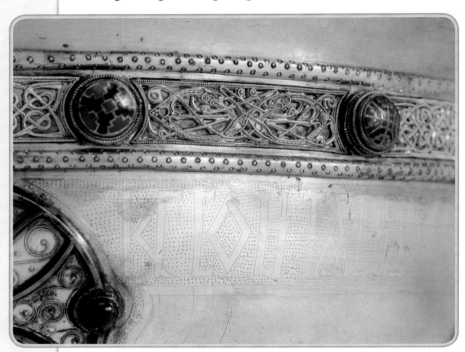

◀ *Detail of the Ardagh Chalice, National Museum – Decorative Arts and History, Dublin*

> **dic·tion·ar·y**
>
> **Enamelling** is a decorative technique which involves heating powdered glass to between 750 and 850 degrees Celsius. The glass melts and can then be poured over metal, glass or ceramic.

DERRYNAFLAN HOARD	
Date	Eighth century
Found	The Derrynaflan Hoard was found on the site of a church in Derrynaflan, Co. Tipperary in 1980. The hoard discovered consists of the chalice, a communion paten, a paten stand and a silver ladle strainer.

Derrynaflan Chalice

The Derrynaflan Chalice is 19.2 cm in height and 21 cm in diameter and is made of gold, silver, amber and glass. It has two handles attached at opposite sides to the rim of the bowl. The chalice consists of over 300 parts soldered together to create the form and decorative elements. A bronze pin holds the bowl to the foot of the chalice through the stem.

- Like the Ardagh Chalice, it is decorated with a band of gold filigree panels running under the rim of the bowl and through the handles.

- The underside of the chalice is also finely ornamented.

▲ *Derrynaflan Chalice, National Museum – Decorative Arts and History, Dublin*

- The bowl of the chalice does not feature the ornamental roundels of the Ardagh Chalice, or the *cloisonné* enamelling.

- The square studs separating the rectangular panels of gold filigree consist of amber stones, glass and mica (mineral found as glittering scales) instead.

◄ *Derrynaflan Hoard, National Museum – Decorative Arts and History, Dublin*

Derrynaflan Paten

It is believed that the paten in the Derrynaflan Hoard possibly originated in the same workshop as the Ardagh Chalice, as there are many similarities in their style of decoration. It is made of silver, glass studs and gold filigree, and is circular in shape with a thick ornamented rim.

- The main central part is made from beaten silver, with a rim consisting of panels of gold filigree separated by studs of cast glass.

- In the detail shown, the filigree panel demonstrates the intricate nature of the craftsmanship. This features two figures kneeling in opposite directions, with a pattern of interlace connecting their hair.

- The side of the paten is also richly decorated, with a central band of thin gold plates showing stamped decoration. These are separated by rectangular *cloisonné* studs decorated with geometric patterns, red and yellow enamel and blue glass. These decorations are bordered by fine silver and copper-wire, knitted-mesh chains.

- Many techniques were used to create this paten. Among them were casting, engraving, wire meshing (knitting silver wire finely together), gold filigree, soldering and enamelling.

Penannular Brooches

During the Christian era, penannular brooches became popular to fasten cloaks of the wealthy and prestigious in Ireland. They consisted of a ring with a gap on one end for a large pin to pass through. Later, ring brooches, called pseudo-penannular brooches, developed. They had a larger ornately decorated ring which was entirely closed, serving as a decorative pin rather than as a brooch. The Tara Brooch is a good example of a ring brooch.

The Function of the Brooch

It is thought that brooches were created in the same workshops where the great religious items were made, due to the fine craftsmanship in their design. We do not know for sure what kind of people wore this magnificent jewellery, but they were undoubtedly wealthy. It is possible that abbots (heads) of monasteries, often laymen from rich and influential families, wore them as a symbol of authority and status. Another function of these brooches may have been to serve as dowries (marriage gifts) or as diplomatic gifts between important figures in Irish society.

TARA BROOCH	
Date	Early eighth century
Found	The Tara Brooch was discovered beside the seashore in Bettystown, Co. Meath in 1850.
Function	To fasten a cloak.

The brooch is made of silver, gold, glass, enamel and amber. It is pseudo-penannular in shape, with a fully closed and richly decorated silver ring through which a large ornamented pin is placed. There is a silver wire mesh chain attached to one side. This indicates that the brooch may have originally been one of a pair, which would fasten on either side of the wearer's cloak.

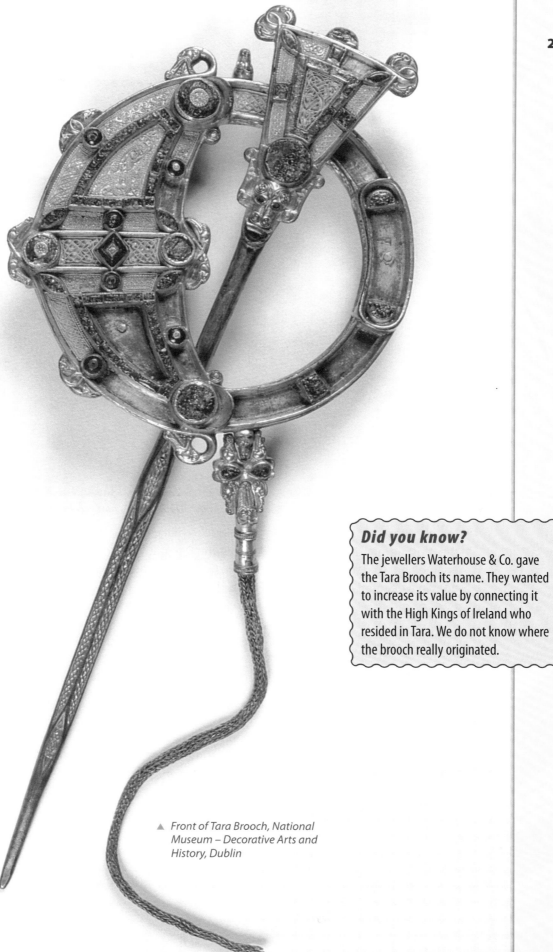

▲ *Front of Tara Brooch, National Museum – Decorative Arts and History, Dublin*

▲ Back of Tara Brooch, National Museum – Decorative Arts and History, Dublin

- Metalsmiths used every available technique to make this brooch, causing it to be one of the most admired items produced in this era. Decorative techniques include gold filigree, enamelling, soldering and wire meshing. *Kerbschnitt* casting, which involved casting the gold in a decorative mould, was also used.

Front of the Brooch

- The front of the brooch is composed of silver with recesses filled with gold filigree work, some of which are now missing.

- The panels of delicate miniscule filigree feature the twisting shapes of animals and complex designs. The fine, beaded wire was carefully soldered onto thin gold plates which were then soldered onto the silver base.

- The image on the previous page illustrates the nature of the filigree decoration. In the triangular section a serpent-like animal assumes a heraldic pose, his body elongated and twisted ornately to form a fabulous abstract design.

- There are a number of studs of amber, glass and enamel placed between the sections of filigree to ornament the brooch further.

Pin

- The head of the pin also features panels of gold filigree, with a fantastical gold head of a beast with jewelled eyes connecting the body of the pin to the head. This was created by the *Kerbschnitt* casting technique.

Back Ring

- On the back of the Tara Brooch, two beautiful *cloisonné* studs decorate the sides of the ring. Two panels of silver decoration fill the triangular sections, featuring spiralling *La Tène* designs (see p. 14).

Chain

- The chain is made of strands of woven silver wire, attached to the main body of the brooch by snake and animal head ornament. This forms a frame for two small human heads made from glass, cast into shape by a mould.

Christian Metalwork Revision Questions

1 Give an account of the nature of the religious items produced during the Christian period, describing their uses and decoration.

2 Compare and contrast the Ardagh Chalice and the Derrynaflan Chalice, with particular emphasis on their form and decoration.

3 The Tara Brooch is considered to be the most beautiful object created during the Christian era. Discuss this statement, describing the nature of ornamentation found on the brooch.

Illuminated Manuscripts

The term 'illuminated manuscripts' refers to early books which combined text with decoration, such as decorated initials or illustrations. The illuminated manuscripts produced in Ireland were based on the Christian Bible and were written on specially prepared calfskin, called vellum. These manuscripts were created in a scriptorium, which was a room specifically designed for this purpose. A scriptorium usually featured a large table in the centre of the room with smaller tables along the walls. Scribes wrote the text and illuminators created the decorative pages. Illuminators also mixed the colour pigments to provide the ink for the illustrations.

▲ *Page from the Lindisfarne Gospels, northern England*

Source and Preparation of Vellum

The pages (leaves) of illuminated manuscripts were made from vellum. The leaves of a manuscript such as those in the Lindisfarne Gospels (from Northern England) were taken from the skins of very young calves. The leaves were cut in bifolia (double pages), so that the skin from the spine of the calf ran across the book horizontally. In the Book of Kells (see pp. 37–43) this varies, with the spine sometimes running vertically. These vellum leaves were taken from older calves, so had thicker pages. Artists preferred to use these stronger leaves for very intricate decorative pages. It is considered that the skins of 185 calves were used to create the Book of Kells.

TURNING CALFSKIN INTO VELLUM

When a monk prepared calfskin for the purpose of creating suitable vellum, he had to go through a number of steps:

1 First the skin was dipped in lime to loosen the hair from the hide.

2 It was then scraped with a knife.

3 The skin was stretched on a frame and the craftsman picked out the remaining hair with a luna (a semicircular knife).

4 The leaves were cut out of the vellum to an equal scale.

5 The manufacturer cut marks with the point of a sharp knife on the edges of the leaves to assist the ruling of the pages for decoration and script.

6 The artist ruled the pages with a ruler made of wood or bone. The layout of the decorative and narrative pages was worked out using measuring implements such as set-squares, dividers, compasses and templates. Mistakes were erased by scratching them from the leaf with a knife. Artists may have used cut crystals to magnify sections of miniaturised detail.

The Nature and Origin of Pigments

The pigments used for colouring the manuscripts came from minerals and organic materials such as plants and insects.

- **Deep blue** came from the mineral lapis lazuli, mined in Afghanistan. It was very difficult and expensive to obtain.
- **Blue** – deep indigo came from an oriental plant. Other shades of blue came from woad, a northern European plant.
- **White** came from chalk and white lead.
- **Purple and mauve** came from *Crozophora tinctoria,* or the litmus plant, which came from the Mediterranean.
- **Yellow** came from arsenic sulphide (the mineral yellow orpiment), and was used to create the gold-coloured decoration.
- **Scarlet** and **orange** came from red lead.
- **Deep red,** known as Kermes, came from *Kermoccocus vermilio, a Mediterranean insect*.
- **Green** came from copper.

Scribes wrote text using a deep brown-black ink called iron gall, created by mixing iron sulphate, ground apples, glue gum and water. Egg white was used to bind the pigments in the Book of Kells. This manuscript differs from other books of a similar kind in that the artists sometimes added a three-dimensional effect by layering the pigments in thin washes.

Quills and Brushes

The scribes used feather quills and sharpened reeds to write the narrative (story) pages of the manuscripts. They used brushes of different sizes to create the decorations and illustration, depending on the scale of the work. Brushes were made from fine fur from animals such as the pine marten.

▶ *Pine marten*

THE BOOK OF DURROW

Date	Seventh century	Found	Durrow, Co. Offaly

The Book of Durrow is considered to the oldest surviving manuscript of the Gospels in Ireland, although it is not thought to be the first made. It was produced in the late seventh century, more than a hundred years before work began on the Book of Kells. Although it cannot be proved beyond doubt, it is believed that the Book of Durrow was produced in the monastery of Durrow, situated 6 km from Tullamore, Co. Offaly. The monastery was built by **Saint Colum Cille** after 585. The name Durrow comes from the Irish for 'The field of oaks,' as oak trees were plentiful in the area. The book originally resided in a shrine which was lost in 1689. The size of the book and the fact that it was enshrined leads us to believe that it was set on the church altar and only used on important occasions. In the years between 1621 and 1623, the bishop of Meath, James Ussher (1581–1656), examined and arranged the Gospels, comparing them with those in the Book of Kells. The book later found a home in Trinity College in Dublin, presented as a gift by Henry Jones (1605–82), the then bishop of Meath.

biography

SAINT COLUM CILLE (521–597), meaning 'dove of the churches', was born in Donegal. He became a monk and founded several monasteries in Ireland, before leaving for Scotland to set up an important monastery in Iona. Here, he converted many pagans to Christianity.

Contents of the Book of Durrow

- The Book of Durrow consists of 248 **folio** pages, which measure 245 mm by 145 mm.
- The book is divided into the four Gospels of the **Four Evangelists**, Matthew, Mark, Luke and John.
- In front of each Gospel is a page featuring the symbol of the Evangelist, followed by a **carpet page** of abstract decoration.
- The first page of text was introduced by decorating the opening words. Canon tables (lists of Gospel passages) were also included to indicate where the verses and readings could be found in the book.

dic·tion·ar·y

A **folio** is a sheet of paper or parchment which is folded in half to make two pages in a book.

The **Four Evangelists** (meaning proclaimers of good news), Matthew, Mark, Luke and John wrote the New Testament of the Bible.

Carpet pages are purely decorative, consisting mainly of geometric designs or intricate interlace.

Canon Tables

The canon tables were based on the scheme laid out by the **Bishop of Caesarea** in 315, when he divided the four Gospels into sections so they could be easily accessed:

- The Gospel of Matthew had 355 sections.
- The Gospel of Mark had 233.
- The Gospel of Luke had 342.
- The Gospel of John had 232.

The layout of the canon tables was created in a grid formation.

biography

EUSEBIUS (c. 263–339) was the Bishop of Caesarea. The ruins of this Roman city can be seen in present-day Israel. Eusebius wrote books on the history of the Church and compiled information on the lives of the saints and martyrs.

Portrait Pages

The portrait pages featured before each Gospel of the Evangelists showed a symbol of the saint.

- Saint Matthew's motif, shown on the opposite page, was a man placed in the centre of the page. The drawing is simplified and stylised with the shape of his cloak resembling the bell shrines prevalent in metalwork at the time. Bell shrines housed the bells used in Mass.

- His neck and arms are covered by the cloak which is decorated with squares, lozenges, circles and crosses.

- His face indicates that the artist had some knowledge of realistic representation as it has tiny red dots to convey shading and tone.

- The hair and beard are made up of directional lines, while his feet, facing to the right, are enclosed in high-backed boots.

- A patterned border surrounds the figure, decorated with flowing ribbon interlace, which echoes the stone carving techniques in crosses and standing stones (see pp. 44–51). Within the loops of interlace, small triangles appear.

Carpet Pages

Carpet pages were used to separate the Gospels, but their interlace patterns may have also served a magical purpose in medieval Ireland. Interlaced knots were used in European culture to ward off evil spirits. Interlace design appeared in church doorways and on book shrines to protect the contents of the book.

- It is believed that the carpet page shown was originally intended to be placed before the Gospel of Saint Matthew.

- In the centre of the folio are two large circles adorned with trumpet shapes and spirals. Above and below these are two more pairs of smaller circles. All of the circles are connected through the use of trumpet shapes and floral patterns, interspersed with small circles.

- The borders (the top of which are lost) have ribbon interlacing in six strands, with four knots in the centre of each circular roundel.

- There are 42 spirals on the page, which relates to the number of animals featured in the book and the 42 generations of Christ. In his Gospel, Matthew states the there are 42 generations between Abraham and Christ.

▲ *Carpet page, Book of Durrow, Trinity College, Dublin*

◄ Initial page, Book of Durrow, Trinity College, Dublin

Designs of Initial Pages

The initial pages preceded the rest of the Gospel text. The most beautifully executed is found at the beginning of Saint John's Gospel.

- The opening lines IN PRINCIPIO ERAT take up the top of the page. Three large stems of the I and the first leg of the N combine to run vertically down the left of the page.

- The letters I and N are ornamented with spirals, circles and interlace.

- The other letters in the three lines in the top left of the page are decorated with panels of pen and ink and yellow orpiment and are surrounded by a pattern of small red dots.

- The three lines below these are smaller in size and are also surrounded by red dots. The eight lines towards the bottom are written in the usual majuscule script (see below).

Script

The writing seen in the text of the Book of Durrow is a form of majuscule script, which was similar to our use of capital letters and was used between the sixth and ninth centuries. The earlier form was known as miniscule. Throughout the text, the scribes added decoration to the pages and the script itself to embellish the folios. The opening word of a section was usually enlarged and decorated with red dots. In lines where the sentence ended before the edge of the page, red scrollwork was applied, and in some parts the ends of initial letters ended in a spiral shape.

◄ Narrative page, Book of Durrow, Trinity College, Dublin

THE BOOK OF KELLS

Date	Begun c. 807	Found	Unknown but thought to be Co. Meath or Iona

The Book of Kells is renowned as the most beautiful of all the illuminated manuscripts produced in Ireland or even the world, and has been likened to the work of angels by historians and scholars. A mystery surrounds the location where it was produced but its place of origin has been narrowed down to monasteries in Kells, Co. Meath, and Iona, an island off the coast of Scotland. Saint Colum Cille founded the monastery in Iona in 561 and has always been linked with the Book of Kells. After Viking raids on Iona monastery, Columban monks arrived in Co. Meath in 807. Experts believe that this was when the book was begun. In 1007, a manuscript matching the description of the Book of Kells was stolen from the monastery in Kells and discovered buried three months later. Its original gold and jewelled book cover was never recovered. In the twelfth century, the reform of the Church resulted in the abbey falling into a state of disrepair. When **Cromwell** arrived in Ireland, leading to the dissolution of the abbeys, the Earl of Cavan sent the manuscript to Dublin to safeguard it in 1653. The fame of the treasure spread and in 1849, the book was displayed for Queen Victoria of England (1819–1901). In the nineteenth century the Book of Kells took up residence in Trinity College's Long Room in the library where it can be seen to this day.

biography

OLIVER CROMWELL (1599–1658) was an English military leader who won the English Civil War and invaded and conquered England and Scotland. He was strongly anti-Catholic and persecuted Catholics in Ireland.

Contents of the Book of Kells

- The Book of Kells consists of 339 pages, made up of the four Gospels from the New Testament. It is thought that there might have been as many as 368 vellum leaves originally, as some are missing from the Gospels of Saint Luke and Saint John. The size of the pages was also altered through time – in the nineteenth century, while binding the book, the leaves were cropped.

- The manuscript includes pages of Latin script decorated with symbols and ornament, elaborate initial pages which precede the Gospels and many beautiful decorative pages, including portraits of the Four Evangelists, Christ, and the Virgin and Child.

- It is believed that each Gospel was preceded by a page of Evangelist symbols, then a portrait page of the Evangelist whose Gospel it was, and then a page illustrating the opening initial of the Gospel. However, some of these pages, such as portraits of Saint Mark and Saint Luke, are now missing.

- The book also contains a fragment of Etymologies (origins and meanings) of Hebrew names.

- Canon tables can be found in two or more of the Evangelists' Gospels.

- Shortened versions of the Gospel narratives (*Breves Causae*) also appear in the book.

- *Argumenta* (prefaces of the Evangelists) are set before each Gospel.

Function of the Book of Kells

It is thought that the Book of Kells was originally intended as an altar book used for special ceremonial occasions. The exquisite decoration was created for many reasons: first, to honour the Word of God, second, to illustrate the script. Another very significant use of art in those days was to educate and preach, as most people in the country were illiterate, but were aware of the symbols and images associated with Christ and the saints. Such a magnificent volume of craftsmanship could not fail to impress.

Artists and Scribes

Historians are unsure of the exact number of artists and scribes who worked on the Book of Kells, although Françoise Henry (a specialist in early Irish art) identified three main artists' hands at work. It is thought that they were influenced by the *cloisonné* enamel work seen in items such as the Ardagh Chalice (see pp. 24–6), the Tara Brooch (see pp. 28–31), and by carved stonework.

1   **The goldsmith:** This artist was reportedly responsible for the 'Chi-Rho' page and the page featuring the eight-circle cross amongst others. He was given the name because of the metallic colours he used and the similarity of his designs to that of Irish metalwork.

2   **The illustrator:** This artist is thought to be the person who decorated the leaves portraying the arrest of Christ, the temptation of Christ and the page of Evangelist symbols.

3   **The portrait painter:** The third artist identified is the portrait painter, thought to have created the portraits of Christ, Saint Matthew and Saint John.

Symbols of Christ

Animal symbols of Christ appear continuously throughout the manuscript, taking different forms to represent different stages of his life and different facets to his character. The four symbols were the fish, the lion, the snake and the peacock.

1   **The Fish:** The symbol of the fish to represent Christ dates back to the second century. It stems from the initials of 'Jesus Christ, Son of God, Saviour' in Greek, spelling the word *icthus*, the Greek word for fish. The fish is also associated with the waters of baptism and conversion to Christianity. The fish is generally shown alongside Christ or his name in the book, and is usually portrayed looking similar to a salmon.

2   **The Lion:** The lion represented Christ's Resurrection. In the fifth century, Greek naturalists believed that the young of the lion were stillborn (born dead), but on the third day after their birth they were revived to life by the breath of their father, creating a parallel to the death and subsequent Resurrection of Jesus. The lion was also a symbol of the House of Judah, the ancestors of Jesus, chosen for the strength, power and majesty which were seen to be characteristic of this animal.

3   **The Snake:** This reptile was used for two purposes in the Book of Kells. One of these was to symbolise the Resurrection, stemming from the idea that the snake is reborn when it sheds its skin. The second use for the snake was to symbolise evil, reminding us of the serpent in the Garden of Eden, who tempted Eve with the apple, causing humankind to be evicted from Paradise. The snake can sometimes appear in an abstract form, often adopting the characteristics of other animals, such as a fish's tail or a duck's beak. Snakes were used in borders of leaves in the book and to form the letter 'S.'

4   **The Peacock:** The symbol of the peacock was used to represent the incorruptible nature of Christ when he was tempted in the desert. This was because of a belief that the flesh of a peacock did not rot after its death. Saint Augustine (354–430) tested this by cooking a peacock, leaving the meat for a month and waiting to see if it would rot. He noted that there was very little decay and no bad odour.

Portrait Pages

Some of the most intricately designed work in the Book of Kells is to be seen in the portrait pages, particularly those depicting the Evangelists. It is perhaps best to examine one of the Evangelist symbols pages to understand the meaning behind some of the images of the Evangelists who wrote the Gospels.

Evangelist Symbol Page

This page appeared in front of the Gospel of Saint Mark and is the most elaborate of all of the portrait pages.

- Saint Matthew is represented by the image of a **man**, as his writing gave insight into the humanity of Christ.

- The **lion** symbolises Saint Mark, who emphasised the royal, powerful side of Christ.

- Saint Luke is portrayed as an **ox**, chosen to portray the sacrificial nature of priesthood, which was the focus of his Gospel.

- The **eagle** represented Saint John, who was considered to have a keen eye for truth.

- The symbols also reflected the life of Christ. The man was a symbol of his birth, the sacrificial calf of his death, the lion of his Resurrection and the eagle of his Ascension into heaven. The Evangelist page shows golden halos surrounding each Evangelist.

- The images are arranged around the shape of a **Saint George's cross**. At the bottom of the page the T-shape at the end of the cross has unequal lengths – perhaps one of the few aesthetic mistakes in the Book of Kells.

- Each section is not fully devoted to a specific Evangelist. A calf and eagle appear underneath the circle around the lion, while a calf and eagle are above the symbol for Saint Luke. The eagle is accompanied by the calf and the lion. This could reflect the similarity of content and intention behind the four Gospels despite their differences.

- In each panel there are two sceptres with heads in the shape of flowers.

▲ *Evangelist Symbol Page, the Book of Kells, Trinity College, Dublin*

dic·tion·ar·y

Saint George's cross is the cross used on the national flag of England. The horizontal arms are of equal size and are longer than the equally sized vertical arms.

▲ *Portrait of Saint John, the Book of Kells, Trinity College, Dublin*

Portrait of Saint John

This page appears before Saint John's Gospel and shows the Evangelist seated on a throne, holding a book and a quill to illustrate his function as a scribe.

- His head is surrounded by a large geometrically designed halo, with three circles intersecting it. The border has four cross shapes with interlace decoration.

- Unlike the other portrait pages there is no arch over the head of the saint, the large scale of the halo compensating for this.

- One of the most intriguing aspects of this image is the figure who stands behind the border (look for his hand protruding on the left, and the feet at the bottom).

- When the leaves of the book were cropped in the nineteenth century, part of the head at the top was removed. It is not known exactly who this figure represents, although it is thought that it could portray either the Crucifixion or the all-embracing figure of God the Father.

The Arrest of Christ

This page is particularly interesting as it portrays a moment in time rather than a straightforward representation of a saint or Christ himself.

▲ *The Arrest of Christ, the Book of Kells, Trinity College, Dublin*

- The large figure of Christ dominates the composition. The guards arresting him appear much smaller in comparison, showing the importance of Christ in relation to his captors.

- The figures are stylised, the two guards shown in profile seeming almost identical, with red moustaches, pointed black beards and elaborately designed red hair.

- Christ by contrast breaks from the stylisation of the characters with his wide-eyed expression of dismay, his hands spread to reflect an attitude of entreaty and also to remind us of his fate on the Cross.

- The images are arranged within a decorated arch, with the words 'And when they had sung a hymn, they went out to the Mount of Olives' appearing under the arch.

- Symbols of Christ appear to highlight the scene, with snake decoration in the lower panels of the arch and crosses holding up the archway.

- Two animal heads, possibly lion-shaped, meet at the top of the page. The curved trefoil (three-leafed) tendrils around the script symbolise the olive gardens of Gethsemane.

Narrative Pages

The script used by the scribes of the Book of Kells was known as insular majuscule, which consisted of mostly lower-case letters with some capitals. It is possible that either three or four scribes were responsible for the creation of the narrative pages and script. There are obvious similarities in their style – they all employ the 'turn-in-the-path' or 'head-under-wing' technique, which means a line of script sometimes finishes on the line above. However, there are also differences which help us to tell them apart.

- The first scribe's style is quite conventional, without showing a lot of decoration. An example of his style is seen at the beginning of Saint Mark's Gospel.

- The second scribe has a more elaborate, flamboyant style, adding colour to his lettering and also tiny details to the ends of his script. He is thought to have worked on Saint Matthew's and Saint John's Gospels.

- The other one or two scribes did most of their work in the Gospels of Matthew, Mark and Luke. They also decorated the pages with their own designs to illustrate them.

Script from Saint Mark's Gospel

The passage above from Saint Mark's Gospel tells of the Crucifixion of Jesus. It is 17 lines long with beautifully executed coloured initials on the left of the page to begin some of the sentences. Some of the letters in the script are filled with colour. The unity between the script and the decorations lead experts to believe that they were both created by one scribe.

Script from Saint Matthew's Gospel

These 17 lines are verses 19 to 24 from Saint Matthew's Gospel. Six of the lines begin with decorated capital letters, some with animal and human images. At the end of the 11th line there is a depiction of the peacock, a reference to Christ.

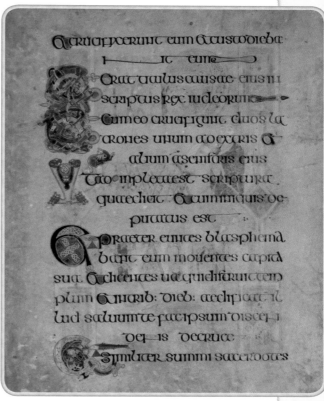

▲ Script from Saint Mark's Gospel, the Book of Kells, Trinity College, Dublin

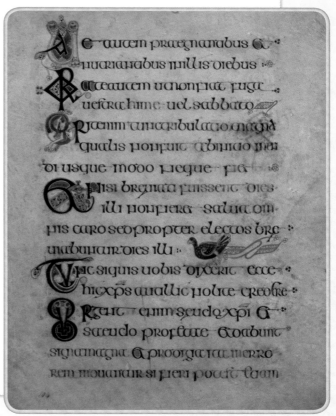

▶ Script from Saint Matthew's Gospel, the Book of Kells, Trinity College, Dublin

Initial Pages

At the beginning of each Gospel in the Book of Kells, the first line took up an entire page, with the decorated capital letter of the first word dominating the format.

CHI-RHO PAGE

This is the most famous of the initial pages, and is also called the Incarnation Initial or the Monogram Page. The line comes from the Gospel of Saint Matthew, and reads 'XRI B GENERATIO' (*Christi autem generatio),* which means 'Now the birth of Jesus Christ...' The large letters are almost unrecognisable in their ornate state.

- The largest of the letters, the X, takes up the left and top of the page.

- Underneath it is a stylised R intertwined with the I and decorated with the head of a man in the centre. This page is recognised as the most exquisitely designed of the entire book because of its wealth of Celtic design, which echoes the metalwork of the age. The pattern of red dots over the lettering on the bottom is reminiscent of the incised dots appearing below the filigree border on the Ardagh Chalice (see p. 24).

> ### dic·tion·ar·y
>
> **Chi-Rho** is a recognised symbol of Christ, which combines the first two letters of Christ when it is spelled in the Greek language. 'Chi' stands for 'Ch' and 'Rho' Stands for 'r.' The Chi-Rho symbol is generally depicted in a cruciform shape to remind viewers of Christ's death on the Cross.

- Animal and human designs can also be seen in the decoration. Three stylised angels lie vertically beside the left bottom leg of the X. Moths are also featured underneath the curve of the left, top leg of the X.

- A chrysalis is shown between them, symbolising new life or resurrection.

- In the bottom of the composition two rats are shown eating a disc representing the Eucharist, watched by two cats with two rats sitting on their backs. Experts are unsure of the meaning of this. It is thought that it might simply represent the problems involved in safeguarding the Eucharist from rats in churches.

- Beside this image is an otter leaning down to take a fish in its mouth, another symbol of Christ.

◀ *The Chi-Rho Page, the Book of Kells, Trinity College, Dublin*

Illuminated Manuscripts Revision Questions

1 Give an account of the creation of an illuminated manuscript. In your answer describe the materials and the techniques used in its making.

2 Describe the types of decoration found in the Book of Durrow, with a detailed description of one page.

3 Describe the symbols and motifs used to decorate the Book of Kells, referring to their appearance and function.

4 Compare and contrast the functions and stylistic decorations of the Portrait, Narrative and Initial pages of the Book of Kells.

The High Crosses

Beautifully carved and imposingly large, high crosses can be seen standing across Ireland to this day. Along with the manuscripts and metalwork produced at this time, they are a reminder of a time in Ireland's history when craft and art were at a peak of achievement. They were mostly created between the ninth and twelfth centuries.

Structure

How do you identify a true high cross? They largely followed the same design in their general structure. They were cut in a cruciform shape with a long shaft. The cross is symbolic of the most significant point in Christian history: the death of Christ. The head of the cross was usually encircled by a ring, a shape derived from a pre-Christian pagan symbol called a sun-cross which consisted of equally sized arms placed at right angles to each other within a circle. High crosses were set upon a wide base and topped with a stone, called a capstone.

Decoration

The decoration on the crosses was almost always based on scenes from the Bible, with the Crucifixion and the Last Judgement being the preferred scenes for the main panels. Other figures that appear continuously are those of Adam and Eve and the hermit saints **Saint Paul** and **Saint Anthony**, who were probably chosen by the monks who created the crosses as a good example of monastic solitude. The decoration looked similar to that of the other Irish crafts, although they differed in some areas. At the time figures were always simplified and shown in a very stylised, two-dimensional manner. By contrast, some of the figures seen on the crosses had an almost naturalistic appearance, showing the influence of Roman art on the sculptors.

> **biography**
>
> **SAINT PAUL** (c. 228–341), not to be confused with the apostle of the same name, is acknowledged as being the first hermit. He was born to wealthy parents but as a young man fled to the desert, where he lived until his death at the age of 113. A raven, sent by God, brought him bread to eat. **SAINT ANTHONY** (c. 251–356), also from a wealthy family, gave away all his money and became a hermit. He met Saint Paul in the desert and buried him when he died.

Function

There were three main functions of the high crosses:

1. The first was a practical one – the crosses acted as boundary markers for landowners.

2. The second function was to inspire devotion in the local people by the beauty of the sculpture.

3. The third and probably most important function of the crosses was to educate the illiterate peasants about the moral tales from the Bible.

CROSSES AT AHENNY	
Date	Originally thought to be eighth century; now considered mid-ninth century
Found	The two crosses stand in a graveyard, which is situated in a field in Ahenny, Co. Tipperary. They lie 15 km south of the town of Calla.
Height	North Cross 3.13 m; South Cross 3.9 m.

Both of these crosses are made of sandstone. Their shafts are shorter than usual, topped with rounded capstones. The bases of the crosses are wide and sturdy. The wheel heads (rings) of both crosses are large in comparison to the shafts.

- Both crosses are heavily influenced by metalwork crosses created in the period, with intricate patterns of geometric ribbon or rope interlacing and large bosses in the centre and on each arm of the cross.

- The bases of the crosses feature stylised animal and human relief sculptures. A panel on the North Cross also has human interlacing – a pattern consisting of interwoven cords ending in representations of human heads, hands or feet.

North Cross at Ahenny

There are four sculpted relief panels on the base of this cross, which can be divided into two groups of two. The panels which have a significant relationship to each other are placed back to back.

- One panel portrays Christ in the centre facing outwards, flanked by three apostles on either side facing inwards towards him.

- On the opposite side a man is shown surrounded by birds and animals. This represents Adam, who was given precedence over the other creatures who inhabited the Earth.

- The other two back-to-back panels show the story of David and Goliath. David was a biblical character who, against all odds, defeated the giant Goliath, armed only with a slingshot. In one panel David is shown in a chariot going into battle, while the other shows his return, bearing the head of the giant. Goliath's body, carried by a pony, is being feasted upon by crows.

South Cross at Ahenny

The sculpture work on the South Cross is created in lower relief than the north cross. It is also more difficult to decipher. The cross bisects (cuts in half) the scenes on both sides.

- On the east face a panel contains a scene from the Bible story of Daniel in the Lions' Den. The story tells that Daniel was thrown to the lions for his beliefs but survived untouched, protected by an angel.

- To the right of this is an image of Christ raised from the dead.

- The lions appear again, possibly as a symbol of Christ's royalty and power.

- On the other three sides more men, horses and animals feature, but it is difficult to figure out the meaning of the scenes portrayed due to the erosion of the stone.

North Cross at Ahenny, Co. Tipperary

NOTE: The figure sculpture on both crosses is only possible to make out in very clear light.

South Cross at Ahenny, Co. Tipperary

CROSS OF MOONE	
Date	Ninth century
Found	In a graveyard in Co. Kildare, which at one time may have been connected to a Columban monastery. It is 7.5 km north of the town of Castledermot.
Height	7.04 m – the second-tallest of the high crosses.

This cross, made of granite, is an unusual shape for a high cross:

- It has a very elongated shaft and a small wheel head on the top.
- The base of the cross is slim and long.
- There is no capstone on the wheel head.

East Face

There are three relief panels on the base of the cross representing Old Testament characters from the Bible:

1. Adam and Eve in the Garden of Eden
2. The Sacrifice of Isaac by his father Abraham
3. Daniel in the Lion's Den.

In the centre of the wheel head on this side is the figure of Christ. The shaft of the cross features five panels decorated with animals and protruding bosses.

South Side

The three panels of decoration on the base of the cross show:

1. Three children situated under an arch, which represents the Children in the Fiery Furnace. In this Bible story, three children are thrown into a fire for refusing to worship false gods. They miraculously survive.

2. The Flight of the Holy Family into Egypt. Mary is seen seated on the donkey holding the Christ-Child, while Joseph walks in front, holding the reins.

3. The Miracle of the Loaves and Fishes, in which Christ manages to feed 5,000 people with five loaves and two fishes. Two fishes face each other over five circular loaves.

West Face

On the base of the west face the 12 apostles stand in three rows of four figures. Over them is a scene from the Crucifixion, while the shaft above has some animal decoration.

▲ *Cross of Moone, east face*

▶ *Detail from south side showing the Flight into Egypt (top) and the Miracle of the Loaves and Fishes (bottom)*

North Side

On the north side of the cross three panels on the base represent more biblical scenes:

<u>1</u> The hermit saints Paul and Anthony are shown being visited by a raven that brought them food.

<u>2</u> The Temptation of Anthony. He was constantly tormented with visions of temptations sent by the Devil to lure him away from his religious, contemplative life.

<u>3</u> A monstrous creature with six heads, which is probably inspired by the Book of Revelations.

MUIREDACH'S CROSS, MONASTERBOICE	
Date	Early tenth century
Found	In the grounds of the old monastery at Monasterboice, Co. Louth, 8 km northwest of the town of Drogheda
Height	5.2 m

The name of this sandstone cross comes from the text inscribed on its base. It is believed that it was erected by one of the abbots of the monastery, a few of which were named Muiredach.

- This cross has a perfectly proportioned shaft, wheel head, base and capstone.
- The capstone is shaped like a tiled roof, similar to the shape seen in relic shrines.
- The east and west faces of the cross are decorated with sculpted **figurative** panels.
- The bases, shafts and heads of the two sides are also decorated.

> dic·tion·ar·y
>
> **Figurative art** means art which is representative of real people, animals or objects.

East Face

In the centre of the head of the east face of the cross is a Last Judgement scene, showing Christ holding a staff and a sceptre (a symbol of royalty).

- Above his head is an eagle; on his left is the figure of David, shown over a harp and with a dove (symbolic of the Holy Spirit).
- To the left of David is an angel recording the names of the mortals entering heaven.
- On the right are the souls of the damned being goaded by Satan.
- Under this scene is the image of Saint Michael the Archangel using scales to weigh a soul.
- Over the Judgement scene is a small panel showing Christ surrounded by two angels.
- On the shaft of the cross are four biblical scenes:

  <u>1</u> The top panel shows four figures representing The Adoration of the Magi (the three Wise Men).

  <u>2</u> There is a scene showing Moses striking a rock to release water for the Israelites to drink.

▲ *Detail of east face showing Moses giving water to the Israelites*

3 There is a scene from the story of David. David has slain the giant Goliath, who is seen on his knees. Saul, the king at the time, is shown seated on a throne.

4 This panel shows two Old Testament scenes. One of these is Adam and Eve with the apple representing their downfall in the Garden of Eden, while the other depicts their son Cain killing his brother Abel.

South Side

➤ The head of the cross features human heads with snake ornamentation.

➤ A panel under the arm of the cross features two animals, and a scene portraying Pontius Pilate (Roman governor of Judaea) washing his hands after sentencing Jesus to death.

➤ On the top is a horseman, who is thought to be one of the Four Horsemen of the **Apocalypse**.

➤ The shaft has panels featuring a **vine scroll**, decorative bosses and human interlacing. Over the base are two intertwined animals.

➤ A chariot procession decorates the base.

> ### dic·tion·ar·y
> A **vine scroll** is a curved linear pattern which includes stylised vine leaves.

> ### Did you know?
> The word 'apocalypse' comes from a Greek word which means 'lifting of the veil,' and signifies a revelation of something hidden. Today, it is often used to describe the end of the world.

West Face

The Crucifixion of Christ is the main image in the centre of the head of the west face.

▲ *Detail of west face panel showing the Mocking of Christ*

➤ On one side of Him is the figure of Stephaton, a Roman soldier who was present at Christ's Crucifixion. He gave Jesus a sponge soaked with vinegar to drink and is shown here holding a cane with a cup.

➤ On Christ's other side is Longinus, the soldier who pierced his side.

➤ Beside Longinus is a seated figure, facing inwards, while beside Stephaton is a figure with its back turned. These may symbolise the sun and moon.

➤ To the left of this scene is the Denial of Peter, in which Saint Peter denied knowing Christ three times. On the right is the Resurrection, depicting Christ ascending over the tomb, which is guarded by two soldiers.

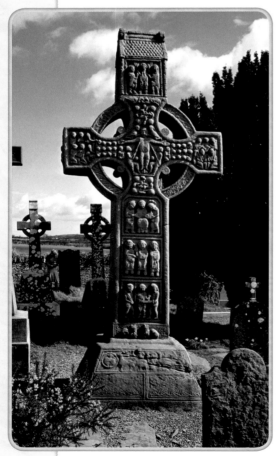

▲ *Muiredach's Cross, west face, Monasterboice, Co. Louth*

The scene at the top features the Ascension of Christ into heaven. The shaft of the cross has three main panels, with another narrower one below:

1. Christ is shown giving the New Testament to the apostle Saint Paul and the key to Saint Peter, the first pope.

2. Peter and Paul accompany the raised Christ.

3. This is a representation of Christ being jeered at by the soldiers, who called him 'The King of the Jews,' giving him a robe, sceptre and crown of thorns. It is called the Second Mocking of Christ.

North Side

At the base of the west face, over the inscription to Muiredach, are two cats, one with a kitten and one with a bird.

- The heads with snake embellishment feature again on the north side of the cross, with the **Hand of God** seen underneath the arm.

- There is a scene showing the First Mocking of Christ, when the Jewish people asked him why he, who saved others, could not save himself.

- On the top are Saint Paul and Saint Anthony, the hermits, receiving bread from a raven. At their feet is a chalice to emphasise the Eucharist as the bread of life.

> **dic·tion·ar·y**
>
> The **Hand of God** is used in Christian art and architecture as a symbol of God the Father. It symbolises God's ownership and care of all his creatures.

▲ *Detail of north side showing the Hand of God*

CROSS OF KELLS	
Date	Ninth and tenth centuries
Found	In the cemetery of Saint Columba's Church of Ireland, Kells, Co. Meath
Height	South Cross 3.3 m; West (headless) Cross 3.5 m; Unfinished Cross 4.75 m; Market Cross 3.35 m.

Kells in Co. Meath is one of the most significant high cross sites in the country. The Columban monastery where it is thought the Book of Kells was created is situated here, as are a round tower and Saint Colum Cille's house. Four high crosses stand on the site; one is unfinished, one is missing its head, while the other two, the South Cross and the Market Cross, are almost intact. Here, we will discuss the Unfinished Cross and the Market Cross.

Unfinished Cross

The Unfinished Cross gives us an insight into the production of the high cross, as it features only some rough preliminary carving as decoration. The head of the cross on the east face has a Crucifixion scene, while on the north arm there is an image which could represent a scene after the Resurrection, when an angel appeared to the women mourning Christ's death.

▶ *The Unfinished Cross, Kells, Co. Meath*

The Market Cross of Kells

This high cross, currently situated outside the Heritage Centre in Kells, Co. Meath, dates from the ninth century. It is not known where it was originally located, but it was re-erected on this site in 1688 and given the name 'The Market Cross' in the nineteenth century. It stands at 3.35 m high and is constructed in the traditional shape, with a ringed cross at the head of a long shaft and a broad base. The top of the wheel head and the capstone are now missing. The cross features carved scenes from the Bible with spiral and animal ornament.

East Face

- At the head of the cross, in the centre, is Daniel in the Lions' Den.
- The Sacrifice of Isaac is on the left arm, and the Temptation of Anthony on the right arm.
- Above the Lions' Den is a representation of Adam and Eve, while below it is David playing his lyre, which he did to help banish evil spirits from King Saul.

▲ *Detail from east face showing Adam and Eve, and Cain slaying Abel*

The shaft is split into three panels:

1. There are two scenes in this panel. The first shows Adam and Eve before they were thrown out of the Garden of Eden. The second depicts their son Cain killing his brother Abel.

2. This panel shows David as king, and his subjects, the Israelites.

3. The third panel depicts soldiers guarding the body of Christ who is laid in the tomb.

4. On the base is a depiction of four men on horses, possibly the Four Horsemen of the Apocalypse.

North Side

The panels on this side of the cross are difficult to interpret; the only one identified being the raven delivering food to the hermits, Paul and Anthony. Others include animal decoration such as centaurs (half-man, half-horse), birds and fish.

West Face

The Crucifixion is central to the head of the cross. Above this scene is the Crown of Thorns, and below it is one of the holy women bringing ointment to the tomb. To the left of Christ is an image of a bird and on his right is the figure of a man. It is thought that these refer to Saint Peter's denial of Jesus three times before the cock crew. On the left arm is Saint Anthony

▲ *The Market Cross of Kells, west face, Kells, Co. Meath*

stabbing the foot of the Devil, who is disguised as a woman to tempt him. Saint Anthony appears again on the other arm, along with Saint Paul as they wrestle with the Devil.

There are four sections on the west shaft:

1   The Miracle of the Loaves and Fishes.

2   This panel shows one of the miracles of Jesus. In it, he cures a servant of a centurion (a leader in the Roman army).

3   The third panel depicts a seated Christ, speaking to children.

4   We do not know what was originally on this panel as it was removed to make place for an inscription in 1688. It now gives the name of Robert Balfe (sovereign of the Corporation of Kells) and the date.

At the base of the west face are carvings of a deer hunt or a man herding animals.

South Side

On the shaft of the south side are four panels:

1   A portrayal of Moses and the Israelites being led across the desert to freedom from the Pharaoh by the Hand of God.

2   The second panel shows the prophet Samuel anointing David to be king of Israel.

3   This panel shows two soldiers holding a figure upside down. It is thought that it could be derived from the **Judgement of Solomon**.

4   The fourth panel depicts a stag being speared by a man.

The fifth panel is on the side of the arm of the cross. It shows David killing a lion. The base of the cross has a scene of soldiers in battle with swords and shields.

The **JUDGEMENT OF SOLOMON** is an Old Testament Bible story. Solomon was a king who was renowned for his fair judgement and wisdom. Two women came before Solomon claiming that they were both the mother of a child. Both women had children of a similar age and one of the children had died during the night. The grieving mother swapped the children, but her trickery was quickly found out by the other mother who recognised her own child. Solomon decreed that the child must be cut in two and equal shares given to both women. One of the women immediately gave up her rights to the child rather than harm him. Solomon then declared that she was the mother as she cared more about his welfare.

The High Crosses Revision Questions

1   Trace the emergence of the high crosses, by discussing the developments in structure and decoration.

2   Describe in detail one of the following high crosses, giving an account of its form, function and decoration: a) The Cross of Moone, b) Muiredach's Cross, c) The Market Cross of Kells.

The Viking Invasions

In 795, a group of warlike, skilled farmers, craftsmen and traders invaded Ireland, and were to have a huge impact, both good and bad, on the island. They were the Vikings (also called Norse people), pagans who came from Norway, Sweden and Denmark, in search not just of conquest, but of good farming land. They continued to raid Ireland frequently throughout the ninth and tenth centuries. The Irish monasteries – with their treasuries of altar vessels, shrines and manuscripts – suffered the most from these invasions. Clonmacnoise alone (see below) was attacked eight times between 834 and 1013. Although the devastation caused by these invasions was severe, the monasteries were very often attacked by the Irish themselves, as annals at Clonmacnoise show; they record 13 Irish attacks between 832 and 1100.

Effects on Irish Society

The Vikings founded the first towns in Ireland by the late eleventh century. These were Dublin, Wexford, Limerick and Waterford. They began to settle in Ireland in large numbers, and at first antagonised the native Irish by capturing some of them as slaves and attacking their places of worship and importance. Continuous battles with the Vikings caused internal power struggles within leading Irish families, and led to the breakdown of the small kingdoms which had previously formed the political structure of Irish society. Out of this chaos emerged powerful Irish dynasties who took over great portions of land. Later, the Vikings became more integrated into Irish society, and intermarriage between the two races helped to forge a bond. The Irish princess Gormflaith (c. 960–1030) married the Norse ruler Olaf (c. 926–981), who converted to Christianity. After his death, she married Brian Boru (c. 941–1014), who died at the Battle of Clontarf in 1014.

Advantages of the Viking Invasion

Although the arrival of the Norse invaders brought about political upheaval and widespread devastation throughout the country, it also brought many advantages:

- The Vikings founded the first towns.
- They encouraged trade between Ireland and Europe.
- They introduced the first coinage.
- They introduced advances in weaponry and shipbuilding.
- They introduced stirrups for better control of horses.
- They brought with them a wealth of knowledge in the fields of metalwork.

Introduction of New Styles and Techniques

In metalwork, the Ringerike and Urnes techniques came from the Vikings, and quickly became incorporated into Irish art, spurring the Irish-Romanesque style (see p. 58).

Ringerike

This was the earlier style of ornament brought over by the Vikings. It is first seen in wood carvings and designs on bone, and these objects now are grouped together under the 'Dublin Style' of Ringerike design. The style, which involves patterns of serpent-like animals with ribbon-shaped bodies, looping into figure-of-eight shapes, was later developed into metalwork, such as in the Crosier of the Abbots at Clonmacnoise (see pp. 55–6).

Urnes

The Urnes style was a later development on the Ringerike style. It continued to use animal ornamentation, but introduced slim, curved tendrils between the animal shapes. This can be seen in the Cross of Cong. The term 'Urnes' comes from a site in Norway, where the door jambs (sides) and lintels of the church are decorated in this technique.

The Fashion for Silver

The Vikings' love of silver filtered into the artwork and jewellery made by Irish craftsmen during this time. Silver was imported into Dublin in vast amounts after the Vikings constructed the port in 841, and it may have been mined in areas south of the city. The influx of silver to Ireland caused metalsmiths to begin working more with this metal than they had previously. Among the multitude of ornaments fashioned from silver in this era were thistle brooches, kite brooches, bossed penannular brooches, arm rings, necklaces and rings.

▼ *Bone motif pieces, National Museum – Decorative Arts and History, Dublin*

> ### Did you know?
> Bone motif pieces were thought to have been used by craftsmen to try out their techniques before working in bronze or silver. In this case 'motif' means trial.

▲ *Silver-bossed penannular brooch, National Museum – Decorative Arts and History, Dublin*

▶ *Thistle brooch, National Museum – Decorative Arts and History, Dublin*

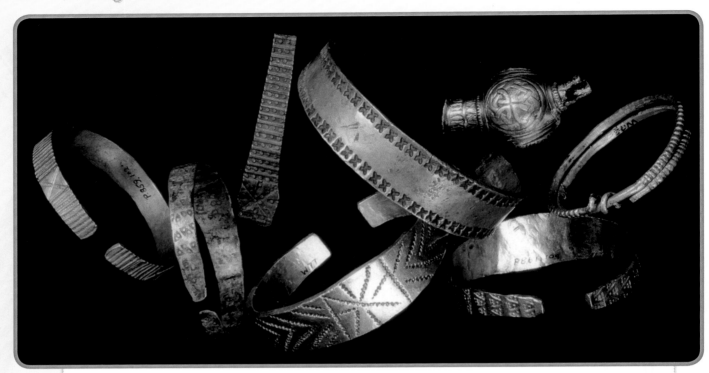

▲ *Silver arm rings, National Museum – Decorative Arts and History, Dublin*

▼ *The Cross of Cong, Cong, Co. Mayo*

THE CROSS OF CONG	
Date	Early twelfth century, created during the end of the Irish-Norse/Romanesque period.
Found	Cong, Co. Mayo. The cross was probably made in Tuam, Co. Galway, or Roscommon.
Function	The cross was used for religious processional purposes and display. It was made to house a relic of the True Cross, which the High King of Ireland, Turlough O'Connor (1088–1156), had obtained in 1122.

This reliquary is made from bronze, gold, silver, **rock crystal, niello**, glass and oak.

dic·tion·ar·y

Rock crystal is a clear, translucent quartz.

Niello is a black enamel alloy which is made by mixing sulphur with either silver, copper or lead.

- It is structured in a cruciform shape with a long shaft, and a large rock crystal in the centre. The crystal was placed there to protect the relic of the True Cross.

- The cross is mounted on a conical base surrounded by gold flanging. The cross itself is made of oak, overlaid with bronze panel work.

- The cross is decorated with cast openwork (see-through) bronze plates. These feature evidence of the Urnes style brought to Ireland by the Vikings, represented in the curved S-shaped animals and slim ribbons representing snakes.

- There are eight panels of decoration on each arm of the cross and the upper part of the shaft. The lower shaft contains 14 panels.

- At the centre, four panels of gold filigree support the huge, clear rock crystal.

- The cross's mount is ornamented with gold filigree work and raised bosses of blue and white glass and niello.

- The mount is joined to the body of the cross by the carved heads of dragon-like animals locking their jaws into it. These animals, with blue glass eyes set into them, have scale-like decoration on the tops of their heads.

▼ *Clonmacnoise Crosier, National Museum – Decorative Arts and History, Dublin*

THE CROSIER OF THE ABBOTS OF CLONMACNOISE

Date	Eleventh century
Found	Clonmacnoise, Co. Offaly
Function	The crosier (hooked staff) is thought to have belonged to the abbot of the Clonmacnoise monastery (see pp. 60–4). He would have used it during religious ceremonies, proclaiming his status as head of the monastery.

- This crosier, made from bronze, silver, niello and wood, was formed by wrapping two sheets of bronze, shaped like a tube, around a wooden staff.

- The crook of the staff is hollow and was cast in one piece. On the top of the crook is a crest made up of a row of five dogs, each one gripping the back of the dog in front with its jaws. This is openwork decoration, in which the designs have been cut into the metal. The figures are almost free-standing.

- The sides of the crook feature the ringerike style of ornament, with ribbon-like snakes with curved jaws, twisting in figure-of-eight patterns. These are created in bands of silver surrounded by borders of niello.

- More animal ornament appears where the staff meets the crook, this time in an openwork band. Four cat-like animals with clawed feet circle the top of the staff, their tails twining around each other to form interlace patterns.

- Between the cat-like figures are other animal heads which interlace with the tails.

- Some of the decoration on the crosier was added in the fifteenth century, including the openwork figure on the front of the crook of a bishop with mitre (pointed cap) slaying a monster.

THE SHRINE OF SAINT PATRICK'S BELL	
Date	c. 1100
Found	Armagh, Co. Armagh
Function	The shrine protected an iron bell coated in bronze, which was made in an earlier period and was believed to have once belonged to Ireland's patron saint, Patrick.

◀ *Shrine of Saint Patrick's Bell, side view, National Museum – Decorative Arts and History, Dublin*

This shrine is made from bronze, gold, silver, crystals and niello. The inscription is in Irish and asks the viewer to pray for four people. The first is Domhnall O'Lochlainn, who was the High King of Ireland, the second is the Bishop of Armagh, Domhnall MacAmhalgadha. The third person is Chathalan O'Maelchallan, the 'Keeper of the Bell,' and the final person is Cudilig O'Inmauien, the craftsman who created the shrine.

- The bell shrine is made up of four **trapezial** shapes with an elaborately decorated curved mount on top.

> **dic·tion·ar·y**
>
> A **trapezium** is a four-sided shape with two of the sides parallel to each other.

- Rings on the side of the shrine allowed it to be carried easily.

- The front panel of the shrine originally held 30 panels of gold filigree, four of which are now missing. The panels are arranged around a ringed cross shape with panels of filigree and six stones making up the border.

- There are four large panels surrounding the central rock crystal, two of which are decorated with gold filigree animals twisting into figure-of-eight patterns.

◈ The patterns were created using incredibly intricate craftwork. First, beaded bronze wire was set on a background of gold foil sheets, then a layer of gold beaded wire was placed over the shapes. The borders of the panels were also formed with beaded gold wire decoration.

◈ The silver back plate of the shrine overlays a bronze background and is decorated with openwork designs. These include interlocked circles and the inscription which runs around the edges.

▲ *Shrine of Saint Patrick's Bell, front view, National Museum – Decorative Arts and History, Dublin*

▲ *Shrine of Saint Patrick's Bell, back view, National Museum – Decorative Arts and History, Dublin*

The Viking Invasions Revision Questions

1 Discuss the changes that occurred in Ireland as a result of the Viking invasions. Include in your answer the metalwork techniques they introduced.

2 Describe the form, function and decoration on two of the following: a) The Shrine of Saint Patrick's Bell, b) The Clonmacnoise crosier, c) The Cross of Cong.

Irish-Romanesque Architecture and Sculpture

The term 'Romanesque' generally refers to the type of architecture that was common across Europe between the seventh and twelfth centuries. The Romanesque architectural style became popular in Ireland after the building of the first Romanesque church in Cashel, Co. Tipperary. Although Irish architects adopted some of the Romanesque traditions such as arcaded walls (with repeated archways) and columns, and ornamental sculpture, Irish churches continued to be built on a smaller scale than those found in Europe. The monastic communities built small churches with chancel arches (separating the eastern end of a church from the rest of the building) and ornately carved doorways. Most of these doorways feature rows of sculpted archways supported by columns and pilasters (flat columns set into a wall). The semicircular recessed area (called a tympanum) constructed over Romanesque doorways in Europe was mostly absent from Irish-Romanesque architecture. Monasteries also began to create high crosses again (see pp. 44–51) during this period. It is believed that the sculptors were influenced by their new knowledge of foreign techniques and designs, but blended this information with decorative motifs based on Irish sources such as the Book of Kells (see pp. 37–43) and the Irish/Urnes style prevalent in metalwork (see p. 53). It is also suggested that some carving was incised to act as guidelines for painted decoration found on religious buildings.

The Spread of the Romanesque Style

The rapid growth of the Romanesque style was largely due to the feudal system which was widespread across Europe at the time. In this system, lords gave lands to the lower classes in return for military service. The lords brought them travelling on **crusades** between 1095 and 1272. The craftsmen and builders travelling with the nobility helped to pass on their techniques and styles. During the crusades, a vast number of pilgrims (Christians visiting holy shrines) travelled to the larger churches to pay homage to the relics of saints which they housed. Abbeys and towns grew up along the routes to the cathedrals to accommodate these pilgrims. The most famous routes ended at the site of Santiago de Compostela in northern Spain (see p. 96), two of them crossing the Pyrenees.

dic·tion·ar·y

The **Crusades** were military campaigns which took place between 1095 and 1272. The Muslims from the Middle East had captured Jerusalem as it had been an important site in the history of their most revered prophet, Mohammed. Christian soldiers then began to wage war on the Muslims to gain back the birthplace and home of Christ. These Christian Crusades often included wars against pagan enemies and countries of other faiths.

Characteristics of the Romanesque Style

Buildings in the Romanesque style shared a number of features. One of the main common features is that they were all very large.

➡ **Thick walls and small windows:** Walls were solid and wide with small openings for windows. Very little natural light came in through the windows, which made the interiors quite dark.

- **Piers:** Large stone piers supported arches and were square or rectangular in shape.

- **Columns:** Classical Roman columns were taken from ancient sites and reused in some Romanesque buildings in Italy. Elsewhere in Europe, columns were built on a massive scale to help support the heavy roofs.

- **Carved capitals:** Corinthian capitals (tops of columns) which had foliage decoration, were most commonly found surmounting the columns.

- **Sculpture:** As most of the pilgrims and population of Europe were illiterate and the Mass was celebrated in Latin instead of the native language of the countries, one way to communicate the Word of God effectively to the congregation was through sculpture. Sculpture portrayed Bible scenes and also grotesque demons which were used to frighten believers into a holy way of life.

- **Rounded arches:** Romanesque arches are semicircular and rounded. Doorways have archways above them as do the larger windows. Some doorways were set into recessed decorative arches.

- **Cruciform layout:** The plan of a Romanesque church is based on the Latin cross – with a long nave (main body of the church) including a wide central aisle – hence the term 'cruciform.' It has two shorter transepts (wings on either side of the main aisle) with a semicircular apse (niche) behind it.

- **Vaulted roofs:** In previous times churches had wooden roofs which caught fire easily. During the Romanesque era, vaulted (arched) stone roofs became more common. Three types of vaults were used at this time:
  1. The barrel vault is the most basic and needs very solid walls to support the single arch.
  2. The groin vault is a square roof space composed of two arches which intersect at right angles.
  3. The ribbed vault is the most complicated vaulting system, with diagonal stone ribs coming together in the middle of the roof space to create a dome-like effect. It was not used as much as the first two, but became more widespread in the Gothic period (see pp.110–26).

▼ *Groin vault*

▼ *Ribbed vault*

Irish-Romanesque Monasteries

In 1169 Ireland was invaded by the Anglo-Normans from England, who brought with them the feudal system and new developments in architecture. Around the time of the invasion, the great western European religious orders began to arrive, setting up communities all over the country. The most significant of these were the Cistercians, the Franciscans, the Dominicans and the Augustinians, who began to construct churches and monasteries on a larger scale than any previously built in Ireland. Other orders such as the Carmelites and the Benedictines also created monasteries but in lesser numbers. The monastic sites consisted of a cloister, usually square or rectangular in shape, with open arcaded sides. Around this were situated the church, round tower, dwellings, refectory (eating hall) and kitchen, surrounded by walls for protection.

CLONMACNOISE

Style	Irish Romanesque	Place	Co. Offaly	Date	Founded 545	Founded by	Saint Ciarán (c. 516–549)

Clonmacnoise is one of Ireland's most famous historic monastic sites, situated beside the River Shannon in Co. Offaly and bordering the provinces of Leinster, Munster and Connaught. It was founded in 545 by Saint Ciarán who received his early religious training from Saint Diarmuid of Clonard and Saint Finian, who was famous for teaching Irish saints. He then studied on the island of Inis Mór, Co. Galway, under Saint Enda. After he moved to Clonmacnoise, Ciarán met Prince Diarmuid MacCerbhaill who was later to become the first Christian High King of Ireland. With the prince's help, Saint Ciarán built the first church in the settlement, but did not live to see the completion of the monastic site as he died of the yellow plague a year later. The original buildings were constructed from wood but none of them has survived. Most of the buildings standing today were built in the Romanesque style during and after the tenth century. These buildings now lie in ruins but the site contains three high crosses, one cathedral, two round towers and seven churches.

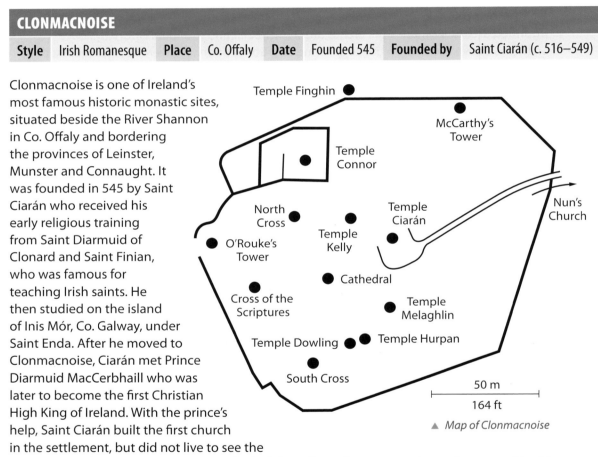

▲ Map of Clonmacnoise

The rapid growth of the site was mainly due to its central location beside the river which made it easily accessible for trade and transport. As a result, Clonmacnoise soon became one of the most important centres of learning and craftsmanship in the country, creating beautiful metalwork and illuminated manuscripts. The wealth and riches accumulated in the monastery were frequently under attack: six times by the Anglo-Normans eight times by the Vikings, as well as many raids by the Irish themselves.

The Nun's Church

The Nun's Church visible at Clonmacnoise was not the first nunnery to be built on this site – an older one dates back to 1026. The present structure was commissioned by Queen Dervorgilla of Breffny in 1172 and was completed in 1180. The queen ordered the building of the church after her husband had been killed in battle. The church is situated a little apart from the site of the monastery, with a stone-lined **causeway** leading it to the centre. The nave of the church is 10 m long and 6 m wide, with the chancel measuring 4.3 m in length and 4.2 m in width.

> **dic·tion·ar·y**
> A **causeway** is a pathway which has been trodden down to create a hard surface.

The large west doorway is adorned with three tiers:

1   The first has recessed and beaded chevrons.
2   The second order consists of the carved heads of beasts holding roll moulding (circular in profile) between their jaws.
3   The third order has richly carved foliar (leaf) decoration.

The piers on either side of the door have running chevron ornamentation which end in carved serpent heads. The hood moulding (designed to throw off water) holds another carved serpent, its head facing north and its tail pointing south.

The chancel arch (arch that spans the space around the altar) also has three orders. It is decorated with:

1   Deeply incised chevrons
2   Double chevrons
3   Fantastical carved heads.

▼ *Detail from the Nun's Church, Clonmacnoise, Co. Offaly*

Temple Mór

This cathedral is the largest ecclesiastical (religious) building on the Clonmacnoise site. It is 19 m long and 8.5 m wide. The cathedral is known by many names:

- Clonmacnoise Cathedral
- The Great Church
- The Church of the Kings
- MacDermott's Church
- Coghlan's Church.

Many influential Irish people were involved in the construction and reconstruction of the building. Building began in 909 under the patronage of Flann, the High King of Ireland (died 964) and Colman, the Abbot of Clonmacnoise and Clonard (died 926). After two fires, which took place in 985 and 1020, it was in need of rebuilding. This was undertaken by Flaithbertach O'Loinsig, the Abbott of Clonmacnoise from 1100 to 1109. Rory O'Connor, the last High King of Ireland was buried in the northeast corner of the chancel in 1198 and his predecessor Turlough was interred in the southwest corner.

- There was a **sacristy** attached to the southern part of the chancel which had a pointed portal (door) and two windows. It was approximately 6 m long and 6 m wide with two small windows and a pointed arched doorway. Above the lower level there was a living space.

> **dic·tion·ar·y**
> A **sacristy** is a room attached to a church where sacred vessels such as chalices are kept.

- There are distinct stylistic differences within the church itself; the west portal was constructed in the Romanesque style whereas the north doorway was created in the Gothic tradition with its intricate moulding and pointed archway.

- Above the north portal are three figures representing Saint Francis, Saint Dominic and Saint Patrick. These date back to 1460.

- Smaller figures carved above the archway represent the four Gospel scribes: Matthew, Mark, Luke and John.

Temple Finghin

Temple Finghin is rectangular building with a round tower attached, constructed at Clonmacnoise in the twelfth century. A Romanesque chancel arch is one of its finest features. The church incorporates a round tower which was built at an earlier date.

◀ *Temple Finghin and McCarthy's Tower, Clonmacnoise, Co. Offaly*

McCarthy's Tower

This tower was built in the twelfth century and funded by Cathal Conchubhair who was the king of Connaught. It is 15.2 m high with a conical roof and is situated in the northwest of the cemetery.

Temple Melaghlin

The name of this church comes from the Melaghlin family who were the kings of Meath. It is also known as Temple Rí – Rí is the Irish word for 'king'. It was built in the thirteenth century and is constructed in the Irish style, popular in the west of Ireland. There are two round-headed windows set into the east wall and the eastern side of the south-facing wall. There is moulding around these windows and corbels at the external corners of the roof. A doorway is situated in the south wall which may have been reconstructed at a later stage.

▲ *Temple Melaghlin, Clonmacnoise, Co. Offaly*

Temple Dowling

This ninth-century church is one of the oldest buildings in Clonmacnoise. It is small, measuring just 9.4 m in length and 4.8 m in width. A large round-headed window is placed in the east wall and is carved from one stone. The three other windows are very narrow in shape. There is a panel made of stone with a carved inscription and coat of arms. It was partially restored in 1869. Outside stands a high cross called the South Cross.

Temple Kelly

This church, situated northeast of the cathedral, is one of the more ruined buildings. It is thought that it was built to replace the wooden oratory which originally stood on this site. It dates back to 1167.

Temple Connor

Temple Connor measures almost 11 m in length by 6 m in width. It is rectangular in shape, with an arched doorway dating from the twelfth century set into the western wall. Like MacCarthy's Tower, it is thought to be associated with the kings of Connaught.

▲ *Temple Dowling, Clonmacnoise, Co. Offaly*

▲ *Temple Connor, Clonmacnoise, Co. Offaly*

O'Rourke's Tower

O'Rourke's Tower is constructed from large limestone blocks and was begun in the tenth century. The benefactor for this building was another Connaught king – Fergal O'Rourke (died 964). The tower was not completed until 1124, long after the death of the king. It was struck by lightning in 1135 and the upper part of the building had to be rebuilt at a later stage. It is situated in the northwest of Clonmacnoise with a high doorway set 3.3 m above ground level.

▶ *O'Rourke's Tower, Clonmacnoise, Co. Offaly*

Temple Hurpan

Temple Hurpan is a small church, 6.7 m long and 3.6 m wide, attached to the east end of Temple Dowling. There is a large window facing east. Over the door there is an indented niche which may have been designed to bear an inscription. In the inside of the north wall there is a grave slab which came from the original church on the site. The slab is inscribed in Irish and reads 'A prayer for Dithraid.'

◄ *Temple Hurpan, Clonmacnoise, Co. Offaly*

GLENDALOUGH							
Style	Irish Romanesque	**Place**	Co. Wicklow	**Date**	Founded in sixth century	**Founded by**	Saint Kevin

The site at Glendalough, Co. Wicklow was once a very important religious centre of learning and was founded by **Saint Kevin** (c. 498–618). The name comes from the Irish name meaning 'glen of the two lakes.' Saint Kevin crossed the mountains to Glendalough to find a peaceful retreat which would serve as a site for monastic development. The track he took was later named Saint Kevin's Way and became the customary route for pilgrims seeking the monastery. It is thought that the original development took place on the southeast of the upper lake where the Reefert church is now situated (built in 1100; now in ruins). This is possibly because this was the place where kings and chieftains were traditionally buried. By the time Saint Kevin died, the monastery and its community were flourishing. It is believed that, apart from the religious population, there were between 500 to 1000 lay people (non-clergy) living in the area. These would have served the monastery, tending the farmland and the stock owned by the monks. They would also have helped to rebuild the monastery and ecclesiastical buildings after the many raids from local chieftains and Norse invaders (see p. 52). The decline of the monastery happened at the same time as the arrival of the Normans in Ireland (see p. 60). The site was destroyed by a Norman invasion in 1214 and never fully recovered. Another factor in its deterioration was the joining of the **diocese** of Glendalough with the diocese of Dublin. This made it less important. Reconstruction of the site began in 1875 and continued until the beginning of the twentieth century.

biography

SAINT KEVIN is thought to have been descended from one of the kings of Leinster. As a young boy, he was taught by three holy men: Eoghan, Lochan and Eanna. There are a number of legends associated with Saint Kevin as a young man. One of these claimed that as Kevin tended sheep for his parents a group of poor beggars approached him. He was so touched by their poverty that he gave them four of his sheep. That evening when the sheep were being counted it was discovered that he still had the right amount of sheep. He later went to live in quiet solitude as a hermit at Glendalough. His severe lifestyle inspired others to follow his example and a religious settlement built up in the area. Saint Kevin lived separately from the rest of the community in Saint Kevin's Cell for four years. During this time he saw nobody, survived on fruit and berries growing in the area and wore only coarse rags to keep warm. It is claimed that he lived for 120 years.

dic·tion·ar·y

A **diocese** is a region consisting of several parishes presided over by a bishop.

Trade and Travel Routes

The development of the early roads in the Glendalough area began in the Late Bronze Age (see pp. 9–12) to accommodate trade between the communities living around the mountains and to allow access to the coast. Four major routes were built for these purposes:

1   One of the roads led from Newcastle beside the coast and wound through the Sally Gap in the mountains to Wicklow, extending as far as Naas.

2   The second road followed a southeasterly route from Wicklow and went around Carrick Mountain, where it veered north to Parkmore and then turned east to Glendalough. After Glendalough the track followed a route carved out by glaciation in the Wicklow Gap as far as Dunlavin. This road was so well-travelled that improvements were made to assist the pilgrims and tradesmen using it. Large granite stones paved the way and small churches and crosses were built by the roadside to help direct pilgrims on their way.

3   Another route started at the coast in Brittas Bay and wound from Glenmalure to Mullamast in Co. Kildare. Here, there are two **ringforts** and a standing stone, which give evidence that a community lived there.

4   The fourth route wound around the southern part of the Wicklow Mountains and ran from Arklow to Rathvilly in Co. Carlow.

> dic·tion·ar·y
>
> **Ringforts** were ancient farmsteads which were fortified by a circular wall or earthen bank surrounding them.

▼ *One of the early roads in the Glendalough area passed through the Sally Gap, Co. Wicklow*

The Gateway to Glendalough

This is the only gateway to an ancient monastic site still in existence. It is situated beside the bridge over the Glendassan River, which runs through Glendalough. The gateway was built at a later date than the rest of the settlement and consists of a gatekeeper's lodge, a tower and a deep double archway. The inner arch is higher than the outer one to counterbalance the ground's rise in slope, and both are supported by granite piers. It is thought that the entrance to the gatekeeper's lodge was situated high above ground level in one of the side walls. On the inside west wall there is a large slab measuring 1.5 m in height and 2.3 m in width. A cross is carved into this slab. This type of incised cross was often found in other ecclesiastical settlements and its function was to let travellers know that they could seek refuge within the walls of the monastery.

▲ *Gateway to Glendalough, Co. Wicklow*

Saint Saviour's Church

Saint Saviour's Church, in the eastern side of Glendalough, is good example of a typical Romanesque building.

- Its nave is 12.5 m long and 6.2 m wide.

- The chancel (where the altar is situated) is 4.26 m by 3.5 m, and has a beautifully decorated chancel arch.

- One of the capitals on the piers surrounding the door has carved decorations of a wolf and a human head. The wolf's tail is intertwined with the human's hair.

- The door jambs (sides) are also carved with animal and human sculptures, with fantastical dragons and a raven shown devouring a human head.

▶ *Saint Saviour's Church, Glendalough, Co. Wicklow*

Saint Kevin's Kitchen

This small building is an oratory dedicated to Saint Kevin. Rising over the west end of the structure is a small version of a round tower. It is called Saint Kevin's 'Kitchen' because the bell turret resembles a big chimney, which might have been used in kitchens at this time. The turret actually may have served as an oratory.

▲ *Saint Kevin's Kitchen, Glendalough, Co. Wicklow*

- The doorway faces west and has a semicircular relieving arch (an archway that bears the weight of the roof).

- Part of the building now lies in ruins – the surviving foundations reveal that a chancel was originally there.

- The roof is supported by a barrel-vaulted ceiling with a small vaulted room above.

Saint Kevin's Cell

This is the cell was where Saint Kevin spent four years living completely alone without contact with anyone from the community. During this time he survived only on food gathered from the land around him. The cell was built away from the main monastic site, looking out over the upper of the two lakes, and is similar to beehive huts constructed at **Skellig Michael** in Kerry.

> ### dic·tion·ar·y
>
> **Skellig Michael** is a seventh-century monastery built on the island of Skellig Michael, off the southwest coast of Ireland. There, monks lived in small stone cells clustered around a little church.

- It is made of stone and circular in shape, with thick walls 0.9 m wide.

- The cell is 3.6 m wide. The roof is now missing but it is believed that is was originally roofed in stone like a traditional beehive hut.

- A small cross shape is in the middle of the cell.

▼ *Saint Kevin's Cell, Glendalough, Co. Wicklow*

Saint Kevin's Bed

Saint Kevin's Bed consists of a cave cut into a rock beside the mountains and a passage leading into it which is 0.9 m high and 0.7 m wide. The cave, set 10 m higher than ground level, is only 0.9 m high and 1.2 m wide and could only have been used as a sleeping place or a place of prayer.

The Priest's House

This small church was possibly used to house relics and reliquaries. It may also have been where objects became relics. Pilgrims may have brought items and touched Saint Kevin's body with them through a niche in the wall, thus making them holy. There is a lintel over the doorway which had carvings of a king and a priest holding a bell incised on it. The building has been renovated extensively – the east end was entirely rebuilt in 1870.

Glendalough Cathedral

The cathedral which now stands in Glendalough dates back to 1000, but within its walls lie the remains of an even older and smaller church. Part of this earlier church still exists, its original west portal altered in height to suit the rest of the later structure. In the late 1100s the church was extended. A new doorway in the northern end of the cathedral was added, along with a chancel arch and a sacristy.

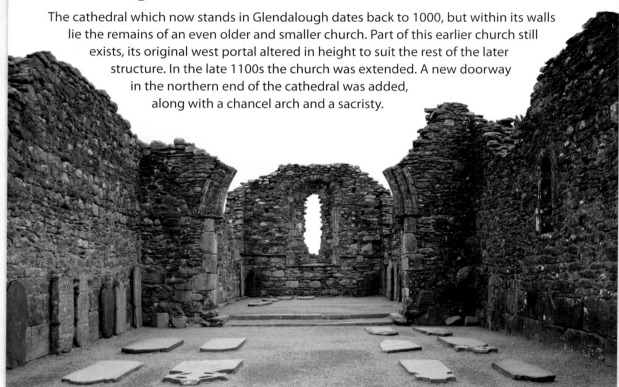

▲ *Glendalough Cathedral, Glendalough, Co. Wicklow*

CLONFERT CATHEDRAL							
Style	Irish Romanesque	**Place**	Co. Galway	**Date**	Founded 563	**Founded by**	Saint Brendan

The Cathedral of Saint Brendan in Clonfert, Co. Galway has the most beautifully ornate doorway of all the Irish-Romanesque churches. The church was built in 1164 and is situated on the west bank of the Shannon River, 8 km northwest of Banagher, Co. Offaly. The cathedral itself is small, only 25 m long, but the doorway is the tallest of its kind. In the fifteenth century, the chancel arch and the innermost order of the doorway were added, both decorated with Tudor foliar designs (rose-shaped) and made of limestone. The older part of the doorway is made from sandstone.

biography

SAINT BRENDAN (c. 484–577) was born near Tralee in Co. Kerry. He went on a voyage in search of Paradise, and later founded several monasteries in Ireland.

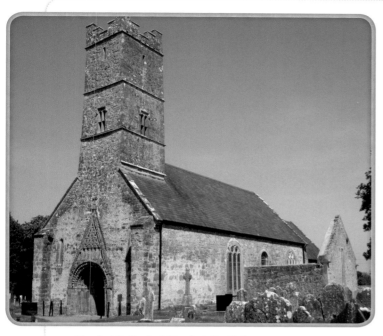

▲ *Clonfert Cathedral, Clonfert, Co. Galway*

▲ *Detail on Clonfert Cathedral doorway, Clonfert, Co. Galway*

Arch Rings

There are five original recessed **arch rings** above the door, each carved with different decorations:

1. The inner arch ring is decorated with foliar patterns of six-petal palmettes (motifs like palm leaves).

2. On the second, carved dogs' heads are shown biting into arris (sharp edge) moulding.

3. The third order has patera (shallow and circular) shapes surrounded by two rows of moulding.

4. The fourth ring features pateras again, this time with one row on the outer ring, and another row in the recess.

5. The outer arch has large stone bosses in horseshoe forms.

▶ *Arch rings on Clonfert Cathedral doorway, Clonfert, Co. Galway*

dic·tion·ar·y

Arch rings are curved concentric half rings (with the same centre) set back behind each other, supported by their own columns.

Columns

Flat decorative pilasters frame the sides of the round and octagonal-shaped columns which support the arch rings. The shafts of the columns are decorated with a number of motifs:

- Lozenges
- Chevrons
- Palmettes
- Circles
- Rosettes (motifs like roses).

These are topped by square capitals, which have scroll foliage carvings. Underneath these are rows of small animal heads.

The columns are set on top of square bases.

▲ *Detail of columns, Clonfert Cathedral doorway, Clonfert, Co. Galway*

Pediment

- The triangular pediment (gable over a door) sits on top of the arch rings and is steep in form.
- Around the edges of the pediment runs decorated rope moulding (resembling a twisted rope).
- Underneath the point of the pediment are five rows of alternating recessed and raised triangles.
- The raised triangles feature carved foliage, while each recessed panel holds a carved human head – ten in all, seven of which are bearded.
- Between the rows of triangles and the arch rings is a row of arches forming a blind arcade – a series of arches supported by columns set against a wall. Underneath each arch is a human head.
- The columns of the arcade all feature different decoration, including stylised herring-bone designs, concentric circles and zigzags.

Irish-Romanesque Architecture and Sculpture Revision Questions

1 Give an account of Irish-Romanesque architecture, with particular reference to two buildings.

2 Discuss the settlement at Clonmacnoise under the headings: a) history, b) buildings.

3 Give an overview of the monastic settlement at Glendalough with particular emphasis on two of the buildings.

4 Describe the decoration on the doorway of Clonfert Cathedral. Include sketches in your answer.

Ancient Art in the Modern World

During the nineteenth century there was a growth of interest in Ireland's Celtic past and a desire for a national identity. This grew from a need felt by many Irish people for political freedom from English rule. In 1829, the **Catholic Relief Act** gave civil rights to Catholics (known as Catholic Emancipation) and instilled in many a desire for a separate cultural identity. To find this, the leaders in the areas of art and

> **Did you know?**
> Before **CATHOLIC EMANCIPATION**, the Penal Laws imposed by the British government prohibited Catholics from holding public office, being elected to parliament, and practising their religion. It also excluded most Catholics from voting.

literature looked back to the early cultures to embrace their Celtic heritage. They studied ancient manuscripts to help provide them with details of the everyday lives and customs in ancient Ireland. Objects of fine craftsmanship and architecture also served as inspiration for a revival of ancient traditions.

Irish Emblems

The use of emblems to symbolise Ireland became popular. The most common of these were:

- The shamrock
- The harp
- The wolfhound
- The round tower.

The Shamrock

This is possibly the most enduring emblem associated with Ireland. One legend states that Saint Patrick used the three leaves of the shamrock to explain the Holy Trinity of God the Father, God the Son, and the Holy Spirit. Later, in the sixteenth century, an English report stated that it formed part of the Irish diet. As this was around the time of the Great Famine, it may have had some basis in truth. The symbol was used on commemorative medals in the nineteenth century.

The Harp

The harp originated as a symbol of Ireland during the reign of Henry VIII of England (1509–47). It featured on the British coat of arms to represent Ireland. In the nineteenth century the most common form of the harp was a design based on Brian Boru's harp and was found reproduced in jewellery such as brooches from 1850. In 1862, the Guinness Brewery adopted the motif.

The Wolfhound

The Irish wolfhound is famous for being the tallest breed of dog in the world and has long been a source of pride in Ireland. Wolfhounds were bred for the hunting of deer and as protection from wolves. Ancient heroic sagas tell tales of the bravery of the wolfhound in the stories of **Fionn MacCumhaill**

and **Cúchulainn**. They were famous throughout Europe – as early as the fourth century some wolfhounds were transported to Rome to show off their skills. In 1885 the Irish Wolfhound Club was founded by Captain Graham, a Scottish soldier. Wolfhounds also appeared in many paintings and emblems accompanied by a female figure representing Ireland.

The Round Tower

The round tower was chosen as a symbol of Ireland because it was a building entirely unique to the island. It wasn't until the mid-nineteenth century that the connection between the monasteries and the round towers was made. Before this their function had been a mystery.

The Revival of Irish Antiquities

In 1828, the antiquarian George Petrie (see p. 17) became a member of the **Royal Irish Academy** and was elected to the council within a year. He had a deep interest in the craftsmanship of ancient Irish culture and was instrumental in organising and displaying the objects in the Academy's museum. Most importantly he added valuable contributions to the collection, acquiring the Cross of Cong in 1839 (see pp. 54–5) and the Tara Brooch and the Ardagh Chalice in 1868 (see pp. 24–6). The beauty and intricate workmanship of these pieces had a huge impact on the public, spurring on the development of a national pride and identity.

Celtic Art in the Twenty-First Century

The traditional Celtic imagery and symbols are still very much a part of Irish culture. They are used in many different ways, from painting and illustration to jewellery and fashion. Celtic art is also used to emphasise Ireland's cultural heritage in the fields of tourism and music. There is a fine line, however, between nostalgic images of Irish cultural identity and tasteless sentimentality. Sometimes people abroad think of the Irish as picturesque fun-loving peasants, believing in leprechauns and living in thatched cottages. These stereotypical images of Irish people and Irish customs are particularly evident in Saint Patrick's Day parades celebrated abroad, which are far removed from present-day Ireland.

◀ *A reveller throws himself in to Saint Patrick's Day celebrations in New York, USA.*

Jewellery

Probably the most common form of Celtic art today is seen in traditional jewellery. Celtic symbols such as the ring-wheeled high cross, Celtic knots (such as the eternity or lovers' knots), spirals and interlace adorn many different types of jewellery including rings, brooches, necklaces and bracelets. Some of the designs are not strictly Celtic in design but have their roots in Celtic culture. An example of a very popular item is the **Claddagh ring**, which is composed of a heart held by a hand on either side, symbolising friendship.

Celtic Symbols in Jewellery

Celtic symbols have been used for hundreds of years and their meanings may have changed or developed over time.

- **Knots and interlace:** These symbolise the intertwining of our spiritual and physical lives. Examples of these are the lover's knot, which is often used on wedding ring; the eternity knot, which symbolises continuity; and the more recent heart knot, in which interlacing ribbons entwine around a heart shape.

- **The Celtic cross:** The wheeled cross in modern design takes its inspiration from the high crosses (see pp. 44–51). The circle is often interpreted as a halo or a symbol of eternity.

- **The Evangelist symbols**: These symbolise the four Gospel scribes.
  The Man – Saint Matthew
  The Lion – Saint Mark
  The Calf – Saint Luke
  The Eagle – Saint John
  Another explanation for the use of these symbols is that they could symbolise the four stages in the life of Christ. He was born as a man, the calf is a motif for his sacrifice, he was a lion in his Resurrection and the eagle represents his Ascension into heaven.

- **Spirals:** Spirals are commonly found in nature, for example in whirlpools or snail shells. They are also the most recognisable of Irish emblems. They are thought to represent blessings and harmony with nature.

> **dic·tion·ar·y**
>
> **Claddagh rings** originated in Claddagh, Co. Galway and are mostly given as a token of friendship or love. The design consists of two hands holding a heart which is topped by a crown. The hands are thought to symbolise friendship; the heart, love and the crown, loyalty. If the ring is worn with the heart facing inwards the person wearing it is in love.

Music Design

Irish traditional music in the twentieth century makes great use of Celtic design, using Celtic fonts (styles of type) for the lettering on CDs and often showing famous ancient landmarks and sites in the artwork. The success of the Irish dancing-based show *Riverdance* brought Celtic design and culture to the attention of the world in recent times.

Art

Some artists use the ancient Irish sagas such as tales of Fionn MacCumhaill as inspiration for their work, drawing upon Celtic designs and patterns to enhance the cultural significance of their work. Jim Fitzpatrick (born 1945) is one of Ireland's most popular living artists. His work is known throughout the world and combines a fluid, linear drawing style with vibrant colours and intricate details. His work is mostly figurative and often includes Celtic patterns and emblems.

Illustration for *The Book of Conquests, 1978*

The inspiration for Jim Fitzpatrick's illustrations in *The Book of Conquests* is derived from the sagas about Nuada who was the king of the **Tuatha dé Danann** in Irish mythology. Fitzpatrick's earlier work was influenced by **Aubrey Beardsley's** graphic style but he became gradually more inspired by early Christian illuminated manuscripts and Japanese prints.

Body Art

Another increasingly popular form of Celtic art and design can be witnessed in the rise of Irish symbols and patterns in body art. Tattoo designs include intricate knot work and interlace designs, animal motifs inspired by the Book of Kells, and Celtic crosses.

State Documents

The government of Ireland uses Irish motifs in their documents, such as passports, which feature the symbol of a harp. The harp is also used on the uniforms of Government officials, such as the Garda and army uniforms.

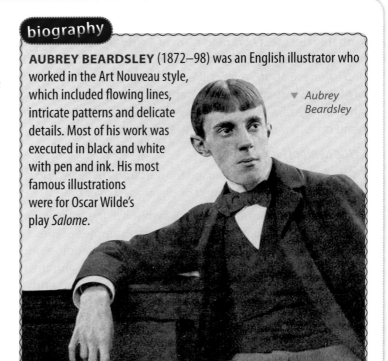

biography

AUBREY BEARDSLEY (1872–98) was an English illustrator who worked in the Art Nouveau style, which included flowing lines, intricate patterns and delicate details. Most of his work was executed in black and white with pen and ink. His most famous illustrations were for Oscar Wilde's play *Salome*.

▼ *Aubrey Beardsley*

dic·tion·ar·y

The **Tuatha dé Danann** are a mythological race of godlike beings that were said to have lived in Ireland in ancient times. They are believed to have settled around the Boyne valley and legend often links them to the historic landmarks in the region such as Newgrange.

Tourism

In almost any town in Ireland it is possible for a tourist to purchase a keepsake of Irish Celtic design in the forms of jewellery, small-scale models of local landmarks and fashion. There is also a broad range of everyday objects available, ornamented with Celtic motifs, including T-shirts, key-rings, mugs or other everyday items. This helps to spread the cultural identity of Ireland abroad.

Ancient Art in the Modern World Revision Questions

1 Discuss the growth of interest in Celtic design in Ireland during the nineteenth century. Trace its influence in the work of artists and designers to the present day.

▶ *'The Coming of Lúgh the Il-Dána,' a Tuatha dé Danann warrior, Jim Fitzpatrick*

Early Irish Art Bibliography

1 Wallace, Patrick F. and O'Floinn, Raghnall: *Treasures of the National Museum of Ireland*, Gill & Macmillan Ltd., 2002

2 Mackworth-Praed, Ben: *The Book of Kells*, Random House UK Ltd, 1993

3 Meehan, Bernard: *The Book of Kells*, Thames & Hudson, 1994

4 Meehan, Bernard: *The Book of Durrow*: A Medieval Masterpiece, Townhouse Ltd, 1996

5 De Breffny, Brian: *Heritage of Ireland*, Weidenfeld & Nicolson, 1980

6 Ryan, Michael: *Early Irish Communion Vessels*, Townhouse & Country House Ltd, 2000

7 Herity, Michael, *Irish Passage Graves*, Irish University Press, 1974

8 De Breffny, Brian, and Mott, George: *The Churches and Abbeys of Ireland*, Thames & Hudson, 1976

9 Rothery, Seán: *A Field Guide to the Buildings of Ireland*, Lilliput Press Ltd, 1997

10 Sheehy, Jeanne: *The Rediscovery of Ireland's Past*, Thames & Hudson, 1980

11 Edelstein, Teri: *Imagining an Irish Past: The Celtic Revival 1840–1940,* University of Chicago Press, 1992

12 Ryan, Michael: *The Illustrated Archaeology of Ireland,* Town and Country House, 1991

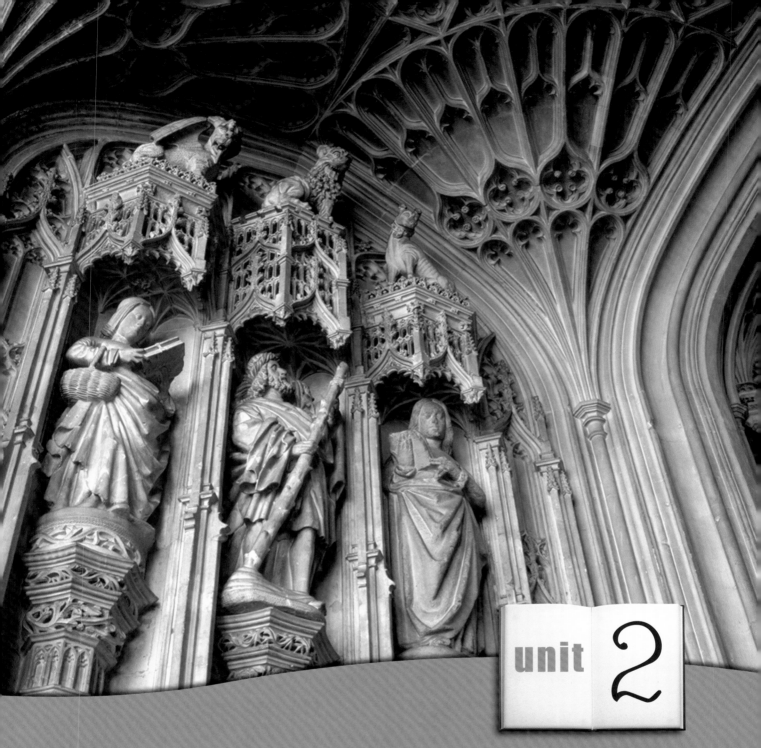

unit 2

Romanesque and Gothic
Art and Architecture
c. 1000–c. 1520

Introduction

Romanesque architecture is the term used to describe the style of buildings which were constructed in western Europe from the seventh century through to the twelfth century. It later developed into Gothic architecture. Romanesque architectural features consist of thick walls, semi-circular arches, strong piers, barrel vaults and groin vaults. Gothic architecture would develop all of these elements and add more to create even more amazing architecture. It is interesting to note that cathedral building surpassed the building of castles and large houses during this era. The glory and beauty of these cathedrals can still be experienced to this day.

Building in the Middle Ages

Many of the castles, churches, cathedrals and monasteries that we can visit today are evidence of the huge amount of building that took place during the **Middle Ages** in Europe. Generous donations from kings and wealthy families made this architecture possible.

The Feudal System

Society during the Middle Ages was organised into a 'feudal' system, in which land was given out in return for military service. The **Anglo-Normans** brought the feudal system with them to Ireland. At the top of the feudal scale was the king. He gave land to his most powerful subjects, the barons and the bishops. They then became the king's vassals (servants). The barons and bishops, in turn, divided their lands between knights. Knights were bound by oath (a promise) to serve their masters and could be ordered to battle at any time.

Castles

A castle is really a fortified (strengthened against attack) home. Many castles were built during the Middle Ages, and they served several purposes in society:

dic·tion·ar·y

The term **Middle Ages** covers the period between the fall of the Roman Empire in the fifth century to the end of the fifteenth century, when the Renaissance swept across Europe. The Middle Ages are referred to as the 'medieval' period.

Anglo-Normans were the descendants of the Normans who ruled England following the conquest by William of Normandy in 1066. They came to Ireland in 1169, bringing with them the feudal system.

▼ *Slane Castle in Co. Meath*

- To display the wealth and power of the owner – only kings or wealthy landlords could afford to live in castles.

- To provide a comfortable dwelling for the owner.

- To protect all the inhabitants, as well as the riches of the owner, from military attacks by enemies in times of war.

- To be a venue for social events, where all society could gather and celebrate.

- To make a statement to outsiders about the owner – this made the originality of the design important.

▲ *Durham Castle, northern England, began in 1072 as a defensive mound*

Motte and Bailey Castles

Over the years castle design changed with new developments in building techniques, technological advances and new materials. The first castles to be built were known as motte and bailey castles.

- **Motte:** A motte was a flat-topped mound of earth and stone, topped with a timber tower and enclosed with a wooden fence called a palisade. The carpentry of the tower required skilled labourers.

- **Bailey:** At the foot of the motte lay a crescent-shaped, D-shaped or U-shaped courtyard called a bailey, which was also enclosed with a palisade and then surrounded with a ditch. It was easy to create this surrounding ditch when workers (usually unskilled) dug the earth out to build up the motte.

▶ *Diagram of a motte and bailey*

Water

Motte

Bridge

Upper bailey

Mottes and Baileys in Ireland

Early in the twelfth century many Irish people had travelled to England and France where they saw fortified castles for the first time. They saw how these fortified castles proved a success to the Anglo-Normans in their warfare and the rulers in Ireland began to build the same type of castle. The Anglo-Normans constructed many motte and bailey castles in the last decade of the twelfth century in Ireland. You can still see mottes in Ireland, some of which still have the outline of the bailey. One of the best-preserved mottes is Knockgraffon motte, Co. Tipperary, built in 1192. On this medieval site there is also a bailey, a church and a castle. The motte at Granard in Co. Longford is said to be the highest in Ireland, at 166 m above sea level. You can clearly see the outline of the bailey protected by a ditch and bank. This motte and bailey were built by Richard Tuite, Lord Chief Justice of Ireland, (died 1210) in 1190. There is a statue of Saint Patrick, erected in 1932, on top of the motte.

▶ *The modern-day remains of a motte, dating from the eleventh century, Norfolk, England*

Keeps

The Anglo-Normans soon realised that if they were to maintain their position in Ireland and expand their control it was necessary for them to build more permanent and defensible fortresses. They had superior weapons and military techniques, but the Irish had superiority in numbers and were fierce and reckless in war. The Anglo-Normans knew that a castle could be better defended if it had a simple, strong stone-built tower, called a keep, and a strong surrounding (curtain) wall. If possible they built the castle on an important headland or site with a commanding view of all roads approaching the castle.

▲ *The castle of Dunamase, Co. Laois, is an excellent example of a hilltop site.*

Carrickfergus Castle, 1177

This castle in Co. Antrim, Northern Ireland, is one of the best-preserved Anglo-Norman buildings in the country. It has a rectangular keep within a curtain wall, built on a low rocky headland on Belfast Lough.

▼ *Carrickfergus Castle, Co. Antrim*

Did you know?
Stone towers are now known as keeps, but back in the Middle Ages they were called **great towers** or **donjons**.

▲ *Nenagh Castle, Co. Tipperary, is an example of a thirteenth century keep*

Gatehouses

A gatehouse is a house built at the gates of a castle. It would have been occupied at all times, usually by a family, and was another security measure for the castle. The people who lived in the gatehouse opened the gates when the king, lord or lady was approaching. There is a fine example of a gatehouse at Birr Castle, Co. Offaly.

Birr Castle, 1630

This castle was the medieval stronghold of the O'Carroll family. It sits 55 m to the northwest of the present castle at Birr. When Sir Charles O'Carroll died in 1619, an opportunity arose for the English Government to declare this land property of the crown and assign it for **plantation**. Much of the land was given back to its former Irish owners, but some was given to English families in the hope that they would bring English rule to the area. In 1620 Birr castle and its 1000 acres of land was allotted to Sir Laurence Parsons, who served as attorney general for Munster. Sir Laurence took great interest in the gatehouse, and flanked it with freestanding towers.

▲ *Birr Castle, Co. Offaly*

Churches

During the Middle Ages the Catholic Church was the only recognised church in Europe, and was ruled by the Pope from Rome, Italy. It was the most important influence in society, and played a huge role in people's day-to-day lives.

1   One of the main roles of the Church was to instruct the people in the teachings of God. As 90 per cent of people were illiterate, they learned about religion at Mass and from Bible stories told through artwork such as statues, stained glass windows and frescoes (large paintings drawn on walls or ceilings). The Church had complete control over the subject matter: craftworkers and artists were told what to create, and what materials and colours to use. Often images were grotesque, to frighten the people into leading good lives for fear of going to hell. The artists saw themselves as instruments of God and not as individuals – as a result, much of the artwork from this era remains anonymous.

2   People in the community saw the church as a place where they could go to receive forgiveness for their sins, to pray for the sick and dead, and also to celebrate events such as weddings and christenings.

3   During the Middle Ages many people went on pilgrimages (visits to holy shrines; see p. 93). As Christianity spread across Europe more pilgrimage sites containing holy **relics** sprung up. In order to facilitate the growing demand for pilgrimages, new churches were built along their routes.

dic·tion·ar·y

During the sixteenth and seventeenth centuries, **plantations** were established throughout Ireland. Under the command of the English crown, English soldiers took away Irish lands, which were owned by Irish and Norman clans. The king gave this land to colonists, called 'planters,' from England. Lots of families were imported into Ireland from England, Scotland and Wales. The plantations took place mainly in Ulster and Munster.

A **relic** is a part of a saint's body, such as a lock of hair or a fragment of bone, or a piece of his/her clothing, which has remained intact over hundreds of years. Christians believe that relics are very holy.

The Wealth of the Church and its Sources

The growth in the number of churches was made possible by the increasing wealth of the Church. A new wave of prosperity swept over Europe, and a social and religious change took place:

- The established royal kingdoms became wealthier, larger, and more secure.

- The Church benefited from this wave of prosperity. It received substantial property donations from kings and gentry, enabling it to build monasteries and cathedrals in prime locations throughout Europe.

- The Catholic Church carried out reforms which included the creation of new monastic orders. The most famous of these was the Benedictine order, which had its main house at Cluny, France (see p. 88). The Cluniac order was a subset of the Benedictines. The order became very powerful through generous donations and gifts of land from kings, gentry and pilgrims.

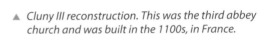

▲ *Cluny III reconstruction. This was the third abbey church and was built in the 1100s, in France.*

Features of Church Design

All church and cathedral designs at this time were similar. They mostly had a **cruciform** shape to symbolise the cross on which Jesus died. They consisted of:

- A **nave:** The main body or aisle of the church. It was quite wide to allow people to approach the altar easily.

- A **transept:** In a church with a cruciform shape, the wings on either side of the main aisle are referred to as transepts. This space allowed extra seating for the congregation.

- A **chancel:** The altar was contained in the eastern end of the church, commonly known as the chancel. This was the main focus for the people and was prominently placed for all to see.

- An **apse:** A large semicircular niche (recess) terminating the chancel at the eastern end of a church.

- A **crypt:** An underground chamber. This was where bishops and important people were buried.

dic·tion·ar·y

Cruciform means shaped like a cross.

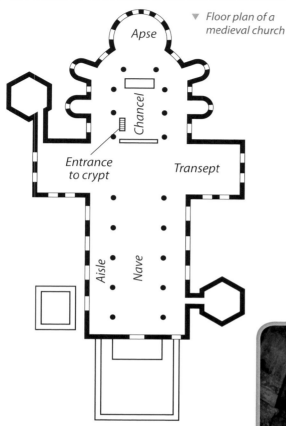

▼ *Floor plan of a medieval church*

Apse

Chancel

Entrance to crypt

Transept

Aisle

Nave

An outstanding example of church design in this era is Cormac's **Chapel**, Cashel, Co. Tipperary, Ireland. It was founded by the king-bishop Cormaic Mac Carthach during his reign, 1122–38, and was consecrated (blessed) in 1134. This impressive rock site was initially a fortress palace and a monastery, until in 1101 King Murtagh O'Brien (c. 1050–1119) gave it to the church exclusively.

dic·tion·ar·y

A **chapel** is a building or room in or attached to a college, castle, monastery or great house, designated as a place of worship.

Monasteries and Cathedrals

Thousands of cathedrals were built across Europe during the Middle Ages. Cathedrals provided an inspirational place, filled with light and colour, in which to worship God. They also promoted art and architecture. Numerous monasteries were also founded at this time. Here, monks could live, work and pray together in peace and calm. Monasteries were also important centres of learning and culture.

▲ *Door of Cormac's Chapel, Cashel, Co. Tipperary*

Building in the Middle Ages Revision Questions

1 Explain in detail what the feudal system was.

2 Describe the purpose and principal features of a medieval castle. Give examples.

3 Outline the place of the Church in society at this time.

4 Describe the principal features of a medieval church. Give examples and draw a sketch.

Monasteries

> **W**ith silent fervour for solitude in their remote retreats perched on craggy precipices overlooking the windy ocean, the Irish monks dwelt like human amphibians between land and sea, so that, as one early poet reflects – 'I may see its heavy waves over the glittering ocean as they chant a melody to their eternal course.'
>
> *(extract from K. Jackson,* Studies in Early Celtic Nature Poetry, *Cambridge, England, 1935)*

Monasteries and convents were very popular in medieval times. Many were dotted around Europe, founded by religious orders such as the Franciscans, Dominicans, Augustinians, Carmelites and Columbans. Each order had its own individual ideals. Monks living in the community followed Saint Benedict's Rule, a code set up by Saint Benedict who founded the first monastery (see p. 86).

▲ *Monks' cells and monastery remains at Skellig Michael, Ireland*

Monastic Life

- For each monk the purpose of monastic life was to dedicate himself to God, by living in a monastery surrounded by people of equal devotion to God.

- Monasteries such as **Cluny** in France and **Skellig Michael** in Ireland were enclosed. This meant they were cut off from and uninterrupted by the distractions of the outside world, giving the monks time to pray for the sinners outside.

- Another important purpose of monastic life was the production of handcrafted manuscripts, beautifully illuminated (decorated) with paints and gold leaf. The Lindisfarne Gospels, produced in northern England in the late seventh century, are a fine example of an illuminated manuscript.

▶ *Carpet page from the Lindisfarne Gospels. Carpet pages were used to separate the different Gospels.*

IDEALS AND EFFECTS OF DIFFERENT MONASTIC ORDERS

ORDER	IDEALS	EFFECTS
Benedictine	Saint Benedict (c. 480–543) of Nursia, Italy, founded the order and the first monastery at Monte Cassino, Italy, in 529. The order pioneered Saint Benedict's Rule: 'To walk in God's ways, with the Gospel as our guide.'	They made a great contribution to monastic life, education, and the government and economics of western Europe.
Franciscan	Order founded in 1209 in Italy by Saint Francis of Assisi (c. 1181–1226). The order insisted on poverty for its followers. Their missionary monks travelled to non-Christian lands in an attempt to gain converts.	Through their missionary work, Franciscan friars converted a lot of New World natives (people from the Americas).
Dominican	Order named after Spanish-born Saint Dominic (1170–1221). He was canonised (sainted) in 1234. This order preached against heresy (beliefs against the Church's teachings). Saint Thomas Aquinas was a Dominican.	They became educators and theologians (religious scholars).
Augustinian	Founded in Algeria by Saint Augustine (354–430). There were two groups: Augustine Canons and Augustine Hermits. They gave up all their goods and private property to live communally.	Saint Augustine is considered one of the key figures of the theology of western Europe.
Carmelite	Founded c. 1155 by a group of pilgrims near Mount Carmel in Palestine. They had strict vows of silence, poverty and seclusion. They supported themselves through donations from the public.	Carmelites prayed for people's intentions and the sins of the world. The most famous Carmelite was Saint Thérèse of Avila.
Columban	Saint Columban (540–615), born in Ireland, founded a monastery at Bobbio, Italy.	The Columbans were famous for their missionary work and teaching.
Cistercian	Robert of Molesme (1027–1111) founded this enclosed order in 1098 near Dijon, France. It encouraged a return to the literal observance of Saint Benedict's Rule.	The Cistercians provoked a return to manual labour, and especially to field work, which became a special characteristic of Cistercian life.

Layout of a Monastery

Monastery buildings were cleverly planned. The layout was designed in a particular way for practical reasons:

1 To provide security for the monks.
2 To protect the monks' privacy.
3 To allow them to pray in calm, peaceful interiors and exteriors.

Every building was in a certain place depending on its day-to-day function and importance. Look at the sketch of Saint Gall Monastery and note the location of the church, refectory (dining hall), school, garden and infirmary (sick room). You can also see quarters for animals and servants. Everything is contained within the walls so that the monks would not have to leave unless instructed to do so.

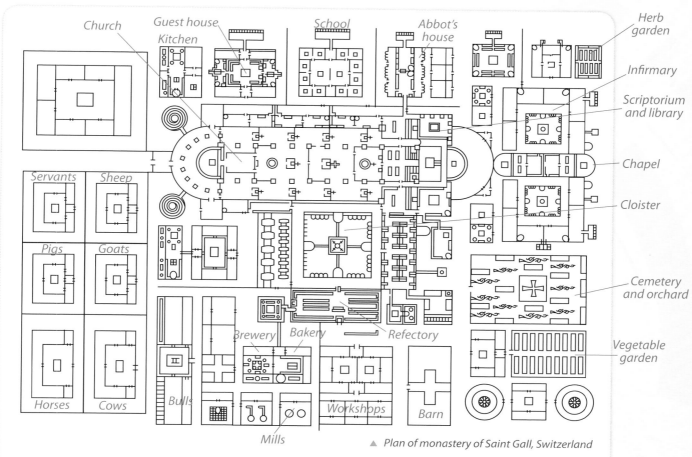

Church Guest house School Abbot's house Herb garden

Kitchen

Infirmary

Scriptorium and library

Chapel

Cloister

Servants Sheep

Pigs Goats

Horses Cows

Bulls

Mills

Brewery Bakery Refectory

Workshops Barn

Cemetery and orchard

Vegetable garden

▲ *Plan of monastery of Saint Gall, Switzerland*

Cloisters

A cloister is a sheltered passageway which can be open on one side, it is a private place to walk, pray and think. It can be roofed or partially roofed. The cloister occupied the central position of the monastery grounds and played an important part in the daily lives of the monks. It was a sacred and quiet space, reserved for the monks to pray, reflect and meditate. The advantage of the cloister was that it served as a link between the different monastic buildings, such as the **chapter house** and the refectory. There were seats in the cloister for resting and there was often an area where the monks could wash their hands before entering the refectory.

> **dic·tion·ar·y**
>
> A **chapter house** is a building attached to a monastery or cathedral in which meetings are held.

SAINT GALL MONASTERY

Country	Switzerland	Date	612	Order	Benedictine

The idea behind the monastery of Saint Gall was to create a self-sufficient town. Although closed and cut off from the outside world, it would accommodate pilgrims and royal guests, in keeping with Benedictine tradition. The floor plan of Saint Gall survives today in the form of five sheets of vellum preserved in the abbey library of Saint Gall in Switzerland. It was drawn up as the perfect Benedictine community. At synods (meetings of clergy) held between 816 and 817, the Benedictine order agreed that the plan of Saint Gall would become the model on which all the order's other monasteries would be based.

- The monastery is laid out according to a simple grid system.

- In the centre is the cloister.

- On the north side of the church is accommodation for royal guests, visiting monks and pilgrims. Beside that are the school and the abbot's house.

- Near the abbot's house is the library, the **scriptorium** and the large kitchen.

- To the south, behind the monks' refectory and kitchen, is the area for the lay workmen, craftworkers, kilns, mills, brewery and bakery.

- The cemetery and the orchard, along with the vegetable garden, can be found in the southern corner.

- To the east beyond the apse of the church, there are rooms for the monastic doctor, the infirmary and the chapel (not visible in the diagram).

> **dic·tion·ar·y**
>
> A **scriptorium** is the name given to a room where monks wrote and decorated holy books, for example The Book of Kells.

CLUNY ABBEY

Country	France	Date	910	Order	Benedictine

The Benedictine monks were presented with farmland in the valley of the Grosne River, France. Abbot Berno built a modest church called Cluny in 910. Over the years 910–916 Cluny grew from its humble beginnings to be the biggest, most powerful and culturally rich monastery in Europe.

Cluny underwent three developmental stages:

1. Cluny I was a modest building, 30 m long, and barn-like in structure. It was dedicated to Saint Peter and Saint Paul.

2. With the popularity of the monastery and the ever-increasing number of visitors, the monks had to build another new church, Cluny II. The project was overseen by Abbot Mayeul (elected abbot in 965) and Abbot Odilo (962–1048). The church boasted an additional porch, and there were two towers built into the façade, making Cluny the most impressive monastery in northern Europe.

3. In 1083 there were only 12 monks living at Cluny hall. This community grew quickly and another new church was needed. Built during the 1100s, this came to be known as Cluny III:

- It was the largest and most glorious church in Europe.

- It was built entirely of stone.

- It was 188 m long.

- Its walls were over 2 m thick.

- Its vaults soared to a massive 29 m.

Cluny III was demolished after the French Revolution (1789–99) and was not renovated until 1928.

▶ *A view of Cluny Abbey as it looks today*

FONTENAY MONASTERY

Country	France	Date	1118	Order	Cistercian

Fontenay Monastery was founded by Saint Bernard of Clairvaux (1090–1153). It is one of the oldest Cistercian monasteries in France and its buildings remain in fine condition. Fontenay consists of a cloister, a church, a refectory, a monks' dormitory, an ironworks and a bakery. All can be viewed today almost in its original state.

SKELLIG MICHAEL MONASTERY

Country	Ireland	Date	588	Order	Augustinian

This seventh-century monastery was built on an island called Skellig Michael off the southwest coast of Ireland. This location provided complete privacy for the monks to devote themselves to God. The monastery was named after the archangel Michael. Legend says that Michael appeared to Saint Patrick on Skellig Michael to help him banish the snakes from Ireland. Although the island was attacked by Vikings three times the monastic community continued to thrive.

▲ *Skellig Michael, off the southwest coast of Ireland*

- The monks lived in small stone cells clustered around the small main church.
- Each cell had walls 2 m deep to protect the monks from the island's harsh maritime climate. Medieval pilgrims traditionally climbed this island and kissed the rock, which was a prehistoric **standing stone** decorated with Celtic designs.
- The monastery is Irish Romanesque (see pp. 104–7) in style.

dic·tion·ar·y

A **standing stone** is a solitary upright stone set into the ground.

JERPOINT MONASTERY

Country	Ireland	Date	1180	Order	Cistercian

Jerpoint Monastery is located on the banks of the river Arrigle, Co. Kilkenny. It is Romanesque in style). Jerpoint was totally self-sufficient, as were the above-named monasteries. It had its own watermills, garden, cemetery and granary.

- The Jerpoint cloister design was very detailed and beautiful.

- It had webs between the pillars decorated with high-relief carvings of apes, dragons and religious designs. The inspiration for these carvings came from drawings in manuscripts and designs on tombstones.

- Jerpoint Abbey's transepts and chancel are the oldest part of the abbey, and their design is Irish Romanesque. Designs are still evident on the transept and chancel.

- The abbey arches are rounded and semicircular with capitals and bases which are thirteenth century in style.

- Jerpoint Monastery boasts the finest **crossing towers** in Ireland. These towers have stepped Irish **battlements** rising to stepped corner turrets.

- The Abbey's beautiful east window dates back to the fourteenth century.

▲ *Jerpoint Monastery, Co. Kilkenny*

dic·tion·ar·y

A crossing, in religious architecture, is the junction of the four arms of a cruciform church. **Crossing Towers** were constructed and supported directly above the crossings.

A **battlement** is a parapet (wall-like barrier) with indentations.

Monasteries Revision Questions

1 Outline the purpose of monastic life.

2 Outline the ideals and effects of the following orders: Franciscan, Benedictine, Cistercian, Dominican, Augustinian, Carmelite, Columban. Use a grid for your answer.

3 Describe and sketch the layout of a monastery (Saint Gall).

4 Describe the layout of a cloister, and explain its role.

5 Do a case study of the following monasteries: Cluny Monastery, Fontenay Monastery, Skellig Michael Monastery, Jerpoint Monastery. Mention in your answer the location, date built, and order of monks who lived there. Draw sketches.

Medieval Cathedrals

During the twelfth century many cathedrals were built across Europe. They were bigger than churches in order to accommodate the growing population of Europe and the increasing flow of pilgrims (see pp. 93–7). At this time, Catholic lands were divided into diocese (sections) overseen by bishops, and each diocese had a cathedral at its centre, also overseen by a bishop. Within each diocese were several parishes, and every parish had its own parish priest.

Architectural Requirements of a Cathedral

- It had to be big enough to accommodate and support the large crowds coming to worship.
- It needed to be cleverly designed to allow an easy flow of people through the cathedral.
- It had to be religiously decorated to make it look attractive to worshippers, and also to instruct the illiterate. Even though these worshippers could not read, they could understand Bible stories illustrated on the cathedral's walls.

Irish Cathedrals

The big Irish churches built at this time were smaller than their European counterparts, but they still reflected the Romanesque style. This was the common and popular style of architecture at this time in Europe and featured a cruciform plan, with rounded arches and decorative mouldings. Irish architects and craftsmen adapted this style and here, it became known as Hiberno Romanesque (*Hiberno* means 'Irish' in Latin), or Irish Romanesque (see pp. 104–5). From the twelfth century and well into the thirteenth century, many Hiberno-Romanesque cathedrals were constructed.

THE CHURCH OF AGHADOE

Style	Irish Romanesque	**Place**	Killarney, Co. Kerry	**Date**	1158	**Built by**	Amhlaoibh O'Donahue

Architectural Features

- The west doorway is Romanesque in style and decoration.
- In the thirteenth century the eastern part of the church was added, and a section of this may have served as living quarters.
- The east window features flower and head motif decoration. It was also added in the thirteenth century.
- There is an **ogham** stone on top of the south wall bearing the inscription BRRUANANN – a simple name, possibly used as a grave marker.
- The round tower is 6.7 m high.

> **dic·tion·ar·y**
>
> **Ogham** is an ancient Irish writing system. The ogham was carved in stone and read from bottom to top.

◄ *Church of Aghadoe, Killarney, Co. Kerry*

SAINT DECLAN'S CATHEDRAL

Style	Irish Romanesque	Place	Ardmore, Co. Waterford	Date	Twelfth century	Built by	Meolettrim O'Duibh-Rathra (died 1203)

Architectural Features

- The west front of the cathedral is in the Romanesque style. It displays fine sculptural work, arranged in a series of arcades (arches supported by columns or piers). The sculpture displays the archangel Michael weighing souls, Adam and Eve, the Judgement of Solomon and the Adoration of the Magi (the Three Wise Men).
- It has a recessed (set back) west window which is also Romanesque in style.
- It has arcades on the interior walls.
- It has a pointed chancel arch.
- It has pointed arches, which are also features of the Late-Gothic style (see pp. 126–27).

▲ *Saint Declan's Cathedral, Ardmore, Co. Waterford*

- There is a small building to the east of the church known as Saint Declan's oratory. It is believed that Saint Declan (born in the fifth century) is buried here.
- The cathedral has a well-preserved round tower which is 29 m high.
- It has two ogham stones inscribed as follows:
  First stone: LUGUDECCAS MAQI COI NETA-SEGAMONAS. This is a commemorative reference to NiaSegmon (son or grandson).
  Second stone: AMDU. This means 'the loved one.'

SAINT FLANNAN'S CATHEDRAL

Style	Irish Romanesque	Place	Killaloe, Co. Clare	Date	1185–1225	Built by	Donal Mór Ó Briain, King of Thomond (reigned 1168–94)

Architectural Features

- The cathedral has no aisles, only a north transept and a south transept.
- It has a bell tower.
- The transepts, the nave and the chancel intersect to form the usual Romanesque cruciform-shaped church.
- On the right-hand side of the entrance there is a beautiful Romanesque doorway.
- There is a stone standing before the doorway with ogham inscriptions.

▶ *Saint Flannan's Cathedral, Killaloe, Co. Clare*

: **Medieval Cathedrals Revision Questions**

  1 Discuss the purpose of a medieval cathedral in society.

  2 Explain the role of the bishop, and define 'diocese'.

  3 Name two medieval cathedrals. Supply the following information for each: who built them, dates built, and architectural features and decoration.

Pilgrimage

Many medieval Christians went on a pilgrimage at some stage of their lives. A pilgrimage is a visit to a holy **shrine**, and these visits were hugely important to believers at that time.

- By going on a pilgrimage, medieval Christians believed they were getting closer to God.
- They went on pilgrimage to ask forgiveness for their sins, pray for the sick, and give thanks to God for all the gifts he had bestowed on them.
- They believed that by touching the holy relics at each pilgrimage location they would have great blessings bestowed on them and even experience miracle cures.
- There was always the chance that they might see a holy vision during a pilgrimage.
- The medieval Christian felt revived and cleansed after a pilgrimage.

> **dic·tion·ar·y**
>
> A **shrine** is a place of worship that has been made holy by the presence of a sacred person or object. It may also be the tomb of a saint, or a container in which holy relics are kept.

Favourite Pilgrimage Destinations

The most popular destinations for pilgrims to travel to were:

1 **Rome in Italy:** As the headquarters of the Pope, and also the resting place of deceased popes, Rome was a major pilgrimage site. Pilgrims might be lucky enough to attend Mass celebrated by the Pope, and also feast their eyes on the art and architecture.

2 **Jerusalem in the Holy Land:** Here, pilgrims could see the sites where Jesus was born, crucified and buried, and view the holy sepulchre (tomb).

3 **Santiago de Compostela in Spain:** The tomb of Saint James, one of Jesus's apostles, was housed here. Pilgrims believed that if they touched his relics, they would receive great blessings.

▲ *Saint Peter's Square, which is in front of Saint Peter's Basilica, in the Vatican City*

Impact on Architecture and Sculpture

Pilgrimage tours had a big impact on medieval architecture and sculpture. With huge crowds travelling around Europe to worship, bigger and more durable churches were needed to facilitate them. In turn, sculptors needed to create pieces that would tell the Bible stories to pilgrims, most of whom were illiterate. For these reasons, Romanesque architecture and sculpture developed rapidly in the last decade of the eleventh century.

The beauty of pilgrimage churches can be fully appreciated and experienced today at Saint-Sernin in Toulouse, southern France. The cathedral is large, with unique double aisles. Apart from the double aisles feature, Saint-Sernin is a copy of Santiago de Compostela (see p. 96).

www.ericpouhier.com

▲ *Crypt of Saint-Sernin Basilica, Toulouse, France*   ▲ *View of the back of Saint-Sernin Basilica*

Pilgrimage Routes

The only way for medieval pilgrims to cover the huge distances involved in visiting a site was on foot or horseback. The routes were so long that the Catholic Church had to build churches along them to break up the journey. This allowed the travellers time to rest, pray and reflect on their journey. One of the most popular pilgrimage sites was Santiago de Compostela in northern Spain. Thousands of pilgrims visited each year from as far away as eastern Europe and Ireland. There were four routes from France to Compostela. There was even a little travel guide, written by a priest called Aymery Picaud, which details the four routes.

▼ *Map of the four routes to Santiago de Compostela, Spain*

- **First route:** Beginning in Paris and Chartres and passing through Tours, Poitiers and Bordeaux.
- **Second route:** Beginning in Vézelay and going via Limoges and Périgueux.
- **Third route:** Beginning in Le Puy and going south-west through Conques and Moissac.
- **Fourth route:** Beginning in Arles and passing through Saint-Guilhelm and Toulouse before crossing the Pyrenees.

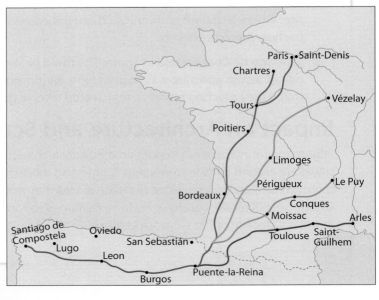

Along these four routes in the eleventh century, five great churches were built to provide pilgrims with places to take a break, along the four routes:

1 Saint-Martial in Limoges, dedicated in 1095, still remains.

2 Saint-Martin in Tours, c. 1050, no longer exists.

3 Saint-Sernin at Toulouse, c. 1080, still remains.

4 Santiago de Compostela, c. 1075, still remains.

5 Sainte-Foy at Conques, c. 1050–1130, still remains.

Relics, Reliquaries and Shrines

All pilgrimage churches were built on holy ground, usually beside a saint's burial ground or where the saint died. As a result of this, many relic and reliquary shrines of the saints are found in pilgrimage churches.

Relics

Relics are extremely sacred, treasured, highly respected and carefully guarded items. Two examples of important relics are:

- The relic remains of Saint James in the cathedral of Santiago de Compostela, Spain. Saint James was believed to have been buried at the site several centuries before the cathedral was built.

- The relic remains of Saint Anthony, in the basilica of Saint Anthony, Padua, Italy.

Reliquaries

A reliquary is a very precious metal vessel for holding sacred relics. Two examples of reliquaries are:

- The beautifully crafted reliquary metal box which housed the Saint Patrick's Bell (see p. 56), at the National Museum – Decorative Arts and History, Ireland.

- The reliquary vessel for the **Shroud of Turin** which is kept in the chapel of the Holy Shroud, Turin, Italy. The church was specially designed for the vessel by Italian architect Camillo-Guarino Guarini (1624–83). The chapel is domed and in the centre of Turin, emphasising the importance of the relic it contains.

Shrines

Sacred relics were also held in shrines. In this context a shrine was a tomb, altar or case. Two examples of important shrines are:

- The shrine of Saint Ursula, 1489, by Hans Memlinc (c. 1430–94), in the Hôpital Saint-Jean, Bruges, Belgium.

- The shrine of the Holy Sacrament, 1370–80. It is recessed into the wall behind the high altar in the church of Saint Sebaldus, Nuremburg, Germany.

dic·tion·ar·y

▲ *The Shroud of Turin, Italy*

The **Shroud of Turin** is a linen cloth, centuries old, displaying the image of a crucified man. Many believe that the man is Jesus of Nazareth.

▶ *The shrine of the Holy Sacrament, Saint Sebaldus, Nuremburg*

SANTIAGO DE COMPOSTELA: A TYPICAL PILGRIMAGE CATHEDRAL

Style	Early Romanesque	Place	Spain	Date	1075	Built by	Unknown

All four pilgrimage routes led to Santiago de Compostela, so it is no surprise that its cathedral has the most elaborate architecture and sculpture of all those built during the Middle Ages. Below is a detailed description of its features:

FEATURE	DETAIL
Cruciform design	The ground plan of this cathedral has the same cruciform design as Saint Peter's in Rome. Here the design is more sophisticated, because the two-towered façade boasts a western foundation.
Apsidioles (apse-chapels, projecting from a larger apse)	Coming from the huge semicircular aisle are the transept arms with apsidioles attached.
Groin vaults (see p. 102)	Groin vaults encircle the apse.
Semicircular aisle	Half-shaped apses.
Pilgrimage choir (the part of the church where services are sung)	The pilgrimage choir is made up of additional apses with altars along the passageway known as the ambulatory.
Ambulatory	The ambulatory gave the pilgrims access to the shrines behind the main altar.
Additional altars	Additional altars were necessary to display the increase in relics on display. There was a relic at each altar.
Priests' residence	Area where the priests lived. This was necessary, as the church required priests in residence to perform Masses for the ever-growing numbers of pilgrims.
Nave aisles	To provide more space for the pilgrims, the aisles of the nave were made bigger and extended around the transept arms.
Coro	This was a high wall which blocked off the choir from the nave. Its function was to separate the priests from the massive pilgrimage crowds.

> **Did you know?**
> 'Santiago' means 'Saint James' in Spanish, hence the cathedral is also known as Saint James's Cathedral.

The Portico of Glory (1168–1217)

▲ Detail of The Portico of Glory, Santiago de Compostela

The artist, Mateo of Santiago, was a great Spanish sculptor. He was employed in 1168 and continued to work for the cathedral up to 1217. The massive entrance of the cathedral is signed and dated 1188. The triple entrance is known as the *Portico de La Gloria* (Portico of Glory) in the narthex (entrance area) end of the church.

- All three doorways have column figures, distinct evidence of French artistic influence.
- Traces of polychromy (decoration using a variety of colours) are still visible.
- On the central door **Christ in Majesty** is on the high tympanum (recessed area over a doorway).
- On this door there is also a carving of the tree of life and the figure of Saint James, the patron saint of the cathedral.

▶ The Portico of Glory, Santiago de Compostela

> **dic·tion·ar·y**
>
> **Christ in Majesty** means that he is seated on a throne in the centre of a composition, surrounded by saints or other figures.

CATHEDRAL OF SAINTE-FOY AT CONQUES			
Style	Early Romanesque	**Place**	France
Date	1050–1130	**Built by**	Begun by Abbot Odolric (1031–65)

Sainte-Foy in France was one of the five great churches built along the four routes to Santiago de Compostela. Pilgrims visited Conques mainly to see the remains of a martyred young woman from the fourth century. Below is a description of sculptural work at Sainte-Foy.

The Tympanum

The tympanum at Sainte-Foy shows resurrected souls arising on Christ's left and the damned being dragged down on his right. Below the feet of Christ, Saint Peter holds a pair of scales, for weighing the good and evil souls. Although this scene had been carved on several capitals (tops of columns) and on the side of portals (important doorways), this is the first time it was depicted in a central position, that is, on the tympanum. This theme of the resurrection of good souls and the damnation of bad souls was very popular at the time.

▲ *Interior image of Sainte-Foy at Conques, France*

◄ *The tympanum at Sainte-Foy, Conques, France*

Pilgrimage Revision Questions

1. Describe the importance of pilgrimage for the medieval Christian.

2. What were the three main pilgrimage destinations? Name them and explain their attraction.

3. Outline the impact of the pilgrimage tradition on architecture and sculpture, giving reasons for your answer.

4. What were the four main routes to Santiago de Compostela? Outline, and draw a sketch of the routes.

5. Name the five great churches built on these routes. Explain their purpose.

6. What is a relic? Give examples.

7. Explain what a reliquary is. Give examples.

8. What is a shrine? Give examples, and draw a sketch.

9. Do a case study on the cathedral of Santiago de Compostela and the cathedral of Sainte-Foy at Conques. Outline date, country, style and architectural features. Draw sketches.

The Romanesque Style of Architecture

One style of architecture dominated the early medieval world. It was known as Romanesque, because it often imitated Roman architecture and was influenced by Roman style elements.

Features of the Romanesque Style

The main features of the Romanesque style were:

- Cruciform layout
- Massive vaults
- Rounded arches
- Engaged columns
- Carved capitals
- Piers
- Decorative doorways
- Small windows.

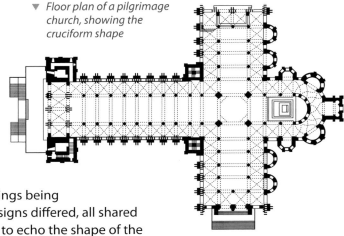

▼ *Floor plan of a pilgrimage church, showing the cruciform shape*

Cruciform Layout

Cathedrals were the main types of buildings being designed at this time. Although their designs differed, all shared the same floor plan – a cruciform shape, to echo the shape of the cross on which Christ died.

Massive Vaults

A vault is an arched ceiling or roof made of brick or stone (see p. 102). Vaults were a common feature of the Romanesque style.

Rounded Arches

An arch is a curved structure that spans an opening. It is formed by wedge-shaped blocks of brick or stone that hold each other in place by lateral (sideways) pressure. The top of the arch, known as the vertex or crown, holds the **keystone**. An arch can either carry a lot of weight from the building or transfer a lot of weight onto piers or columns. The inside curve of the arch is called the intrados, while the outside curve is called the extrados. There are many different types of arches, but in this section we will focus on the Romanesque semicircular arch.

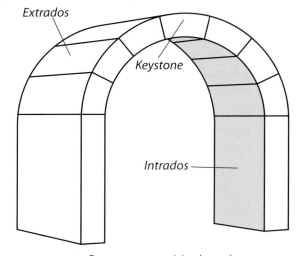

Extrados

Keystone

Intrados

▲ *Romanesque semicircular arch*

dic·tion·ar·y

The **keystone** is the central wedge-shaped stone at the crown of an arch that holds the structure together.

Engaged Columns

A column is a pillar which can either be free standing or can help to support an architectural structure. When a column is attached to a wall or a pier, it is called an engaged column. These types were the most common in Romanesque architecture. A column is made up of:

1 A base

2 A shaft

3 A capital

There were three main classical orders (types) of column design (see also p. 165):

1 **Doric:** this type of column has no base. It has a fluted shaft, and a plain capital.

2 **Ionic:** this column has a base, a fluted shaft (with grooves), and a volute (spiral or scroll shape) capital.

3 **Corinthian:** taller and more elegant than the preceding two, this consists of a base on a plinth, a tall fluted shaft and an ornate capital.

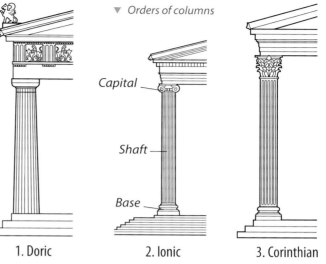

▼ *Orders of columns*

Capital

Shaft

Base

1. Doric   2. Ionic   3. Corinthian

Carved Capitals

A capital is the name given to the top of a column. Capitals were usually decorated. In Romanesque architecture, the Corinthian capital was the most popular. There are 60 carved capitals to be seen at Saulieu Basilica in France. Here, in one of the ten narrative capitals, 'The Temptation of Christ' shows a devil on the left tempting a seated Christ on the right, who is holding a book and accompanied by an angel.

▲ *A Corinthian capital at the basilica at Saulieu, France, built in the twelfth century*

Piers

Piers, not to be confused with columns, were heavy stone supports, usually square or rectangular in shape.

Decorative Doorways

Romanesque artists took great pride in decorating cathedral doorways with hand-crafted patterned designs. Chevron motifs (zig-zag designs) were popular, as were leafy patterns. The designs were usually carved in high relief (raised) on the doorway or over the doorway.

▶ *Doorway of church of Saint-Michel d'Aiguilhe, Le Puy, France, built in the twelfth century*

Tympana

Artists could create more elaborate designs on the tympanum, a semi-circular space or section which was located above a door. Most tympana designs followed the style of the one at Sainte Marie-Madeleine, Vézelay, France.

Small Windows

Romanesque windows were very small, letting in little natural light and making cathedrals very dark. The windows were located at the very top of the cathedral above the **triforium**, and were filled with thick glass and oiled linen. Window decoration was not ornate. One such Romanesque window decoration can be found at the cathedral of Saint-Pierre, Santonge, built in the twelfth century. Here we can see sculptural decoration on the exterior part of the window.

▲ *The tympanum at Sainte-Marie-Madeleine, Vézelay, France, shows the Ascension and Pentecost.*

dic·tion·ar·y

A **triforium** is a passage in the wall of the nave between the main arcade and the clerestory (upper part of the walls).

Overall Effect

The above elements all came together to create the Romanesque style. It is believed that the architects and sculptors at the time, who worked together to implement the style, were influenced by Neoplatonic ideas. The Neoplatonic students shared the following beliefs:

- The mystical body of Christ was represented in the stone, wood and glass of the physical cathedral.
- The columns and the piers symbolised the apostles and the saints.
- The glazed windows were the doctors of the church, letting in the light of true belief.

◄ *Detail of window decoration at the cathedral of Saint-Pierre, Santonge, France*

BASILICA OF SAINTE-MARIE-MADELEINE, VÉZELAY

Style	Romanesque	**Place**	France	**Date**	1104–32	**Built by**	Abbot Geoffray

Vézelay is a small town in France, made famous by the pilgrimage cathedral of Sainte-Marie-Madeleine. Pilgrims journeyed there to visit the relics of Saint Mary Magdalene, thought to reside there. The cathedral has a large nave divided into two bays by transverse arches in alternate red and white stone. The groin vaulting (see p. 102) in the cathedral is characteristic of the Romanesque era. Bible stories are carved in low relief (into the background) on the tympanum and on the capitals. This sculpture played an educational as well as a decorative role in the cathedral.

▲ *Detail of Christ in the tympanum at Vézelay, France*

Vézelay's Tympanum

- The theme of Vézelay's tympanum is a combination of the Ascension of Christ into heaven and the descent of the Holy Spirit on the apostles (Pentecost).

- His hands are raised from the frame of the tympanum, in order to release fire onto the heads of the apostles.

- The upper half of Christ's body is facing forwards. The artist added great atmosphere to Christ by placing his knees to the right-hand side, causing his robe to fall into creases.

- The large figure of Christ, accompanied by the 12 apostles, takes up the central compartment of the tympanum.

- The outer part contains smaller compartments. Each one contains a group of figures who are communicating with one another with great sincerity.

- A group of creatures, appearing to quiver with emotion, cross the lintel (supporting beam that spans an opening).

Romanesque Construction

Building a Romanesque cathedral was a huge feat. A lot of money was needed, and this came from the many contributions people had to make to the Church during their lifetimes. Working conditions were very poor and a lot of men died during construction. The process began with an architect, who was in charge of hiring several skilled craftsmen:

- A master quarryman
- A master stonecutter
- A master mortar maker
- A master sculptor
- A master mason
- A master blacksmith
- A master glassmaker
- A master carpenter
- A master roofer

Constructing a Romanesque cathedral involved several elements which all came together in the final building:

- Quarried stone
- Stone vaulting
- Timber roofing
- Early methods of buttressing.

Quarried Stone

Romanesque builders needed large stones of a similar type and a specific size particularly for vaulting, so there was a lot of work to do in quarries before the building could start. While the foundations were being laid, the master mason gave the master quarryman templates (plans) of the special large stones to be cut from the quarried stone. The master quarryman then supervised 300 men in the exact cutting of the stone for the cathedral. Each stone was carefully marked by the master mason to show where it would be located and then, once the construction started, carefully transported and put in place.

> ### dic·tion·ar·y
>
> **Quarries:** open excavations in the ground from which stone is taken

Timber Roofs

In early Romanesque architecture timber roofs were commonplace. Stone roofs were more difficult to build and needed very thick walls to hold them up. However, timber roofs were a fire hazard. Many Romanesque churches burned down because of their timber roofs.

Vaults

Stone or brick arched vaults replaced the timber arched ceilings or roofs during the Romanesque era. Masons from Lombardy in northern Italy designed three different types of vaults:

1. A barrel vault is a single round-arched structural vault.
2. Groin vaults are two barrel vaults intersecting each other to make an X shape.
3. A rib vault is a groin vault with pointed arches. It was more common during the Gothic era (see p. 110).

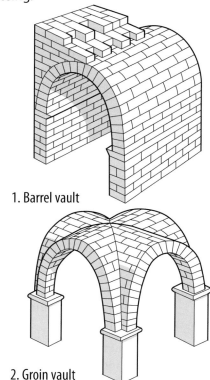

1. Barrel vault

2. Groin vault

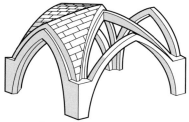

3. Rib vault

▲ *Barrel and groin vaults were mainly used during the Romanesque era.*

There were both practical and spiritual reasons for vaulting churches:

- They gave the church added strength, and increased the structural safety of the roof.
- With vaulting, Romanesque builders could raise the height of the church, making it look more impressive.
- Visiting pilgrims were astounded by the height and volume of the cathedral once entering its front door. It showed them the strength and power of the Catholic Church and the overall power of God – a huge goal during the Middle Ages.

> ### Did you know?
> In an effort to build higher and higher churches, sometimes the builders went too far, putting too much pressure on the vaults. With nothing to sustain this pressure, some churches collapsed.

Early Methods of Buttressing

Buttressing was not widely used in architecture until the Gothic era (see pp. 110–12), but there are a few examples of early methods of buttressing in the Romanesque era. A buttress is a structure that supports a building at a point of pressure, for example an arch, the roof or a vault. It was usually found on the outside of the cathedral. The buttress support can be vertical or arched (flying). Flying buttresses were very common in Gothic architecture.

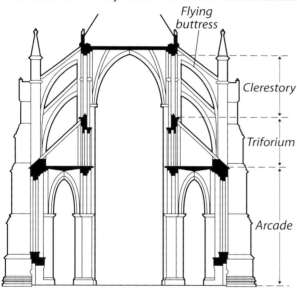

Flying buttress

Clerestory

Triforium

Arcade

▲ In this cross-section diagram through the aisles and nave of a cathedral, we see all the elements of Romanesque architecture.

▲ The basilica of Saint-Sernin, Toulouse, France is a practical example of how the elements of Romanesque architecture combined to produce fine buildings.

DURHAM CATHEDRAL							
Style	Romanesque	**Country**	England	**Date**	1093–1140	**Built by**	Unknown

Romanesque architecture was brought to England by the **Normans**, who conquered the country in 1066. Because of this, Romanesque style in England also came to be called the Norman style. The English cathedrals, abbeys and parish churches took on the new style of architecture.

dic·tion·ar·y

The **Normans** were a people from Normandy in northwest France. They were the driving force behind the Crusades (religious wars) of the eleventh century onwards. They had many military victories and introduced the feudal system into the countries they conquered (including England and Ireland).

Enormous cathedrals were built as a result, including those at Canterbury (1070) and Winchester (1079). One of the most impressive examples of Romanesque architecture in England is Durham Cathedral.

Architectural Features

- Rounded columns make a pattern across the nave and up into the transepts.
- The choir has fluting chevrons, with hatching and swirling motifs (designs).

▲ *Durham Cathedral nave, England*

- The triforium has extremely delicate mouldings (ornamental edging). Perhaps the Romanesque builder wanted the Christian to be astounded by the impressive nave and then, on looking higher, further impressed by the gentle view of the rounded nave.

The Romanesque Style of Architecture Revision Questions

1 Outline the main features of Romanesque architecture. Describe each feature and draw sketches.

2 Describe the architectural features and draw sketches of: a) Basilica of Sainte-Marie-Madeleine, Vézelay, and b) Durham Cathedral, England.

3 List the many types of master craftsmen who were involved in making a Romanesque cathedral. Why was quarried stone used?

4 Explain why churches were vaulted, and draw sketches of the different types of vaults. Explain what is meant by buttressing, giving examples.

Romanesque Architecture in Ireland

The Romanesque architectural style influenced most of Europe, including Ireland. However, Irish Romanesque was a distinct style, different from that of the rest of Europe.

Features of Irish-Romanesque Architecture

Although Ireland's cathedrals and abbeys were not as big as those of its European neighbours such as France and England, they were richly decorated. Irish-Romanesque architecture featured a lot of sculptural decoration, particularly on doors and arches.

◀ *The Nun's church, west doorway and chancel arch, Clonmacnoise, Co. Offaly*

Sculpture

In the Irish-Romanesque era, it was easier for the architect and sculptor to work together. They integrated their ideas into a single project such as Cormac's Chapel and the west door of Clonfert Cathedral (see p. 107). Irish-Romanesque sculpture was different too. It evoked a feeling of magic and fantasy, which can be experienced in the remains of Annaghdown Cathedral, Co. Galway.

Portals and Arches

Intricate designs on portals (doors) and arches were a notable feature of Irish-Romanesque architecture. Cormac's Chapel in Co. Tipperary has a fine example of this. The chapel looks out onto a triangular courtyard. Its majestic north doorway has great depth, with a tunnel-like archway. The portal has two outer orders of pillar and arch and supporting pillars. A wide deep gable (triangular feature) with a repeating chevron pattern sits above the portal.

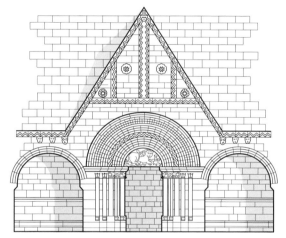

▶ North porch, Cormac's Chapel, Cashel, Co. Tipperary

Decoration of Churches

During the Irish-Romanesque era, the decoration of churches and monasteries was almost as important as the architecture. Artists took extreme care to choose the right pattern designs. In the diagram below you can see a breakdown of the motifs which decorate the west doorway of Clonfert Cathedral, Co. Galway. On the right is a selection of decorative details from Annaghdown Cathedral, Co. Galway.

▲ Annaghdown Cathedral, east window, showing richly decorated frame

▲ Close-up view of window frame showing floral motifs in triangular panels

▲ This shows the motif on the base of the window jamb (side). The motif depicts the head and tail of a beast.

▼ Diagram of motifs on West doorway, Clonfert Cathedral, Co. Galway
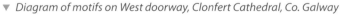

Chevron motif　　*Circular and square motif*　　*Knot motif*　　*Decorative motif*

CORMAC'S CHAPEL

Style	Irish Romanesque	Place	Cashel, Co. Tipperary	Date	1127–34	Built by	King-Bishop Cormaic Mac Carthach

Cormac's Chapel is the fourth and last construction on one of the most impressive archaeological sites in Ireland, the Rock of Cashel. The site, which is surrounded by a large stone wall, consists of four structures:

1. A round tower
2. The cathedral
3. The hall of the vicar's coral (a meeting room)
4. Cormac's Chapel.

Architectural Features

- It has a nave and chancel.
- A large archway joins the nave to the church.
- Towers flank the nave at its east end.
- It has the highest chancel archway in Irish-Romanesque architecture, it was possibly influenced by European design.
- Its columns are decorated with representations of human heads, masks and twisted designs.
- The vault has groin ribs coming from engaged pillars.
- The north doorway is the most striking feature of this church (see p. 105).
- The church is very dark inside.

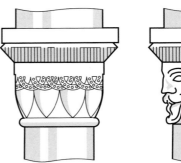

▲ *Capital decoration from the north doorway in Cormac's Chapel, Co. Tipperary*

▶ *South side of Cormac's Chapel, Cashel, Co. Tipperary*

CLONMACNOISE CATHEDRAL

Style	Irish Romanesque	Place	Co. Offaly	Date	Founded 545	Built by	Saint Ciarán (c. 516–549)

Did you know?

Saint Ciarán had a special bond with animals and preserved in Clonmacnoise is a precious relic of the hide of a cow. The story is told that this cow followed Saint Ciarán when he left home.

Clonmacnoise was built beside the river Shannon in Co. Offaly. It was a very famous monastery and one of the greatest centres of Celtic Christianity and learning. It has the ruins of eight churches, two round towers and great stone crosses. The first cathedral was built early in the tenth century. In the late eleventh century this was replaced by the present building. In 1189, the last high king of Ireland, Brian Boru, was buried in the old **sacristy**.

dic·tion·ar·y

A **sarcristy** is a room attached to a church where sacred vessels such as chalices are kept.

Architectural Features

- The cathedral is a single chamber church with **antae** at both ends.
- Its earliest feature is its fragmented west door.
- The north door, inserted in 1460, has mouldings of the figures of Saint Dominic, Saint Patrick and Saint Francis above the arch.
- To the east of the cathedral is the Nun's Church, which has fine Romanesque carvings in the door and chancel arch.
- There is also a Romanesque church and a round tower known as Temple Finghin.

> ### dic·tion·ar·y
>
> An **anta** is a square or rectangular pier formed by the thickening end of a wall.

Other Structures Built Close to the Cathedral

- Outside the cathedral is a tenth-century cross of the scriptures and a round tower known as O'Rourkes' Tower.
- There is a very small oratory in which Saint Ciarán is said to be buried. During excavation two crosiers (hooked staffs of a bishop) were found here.

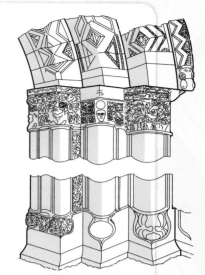

▲ *Decorative details of the chancel archway in Clonmacnoise Cathedral, Co. Offaly*

CLONFERT CATHEDRAL

Style	Irish Romanesque	**Place**	Clonfert, Co. Galway	**Date**	Founded 563	**Built by**	Saint Brendan (c. 484–577)

Clonfert is an area in south Galway which is renowned for its many monastic settlements. It was frequently attacked by vikings from Denmark who burned it down on a few occasions.

Architectural Features

The main feature to study in Clonfert Cathedral is its doorway, called the West Door. The visitor has to stand back from the door to appreciate its six large arcs containing several stylistic motifs:

NOTE: See p. 69 for more detailed pictures of the West Door.

- The door has a triangular **pediment**.
- The human faces of the redeemed (saved) are etched onto the door. Their faces project out above carvings of animal heads.
- The door is set into a mortar-rendered wall.

◄ *West Door, Clonfert Cathedral, Co. Galway*

> ### dic·tion·ar·y
>
> A **pediment** is a low-pitched triangular gable with a sloping roof on both sides and a cornice under the base. Pediments are usually found over doors and windows.

Romanesque Architecture in Ireland Revision

1 What were the main features of Romanesque architecture in Ireland?

2 Explain how the Irish-Romanesque style was implemented into the following buildings:
a) Cormac's Chapel, b) Clonmacnoise Cathedral, c) Clonfert Cathedral. Use sketches.

Romanesque Sculpture

As in Roman times, sculpture played a big part in architecture in medieval times. Why was sculpture important? It served to teach Bible stories to medieval people, who were usually uneducated. It also helped them to live better lives – when they looked at strong images of hell they thought about what would happen to them if they sinned.

Features of Romanesque Sculpture

- It was mostly located in cathedrals, churches and abbeys.
- Sculpture in Romanesque churches was mainly found in doorways and tympana and on capitals.
- Subjects portrayed included Bible stories, Greek myths, **abstract imagery** and monsters.
- The style of this sculpture involved interlacing designs. Figures depicted were simple dancing characters.
- The design was geometrical in form. Each was organised around an abstract pattern of circles and triangles.
- Although it followed the classical orders, Romanesque sculpture did not use **classical proportions**.
- Romanesque sculptural artists generally remained anonymous (unknown).

> ### dic·tion·ar·y
>
> **Abstract imagery** is not pictorial – the image is hard to make out or understand as it involves just shapes and colours.
>
> The ancient Greeks worked out rules for proportioning mouldings. These rules were called orders of architecture, namely the Doric, Ionic and Corinthian orders (see p. 99). All of these orders had **classical proportions**, which refers to the proportion of the capital in relation to the shaft and base of a column.

Types of Subjects Portrayed

The main theme selected and portrayed by Romanesque sculptors was a religious one. The subject of Christ was very popular and was almost always portrayed in the tympana. The subjects of Mary and the saints were as frequently shown in Romanesque cathedrals. Alongside spiritual and saintly subjects, there were also gruesome images of hell, designed to warn people against committing sin.

The Expressive Qualities of Romanesque Sculpture

Romanesque sculpture had to be expressive. This served a dual purpose: to convey happy and joyful Bible stories, and also serious and thought-provoking Bible stories. We can clearly see these strong expressive qualities in the work of the French Romanesque sculptor Gislebertus.

TYMPANUM AT CATHEDRAL OF SAINT-LAZARE, AUTUN							
Style	Romanesque	**Place**	France	**Date**	1120–35	**Built by**	Gislebertus

The rare thing about this tympanum is that we know the name of the artist who created it. Gislebertus (flourished c. 1120–40) had an unusual style, and his use of iconography (symbolism) is unique. He occasionally used models as an aid to accuracy. He had great artistic vision, and wanted this tympanum to express a feeling of great emotion. He also took inspiration from **Byzantine** manuscripts.

> ### dic·tion·ar·y
>
> The **Byzantine** style (300–1453) was the type of art produced by artists of the Byzantine Empire. At the empire's centre was the glittering city of Constantinople, renamed from the Greek Byzantium, and now called Istanbul in present day Turkey. The style was originally influenced by classical Roman art, but became much more abstract and symbolic, concentrating mainly on religious subject matter, including icons (depictions of sacred images), and paintings of emperors.

Sculptural Features

- The theme of this tympanum is 'The Last Judgement'.
- Christ's body is arranged around a central vertical axis.
- Christ is seated in the centre of the tympanum, which is a mark of respect and honour.
- His hands are outstretched in judgement, and the pose of his body is very severe.
- He is facing forwards.

▶ *Tympanum at Saint-Lazare Cathedral, Autun, France, showing 'The Last Judgement' by Gislebertus*

CAPITAL AT CHURCH OF SAINT-BÉNIGNE, DIJON

Style	Romanesque	**Place**	France	**Date**	1007–17	**Built by**	William of Volpiano

Sculptural decoration on capitals was popular in Romanesque times (see p. 99). Saint-Bénigne Church, one of the first Romanesque churches, was designed by architect William of Volpiano (962–1031). Its carved capitals display figurative, decorative, adventurous and playful sculpture techniques.

- This capital displays four cubic faces. Each face depicts a very serious-looking bearded man.
- The figures are gazing forwards.
- At the four top corners of the capital their hands meet diagonally, back to back.
- This sculptural decoration is in low relief, with little sense of volume.
- There is a decoration of palmate (shaped like an open hand) leaves.

◀ *'Capital with Bearded Figure' at Saint-Bénigne Church, Dijon, France*

Romanesque Sculpture Revision Questions

1 What were the main features of Romanesque sculpture?

2 Outline the types of subjects portrayed and the reasons for their selection. Use sketches.

3 What was the purpose of sculpture in medieval times? Explain.

4 Discuss the work of Gislebertus of Autun. Draw a sketch.

5 Write about the tympanum at the Cathedral of Saint-Lazare, Autun.

The Gothic Style of Architecture

During the twelfth and thirteenth centuries a style of art and architecture grew in the northeast of France and spread throughout Europe. It was known as Gothic, and was very different to the Romanesque style. People could afford to build bigger churches because there was more money available. The roofs were now stone instead of wood, meaning that fewer churches burned down. The aim of Gothic architecture was to create a soaring, light-filled space that would inspire awe in the faithful and make them feel they had been transported into a heavenly, place of worship.

Gothic art can be divided into three stages:

1   Early Gothic: 1140–1200
2   Middle Gothic: 1200–50
3   Late Gothic: 1250 onwards

Gothic architecture often involved rebuilding Romanesque structures that had been destroyed by fire, for example:

- Canterbury, England (burned 1174)
- Chartres, France (burned 1194)
- Rheims, France (burned 1211)

▲ *Chartres Cathedral, France*

Features of the Gothic Style

The most obvious difference between Gothic and Romanesque architecture is the shape of the arches – they are pointed instead of round. In addition to these, Gothic architecture featured ribbed vaults, flying buttresses, large windows with stained glass, and delicate architectural details such as mouldings and tracery (see p. 112). The overall impression of height was emphasised by a linear and vertical style of architectural decoration.

Pointed Arches

Gothic architects wanted to create a lighter, more vertical arch that pointed towards heaven. Magnificent examples of these pointed arches can be found in Chartres Cathedral and Saint-Denis Cathedral, both in France.

Ribbed Vaults

When constructing vaults in the Romanesque era, (pp. 102–3), builders put the emphasis on strength and solidity. By contrast, Gothic architects wanted to create a type of frame that would increase the height of the cathedral and allow more light in. They achieved this by using ribbed vaulting instead of solid stone vaults. A ribbed vault is criss-crossed by 'ribs' that provide a skeletal frame to support the vault. The new type of vault made further changes possible:

- It was possible to build to much greater heights than before.

- Because the ribbed vaults were lighter, they did not need massive stone walls to support them. Architects could therefore make the walls less thick.

- This in turn made it possible to open large spaces in the walls for windows.

Flying Buttresses

Flying buttresses were the most frequently type of buttress used during the Gothic era. A flying buttress is made up of an arched structure extending out from the upper part of a wall to a massive pier. Its purpose is to support the wall by transferring the outward thrust of the vault downwards to the ground. This allowed the walls of a cathedral to be higher and thinner.

▲ *In this section of a nave bay of Amiens Cathedral, France, we can see rib vaulting, flying buttresses and pointed arches.*

Large Windows Filled with Stained Glass

The great height and thinner walls of Gothic cathedrals meant that lots of tall windows could be installed to allow light to stream in. Many of these windows featured colourful stained glass. This had been in use for centuries but during the Gothic era stained glass came into its own. Gothic architecture featured some of the most wonderful examples of stained glass in the whole history of art.

▶ *Stained-glass window, Chartres Cathedral, France*

Mouldings and Tracery

Moulding is an ornamental edging or band, often enriched with decorative carving, sticking out from a wall or other surface. Tracery is the ornamental patternwork in stone which fills the upper part of a Gothic window. Both were widely used during the Gothic era.

CATHEDRAL OF SAINT-DENIS							
Style	Gothic	**Place**	France	**Date**	1140–44	**Built by**	Abbot Suger

▲ *West front of Saint-Denis, near Paris, France*

The cathedral of Saint-Denis, situated just outside Paris, was the first truly Gothic building. Several churches were built on the site where Saint Denis, the first bishop of Paris, was buried in the third century. The man responsible for building the church in the Gothic style was Abbot Suger (c. 1081–1151), a French abbot-statesman and historian. He believed that more space was needed to accommodate the increasing number of pilgrims who were flocking to visit the relics of Saint Denis. There was great competition between towns to have the largest most beautiful church. Suger referred to the cathedral of Saint-Denis as 'some strange region of the universe which neither exists in the slime of earth nor entirely in the purity of heaven.'

Architectural Features

- Saint-Denis is a magnificent combination of Gothic architecture with sculpture, stained glass, gold-smithing and painting.
- The **rose window** is constructed in bar tracery. This allowed for thinner bars between the glass and meant that the window was structurally independent of the wall.
- The interior of the cathedral is decorated with marble pillars, colourful hangings and decorative archways.

> dic·tion·ar·y
>
> A **rose window** is a circular window, such as those found in Gothic cathedrals. It is divided into segments by stone mullions (slender posts) and tracery.

- The choir chapel in Saint-Denis is decorated in a very elegant fashion. There are five radiating chapels (spreading out from a central point), illuminated by stained glass.

- There are three portals (doors), with the largest in the centre. Each door is topped by beautifully decorated tympana which are supported by large pillars. The tympanum over the main entrance shows 'The Last Judgement.' The doors are made of gilded (covered in gold leaf) bronze.

- The exterior façade has a combination of Romanesque and Gothic features.

- The spires on the cathedral were designed as defensive towers.

CHARTRES CATHEDRAL

Style	Gothic	Place	France	Date	First Gothic version was built in twelfth century	Built by	A local bishop (name unknown)

This amazing Gothic cathedral, located in the French city of Chartres, went through several phases of development:

1 In 1020 the first cathedral burned down and was rebuilt.

2 This structure was destroyed by fire in 1134.

3 In 1145 its rebuilding began.

4 In 1194 it was again hit by a devastating fire.

5 In 1220, it was rebuilt again.

Chartres Cathedral was a very popular pilgrimage church as it housed a sacred relic, believed to be the garment worn by Mary when she gave birth to Jesus. The cathedral is notable for its vast nave, its porches adorned with fine sculptures, and its awe-inspiring stained glass windows.

Architectural Features

- The **martyrum** beneath the choir is the oldest part of the Cathedral. It dates back to the ninth century.

> ### dic·tion·ar·y
> A **martyrum** is a circular structure like a tomb, built over the burial place of a Christian martyr.

- An eleventh-century crypt, designed by French scholar, teacher and bishop Fulbert (bishop of Chartress 1006–28), is constructed around the martyrum.

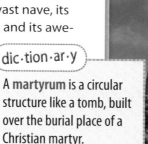

▲ West front and rose window of Chartres Cathedral, France

- In 1020 long, groin-vaulted pilgrimage galleries were built beneath the aisles.

- Chartres has radiating chapels and an **ambulatory**.

- It has three semicircular apsidal chapels (small chapels projecting out from a larger apse).

- There are Romanesque and Gothic chapels in the crypt.

> ### dic·tion·ar·y
> An **ambulatory** is a place in a cathedral in which to walk, usually between the sanctuary and the chapels.

- The stained-glass windows cover a surface of more than 2,000 square metres. They depict biblical scenes such as 'The Last Judgement' in the west rose window (see p. 113).

- In the twelfth century the Royal Portal, with its three **lancet** windows and towers on either side were built.

- Sculpture played an important role in the cathedral. The image on the right shows the prophets Isaiah, Jeremiah, and Simeon (holding baby Jesus). They are jamb statues from the right side of the central portal, north transept.

- The north tower, dating back to 1130, has traditional Romanesque capitals with mythological beasts and hunting scenes. The tower narrows at the rose window level. It is supported by buttresses that become gradually smaller. These were built to support the wooden steeple, burned in 1194.

▲ *Sculpture of Isaiah, Jeremiah and Simeon, Chartres Cathedral, France.*

- The south-west tower has capitals that are more solemnly decorated with prickly foliage. The tower narrows steadily and it has disguised fluted columns that emphasise its height.

- Gothic builders expanded the cathedral in two ways: they added a very wide transept so that the ground-plan was altered from a U shape to a cruciform plan. They built a much bigger interior which was divided into three parts:

  1 **The arcade:** The lower storey, called the arcade, is made up of a series of pointed arches in the nave, transept and choir.
  2 **The triforium:** The triforium is a narrow horizontal gallery with a row of elegant columns creating a vertical look. This style replaced the heavier platform of earlier cathedrals, for example Durham Cathedral.
  3 **The clerestory:** Above the triforium is the clerestory, which is lit by a series of double lancet windows.

> ### dic·tion·ar·y
> A **lancet** window is a tall, narrow window with a pointed arch at its top.

- Gothic builders also introduced rectangular quadripartite (divided into four sections) vaults along the flying buttresses. This innovation made it possible to build higher and open up the walls to fill them with beautiful stained glass to a degree never seen before.

The Gothic Style of Architecture Revision Questions

1 Write a paragraph explaining the meaning of 'Gothic' in terms of architecture.

2 Describe the features of Gothic architecture, using sketches to illustrate your answer.

3 Describe how it is different to the Romanesque style.

4 Describe the architectural features of the Cathedral of Saint-Denis, near Paris. Use sketches in your answer.

5 Describe the architectural features of Chartres Cathedral. Use sketches in your answer.

Stained Glass

The use of stained, or coloured, glass as an artistic and educational tool reached a high point in the Gothic era. In contrast to Romanesque churches, which were dark and gloomy inside, Gothic churches were filled with light and space. When worshippers saw coloured light streaming though huge windows, it may have given them a spiritual lift, made them feel closer to God, and inspired them to lead better lives. In turn, when they looked closely at the scenes depicted on the windows, they received moral lessons, saw miracles depicted, and interpreted religious symbols.

Selection of Subjects

Careful consideration was given to the selection of subjects for the stained-glass windows:

- If the church was dedicated to Mary, Jesus or a particular saint, key moments in the individual's life were shown on the windows.

- Themes were mostly religious, and were laid out carefully in sequential order.

- Good scenes and bad scenes from the Bible were portrayed. The good scenes inspired pilgrims to lead good lives, while bad scenes warned them against living sinful lives.

Methods of Stained Glass Manufacture

The manufacture of stained glass has changed little since the Middle Ages, although techniques have been greatly developed. Much of what we know is thanks to the German monk **Theophilus** (c. 1070–1125). He had a recipe for stained glass: two parts wood ash (to provide potassium), and one part river sand. The result was a glass that lacked toughness and degraded easily in damp weather as it was silica-free. This is one of the reasons why the glass in medieval windows deteriorated and darkened.

▲ *'The Tree of Jesse' is depicted in a stained glass window at Chartres Cathedral, France*

Colouring Glass

Glassmakers added metal **oxides** to molten glass to give it colour. Oxides of iron, copper and manganese were most commonly used in the Middle Ages, to produce colours. Below are some examples of colours obtained from different metal oxides:

- Blue – cobalt and chromium
- Red – selenium and copper salts
- Yellow – selenium and chromium with cadmium salts
- Green – copper and chromium salts
- Purple – manganese and cobalt.

Did you know?

Theophilus, himself an artist and metalworker, studied glaziers (glass workers) and painters at work, and wrote a handbook for craftsmen in the twelfth century.

dic·tion·ar·y

An **oxide** is a chemical compound in which oxygen is combined with another element.

Flashed-Glass Colour Technique

At the end of the thirteenth century the use of 'flashed' or 'plated' glass became very popular. This glass was made up of several layers of which two were different colours. The surface colour was scraped off using hydrofluoric acid on the glass, displaying the underlying colour.

Constructing a Stained-Glass Window

Constructing a stained-glass window is a bit like putting a fragile jigsaw puzzle together. It follows the following format:

1. Design the window.
2. Produce the full-sized cartoon (sketch).
3. Cut the glass.
4. Paint the glass.
5. Fire in the kiln.
6. Assemble the pieces.

Design

The artist's first task was to make a design for the stained-glass window. The subject of the window was decided by the patron (person paying for the art). The artist worked closely alongside the patron, the architect and the sculpture mason to make sure their themes and ideas for the cathedral worked together. Once the subject was decided, the glazier prepared a small sketch.

The Full-Sized Cartoon

A full-sized cartoon was produced from this sketch and was moved to a large bench, which served as a template for assembly. The template (a pattern for cutting shapes) included all the lead lines which were in turn shaped to the pieces of glass that made up the design.

Cutting

Working from the cartoon, the artist cut pieces of glass to fit the design. These glass pieces were cut with a red-hot iron and trimmed with a hook-shaped tool called a grozing iron.

▲ *A modern-day glazier works on a stained-glass piece*

Painting the Glass

The artist painted each piece of glass, and did shading in black.

Firing in the Kiln

These pieces of glass were fired in a kiln to fuse the design to the glass.

Assembling the Pieces

The last step involved assembling the pieces of glass. This was done on a table. The pieces were fitted into a lead framework, then soldered (joined using molten metal) together and fitted into an iron armature (frame).

THE STAINED GLASS OF CHARTRES CATHEDRAL

The making of stained glass peaked between the twelfth and the fourteenth centuries, and featured in many European cathedrals. Some of the most exquisite examples of stained glass can be found in Chartres Cathedral, France.

The North Rose Window and Lancets

This window carries the theme of Christ in the prophesies of the Old Testament and the theme of the Glorification of the Virgin. Details on the window include:

- Mary and the Child Jesus
- Saint Anne with Mary
- Priest-King Melchizedek
- King Nebuchadnezzar (king of Chaldean Empire)
- David with his ten-stringed harp
- David's son, Solomon
- Moses.

The Blue Virgin Window

In this window, Mary can be seen seated facing the viewer, crowned and enthroned with the Child Jesus upon her knee and numerous angels holding her throne. Under her throne there are six scenes which tell the story of 'The Marriage at Cana,' where Jesus turned water into wine.

- The background colour is a rich ruby red and Mary's halo and clothing are a luminous blue.
- A dove decends on Mary from above, its beak connecting with her halo by three blue rays.
- Each angel swings a censer (a vessel for burning incense) and holds a candlestick.
- This window is situated in the south ambulatory.
- It dates from the thirteenth century.

▲ *This image shows a detail from a lancet beneath the North Rose Window, Chartres Cathedral. It depicts King David playing his harp.*

▼ *The Blue Virgin Window at Chartres Cathedral, France*

Stained Glass Revision Questions

1 Describe the methods of stained-glass manufacture.

2 Describe the flashed glass technique.

3 Outline the construction of a stained-glass window.

4 Outline how subjects were selected for stained glass.

5 Discuss the location and integration of stained glass and the type of subjects depicted in Chartres Cathedral. Describe how it may have impacted the viewer then and today.

Gothic Sculpture

It is easy to see the difference between Gothic and Romanesque sculpture. Where Romanesque figures were squat and chunky, Gothic figures were elongated (longer than normal) and elegant. They also had a naturalistic (realistic) feel, by contrast to the abstract (unrealistic) feel of Romanesque figures. The favourite place to put Gothic sculptures was in the tympana and on either side of the portals (doors).

Naturalism and Idealism

The concept of naturalism in Gothic sculpture was very important. The sculpture drew inspiration and ideas from the natural world around it and from **humanism**. Religious teaching during the Gothic era concentrated on a generous and forgiving God. During the Romanesque era, the idea of a more fearsome God had been promoted.

Idealism also played a big part in Gothic sculpture. Artists wanted their work to look as perfect as possible, while at the same time retaining a natural look. The sculpture was very serene, with lots of elongated and vertical poses.

dic·tion·ar·y

Humanism is a type of philosophy that concentrates on human effort rather than on religion.

The term **idealism** refers to a person or thing regarded as perfect or as a standard to aim to.

Choice of Subjects in Gothic Sculpture

Just like subjects used in stained glass and in the Romanesque era, those used in sculpture were mainly religious. This is because the Church remained the chief patron of the arts, and cathedral decoration was the main source of employment for medieval artists. Therefore the clergy decided which religious subjects they wanted, leaving the artist with little say in the matter.

Gothic Carving Techniques and Tools

Sculptural carving was a very important feature of Gothic architecture. It was clearly evident throughout Gothic cathedrals from the impressive tympana and carved capitals to the statues.

Did you know?

After the Roman Empire there were no free-standing sculptures as they were seen as a worship of false gods. Gothic sculpture saw the return of free-standing sculptures such as a small Madonna and Child.

CARVING TECHNIQUES USED BY SCULPTORS

- **Intaglio carving:** Incised (cut) decoration which is cut into a stone in a linear style. Sculptors used a sharp-pointed chisel for this type of carving.
- **Low-relief carving:** Sculpture which is slightly raised from a two-dimensional background.
- **High-relief carving:** More three-dimensional relief, which is almost but not quite independent from the surface. Relief sculpture was carved from a thick slab of stone, beginning with a preliminary sketch on the surface. The form would appear out of the stone after chipping into the block with a hammer and chisel. Relief work can be found on tympana and on the archways in Gothic cathedrals.
- **Free-standing carving:** The sculptures are fully three-dimensional and can be viewed from all sides and balance without assistance. To achieve this effect, sculptors used hammers and a variety of different sizes of chisels. The original design for the statues was moulded from clay or carved in wax. Examples of this type of carving can be found in Chartres Cathedral and Rheims Cathedral, both in France.

GOTHIC SCULPTURE IN CHARTRES CATHEDRAL

Chartres Cathedral is a landmark in the history of sculpture. It has 200 statues featured in 41 different scenes. The sculptures mark a clear division between the Romanesque and Gothic styles. The essence of early Gothic sculpture is captured by the statues that decorate the three portals of the western façade, known collectively as the Royal Portal.

The Royal Portal

The Royal Portal was built between 1145 and 1555. Originally it featured 24 statues, but only 19 have survived. Sculptors from at least three schools of sculpture came and worked on the Royal Portal, including the School of Saint Denis and School of Etampes. The master sculptor of Chartres completed the central portal.

▲ *Old Testament figures from the right bay of the Royal Portal, left jamb, Chartres Cathedral, France*

- The sculpture on the central portal (west façade) depicts religious and royal imagery, including stories of the life of Christ, Christ's Ascension into heaven, and stories of saints and apostles.

- Below the religious figures are statues of kings and queens – hence the name 'The Royal Portal.' These statues are based on figures from the Old Testament. By placing these statues near the religious statues, a close relationship between the kings and God was implied.

- The statues on the portal are elongated and elegant.

- The sculpted statues on the porches stand stiffly, their heads raised ready to proclaim a great prophecy.

- The left part of the portal focuses on events in the the life of Mary, for example 'The Annunciation,' 'The Visitation' and 'The Nativity.' Other themes on this section are 'The Annunciation to the Shepherd,' 'The Adoration of the Magi,' and 'The Flight into Egypt.' A lot of these scenes are repeated in the stained glass of the central lancet window (see p. 117).

- The right part of the portal focuses on the death and Resurrection of Jesus. Again this is repeated in the stained-glass window above it.

- On the outer section of the portal the statues have been deliberately elongated. The crowned figures represent the kings and queens of Judah. Their facial expressions are serene and dignified.

- On the right bay of the Royal Portal, left jamb, are Old Testament figures. They appear to be smiling, with their right hands raised to their chests. Heads are raised and looking forward.

- The tympanum was the point of focus to all church goers. For this reason Christ was always present there. In the Royal Portal, Christ is sitting in the centre of the tympanum, surrounded by his 12 apostles. He is portrayed as a peaceful, elegant figure.

The Central Portal

Another fine example of Gothic sculpture from Chartres Cathedral can be found in the central portal, north transept, which depicts Abraham, the founder of Hebrew peoples and his son Isaac. His head is turned to listen to God's message.

▶ *Sculpture of Abraham with Isaac in the central paortal of Chartres Cathedral, France*

GOTHIC SCULPTURE IN RHEIMS CATHEDRAL

Built in the thirteenth century, Rheims Cathedral in France is a major example of the classic High Gothic style. It was a coronation cathedral for French kings, so enjoyed superior status. A good example of its beautiful sculpture can be seen on the West Portal.

The West Portal

Once the king was crowned inside the church he would leave through the west portal. The portal is made up of three entrances, located on the west wall, joined together almost as if to form a triumphal arch. Instead of sculpture, the high tympanum has a rose window. In the gables above the doorways its sculptural subjects, thought to be masterpieces of the thirteenth century, are:

- The Coronation of the Virgin in the middle accompanied by figures representing scenes from the Bible
- The birth and childhood of Christ
- The Annunciation and The Visitation, to the right of this
- The Last Judgement, featuring Christ, on the left of this
- The Presentation in the Temple
- The Crucifixion.

▲ *The west portal at Rheims Cathedral, France*

▼ *'The Visitation' from the West Portal at Rheims Cathedral*

The Visitation

Of the themes listed above, 'The Visitation' is the most important. It depicts Mary and Elizabeth, who are portrayed with concerned looks. They are in **contrappostal** poses. They are situated before the tomb's columns but do not appear to be supported by them. Elizabeth waves hello to Mary and the sculpture work is so realistic, you get the feeling that Elizabeth is waiting for Mary to turn to her.

Their garments are draped around their bodies in deep folds which gives the appearance of lots of movement.

> **dic·tion·ar·y**
>
> *Contrapposto*, meaning counterpoise, describes a figure standing with its weight resting on one leg and the upper part of the body and arms twisted. This serves to create a natural looking pose.

Gothic Sculpture Revision Questions

1 Describe the difference between Romanesque sculpture and Gothic sculpture. Give examples and sketches.

2 Explain the concepts of naturalism and idealism in Gothic sculpture.

3 Explain the choice of subjects used. Draw sketches.

4 Explain the tools and techniques used in Gothic sculpture.

5 Do a detailed study of the sculpture of Chartres Cathedral. Draw sketches.

6 Describe the sculpture on the West Portal of Rheims Cathedral. Draw sketches.

Gothic Architecture in England

While flourishing in mainland Europe, Gothic architecture was also establishing strong roots in England. However, there was a difference in approach: English Gothic architects put more emphasis on the decoration of the cathedral rather than on its height.

Contrast Between English Gothic and French Gothic Styles

During the second half of the twelfth century, England was one of the first countries to adopt certain features of French Gothic architecture. However, there is a distinct difference between the two due to rivalry between the countries. The table below highlights the differences between the English and French Gothic styles. Here, we compare Amiens Cathedral in France with Salisbury Cathedral in England.

Amiens Cathedral, France	Salisbury Cathedral, England
The French Gothic architect's main concern was the height of the cathedral. Amiens Cathedral is 43.5 m high.	The English architect's main concern was the decoration of the cathedral. Salisbury Cathedral, at 25.6 m high, is dwarfed by Amiens.
The cathedral was located in the town.	The cathedral was located in a rural area.
Amiens Cathedral has twin towers.	Salisbury Cathedral's façade is a screen façade with a large crossing-tower.
This cathedral has thin walls.	This cathedral has thick walls.
This cathedral has large window openings.	The cathedral has small window openings.
The cathedral has open (visible) buttressing.	The buttressing on this cathedral is hidden.

Marble

During the Gothic era artists used vast quanties of marble to decorate cathedrals. Purbeck marble was very popular in England, and it is visible in the nave of Salisbury cathedral, and in most of the cathedrals in southern England, from columns to flooring. This marble is a sedimentary limestone quarried from the Isle of Purbeck, in the south of England. Although not true marble, it can be polished like marble.

SALISBURY CATHEDRAL

Style	English Gothic	**Place**	Salisbury	**Date**	1220–58	**Built by**	Unknown

The official name for this cathedral is the Cathedral of Saint Mary. It took only 38 years to build. It has many impressive statistics – it has the tallest church spire in England, at 123 m high, and the largest cloister and park in England (80 acres).

Architectural Features

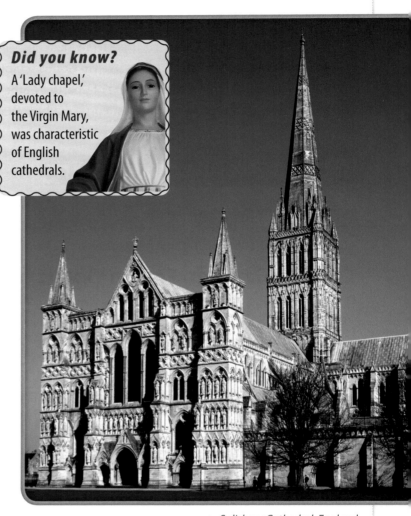

Did you know?

A 'Lady chapel,' devoted to the Virgin Mary, was characteristic of English cathedrals.

▲ *Salisbury Cathedral, England*

- North of Salisbury Cathedral there was a free-standing clock tower, which was demolished in 1792. The clock itself still survives and is the world's oldest clock.

- South of the cathedral there is a cloister surrounded by a high octagonal central building, called the chapter house.

- Salisbury Cathedral is made up entirely of rectangles, with a large transept dividing the building in the middle.

- The choir is made up of a number of buildings: a high choir, a rectangular ambulatory and a low eastern chapel.

- Only the nave was accessible to the laity (lay people). A choir screen separates the choir area (which was reserved for the clergy) from the nave.

- The east chapel, known as the 'Lady chapel,' was used as a place of adoration to the Virgin Mary. Here, there were daily Masses to Mary.

- The exterior of Salisbury Cathedral has none of the open buttressing which is evident in French Gothic cathedrals. English Gothic architects hid their buttressing.

Gothic Architecture in England Revision Questions

1. Outline the contrasts between English Gothic architecture and French Gothic architecture.
2. Discuss the architectural features of the English Gothic cathedral at Salisbury. Use sketches.

Gothic Architecture in Ireland

The Normans were responsible for bringing Gothic architecture to Ireland. When they invaded and settled in Ireland (from 1169), they built churches, monasteries and cathedrals. Due to trade, the Gothic style flourished on the east coast of Ireland. By contrast, the Romanesque style continued to thrive on the west coast. Irish-Gothic buildings featured pointed arches, high ceilings and flying buttresses. There were also stained-glass windows and lifelike sculpture depicting religious themes, people, animals and architecture.

BALTINGLASS ABBEY

Style	Irish Gothic	Date	1148	Place	Baltinglass, Co. Wicklow	Built by	Diarmaid Mac Murchadha, King of Leinster

This is the first example of Gothic architecture in Ireland. It was begun in 1148 when Diarmaid Mac Murchada brought Cistercian monks from Mellifont Abbey, Co. Louth, to found a new monastery in Baltinglass. The original building was completed by 1170.

▲ *Baltinglass Abbey, Co. Wicklow*

Architectural Features

- The building is made up of a nave with aisles, a chancel and two transepts.
- The abbey floor plan is cross shaped.
- It has both round and square columns.
- In the twelfth century three west windows were added.
- In the nineteenth century the east windows and the tower were added.
- Joining the south aisle to the cloister is a twelfth-century doorway.
- The abbey displays beautiful decorative stonework.

CHRIST CHURCH CATHEDRAL

Style	Irish Gothic	Date	1038	Place	Dublin	Built by	Archbishop O'Toole and Strongbow

Christ Church Cathedral was begun in 1038 by King Sitric Silkbeard, who was king of Dublin at that time. In 1171 Anglo-Normans seized Dublin and their leader Strongbow, together with the archbishop Laurence O'Toole (1128–80), decided to rebuild the cathedral. In 1561 the south side of the nave collapsed due to fire. Its reconstruction was carried out by the architect George Edmond, and he rebuilt it in the style of the north nave.

Architectural Features

- The transept and the crypt are the only remaining features of the church of Saint Laurence O'Toole, added in the 1200s. He requested that his heart be sent back to his cathedral, which is preserved in a heart-shaped box in the chapel of Saint Laud.

- The crypt is very well preserved and is a clear example of the Irish-Gothic style.

- The north side of the nave is rich in carvings. It was built between 1212 and 1235. The stone used here was quarried at Dundry, England and shipped to Dublin.

- The triforium is joined together with the clerestory. This is done by marble shafts which rise from the openings of the triforium up to the clerestory level. There is a trefoil (three-leafed) headed arch in the triforium and a trefoil-headed arch in the clerestory.

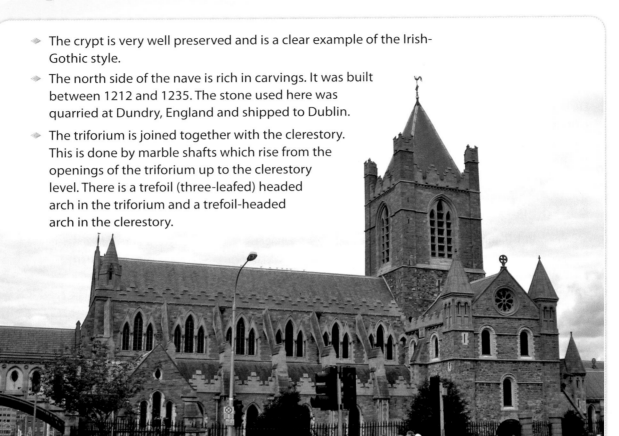

▲ *Christ Church Cathedral , Dublin*

▼ *Internal view of Christ Church Cathedral , showing three pointed stained-glass windows*

SAINT PATRICK'S CATHEDRAL

Style	Irish Gothic	**Date**	1200–70	**Place**	Dublin	**Built by**	Archbishop John Comyn

Saint Patrick's Cathedral is so called because it was built on the site of a holy well used by Saint Patrick for baptisms. A wealthy donor, Sir Benjamin Guinness, paid the sum of £16,000 for a huge restoration project between 1860 and 1870.

Architectural Features

The best examples of Gothic architecture which survive in the cathedral are:

1 The eastern bays of the north side of the nave

2 Vaulting of the south transept

3 The eastern wall and aisle

4 The north and east walls of the choir

- The high north-west tower, built in the fourteenth century, is capped by a spire and stepped battlements.

- Inside the cathedral there is a series of 18 standing marble figures up the north aisle of the nave. One example is the bust of author Jonathan Swift (1667–1745), dean of the cathedral for many years. It bears the words 'Swift has sailed into his rest/ savage inignation there cannot lacerate his breast.'

- Crests and swords of the now ceased order of Saint Patrick decorate the stalls in the choir, accompanied with bright banners overhead.

- The 'Lady Chapel,' said to be influenced by that at Salisbury Cathedral (see p. 122), was consecrated in 1224.

▲ *Saint Patrick's Cathedral, Dublin*

▼ *Interior of Saint Patrick's Cathedral, Dublin*

Gothic Architecture in Ireland Revision Questions

1 Describe the features of the Irish-Gothic style.

2 How did the Norman invasion affect Ireland's architecture?

3 Describe the Gothic architectural features of Christ Church Cathedral. Use sketches.

4 Describe the Gothic architectural features of Saint Patrick's Cathedral. Use sketches.

The Late-Gothic Style

The Late-Gothic style, which was the final stage of the Gothic era, spanned the fourteenth and fifteenth centuries. It is best known for its smaller-scale buildings and **flamboyant** style of ornamentation, particularly in its tracery.

Characteristics of the Late Gothic Style

In the Late Gothic style, gone was the obsession with the size and height of cathedrals. It was replaced by a desire for more ornamentation, especially on windows and vaults.

Window Tracery

Tracery is simply the division of panels, screens, vaults or windows. It involves ornamental stonework in patterns, like the web of stonework in the upper part of Gothic rose windows (see p. 111). It was later developed to include raised decoration on wall surfaces. Window tracery was usually made up of a crown supported by mullions (see below). Another element in tracery design was foil (metal in a paper-thin sheet) detail.

There are three different types of foil used in window tracery:

1 Trefoil – three-leafed
2 Quatrefoil – four-leafed
3 Multifoil – many-leafed

> **Did you know?**
> The word 'flamboyant' is often used to describe the components of the Late Gothic style. It comes from the French word for 'flame-like.'

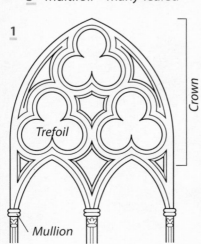
▲ Trefoil tracery

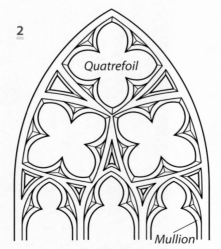
▲ Quatrefoil tracery

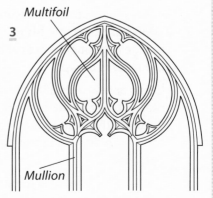
▲ Multifoil tracery

VAULTING PATTERN AND DESIGN

By the late Gothic era vaults were extremely well developed. The fan vault, which is an ornate version of the rib vault (see p. 102), was introduced at this time. All ribs in a fan vault were curved the same way. The vault design was a challenge as there were several types (see below). Working at extraordinarily dangerous heights, the mason had to construct an arch in the ceiling of the cathedral, with a depth that was greater than the width. As vault designs became ever more beautiful, their construction became ever more difficult. The vaults were usually made of concrete or stone, and all the materials had to be hoisted in place, a big task in itself. Then skilled craftsmen set to work on constructing the vaults.

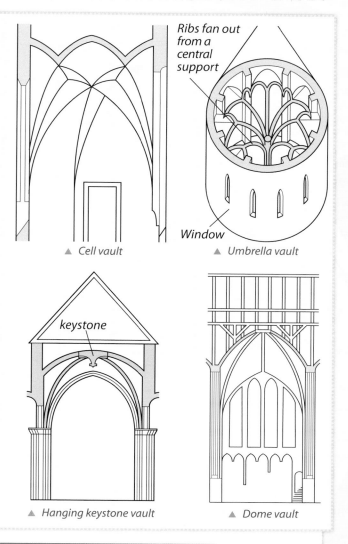

▲ Cell vault

Ribs fan out from a central support

Window

▲ Umbrella vault

keystone

▲ Hanging keystone vault

▲ Dome vault

- A dome vault is a circular-based vault of even curvature.

- A cell vault is one of the compartments of a rib vault.

- An umbrella vault is an advanced form of a domed vault.

- A hanging keystone vault is where the keystone (top stone) 'hangs' from the vault and gives the impression that it is being suspended rather than supporting the load.

KING'S COLLEGE CHAPEL

Style	Late Gothic	Date	1446–1547	Country	England	Built by	Henry VI

King's College Chapel in Cambridge, England, was founded by King Henry VI (1421–71). It took more than a century to build, in four different phases:

1. First building phase: 1446–62

2. Second building phase: 1477–84, saw a notable change in colour of stone.

3. Third building phase: 1508–15, showed innovations such as stained and painted glass windows.

4. Fourth building phase: completed in 1547, involved addition of woodwork and windows

Architectural Features

- The layout is very simple, with a long 'narrow' high central nave divided into a chapel and an ante-chapel.

- The external façade has a strong pattern of windows and buttresses. The west front of the cathedral has octagonal corner turrets which cover the side chapels.

- Some of the decorative features include pierced parapets (low walls) and chapel windows showing two different tracery patterns.
- Inside, the chapel has original **Flemish Renaissance** stained-glass windows – one of the finest examples of stained glass from the sixteenth century.

> ### Did you know?
> The **Flemish Renaissance** took place during the sixteenth century in Northern Europe. Flemish Renaissance artists were influenced by the innovations of Italian Renaissance painting and the local traditions of the early Netherlandish artists.

Vaults

There are two important factors to note in the vaults of King's College Chapel:

1. The height and span of the church made it necessary to build three encircling bands of ornament. This was to prevent:

    (a) The introduction of unnecessary intermediate ribs high up

    (b) Too large an area of plain vaulting which would have spoiled the overall look of the chapel.

2. Each conoid (a form resembling a cone) of each vault is divided into two segments by four centred transverse arches. This in turn increases the width of the nave. Continuity is added to the vaults with a series of concentric rings of decoration (rings within rings). These appear over the whole surface of the vault and this adds a sense of movement.

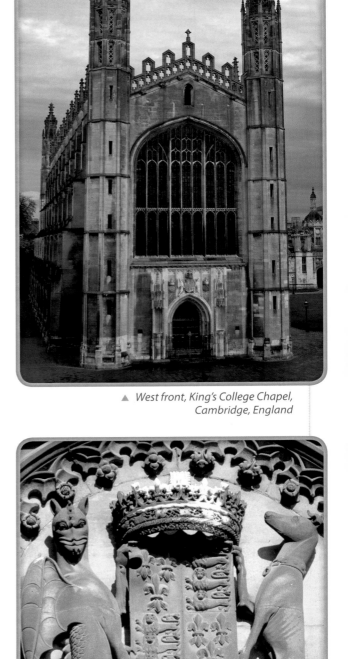

▲ *West front, King's College Chapel, Cambridge, England*

▶ *The Royal Arms of England carved above a door, King's College Chapel, Cambridge*

CHAPEL OF HENRY VII AT WESTMINSTER

Style	Late Gothic	Date	1503–19	Country	England	Built by	Sir Reginald Bray (1440–1503)

The Chapel of Henry VII (1457–1509) at Westminster, also called the Lady Chapel, is situated at the far eastern end of Westminster Abbey in London. With its beautifully and richly decorated interior, it is the most impressive example of Late-Gothic architecture in Europe.

▲ *King's beasts gaze out from canopies above the saints, Henry VII Chapel, London*

▶ *Exterior of Henry VII Chapel, London*

Architectural Features

- The apsidal (in the apse) chapel has lavish wall decoration, with 95 statues of saints surmounted by **heraldic** motifs of king's beasts (regal-looking beasts).

- The tombs of Henry VII and his wife, Elizabeth of York (1466–1503), are in the centre of the chapel, behind the altar, enclosed by a bronze grille. They consist of a stone coffin topped by superb gilt bronze effigies showing the couple in repose, and were designed by the Italian sculptor Pietro Torrigiano (1472–1528).

- Brightly coloured heraldic banners of living knights hang above the oak stalls in the chapel.

- The apsidal chapel and aisle windows are at different angles.

- Externally you can see the unity of windows and buttresses. Cupolas (domes) crown the octagonal buttress piers.

dic·tion·ar·y

Heraldry relates to coats of arms. These were originally used to identify knights in combat, whose faces were hidden by helmets, by symbols on their shields.

Vaults

The chapel has a lacy web of fan and **pendant vaults** adorning its ceiling. Pendant vaults are very difficult to construct. First strong transverse arches provide the foundation. Then by extending one of the wedge shapes a pendant fan is formed, thus the *voussoirs* are shaped downwards and finally a conoid is constructed around it. In simple terms, the final result resembles a half-open umbrella hanging upside down from its handle and stopped from opening fully by spokes from other umbrellas around it.

> **dic·tion·ar·y**
>
> A **pendant vault** is a vault supporting one or more dependant structures.
>
> A *voussoir* is a wedge-shaped block used to make up an arch.

The Late-Gothic Style Revision Questions

1 What were the features of the Late-Gothic style?

2 What does tracery mean? Give examples.

3 Describe the architectural features of King's College Chapel. Draw sketches.

4 Describe the architectural features of the Chapel of Henry VII at Westminster. Draw sketches.

5 Why is vaulting so important in Gothic architecture? Give examples of Gothic vaulting and draw sketches.

The Late-Gothic Style in Ireland

The Late-Gothic style flourished in Ireland too, but differed from that of the rest of Europe. For example, Irish Late-Gothic cathedrals were:

- Simpler in design and detail
- Smaller, longer and lower
- Lacking the spectacular rib vaulting of European cathedrals (see p.111).

This was mainly due to the lack of funds and building materials.
Irish Late Gothic buildings often featured:

- A tower house
- Wide traceried windows
- Increased carvings on doorways and seats.

Components of Irish Late-Gothic Architecture

The main types of buildings being constructed during this period were monasteries and churches, tower houses, and castles. Private houses were also built.

Monasteries and Churches

During the Late-Gothic period in Ireland, the Franciscan order of monks created some of the finest Irish monasteries, for example Quin Friary in Co. Clare (see p. 132).

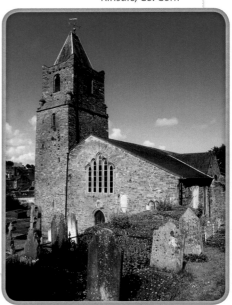
▼ *Church of Saint Multose, Kinsale, Co. Cork*

During the period 1400–1535 churches were given a facelift.

- New doors were installed.
- Old narrow lancet windows were blocked up or replaced by wider traceried windows which allowed more natural light into the church, for example the Church of Saint Multose in Kinsale, Co. Cork.
- This renovating work ended when King Henry VIII (1491–1547) and Oliver Cromwell (1599–1658) confiscated (took away) lands and looted (stole from) many churches and monasteries.

Tower Houses

During the Middle Ages, there were approximately 8,000 tower houses in Ireland. Today, there are more than 2,000 left – some inhabited, others in ruins. Towers were often several stories high and had **gabled** roofs. Most towers were rectangular in shape but there were some round ones. A tower house had several functions:

- To house the church bell
- To be a lookout point against invasion
- To decorate the church grounds.

The way a tower was designed very much suited its function:

- A tower was approximately 30–46 m in height which made it a good point for viewing the surrounding countryside in case of attack.
- At the top of the tower there were windows to the north, south, east and west, giving a clear view of all directions at all times. In addition to this, each floor had a window facing alternately to the north, south, east or west. The windows varied in size and shape from tower to tower across the country.
- In the early days of tower-house building the windows were narrow and pointed. The later tower house windows were squared with projecting **drip mouldings** and sometimes mullions (see p. 112).
- The tower door was usually slender in form, possibly to restrict access to the tower house.
- The tower house was mostly built in the middle of a courtyard surrounded by a **bawn** wall with one or more **turrets**.

dic·tion·ar·y

A **gable** is the triangular upper part of an outside wall between the top of the side walls and the slope of the roof.

Drip mouldings were mouldings above a window that allowed rainwater to drip down.

A **bawn** is a defensive wall built around Irish tower houses.

A **turret** is a round tower which sits vertically out from the wall of a medieval castle.

Castles

Examples of castles built during this period were:

1. Bunratty Castle, Co. Clare – built by the MacNamara family in c. 1425.
2. Blarney Castle, Co. Cork – built by Cormac MacCarthy, King of Munster, in c. 1446.
3. Cahir Castle, Co. Tipperary – built by Conor O'Brien, Prince of Thomond, in 1142.

▼ *Bunratty Castle, Co. Clare*  ▼ *Blarney Castle, Co. Cork*  ▼ *Cahir Castle, Co. Tipperary*

Houses

Houses from the Late-Gothic era adopted elements of the kind of urban architecture that was common in England in the second half of the sixteenth century.

Rothe House

Rothe House in Kilkenny, a wealthy merchant's townhouse, is a good example of the Late-Gothic style.

▲ *Rothe House, Kilkenny*

- Rothe House was built between 1594 and 1610.
- It has been restored to its original glory and is now a museum.
- It features arcades on the ground floor opening on to the street.
- The first floor has a living room lit by mullioned windows.
- A central arch leads into two successive courtyards.
- The garden at the back, reconstructed in 2008, is a typical early seventeenth century town garden.

FRIARIES

Friars were members of certain religious orders of men. They lived lives of poverty, serving the community. The most important requirement of a friary (a monastery of friars) was that it be built near a large town, for example Kilkenny, Drogheda or Athenry. Many Late-Gothic friaries still survive – in the west of Ireland alone 12 well preserved friaries remain. This cannot be said for the rest of Europe: in England few remain.

Cloister Layout

The size of the cloister in a friary made up one third of the total length of the church. It was usually located in the western section. Friary cloisters were divided into two equal parts. One part had light so that literate friars could read their service books. The other had no light for those who could not read. Some friaries show gable-ended architectural structures, with several levels rising up to a long thin tower. It was usual to find lots of Gothic motifs on this structure.

Friary Towers

Friary towers were usually fifteenth-century additions. They were always tall and thin, narrower than the church and built of stone. The towers were generally built running north to south. In Muckross Friary, Killarney, there is an example of an oblong tower which was a rare sight. It runs from east to west.

QUIN FRANCISCAN FRIARY						
Style	Late Irish Gothic	**Date**	1433	**Place**	Co. Clare	**Built by**	Sioda MacNamara

This Franciscan friary was founded by Sioda MacNamara (chieftain of the MacNamara clan). It incorporates part of an earlier Anglo-Norman castle belonging to the DeClares, the wealthiest clan in Ireland during the thirteenth century. The friary took about 20 years to build.

Architectural Features

▲ *Quin Franciscan Friary, Co. Clare*

- The friary is divided by a narrow tower into the chancel and nave.

- There is a large transept in the middle of the south wall of the nave.

- The choir windows are sunk into deep recesses. This is as a result of the thick walls of the previous castle within which the friary was built.

- It has a tall, thin tower, typical of Irish friaries at the time, especially in the west of Ireland.

- It had three round towers, the bases of which can still be seen.

- Quin Friary had five altars – a high altar, two more in the nave and a further two in the transept. All five altars remain in good condition.

- It is not a perfect square, and we can see the location of the cloister chapel (see diagram below). There is a detached ablutionary (for washing) block to the north of the refectory (for eating), reached by a bridge.

- It has six double bay windows facing in one direction and several more facing in another direction. It also has big arches.

- The buttresses are extremely narrow and deep and lie into the walls.

- The columns and bases at Quin Friary are different from each other, with beautiful twist patterns.

- The east window, which is set back into the wall, displays beautiful tracery. It is made up of three intersecting bars following the same curve as the window arch. The lower bars are completed with trefoil arches (see p. 126).

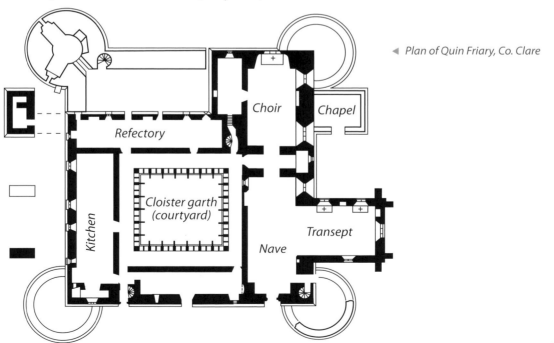

◀ *Plan of Quin Friary, Co. Clare*

The Late-Gothic Style in Ireland Revision Questions

1 What were the main features of the Late-Gothic style in Ireland?

2 What was a friary?

3 What was a cloister? Explain its layout.

4 Describe the function and purpose of a tower house. Use a sketch in your answer.

5 Describe the architectural features of Quin Friary. Use a sketch in your answer.

The Gothic Revival

During the second half of the eighteenth century, British architects began to design buildings in the Gothic style again. This was known as the Gothic Revival, and it carried on throughout the nineteenth century. The style became fashionable and quickly spread across Europe and America.

Medieval Buildings Versus Gothic-Revival Buildings

To copy an original Gothic building took a lot of work, research, time and patience. In the initial stages of the Gothic Revival these copied Gothic buildings were not very convincing in archaeological terms and did not resemble the original medieval buildings. In England there were several simple commissioned buildings with basic perpendicular or pointed windows that pretended to be Gothic. To get the original Gothic effect people from each area of the building industry such as builders, manufacturers and craftsmen had to be retrained. They learned skills such as carving and stained glass manufacture.

▲ *Hawksmoor's All Souls' College, Oxford, 1716 –35. This was rebuilt by English architect Nicholas Hawksmoor (1661–1736). He built it in the Gothic style , blending it in perfectly with the existing medieval buildings.*

▶ *The western towers of Westminster Abbey, London. These were begun in 1722 and finished in 1745, to a design by Nicholas Hawksmoor.*

Types of Gothic Revival

The Gothic Revival can be split into two periods:

1 **Early Neo-Gothic**: Architects of this era used only elements of Gothic decoration. Their churches were frequently plastered and used false materials in their production. Early Neo-Gothic architects looked to the English-Gothic style for inspiration.

2 **Neo-Gothic**: Architects of this era understood the techniques needed to build and decorate a true Gothic church. They wanted to recreate the entire church as a replica of the original Gothic style, and looked to the French Gothic style for inspiration.

Reasons for the Gothic Revival

The Gothic style went through a revival during the eighteenth and nineteenth centuries for a number of reasons:

- Architects saw the style as spiritually pure.

- It was considered to have more artistic merit than the plainer **Neoclassical** style which had gone before.

- The amount of decoration involved was seen as a refreshing change from the simplicity of the ornament on the contemporary architecture, particularly on industrial buildings.

> dic·tion·ar·y
>
> The **Neoclassical** style came before the Gothic Revival. It was characterised by an interest in ancient Greek and Roman styles of building.

New Uses of Romanesque and Gothic Buildings

Some of the existing Romanesque and Gothic buildings were converted and used as schools, colleges, country houses and civic (public) buildings. The restoration of medieval buildings throughout Europe was prompted partly by national pride and partly by a religious revival. This encouraged accurate surveys of exact Gothic building designs. As architects' experience and knowledge grew, Gothic revival buildings became more authentic.

STRAWBERRY HILL							
Style	Neo-Gothic	**Date**	1747–92	**Place**	Twickenham, England	**Built by**	Horace Walpole

Horace Walpole (1717–97) took this modest house, built in 1698, and transformed it into the Gothic Revival masterpiece that it is today. He carried out this transformation with the help of two friends, John Chute (1701–97), and draughtsman Richard Bentley (1708–82). All three did research by looking at good examples of architecture in England, for example the chapel at Westminster Abbey (see p. 134) inspired the fan vaulting of the gallery.

- Walpole made it twice the size.

- He added towers and battlements.

- He decorated it with beautiful treasures.

- Gothic decorations included papier-mâché (made of paper mixed with paste) mouldings on the ceiling.

◄ *Strawberry Hill, Twickenham, England*

FONTHILL ABBEY

Style	Neo-Gothic	Date	1795–1813	Place	Wiltshire, England	Built by	William Thomas Beckford

This was built by William Thomas Beckford (1760–1844) as a country residence. Beckford was a politician, novelist and art critic. In 1822 Beckford was forced to sell Fonthill for £30,000.

▲ *Fonthill Abbey in Wiltshire, England, before it was destroyed.*

- Fonthill Abbey had a tower which collapsed. A second tower was built six years later and this also collapsed. The reason for this remains unknown.
- The abbey section was decorated in silver, gold, purples and reds.
- The front doors were 10 m tall.
- Four long, radiating wings came from the octagonal central room.
- The abbey was later demolished – all that remains today is a small gate house and a small section of the north wing.

CASTLEWARD HOUSE

Style	Neo-Gothic	Date	1756	Place	Strangford, Co. Down, Northern Ireland	Built by	Bernard Ward

This was designed for Sir Bernard and Lady Anne Ward. Bernard (1719–81) was the first Viscount of Co. Down, known as the first Viscount Bangor. It is situated on the southern shores of Strangford Lough, near Belfast, and is one of Northern Ireland's finest estates.

- The house has two distinctive architectural styles – neoclassical and Gothic, both inside and outside.
- It has an exotic sunken garden, an artificial lake and an old farmyard with a seventeenth-century keep.
- It is still in excellent condition.

▼ *Castleward House, Co. Down, Northern Ireland*

THE BRITISH HOUSES OF PARLIAMENT

Style	Neo-Gothic	Date	Following a fire in 1834, the Houses of Parliament were rebuilt, and took 30 years to complete.	Place	London, England	Built by	Architects Charles Barry (1795–1860) and Augustus Pugin (1812–52)

The British Houses of Parliament are also known as the Palace of Westminster. The British parliament, composed of the House of Lords and the House of Commons, meet up in the Houses of Parliament.

▲ *The British Houses of Parliament, London*

- This is a fine example of the Neo-Gothic style in a civic building.
- It is built in the perpendicular Gothic style, popular during the Gothic Revival.
- The exterior is very ornately decorated featuring spires and turrets.
- The stonework had to be changed and improved several times. The first stone used was Anston, a sand-coloured limestone. Pollution caused this stone to decay and in 1928 Clipsham stone, a honey-coloured limestone replaced the Anston. Pollution began to decay this stone as well so in 1981 the building was restored again, and completed in 1994.
- It has several towers, including the Victoria Tower and Saint Stephen's Tower.
- The clock tower, which contains the bell, is called 'Big Ben,' and stands at 96.3 m tall.
- Inside, the building has 1,100 rooms, 100 staircases, and 4.8 km of passageways set out over four floors.
- The Victoria Tower Gardens, located beside the Houses of Parliament are open to the public.

SAINT FIN BARRE'S CATHEDRAL

Style	Neo-Gothic	Date	1879
Place	Cork, Ireland	Built by	William Burges

This monastery cathedral cost £10,000 to build and decorate. At the time, this was a huge amount. It was designed by English architect and designer William Burges (1827–81).

Architectural Features

- It has intricate stonework and woodwork, delicate metalwork and beautiful stained glass.

▶ *Saint Fin Barre's Cathedral, Cork*

- There is a strong relationship between sculpture and architecture in the cathedral, which was deliberate on the part of the architect.
- There are 1,260 pieces of sculpture in the cathedral. A fine example of this can be seen on the west doorway.
- The exterior and the interior of Saint Finbarr's looks larger than it is as a result of the impressively ornate decoration.

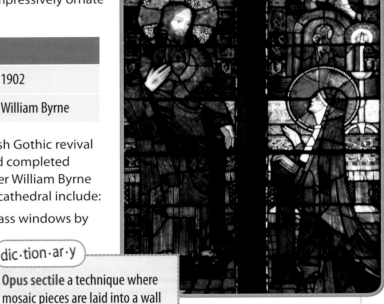

SAINT BRENDAN'S CATHEDRAL			
Style	Neo-Gothic	**Date**	1902
Place	Loughrea, Co. Galway	**Built by**	William Byrne

This cathedral is a shining example of Irish Gothic revival architecture and art, started on 1897 and completed five years later. The architect was Dubliner William Byrne (1844–1917). Examples of art inside the cathedral include:

- A magnificent series of stained-glass windows by modern artists from the time, including Evie Hone (see p. 141).

dic·tion·ar·y

Opus sectile a technique where mosaic pieces are laid into a wall to make a design or picture.

- Stations of the Cross created by artist Ethel Rhind (1844–1917) in **opus sectile.**

▲ *A stained-glass window in Saint Brendan's Cathedral, Loughrea, Co. Galway*

COBH CATHEDRAL							
Style	Neo-Gothic	**Date**	1868–1915	**Place**	Cobh, Co. Cork, Ireland	**Built by**	George Ashlin, Thomas Coleman, E.W. Pugin

This cathedral is dedicated to Saint Colman who founded the diocese in 560. It took 47 years to build, and was completed in 1915. E.W. Pugin (1834–75) was the eldest son of Augustus Pugin (see p. 137). George Ashlin (1837–1921) was born in Co. Cork, and worked on around 25 religious buildings with Pugin. Thomas Coleman (1865–1952) made up the architectural trio. Cobh Cathedral is the best example of the Gothic Revival in nineteenth-century Ireland.

Architectural Features

- It has an aisled nave which has seven bays, a triforium and clerestory.
- It has transepts with eastern chapels, and an apsidal chancel.
- There is a tower and a spire at the southwest corner of the nave.
- Rose windows are set within high, pointed arches.

▶ *Cobh Cathedral, Co. Cork*

- Gothic carvings recall the history of the church – from the time of Saint Patrick to the present day.

- There is a spiritual ambience, which is enhanced by the gentle lighting and the radiance of the stained-glass windows.

- In 1916 a **carillon** of bells was fitted in Cobh Cathedral.

- The baptistry is located at the entrance to the north side. It is enclosed by a low rail of white Italian marble. The octagonal font is white marble and the domed cover is made of brass.

> **dic·tion·ar·y**
>
> A **carillon** is a musical instrument that consists of at least 23 bells. They can play melodies or chords.

▲ *The baptistry, Cobh Cathedral, Co. Cork*

▲ *Tympanum at Cobh Cathedral, Co. Cork*

- On the west portal is a beautifully carved tympanum entitled 'Christ enthroned.'

- A sculpture of the Virgin and Child is at the trumeau (stone pier supporting the tympanum) of the west portal.

◀ *The trumeau of the west portal, Cobh Cathedral, Co. Cork*

The Gothic Revival Revision Questions

1 What was the Gothic Revival? Why did medieval styles become popular in the eighteenth and nineteenth centuries?

2 Give two examples of Gothic Revivalist architecture.

3 Describe the architectural features of Saint Finbarr's Cathedral, Cork. Use sketches in your answer.

4 Describe the architectural features of Cobh Cathedral, Cork. Use sketches in your answer.

Rediscovery of Stained Glass in Ireland

In 1903 Sarah Purser, a portrait painter, founded *An Tur Gloine* which means 'The Tower of Glass.' This was a cooperative workshop for stained glass, mosaics and other crafts, and heralded a rediscovery of stained glass in Ireland. Members included fellow artists Catherine O'Brien, Michael Healy, Wilhelmina Geddes, Evie Hone and Harry Clarke. Other important developments in stained glass in Ireland included the opening of a stained-glass department in the Metropolitan School of Art in Dublin. The department had a very high standard of work which was overseen by the artist A.E. Child. Two artists contributed greatly to Ireland's reputation for beautiful stained glass: Harry Clarke and Evie Hone.

HARRY CLARKE	
Style	Symbolist
Place	Dublin
Date	1889–1931

Harry Clarke took night classes in stained glass at the Metropolitan School of Art in Dublin. He won a scholarship to study there full-time, which he did from 1911 to 1913. His first public commission was for the Honan Chapel, in Co. Cork. He loved literature, for example work by Irish poet W.B. Yeats (1865–1939) and English Romantic poet John Keats (1795–1821), and used this influence in his stained-glass. He died of lung disease tuberculosis at the age of 41 in Switzerland.

▶ *'Saint Declan with Ruanus,' the Honan Chapel, Co. Cork*

Saint Declan with Ruanus, 1916

- Clarke's stained-glass windows show his mature style.

- The main panel shows Saint Declan, an Irish saint who lived in the fifth century. He is shown holding a model of the cathedral he founded at Ardmore, Waterford. His disciple, Ruanus, is also shown. Legend says that Ruanus once left Declan's sacred bell in Wales. When they missed the bell on the way home by boat, the saint prayed to God and the bell miraculously appeared before them, borne on a boulder. It then guided them safely home.

- Saint Declan is shown holding a detailed model of his monastic settlement, with a cathedral and a round tower.

- He carries a Celtic motif staff (special stick) and a flame motif. These symbolise another story from the life of Saint Declan, in which he throws his staff at a burning chieftain's house, miraculously putting out the fire.

- The lower panel depicts Saint Declan meeting Saint Patrick on his return home from his consecration by Pope Leo I (c. 390–461) in Rome.

- Clarke portrays his saints as elegant figures in richly ornamented clothes.

- Strong vibrant colours and attention to detail are a major characteristic of the stained glass-work of Harry Clarke.

▲ *Panel showing Saint Declan meeting Saint Patrick, Honan Chapel, Co. Cork*

EVIE HONE					
Style	Expressionist	**Place**	Dublin	**Date**	1894–1955

Evie Hone was born in Dublin. She contracted the viral disease polio at a young age which resulted in her needing medical treatment throughout her life. She trained at the Westminster School of Art in London and later in Paris at the André Lhote Academy. Lhote (1885–1962) was a painter, sculptor and writer who set up his own school. In Paris, Hone worked closely with painter and printmaker Albert Gleizes (1881–1953), and her early work was quite similar in style to his. Although her first exhibition in Dublin (1924) was not a big success, she went on to become recognised as a great *avant garde* artist. In 1930 Hone began to specialise in stained glass. She was greatly influenced by French painter George Rouault (1871–1958), Spanish artist El Greco (c. 1541–1614) and Giotto (see p. 156). She converted to Catholicism in 1937, which resulted in her work becoming more religious in content. In her lifetime she completed more than 50 pieces of art.

dic·tion·ar·y

Early in the twentieth century the term *avant garde* was used to describe cultural innovators.

▲ *'The Last Supper of Christ and the Washing of the Feet,' Manresa House, Dublin*

▶ *Detail from 'The Last Supper of Christ and the Washing of the Feet'*

The Last Supper of Christ and the Washing of the Feet, 1946

- ❧ Evie Hone designed this stained-glass window which was made in 1946 for the chapel of the Jesuit College at Rahan, Tullabeg, Co. Offaly. It is on view in the chapel at Manresa House in Dublin.

- ❧ It was based on an extract from the Bible – John 13: 1–11.

- ❧ The top part of the window depicts 'The Last Supper.' Jesus is the central figure in the composition, surrounded by his apostles. He has a calm and peaceful expression on his face. The chalice holding the 'blood' of Christ is in front of him and the 'body' of Christ is in a basket slightly to the left of Judas. John is leaning on Jesus's right shoulder asking him to tell them who will betray him. Judas is at the bottom right corner holding a piece of bread given to him by Jesus.

- ❧ The bottom part of the window (below) depicts 'The Washing of the Feet.' Jesus's facial expression has changed to one of sadness.

Recent Irish Stained-Glass Artists

Today, many stained-glass artists work in contemporary and traditional designs. In summer 2007 a unique stained-glass art exhibition took place in the National Craft Gallery, Kilkenny, to celebrate contemporary artists. The exhibition featured stained glass, painted glass and etched glass. Some of the artists who exhibited their work were George Walsh, Patrick Muldowney, Eva Kelly and Peter Young.

GEORGE WALSH

Style	Modern	**Place**	Dublin	**Date**	Born 1939

George Walsh was born in Dublin, and studied stained-glass manufacture in Dublin and Belfast. His father was also a stained-glass artist and worked in the studio of Harry Clarke. Walsh worked in America for several years which gave him great experience. He is currently based and working in Dublin. Walsh has exhibited across Ireland in galleries including the Royal Hibernian Academy, Dublin, Kenny Gallery in Galway and Kilcock Art Gallery, Co. Kildare.

> Although...most stained glass is ecclesiastical (religious) in form, new buildings (and sometimes poor architectural spaces) can be enhanced by the introduction of a glass wall or piece of work. ...glass is such an underrated material in our society. Stained glass can transport us back to the Middle Ages. It can give an atmosphere to a space both spiritual and contemplative. As in the words of Abbot Suger in 1200: '...to illuminate men's minds so that they may travel through light to an apprehension of God's light...'
>
> *George Walsh*

STEPS IN CREATING A MODERN STAINED-GLASS PIECE

1 A commission for glass usually starts with the client, his or her committee and an architect.

2 When the committee has a feeling for the location, the artist presents suggestions in the form of scaled sketches.

3 After approval the artist can proceed to create full-size drawings (cartoons) for the work.

4 From the full-size drawings, glass is selected, cut, painted and fired in a kiln.

5 Lastly, the glass panels are leaded and weather-proofed and installed in position.

This process can take several weeks to complete, depending on the detail in the piece.

▲ *George Walsh at work on cartoons in the gymnasium of Sandford National School, Dublin.*

▲ *Close-up of a window designed by George Walsh for the Royal College of Surgeons, Edinburgh. Architect: Mr Richard Hurley.*

Church of the Holy Family, Belfast

A new Catholic church was built for the Holy Family parish in north Belfast, and dedicated in March 2007. It was designed by architect Eamon Hederman as a symbol of forgiveness and reconciliation between Catholics and Protestants, in what was a very troubled area of Belfast. George Walsh designed the stained-glass window for the church.

- The tabernacle is built into the stained-glass window.

- The window is lit from behind.

- It runs from ceiling to floor.

- The theme of the window is a bridging of the divide between Protestants and Catholics.

- Walsh used a mixture of cool colours, such as blues and greens, and warm colours, such as reds and yellows, in his window.

▶ *View of stained-glass window on entering the Church of the Holy Family, Belfast*

▲ *Tabernacle and screen, Church of the Holy Family, Belfast*

In addition to featuring in private collections worldwide, Walsh's work can be found in the following places:

- The Royal College of Surgeons, Dublin
- Galway Cathedral
- NUI Galway – New University Chapel
- Dublinia, Christ Church Cathedral, Dublin
- Black Abbey, Kilkenny
- Church of the Irish Martyrs, Ballycane, Naas, Co. Kildare
- Our Lady of Lourdes Parish Church, Kilcummin, Co. Kerry.

◀ *Detail of an exhibition piece by George Walsh*

Rediscovery of Stained Glass in Ireland Revision Questions

1 Explain the effect Sarah Purser had on Irish stained glass.

2 'Harry Clarke is one of Ireland's foremost stained-glass artists.' Discuss this statement in relation to one of his works. Use sketches in your answer.

3 'Evie Hone has influenced stained-glass art.' Discuss this statement in relation to one work of art by her. Use sketches in your answer.

4 List some of the pieces created by Irish stained-glass artist George Walsh.

Bibliography

Romanesque Section

1 Atroshenko, V.I. and Collins, Judith: *The Origins of the Romanesque*, Lord Humphries, 1985

2 Craig, Maurice: *The Architecture of Ireland from the Earliest Times to 1880*. B.T. Batsford Ltd, 1982

3 De Breffny, Brian: *Castles of Ireland*, Thames and Hudson, England, 1977

4 De Breffny, Brian and Mott, George: *The Churches and Abbeys of Ireland*, Thames and Hudson, 1976

5 Snyder, James: *Medieval Art: Painting, Sculpture, Architecture 4th–14th century*: Harry N. Abrams, 1989

Gothic Section

1 Brisac, Catherine: *A Thousand Years of Stained Glass*, MacDonald Books, 1984

2 Camille, Michael: *Gothic: Art*: George Weidenfield and Nicolson Ltd, 1996

3 Craig, Maurice: *The Architecture of Ireland from the Earliest Times to 1880*, B.T. Batsford Ltd, 1982

4 Miller, Malcolm: *Chartres Cathedral*, ABC Printers, 1985

5 Toman, Rolf: *Gothic Architecture, Sculpture and Painting*, Konemann, 1988

6 Swann, Wim: *Art and Architecture of the Late Middle Ages*, Omega Books Ltd, 1982

unit 3

European Art During the Renaissance c. 1300–c. 1520

Introduction

The word 'Renaissance' is the French term for 'rebirth,' and is used to describe a period of time in European history between the fourteenth and sixteenth centuries. During this time, great changes and innovations took place in the arts and in learning. The birthplace of this movement was Italy, but it quickly spread to the rest of Europe. There were several factors involved in the dawn of the Renaissance:

- Classical art and literature
- Humanism
- Patronage
- Heightened social status of artists
- Portrait painting
- Narrative painting
- Landscape painting.

Classical Art and Literature

There was a renewed interest in the legacy of ancient Greece and Rome, and artists began to use **classical** art as an inspiration for their own work. One of the reasons the Renaissance began in Italy is because there were so many relics from this era, from monuments, buildings and sculptures to carved sarcophagi (tombs). Scholars and artists alike began to read about the myths and legends of ancient Greece and Rome, instead of concentrating only on religious themes.

Humanism

Coming out of the rediscovery of Latin and Greek texts was a new movement, called **humanism**. These texts gave a different vision of life and humanity than that of previous centuries, which had been dominated by Christian interpretations. Artists became interested in the physical and natural world around them, including the anatomy and proportions of the body, science, astrology and nature. Previously, artists were only interested in portraying biblical scenes. While religious painting was still very popular during the Renaissance, elements of humanist teachings and beliefs slowly crept into the artists' work.

> dic·tion·ar·y
>
> **Classical** refers to the civilisations of ancient Greece and Rome.
>
> **Humanism** is a type of philosophy that concentrates on human effort rather than on religion.

Patronage

Patronage, meaning support, often financial, by an institution was very important for artists during the Renaissance. There were three types of patronage:

1. **The Catholic Church:** Still extremely influential, commissioning frescoes and altarpieces for their chapels.

2. **Civic commissions:** Local governments and princely states (ruled by a *signore*, or lord) competed with each other to employ the leading artists of the time to decorate their town halls and city buildings.

3. **Private commissions:** Wealthy merchants and bankers became valuable patrons of the arts, commissioning portraits, frescoes and even furniture decoration. The most notable of these patrons was the influential Medici family (see p. 149).

Heightened Social Status of Artists

During the Middle Ages, sculptors, painters and architects had only been regarded as skilled tradesmen, often not even acknowledged for their work. During the Renaissance, however, they became valued as learned scholars, with extensive knowledge of art, literature, science and philosophy and were allowed to be more creative in their work.

Portrait Painting

Artists painted their patrons either in traditional portraits or included them in a religious painting. They were expected to portray a patron in the way they wished to appear, as sophisticated, learned aristocrats of noble birth and extensive property. Wealthy patrons often had their own private chapels in churches which would be decorated with religious frescoes. The patrons were sometimes shown as onlookers in these paintings, establishing them as pious and upstanding citizens. Artists developed an interest in individual facial expressions and the realistic portrayal of the face and figure.

Narrative Paintings

These were paintings that told a story, either from the Bible or from mythology or history. They were considered important as they could also teach morals.

Landscape Paintings

Landscape painting was approached in a new way. Instead of being simply treated as a symbolic or decorative surround for the figures in the painting, it was painted in a more naturalistic manner, incorporating the rules of perspective to add depth and realism to the work.

Trecento Architecture

The term 'Trecento' comes from the Italian phrase *mille trecento* meaning 1300s. This period was also known as the Proto-Renaissance and marked the beginning of the Renaissance in Italy. Architecture in this period was also to undergo a change, from the flamboyant Gothic style to the more restrained, classical style which drew its inspiration from ancient Greece and Rome.

Florence and the Medicis

It is generally recognised that the Renaissance first flourished in Florence, in southern Italy. The city had been successful in a struggle for power, raging since the decline of the Roman Empire, (c. 476), between the northern Italian states. As a result, its wealth and dominance was greater than any other city in the region. Most of the wealth was managed by a small number of influential families, in particular the Medici dynasty. The Medicis were a distinguished, well-educated and cultured banking family who were to become the most famous art patrons in history. Cosimo de'Medici (1389–1464), the head of the dynasty, built the first public library since ancient Greek and Roman times, which was further expanded by his grandson, Lorenzo the Magnificent (1449–92). Although the family were ruthless in matters of business, they had a huge appetite for expanding their knowledge, and used their wealth and influence to draw poets, artists, writers and philosophers to them. Throughout the fifteenth century, art and culture thrived in Florence, ending only after the death of Lorenzo de'Medici. His second son Giovanni, a cardinal at only 13, later built Rome to be the new cultural centre of of the Renaissance. This reached its apex during his papacy as Pope Leo X (from 1513 until his death in 1521).

Lorenzo de'Medici ▶

Gothic Architecture

Before we examine Renaissance architecture it is important to know about the ecclesiastical style (architecture of religious buildings) which preceded it. The Gothic style, which featured religious buildings, had swept across Europe from the mid twelfth century to the fifteenth century. Evidence of the style can be seen in almost every country in Europe to this day.

- There was a strong emphasis on the vertical in Gothic architecture, with high soaring spires and pointed arched windows filled with dramatic stained-glass depictions of Bible stories.

- The western façades of Gothic buildings were very ornate. They featured stone tracery and sculpture, and had three large pointed portals (doors). The middle one was topped by a tympanum (semicircular area above a door) showing **Christ in majesty**.

- The slim walls and vaulted (arched) ceilings were supported by flying buttresses (stone structures used to help take weight), allowing larger windows to be accommodated.

During the Renaissance, architecture departed from this ornate and embellished style. It owed more to the architecture of ancient Rome, which valued regularity and symmetry over flamboyant decoration and construction.

Architecture in Florence

Architecture in Florence combined the classical style of ancient Greece and Rome with modern innovations. One of the most important Renaissance architects, Alberti (see p. 164), wrote a book on ancient architecture, which helped his fellow architects to understand the basic structures, decoration and proportions of classical buildings, as well as introducing new techniques to enhance the style. During the Renaissance architects placed value on proportion and symmetry, using classical elements in their designs such as columns both as decoration and as a means of support to structures, and flat **pilasters** to decorate walls. Lintels and semicircular arches surmounted doorways and windows and semicircular domes were created on the roofs of churches.

dic·tion·ar·y

Showing **Christ in majesty** means that he was seated on a throne in the centre of a composition, surrounded by saints or other figures. ▼

A **pilaster** is a low-relief rectangular support with a base on the bottom, and a shaft and capital on the top. It projects slightly from the wall and can be used as a support or just for decorative effect.

SANTA CROCE			
Style	Trecento	**Country**	Italy
Date	1385	**Built by**	Arnolfo di Cambio, Niccolò Matas

Building of this Franciscan church began in 1294, from a design by Florentine architect Arnolfo di Cambio (c. 1240–1305). It was originally planned to rival the Benedictine Santa Maria Novella (see p. 151), but although the church was completed in 1385, the façade remained unfinished until the 1850s. Niccolò Matas (1798–1872) was the architect responsible for this, and it is thought that he used drawings and references from di Cambio.

Architectural Features

- The façade includes many Gothic elements, for example the pointed arches above the three portals and the large round window above the main entrance. Vertical rectangular marble inlays decorate the harmonious, symmetrical (even) face of the church.

- The interior of Santa Croce is a fine example of Florentine Gothic architecture, with a wide nave (central aisle), high broad pointed arches separating the nave from the aisles and long narrow windows. The ceiling timbers are exposed without vaulting of any kind. Many wealthy and influential Florentines are buried here, including Ghiberti (see p. 181) and Michelangelo (see pp. 194–208).

- The beautifully decorated Capella Maggiore is the main choir chapel in Santa Croce. Frescoes (see p. 155) by painter Agnolo di Taddeo Gaddi (c. 1350–96), based on the Legend of The **True Cross,** adorn the walls. Saints are portrayed on the tabernacles (which house the chalice and Eucharist). Two other chapels in Santa Croce, Cappella Bardi and Cappella Peruzzi, feature frescoes by Giotto (see p. 156).

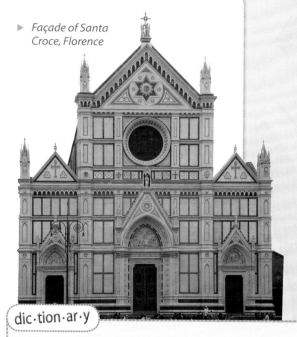

▶ *Façade of Santa Croce, Florence*

dic·tion·ar·y

The **Eucharist**, also called Holy Communion, is the Christian sacrament in which bread and wine are blessed to commemorate Christ's Last Supper.

Did you know?

The **TRUE CROSS** is said to be the cross on which Christ was crucified. Legend says that the tree the wood came from grew from a seed of the Tree of Life in the Garden of Eden. The seed, put into Adam's mouth before he was buried, grew into a tree, and many years later its wood was used to make the cross.

◀ *Interior of Santa Croce, Florence*

SANTA MARIA NOVELLA			
Style	Trecento	**Country**	Italy
Date	1456–70	**Built by**	Leone Battista Alberti

The façade of this Dominican church was designed by architect Leone Battista Alberti (1404–72) for textile merchant Giovanni di Paolo Rucellai (1403–81) in around 1456, replacing the original façade. Alberti was inspired by Santa Miniato al Monte, an earlier building in Florence created during Romanesque times. The building is a wonderful example of Florentine Renaissance architecture, mixing elements of Roman, Gothic and contemporary styles with perfectly balanced proportions.

Architectural Features

* The Gothic parts of the façade, for example the two smaller doors and circular window, were part of the original design which Alberti had to incorporate into his ideas.

* There are three portals (doors) at the front of the building, the largest in the centre capped by a large semicircular tympanum with pedestals on either side. Gothic pointed arches crown the two smaller doors and six wall niches (recessed areas) are positioned in the remaining wall space. These are equally placed within four arcades (series of supported arches) on each side of the main portal.

* An **entablature** separates the lower section of the façade from the upper, topped by a broad band decorated with geometric square inlays. Above this is the central Gothic round window, which is echoed in the circular designs on both volutes (scrolls used to connect horizontal and vertical design elements) and also in the richly ornamented triangular **pediment** situated on top of the structure.

▲ Façade of Santa Maria Novella, Florence

dic·tion·ar·y

An **entablature** is the section of a classical building that lies between the tops of the columns and the roof. It is divided into three sections. The architrave is the lowest horizontal part, the frieze is in the middle and is usually decorated, and the cornice is in the upper section.

A **pediment** is a low-pitched triangular gable with a sloping roof on both sides and a cornice under the base. Pediments are usually found over doors and windows.

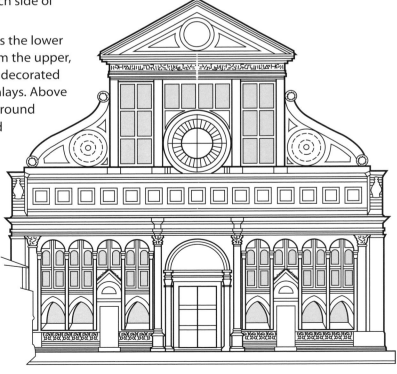

▶ Diagram of Santa Maria Novella, Florence

THE BARGELLO

Style	Trecento	Country	Italy
Date	1255; third storey added 1323	Built by	Lapo Tedesco, an architect presumed to be Arnolfo di Cambio's father

The majestic Bargello building was originally built for the use of the mayor of Florence and was then transformed into a prison. In 1574 police headquarters were based there and later still, in 1865, it became a museum for exhibiting sculpture and craftwork. Many famous sculptures are housed here, including Michelangelo's Bacchus (a marble sculpture of the god of wine) and Donatello's David (see p. 188).

Architectural Features

The Bargello is a sturdily built structure, its small windows and formidable battlements creating the sense of a defensive fortress. It has three storeys and a large square bell tower incorporated in the right of the façade which was built originally to sound warnings to the townspeople.

- Biforate windows (two windows placed closely together under an arch) are set above the entablature on the first floor. Smaller rectangular windows are situated directly over them on a higher layer.

- The top storey is built from roughly cut stone and crowned by an arched **console** with a **crenellated** parapet.

- The inner courtyard is spacious and grand with an open staircase and large, curved arches supported by heavy columns. It is decorated with the coats of arms of the mayors and judges who worked in the building throughout the ages.

▲ The Bargello, Florence

◀ Courtyard of the Bargello, Florence

dic·tion·ar·y

A **console** is a type of bracket, shaped like a scroll, which can be used to support a sculpture, shelf or cornice.

Crenellation is the name for the notched pattern that appears at the tops of the walls of many medieval castles. Crenellations are also called battlements.

PALAZZO VECCHIO

Style	Trecento	**Country**	Italy
Date	1299–1314	**Built by**	Arnolfo di Cambio

A palazzo is a multi-storied, fortress-like building. The Palazzo Vecchio is one of the most important civic (public) buildings in Florence, designed by architect Arnolfo di Cambio. It has been used for many different reasons throughout the ages. At the time it was built it was used by the Florentine city council who met in the richly decorated audience hall, which features frescoes by painter Francesco Salviati (1510–63).

Architectural Features

- This building is similar to a barracks or fortress, with its small lower windows and heavy rusticated (roughly cut with deep grooves between blocks) stonework. It is cube shaped, with three storeys and a crenellated parapet, supported by a console.

- A 94 m tower dominates the front of the main façade, and is a symbol of the Republic of Florence.

- The windows on the first and second floors are biforate and arched.

- The courtyard, a feature common in large Florentine buildings, is medieval in design. Architect and sculptor Michelozzo (c. 1391–1472) is responsible for the beautifully ordered and elegant arched inner courtyard. The fountain with cherub and dolphin in the centre is by Andrea del Verrochio (c. 1435–88), a sculptor and painter in the Medici court. The courtyard was fabulously decorated for a royal wedding in 1565. Panoramic landscape paintings were added to the walls and the pillars were adorned with gilt.

◄ *Courtyard of the Palazzo Vecchio, Florence*

Trecento Architecture Revision Questions

1 Describe the developments made in ecclesiastical architecture during the Early Renaissance, by discussing two churches, and with the use of sketches to illustrate your answer.

2 Discuss the rise of civic architecture in Early Renaissance Florence under the headings: a) function, b) façade, c) decoration, d) layout of the interior.

Trecento Painting

During this time the International Gothic style of painting was the traditionally accepted art form, involving brilliant colours, elegant figures, and great attention to detail. It began in Burgundy in present-day France and flourished throughout Europe. However, artists such as Giotto (see p. 155) developed a less decorative and more realistic approach, which influenced other artists. There was also a revival of fresco painting, which had been popular during ancient Greek and Roman times.

Frescoes

Fresco painting involved painting straight onto the plaster of a wall or ceiling. There are two methods:

1 *Fresco secco:* In this technique, the artist mixed pigment with a binding agent and painted on dry plaster. This method was not as durable (lasting) as true fresco painting.

2 *Buon fresco:* Here, the artist painted his picture on a layer of lime plaster before it dried, incorporating the paint with the plaster. This gave a more long-lasting finish. However, this technique was not without drawbacks. The plaster dried very quickly, giving the artist only one day to complete a painting, so frescoes were created section by section. These paintings became known as *giornate*, which is the Italian for 'day.'

GIOVANNI CIMABUE (CENNI DI PEPO)

Date	c. 1240–1302	**Patrons**	The Catholic Church
Cities	Florence, Rome, Pisa	**Themes**	Religious
Apprenticeship	Florence Baptistry mosaic workshop	**Style**	Dignified, decorative, serene
Influences	Pietro Cavallini (c. 1250–1330), Byzantine style		

Cimabue, whose real name is *Cenni di Pepo*, was born in Florence and died in Pisa. He is often referred to as the first great master of Italian Renaissance painting, and the last to work in the **Byzantine style**. Giotto di Bondone was his student. While his work shows Byzantine features, it also reflects his interest in classical art and was to influence a new generation of Florentine painters.

▲ *Byzantine reliquary of the True Cross, c. 800*

The **Byzantine style** (300–1453) was the type of art produced by artists of the Byzantine Empire. At the empire's centre was the glittering city of Constantinople, renamed from the Greek Byzantium. The style was originally influenced by classical Roman art, but became much more abstract and symbolic, concentrating mainly on religious subject matter, including icons (depictions of sacred images), and paintings of emperors.

Madonna and Child Enthroned with Eight Angels and Four Prophets, c. 1281

- This painting has a strong central composition, with the figures of the Madonna (Mary) and Child (Jesus) dominating the picture space.

- They are shown seated in a decorative, architectural setting, which demonstrates Cimabue's interest in classical art.

- The exaggerated size of Mary and Jesus is in keeping with the symmetrical Byzantine style of Constantinople, as is his use of gold leaf in the background.

- The idealised (portrayed as perfect) faces of the angels, Madonna and Jesus are in contrast with those of the prophets shown beneath, who appear to be more realistic with individual characteristics.

▶ 'Madonna and Child Enthroned with Eight Angels and Four Prophets,' Uffizi Gallery, Florence, Cimabue

GIOTTO DI BONDONE			
Date	c. 1267–1337	**Patrons**	Robert d'Anjou (son of Charles I), Giovanni Peruzzi (from a Florentine banking dynasty), Enrico degli Scrovegni
Cities	Florence, Rome, Padua, Naples, Milan		
Apprenticeship	Cimabue	**Themes**	Religious
Influences	French Gothic statues, classical art	**Style**	Narrative, realistic, expressive

Cimabue discovered Giotto at a very young age, drawing his father's flock of sheep. Giotto later joined Cimabue's workshop. He quickly developed his own distinctive, realistic style of painting. He has often been referred to as 'The Founder of the Renaissance' as a result of his innovative style and techniques, which were to influence later artists. He introduced and developed many exciting new ideas in his dramatic narrative scenes using **foreshortening** of limbs, vibrant colour, emotive and realistic facial expressions and carefully constructed compositions.

dic·tion·ar·y

Foreshortening is the technique artists use to create the illusion that an object is extending backwards into space. It is achieved by making the nearest part of the object larger in comparison to the rest of the object, which reduces in size as it recedes.

Arena Chapel, 1303–06

Giotto's best-known work was a series of frescoes painted in the Arena Chapel in Padua. Enrico degli Scrovegni, a wealthy nobleman, commissioned the paintings using money inherited from his father, Reginaldo, who had been a corrupt moneylender. Enrico hoped the commission would atone for his father's sins and restore the family dignity. At this time, the patron believed that by supporting art which celebrated the lives of the saints, he was ensuring his place in heaven and gaining respect on earth for his religious piety. The paintings, which number 38 in all, depict the lives of Jesus Christ and the Virgin Mary.

- The Gospels and 'The Golden Legend,' a book on the lives of the saints by writer Jacobus de Voragine (c. 1230–98), provided the literary source for the paintings.
- The series of frescoes begins on the upper left side of the Chapel and runs in a clockwise direction around the chapel in three further tiers.
- The top tier shows the Annunciation, the lives of the Virgin's parents, called Joachim and Anna, and the life of Mary.
- The second tier depicts the life of Christ, from infancy through to his miracles and teachings.
- The third tier shows the end of Christ's life, from the Last Supper to his Crucifixion.
- On the fourth tier, right-hand side, Christian virtues are depicted. The left side shows vices.
- 'The Last Judgement' is the largest fresco in the Chapel. It covers the entire entrance wall and is the last image visitors see as they leave.

The Betrayal of Christ

- This fresco shows the moment of Judas's treachery, giving Christ a kiss as a signal for the soldiers to arrest him.

- It is a very busy and cluttered composition, demonstrating Giotto's narrative style with the figures at the edges of the painting being cut off to emphasise the continuous action of the story.

- The angles of the weapons held above the heads of the characters direct the viewer's eye to the head of Jesus, as do the pointing gestures of the men on either side.

- The rich gold of Judas's robes and the strong diagonal lines of the creases provide a focus for the eye.

▲ *'The Betrayal of Christ,' Arena Chapel, Padua, Giotto*

- The serene, resigned face of Jesus is in direct contrast to the violent expressions of the soldiers and the guilt-ridden Judas.

- On the left we see Peter cutting the ear off Malchus, the High Priest Caiaphas's servant.

The Lamentation

- This shows the reactions of Christ's followers, after his body has been taken down from the cross.
- Giotto draws our attention to the face of the dead Christ by the direction of the subjects' gazes and the inclination of their bodies. The line of the hill in the background also serves as a compositional device.
- This is a highly emotive painting - every face shows a different emotion, which was a huge departure from the serene Gothic style.
- Giotto's women display their grief openly, their faces distorted in despair, whereas the men's sorrow is more controlled, with the exception of John, who throws his arms wide in a gesture of hopelessness. This pose was particularly important as it introduced foreshortening of the limbs.
- The angels are depicted as inconsolable their mouths open in wails of agony.

▲ *'The Lamentation,' Arena Chapel, Padua, Giotto*

Sienese Artists

Although it is generally believed that Florence was the birthplace of the Renaissance, Siena, a city close to Florence, also contributed greatly to the Early Renaissance. The father of Sienese painting was Duccio di Buoninsegna (c. 1255–c. 1318). He worked at the same time as Giotto, and like the Florentine master, developed a new style. He explored the notion of perspective in his paintings as did Giotto, but his figure painting was more linear and had less volume. The Sienese School was very significant in the development of the International Gothic style and brought a poetic and expressive quality to art.

SIMONE MARTINI			
Date:	c. 1284–c. 1344	**Patrons:**	Merchants of Siena, Robert d'Anjou
Cities:	Siena, Naples, Avignon		
Apprenticeship:	Duccio	**Themes:**	Religious
Influences:	Duccio, Giotto, Pisano (an Italian architect and sculptor, see p. 179), French art	**Style:**	Elegant, sensitive

Although Martini was influenced by Giotto, particularly by his use of space in his compositions, he had his own very distinctive style. This is evident in his brilliant use of colour, which is both radiant and subtle. One of his most famous paintings, 'La Maesta,' is in the Palazzo Pubblico (town hall) in Siena.

La Maesta, 1315

- The figures in the painting are very large, and are painted with great delicacy.
- The throne on which the Virgin is seated is ornate and richly gilded. This takes its form from Gothic architecture.
- The painting has a reverent (holy) atmosphere, mainly because the saints are kneeling in submission before the throne.

▼ *'La Maesta,' Siena Palazzo Pubblico, Martini*

THE LORENZETTI BROTHERS

Date:	c. 1280–1348 (Pietro); c. 1290–1348 (Ambrogio)	**Patrons:**	The Church, civic commissions
Cities:	Siena, Florence	**Themes:**	Religious
Apprenticeship:	Duccio	**Style:**	Naturalistic, three-dimensional
Influences:	Duccio, Giotto, Pisano		

The brothers Pietro and Ambrogio Lorenzetti were extremely influential Sienese artists. They were most likely pupils of Duccio and followed his tradition of creating solid forms and exploring expressive emotions in their subjects. They were also influenced by Tuscan sculptor Giovanni Pisano (c. 1250–1315) and by Giotto. Ambrogio, probably the younger brother, is considered to be the more creative and inventive of the two. He spent some time in Florence and was aware of the developments in art being made by Giotto.

'Allegory of Good Government', 1337–39, Ambrogio Lorenzetti

Ambrogio painted a series of frescoes for the Sala dei Nove in Siena's Palazzo Pubblico. The theme of the frescoes, which are allegorical, is 'Good and Bad Government.' Allegories use symbols to convey a moral meaning, and in these paintings they depict things that happen if a country is ruled in a good way, such as prosperity, wealth and happiness. By contrast, bad

▲ 'Allegory of Good Government', Siena Palazzo Pubblico, Ambrogio Lorenzetti

ruling shows war, crime and poverty. The paintings are an important landmark in art history for two reasons. They give prominence to the landscape, which is used to create atmosphere. They also have a secular (non-religious) theme.

- The painting shown is the 'Allegory of Good Government' and is composed of three horizontal bamds. The foreground shows a progression of Sienese councillors. Behind them, on a stage, there are allegorical figures in two groups, connected by the procession. The upper band indicates the heavenly sphere with floating figures of justice.

- The woman seated on the left personifies justice. She gestures to scales of balance, held by a winged figure symbolising wisdom.

- The man on the throne signifies Siena and the good government. He is flanked by personifications of virtues such as prudence and fortitude. The reclining figure in white on the left represents peace.

- At Siena's feet the two children playing are the sons of Remus, Ascius and Senius, who, according to Roman legend, founded the city of Siena.

The Birth of the Virgin, 1320, Pietro Lorenzetti

- This painting is situated on the altarpiece in the church of Santa Maria Della Pieve, in the Tuscan town of Arezzo.

- Although it was in some part influenced by the work of Simone Martini in its composition, the style of the figures is very different.

- There is volume in the bulky bodies and a solemn expression on the face of the Virgin.

- Unusually, Pietro incorporates the frame into the painting, the pillars serving as a frame and also as part of the structure of the building in which the Virgin is seated.

◄ 'The Birth of The Virgin,' Church of Santa Maria Della Pieve, Arezzo, Pietro Lorenzetti

Trecento Painting Revision Questions

1 Discuss the influence of Giotto di Bondone on Renaissance artists under the headings:
a) colour, b) form, c) expression, d) gestures, e) background.

2 Discuss the layout of the Arena Chapel frescoes by Giotto. Describe one fresco in detail.
Include sketches in your answer.

3 Describe the developments in style and technique made in Siena in the Early Renaissance,
with reference to one artist in particular.

Quattrocento Architecture

During the Quattrocento period (1400s), also referred to as the Early Renaissance, there were
further developments in architecture. Although architects wished to create the harmonious
symmetry of buildings from ancient Rome, there were no templates (models) from that time for
Christian churches or modern palaces for wealthy patrons. These had to be developed by the
Renaissance architects, by examining the ancient orders and recreating them to utilise them in a
modern way.

Ecclesiastical Architecture

The term 'ecclesiastical architecture' is used to describe religious buildings, and it is by looking at
these types of buildings that we can get a real idea of Quattrocentro architecture. Renaissance
churches were planned along geometric shapes, such as squares and rectangles, and the size and
proportions of a church were determined by the width of its aisle. Church façades, usually square
in shape, were generally decorated by pilasters, entablatures and arches. Above the façade was a
pediment, and domes were incorporated into the roof that was over the altar.

THE DOME OF FLORENCE CATHEDRAL			
Style	Quattrocento	**Country**	Italy
Date	1419–36	**Built by**	Fillippo Brunelleschi (1377–1446)

▼ *Florence Cathedral, showing Brunelleschi's Dome*

The construction of the dome of this Renaissance cathedral presented a lot of problems. The sheer size of the base made it difficult to design a dome which could support its own weight. The dimensions were 45 m wide in diameter, by 101 m at its highest point, and were octagonal in shape. In 1418, the problem of the dome construction was outlined and architects were asked to provide a solution. One idea was to fill the space with earth mixed with coins and then build the dome over this. Poor citizens and children would then take out the clay and keep the money. The Florentine architect Fillippo Brunelleschi won the commission. His great mathematical skills, combined with his vast knowledge of ancient Roman architecture, finally solved the dilemma.

Did you know?
Fillippo Brunelleschi started his career as a goldsmith. No-one knows for sure when he became an architect, but he became one of the greatest Renaissance architects.

Construction of the Dome

1   Brunelleschi designed two brick shells, which were held securely together by eight huge longitudinal stone ribs. Pairs of smaller ribs were placed between these, which were in turn supported by smaller horizontal ribs.

2   He suspended a portable scaffold (platform from which to work) from the ribs for his builders to work from. This was moved upwards as the dome grew higher.

3   He used light building materials to put less pressure on the structure.

4   The herringbone technique, which involves interlocking bricks to create a spiral structure, was used for the masonry (stonework) of the dome.

PAZZI CHAPEL			
Style	Quattrocento	**Country**	Italy
Date	c. 1442–70	**Built by**	Fillippo Brunelleschi

This elegant building is the **chapter house** in a **cloister** of the church of Santa Croce, Florence (see p. 150). It was commissioned by the wealthy Florentine Pazzi family in 1429. It is one of Brunelleschi's most beautiful and famous designs, although he never lived to see it completed.

dic·tion·ar·y

A **chapter house** is a building or chamber used to hold meetings in a cathedral.

A **cloister** is a courtyard with four corridors surrounding it.

▲ *The Pazzi Chapel, Florence, Brunelleschi*

Architectural Features

Exterior

◈   A barrel-vaulted vestibule (entrance area) in front is supported by six slim Corinthian columns (see p. 165). Barrel vaults are semi-cylindrical in shape.

◈   Above these on the attic are double Corinthian pilasters, (see p. 165)

◈   There is a high, wide entrance arch before the portal.

Interior

▲ *Interior of the Pazzi Chapel, Florence, Brunelleschi*

- A large ribbed dome dominates the ceiling of the chapel.
- Brunelleschi used geometric linear designs to decorate the interior.
- The grey stone pilasters and tondi (circular sculptural reliefs) of the 12 apostles, created by sculptor Luca della Robbia are in wonderful contrast with the plain white-plastered walls.
- Even the pattern on the floor complements the regular symmetrical shapes and layout of the room.

Civic Architecture

Civic, or public, buildings were owned by the state or by private patrons. They included palaces owned by wealthy businessmen and aristocratic families or functional buildings such as the Hospital of the Innocenti. Large city palaces were rectangular in shape with regularly spaced windows and a central doorway decorated with rustication. The stonework on the lowest storey was also rusticated, using large rough stones. As the storeys progressed upwards the stonework became smoother. The palaces were often surmounted by a cornice.

HOSPITAL OF THE INNOCENTS			
Style	Quattrocento	**Country**	Italy
Date	1419–24	**Built by**	Fillippo Brunelleschi

This building in Florence is also known as the Foundling Hospital and was the first orphanage in the world. It was commissioned by the silk merchants and goldsmith guilds.

▶ *The Hospital of the Innocents, Florence, Brunelleschi*

Architectural Features

- The façade of the building is the most notable feature, incorporating many Renaissance architectural elements. These are derived from both **Tuscan Romanesque** styles and also ancient Roman buildings.

Classical Features

- The loggia (the structure supported by columns).
- Round arches and classical columns.
- Square domed bays (recesses) supported by the columns and corbels (stone structures jutting out from a wall).
- Capitals adorning the tops of columns.

Romanesque Features

- Dosserets (areas between the capitals and the base of vaults).
- Curved architrave, seen sloping downwards at the ends of the building.

> **dic·tion·ar·y**
>
> **Tuscan Romanesque** churches showed the influence of Byzantine culture, with their use of white and coloured marble on the façades. They generally feature arcades over flat pilasters projecting from the walls.

PALAZZO RUCELLAI			
Style	Quattrocento	**Country**	Italy
Date	1450	**Built by**	Leone Batista Alberti

This building was designed by Alberti, a highly influential figure in the Florentine Renaissance. Architect Bernardo Rosselino (1409–64) constructed the palazzo to be a city dwelling for wealthy wool trader Giovanni Rucellai (see p. 151).

▼ *Diagram of the Palazzo Rucellai, Florence, Alberti*

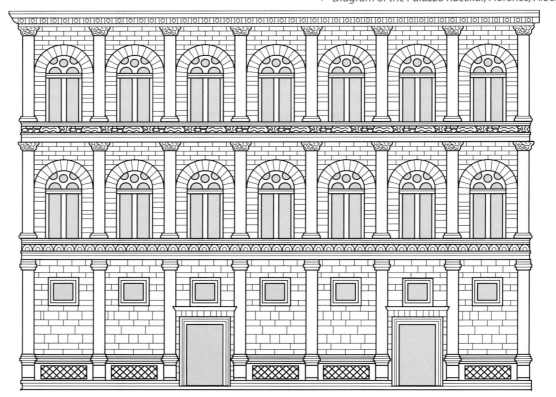

Architectural Features

- The façade incorporates elements of ancient Roman architecture with contemporary Florentine design.

- Smooth rusticated stone was used to build the façade of the Palazzo Rucelli. This was typical of Florentine palazzo architecture of the time.

- A bench runs along the bottom of the building, another typical Florentine feature.

- Like Brunelleschi's Hospital of the Innocenti, it has a very symmetrical design.

Classical Features

- Alberti used the orders of columns which had been in use in the classical era. In this palazzo, he followed the example of those used in the Roman Colosseum (a huge circular amphitheatre built in 80).

- He used purely decorative pilasters instead of pillars between the windows, which are surrounded by arches in the Roman style.

- The ground floor has Doric capitals, the second Ionic, the third, Corinthian.

- The storeys are separated by varied ornate entablatures topped by a roof cornice.

▲ *Palazzo Rucellai, Florence, Alberti*

COLUMN ORDERS

The first three orders of columns originated in ancient Greece while the last two were created in Rome.

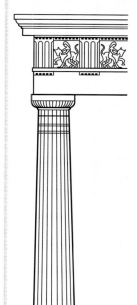 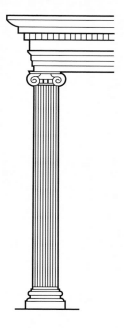 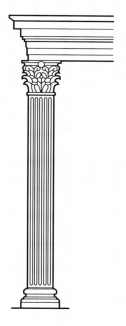 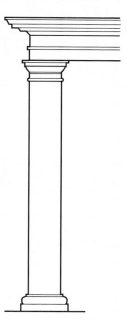 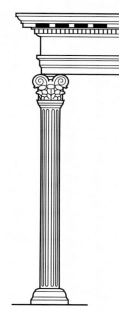

1 *Doric:* Fluted (grooved) column, plain capital.

2 *Ionic:* Fluted column, capital decorated with volutes (scroll shapes).

3 *Corinthian:* Fluted column, capital decorated with foliage.

4 *Tuscan:* Plain column, capital similar to the Doric.

5 *Composite:* Fluted column, a mixture of Ionic and Corinthian, combining scrolls with foliage.

Quattrocento Architecture Revision Questions

1 Discuss the problems involved in building the dome of Florence Cathedral and its solution.

2 Discuss one civic building in Renaissance Florence and describe how the architect was influenced by classical architecture, while maintaining Florentine tradition.

3 What are the main elements of palazzo design? Give examples and draw diagrams to illustrate your answer.

Quattocentro Painting

Artists in Florence were heavily influenced by the work of Giotto and also the humanist teachings of Trecento scholars such as **Petrarch** and **Dante**. They looked to ancient Greece and Rome for inspiration and studied nature to develop a better understanding of anatomy, botany and perspective. The most significant artists of this time period were Masaccio, Botticelli and Piero della Francesca. The Catholic Church continued to influence and commission painting, sculpture and architecture, resulting in some of the most spectacular achievements of the era such as Michelangelo's Sistine Chapel frescoes in Saint Peter's Basilica in the Vatican City, Rome (see pp. 202–7).

biography

PETRARCH (1304–74) was one of the earliest humanist philosophers as well as being an accomplished writer and poet. He created the Petrarchan sonnet which was later used and further developed by Shakespeare.

DANTE (c. 1265–1321) was a Florentine poet who is most famous for writing 'The Divine Comedy,' often considered the finest work in Italian literature.

Christian Subject Matter

Although there was a growing interest in classical mythological themes during the Renaissance, the Catholic Church still remained the most influential and powerful patron of painting. Artists were commissioned to paint large-scale frescoes and altarpieces for churches celebrating the life of Christ. Wealthy patrons such as the Medici family also commissioned religious paintings to adorn their private chapels.

FRA ANGELICO			
Date	c. 1387–1455	Patrons	The Catholic Church, the Medici family
Cities	Florence, Rome		
Apprenticeship	Unknown	Themes	Religious
Influences	Masolino da Panicale (c. 1383–1447)	Style	Spiritual, colourful, delicate

Fra Angelico was a Dominican friar who had an amazing talent for painting religious subjects. He was born Guido di Pietro, but later became known as Fra Angelico, meaning 'angelic brother.' Angelico started his artistic career illuminating manuscripts. Later he painted frescoes in monasteries and churches.

Convent of San Marco

The Convent of San Marco in Florence was built between 1437 and 1452 by Michelozzo. It is most famous for its frescoes by Fra Angelico in the cloister of Saint Anthony. His paintings are serene and spiritual, reflecting his own life as a deeply religious Dominican friar.

San Marco Altarpiece, c. 1438–40

- This wood panel was commissioned by the Medici family for the San Marco altarpiece and was dedicated to the saints Cosmas and Damian, seen kneeling in the foreground.

- The face of Saint Cosmas (believed to be a portrait of Cosimo de 'Medici) is turned towards the viewer, while his hand directs us towards the centrally placed figures of the Virgin and Child.

- Angelico has made efforts to use the rules of perspective to create pictorial depth, visible in the detail of the patterned carpet, but the figures of the saints leading the eye to Mary and Jesus are not placed in the space in a convincing manner.

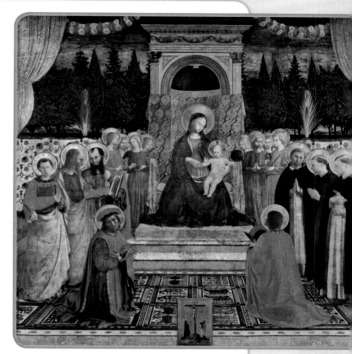

▲ *San Marco Altarpiece, main painting, Convent of San Marco, Florence, Fra Angelico*

MASACCIO			
Date	1401–28	**Patrons**	The Catholic Church
Cities	Florence, Rome	**Themes**	Religious
Apprenticeship	Unknown	**Style**	Realistic, narrative, master of spatial perspective
Influences	Masolino da Panicale		

This painter was born Tommaso Cassai but later became known as Masaccio, which is a pet name for Tommaso. He is most famous for his expert use of central perspective in his paintings, which was a technique developed to create the illusion of depth and space by Ghiberti (see p. 181) and Donatello (see p. 186) in relief sculpture.

PERSPECTIVE

Perspective is the representation of three-dimensional objects on a two-dimensional flat surface. In painting, this means that the artist represents objects, figures and backgrounds in accordance to the optical illusions we perceive in reality. Objects in the distance, for example, appear smaller.

Developments in Central Perspective

1 The artist began by drawing a grid (network of horizontal and vertical lines) and sketching the objects and figures on to it.

2 He then chose a standpoint of the viewer in the centre of the painting. This is called the vanishing point or centre of perspective.

3 Using thread, he then measured lines outwards from the vanishing point to the objects and figures. This informed him of the depth of the objects within the painting. From this, he could figure out the sizes and dimensions of objects giving the impression they are receding into the distance or appearing close up.

Holy Trinity, c. 1427

In this fresco, Masaccio became the first painter to apply central perspective in its most correct and consistent form. This makes it one of the most notable in the history of painting. It is located in the church of Santa Maria Novella, in Florence.

▲ 'Holy Trinity', Santa Maria Novella, Florence, Masaccio

- The figure of Christ can be seen hanging from the cross in the centre, with his feet as the vanishing point for the entire composition.

- The two figures shown beside the cross are the Virgin and Saint Joseph, with God the Father appearing behind the body of Jesus.

- The patrons of this fresco, two members of the wealthy Florentine Lenzi family, are shown kneeling to either side, as a sign of their piety and devotion.

- The great sense of perspective is achieved mostly by the portrayal of the vaulted ceiling framed by the pilasters on each side. Some people believe that Brunelleschi was involved with the design of this painting because of the similarities to his architecture (see p. 161).

The Brancacci Chapel Frescoes, 1424–85

The frescoes that adorn the walls of the Brancacci Chapel in Florence are among the most famous of the entire Renaissance period. They are the result of contributions from a number of artists, including Masaccio.

- Masolino da Panicale began the paintings in 1424, assisted by a young Masaccio.
- Masaccio took over the project in 1425 until his death in 1428.
- Filippino Lippi (c. 1458–1504) then completed the paintings between the years 1481 and 1485.
- The frescoes were restored over a period of nine years starting in 1981.

> ### Did you know?
> The Brancacci Chapel is part of the Florentine church of Santa Maria del Carmine. It is sometimes referred to as the Sistine Chapel (see p. 202) of the early Renaissance because of the quality of its frescoes.

The Tribute Money, c. 1425

▲ *'The Tribute Money,' Broncacci Chapel, Florence, Masaccio*

This fresco incorporates three scenes telling the story of how Jesus and his apostles received money to pay a tribute to the temple. It is an unusual and very effective composition set against a background showing Masaccio's use of perspective.

- The story begins in the centre of the composition, with Jesus telling Saint Peter to look in the mouth of a fish in the lake for coins to pay the tax collector.
- The next part of the story is on the left showing Peter taking the money from the fish's mouth.
- The concluding episode showing the coins being handed over is on the right.

Masaccio's Use of Perspective

- Masaccio uses central perspective to draw the eye to the figure of Jesus in the middle. All of the diagonal perspective lines from the architecture of the temple on the right meet at the vanishing point behind Christ's head.
- Aerial perspective is also used to let the figures emerge from the background. The cool greys and blues of the mountains fade as they recede, creating the illusion that they are in the distance. By contrast, the robes of the men are mainly warm reds, oranges and crimsons which leap to the viewer's eye.

The Expulsion from Paradise, c. 1425

This painting portrays Adam and Eve being cast out from the Garden of Eden (Paradise) by an angry angel (seen at the top of the picture), after their fall from grace. It is a highly dramatic scene, showing Masaccio's vast knowledge of anatomy, light and shade and narrative skills. The figures of Adam and Eve show their individual remorse in an innovative and moving way.

▶ *'The Expulsion from Paradise,' Broncacci Chapel, Florence, Masaccio*

- Adam covers his face in despair, his shoulders slumped in dejection. He symbolises man's horror at his own actions which lead to terrible consequences.

- Eve has a more obvious reaction than Adam, her head thrown back in anguish, her features contorted in agony. She attempts to cover her nakedness, indicating physical shame.

PIERO DELLA FRANCESCA			
Date	c. 1420–92	Patrons	The Catholic Church
Cities	Florence, Rome, Urbino, Ferrara, Arezzo	Themes	Religious
Apprenticeship	Domenico Veneziano (c. 1410–61)	Style	Atmospheric, figurative style, use of perspective
Influences	Domenico Veneziano, Andrea del Castagno (c. 1421–57)		

Piero della Francesca was one of the most prominent Early Renaissance artists, celebrated for the combination of precise symmetrical compositions and tranquil peaceful images in his paintings.

The Baptism of Christ, c. 1450

- This wood panel depicting the baptism of Christ shows della Francesca's interest in the portrayal of light and the harmony of man and nature.

- Almost every part of the painting appears to be designed around the central figure of Christ, whose anatomy is modelled subtly in pale glowing light.

- The horizontal shapes of the hovering dove above his head and the clouds harmonise with the vertical shapes of the figures and trees to create a still and serene scene, only slightly offset by the more relaxed figures of the angels to the left of the composition.

▲ 'The Baptism of Christ,' National Gallery, London, Piero della Francesca

ANDREA MANTEGNA

Date	c. 1431–1506	Patrons	Gonzaga Dynasty (rulers of city-states Matua and Montferrat), the Catholic Church
Cities	Padua, Mantua		
Apprenticeship	Francesco Squarcione	Themes	Religious
Influences	Donatello (see p. 186), Andrea del Castagno, Jacopo Bellini (c. 1396–1457)	Style	Detailed, anatomical precision

Andrea Mantegna is famous for his rugged landscapes which play an important part in his paintings and create a sculptural three-dimensional effect in his work. The figures in his pictures are monumental and statuesque with rigidly folded draperies enveloping them. He began his career in Padua as an apprentice to Francesco Squarcione (c. 1397–1468), but was later influenced by Florentine art. He is also well known for his very successful print workshop.

The Crucifixion, 1456–60

* This painting was originally one of three **predella panels** for the altarpiece of the basilica of San Zeno in Verona.

* The many figures featured in the picture show his knowledge of the great developments being made by Masaccio and Donatello in anatomical accuracy.

* The bodies are elongated, giving the characters more power in this small panel.

* The composition of the painting is based around central perspective, with the figure of Christ in the middle, flanked by the diagonally placed crosses of the thieves in the foreground.

* The background, showing a city scene on a hill, is painted in softer tones to imply aerial perspective, giving the illusion of depth in the painting.

* The figures are placed in groups exhibiting various different emotions. On the left we see the despair of the mourners, while on the right, soldiers play dice over ownership of Christ's clothing.

▲ 'The Crucifixion,' Musée du Louvre, Paris, Mantegna

dic·tion·ar·y

Predella panels were usually situated under the main painting of an altarpiece. They often featured narrative scenes from the life of Christ or the saints.

▲ 'Saint Sebastian,' Musée du Louvre, Paris, Mantegna

Saint Sebastian, c. 1480

- This wood panel portrayal of Saint Sebastian is the middle of three painted by Mantegna. It was originally in San Zeno but now hangs in the Louvre museum, Paris.

- It differs greatly from other contemporary pictures on the same theme, as it shows the saint as a middle-aged man instead of a beautiful youth.

- He was traditionally shown with arrows protruding from the front of his body, but in this painting, he has been shot in the sides.

- The elegant *contrapposto* pose of the figure and the delicately rendered classical column behind it contrast deeply with the menacing cliffs in the background and the harsh faces of the executioners in the foreground.

Did you know?

Mantegna painted three works on the subject of Saint Sebastian, who was considered a protector against plagues, a frequent occurrence in Mantegna's time. Sebastian was usually portrayed tied to a post and shot with arrows.

dic·tion·ar·y

Contrapposto, meaning 'counterpoise,' describes a figure standing with its weight resting on one leg and the upper part of the body and arms twisted. This serves to create a natural-looking pose.

The Lamentation Over the Dead Christ, c. 1480

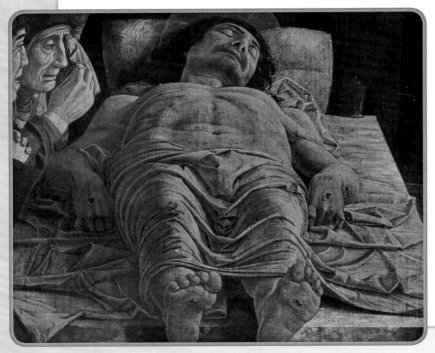

- The Dead Christ was an extremely unusual painting for its time, focusing on the foreshortened figure of Jesus lying prone on a slab, with the close-up profiles of two weeping women lamenting on the left.

- Although the foreshortening of the limbs is very well planned, the painting is still not entirely convincing, possibly because Mantegna did not take into account the optical illusion that objects appear larger when closer; the feet seem too small.

◄ 'The Lamentation Over the Dead Christ,' Pinacoteca di Brera, Milan, Mantegna

- This picture has also been praised for its beautiful use of light and shade, creating an atmosphere of pathos and melancholy.
- It was found in Mantegna's studio after his death and now resides at the Pinacoteca di Brera, an art gallery in Milan.

Mythological Subjects

People became interested in classical literature and mythology from ancient Greece and Rome during the Renaissance. Artists such as Botticelli were commissioned to paint scenes featuring gods, goddesses, nymphs and satyrs.

SANDRO BOTTICELLI			
Date	1445–1510	**Patrons**	The Catholic Church, the Vatican, the Medici family, Florentine merchants
Cities	Florence		
Apprenticeship	Filippino Lippi	**Themes**	Mythological, religious
Influences	Domenico Ghirlandaio (1449–94), Perugino (1446–1524), Verrocchio (c. 1435–88), humanism	**Style**	Graceful, animated, linear compositions

Born Alessandro di Mariano Filippi, this painter's work sums up the spirit of the Renaissance for many people. He started his career as a goldsmith, then became a student of Filippino Lippi. He spent all his life in Florence except for a year in Rome spent painting frescoes in the Sistine Chapel.

The Primavera, c. 1478

- This painting's theme is the arrival of spring and the happiness of the wedded state. It was said to have been painted for a private villa in Florence belonging to one of the Medici family, but is now in the Uffizi Gallery in Florence.
- The nymph Chloris is seen at the right being attacked by the wind god Zephyrus, who turns her into Flora, the goddess of spring.

▼ 'The Primavera,' Uffizi Gallery, Florence, Botticelli

- Flora is painted to the left of Chloris. Her gown, beautifully embroidered with delicate flowers, symbolises eternal springtime.

- Venus, the goddess of love, is in the centre.

- Mercury is featured in the right of the picture, keeping bad weather at bay.

- The Three Graces dance in the left of the painting, celebrating the beginning of spring. They are also thought to symbolise the three stages of love: beauty, desire and consummation.

- Cupid points an arrow at one of the three graces above.

The Birth of Venus, c. 1485

▲ *'The Birth of Venus,' Uffizi Gallery, Florence, Botticelli*

- This painting shows the goddess of love, Venus, arriving on the shore of Cythera, Greece. It was originally in the same villa as the Primavera, and now is in the Uffizi Gallery, Florence.

- Venus is portrayed as the ideal of feminine beauty. She is modest and serene, her body slightly elongated and leaning on one leg as she balances on the seashell which has brought her ashore.

- The wind gods Zephyrus and Aurora are on the left of the picture. On the right one of the attendant nymphs prepares to wrap Venus in a floral embroidered robe.

- The sea is painted in a very stylised (unrealistic) manner, as are the leaves on the trees behind the nymph.

Civic Painting

During the Renaissance, artists were often commissioned to create frescoes and paintings to decorate public buildings. These were intended to inspire and educate the public and generally were large-scale history paintings featuring either military victories or the state or heroic tales from classical sources.

PAOLO UCCELLO

Date	1397–1475	**Patrons**	The Medici family
Cities	Florence	**Themes**	Historical, civic and religious
Apprenticeship	The workshop of Lorenzo Ghiberti (see p. 181)	**Style**	Colourful, patterned, innovative use of perspective
Influences	Masaccio, Donatello		

Named Paolo di Dono at his birth, this painter was nicknamed *Uccello* meaning 'bird.' This came from his fondness for painting animals. He had a big interest in the use of perspective. He painted 'The Battle of San Romano' for the Palazzo Medici in Florence. It consists of three paintings, each more than 3 m long, about the battle, one of which is featured below.

Niccolò Mauruzi da Tolentino at the Battle of San Romano, c. 1438–40

▼ *'Niccolò Mauruzi da Tolentino at the Battle of San Romano,' National Gallery, London, Uccello*

- ➥ This painting represents the historical battle of San Romano, portraying the victory of Florence over Siena, and demonstrating knowledge learned from Giotto's work of the mathematical uses of perspective.
- ➥ Niccolò Mauruzi da Tolentino leads the battle, seated on a white horse and wearing a red and gold hat. Da Tolentino (c. 1350–1435) was an Italian *Condottiero* (mercenary soldier).

- The most striking aspect of this painted mural is the rigid construction of space and perspective. However there seems to be little connection between foreground and background, which creates an impression of a backdrop and props as in a stage set.
- The figures and horses add to this effect by the geometrical decoration on the harnesses and bridles on the horses, and the main figure's turban.
- The two-tone shading on the horses' bodies gives them the appearance of clockwork toys.
- Uccello created the illusion of depth and space by aligning broken shards of lances and helmets along perspective grid lines leading to a central vanishing point.
- A foreshortened fallen soldier to the left of the painting adds to this slightly exaggerated composition.

BENOZZO GOZZOLI			
Date	c. 1420–97	**Patrons**	The Catholic Church, the Medici family
Cities	Florence, Rome, Pisa		
Apprenticeship	Unknown	**Themes**	Civic, religious
Influences	Ghiberti, Fra Angelico	**Style**	Narrative, colourful frescoes

Benozzo Gozzoli moved from Sant'Ilario a Colombano to Florence in 1427 where he worked as an apprentice and assistant to Fra Angelico until 1449. His work is most admired for its bright and lively colours.

The Journey of The Magi, c. 1460

- Gozzoli painted a series of highly colourful, imaginative and detailed frescoes in a small chapel in the Palazzo Medici Riccardi in Florence. The theme is the procession of the Magi (Three Wise Men) to Bethlehem to visit the newly born Jesus.
- The Procession of King Caspar is situated on the west wall and the Procession of King Balthazar is on the eastern side.
- Gozzoli's attention to detail can be seen in the intricate patterns on the clothing, the leaves and fruit on the trees and coats of the many animals in the background.
- An early attempt at perspective can be seen in the winding roads leading the viewer's eye to the grouped figures in the foreground.
- However the varying sizes of the animals and trees in the middle of the frescoes show the artist's incomplete understanding of the art of perspective.
- Members of the Medici family, as well as a self-portrait of the artist, can be seen among the followers in the convoy.

▶ *Procession of King Caspar, 'The Journey of The Magi' Florence, Gozzoli*

GENTILE DA FABRIANO

Date	c. 1370–c. 1427	Patrons	The Church, Civic commissions
Cities	Venice, Florence, Siena, Orvieto	Themes	Religious, history painting
Apprenticeship	Allegretto Nuzzi (c. 1315–73)	Style	International Gothic style
Influences	International Gothic style (see p. 155)		

Gentile da Fabriano's early career is mostly unrecorded but his first major work is believed to be an altarpiece in Venice painted in 1408. His work is renowned for its rich colour and use of gold to create very decorative compositions.

Adoration of the Magi, 1423

- This painting was commissioned by the wealthy Strozzi family for their private chapel in the Santa Trinita Church, Florence.

- It is filled with rich decoration, and embellished with **lapis lazuli** and gold leaf which can be seen on the bridles of the horses and on the crowns of the wise men.

- The Three Wise Men are depicted paying tribute to the Holy Family.

- Their followers are shown in a long procession, winding back in perspective.

> ### dic·tion·ar·y
>
> **Lapis lazuli** is a semi-precious blue stone crushed to create a deep blue hue. It was usually used to paint the Virgin Mary's blue robes.

▲ 'The Adoration of The Magi,' Santa Trinita Church, Florence, Gentile da Fabriano

Quattrcento Painting Revision Questions

1 Discuss the use of perspective and the role of the patron in Masaccio's painting 'The Trinity.'

2 Describe 'The Tribute Money' by Masaccio under the following headings:
a) narrative, b) perspective, c) colour.

3 Discuss the portrayal of mythological subjects and symbolism in the work of Sandro Botticelli.

4 Discuss the art elements of pattern, texture, colour and movement in 'The Primavera' by Botticelli.

5 Compare and contrast 'The Journey of the Magi' by Benozzo Gozzoli with 'Adoration of the Magi' by Gentile da Fabriano.

Quattrocento Relief Carving and Sculpture

During the Renaissance both painters and sculptors looked to sculptures from ancient Greece and Rome for inspiration for their work. Classical sculpture originated in Greece in the sixth century B.C. Sculptors began to study the movements and stance of the human body to create more realistic sculptures. They looked at how shifting weight onto one leg and twisting the body affected the positions of the limbs creating the first sculptures to exhibit *contrapposto* (see p. 172). The features of the statues became more defined and naturalistic. The function of sculpture also changed during the classical period. Statues were first used to adorn temples and represent the gods. As time passed, sculptors were gradually commissioned to create sculptures for private patrons. These included busts of the head and shoulders, which were popular to commemorate a general; tomb statues, and full-size statues of wealthy people to be placed in temples as a sign of their piety.

This tradition of realistic sculpture was admired by the Romans, who began by copying the Greek style. They later developed their own form of classical sculpture by focusing their attention more on the individual qualities of the subject. This is visible in the many statues of Roman emperors.

In this section, we will discuss two main types of sculpture – relief and free-standing.

- In relief sculpture, the sculpture is still attached to a background.
- In free-standing sculpture, the sculpture is surrounded by space on all sides.

Bronze Casting

This technique was first used in classical times and later adopted during the Renaissance. It was commonly called the 'lost-wax casting method,' allowing objects to be produced in either solid or hollow form. Hollow casts were more popular for a number of reasons:

- They were easier to transport as they were lighter.
- They used less expensive material.
- They were less likely to crack as they cooled.

LOST WAX METHOD

1 The artist began by making a sculpture out of wax or clay.

2 They then moulded plaster around the sculpture. If it was a very large sculpture, more than one mould was used.

3 When the mould hardened it was removed from the wax or clay sculpture.

4 The artist poured wax into the mould, creating a layer inside it. The inside was left hollow.

5 The hollow wax sculpture was taken from the mould and polished to remove any imperfections.

6 The artist then dipped the wax sculpture first into liquid silica, then into a dry crystalline silica, which dried into a ceramic shell.

7 The shell was then heated in a kiln to harden it. The wax melted and ran from the shell (hence the 'lost wax' term).

8 The artist poured melted bronze into the shell.

9 When the bronze cooled, the shell was hammered off, leaving the bronze sculpture.

10 With a last polish, the bronze sculpture was completed.

Doors of Saint John's Baptistry

Saint John's Baptistry is a religious building situated in the Piazza del Duomo in Florence, Italy. It was originally thought to have been built during the age of the Roman Empire, but construction actually began in c. 1059 and was completed for the most part by 1128. Although famed for its octagonal structure and domed roof, its most famous features are the three spectacular bronze panelled doors. The sculptors responsible for these are Andrea Pisano and Lorenzo Ghiberti.

ANDREA PISANO			
Date	1290–c.1349	**Patrons**	The Catholic Church
Cities	Florence	**Themes**	Religious
Apprenticeship	Goldsmith, Giotto	**Style**	Late Gothic, clear, concise
Influences	Giotto		

South Baptistry Doors, 1330–36

Quatrefoil Panels, 53 cm x 40 cm

dic·tion·ar·y

Meaning 'four leaves,' a **quatrefoil** is a symmetrical shape which was often used in Gothic and Renaissance architecture. It forms the overall outline of four circles of the same diameter that overlap slightly.

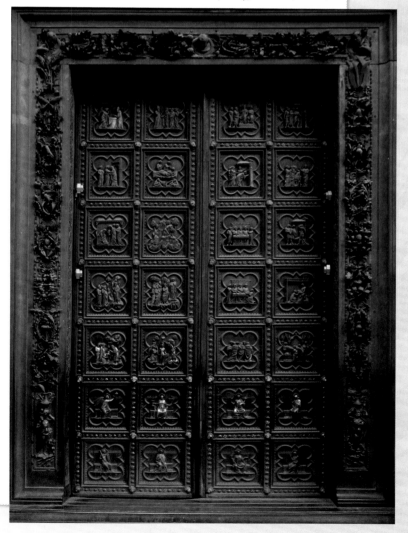

▼ *South Doors of Saint John's Baptistry, Florence, Pisano*

The sculptor Andrea Pisano, recommended by Giotto (see p. 156), won the commission to design the first set of doors (South Doors) for the baptistry. In his design, he used panels in the shape of Gothic quatrefoils to frame the relief castings. The castings were first moulded out of wax in 1330 and then cast in bronze in Venice by craftworkers. Some parts were later gilded (covered in gold) to emphasise prominent details. There were 28 panels in all on the doors. Twenty of the panels feature scenes from the life of Saint John the Baptist, while the lower eight depict the virtues of Christianity. Saint John was Jesus's cousin who baptised him.

▶ *Explanation of scenes depicted on the South Door of Saint John's Baptistry, by Andrea Pisano. The main theme of these doors was the life of Saint John the Baptist.*

Saint John Baptises

This panel shows Saint John baptising a kneeling man.

- The figures standing on the left draw attention to the main action by the direction of their gaze and the inclination of their bodies.

- They are gilded, as is a small bird watching from the mountains carved in low relief in the background.

- Saint John is featured wearing his traditional fleece garment, indicating his role as a shepherd of Christ.

▶ *'Saint John Baptises,' South Baptistry Doors, Florence, Pisano*

Dance of Salome

Salome convinced Herod to give her the head of John the Baptist by performing the dance of the seven veils.

- Pisano again focuses the viewer's attention on the event by turning all the figures' heads toward Salome as she dances.

- The movement of the people is restrained and formal.

- The background, a plain curtain suspended from a rail, is simple and uncomplicated.

▶ 'Dance of Salome,' South Baptistry Doors, Florence, Pisano

LORENZO GHIBERTI				
Date	1378–1455	Patrons	The Merchants' Guild, the Church, the Bankers' Guild, The Wool Guild	
City	Florence			
Apprenticeship	Goldsmith in workshop of Bartolo di Michele (his stepfather)	Themes	Religious	
Influences	Andrea Pisano, classical art and architecture	Style	Elegant, expressive, innovative	

North Baptistry Doors, 1403–24

Quatrefoil Panels, 39 cm x 39 cm

A competition was held to find a designer for the second set of doors for the baptistry. Among the competitors were Lorenzo Ghiberti and Filippo Brunelleschi (see p. 161). Each competitor was required to make a sample panel for the doors, based on the theme 'The sacrifice of Isaac' and in keeping with the designs previously set in place by Pisano. Ghiberti was only 23 years old when he won. It is thought that a key factor was his development of casting the low-relief background and high-relief figures together, creating a much more economical method. The design of the doors themselves were based closely on Andrea Pisano's. Like Pisano's, there were 28 panels; the top 20 on the life of Christ and the bottom eight on the **Four Evangelists** and the **Church Fathers** Saint Ambrose, Saint Jerome, Saint Gregory

dic·tion·ar·y

The **Four Evangelists** (meaning proclaimers of good news), Matthew, Mark, Luke, and John wrote the New Testament of the Bible. ▼

The **Church Fathers** were early Christian writers.

▲ *North Baptistry Doors, Florence, Ghiberti*

Jesus Carries the Cross	Crucifixion	Resurrection	Pentecost
Garden of Gethsemane	Jesus is Taken Prisoner	Flagellation	Pontius Pilate Washes his Hands
Transfiguration	Jesus raises Lazarus from the Dead	Jesus enters Jerusalem	Last Supper
Baptism of Jesus	Temptation of Jesus	Chasing the Merchants from the Temple	Jesus Walks on Water
Annunciation	Birth	Adoration of the Magi	Dispute With the Doctors
Saint John the Evangelist	Saint Matthew the Evangelist	Saint Luke the Evangelist	Saint Mark the Evangelist
Saint Ambrose	Saint Jerome	Saint Gregory	Saint Augustine

▲ *Explanation of scenes depicted on the North Doors of Saint John's Baptistry, by Lorenzo Ghiberti. The main theme of these doors was the New Testament.*

Dispute With the Doctors

This panel concentrates on the young Christ in the temple preaching to the scribes and elders.

- Ghiberti places Jesus in the centre of the composition surrounded by attentive scribes clothed in exquisitely formed drapery.
- They are set in an architectural background which shows his knowledge of perspective.

▶ *'Dispute With the Doctors,' North Baptistry Doors, Florence, Ghiberti*

Chasing the Merchants From the Temple

This scene is a much more dynamic and dramatic one focusing on an outraged Jesus driving the moneylenders and traders from the House of God.

- There is a great contrast between the tumbling, energetic figures and the clean straight lines of the architecture carved in low relief in the background.

▶ *'Chasing the Merchants From the Temple,' North Baptistry Doors, Florence, Ghiberti*

East Baptistry Doors 'The Gates of Paradise,' 1425–52

Rectangular Panels, 80 cm x 80 cm

The East Doors of the baptistry are the most famous of all the doors, described by Michelangelo (see p. 194) as 'The Gates of Paradise.' They were also hailed as the most beautiful work of art on earth by Vasari (1511–74) who wrote famous biographies of the Renaissance artists. Ghiberti was commissioned to create these after the success of his previous doors and this time was allowed to design his own composition of the panels and the overall layout. He designed the doors very differently to his previous ones.

- The East Doors had only ten rectangular panels, each one portraying more than one biblical scene from the Old Testament.

- The panels were twice the size of the ones on his last set of doors, giving Ghiberti greater scope to create lavish and astounding detail on each one.

- The scenes were no longer contained within the quatrefoil shape of the South and North Door scenes.

▶ *Explanation of scenes depicted on the East Doors of Saint John's Baptistry, by Lorenzo Ghiberti. The main theme of these doors was the Old Testament.*

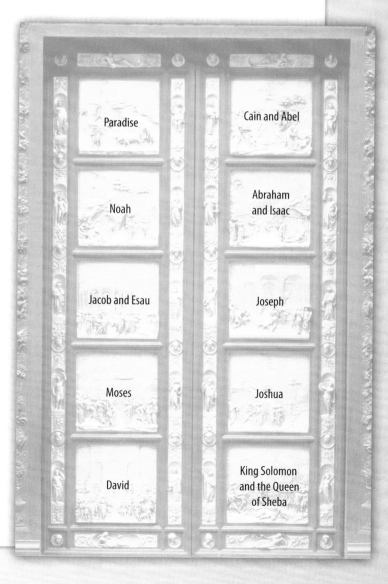

Paradise	Cain and Abel
Noah	Abraham and Isaac
Jacob and Esau	Joseph
Moses	Joshua
David	King Solomon and the Queen of Sheba

The Story of Noah

There are various aspects from the life of Noah to be found in this panel.

- The pyramid shape carved in low relief in the background symbolises the ark he built to transport the animals from the flood.

- We see him offering thanks to God on the front right-hand side.

- Noah's sons are shown reproaching him for his drunken state and nudity while attempting to cover him up.

- Noah and his family emerge from the ark after the long voyage. Lions, a bear, a stag and elephant walk around, while birds out of the top windows.

▶ *'The Story of Noah,' East Baptistry Doors, Florence, Ghiberti*

The Story of Joseph

This is composed of scenes from the life of Joseph whose brothers sold him into slavery in Egypt because he was the favourite of his father, Jacob. After several years he became the Pharoah's top governor because of his skill in interpreting dreams.

- It shows Ghiberti's growing mastery in the art of perspective by his detailed carving of the temple.

- The lifelike figures seem almost free-standing, as if they are on the verge of escaping from their frame.

- The scene in the upper right shows Joseph being thrown into a well, then sold into slavery.

- In the left foreground is the King's gold cup being hidden in a sack of grain, a trick played on Joseph on his brothers.

- The upper-left scene shows Joseph's revelation of himself to his brothers.

▲ *'The Story of Joseph,' East Baptistry Doors, Florence, Ghiberti*

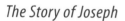

◀ *East Baptistry Doors, Florence, Ghiberti*

DONATELLO			
Date	1386–1466	Patrons	The Catholic Church
Cities	Florence, Siena, Rome, Padua	Themes	Religious
Apprenticeship	Lorenzo Ghiberti, sculptor Nanni di Banco (c. 1384–1421)	Style	Innovative, realistic, thought to be the greatest fifteenth-century sculptor
Influences	Classical sculpture		

Donatello was one of the most famous sculptors of the Early Renaissance. He sculpted both three-dimensional statues and also relief sculpture that is renowned for its illusion of perspective and depth. The most famous of these relief sculptures 'The Feast of Herod' is situated on the baptismal font in the Baptistry of Siena.

The Feast of Herod, 1423–27

Gilded Bronze, 60 cm x 60 cm

- The head of John the Baptist is presented to Herod by a soldier, while Salome, who requested his beheading, is shown on the right.

- This is the most intricate and adventurous of Donatello's reliefs, using perspective to create depth of space within the composition. This was achieved by combining high-and low-relief carving with incised (engraved) decoration.

- This is a highly dramatic scene, demonstrating Donatello's interest in conveying human emotions through facial expressions and gestures.

- The most flamboyant of the characters is Herod himself, who is leaning away in horror, his face contorted in dismay.

▲ *'The Feast of Herod,' Siena Baptistry, Donatello*

Quattrocento Free-Standing Sculpture

The art of realism in sculpture was first introduced in ancient Greece and continued by the Romans. These skills were almost entirely lost until the Renaissance when there was a renewed interest in classical art. Sculptors began to study both ancient sculpture along with human anatomy to create three-dimensional realistic statues celebrating the humanist values of the beauty, intellect, and ambition of humankind.

THE ORSANMICHELE			
Style	Gothic	**Built by**	Architects Benci di Cione, Neri de Fioravante and Francesco Talenti.
Date	1337		
Country	Italy		

The Orsanmichele was built in Florence in 1337 as a guildhall. It is most famous for the statues standing in the 14 niches on the exterior of the first floor of the building. These statues were commissioned by the major guilds in Florence and were created by the prominent sculptors of the era, including: Donatello, Lorenzo Ghiberti, Nanni di Banco and Niccolo di Pietro Lamberti (c. 1370–1451).

Saint John the Baptist, 1414, Ghiberti

Bronze, 2.55 m

Ghiberti completed three sculptures for the Orsanmichele portraying the saints Matthew, Stephen and Saint John the Baptist. This was one of the first larger-than-life sculptures to be made since ancient times.

- The robes of this commanding figure are sweeping and deeply carved, the folds lifted by the left hand hinting at the *contrapposto* position of the body beneath.

- The ornate texture of the beard and hair frame an expressive and powerful face.

- The saint's traditional garb of a sheep's fleece (seen under the robe) is particularly apt as this statue was commissioned by the guild of wool refiners.

▲ *'Saint John the Baptist,' Orsanmichele, Florence, Ghiberti*

Saint Matthew, 1419–21, Ghiberti

Bronze, 2.69 m

Before Saint Matthew met Christ he was a tax collector. This made him a suitable patron saint of the Bankers' Guild, who commissioned this sculpture.

- The saint is portrayed with his weight resting on his left leg, with his eyes gazing out to the right.

- The flowing drapery moulded around the body enhances the realistic weight and monumental stance of the statue.

- The folds of the robes are less stylised as is the body of the saint which is clearly defined underneath his clothing.

- He points to the book he holds in his left hand, indicating his role as a Gospel scribe.

▶ *'Saint Matthew,' Orsanmichele, Florence, Ghiberti*

Saint George, c. 1417, Donatello

Marble, 2.09 m

This is a statue of George, the saint and martyr who was famous for his legendary slaying of a dragon. The statue in the Orsanmichele is a copy of the original which is now located in the Bargello museum (see p. 153).

- The figure of Saint George is sculpted as a young soldier, his determination and taut, controlled energy visible in his stance.
- The feet are planted firmly apart, his right fist clenched as it falls to his side. His face, slightly angled from his body, shows a decisive and strong-willed nature.
- Underneath the sculpture is a relief of Saint George fighting the dragon which is almost as famous as the sculpture itself. It shows Donatello's innovative use of a technique called *rilievo schiacciato* which means 'layers of surfaces.' This created the effect of perspective in relief carving.

David, c. 1425–30, Donatello

Bronze, 1.58 m

This sculpture depicts the boy David, a biblical character who defied all odds by defeating the giant Goliath, armed only with a slingshot. This was the first free-standing nude sculpture since ancient Greece and Rome and created a scandal at the time. The statue originally belonged to Cosimo de'Medici, and is now in the Bargello, Florence (see p. 153).

- Donatello's David is balancing his weight on his right leg while the other rests on the head of Goliath.
- The thoughtful, downcast face of David contrasts with his jaunty pose with his hand on his hip and his helmet adorned with a laurel wreath to symbolise his victory.
- The lithe graceful body of David is beautifully crafted showing Donatello's knowledge of anatomy and mastery of technique.

▲ *'Saint George,' Florence, Orsanmichele, Donatello*

▼ *'The Penitent Mary Magdalene,' Orsanmichele, Florence, Donatello*

◄ *'David,' Bargello, Florence, Donatello*

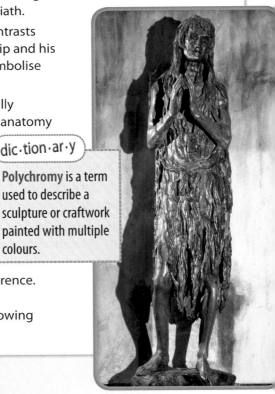

dic·tion·ar·y

Polychromy is a term used to describe a sculpture or craftwork painted with multiple colours.

The Penitent Mary Magdalene, c. 1455, Donatello

*Wood with **Polychromy** and Gold, 1.88 m*

This statue is now in the museo dell'opera del Duomo in Florence. It portrays Saint Mary Magdalene, a biblical character who repented of her sins as a prostitute and adulterer. It is a harrowing and moving portrayal of a woman in deep spiritual anguish.

- The figure of Magdalene is clothed only by her long tousled tresses of hair, referring to the hair shirts worn by penitents (repentant sinners) in biblical times.
- Her body is frail and thin, and her hands are clasped together in a prayerful pose.
- The face of Magdalene is not that of a beautiful temptress, but of a gaunt poignant sinner.

Quattrocento Relief Carving and Sculpture Revision Questions

1 Describe Andrea Pisano's doors for Saint John's Baptistry with particular reference to two panels. Use diagrams to illustrate your answer.

2 Discuss the developments in relief carving by Ghiberti in his work 'The Gates of Paradise' under the headings:
a) method of relief carving, b) narrative style, c) use of perspective.

3 Describe the use of perspective, expression, and realism in 'The Feast of Herod' by Donatello.

4 Trace the development of Renaissance sculpture by referring to the sculptures in Orsanmichele.

5 Discuss the importance of realism, anatomical accuracy and expressiveness in the works of Donatello.

The High Renaissance

The Early Renaissance, rooted in Florence, and inspired by ancient Greece and Rome, matured into the High Renaissance between the years 1450 and 1527. During this time, viewed as the climax of the Renaissance period, an explosion of creative genius occurred in Italy. The centre of the explosion moved from Florence to Rome, the home of the Pope. This was due to the patronage of Pope Julius II. Three great artists dominated this period: Leonardo da Vinci, Michelangelo Buonarroti, and Raphael Sanzio.

LEONARDO DA VINCI			
Date	1452–1519	Patrons	King Francis, private patrons, the Catholic Church
Cities	Florence, Milan, Rome, Mantua, Venice	Themes	Religious, portraiture
Apprenticeship	Andrea del Verrocchio	Style	Tonal, technical, imaginative, innovative
Influences	Andrea del Verrocchio		

Leonardo da Vinci is perhaps most deserving of any artist working at the time of the title 'Renaissance man.' This was the ideal that a man could excel at many different things at once. He was born in Vinci near Florence, an illegitimate child of a notary (solicitor) and a peasant girl. He lived with his father where he studied intellectual texts.

Leonardo's Career Development

At the age of 15 he became an apprentice of Andrea del Verrocchio, an influential Florentine sculptor, goldsmith and painter (see p. 154). His early genius was immediately recognised and after painting an angel in one of his master's paintings, 'The Baptism of Christ,' Verrocchio was apparently so disheartened by the comparison between his own work and his pupil's that he vowed never to paint again. In 1482 Leonardo began a 17-year period working in Milan under the patronage of the duke of Milan, Duke Ludovico Sforza (1452–1508). This marked the beginning of Leonardo's multi-faceted career as an engineer, mathematician, architect, painter and scientist. The duke encouraged all aspects of his talent and during this time Leonardo designed many inventions, from submarines to new innovations in canal engineering.

Move to Rome

From 1490 to 1495 he began keeping notebooks to research and develop the many ideas which preoccupied him, giving us a great insight into the workings of his mind. In 1499, after the duke's fall from power, Leonardo spent sixteen years travelling around Italy, working for numerous patrons, among them **Cesare Borgia**, who employed him as a military engineer. A year after he began the 'Mona Lisa' (see p. 191) in 1503, his father died. He was left no inheritance, but the death of his uncle soon afterwards left him wealthy and with the use of his home and land. He moved to Rome in 1513 where he stayed for three years under the patronage Giuliano de'Medici (1479–1516).

biography

CESARE BORGIA (1475–1507), the Duke of Valentinois and Romagna in Italy, was from a notorious and powerful political family. He had a distinguished military career.

Patronage of François I

His last patron was the king of France, François I, who gave him the title Premier Painter and Architect of the King. He was a trusted and valued friend to François and the king gave him the use of a house near the royal palace in Amboise, France. Leonardo's studies and painting continued to flourish in these surroundings, even though he had developed paralysis in his right hand. He died on the 2nd of May in 1519, with the king of France by his side.

▼ *'Anatomy Sketches,' Leonardo da Vinci*

Leonardo's Artistic and Technical Developments

Leonardo's many sketchbooks provide a valuable insight into the mind of a genius, showing many detailed drawings on a vast number of subjects. He devised a crafty system to prevent others from easy access to his ideas, writing his notes backwards so they could only be read with the use of a mirror. Ideas covered included:

- Inventions, including aeroplanes, helicopters, armoured tanks and diving suits, all of which were extremely advanced ideas for his time.
- Studies of anatomy, ranging from human skeletal and muscular structure to birds in flight and the movement of animals.
- Architecture, which included everything from fortresses to churches and civic buildings.
- Painting, where he devised new techniques to enhance his work.

He also developed artistic techniques that had not been used before:

- From the Italian word, meaning 'to cover in smoke,' *sfumato* was a technique developed by Leonardo to soften the edges of forms by gradually shading tones and colours into one another.
- *Chiaroscuro* involved using light and shade to make objects appear three-dimensional.

Leonardo's Paintings

▼ *'Design for an Armoured Chariot,'
Turin, Leonardo da Vinci*

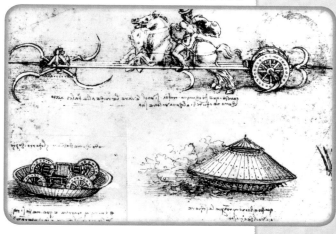

Although Leonardo da Vinci is probably the most famous and respected artist in the world, he finished only a small number of paintings in his long career:

- Annunciation
- Ginerva de Benci
- The Madonna of the Rocks (two versions)
- The Last Supper
- The Madonna and Child with Saint Anne
- Bacchus
- Mona Lisa

Mona Lisa, begun c. 1503

The identity of this mysterious woman has been the subject of much speculation, but has never been confirmed. It is thought to be a portrait of La Giaconda, a wealthy Florentine merchant's wife, but another controversial theory suggests that it is a self-portrait in female form. The pose of the figure, set obliquely in a triangular composition, with the face slightly directed towards the viewer, has been widely copied and is to this day the typical model for photographic portraiture.

- The ambiguous expression on Mona Lisa's face is perhaps the reason for the world's enduring fascination with this painting.

- Although the edges of the mouth are slightly lifted in a smile, the *sfumato* around the lips and eyes and the lack of distinct eyebrows make the expression hard to read.

- The relaxed muscles in the cheeks do not correspond with a smile, a fact which would be known to Leonardo, a master of anatomy. This leads us to believe that he used a deliberate technique to puzzle the viewer.

- This theory is further advanced when studying the background, as the scene on the right contradicts that on the left, appearing to have a higher horizon line.

- The colours in the picture are dark and muted, with the face, skin above the neckline, and hands highlighted in warm golden tones.

▶ *'The Mona Lisa,' Musée du Louvre, Paris, Leonardo da Vinci*

The Last Supper, c. 1495–98

Da Vinci was commissioned to paint this fresco on the back wall of the dining hall of the Santa Maria delle Grazie Church in Milan. The long supper table with the apostles and Christ seated facing the viewer was a traditional device used by painters at the time, but Leonardo added new life to the subject. He did this by capturing a specific moment in time and recording the contrasting emotions on the faces of his characters. It is the moment after Jesus revealed that he would be betrayed by one of his apostles. Leonardo spent a lot of time determining the features and gestures of the individual figures. His rough preparatory cartoons indicate that he worked from live models.

➤ The reactions of the disciples range from fury (Peter) and sorrow (John), to the guilt of Judas. He is shown distancing himself by leaning back and clutching a bag of coins, his reward for

betraying Jesus. These contrast with the resigned pose of Christ, eyes downcast and hands outstretched.

- Christ is placed in the exact centre of the painting, his head framed by the doorway in the background, serving as the vanishing point for the perspective lines which radiate outwards to the edges of the composition. These are visible in the lines of the architecture of the room in which they are seated.

- The ceiling is dramatically foreshortened, whereas the figures are presented at eye level, leading us to believe that the room is long and the doorway and windows in the distance huge in size.

- Colour also plays a part in focusing the viewer's gaze on the centre with the rich red and blue of Christ's robes highlighted by the faded background seen through the doorway.

▼ *'The Last Supper,' Santa Maria delle Grazie Church, Milan, Leonardo da Vinci*

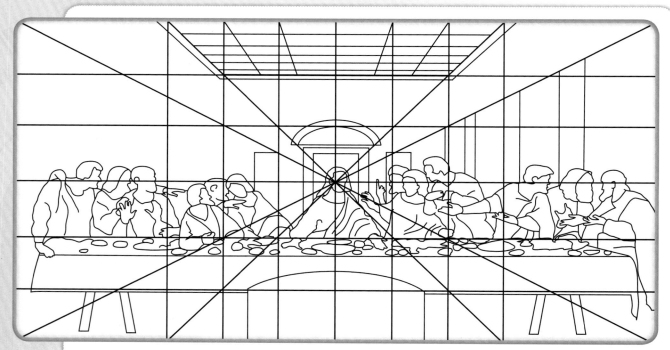

▲ *Diagram of 'The Last Supper,' da Vinci*

Characters from left to right: Bartholomew, James Minor, Andrew, Judas, Peter, John the Evangelist, Christ, Thomas, James Major, Philip, Matthew, Jude Thaddeus, Simon.

MICHELANGELO BUONARROTI			
Date	1475–1564	**Influences**	Classical sculpture, Masaccio
Cities	Caprese, Florence, Rome	**Patrons**	The Medici Family, Pope Julius II
Apprenticeship	Francesco Granacci, Domenico Ghirlandaio	**Themes**	Religious
		Style	Energetic, vibrant, anatomical perfection

With his huge skills in painting, sculpture, architecture, writing and engineering, Michelangelo Buonarroti rivalled Leonardo da Vinci for the title of true Renaissance Man.

He was born on 6 March 1475 in Caprese, Tuscany to Lodovico di Leonardo and Francesca Buonarroti. The family owned two homes, one in Tuscany and the other in Florence. When Michelangelo was six years old his mother died. This was also the year he received his first drawing lessons from Florentine painter Francesco Granacci (c. 1469–1543).

Michelangelo's Career Development

In 1488 Michelangelo moved to Florence and became an assistant to the artist Domenico Ghirlandaio (1449–94). As with all Renaissance artists, he depended on wealthy patrons. The most prestigious patrons who commissioned work from him were the Medici Family and Pope Julius II. Michelangelo was a fiery and fervent character and had very different relationships with these patrons.

Patronage by the Medici Family

In 1489, his talent and flair in the workshop of Ghirlandaio were noticed by Lorenzo de'Medici (see p. 149) and he was invited to his court. There, Michelangelo was surrounded by prominent painters, poets and sculptors within a setting which boasted many classical statues and works of art from antiquity. He taught himself to sculpt in clay by drawing these sculptures and also by studying anatomy of bodies in a local church. He maintained a lifelong friendship with the Medici family. Following his death, Duke Cosimo de'Medici orderedthe theft of his body from Rome and placed it in a marble tomb in Santa Croce, Florence, designed by Vasan.

Patronage of Pope Julius II

Pope Julius II (1443–1513) was a member of a powerful rival family of the Medicis, and was famed for his authoritative manner. Michelangelo had many arguments with him over control of his projects, but they eventually grew to appreciate each others' talents. Pope Julius commissioned his own tomb, and the frescoes in the Sistine Chapel in Rome (see pp. 202–7) from Michelangelo.

▲ *Pope Julius II*

Final Years

After the death of Julius II Michelangelo was employed by Pope Leo X (see p. 149) and his successor Pope Clement VII (1478–1534). After he died in Rome his body was brought to Santa Croce, where he was buried (see above).

Michelangelo's Sculpture

David, 1501–04

Marble, 5.17 m

This vast sculpture was commissioned by the Republican government of Florence as a symbol of strength and courage in the face of adversity. This echoed the state of Florence, which was surrounded by powerful states competing for power in northern Italy. It is sculpted from one large piece of marble which shows Michelangelo's confidence and ambition. It portrays the Biblical character David, who famously killed the giant Goliath (see also Donatello's David, p. 188).

▶ *'David,' Galleria dell' Accademia, Florence, Michelangelo*

- The head and hands of the figure are disproportionately large, indicating that he used an adolescent boy as his model.

- Despite these attributes of an inexperienced and youthful boy, Michelangelo adds strength and power by giving David a muscular frame.

- The tendons on the hands and neck show the tension of the figure as he waits for Goliath to appear. The classically beautiful features are set in an expectant and alert expression which shows in the anxious furrows on his brow.

- This contrasts with the relaxed pose of the body, balanced to perfection as he leans on one leg, his slingshot hanging casually over his shoulder.

Comparison of Michelangelo's David with Donatello's David

Although Michelangelo used the same biblical source as Donatello, there are marked differences in his treatment of both the body and the subject.

DONATELLO'S DAVID	MICHELANGELO'S DAVID
• Donatello's David, poised over the head of Goliath, has already overcome the giant and assumes a relaxed pose, his eyes cast downward and his lips smiling.	• Michelangelo's David is shown before the battle, looking determinedly outwards at an enemy we cannot see.
• The statue is totally self-contained. We see the connection between David and Goliath by the direction of his gaze.	• Although at first he appears to assume a relaxed *contrapposto* stance, similar to Donatello's statue, there is an underlying tension and purpose shown in the tendons, muscles and features.
• Donatello's additions of helmet, leg armour and sword proclaim the victorious conqueror.	• Michelangelo's nude portrays a noble vulnerability.

The Pietà, 1498–99

Marble, 1.74 m x 1.95 m

The word *pietà* comes from the Italian word meaning 'pity.' It is traditionally a sculpture of Mary with the body of Christ taken down from the cross. Michelangelo created a lot of Pietàs, but the most famous resides in Saint Peter's Basilica, Vatican City, Rome.

- Mary is portrayed with the beautiful, sorrowful appearance of a young woman, reflecting her chaste life.

- Her eyes are lowered, her left hand held upturned in a gesture of entreaty to God.

▶ *'The Pietà,' Saint Peter's Basilica, Rome, Michelangelo*

- Michelangelo resolved the difficulty in balancing a fully grown man across the lap of a woman by making Mary's robes fall in full, heavy folds to support the body of Jesus.

- Christ's reclining figure is classically perfect, demonstrating Michelangelo's complete understanding of human anatomy.

- The sash placed across Mary's chest reads: 'Michelangelo Buonarroti, Florentine, made this,' indicating his pride in this work.

The Medici Tombs

The chapel of San Lorenzo in Florence was the private chapel of the Medici family. In 1520 Michelangelo was asked by the Medici pope, Pope Leo X (see p. 149) to create a new **sacristy** attached to it, to accommodate four tombs for the family. The tombs were to house the bodies of Lorenzo de'Medici and his brother Giuliano de'Medici, and their relatives, Lorenzo, Duke of Urbino, and Giuliano, Duke of Nemours. The first two were never completed. The tombs of Lorenzo, Duke of Urbino, and Giuliano, Duke of Nemoirs, incorporate both religious and mythological themes. The tombs face each other in front of a statue of the Madonna and Child.

> dic·tion·ar·y
>
> A **sacristy** is a room attached to a church where sacred vessels such as chalices are kept.

Tomb of Lorenzo de'Medici, Duke of Urbino, 1526–31

Marble, 6.3 m x 4.19 m

- A statue of Lorenzo is seated in an alcove above figures representing Twilight and Dawn, who are reclining on top of the tomb.

- The statue, dressed in Roman body armour, is thoughtful and solemn, his features idealised in the style of classical sculpture.

- Twilight and Dawn represent human mortality. Dawn is portrayed as an awakening female, her head lifted to symbolise the rising of the sun, while the band around her chest and her veil suggest mourning.

- Twilight, on the other side, is shown as an older male, with head downcast to convey sorrow and the setting of the sun.

Tomb of Giuliano de'Medici, Duke of Nemours, 1520–34

Marble, 6.3 m x 4.19 m

- The figure of Giuliano appears much more alert and shows more movement than that of Lorenzo.

- He is shown wearing detailed body armour and has the regular features and elaborately curled hair of classical times.

- He is seated above the reclining figures of Night and Day, who are again portrayed as female and male.

▶ *'Tomb of Lorenzo de'Medici,'*
San Lorenzo Chapel, Florence, Michelangelo

- Night is shown sleeping: symbolic of death, wearing a crown decorated with the moon and stars, her open relaxed pose making her appear vulnerable.

- Day's body is twisted away from the viewer in a defensive manner and is awake: symbolic of life.

▲ 'Tomb of Giuliano de'Medici,' San Lorenzo Chapel, Florence, Michelangelo

▲ 'The Tomb of Julius II,' San Pietro in Vincoli, Rome, Michelangelo

Tomb of Pope Julius II, 1542–59

Originally the design for this tomb was much more elaborate than the finished one, intended to have over 40 statues adorning a three-storied monument. However over the 42-year period in which it took to complete the project, it was simplified down to three marble statues. These depicted the Biblical characters Moses, **Rachel** and **Leah**.

- The charismatic figure of Moses (2.35 m high) combines the features of the Pope and Michelangelo himself, idealised in a classical style.

- His body is strong and muscular and double life-size, with a commanding expression on his rugged face.

- The reason for his huge size is because he was initially intended to be seated on top of a 15.2 m structure.

- The tablets underneath his right arm are the Ten Commandments.

- The other statues are based on Rachel and Leah, who symbolise the contemplative and active life.

biography

RACHEL and **LEAH** were sisters who appeared in the Book of Genesis in the Old Testament. Rachel became engaged to the prophet Jacob who had agreed to work for her father for seven years in return for her hand in marriage. Her father tricked Jacob into marrying Leah instead and the sisters spent the rest of their lives competing with each other for Jacob's affections.

Slave Sculptures

Michelangelo began a series of 12 slave sculptures for the tomb of Pope Julius II. Few were finished, but the incomplete slaves provide an insight to the artist's methods and techniques.

The Dying Slave, 1513–16

- This slave is leaning in a relaxed *contrapposto* pose, his head tilted back, left arm raised above it, while the right hand rests on his chest in a languid manner.

- The slave appears to be in a gentle slumber rather than in the throes of death.

The Awakening Slave 1520–30

- The unfinished state of this sculpture creates a powerful image of a muscular form struggling to free himself from the marble he is encased in.

- The only sculpted details are that of the torso, hips, right leg and part of the right shoulder and arm.

▲ *'The Awakening Slave,' Accademia di Belle Arti Firenze, Florence, Michelangelo*

◀ *'The Dying Slave,' Musée du Louvre, Paris, Michelangelo*

MICHELANGELO'S STONE CARVING TECHNIQUE

1. He made a wax model to help him visualise the finished sculpture.

2. He then drew the outline of the figure on to the front of a block of marble in charcoal.

3. He chiselled from the front of the marble and worked inwards towards the back using chisels of different sizes.

Michelangelo's Architecture

In the Middle Ages, Romanesque and Gothic architecture and sculpture went hand in hand, creating a unified appearance. During the Renaissance, however, architects, sculptors and artists worked independently of each other. When Michelangelo was commissioned to design the San Lorenzo Church sacristy in its entirety, along with the sculpture and tombs, he was delighted. This gave him the opportunity he craved – to create pure harmony of sculpture and architecture which was to pave the way for the Baroque era (1590–1680). Even though the sacristy was unfinished at the time of Michelangelo's death, we still have some idea of his desired result. Michelangelo tied his design in with the old sacristy in the church, designed by Brunelleschi almost a century before (see. p. 162).

San Lorenzo Church Sacristy, c. 1520–50

There are three tiers to the building. The first and second storeys have windows surmounted by classical pediments. On the second storey Michelangelo created an added impression of height by decreasing the width of the windows towards the top.

- The sacristy is a basic square room, with four walls, each with two doors. Only three are functioning doors – the others were added to balance the symmetry of the room.
- Over each doorway there are recessed niches which are set under arches.
- The sacristy walls are made of white marble and decorated with cornices, pilasters and pediments sculpted from a fine, dark-grey sandstone known as *pietra serena* (serene stone).
- The two Medici tombs are positioned at opposite sides of the room. At one of the other walls stand three statues, the largest central statue being the Madonna and Child. The sculptures on either side represent Cosmos and Damian, who were the Medicis' patron saints. These three statues were done by Michelangelo's students.
- These statues, originally intended for the double tomb of Lorenzo the Magnificent and his brother Giuliano, are placed where this tomb was planned to be.
- The other side of the room houses the altar of the little chapel.

The Laurentian Library, c.1524–34

The Medici pope, Clement VII (see p. 195), commissioned Michelangelo to design and build the Laurentian Library. The library is situated above the refectory (eating hall) in the San Lorenzo Basilica, Florence. The addition of the library after the building of the refectory meant that Michelangelo had to be aware of any structural difficulties. The construction had to be light enough to prevent any impact on the building below. He used light materials with relatively thin walls, creating the decorative elements from *pietra serena*.

▼ *The Reading Room' Laurentian Library, Florence, Michelangelo*

Libraries were traditionally positioned on the second level of buildings to avoid damp and flooding. In addition to this, more windows could be set into the walls to let in more light, thus reducing the need of candles and therefore the risk of fire.

The Reading Room

- This wall decoration was made up of flat pilasters between each window, the window frames, the cornices and the frames of the false blank windows. The remaining areas of the walls are painted a plain white **stucco**.

- It is a long, narrow room with a wide aisle running through the centre.

- Along each side run rows of wooden desks, which are tilted to make reading and writing easy. These are intricately carved, as are the panels of the ceiling above.

Entrance to Library

- The entrance to the Laurentian Library was designed at the same time as the reading room, but completed at a later date.

- It is decorated in much the same way as the reading room, with white stucco walls and *pietra serena* pilasters and window frames.

- The large pairs of columns flanking the doorway and niches are actually placed there to support the structure of the building, although they look as if they are merely present as decoration. This is because they seem to blend into the wall.

The Staircase

- The staircase, situated in the vestibule (entrance hall) is unusually constructed. After the first five stairs leading down from the library, it divides into three separate stairways.

- This division flows organically, helped by the curved scrolls connecting them.

- Although the outer stairways are rigidly geometric, the central stairs have curved steps. The last three steps are completely oval in shape.

> **dic·tion·ar·y**
>
> **Stucco** is a cement mixture of water, sand and lime used as a coating for interior walls and decoration.

▶ *The Staircase, Laurentian Library, Florence, Michelangelo*

The Completion of Saint Peter's, Rome

After the death of Bramante (1444–1514), who was the original architect of Saint Peter's Cathedral, Rome, a series of architects were approached to continue his work on the unfinished dome. Michelangelo accepted the commission to complete the dome for no fee, but purely to present himself with a challenge. Although he respected Bramante's original design, he did make some changes to make the design more practical and classical:

▲ *The Dome of Saint Peter's Basilica, the Vatican City, Rome, Michelangelo*

- He created a Greek cross shape (a cross with arms of equal length) intersecting a rigid square as the basis for his design.

- He originally intended to build a high dome, similar to Brunelleschi's dome on Florence Cathedral (see p. 161). He then changed his mind, opting instead for a shallower, semicircular version. He thought that this would balance out the high vertical lines of the architecture below.

Michelangelo died before construction began on the dome and Giacomo della Porta (c. 1533–1602), an architect from Lombardy, took over his work. He decided to revert back to Michelangelo's first design of a high dome as it was less experimental and easier to build.

Michelangelo's Paintings

Although Michelangelo regarded himself above all as a sculptor, it is perhaps surprising to learn that he reached the peak of his achievement on a painting project.

The Sistine Chapel

The Sistine Chapel in **The Vatican City**, Rome, was named after Pope Sixtus IV (1414–84), and was used for meetings of the Papal Council. Although many other artists have decorated this chapel with frescoes, including Botticelli and Ghirlandaio (see p. 173) it is most renowned for the spectacular ceiling frescoes painted by Michelangelo. He did not originally want to accept the commission, given by Pope Julius II, but did so when he was given full control of the subject matter and design of the project. Years later, another pope, Clement VII, commissioned Michelangelo to paint another fresco for the Sistine Chapel - this time on the altar wall.

> dic·tion·ar·y
>
> **The Vatican City**, situated in Rome, is the smallest independent state in the world and is ruled by the Pope of the Catholic Church.

The Ceiling Frescoes, 1508–12

The main narrative of the paintings is the story of Noah and the Creation. It consists of nine pictures set in a strip down the middle of the ceiling, divided by painted pilasters. These pictures are not all of equal size – the smaller ones are framed in a painted marble effect.

▶ *The Ceiling of The Sistine Chapel, Rome, Michelangelo*

- 20 *Ignudi* (seated male nude figures), are situated in the corners of the narrative panels, symbolising the ideal form of beauty.

- Where the vaulted ceiling meets the walls, the frescoes are divided into eight triangular spandrels along the side walls and four larger ones, one in each corner of the chapel. These focus on the ancestors of Christ.

- The 12 panels situated between the spandrels and under the main narrative panels are based on the prophets and sibyls (wise women) from the Old Testament.

- The sibyls are depicted as muscular and powerful, indicating that Michelangelo probably used a male life model for his female figures.

▶ *'Studies for a Flying Angel for the Last Judgement,' Sistine Chapel, Rome, Michelangelo*

▼ *Plan of Sistine ceiling*

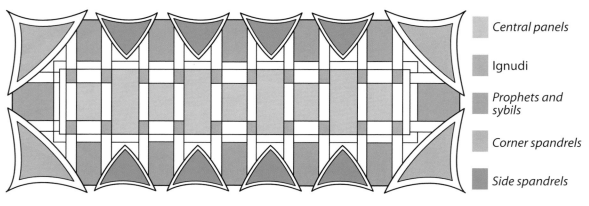

Central panels

Ignudi

Prophets and sybils

Corner spandrels

Side spandrels

The Creation of Adam, 1508–12

This is the most famous and striking of all the main panels in the chapel. The reason for this is because Michelangelo let the figures dominate the picture space, and painted minimal details in the background to draw attention to the subject.

- It is a moment filled with majesty and power, the fingers of God and Adam almost, but not quite touching, create an apprehensive atmosphere.
- The nude figure of Adam is classically perfect.
- The energy of the picture comes from the diagonal movement of God, his flowing robe, and the angels arranged dynamically around his body.

▲ *'The Creation of Adam,' Sistine Chapel, Rome, Michelangelo*

The Fall of Man and the Expulsion from Paradise, 1508–12

This panel tells the story of Adam and Eve's expulsion from the Garden of Eden (Paradise).

▲ *'The Fall of Man,' Rome, Sistine Chapel, Michelangelo*

- On the left we see a standing Adam reaching for the apple from the centrally placed tree. Eve, seated at his feet, turns to receive the forbidden fruit from the serpent, which is shown in human from with a serpent's tail wrapped around the tree trunk.

- Unusually, Satan is depicted here as a female seductress, emphasising the Biblical notion that the Fall of Man was a direct result of a woman's actions.

- On the right, a shamed Adam and Eve are forced to leave Paradise by a scarlet-clad angel. The portrayal of the couple appears to have been inspired by Masaccio's 'Expulsion from Paradise' which Michelangelo would have known well from Florence's Brancacci Chapel (see. p. 169).

- Michelangelo was obviously more interested in portraying the characters and observing their anatomy than the background. This is sparsely represented in strong contrast with other artists' depictions of the garden's beautiful scenery and green foliage.

The Flood, 1508–12

Many art experts believe this to be the first of the nine panels completed by Michelangelo as it is smaller in scale, more detailed and contains smaller characters than the others. It shows various scenes from the Old Testament Bible story of Noah's Ark.

- In the left foreground a group of figures scale a hill to reach safety, carrying children and possessions. A dramatic element is added by the terrified man gripping a tree to anchor himself against the strong gusts of wind.

- In the centre of the panel people battle desperately to maintain their positions on a boat and on the Ark, which can be seen in the background.

- On the right another group are gathered on a rocky outcrop, extending offers of help to other victims of the flood.

▲ 'The Flood,' Sistine Chapel, Rome, Michelangelo

The Last Judgement, c. 1535

This fresco takes up the entire wall behind the altar of the Sistine Chapel and was the first work of this size to be undertaken by a single artist.

- Christ is positioned in the centre of the painting with the Virgin by his side, surrounded by an inner ring of apostles and saints who have already ascended to heaven.

- The figures on the right are of those condemned to hell, while those on the left are destined for Paradise.

- Jesus is depicted here, not as a gentle and forgiving saviour, but a ruthless and determined young man, with a powerfully built, muscular frame.

- The main movement of the fresco, beginning with the figures, reinforces its theme, which appears to be that it is not easy for everyone to enter heaven. (Beginning with the figures on the bottom left rising from the dead.)

- The next part of the sequence is the journey to heaven, followed by the descent to hell on the right.

▶ *'The Last Judgement,' Sistine Chapel, Rome, Michelangelo*

The Pauline Chapel

After Michelangelo finished 'The Last Judgement,' he was approached by Pope Paul III (1468–1549) to paint another series of frescoes in his own private chapel in the Vatican. This chapel, known as the Pauline Chapel, was also where the popes were selected by the cardinals.

The Conversion of Saul, 1542–45

This painting was created to celebrate the life of the Pope's namesake Saint Paul. In the Bible story, the young Saul was travelling on horseback on the road to Damascus when he was converted to Christianity by an apparition from the heavens. From then on he was known as Paul. Michelangelo depicts the saint here as a much older man, likening him to his patron the Pope.

- At the top of the painting we see the sky opening up to reveal Christ and his angels.

- A bolt of light that seems to come from Christ's hand illuminates the scene and leads the eye down to the figure of Saul which lies on the ground.

- Saul is shown shielding his eyes from the light as he gazes upwards.

- This is a dramatic scene, accentuated by the dynamic figure of Christ, the rearing horse and the terrified responses of the people surrounding the saint.

▲ *'The Conversion of Saul,' Pauline Chapel, Vatican City, Michelangelo*

The Crucifixion of Saint Peter, 1546–50

This painting shows Saint Peter about to be crucified. The Bible story states that he was hung upside-down on a cross. Saint Peter was chosen as a fitting subject for this room as he was the first pope appointed by Christ to lead his people.

- The composition of the painting is based around a diagonal bisecting (cutting in half) a circle. The diagonal is created by the wooden cross and body of the saint in the foreground, with the circle constructed by the crowd gathered around him.

- Saint Peter is the figure we are immediately drawn to, as the other characters focus their gazes in his direction and gesture towards him. Michelangelo's use of concentrated light on the figure also helps focus the eye on him.

- This is a powerful painting, dominated by the muscular and fierce depiction of Saint Peter. He twists his body and turns his head to fix us with a fierce glare as if reproaching us for our human sins of violence and lack of belief.

◄ *'The Crucifixion of Saint Peter,' Pauline Chapel, Vatican City, Michelangelo*

RAPHAEL SANZIO			
Date	1483–1520	Patrons	The Medici Family, the Catholic Church
Cities	Urbino, Florence, Rome	Themes	Religious, portraiture
Apprenticeship	Pietro Perugino, Perugia	Style	Serene, tonal
Influences	Da Vinci, Michelangelo		

Raphael, or in Italian, Raffaello, was the most prominent artist of the High Renaissance in Florence. Although he lacked Leonardo da Vinci's genius in the areas of scientific pioneering and Michelangelo's versatility and drive in all forms of art, he was nevertheless regarded as one of the greatest portrait painters of all time. His Madonna paintings are still revered as some of the most beautiful pictures of the Renaissance.

Raphael's Career Development

Raphael was unlike Michelangelo, whose tempestuous nature could alienate patrons, or Leonardo who did not always finish his work. He was much easier to work with, and had a prolific and successful career.

Patronage of Pope Julius II

Like Michelangelo, Raphael developed working relationships with Italy's most influential patrons: the Popes. His first Papal patron, Pope Julius II (see p. 195) commissioned him to undertake the decoration of the Papal rooms in the Vatican. The Pope found Raphael a much easier artist to work with than Michelangelo, who sometimes had to be persuaded into accepting commissions and was a fiery and argumentative character. Raphael, by contrast, was a pleasant, sociable and handsome young man who enjoyed mingling with the aristocracy and was accepted as a distinguished member of the Papal Court. He had many admirers and was courteous and agreeable to all.

Patronage of Pope Leo X

He struck up a close friendship with Julius II's successor, Pope Leo X of the Medici family, (see p. 149). The Pope appreciated Raphael's scholarly mind and classical ideals.

Raphael's Portraits

Raphael was appointed to produce many portraits of the Pope and his wealthy, influential Roman friends. These portraits not only captured the patrons' looks, they also emphasised their intelligence and nobility

Portrait of Pope Leo X With his Cardinals, c. 1518

The subject of the portrait was Pope Leo X with two cardinals in the background. These were his nephews – Luigi de'Rossi and Giulio de'Medici.

- In painting the faces of these men Raphael broke away from Michelangelo's tradition of idealising his subjects and instead invested each one with separate personalities and personal idiosyncrasies.

- No attempt is made to flatter the strong-willed, dominant features of the Pope who is seen with a book open in front of him, reflecting his interest in humanism and the arts.

- Cardinal Giulio, on the left, looks distracted and dreamy whereas Cardinal Luigi seems stern and austere.
- The attention to detail is more exacting than any Florentine artist had ever achieved before. This can be seen in the silver and gold bell on the table, the illuminated manuscript, and the rich textures of the velvets of the robes. A reflection of the window can be seen on the gold knob on the back of the chair.
- The entire composition is tied together by lush harmonies of colours, including oranges, scarlets and crimsons.

◄ *'Portrait of Pope Leo X With his Cardinals,' Uffizi Gallery, Florence, Raphael*

▼ *'Madonna della Sedia,' Palazzo Pitti, Florence, Raphael*

Christian Subjects

Some of Raphael's most famous and best-loved paintings are his pictures of the Madonna and Child. They are celebrated for the artist's skill in using tone and colour to create a three-dimensional quality to his subjects. People also marvel at their prevailing atmosphere of serene calm and tranquillity.

Madonna Della Sedia (Madonna of the Chair), 1514–15

This is probably the most beloved of Raphael's Madonnas, due to the intimacy of the figures' poses and the gentle gaze of the Madonna involving the viewer in this touching scene.

- The figures occupy most of the picture space, yet do not seem cramped within the circular composition (known as a *tondo*). This is because their forms are presented in profile.

- The circular composition is strengthened further by the curves of the figures' arms in the middle of the painting.

- Raphael has constructed his picture space around the central figure of Jesus, who, if he was standing, would be the exact height of the circle.

- The attention to detail is remarkable, particularly on Mary's garments. The rich red and orange hues contrast beautifully with the green of her shawl.

Mythological Subjects

Although Raphael painted mostly religious subjects, he also portrayed mythological scenes from ancient Greek legends. These paintings celebrated the beauty of the human form in harmony with nature and established him not only as a gifted painter but a learned humanist intellectual as well.

The Triumph of Galatea, c. 1512

In creating this painting Raphael worked from a number of sources:

Artistic Influences

- Roman relief carving
- Sienese marine sarcophagi
- 'The Battle of The Sea Gods' by Andrea Mantegna
- Botticelli's 'Birth of Venus'
- Michelangelo's *contrapposto* technique.

Literary Influences

- A poem on the subject by Poliziano.

Raphael painted this fresco for the Villa Farnesina in Rome. It shows a character from Greek Mythology, Galatea, being deified.

- Galatea, in the centre of the picture, is being pulled along in a shell chariot by fierce-looking dolphins.

- To keep her balance on the shell, her body is twisted diagonally, creating a dynamic and flowing composition.

- Her head is turned to balance this diagonal thrust.

- To the left a triton (half man and half fish) is grasping a sea nymph.

- Behind him another triton plays a shell like a trumpet.

▲ *'The Triumph of Galatea,' Villa Farnesina, Rome, Raphael*

Raphael chose the subject for this painting from a poem by the Florentine poet Angelo Poliziano (1454–94) which had also helped to inspire Botticelli's 'Birth of Venus' (see p. 174).

'The School
of Athens,'
Vatican
Palace, Ror
Raphael

The School of Athens, 1509–11

This painting portrays a gathering of the foremost philosophers and masters of natural science. They are gathered against an imaginary architectural background thought to be the Basilica of Constantine in the Roman Forum. It incorporates Raphael's contemporaries, teachers and fellow artists.

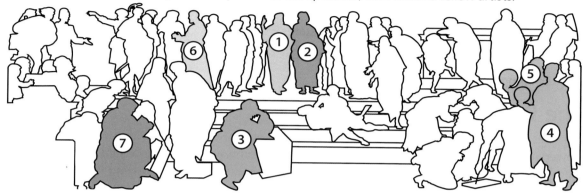

▲ *Outline diagram of 'The School of Athens'*

1 **Plato**, a Greek philosopher (c. 428–c. 348 B.C.). This is the figure in the centre pointing heavenward. It is thought to be modelled on Leonardo da Vinci.

2 **Aristotle**, Greek philosopher and student of Plato (384–322 B.C.). He is to the right of Plato and is pointing towards the earth.

3 **Heraclitus**, a Greek philosopher (c. 535–c. 475 B.C.). Michelangelo is the model for the figure of Heraclitus, shown looking melancholy and thoughtful on the steps in the foreground.

4 **Ptolemy**, a Greek mathematician, geographer, and astronomer (c. 83 B.C.–161 A.D.). This is one of the grouped figures on the right of the foreground, seen with a globe in his hand.

5 **Zoroaster**, a religious reformer from Iran (628–551 B.C.). He is shown beside Ptolemy holding a star-filled globe indicating the universe. Raphael is the young man having a discussion with them; the other man is considered to be Sodoma (1477–1549), an Italian artist who was a contemporary of Raphael.

6 **Socrates**, a Greek philosopher (c. 469–399). He is depicted explaining his theories to the group in the top-left corner.

7 **Pythagoras**, a Greek mathematician (c. 580–500 B.C.). He is shown as a seated figure in the foreground to the left.

The High Renaissance Revision Questions

1 Discuss the developments in painting techniques and the effect of tone by Leonardo da Vinci in his painting 'Mona Lisa.'

2 Describe 'The Last Supper' by Leonardo da Vinci, with reference to perspective, composition, and figure painting. Include a diagram of the painting in your answer.

3 Describe the content and layout of the Sistine Chapel ceiling painted by Michelangelo. Discuss one section of the ceiling in detail.

4 Discuss the importance of portraiture in Renaissance art by referring to the works of Raphael.

5 Discuss a sculpture by Michelangelo with reference to his carving techniques, *contrapposto*, and the influence of classical art.

6 Compare and contrast the tomb of Pope Julius II with the Medici tombs.

The Renaissance in Venice

Although influenced by the Florentine masters and their advances in art, the Renaissance in Venice developed in different ways. This may be due to a number of reasons:

1 Rivalry between the different Italian city-states

2 The increasing influence of Flemish techniques

3 Differing interests in theme.

The Italian States

Italy was a very influential and rich country at the time of the Renaissance, with the balance of power and wealth lying in the north. The Papal state in Rome, as well as Venice, Florence and Genoa were the most densely populated and successful states as a result of their thriving trade links and manufacturing. This included textile industries, glass, printing, mining and metalwork. Their inhabitants were filled with civic pride and attached great importance to their states' identity and power. During the fifteenth century Italy's prosperity waned, with only the Papal state and Venice remaining independent. The other states succumbed to pressure from France and Spain and Venice had to defend itself continually from the onslaughts of the Turkish Empire.

▼ *View from Campanile di San Marco, Venice*

Themes

The subjects of Venetian painting, although dealing with the same forms of portraiture and historical and mythological painting as Florentine art, were treated in a decidedly different way.

FLORENCE AND ROME	VENICE
Artists in Florence and Rome focused on tales of heroic endeavours. They depicted great champions in intellectual ways and glorified classical structures and ideals.	The Venetian artists were more concerned with exploring peoples' relationship with nature and the celebration of the beauty of youth. The mythological themes consisted less of serious and 'worthy' subject matter and concentrated more on revelry and dreamlike images of pastoral pleasure. Venetians were intrigued by the idea of Arcadia which was a mythical paradise where animals and nature lived together in perfect harmony.
The Florentines, were more concerned with masculine than feminine characteristics.	Venetians were interested in portraying and celebrating the female form. Large-scale female nudes were frequently the focus of Venetian paintings.

Style

Unlike the Florentine artists who were absorbed with creating realistic yet idealised form and volume, the Venetians used colour to a much greater extent to create atmosphere and tone. Their work is vibrant and animated, the colours blending harmoniously to complement their compositions. Their developments in colour were probably a direct result of Venice's close connection with Flemish art (see p. 228), and the advances made in oil painting. Oil paint was so much easier to use and vivid in colour that it is no wonder that the new medium inspired artists to experiment with it to create innovative and exciting effects. Venetian artists also explored light and shade to a much greater degree than their contemporaries in Italy. Incandescent (brightly glowing) rays of brilliant light illuminated the scenes and bathed the figures in the paintings with a delicate glow.

GIOVANNI BELLINI			
Date	c. 1430–1516	Patrons	The state of Venice
City	Venice	Themes	Portraiture, religious, Madonnas
Apprenticeship	Jacopo Bellini	Style	Naturalistic, serene
Influences	Andrea Mantegna, Jacopo Bellini		

Giovanni Bellini was the son of the great Venetian master Jacopo Bellini (c. 1396–c. 1470) and brother of fellow artist Gentile Bellini (c. 1429–1507).

Bellini's Career Development

The two brothers worked in their father's workshop until his death, although there is evidence that they also accepted outside commissions. Their father was to have a marked influence on Giovanni's work as did his contemporary Mantegna (see p. 171) who was married to his sister. He was a distinguished teacher in his own right, teaching many successful painters, such as Titian (see p. 219) Giorgione (see p. 217) and Sebastiano del Piombo (c. 1485–1547), and was thus responsible for the emergence and growth of the Venetian style during the Renaissance. He took over his brother Gentile's work in the *Doge's* Palace (see p. 216) in 1479. As a result of his work there, he was appointed Chief Painter to the State of Venice, a position which he retained until his death.

Style and Techniques

Bellini made revolutionary advances in oil painting, which was to become the medium of choice for Venetian artists to follow. He was not only an accomplished religious painter but also an established portrait painter and master of mythological and historical paintings. His portrait style derived inspiration from the Flemish masters, presenting the viewer with a three-quarter view of the sitter, set against the backdrop of a natural landscape. The portraits are realistic and unidealised, celebrating the true nature of the patron. In his later career, he painted large mythological paintings such as 'The Feast of the Gods,' which demonstrate his ability to adapt his style to suit these themes.

The *Doge* Leonardo Loredan, c. 1501

The role of the *Doge* in Venetian society was a very influential one. He was elected as the head of the aristocrats who ruled the state of Venice and was considered to be both a political and spiritual leader. This portrait of the *Doge* Leonardo Loredan emphasises both of these aspects of his position as well as his character as a man.

- Portraits of the nobility in Venice traditionally portrayed the sitter in profile or three-quarter view. This painting depicts the *Doge* from an almost frontal viewpoint, which was more commonly used to portray religious and revered figures.

- His traditional costume is also more reminiscent of holy leaders. These factors emphasise his religious power.

- Bellini creates a sense of movement in the composition by ensuring that the *Doge* is not located in the exact centre of the painting and shifting his body to a slight angle from the viewer.

- The artist uses other subtle means to convey movement in the portrait. Although the face is peaceful and still, the buttons on his robe are asymmetrical in both size and position. The strings of his hat sway as they fall to his shoulders.

- He uses small dabs of colour to indicate the richness of the gold details in the *Doge's* clothing and cap and also the fabric of the costume.

- Bellini treats the face in quite a different manner than he does the body. He uses gradual tonal glazes to create soft undefined contours. The reason he did this was because he wanted the viewer to gaze closely at the face, subconsciously completing and defining the image with their eyes. He had seen and was impressed by Leonardo's 'Mona Lisa' (see p. 191). The blurred edges of the features and the indirect gaze pay homage to this and also give the *Doge* an enigmatic expression.

◀ *'The* Doge *Leonardo Loredan,' National Gallery, London, Bellini*

The Baptism of Christ

This painting explores a very popular Renaissance subject matter: Christ being baptised by John the Baptist.

- The painting is arch-shaped and is divided into four sections. Christ is in the lower middle, Saint John is at a higher level on the right, Christ's followers are to the left and God is in the top section.

- In the background are rolling hills receding into the distance. The diagonal sloping hills on the left draw the eye towards Christ's head.

- There is a quiet and mystical elegance to this painting. Bellini uses aerial perspective in the fading of his colours in the background.

- Our attention is immediately drawn to the figure of Christ as all of the characters in the picture are looking in his direction and because of his central location.

- Even with the dramatic vision of God giving Christ his blessing, there is a sense of stillness and peace about the painting, due to the serene and graceful stances of the figures.

▲ 'The Baptism of Christ,' Church of Santa Corona, Venice, Bellini

GIORGIONE			
Date	c. 1476–1510	Patrons	Private patrons
City	Venice	Themes	Mythological subjects, the harmony between man and nature
Apprenticeship	Giovanni Bellini		
Influences	Titian, Sebastiano del Piombo	Style	Restful, idyllic

Born Giorgio Barbarelli da Castelfranco, this painter remains somewhat of a mystery in Renaissance painting. This is because only a few of his paintings are known for certain to be his work alone. Several of his contemporary artists at the time such as Titian (see p. 219) and Sebastiano del Piombo (see p. 215) are said to have finished some of his paintings. Titian is generally accredited with a lot of artistic innovations in his career, but because we are unsure at what stage he took over some of Giorgione's paintings, we are therefore unsure who was the initial innovator. Although controversy surrounds his career as a result of our lack of absolute knowledge about his paintings, we do know that he was one of the first Renaissance artists to paint small-scale portraits and pictures for wealthy Venetian patrons.

The Tempest, c. 1508

This is one of the few paintings that historians are absolutely positive was painted in its entirety by Giorgione. 'The Tempest' gives us a very good example of how symbolic significance can be lost or misconstrued through time. The subject matter is completely unknown and only conjectures can be made as to what the painting really means. It is not even sure whether the painting is intended to be religious or mythological. Speculations have included the finding of Moses, the gods Mercury and Isis, and the flight by the Virgin and Saint Joseph into Egypt. Examinations made on the painting tell us that another nude female figure was originally painted where the man now stands, which further confuses the speculators. All that we can be sure of is what we see: a mother and child, a soldier, and a rocky landscape with a city in the background.

▲ *'The Tempest,' Gallerie dell' accademia, Venice, Giorgione*

- The mother and child sit in the right foreground while the soldier stands guard in the left. You can see a city behind the ruins where they shelter, while a storm brews overhead.
- It is thought that possibly Giorgione had no real intention to portray a real or mythological event in this painting because of the way in which he deals with the overall image. Perhaps he merely wished to let his imagination take flight in this dramatic scene.
- The people shown in the painting are not depicted as the focal point but simply as elements within the general composition.
- The landscape, sky and nature are given equal dominance by the artist's handling of the details which make up the painting.
- The power and strength of nature are shown by the lightning which illuminates the scene and the ruins in the foreground, overgrown by vegetation. This could symbolise the enduring power of nature as opposed to the transient nature of humans and their creations.

The Sleeping Venus, c. 1510

There is still controversy about whether Giorgione was the only painter involved in the production of this painting. For years it was thought that this was a painting by Titian but it is now generally considered that Giorgione began the painting and after his death Titian completed it.

- The large central figure represents Venus the goddess of love, sleeping peacefully in a beautiful pastoral setting.
- It is thought that Giorgione had intended simply to show the harmonious relationship between the nude figure and the landscape.

* The cupid and the drapery she reclines on are thought to have been added later by Titian.

* These embellishments are thought by some critics to detract from the idyllic dreamlike effect created by Giorgione.

▲ *'The Sleeping Venus,' Gemäldegalerie Alte Meister, Dresden, Giorgione*

TITIAN (TIZIANO VECELLI)				
Date	c. 1487–1576	**Patrons**	Charles V and Philip II of Spain, Pope Paul III, Alfonso d'Este	
Cities	Venice, Padua			
Apprenticeship	Giovanni and Gentile Bellini	**Themes**	Mythology, religious, portraiture	
Influences	Giorgione, Michelangelo	**Style**	Colourful, dramatic, meticulous	

Titian is considered by many to be the father of modern art as he developed his own distinctive style throughout his long career. After the deaths of Giorgione and Bellini, he became the most popular artist working in Venice and received the honour of becoming official Painter to the Republic of Venice in 1516.

Titian's Career Development

His painting 'The Assumption of the Virgin' for the Frari Church in Venice established Titian as the leader of the High Renaissance there. A further distinction to his career happened in 1532 on meeting the emperor Charles V of Spain (1500–58) who was so impressed by his work that he subsequently appointed him as his court painter. His close friendship with the emperor was very different from the usual artist and patron relationship and continued until Charles V's abdication, after which Titian continued to work for his successor Philip II (1527–98). Titian employed a workshop of painters to aid him, one of whom was his own son Orazio.

Style and Techniques

Titian's painting style continued to develop and change throughout his life. His early works show a confident and often flamboyant style, richly coloured with free-flowing movement. The figures within his compositions were well-defined and anatomically correct. During the 1540s a visit to Rome opened his eyes to other Renaissance ideas and inspirations such as classical sculpture and Michelangelo's work in particular. He developed his own style of realism, and used it in a realistically honest portrait of Pope Paul III (1468–1549).

Royal Patronage

His work for the emperor Charles V of Spain mainly took the form of portraiture. The theme of his work changed under the patronage of Philip II, who commissioned mythological subject matter.

Titian's Late Style

The most influential and exciting work came late in Titian's career, when he developed a much more fluid and free style of painting. This was due to the alteration in his techniques:

▲ *Titian painted this self-portrait in 1567, relatively late in life. It is in the Museo del Prado, Madrid.*

1 He began his painting by laying down an undercoat of Venetian red and white lead for mid-tones. Then he used black, red and yellow to build up the tones.

2 After this he would put the painting aside, ignore it for months and then come back to it with fresh eyes.

3 He then began to paint, deliberately not focusing on one section at a time as he wanted all parts of the painting to develop simultaneously.

4 He would repeat this process until he was finally satisfied that it was completed to perfection.

5 He often worked on more than one painting at a time. This method was later to become part of the Impressionist technique, Monet's in particular (see p. 288).

Titian's way of painting was innovative and revolutionary in his time. He lost his interest in defining precise contours and outlines and instead became interested in defining the body by creating shapes in colour, light and shade. His brushstrokes were more fluid and uninhibited and as he grew older he started to use his fingers as brushes more and more. He would dab blobs of colour onto the canvas to highlight or accentuate details and also blend light into dark by blending and smoothing the paint with his fingers.

Bacchus and Ariadne, 1522–23

This is one of the most famous works created in Titian's early style. The theme is derived from ancient mythology and was most likely a subject commissioned by his patron Alfonso d'Este (1486–1534) for his *Camerino d'Albastro* (alabaster chamber).

◆ The picture shows Ariadne, the daughter of King Minos, who had been left by her lover, Theseus on the island of Naxos. The moment captured by Titian portrays the wine god Bacchus coming to her aid, followed by his servants displaying items won from his adventures.

◆ Ariadne is shocked by his sudden appearance and the drama of the event is demonstrated by use of the dynamic movement of the figures and also by the diagonal composition.

◆ It is thought that the painter used the figures of the famous Greek sculpture '**The Laocoon**' as a source for the dark-bearded figure on the right.

- The peaceful idyllic and pastoral setting of the island is shaken by the arrival of Bacchus and his followers.

- Titian's portrayal of Bacchus's energetic figure, full of gestures and expression, make this an exciting and stimulating composition.

- His glowing colours and radiant light infuse the entire work with drama.

Did you know?

'**The Laocoon**' (c. 42–20 B.C.) is an ancient Greek statue thought to have been created by three sculptors, Agesander, Polydorus and Athenodorus, from the Greek island of Rhodes. The sculpture includes the central figure of Laocoon, a priest from Troy, flanked by his two sons Antiphantes and Thymbraeus. They are shown being attacked by serpents. It is now housed in the Belvedere Garden in the Vatican Museum, Rome.

▲ 'Bacchus and Ariadne,' National Gallery, London, Titian

▼ 'The Pietà,' Gallerie dell' accademia, Venice, Titian

The Pietà, 1576

This is Titian's last masterpiece and is a large-scale canvas intended for the altar in the Capella del Cristo (a small chapel in Venice). It was left uncompleted at his death and was finished by painter Palma Giovane (c.1548–1628). Palma made an inscription which claimed that he completed it with respect and dedicated it to God.

- The painting, like other Pietàs, portrays Mary holding the dead Christ in her arms after he has been taken down from the cross.

- Titian painted this as a votive offering to help shield himself and his son from the **plague**. He uses symbolism to give depth and meaning to his work.

- The two statues on either side of the Virgin and Christ are the prophet Moses and a prophetic female figure called a sibyl. The figure of Moses is thought to represent the Old Testament while the sibyl is deemed to signify a foreknowledge of Christ's death and resurrection.

- Beside the grieving Virgin are Saint Mary Magdalen and a man who closely resembles Titian himself. The man is considered to represent either **Joseph of Arimathea** or **Saint Jerome**.

biography

JOSEPH OF ARIMATHEA was a wealthy man who gave up his tomb to place the body of Christ in it after the Crucifixion . ▶

SAINT JEROME (331–420) was a theologian and translator of the Bible from Hebrew to Latin. He is the patron saint of librarians.

- The plinths supporting the two statues are shaped like lions' heads and could indicate the Bible scribe Saint Mark or Titian's own family.

- This is a very different type of painting from 'Bacchus and Ariadne,' not simply because it has a religious instead of a mythological theme. It is executed in Titian's late style, with thickly applied paint strokes smoothed by his fingertips.

- The colour is rich and vibrant and the outlines of the figures and details appear obscured. All of this serves to create a beautifully tragic and moving work.

Did you know?

The bubonic plague, a fatal and contagious illness, swept through Venice during the 1500s. Titian died from the plague when he was 88, and was the only Venetian plague victim to receive a church burial.

JACOPO TINTORETTO

Date	1518–94	**Patrons**	The state of Venice, the Scuola di San Rocco
City	Venice		
Influences	Titian	**Themes**	Religious
Apprenticeship	Titian, Andrea Schiavone (c. 1510–63), Paris Bordone (1495–1570)	**Style**	Vibrant colour and light, mystical and visionary

Tintoretto was the last of the great Venetian Renaissance artists. His early works are unknown but he soon made his stamp in Venice with his painting 'Saint Mark Rescuing a Slave' for the *Scuola di San Marco* in 1548. His work is characterised by his complex and effective compositions which draw the eye all around the work through the use of dynamic groups of figures and contrasts of light and dark. He was influenced by Titian, and had a large workshop of artists to help him complete commissions, among them his own two sons and one daughter.

▼ *'The Crucifixion,' Scuola Grande di San Rocco, Venice, Tintoretto*

The San Rocco Cycle

biography

SAINT ROCCO was born in France and came to Rome during a time of plague and disease. He cured many illnesses and is now known as the partron saint of pestilence.

Tintoretto did the famous San Rocco cycle of paintings as a result of winning a competition. The prize was to be allowed to decorate the rooms of the *Scuola Grande di San Rocco* in Venice. All of the painters who entered the competition were asked to show a drawing of **Saint Rocco** surrounded by angels which was intended to decorate a ceiling in the building. Tintoretto employed the help of a caretaker to attach his own finished painting to the ceiling during the night before the other artists' work could be seen. The ploy worked and three weeks later, much to the alleged frustration of his fellow artists such as Titian and Paolo Veronese (1528–88), he was commissioned to paint all of the paintings required to decorate the interior.

▲ *Façade of the Scuola Grande di San Rocco, Venice*

- The *Sala Grande* and the *Sala dell'Albergo* are the two rooms famous for the large canvases and ceiling paintings created by Tintoretto. Apart from the sheer scale of the work, Tintoretto's vivid imagination and exquisite use of light all make these dramatic and visionary masterpieces.

- In the *Sala Grande* are paintings commemorating the life of Christ while on the ceiling are scenes taken from the Old Testament.

- An entire series of paintings based on the Passion of Christ was designed for the *Sala dell'Albergo* of which the picture 'The Crucifixion' is the most celebrated.

The Crucifixion, 1568

This painting depicts the Crucifixion of Christ on the cross on the hill of Calvary. The painting has the impression of a moment caught in time as a result of the great movement portrayed by the characters and also by Tintoretto's wonderful use of light.

- This is a large-scale painting, covering the entire back wall of a large room. The impressiveness of the painting is not simply due to its size but also to its dramatic composition.

- Christ's cross is shown in the exact centre, with the figure of Jesus at the very top of the picture. On either side are the crosses of the two thieves which are portrayed diagonally, giving the painting an illusion of movement.

- The composition is divided into sections, showing different groups of people. On each side of the foreground are horsemen and soldiers. Huddled at the foot of the cross are the mourners and in the background are further groups of spectators.

- The hills behind the scene slope down towards the centre of the painting bringing the focus of the viewer to the image of Christ on the cross.

- Tintoretto creates an exciting and stirring atmosphere by the bright light surrounding the torso of Christ. It falls dramatically over the scene, casting the mourners and spectators into sharp relief against the background.

- The deep contrasts in light and dark and vibrant colour all serve to heighten the drama of the work as do the seemingly erratic movements and positions of the figures within their groups.

ANDREA PALLADIO

Date	1508–80	**Patrons**	Count Gian Giorgio Trissino (1478–1550)
City	Venice		Daniele Barbaro
Apprenticeship	Bartolomeo Cavazza, a stonemason	**Style**	Classical
Influences	Ancient Roman architecture		

Andrea Palladio was originally trained as a stonemason and began his career as an architect in 1538. He travelled to Rome to learn about classical architecture and this was to influence his work deeply in the future. He was also a very successful author – his book on the principles of architecture reached as far as England and North America in its appeal.

Palladio is most famous for the many villas he designed for the Venetian aristocracy on their country estates. A desire for the quiet contemplative life surrounded by nature had permeated into the cultural and social lives of the nobility, but the wish for a country retreat was motivated by other reasons. As business declined in the city, landowners were gradually forced to rely on their country properties for sustenance, and wished to live in surroundings that suited their station in life.

The Villa Rotunda, c. 1566–70

Palladio designed the Rotunda for Paolo Almerico, a clergyman who had retired and wished to use the villa for entertaining his guests. It is located outside Florence on top of a hill.

- The Villa Rotunda is unusual among Palladio's buildings in that it does not possess secondary functional buildings (such as farm buildings) generally associated with the style. This was because the building was designed as simply a place where people could gather to appreciate the nature which surrounded them.

- The layout is a basic square consisting of four equally sized façades with porches projecting out from each. The centre of the building is the rotunda where Almerico held his social events. Guests were able to choose their views from the four sides of the building.

- The cupola (dome) is associated with religious buildings which could have influenced Palladio in designing this building for a clergyman.

- The four façades of the building are identical to each other and are based on ancient Greek and Roman architecture.

▼ *The Villa Rotunda, Florence, Palladio*

dic·tion·ar·y

The Pantheon, dating from 125, was originally built as a temple of the Roman gods and is now used as a Catholic church. It is the oldest domed building standing in Rome. The term 'pantheon' means a burial place for distinguished people.

- The porches, complete with strong elegant columns and pediments situated in front of a dome, are similar to those of the **Pantheon** in Rome.

The Villa Barbaro, 1557–58

The Villa Barbaro was commissioned by Daniele Barbaro (1514–70), who was a close friend of the architect.

- This is a more typical example of Palladio's work, incorporating secondary buildings with the main personal villa of the patron.

- He has combined an opulent mansion with a fully functioning farmhouse. Palladio took his inspiration from descriptions of classical architecture, although he integrated this with more recent Renaissance developments.

- The building in the middle is the residence of the patron and the two perpendicular wings extending from it house the farming offices and servants' quarters.

▼ *Nymphaeum Statue, Villa Barbaro, Maser, Italy, Palladio*   ▲ *Villa Barbaro, Maser, Italy, Palladio*

The Nymphaeum

This arching, curved wall is situated at the back of the house and was heavily influenced by classical Roman villa design. The wall is inlaid with sculptures depicting spirits of the woods (nymphs). It is not known exactly who is fully responsible for the decoration, as critics are divided in opinion. Some attribute it to Barbaro's brother Marcantonio.

San Giorgio Maggiore, 1565

The church of San Giorgio Maggiore is situated across the canal from the famous Piazza San Marco in Venice.

- The façade for the church is unusual: it combines two façades into one.

- A long, narrow vertical porch is formed by four pillars set on thick rectangular bases and a triangular pediment surmounted by three statues.

- This porch appears to be superimposed over another, lower and wider façade which has a horizontal rectangular shape for a base and a squatter pediment above it.

- A circular tympanum is situated over the centrally placed portal.

- In between each pair of columns is an arched niche which houses a statue.

- Directly above these, on the first floor, are stone carvings and a slab holding an inscription is placed centrally above the tympanum.

- At the ends of the smaller façade are two more niches, one on either side, which hold two more statues. These niches are rectangular and have small columns at the sides and a pediment on top.

Interior

- The domed roof, with windows set into the drum, provides the church with a light and airy atmosphere.

- It has a high vaulted ceiling and combines the essential elements of Renaissance architecture complete with columns, entablatures, carved capitals and classical pediments.

- It is built in the Latin cross design (which echoes the shape of a Christian cross). The western nave of the church is longer than the transepts and apse.

▲ *San Giorgio Maggiore, Venice, Palladio*

▲ *The Interior of San Giorgio Maggiore, Venice, Palladio*

The Renaissance in Venice Revision Questions

1 Describe the work of Giovanni Bellini, referring to both his portraits and his religious work.

2 Compare and contrast the Renaissance in Venice with the Renaissance in Florence. Refer to style, subject matter and use of colour in your answer.

3 Discuss the development of Titian's techniques and style through his career with particular reference to two of his works.

4 Describe the San Rocco cycle by Tintoretto giving detailed analysis of one of the paintings.

5 Describe a building by Palladio under the headings function, layout and style.

The Northern Renaissance

The term Northern Renaissance is used to describe the flourishing of the Renaissance outside Italy and particularly in Northern Europe. This began to happen during the middle of the fifteenth century. It first took roots in France where King Francis I, Leonardo da Vinci's last patron, bought Italian paintings and literature. The ideas were seen here and quickly spread across northern Europe, influencing artists including those from the Netherlands and Germany. Northern Renaissance art was influenced by the Protestant Reformation. This was a movement led by German preacher Martin Luther (1483–1546). He protested against a number of abuses practised by the Roman Catholic Church. He and his followers formed a new church that allowed its priests to marry. Luther also translated the Bible into German. Protestantism swept through Northen Europe, influencing artists' subject matter and approach to their work.

> **Did you know?**
>
> During the Renaissance, the area known as Flanders consisted of regions of three present-day countries: Belgium, France and the Netherlands. The term 'Flemish' which derives from Flanders is often used to describe the art and artists of the Northern Renaissance.

> dic·tion·ar·y
>
> **Latin** was spoken in ancient Rome and was spread throughout Europe by the conquering Romans. It fell out of spoken use but was still used internationally as the language for religion, science and education during the Renaissance and after.

▶ *Johannes Gutenberg*

Printing Press

The printing press was invented in around 1437 by Johannes Gutenberg (c. 1400–68) in Germany. This helped to speed up the progress of Renaissance ideas across the continent as books on scientific and artistic research were now more widely available. This helped particularly as the northern countries used their own languages instead of **Latin**, which made them more widely comprehensible.

Differences Between Northern and Italian Styles

The style of the Northern Renaissance artists was different from that of their contemporary Italian painters. This was due to the lingering International Gothic Style (see p. 155) which was still very popular and also the religious upheaval brought about by the Protestant Reformation. Although the Italians painted religious subjects, they were obsessed with portraying humanity in a realistic way and also looked to ancient Rome as their inspiration. Northern painting was more concerned with spirituality and symbolism.

JAN VAN EYCK			
Date	c. 1390–1441	**Patrons**	Duke Philip the Good of Burgundy
Cities	Maaseyck, Lille, Bruges, The Hague, Ghent	**Themes**	Religious, portraiture
Apprenticeship	Unknown	**Style**	Innovative, technical, realistic
Influences	Hubert Van Eyck		

The Flemish painter Jan Van Eyck started his career in the Hague, Netherlands, in the court of John of Bavaria (1374–1425). He then moved to the court of Duke Philip of Burgundy (1396–1467). He spent the rest of his life living in Bruges, Belgium, in service to the Duke who valued him both as an artist and as a friend. He also accepted commissions from other clients during this time. Van Eyck has often been credited with the invention of oil painting, and while this is not strictly true, he did develop this medium so it became more widely used. He covered the panel with gesso, and then applied opaque paint initially, later adding layer upon layer of fine, translucent coloured glazes to achieve a glowing, richly hued effect.

Portraiture

Van Eyck broke with the exaggerated Gothic Style of portraiture, to create more realistic and precise likenesses of his subjects. He adopted the three-quarter view of the sitter, turning their face toward the light source to model their features naturally in light and shadow. The subjects also have a very direct gaze, fixing the viewer with an unwavering steady look.

The Ghent Altarpiece, 1432

This is one of the first major works accredited to the Dutch master, although his brother Hubert's name is also connected with it. An inscription claims that Hubert Van Eyck began the altarpiece and Jan Van Eyck completed it. Exactly what parts of the work belong solely to Jan is not known – one school of thought maintains that Hubert created the framework for the panels which has since been lost, and Jan was the painter. It was commissioned by a rich merchant banker for his chapel in the Saint Bavo Cathedral in Ghent, Belgium. It is now situated in the main church. This type of many-panelled altarpiece, called a polyptych, was very common in Dutch art and represented the artists' love of concealing hidden meanings behind innocent objects.

▼ *'The Ghent Altarpiece,' Saint Bavo Cathedral, Ghent, Hubert and Jan Van Eyck*

Overall there are 24 painted panels in the altarpiece, 12 making up the outer part and the other 12 the inner part. The panels are hinged and can be closed to create the outer scenes. The closed view portrays the Annunciation on the top layer, with portraits of the donor and his wife flanking two saints, Saint John the Baptist, and Saint John the Gospel scribe. Each panel is painted with great precision and attention to detail. The richness of the fabrics, the burnished sheen of precious metals, the lush pastoral background and the delicacy of the features are all painted with equal care and reverence.

Top Layer: God the Father

God the Father is shown in the central panel wearing a red robe, with a crown on his head which represents the Roman popes and a crown at his feet, symbolising the world.

- He is seated on a throne which depicts motifs of pelicans. The pelican was a symbol of self sacrifice and love, as it was believed that it would shed its own blood to feed its chicks.

- The inscription on the throne proclaims God's generosity and power. The inscription under the lower crown reinforces this message of a forgiving father and loving master.

- In the panel to the left of God is Mary, wearing a deep blue robe and the crown of heaven, symbolised by the twelve stars adorning it. An inscription over her head celebrates her sanctity and virtue.

- John the Baptist is depicted in the panel to the right of God. His inscription honours his role as the prophet who foretold the coming of Christ.

- In the panel on the second left, angels sing about the glory of God.

- Angels appear again beside Saint Cecilia (patron saint of music and musicians) in the foreground of the second-right panel playing an organ.

- A naked Adam is depicted in the panel on the outer left as the origin of the human race.

- On the outer right panel, Eve looks wistfully towards the central panels.

Lower Layer: The Adoration of The Lamb

This is the central panel of the lower part of the altarpiece and the most famous. In the middle of the picture there is a lamb standing on an altar, representing Jesus, the sacrifice made by God to save sinners.

- Blood runs from the lamb's heart into a chalice. In the middle foreground stands the well containing the water of life. The dove, a symbol of baptism, shines radiantly over the altar.

- The four New Testament scribes, Matthew, Mark, Luke and John are shown in the left foreground kneeling with their Gospels open in front of them. Behind them are prophets.

- In the left background are the Holy Confessors, Christians who refused to deny their faith even if they were tortured.

- In the right foreground the Twelve Apostles are accompanied by martyrs who can be spotted by their red robes.

- The Holy Virgins, female saints and martyrs, are in the right background.

The panels flanking the main central panel depict personifications of the four Christian virtues: fortitude, prudence, justice and temperance.

- The knights on horseback shown in the near-left panel personify the virtue fortitude (courage and bravery).

- Judges shown in the outer left panel represent justice (fairness).
- The pilgrims in the near right panel signify prudence (good judgement).
- The hermits in the outer right panel stand for temperance (moderation).

The Arnolfini Wedding, 1434

Giovanni Arnolfini, a merchant from Lucca, Italy, and his wife Giovanna Cenami commissioned this painting to celebrate their wedding. There are various symbolic references in the picture.

SYMBOL	MEANING
Griffon terrier	Fidelity
Lit candle	Presence of God
Clogs	Indicate event is taking place on holy ground.
Beam of light	The Incarnation
Joined hands	Unity
Bed	Consummation of marriage
Bedpost detail	Saint Margaret, patron of childbirth

Clothing

The cherry tree in fruit outside the window indicates that it is summer. However, husband and wife are both heavily dressed in garments not only trimmed, but lined, with fur.

Mirror

The mirror in the background shows extraordinary detail, including the reflection of the window , the subjects and also that of the painter. Above the mirror is an inscription meaning 'Van Eyck was here.' The frame is made up of scenes from the Crucifixion.

▶ *The Arnolfini Wedding,' National Gallery, London, Jan Van Eyck*

The Madonna of Chancellor Rolin, c. 1435

Nicolas Rolin (chancellor of the Duchy of Burgundy) commissioned this painting for his parish church, Notre-Dame-du-Chastel in Autun, France. It can now be seen in the Louvre, Paris. It shows Rolin praying in front of the Madonna and Child, demonstrating his piety.

- Van Eyck developed a new compositional style, incorporating the figures shown high in the foreground above a spreading landscape depicted much lower in the background. This became known as a plateau-type composition, and allowed the artist to explore the relationship between foreground interiors and background exteriors.

- His portrayal of the two figures in the middleground gazing over the parapet was revolutionary.

- The artist's knowledge of perspective is evident in the detail of the tiles on the floor and the columns on either side of the room.

- There is incredible attention to detail. You can see this particularly on the intricate filigree (delicate ornamental work) of the crown, the textures of the clothing and the light shining through the decorative glass windows.

◄ *'The Madonna of Chancellor Rolin,' Musée du Louvre, Paris, Jan Van Eyck*

HIERONYMOUS BOSCH

Date	1453–1516	**Patrons**	The Church
City	s'Hertogenbosch	**Themes**	Religious
Apprenticeship	Unknown	**Style**	Symbolic, moralistic, enigmatic
Influences	Medieval art		

Bosch was born and lived most of his life in the town of s'Hertogenbosch in the Netherlands. He was a very religious man who specialised in portraying peoples' sins and the punishments resulting from these in the afterlife. His work consisted mainly of complex fantasy paintings combining symbolism with hideous demons, fantastical animals and fruit.

The Garden of Earthly Delights, 1505–10

This painting is the centrepiece of a triptych (a painting on three panels, depicting three different but related pictures), and deals with a symbolic representation of Earth, flanked by two panels showing the consequences of man's actions: Paradise and hell.

- The central painting is a strange mix of cavorting animals, people and giant exotic fruits.
- Mythical creatures such as **gryphons** abound in a surreal landscape with dreamlike fabulous structures set in the background, giving the painting a bizarre other-worldly atmosphere.
- A lot of the symbolism is now lost on modern viewers, although it would have been easily interpreted during Bosch's time.
- The women in the picture are often shown with an apple, a symbol of Eve's temptation of Adam. This is particularly evident in the centre of the painting where female figures are shown in a circular pool displaying their charms to the men surrounding them.

> **dic·tion·ar·y**
>
> A **gryphon**, also known as a griffin, is a winged monster with the head of an eagle and the body of a lion.

▼ *'The Garden of Earthly Delights,' Museo del Prado, Madrid, Bosch*

The Wayfarer, 1500–02

This is the second of two paintings by Bosch on the same theme. It differs from the first, the outer panel of 'The Haywain' (c. 1485–90) because it has a circular composition instead of a rectangular one and because its message is portrayed in a more subtle way. The image of the wayfarer was a commonly used symbol at the time representing the Christian's daily struggle against sin and corruption.

- The wayfarer (person on a journey) in the picture is shown as careworn and undernourished with tattered rags for clothing; his worldly possessions gathered into a wicker basket which he wears on his back.

- The painting shows a spiritual pilgrimage which could be corrupted on the way.

- The internal conflict of the wayfarer is easily seen by the indecisive expression on his face which is turned to gaze at the inn in the background. It appears as if he is hesitating about whether to keep going or to turn back and go inside.

- The inn itself represents sin. The embracing couple in the doorway symbolise lust as does the face in the window which is trying to entice the wayfarer to come in and join her. The building itself is falling apart, which shows outwardly the decaying morals of those within.

- At the side of the building is a man relieving himself; a further image of lewd behaviour.

- The pigs eating from a trough indicate the sin of gluttony, while the snarling dog could represent slanderous speech as well as physical dangers.

- The ragged clothes of the wayfarer are also thought to be indicative of his own immoral and sinful nature which has brought about his homelessness and poverty.

▶ *'The Wayfarer,' Museum Boymans–van Beuningen, Rotterdam, Bosch*

ALBRECHT DÜRER

Date	c. 1471–1528	**Influences**	Venetian painting, Mantegna
Cities	Nuremberg, Venice	**Patrons**	Maximilian I of Austria (1459–1519), Charles V of Spain
Apprenticeship	As a goldsmith in his father's workshop; later with painter Michael Wolgemut (1434–1519), and engraver Martin Schongauer (c. 1448–91)	**Themes**	Portraits, nature, religious
		Style	Mixture of northern and Italian styles

Dürer's Career Development

German-born Albrecht Dürer's early introduction to art began in the workshop of his goldsmith father. He was later taught by Michael Wolgemut, who specialised in painting and woodcuts. He travelled to Venice, where he derived considerable inspiration from the artists' work and also the new role the Italian artist had in the world around him.

Interest in Nature

He became interested in science, anatomy, mathematics and Latin and looked for ways to incorporate his knowledge into his art. This was the first time that a German engraver incorporated exceptional realistic detail and anatomical accuracy into his woodcuts. Dürer believed that there was true beauty in every aspect of nature and perhaps more so in those which are generally overlooked. He was more interested in drawing wild, unkempt nature than idealised, cultivated and superficial compositions.

Self-Portraits

Throughout his life, Dürer completed many self-portraits in various media (paintings, woodcuts, engravings). He was an extremely confident artist and took great pride in his appearance.

Self-Portrait, 1484

Dürer created his first self-portrait at the age of 13, demonstrating his already astonishing talent in this area. It was created using a technique called silverpoint, where the artist etched out his design on coated paper using a silver stylus (pen-like object).

Self-Portrait, 1493

In 1493, Dürer's father arranged a marriage for him to Agnes Frey, the daughter of a successful brassworker in Nuremberg. As Dürer was away from home at the time, he sent back a portrait of himself at the age of 22. This accomplished painting shows a fashionably dressed youth gazing out at the viewer. His personal pride can be seen in the fine details of the handsome features and long flowing hair. In his hands, Dürer holds a thistle-like plant, which could symbolise fidelity. This is the first recognised painted self-portrait created solely for the painter's own gratification.

▲ 'Self-Portrait,' 1484, Graphische Sammling Albertina, Vienna, Dürer

▼ 'Self-Portrait,' 1493, Musée du Louvre, Paris, Dürer

Self-Portrait, 1498

This portrait depicts the artist as a cultured and elegant young man. In those days, northern artists were seen as skilled craftsmen, but here we see a refined and poised gentleman. At this time, Dürer was already established as a prominent and successful artist and much in demand as a portrait painter. The blend of northern and Italian styles is demonstrated here in the intricacy of the details, reminiscent of Van Eyck's work (see p. 228), and the subtlety of tone and colour, derived from the Italian masters, in particular Giovanni Bellini (see p. 215).

Woodcuts

The art of woodcuts had been practised in Europe since the 1400s, but Dürer's brought the medium to a new level of sophistication. He drew his designs on soft wood, which was then cut out by expert craftsmen. The raised parts of the block were then inked and printed on paper. Dürer's most famous collection of woodcuts were 'The **Apocalypse**.'

The Apocalypse, 1498

Dürer did a collection of 15 woodcuts on the theme of the final judgement and the end of the world, based on The Book of Revelations from the Bible. This Book consists of prophecies about the second coming of Christ and the final battle between heaven and hell. As many people believed that the world would end in 1500, these depictions were extremely topical and popular.

Style of Apocalypse Woodcuts

- These woodcuts depicted graphic, violent scenes, full of dramatic imagery, and expressive portrayals of suffering and horror.
- This suffering was vividly reflected in the faces and gestures of his characters.
- Dürer used techniques learned from his travels in Italy to give realism and volume to his figures, seen in the linear tones of the bodies.
- He also demonstrated his knowledge of perspective in the backgrounds.

dic·tion·ar·y

The word '**apocalypse**' comes from a Greek word which means 'lifting of the veil,' and means a revelation of something hidden. Today, it is often used to describe the end of the world.

▲ *'Self-Portrait,' Museo del Prado, Madrid, Dürer*

▼ *'The Four Horsemen of the Apocalypse,' British Museum, London, Dürer*

Prints: Copperplate Etching

Dürer was one of the innovators of this technique. It was a complex process:

1 First, the artist melted wax over a copper plate.

2 They then scratched the desired design into the wax with an etching tool, to expose the copper underneath.

3 The plate was then immersed in an acid bath. The acid only ate into the drawing etched, because the wax was resistant to the acid.

4 When the desired depth of design was achieved, the artist dried off the plate, rolled it with ink, and printed it onto paper.

The Fall of Man, 1504

Already aware of the principles of the **Vitruvian Man**, Dürer developed his own formula for the perfect classical proportions of the human body for this engraving. It is also know as 'Adam and Eve.'

- It portrays the idealised, graceful figures of Adam and Eve, surrounded by an exquisitely detailed landscape, rich in symbolism and fine textural qualities.

- The branch in Adam's hand symbolises the Tree of Life, while the parrot stands for wisdom.

▼ *'The Fall of Man,' Staatliche Kunsthalle, Karlsruhe, Dürer*

dic·tion·ar·y

The **Vitruvian Man** was a sketch by Leonardo da Vinci, which demonstrated his understanding of the proportions of the human body. It worked out the proportions mathematically and served as a guide for artists to follow. Examples of these proportions are:

- The length of the upper arm is one-eighth of a man's height.

- The outstretched arms are equal to a man's height.

- The length of the hand is one-eighth of a man's height.

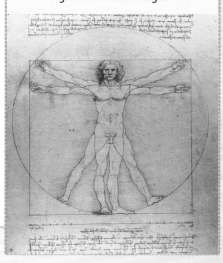

The Knight, Death and the Devil, 1513

This engraving shows a knight riding through a terrifying landscape, surrounded by hideous beasts. It symbolises the Christian virtues overcoming sin and evil.

- ➤ The design of the horse is based on the Colleoni monument by Andrea del Verrocchio (see p. 154) which Dürer saw in Italy. Verrocchio created the monument, which shows a horse and rider, to commemorate Bartolomeo Colleoni, a military captain who won many victories for Venice.

- ➤ This etching demonstrates Dürer's mastery of technique in the finely etched lines, adding volume and texture to the anatomical accuracy of man and horse.

▶ *'The Knight, Death and the Devil,' Staatliche Kunsthalle, Karlsruhe, Dürer*

MATTHIAS GRÜNEWALD

Date	c. 1474–1528	Patrons	Cardinal Albert of Hohenzollern (1490–1545), Archbishop of Mainz, Guido Gaersi
Cities	Mainz, Halle		
Apprenticeship	Holbein the Elder (c. 1465–1524)	Themes	Religious
Influences	Religious writings, **Saint Bridget of Sweden**, Martin Luther	Style	Emotional, spiritual, colourful

The German artist Matthias Grünewald was a unique and individual painter. Unlike many of his northern contemporaries, he was not influenced by the Italian Renaissance artists' developments in techniques and styles. Instead, he worked from his imagination, cultivating his own approach to painting. His works show his interest in depicting far from idealised people, showing real and often disturbing emotions.

The backgrounds of his paintings are not governed by rules of perspective and classical elegance; instead they are usually dark, indistinct and dimly lit. He also used symbols to convey the meanings behind his paintings.

biography

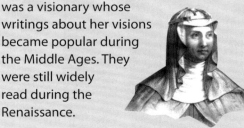

SAINT BRIDGET OF SWEDEN (1303–73) was a visionary whose writings about her visions became popular during the Middle Ages. They were still widely read during the Renaissance.

The Isenheim Altarpiece, 1512–15

This polyptych altarpiece was commissioned by Guido Gaersi, the preceptor (head) at Isenheim, **Alsace**, for this plague hospital and monastery. The central panel focuses on the suffering of the crucified Christ.

The Crucifixion Scene

- Grünewald used a palette of warm, rich reds, oranges and crimsons to create an atmosphere of the suffering Christ endured.

- Christ's contorted body in the centre of the composition instantly commands attention. The graphic depiction of his agonised face, complete with rivulets of blood from the thorns embedded in his forehead, to the sores on his body (which represent an affinity with the plague sufferers in the hospital), and the twisted fingers demonstrate Grünewald's ability to evoke an emotional response from the viewer.

- The Virgin is shown fainting in the arms of Saint John the Evangelist to the left of Christ. Her ghastly pallor and clasped hands eloquently display her overwhelming grief.

- Saint John the Baptist is on the right, pointing towards Jesus. He is prophesying that the death of Christ is not the end; but the beginning of eternal life for all. At his feet is the symbol of Christ, the Lamb. The animal is shown bleeding into a chalice and holding a cross.

- A panel depicting Saint Sebastian is on the right of the central panel. He is included because plague victims prayed to him to ease their pain. He is portrayed with his traditional wounds and arrows, his face full of compassion for the agonies of Christ and the plight of the patients in the hospital. It is often thought that Saint Sebastian is a self-portrait of Grünewald himself.

- The patron saint of Isenheim was Saint Anthony, who can be seen here on the panel to the left of the main Crucifixion scene. The serene Saint Anthony is undisturbed by the demonic figure at the window (top right corner). This demon represents the 'burning sickness' which afflicted the Isenheim patients.

> dic·tion·ar·y
>
> **Alsace** is a region in the east of France, which was originally part of the Roman Empire of the German nation.

▼ 'The Isenheim Altarpiece,' Alsace, Grünewald

The Resurrection

Another panel on the polyptych shows Christ ascending into heaven from the tomb, his delicate robes and floating figure in direct contrast to the clumsy, heavy soldiers at the bottom of the panel.

- This panel demonstrates Grünewald's novel and imaginative colour techniques. Intensely dramatic yellows and oranges frame Christ's head in a luminous halo, which was extraordinary in an era when artists strived simply for realism in their pictures.

- Grünewald used vibrant warm reds and oranges for Christ's flowing robes and most unusually, for a portrayal of Jesus, gave him golden hair. This was obviously for purely aesthetic reasons.

▶ 'The Resurrection,' Alsace, Grünewald

HANS HOLBEIN THE YOUNGER			
Date	c. 1497–1543	Patrons	The English Court, Henry VIII
Cities	Basel, London		
Apprenticeship	His father's studio, Augberg, Germany (Holbein the Elder)	Themes	Portraiture, symbolism
Influences	Erasmus, fifteenth-century Flemish painting, contemporary Italian painting	Style	Realistic, detailed

The work of German artist Hans Holbein demonstrates the technical mastery achieved by the painters of the Northern Renaissance. His close attention to detail and knowledge of anatomy alongside his understanding and correct use of perspective were remarkable. He also made great developments in the realistic applications of colour and tone.

At the Court of Henry VIII

Through his friendship with **Erasmus**, one of the most influential voices during the Reformation, Holbein was introduced to the English Court in London. King Henry VIII (1491–1547) appointed him as court painter in 1526, where he had a very successful career for seven years. As well as completing portraits of the king himself, he painted the monarch's son, Edward VI (1537–53), some of his wives and important political figures such as the statesman Sir Thomas More (1478–1535).

biography

ERASMUS (c. 1466–1536) from Rotterdam, the Netherlands, was the most famous humanist scholar of the Renaissance. He compiled the first published Greek New Testament, which he then translated into Latin. This was to influence the teachings of Martin Luther, although Erasmus did not agree with all of Luther's views.

The Ambassadors, 1533

This is a portrait of two rich and ambitious young Frenchmen. On the left is Jean de Dinteville (1504–55) who, at the relatively young age of 29, was the French ambassador to England. Georges de Selve (c. 1508–41) is portrayed on the right. When the portrait was painted he was not yet appointed the ambassador to Venice in Italy, but was recently ordained as a bishop at the age of 25.

⇨ Holbein includes various instruments and literature in the painting to emphasise the men's extensive learning and knowledge. These were specifically chosen to represent different aspects of their lives, education and interests.

OBJECT	SIGNIFICANCE
The globe 1	A celestial (relating to the sky) globe, showing the ambassadors' knowledge of astronomy
The sundial	A portable device, signifying travel
The quadrant	A mechanism used by astronomers to calculate distances and positions of stars
The many-sided sundial	An apparatus used to tell the time
The torquetum	An object which was used in conjunction with the quadrant to determine celestial measures
The mathematics book	An arithmetic book for travelling merchants
The globe 2	A map of the world
The T-square	An item used for drawing maps
The lute	An emblem of the love of music
The hymn book	A symbol of the Lutheran religion
The flutes	Another representation of music lovers

There are other important symbols almost hidden from the viewer within the painting:

⇨ In the extreme top-left corner is a silver crucifix, partially concealed behind the green curtain. This is a reminder that, despite the ambassadors' earthly knowledge, there is still an underlying desire for life after death.

⇨ This idea is reinforced further by the diagonally positioned object seen in the foreground at the bottom of the painting. It is actually a stretched and distorted skull, which is placed here to represent human mortality.

⇨ This painting sums up Holbein's love of detail and accuracy in interpreting textures and tone. The intricate pattern on the fabric draped over the top shelf and the soft feathery texture of the fur on the men's coats are meticulously observed and rendered.

▶ 'The Ambassadors,' National Gallery, London, Holbein

Portrait of Sir Thomas More, 1527

As a trusted friend and advisor of King Henry VIII, Thomas More was a highly influential man during his lifetime. He attended Oxford University, England, where he gained an interest in humanist beliefs. These were to cause an internal conflict with his own strong religious principles throughout his life. He was appointed as Lord Chancellor of England, a position he held from 1529 to 1532. Sir Thomas had a reputation for being a saintly and learned man, but is also remembered for condemning heretics (people who do not accept the Church's teachings) to be burned at the stake. When Henry VIII appointed himself the head of the Church of England, Sir Thomas More refused to accept him and was arrested and beheaded in the following year. The Roman Catholic Church canonised him as a saint in 1935.

▶ *'Portrait of Sir Thomas More,'*
The Frick Collection, New York, Holbein

- Holbein chose to seat the sitter at an angle so he is not directly facing the viewer, or engaging the viewer with his eyes.
- He appears deep in thought, gazing into the distance.
- The opulent fur trim on his collar and velvet cuffs proclaim the wearer's high and important position in society, although the golden chain symbolises his subservience to the king.
- Holbein's use of the complementary colours red and green heighten the intensity of the portrait.

Portrait of Georg Gisze, 1497

Georg Gisze (1497–1562) was born in Danzig, Germany, and became a wealthy merchant working in London. It is thought that this portrait was commissioned before his marriage. He is portrayed writing a letter to his brother in Germany. His identity is established by the name appearing repeatedly on the documents seen on the wall in the background.

- The merchant is depicted seated behind his desk, which is covered with a finely embroidered cloth. His profession and education is proclaimed by some of the objects shown on the table, such as the pewter writing stand, complete with goose-feather quills, ink, sealing wax and sand.

◀ *'Portrait of Georg Gisze,'*
Staatliche Museen, Berlin, Holbein

- Beside the scissors on the table lie a signet ring and seal, which assert his elevated role.

- In the top-right corner there is a shelf containing numerous keys and signet rings.

- A further reminder of his learning is found in the Latin inscription on the wall behind him which states 'No joy without sorrow.'

- There are symbols arranged naturally in the painting. Among those are the small clock and flowers in the centre, both representing the passage of time. The Venetian glass vase of carnations can also be interpreted as a symbol of an engagement.

- Holbein's portrait is realistic and meticulously accurate in every detail. It not only captures the image of the sitter extremely well, but also tells us a lot about the way he wished to be perceived, as a wealthy, influential and learned man.

Study for the Family Portrait of Sir Thomas More, 1526

This is a pen-and-ink drawing of Sir Thomas More surrounded by his family in his home in Chelsea, London. It was a study for a large-scale painting which was destroyed in a fire in the 1700s. Holbein gave this sketch to More's good friend, the scholar Erasmus, who lived in Switzerland.

- The sketch is particularly interesting in that we can see the working process of the artist.

- He has made notes in German about alterations he was planning for the finished piece, and also included a monkey in the bottom-right corner. Sir Thomas More was known for his love of animals and even had a small zoo, which included a monkey, his favourite pet.

▼ *'Study for the Family Portrait of Sir Thomas More,' Kunstmuseum, Basel, Holbein*

PIETER BRUEGEL THE ELDER

Date	c. 1525–1569	Patrons	Cardinal Granvella
City	Antwerp	Themes	Landscape, peasant life, satiric observations of humanity
Apprenticeship	Pieter Coecke (1502–50)		
Influences	Hieronymous Bosch, de Patiner (1480–1524)	Style	Realistic, comical

Pieter Bruegel, from the Netherlands, is one of the most memorable painters of the sixteenth century. His work not only employed the symbolism so common in northern painting, but combined it with graphic realism, humour and his considerable talent as a landscape artist. His early work is largely devoted to landscape painting, inspired by his two years spent travelling around Italy and by the Flemish countryside where he lived.

Paintings of the Working Classes

His later work shows his interest in humanism, choosing to paint the working classes because they, unlike the higher classes, didn't seek to hide their emotions and as a result revealed a truer representation of humanity. Although these paintings are satirical in nature, showing some of the baser instincts of humanity, he did not simply wish to ridicule peasants' lives, he also wanted to make a social comment on the harshness of their existence. In his series of paintings about peasants he often used symbolism to indicate people's gradual loss of Christian values.

January (Hunters in the Snow), 1565

▼ *'January,' Kunsthistoriches Museum, Vienna, Bruegel*

This painting depicts a winter scene in which hunters and their pack of dogs trudge through the snow back to their village. To their left, we see people building a fire and in the distance, villagers skate over the icy lake or go about their chores. All of the characters in the scene are wearing peasant dress typical of the time. The picture was originally one of six seasonal paintings. It is the only one known to exist still.

- Bruegel's travels in Italy provided him with the source of the craggy mountains in the background, but the rest of the painting depicts a straightforward representation of the Flemish countryside.
- The realism of the scene is heightened by his use of perspective, with the trees and villagers appearing smaller to make them seem further away.
- Bruegel also used aerial perspective, fading the colours and blurring outlines as the objects fade into the background.
- The viewer's eye is drawn into the painting in a very effective manner. The hunters, facing the village, are walking towards the top of the hill, which slants diagonally across the foreground. This leads our attention effortlessly into the background, giving the landscape a dynamic and balanced composition.

The Peasant Dance, 1567

The scene is set in a small Flemish rural village. A peasant dance is taking place to celebrate a saint's day, complete with jugs of wine and bagpipers providing the music. Bruegel has given us a vision of country life at its most lively and boisterous. However, he hid symbols in the painting to provide us with his opinions of the villagers' morals and values.

▼ *'The Peasant Dance,' Kunsthistoriches Museum, Vienna, Bruegel*

- In the foreground, a couple run hand-in-hand from the right towards the dancers in the middleground. These dancers are shown as unrefined and energetic, while to the left of the picture sits the bagpiper, being distracted by a drunken villager.
- At the table behind him a row appears to have broken out between the men and behind these a couple embrace publicly, an act which would have been considered very vulgar at the time.

Hidden Symbols in the Painting

- Firstly, the dancers in the background are all facing away from the church seen in the background. A picture of the Virgin Mary, shown attached to a tree on the right, is ignored by the villagers. This shows us that the artist thinks they have forgotten, or simply do not care, about the fact that they are celebrating a religious event.
- A peacock's feather is a symbol of vanity, while the kissing couple indicates lust, two undesirable vices.
- Northern painters such as Bosch (see p. 232) sometimes used musical instruments to represent Satan, so it is possible that the bagpiper could be seen as the devil instigating sin by playing music.

The Wedding Feast, c. 1567–68

This picture shows us a typical country wedding feast set in a rustic barn. The guests are seated at a long table, being served with bowls of food by the servants in the foreground and serenaded by the bagpipe players on the left. The bride is placed slightly right of the centre of the painting, her position discernible from the rest by the drapery behind her which is embellished by a paper crown.

- Bruegel deliberately gives us an unromantic vision of the peasant wedding – his focus is not to idealise the situation but to present it as it really is.
- The villagers greedily wolf down their food, while the child in the foreground licks its fingers. One of the bagpipers appears more interested in the food being served than in entertaining the guests.
- The bride herself is not depicted as a wistful beauty but as a simple and smug young woman contented with her moment of glory in an otherwise hard and deprived life.

▼ *'The Wedding Feast,' Kunsthistoriches Museum, Vienna, Bruegel*

The Triumph of Death, c. 1562

This is a painting about death and the Last Judgement. Bruegel shows the humans who face death as symbols of different sins and also as representations of varying class levels and occupations. He places this within a sparse and terrible landscape which symbolises Death's domain.

- Bruegel's images of death do not discriminate between rich and poor or the crimes and sins committed. He presents us with a vision of Death's revenge on all mortals for their sins against God.

- The personification of Death is shown in the centre of the painting riding a horse and brandishing his scythe. Beside him a hideous creature resembling a toad represents greed and the worship of false and material gods.

- In the right foreground of the picture we see the symbols of lust, anger, gambling and gluttony.

- In the corner of the left foreground lies a king surrounded by barrels filled with gold. Beside him is the figure of a cardinal. This shows us that Bruegel considers that even elevated figures of high social and religious standing are not immune from the sin of greed.

- Further back in the painting, the artist depicts ordinary criminals and people who have committed suicide.

▼ *'The Triumph of Death,' Museo del Prado, Madrid, Bruegel*

The Northern Renaissance Revision Questions

1 Discuss 'The Arnolfini Wedding' by Jan Van Eyck under the headings: a) theme, b) composition, c) painting techniques, d) symbolism.

2 Discuss the imaginative content of Bosch's 'The Garden of Earthly Delights.'

3 Discuss Dürer's versatility and attention to naturalistic detail in the fields of painting, woodcuts and printing, with reference to specific examples of each.

4 Discuss spirituality and symbolism in Grünewald's 'The Isenheim Altarpiece.'

5 Compare and contrast two portraits by Hans Holbein the Younger.

6 Discuss two works by Bruegel, referring to his subject matters and style.

Bibliography

Renaissance section

1 Battisti, Eugenio, *Cimabue*, The Pennsylvania State University Press, 1967

2 Beek, James H., *Raphael*, Harry N. Abrams Inc., 1976

3 Bennett, Bonnie A. and Wilkins, David G. *Donatello*, Phaidon Press Ltd, 1984

4 Bradbury, Kirsten, *Michelangelo*, Parragon, 2001

5 Colvin, Howard, *Architecture and the Afterlife,* Yale University Press, 1991

6 Copplestone, Trewin, *The Life and Works of Hieronymus Bosch*, Parragon, 1995

7 Garavaglia, Niny, *Mantegna*, George Weidenfeld & Nicolson Ltd, 1971

8 Gibson, Walter S., *Hieronymous Bosch*, Thames and Hudson Ltd, 1973

9 Goffen, Rona, *Giovanni Bellini*, Yale University, 1985

10 Grossman, F., *Pieter Bruegel, The Paintings*, Phaidon Press Ltd, 1964

11 Hale, J.R. *Renaissance Europe 1480–1520*, Wm. Collins Sons & Co. Ltd, 1971

12 Jestaz, Bertrand, *Art of The Renaissance*, Harry N. Abrams Inc., 1995

13 Lightbown, Ronald, *Mantegna*, Phaidon/Christies Ltd, 1986

14 Lowry, Bates, *Renaissance Architecture*, Readers' Union, Prentice Hall International, 1964

15 Murray, Peter, *The Architecture of the Italian Renaissance*, Thames and Hudson Ltd, 1996

16 Pedrocco, Filippo, *Titian, The Complete Paintings*, Thames and Hudson, 2001

17 *The Great Artists Part 26*, Marshall Cavendish Partworks Ltd, 1994

18 *The Great Artists Part 30*, Marshall Cavendish Partworks Ltd, 1993

19 *The Great Artists Part 36*, Marshall Cavendish Partworks Ltd, 1994

20 *The Great Artists Part 45*, Marshall Cavendish Partworks Ltd, 1994

21 Valconover, Francesco and Pignatti, Terisio, *Tintoretto*, Harry N. Abrams Inc., 1985

22 Watkin, David, *A History of Western Architecture*, Laurence King Publishing, 1996

23 Wirtz, Rolf C., *Art and Architecture, Florence,* Konemann, 1999

24 Zampetti, Pietro, *The Complete Paintings of Giorgione*, George Weidenfeld and Nicolson Ltd, 1970

The Age of Revolution:
French Painting
1780–1880

Historical Background

During the eighteenth century, two major, but very different, revolutions took place that were to have a huge influence on the art of the period.

The French Revolution

On 14 July, 1789 hordes of French revolutionaries attacked the Royal Prison in Paris (The Bastille), seeking weapons to fuel their rebellion. At the time, there was huge unrest amongst the poorer classes in French society. They had to pay harsh taxes to the crown, and could barely afford to survive. By contrast, the noble ruling classes did not have to pay any taxes from their vast incomes, and lived in luxury. In addition to this, the country was facing huge national debt from the many was it had waged in the past years. In May 1789 King Louis XVI (1754–93) called a meeting of the **Estates-General**. However, rather than helping to solve the problems, they seized power and abolished the **feudal system** of the nobility. Upper-class families were forced to flee France or face execution by **guillotine**. In 1791, the Royal family was captured and King Louis XVI and his queen Marie Antoinette (1755–93) were eventually put to death. The slogan *Liberté, Egalité, Fraternité* (Liberty, Equality and Fraternity) inspired many artists to follow the cause of the revolutionaries, believing in the importance of equality among men and portraying the leaders of the Revolution in a romantic, heroic light.

The Industrial Revolution

Beginning in about 1760, an industrial revolution began to take place in Europe which would change people's lives forever. Scientists made discoveries in the areas of electricity, combustion and steam power which changed the face of industry, allowing it to leap forward into a new era. The invention of the steam engine made travel more accessible and transportation of goods much more manageable. Floods of workers moved from the countryside to work in new factories in the cities, creating more urbanised societies. The addition of machinery in the workplace dramatically increased the production of manufactured goods leading to growth in economy. The Industrial Revolution had a great impact on the styles of art produced at this time. Many people were working long hours in cities and sought escapism in art which epitomised the beauty of nature, as well as idealising notions of nobility and heroism. Throughout this chapter we will be examining how the new art of photography forced artists to reconsider their role in society and develop new ways of portraying their subjects.

dic·tion·ar·y

The **Estates-General** in France was a government made up of representatives from three estates: the First consiste of the clergy, the Second; the aristocracy and the Third wa made up of the rest of the French people.

In the French **feudal system**, all land was owned by the king who granted land to the aristocracy on condition tha they would swear loyalty to him and provide him with military aid. The aristocracy in turn provided land for their knights in exchange for their military service. The lowest order in the feudal system consisted of the serfs, who were basically slaves with no rights and had to provide th knights with food and services in return for their land.

A **guillotine** was a device used to carry out executions by beheading people. It consisted of a tall frame with a heav blade at the top. The victim had to lean over the bottom o the frame while the blade was dropped with force, severii the head from the body.

THE BEGINNINGS OF MUSEUM ART

The Louvre is an important landmark in the history of art, as it became the first public museum. Previously, art had been accessible to the higher classes of society only. The success of the Louvre led to changes elsewhere in Europe, as new museums opened their collections for public view.

The Louvre: From Royal Palace to Museum of Art

The original Louvre building was constructed in Paris in 1190, and was used primarily as a fortress to protect royal treasure, but also housed prisoners. In 1400, the building's function changed, and it became a royal retreat. King Charles VI of France (r.1380–1422) was the first king to use the Louvre for the purpose of entertainment, hosting state occasions, jousting tournaments and banquets there. Several additions were added, including the Tuileries gardens which housed a number of exotic birds and animals. The Louvre was raided by the English in 1415, and a lot of its treasures were plundered and sold to collectors all across Europe. As a result of the state of disrepair the building had fallen into, the entire structure was demolished in 1527, and a new building was erected on the site during the reigns of Francis I (1494–1547) and Henry II (1519–59). In the years to follow, a succession of French kings added extensions and improvements to the building, taking almost 300 years to complete. The Louvre became the recognised capital of art in the world during the reign of Henry IV (1553–1610). A vast number of craftsmen and artists lived on site, adding to the magnificence of the collection.

▲ *The Louvre, Paris*

Louis XIV's Contribution

When Louis XIV (1638–1715) became king, he promoted the value of art, and purchased and commissioned hundreds of pieces. By the 1700s there were more than 2400 objects of art in the collection. More buildings were erected around the three sides of the quadrangle (rectangular courtyard) to house the works displayed. When Louis XIV moved to the Palace of Versailles (outside Paris) the unused building gradually fell into disrepair.

Public Museum

In 1793, after the French Revolution, the people decided that the Louvre should become a public museum. The interiors and exteriors of the buildings were renovated to house the multitude of artworks collected over the years. During the nineteenth and twentieth centuries many works were donated, making the Louvre one of the largest and most spectacular museums, housing works such as Leonardo da Vinci's 'Mona Lisa' (see p. 191) among others.

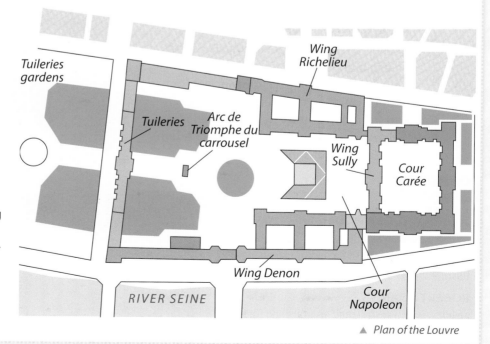

▲ *Plan of the Louvre*

The French Revolution and Neoclassical Painting

A renewal of interest in ancient Greece and Rome coupled with a surge of political activity and upheaval caused artists to combine both of these concerns in their paintings. Art became a medium which was used to promote patriotism, heroism and civic pride.

The Revival of Classical Art

Towards the end of the eighteenth century, artists increasingly derived inspiration from **classical** culture. As a result of the great **political turmoil** sweeping across Europe and the fast-changing nature of industrialisation, philosophers, writers and artists looked back to a time when civilisation was at its peak of refinement and cultural enlightenment. They admired the rational thinking of these ancient worlds, as well as the symmetrical and graceful architecture of the period.

Excavations of Pompeii and Herculaneum

The revived interest in classical antiquity accelerated when the lost cities of Herculaneum and Pompeii near Naples in Italy were excavated in the mid 1700s. They had been covered by ash and volcanic mud since the eruption of the volcano Vesuvius in 79, centuries before. The cities beneath were perfectly preserved, giving valuable insight into the lives, customs and domestic arrangements of an ancient civilisation. A large-scale excavation of the sites unearthed skeletons of people and animals, buildings, paintings, sculptures, pottery, weaponry and silver ornaments. Collectors and museums across Europe bought and displayed a lot of the objects discovered by the archaeologists. The displays and exhibitions stimulated the public's interest in these artefacts from ancient Roman culture, inspiring many different aspects of art including pottery design (**Josiah Wedgewood**), interior design (**Robert Adam**), painting, sculpture and even fashion.

▲ *Pompeii ruins*

◄ *Plaster casts of bodies show the Pompeiians in their dying poses.*

biography

JOSIAH WEDGEWOOD (1730–95) was an English potter who became famous for his ceramic designs and also for his improvements in the manufacture of pottery.

ROBERT ADAM (1728–92) was a Scottish architect who also designed furniture and the interiors of buildings. He based his work on the art and architecture of ancient Greece and Rome.

Historical Paintings

Many large-scale history paintings began to emerge around the time of the French Revolution. Traditionally, these paintings were created to mark an important or pivotal point in political or cultural history. Artists were inspired by the stories of ancient Greece and Rome, believing that by painting pictures of great historical significance about the nobility of humankind and patriotism to one's country, the artist could inspire love of country and desire for an egalitarian (equal) society. The subjects of the paintings were not always the noble of birth, but the noble of spirit, such as great military figures who valued morality, courage and self sacrifice above other virtues. In the context of the troubled times in France these pictures served to glorify the cause of the Revolution, instilling the leaders with civic virtue and heroism.

The Neoclassical Style

Neoclassical painters were absorbed with creating precise, correct depictions of historical, classical and contemporary events. They researched the architectural settings and costumes of their subjects to give a realism and accuracy to their art, feeling that this would lend a gravity and importance to their work. Even in their contemporary paintings they looked to ancient classical sculpture to recreate the heroic gestures, stances and facial expressions they saw there as well as imitating the linear flow of the clothing and the rigid, geometric lines of the architecture. Artists sought to portray contemporary subjects in idealistic ways to equate them with praiseworthy heroes of classical times.

JACQUES-LOUIS DAVID			
Date	1748–1825	**Influences**	French painter Francois Boucher (1703–70), classical art, Renaissance art, the idealism of the French Revolution
Cities	Paris, Rome, Brussels		
Movement	Neoclassical		
Themes	Revolutionary ideals, self-sacrifice, heroism	**Style**	Dramatic, warm, vivid colours

Jacques-Louis David was one of the most influential and renowned Neoclassical French painters. He was born into a privileged and wealthy family and received his artistic education at the Royal Academy in Paris, which was situated in the present-day Louvre. He visited Rome in 1775 and remained there for five years, where he became fascinated by classical art and architecture and also Renaissance art, particularly that of Raphael (see p. 209).

His early work, such as the 'Oath of the Horatii' and the 'Oath of the Tennis Court,' exemplified the qualities of honour, nobility and self-sacrifice to the Republic, which David admired in classical art. He became a strong supporter of the French Revolution, believing it to embody all of these qualities. He continued to paint historical classical subjects which symbolised the ideals of the Revolution but he also painted contemporary subjects such as 'The Death of Marat' and portraits of **Napoleon** who held both his talent and his commitment to the emperor's cause in high regard. In 1804

biography

NAPOLEON BONAPARTE (1769–1821), born in Corsica, was a brilliant military leader. He seized power in France after the French Revolution and went on to become emperor, calling himself Napoleon I. He conquered much of Europe but was finally defeated by Britain and Prussia at the Battle of Waterloo in 1815. He was exiled to the island of Elba, off the coast of Italy. Following this, he was exiled to the British island of St. Helena in the Atlantic, where he died six years later.

David was given the position of official court painter by Napoleon. When the King of France Louis XVIII (1755–1824) was restored to power in 1814 David relocated to Brussels in Belgium, where he painted mythological paintings and portraits of Belgians and French immigrants. He died after being hit by a carriage.

Oath of the Horatii, 1784

This painting is based on historical fact, referring to the war between ancient Rome and Alba in the seventh century B.C., and how the leaders of these cities in Italy proposed to end it. The three foremost champions of Rome, the Horatius brothers, swore an oath to combat the three greatest champions of Alba, the Curatius brothers, in a series of battles to determine the outcome of the war. The great tragedy of the story is the relationship between the two families: the youngest of the Horatius brothers was married to a sister of the Curatii and one of the Horatius sisters was engaged to marry a champion of the defenders of Alba. This historical painting immortalises the moment the Horatii pledge their oath to their city by raising their arms to the swords held in the hand of their father. The themes of the painting include the loyalty and nobility of warriors in contrast to the despair and resignation of the female characters, and the virtue of patriotism.

▲ 'Oath of the Horatii,' Musée du Louvre, Paris, David

Classical Influences

- The influence of ancient classical art can be seen in a number of ways in this painting. The background is deliberately simplified, with three curved archways and a geometrically tiled floor adhering to the rules of perspective set down by Renaissance artists several hundred years before.

- The way in which the characters are placed in the composition also evokes the memory of relief sculpture of ancient times, as they are all situated in the foreground of the picture, modelled in light and shade.

- The weary despairing figures of the women seated in the right of the painting are in direct contrast to the straight defiant stances of the men as they prepare to give their lives in service of their city and people.

Oath of the Tennis Court, 1791

David sought to inspire the French people with revolutionary patriotic zeal by creating a large-scale historical painting based on actual events in the French Revolution. The picture represents the moment when spokesmen for the French lower and middle classes (the Third Estate) rejected the voting policies put forward by the king's governing body, which took place beside a tennis court. The central figure is that of Jean-Sylvain Bailly (1736–93), who would later become the mayor of Paris. The sketch, in pen and brown ink, was commissioned by the Jacobins, a fanatically militant group of revolutionaries. The picture itself was never completed.

> **Did you know?**
> When the deputies of the Third Estate wanted to come together for a meeting to discuss reforms in the government of France, they arrived at their meeting hall, Menus–Plaisirs, to find it locked. The deputies believed that this was an attempt by Louis XVI to end their demands for reform. Refusing to be suppressed by their King, the deputies did not break up. Instead they moved their meeting to a nearby indoor tennis court, hence the term 'Oath of the Tennis Court.'

▼ *'Oath of the Tennis Court,' National Museum of Versailles, David*

- This painting has a very different composition from the 'Oath of the Horatii.' Although the characters are fervent and expressive in their stances and attitudes, there is no classical simplicity of composition with large figures dominating the foreground.

- Here, the picture is crowded with energetic and lively characters jostling for the viewer's attention. David was seeking to demonstrate the excitement and fervour of the moment.

- This can also be seen in the dramatic billowing curtain in the top left corner, and is further demonstrated by the figures leaning in from the windows.

- Despite the multitude of characters, David successfully guides the viewer's eye towards the central figure in the composition by the gestures of the crowds surrounding him.

The Death of Marat, 1793

In this painting, David explores the theme of martyrdom for one's country and ideals. David had become increasingly more involved in the French Revolution, helping to create propaganda to inspire the lower and middle classes to overthrow the dictates of the former kingdom. The subject of the painting, Jean-Paul Marat, was a friend of his. He was a prominent politician and writer who was murdered by Charlotte Corday (1768–93), a fanatical royalist. Marat is depicted having been stabbed in his bath. He worked from a herbal bath daily for medicinal purposes as he had a severe skin condition. No traces of this disease can be seen in this picture; David preferring to create a romantic image of the martyr for the Revolution.

◀ *'The Death of Marat,' Royal Museum of Fine Arts of Belgium, David*

- The composition of this painting is stark and simple. The figure of Marat dominates the foreground of the work, bathed in light and painted in realistic detail, reflecting David's knowledge of the work of Michelangelo (see pp. 194–208).

- He strives to stimulate in the viewer a sense of horror at what has occurred, by graphically showing the stab wound and bloody bath water.

- The knife dropped on the ground beside the bath and the letter in his hand given to him by his murderer give the picture a sense of immediacy, as if Corday has just left the room.

- The dark background also lends the work a bleakness fitting to the subject depicted.

JEAN AUGUSTE DOMINIQUE INGRES			
Date	1780–1867	**Influences**	Antique Greek painting, Jacques-Louis David, Titian (see p. 219), Raphael (see p. 209)
Cities	Paris, Rome, Florence		
Movement	Neoclassical	**Style**	Classic, linear, sensual
Themes	Portraiture, the female nude		

Ingres was originally a student of Jacques-Louis David, but soon distanced himself from his master as a result of disagreements over their drawing styles. Ingres's drawing was more simplistic and linear, reflecting his interest in ancient Greek vase painting. Large figures in the foreground of his paintings reflect the influence of low-relief Greek sculpture on his work. He was also very much influenced by the Renaissance artists; especially Raphael, adopting his serene classical style. He opposed the modern romantic and realistic artwork, considering it to be destructive to the principles laid down by the great artists who had gone before, especially Raphael. Ingres believed that carefully balanced compositions and idealised forms were more artistically pleasing than the extravagantly colourful and expressive romantic paintings.

Paganini, 1819

Niccolò Paganini (1782–1840) was a celebrated violin player of the time, and was also a friend of Ingres, who was a violinist himself and very fond of music. The subject is shown here as a confident and assured gentleman turning to face his audience.

- Ingres's style of clean, linear contour drawing can be observed particularly in the lines of the clothing, hands and violin.

- The face is more detailed and tonal (using different shades) although it still retains a classical simplicity of line. The artist may have idealised the features of his subject to some degree, but there is character and personality evident in this portrait.

- The realistic portrayal of the violinist contradicts his formal pose.

▲ 'Paganini,' the Metropolitan Museum of Art, New York, Ingres

Apotheosis of Homer, 1827

This painting depicts a grouping of the world's finest artists, poets, philosophers and musicians gathering to witness the coronation of the eighth-century Greek poet Homer. It serves to celebrate humanity's greatest geniuses in the fields of art, music, philosophy and poetry. The main characters depicted are:

1 **Horace** (65–8 B.C.), a writer from Ancient Greece. His most famous work was *Satires*.

2 **Virgil** (70–19 B.C.), a Roman poet, known for his epic poem *The Aeneid*.

3 **Raphael Sanzio** (1483–1520), an Italian High Renaissance painter, whose painting 'The School of Athens' (see p. 213) heavily influenced Ingres.

4 **Sappho** (c. 650–590 B.C.), an acclaimed Greek poetess.

5 **Apelles** (c. 352–308 B.C.), a Greek artist.

6 **Orpheus**, a mythological Greek poet and musician.

7 **Homer** (lived during the eighth century B.C.), a famous Greek poet, is shown being crowned by a winged figure (see below).

8 **Nike**, the Goddess of Victory, is depicted crowning Homer.

9 **Pindar** (c. 522–443), a Greek lyric poet.

10 **Plato** (c. 428–348 B.C.), a Greek philosopher.

11 **Socrates** (c. 469–399), a Greek philosopher.

> **dic·tion·ar·y**
>
> An **apotheosis** is the elevation of a normal being to godlike status.

▼ *Outline diagram of 'Apotheosis of Homer'*

12   **Phidias** (c. 480–430 B.C.), a Greek sculptor who carved the **Zeus statue**, is shown holding a hammer to symbolise his craft.

13   **Michelangelo Buonarroti** (1475–1564), one of the most famous Italian High Renaissance painters, sculptors and architects.

14   **Alexander the Great** (356–323 B.C.), a famous Greek king who was a very successful military commander.

15   **Longinus** (lived between the first and third centuries A.D.), an acclaimed Greek literary critic.

16   **Molière** (1622–73), a famous French writer.

17   **Nicholas Boileau–Despréaux** (1636–1711), a French critic and writer.

18   **Jean Racine** (1639–99), a French writer.

19   **Aesop** (620–560 B.C.), the writer of *Aesop's Fables*, a collection of morality tales.

20   *The Odyssey*, a personification of one of Homer's epic poems.

21   *The Iliad*, a representation of one of Homer's epic poems.

22   **Nicholas Poussin** (1594–1665), a French Classical painter.

23   **William Shakespeare** (1564–1616), the most well-known author of poems and plays in the history of the English language.

24   **Mozart** (1756–91), an Austrian composer.

25   **Dante Alighieri** (c. 1265–1321), a renowned Italian writer of epic poetry.

dic·tion·ar·y

At a colossal 12 m tall, the seated figure of **Zeus** was erected by Phidias in the temple of Zeus in Olympia, Greece in c. 432 B.C. Made of ivory and gold-plated bronze, it was one of the Seven Wonders of the Ancient World. No one knows exactly when it was destroyed, but it is thought to have perished in a fire in the fifth century A.D.

▼ *'Apotheosis of Homer,' Musée du Louvre, Paris, Ingres*

- The viewer is immediately involved in the subject of the painting by a number of devices employed by the artist. The main action takes place in the centre of the piece, framed by the architectural backdrop.
- The viewer's eye is engaged by the figures in the foreground that gaze directly out of the painting, and then led back to the focus of the painting; Homer, by gestures and the stances of the figures that face the central group.
- Showing the steps of the temple is another technique Ingres uses to draw our eye towards the figure of Homer.

Influence of Raphael

The influence of Raphael can be easily seen in this work; both in its subject matter and in the manner of its execution.

- The gathering of history's elite philosophers, poets, artists and other revered geniuses recalls 'The School of Athens' by Raphael, as does its classical architectural setting (see p. 213).
- The grand scale of the work is also reminiscent of Raphael's most ambitious work.
- The smooth painting style adopted by Ingres reflects the techniques employed by Raphael to create a serene and idealised scene.

The French Revolution and Neoclassical Painting Revision Questions

1 Describe the impact of the French Revolution on art in France with particular emphasis on two paintings created at this time.

2 Compare and contrast two works by Jacques Louis David: 'Oath of the Tennis Court' and 'The Death of Marat.' Include in your answer a discussion of the themes and compositional layouts of both paintings.

3 'Apotheosis of Homer' is a painting by Jean Auguste Dominique Ingres. Discuss the influence of both Classical and Renaissance art on this work.

Portraiture

The painting of portraits thrived at this time, serving to capture both the likeness and the social station of the sitter.

Formal Portraiture

The most popular form was the formal full-length portrait, which usually showed the person portrayed in a dignified, restrained pose. The sitter was almost always a wealthy person of noble birth who was pictured against a backdrop of idealised nature. The male sitters were often shown with hunting gear, implying that the wonderful pastoral (rural) setting was a part of their large estates and indicating to the viewer that they were the lords of their surroundings. Artists generally painted the figure in a large scale in the foreground of the canvas with the horizon line in the background situated low in the composition.

Informal Portraiture

Some artists sought to create less contrived portraits in order to give a more natural image of the sitter. The viewpoint of the artist moved closer, giving the picture a more intimate feel. The sitter was often portrayed in a more spontaneous pose, caught in the act of moving, or half-turned to smile at the viewer. The models for the portraits were not necessarily from the high-bred nobility, but may have achieved their social standing through literary, artistic or musical achievements. These sitters were often shown in a setting or with props which proclaimed their profession.

Portraits of Napoleon

The French Revolution and the rapid rise of Napoleon marked a new era in French art. Napoleon was fascinated with the emperors of ancient Rome and wanted to copy their passion for great art and architecture to serve as memorials to their importance in world history. He commissioned art as **propaganda** for his own empire and as a social document of the time and also as a celebration of Roman history. These included historical paintings commemorating great landmark moments of ancient Rome, such as victory in battle and conquests of other countries (see 'Oath of the Horatii,' p. 254). There were also large-scale impressive portraits of Napoleon, his family and his advisors. This love of ancient times translated into the kind of architecture he commissioned, such as the classically structured Arc de Triomphe in Paris which was based on a triumphal Roman arch. Napoleon's preoccupation with all things Roman also showed itself in the coins created for the French Republic, with a profile of the emperor on one side and a laurel wreath on the other. Even the colours of his army were based on the Roman legionaries' uniforms. He valued the classical notions of putting heroism, patriotism and the good of society before the needs of the individual. The following paintings demonstrate the various types of portraits of Napoleon created by different artists to honour the emperor.

> **dic·tion·ar·y**
>
> **Propaganda** involves the spreading of information either to damage or assist a cause, movement, or government.

▲ *The Arc de Triomphe in Paris, commissioned by Napoleon*

ANTOINE-JEAN GROS (BARON GROS)				
Date	1771–1835	Themes	Napoleon's military career, heroism
Cities	Paris, Genoa		
Movement	Neoclassical	Style	Dramatic, naturalistic, detailed
Influences	Jacques-Louis David, classical writings, Near-East culture, (relating to the Balkan states in Southeast Europe)		

Baron Gros began his career as a portrait painter, specialising in miniature paintings of his clients. He was inspired by Napoleon's triumphs and ideologies to produce paintings celebrating his career and campaigns. During his career Gros travelled in Italy following the French army, where he was motivated by the idealism he perceived in Renaissance art. Napoleon recognised his commitment and skill and awarded him the title of Baron of the Empire for his services in 1808.

Napoleon at the Pesthouse at Jaffa, 1804

In 1799, the bubonic plague ravaged the Near East where the French were campaigning. This picture captures Napoleon's visit to one of the hospitals caring for soldiers who had caught the fatal and highly contagious disease. Napoleon commissioned this painting from Gros to quash rumours that he had ordered the diseased soldiers to be poisoned a short while after his visit. and to add to the positive propaganda surrounding his rise to success. The painting's themes are nobility, benevolence and the courage and fearlessness of a great leader: in this case, Napoleon.

- Napoleon immediately attracts our attention from his central position in the picture. He is depicted as a fearless benefactor, reaching out to those in need. His calm and noble demeanour is in strong contrast to the other characters around him.

- The victims are shown in despairing attitudes, while the officers accompanying Napoleon appear fastidious, and are shown holding their noses.

- The mythical healing power of the true king is obliquely referred to by the outstretched hand of the ruler to the sick.

- The background is derived from Moorish sources, with its pointed archways and mosque tower.

- The interior is dark and gloomy with a dramatic light shining on Napoleon and his officers as he comforts the afflicted.

▼ *'Napoleon at the Pesthouse at Jaffa,' Musée du Louvre, Paris, Gros*

Napoleon in His Study, 1812, by Jacques-Louis David

This painter, featured on pp. 253–57, also contributed to portraits of the great leader. This is a full-length portrait of the emperor, and is almost life-size, being more than 1.7 m high. Its theme is military leadership, and a celebration of the accomplishments of the emperor Napoleon. David was using the painting to create positive propaganda.

◈ The sheer scale of the portrait serves to enhance the importance of the subject.

◈ The portrait has a casual appearance – Napoleon seems to have just risen from his desk to greet the viewer. Even the carpet is wrinkled as if the chair had been hastily pushed back. However, every item in this work is deliberately included, and tells us a little about the emperor.

Symbolism

There are a number of devices by which David suggests different aspects of Napoleon's greatness. He places objects of significance around the study to influence our opinion on the man.

◈ To the left of Napoleon's head, there are several wall decorations containing symbols related to the artist's view of his subject, including the god **Mercury** (symbolising wealth), the **eagle** (power and victory), and the **Egyptian lion's head** seen on the leg of the table draws a parallel between this ancient civilisation and the new French empire.

◈ The **clock** in the top-right corner states that the time is 4:13, while on Napoleon's desk, the **candles** have almost burned out. This gives us the impression that the emperor has been working until the early hours of the morning.

◈ Another indication that he has been up late is the slight hint of **stubble** on his face, combined with his **tousled hair**.

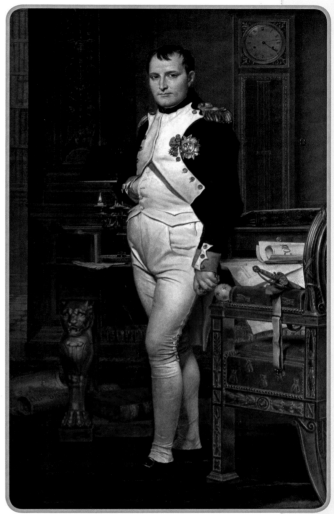

▲ *'Napoleon in His Study,' National Gallery of Art, Washington D.C., David*

◈ A **pattern of bees** on the seat of the chair reinforces the idea of the amount of work Napoleon did (as busy as a bee). The bee was also the symbol of Napoleon's family.

◈ There is a lot of emphasis placed on the emperor's role as a military leader, not simply a figurehead of the Revolution. He is shown in full **uniform**, the **epaulette** (shoulder ornament) signifying the highest military rank, while on his jacket is the **Legion of Honour** medal, which is the highest honour bestowed in France.

◈ Casually left across the chair is a **gold-handled sword**, which conveys the message that the emperor is a courageous warrior.

- The book on the ground under the desk is *Lives* by **Plutarch**, which relates the histories of important historical figures such as Hannibal and Julius Caesar. The fact that it is shown at the feet of Napoleon gives us the idea that the artist is implying that he is far more powerful.

- The scroll on the right of the desktop is part of the **Napoleonic Code** of Regulations.

dic·tion·ar·y

The **Napoleonic Code** was drawn up by Napoleon in 1894. It was based on the Roman law and related to personal status, property and the acquisition of property. Parts of the code are still in use to this day.

biography

PLUTARCH (46–120) was born in Greece and lived in Rome. He was a historian who is renowned for his biographies and essays on Greek and Roman heroes such as Alexander the Great (356–323 B.C.) and Julius Caesar (100–44 B.C.).

Bonaparte as First Consul, 1804, by Jean Auguste Dominique Ingres

▲ *'Bonaparte as First Consul,' Museum of Modern Contemporary Art of Liège, Ingres*

At only 23 years of age, Ingres (see pp. 257–60) received a commission to paint Napoleon. The emperor had presented 300,000 francs as a gift to the town of Liège in Belgium and wished to have the occasion captured in the shape of a full-length portrait. The consul system began in ancient Rome, where two appointed consuls were the most powerful magistrates and military leaders in government. Napoleon used this system in setting up his own government, but appointed three consuls, with himself as the first, and most important one.

- Napoleon is positioned in the exact centre of the painting in his traditional pose – with his hand placed inside his waistcoat. This pose had been previously used in portraits of noblemen in preceding centuries, to indicate refinement and good breeding. However Napoleon was portrayed so frequently in this stance that it became his trademark. His intense gaze is fixed on a point to the right of the viewer.

- His finger points to the decree detailing the gift which lies on a table covered by rich, velvet, olive-coloured drapery.

- A luxuriously upholstered chair stands between Napoleon and the window, through which we can see Liège Cathedral.

⟐ Ingres demonstrates his technical mastery of realistic texture in his depiction of the lustrous velvet curtains and table covering. The shining silken gold tassels, the softness of the quill feathers and the ornate gilding on the chair all give us a very realistic and sumptuous impression.

⟐ Ingres was a master of colour and tone. He deliberately used a restricted palette of colours to tie the composition together. An olive green colour prevails throughout the picture space, helping Napoleon to stand out in his complementary outfit of scarlet red.

⟐ Napoleon's clothing is echoed in the deeper red in the chair inlays. Accents of gold lend a lavish touch, appearing in the tassels, the chair and the embroidery on Napoleon's clothing and hat lying on the table.

Napoleon I on His Imperial Throne, 1806, by Jean Auguste Dominique Ingres

Napoleon looked to ancient Rome to create his imperial image. He had the deepest admiration for the first Christian ruler of Europe, Charlemagne (742–814), and used the same motifs and objects as him to symbolise his ruling:

⟐ The **Sceptre**: The baton of command, a symbol of sovereign authority.

⟐ The **Sword**: A symbol of military power.

⟐ The **Hand of Justice**: A stick with a hand made from ivory which symbolises divinity and a royal blessing.

⟐ The **Orb**: A symbol of the world, representing world dominance.

Even his golden crown closely resembled the laurel wreath worn by Roman emperors. He also had his hair cut short in the style of ancient Rome. Ingres rose to the challenge of depicting France's ruler as a Roman emperor in this painting.

⟐ This is a very different portrait of Napoleon painted only two years later by the same artist.

⟐ Here we are presented with Napoleon as royal leader, supreme ruler of his vast empire. It is a much more formal composition, painted for the glorification of the emperor.

⟐ The more informal nature and composition of 'Bonaparte as First Consul' is gone, replaced by an official, stern representation, from which a confident and self-assured emperor regards us.

⟐ He is shown wearing his crimson coronation robes, trimmed and lined with white **ermine fur** and embellished with lavish golden designs. He holds the symbols of his reign; the sceptre in his right hand and the hand of justice in his left. The sword is tucked under his left elbow.

▲ 'Napoleon I on His Imperial Throne,' Musée de l'armée, Paris, Ingres

Did you know?
ERMINE FUR comes from a type of stoat, which has a brown coat in the summer but a completely white one in the winter (as camouflage for the snowy regions in which it lives). The fur was highly prized and used in Europe as a symbol of nobility and royalty.

Portraiture Revision Questions

<u>1</u> Compare and contrast two portraits of Napoleon by Jean Auguste Dominique Ingres, taking into account the nature of the paintings and the messages the artist wants them to give to the viewer.

<u>2</u> Portraits of Napoleon were commissioned by the emperor to contribute to his revolutionary propaganda. Discuss Baron Gros's 'Napoleon at the Pesthouse at Jaffa' with reference to the above statement.

<u>3</u> Describe the meanings of the symbols seen in 'Napoleon in His Study' by Jacques-Louis David.

Romanticism

Romanticism was a type of painting which flourished between 1750 and 1850. It originated in Germany with literature and folklore collected and compiled by the **Grimm brothers**, and swept throughout Europe. By contrast to the intellectual, rational aims of Neoclassicism, the art created in this time stressed the expression of the imagination of the artist. Romantic artists believed that each individual had their own unique view on life and on politics, and that they should have the liberty to feel and express this view. Painters also explored the darker aspects of the human condition and emotions, often creating nightmarish and dramatic scenes to provoke an emotional response from the viewer.

biography

The **GRIMM BROTHERS** Jacob (1785–1863) and Wilhelm (1786–1859), were born near Frankfurt, in Germany. They became interested in collecting and editing folktales from around Europe, and it is through them that tales such as Cinderella, Hansel and Gretel, and Snow White came into the public domain.

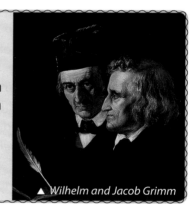

▲ *Wilhelm and Jacob Grimm*

The Line versus Colour Debate

In the late seventeenth century, after the founding of the **Royal Academy of Painting and Sculpture**, a conflict began to grow between artists who believed that contour (outline) and line were the most important elements of any painting and artists who were more concerned with using colour to create drama and animation in their work. Eugène Delacroix (see p. 269), the most famous of the Colourists, rebelled against the strict demands of the Academy to use classical linear techniques and instead used bold colour to create spectacular, striking paintings. The Colourists were considered to be linked politically to revolutionary ideals

dic·tion·ar·y

The **Royal Academy of Painting and Sculpture** was founded in Paris in 1648 by the painter Charles Le Brun (1619–90). To become a member of the Academy an artist had to have a painting accepted and contribute work to the exhibitions which took place every two years. Artists who were members of the Academy were almost guaranteed success in contrast to those painters who were not accepted.

during this time, whereas the Classicists were associated with authoritarian dictatorship. Jean Auguste Dominique Ingres (see p. 257) was the most famous champion of the Classicists' methods. He rejected excessive use of colour and concentrated on creating ideal beauty based on ancient statues. He considered Colourist paintings to be superficial: they served only to please the eye but did not demand a response from the mind.

THÉODORE GÉRICAULT				
Date	1791–1824	**Themes**	Horses, humanitarian issues such as mental illness and poverty	
Cities	Rouen, Paris			
Movement	Romantic			
Influences	Originally Neoclassicism, later Rubens (1577–1640), a Venetian Renaissance artist and Rembrandt (1606–69), a Dutch painter who used vibrant dramatic colours	**Style**	Dramatic, powerful, vividly coloured	

Théodore Géricault began his artistic career as a horse painter, specialising in pictures of cavalry. After visiting Florence and Rome, he became inspired by Renaissance art, particularly the vibrantly coloured and dramatic masterpieces and also the works of Rembrandt. His compassion and interest in humanitarian issues also led him to paint many portraits of mental patients and impoverished city dwellers. He died at the young age of 33 after falling off a horse.

The Raft of the *Medusa*, 1818–19

This painting was based on an actual event. The *Medusa*, a French ship transporting soldiers and colonists to Senegal, North Africa, became shipwrecked on a reef. Because of a shortage of lifeboats, the passengers had to make a raft from the debris of the ship. In the beginning, 150 people were on the raft, but the cold, lack of food and water, and overcrowding soon reduced their numbers. After 12 days at sea only 15 remained, and these became mad through their suffering, having had to survive by becoming cannibals. The captain of the *Medusa* who was appointed by the government was responsible for the shipwreck and took one of the few lifeboats for himself and his officers. When this information became known the people of France were horrified and scandalised by the story. Géricault wished to understand fully the horror and trauma of the ordeal the passengers went through by researching the story in depth before painting the scene. He interviewed some of the survivors of the shipwreck and created a model of the raft to use as a reference for the painting. He even sketched corpses in morgues to attain accurate realism. The theme of this painting is vividly clear: death, despair and the resilience of the human spirit.

- The sheer scale of the work (40.6 cm x 58.4 cm) already commands the attention of the viewer, but Géricault's painting is so full of raw human emotion and dynamic energy that it immediately involves us emotionally in the moment. He wished the viewer to have feelings of outrage at the victims' plight and human empathy for the characters, shown in the throes of despair and death. There is also a glimmer of hope shown in the lightening sky on the horizon and in the last burst of energy by the figures on the right as they signal for assistance.

- The dark colour palette, with its heavy shadows and sombre greenish pallor in the brighter areas all add to the morbid atmosphere of the picture.

Géricault also uses this dramatic painting to draw attention to a cause near to his heart. He was an abolitionist and deeply opposed to slavery. In this work, the foremost character hailing the distant ship is a black soldier named Jean Charles.

The painting is composed around a dramatic X-axis which creates a dynamic, lively effect. The sail on the top left forms the top of one axis ending in the bottom right with the body trailing in the water. The other axis leads from the diagonally placed figure in the bottom left and brings the eye upwards to the waving figure of Jean Charles. The raft itself is at a diagonal to the picture frame, the edge of it jutting out towards us. This was done intentionally to include the spectator in the scene, as the characters appear to be almost about to enter the space outside the painting.

Did you know?

The young Eugène Delacroix assisted Géricault when he was creating the painting by posing as one of the dying figures on the raft.

▲ 'The Raft of the Medusa,' Musée du Louvre, Paris, Géricault

EUGÈNE DELACROIX

Date	1798–1863	Influences	Théodore Géricault, Lord Byron, Flemish painter Rubens (1577–1640), North African culture and landscape
Cities	Paris, Champrosay, Casablanca	Themes	North Africa, politics
Movement	Romantic	Style	Dreamlike, harmonious

Eugène Delacroix is one of the most celebrated Romantic artists. His interest in Romantic painting was first stirred on meeting Théodore Géricault whose work he greatly admired. He developed an interest in politics and demonstrated his views through his art. An example of this is 'Liberty leading the People' (1830, Louvre, Paris) which depicted his support of the 1830 rebellion against King Charles X (1757–1836) and the absolute power of the monarchy. Delacroix travelled to North Africa as a guest of the Ambassador to the Sultan of Morocco. In the six months he spent there he developed a fascination for Arab culture and traditions and introduced them as themes in his work.

Death of Sardanapalus, 1827

▲ *'Death of Sardanapalus,' Musée du Louvre, Paris, Delacroix*

The painting is loosely based on *Sardanapalus*, which was an epic poem by the English Romantic poet Lord Byron (1788–1824). In Byron's poem, the Assyrian king Sardanapalus commits suicide after he hears of the defeat of his armies and the fall of his city, Nineveh. He also orders his servants killed and possessions destroyed. Delacroix's painting portrays this event in a dramatic and violent scene – more violent than that portrayed in the poem. Here, the king's **concubines**, horses and servants are killed as he watches from his luxurious bed. The images depicted are graphically brutal, particularly that of the **harem woman** being stabbed in the foreground. Perhaps the most disturbing image in this work is that of the reclining figure of the Assyrian king who seems only resignedly gloomy even though he is aware of the slaughter of his servants and prized animals, the theft of his jewels and his own imminent death by fire. The painting's themes are exotic drama, destruction and death.

> ### dic·tion·ar·y
>
> A **concubine** is a woman who lives with a man of importance but is not married to him. She may be one of many.
>
> A **harem woman** is a woman who lives in a house or part of a house which is exclusively reserved for the female members of the household.

- The composition of the painting is crowded with turbulent images, writhing figures, vibrant colour and movement.

- The eye of the viewer is led diagonally into the picture space by the effect of light: the figure of the dying woman in the right foreground gazes up at the left corner, where the king, the main focus, is partially lit with a strong dramatic light.

- The light also illuminates the subservient harem girl who throws herself across the bed, arms outstretched in supplication. The upper half of the king is in shadow, giving him an evil aura.

- The colour palette in the painting is gloriously rich and vivid. Deep royal reds pervade the composition, helping to set the scene in the king's bedchamber, with its fabulous extravagance. The colour red traditionally symbolises danger and passion and is also reminiscent of blood.

Romanticism Revision Questions

1 Explain the themes chosen by the Romantic painters and how they are portrayed with reference to two paintings.

2 Discuss how Géricault achieved a sense of drama in his painting 'The Raft of the Medusa,' including the history behind the painting in your answer.

3 Describe Delacroix's 'Death of Sardanapalus' under the following headings:
   a) subject matter b) composition c) use of colour.

Landscape Painting

The growth in landscape painting during the nineteenth century was a direct reaction to the Industrial Revolution. Artists wished to escape the hectic pressures of urban life and portray instead simple, tranquil scenes of the countryside. Landscape painting was not merely a form of escapism and rejection of city life; it was also a rebellion against the studied, artificial landscapes created by the academic studio painters at the time. Artists wished to paint scenes which appeared real and original by capturing wild, untamed scenery. They also sought to celebrate humankind's close relationship with nature.

Plein-Air Painting

The nineteenth century saw great changes in artists' methods and working conditions. New metal tubes for storing oil paint and the invention of collapsible easels permitted painters to travel around with their equipment, rather than staying in a studio. As a result, artists had greater freedom and many chose to paint outdoors, a practice that allowed them to recreate more exactly the effects of light, changes of atmosphere and the structure and colour of the landscape. This became known as *plein-air* painting, a French term that translates as 'open air.' The first artist to use this style of painting in France was Charles-François Daubigny (1817–78). He influenced many painters including the Impressionists (see pp. 286–300) who formed working communities along the banks of the river Seine near Paris.

> ### *Did you know?*
> Before the invention of paint tubes, artists had to prepare their own paint by grinding pigments and keeping them fresh in bags made from leather or pigs' bladders.

JEAN-BAPTISTE-CAMILLE COROT

Date	1796–1875	Influences	The Italian countryside, English landscape painters John Constable (1776–1837) and J.M.W. Turner (1775–1851)
Cities	Paris, Rouen, Fontainebleau, Rome		
Movement	Realism	Style	Dreamlike, harmonious
Themes	The French landscape		

Corot, one of France's foremost landscape painters, began his career later than many painters at the age of 24. He drew sketches straight from observation of a scene and finished his paintings in his studio, attempting to remain as true to the landscape as he could. These realistic and detailed paintings were well-received at the time and he regularly exhibited at the Salon in Paris.

A View Near Volterra, 1838

Corot travelled to Italy in 1825 and was struck by the beauty of the countryside. Here, he first discovered the practice of painting outside. In this painting, he explores idyllic pastoral beauty in a typical Italian landscape. Although Corot was one of the first artists to engage in *plein-air* painting, this landscape was actually painted in his studio from sketches he made at the scene. His method of working was to influence generations of painters.

▲ *'A View Near Volterra,' National Gallery of Art, Washington D.C., Corot*

- Corot's composition is perfectly balanced to reflect the harmony of this rural scene. The bright sunny sky in the top left of the picture is echoed by the sun-drenched, golden pathway and rocks in the bottom right.

- The darker tones in the painting run on a diagonal axis from the trees in the top right to the shady hills and shadows in the left foreground.

- The horseman, who is the main focus of the work, is brought to our notice by the arrangement of the diagonal lines forming the road and the slope of the grass to the left of the figure.

Ville d'Avray, c.1867–70

This is a quiet rural scene with a winding country road on which we see a solitary horseman, with a fisherman on the banks of the lake in the left and a peasant woman with her two children in the right of the foreground. Large trees on the right sweep into the centre of the composition, dominating the painting. A shining, reflective lake is seen in the left middleground, with a glimpse of the white buildings of the rural village of Ville d'Avray lying along the banks of the lake on the other side.

- This was painted many years after 'A View near Volterra' and is a good example of Corot's later works. It retains the peaceful nature of his earlier paintings but this shows a freer style of brushwork.

▲ *'Ville d'Avray,' private collection, Corot*

- The outlines are a little blurred, the foliage on the trees and the bushes in the foreground are indicated by thick daubs of paint, a forerunner to the Impressionistic style.

- The hazy background is indistinct and soft, creating an almost dreamlike tranquillity.

The Barbizon School (c. 1830–70)

The 1830s saw a shift from the Parisian studio to the French countryside. Landscape artists, influenced by Corot and English artists such as Constable, moved to Barbizon, a small village beside the Forest of Fontainebleau (near Paris). There, they worked *en plein air* to achieve greater realism and naturalism in their work. The artists sought to create realistic pastoral scenes directly from nature. Although the main focus of their paintings was the French countryside they also included the rural working classes in their work, portraying them as a vital part of the scenery.

Landscape Painting Revision Questions

1 Discuss the importance of *plein-air* painting on the work of Jean-Baptiste-Camille Corot with particular reference to his painting 'A View Near Volterra.'

2 Compare and contrast an early painting by Corot with one of his later works.

Realism

The Realists were a group of artists who believed in the importance and value of representing ordinary, everyday scenes and objects in their paintings. They considered only what was within their own experience to be 'real,' and historical and mythological subjects to be of no artistic merit as they could not visually or physically witness them. Instead, they focused on the world around them, creating artwork from subjects previously considered unworthy of depiction, such as working-class customs and traditions. These subjects were often dramatised in the style of a history painting.

Social Opinion of Realism

After the French Revolution, the upper and middle classes became more aware of the Socialist Movement among the lower and working classes. This was largely due to a number of educated and vocal men who included French writers Honoré de Balzac (1799–1850), Gustave Flaubert (1821–80) and Émile Zola (1840–1902). In addition to these were English novelist Charles Dickens (1812–70) and German philosopher and revolutionary Karl Marx (1818–83). They demanded an economic equality for all classes and justice for the oppressed. This frightened the more prosperous French people, and caused them to be suspicious of the works of the Realists, who invested their working-class subjects with strength and heroism.

GUSTAVE COURBET				
Date	1819–77	**Influences**	Sixteenth and seventeenth-century art, particularly Italian painter Caravaggio (1573–1610) and Dutch painter Rembrandt (1606–69)	
Cities	Ornans, Paris			
Movement	Realism			
Themes	The French landscape, seascapes, social issues (poverty of the working classes)	**Style**	Spontaneous, realistic, unidealised	

Gustave Courbet was the most famous and controversial of the Realist artists. Although he came from a relatively wealthy farming family he became absorbed with portraying the harsh conditions of working-class rural life instead of the usual themes of rich people in luxurious surroundings. His socialist sympathies led him into trouble in 1871 when he was sent to prison for six months. He was unable to pay the fine which accompanied the sentence and had to flee to Switzerland, where he died.

A Burial at Ornans, 1849

The artist depicts an everyday example of a funeral in the village of Ornans, eastern France, amidst a bleak, gloomy landscape. The large size of the canvas (3.1 m x 6.6 m) and the detail he enters into give it the sense of a history painting. As history paintings previously only immortalised important historical moments, the French critics were shocked to see the burial of an ordinary man given such extravagant treatment. The faces of the people depicted are very realistic – some of them were friends of Courbet. They are also wearing the contemporary clothing of the district, which sets the scene in a particular time and place. The painting's theme is mourning, at a typical provincial funeral.

- The composition of the painting is made up of groups of figures placed close to the front of the picture space.
- Although we can see a bleak, barren landscape behind the crowd, there is little depth to the painting; the emphasis is clearly focused on the characters themselves.
- The dull greens and greys of the background reinforce the solemnity of the occasion.
- The open grave is placed centrally in the foreground and our attention is drawn to this by the artist's use of colour in the vivid red garments of the churchmen.
- Only the faces and bonnets of the mourners on the right stand out against the darkness of their clothes, echoing the white ceremonial church robes on the left.

▲ 'A Burial at Ornans,' Musée d'Orsay, Paris, Courbet

JEAN-FRANÇOIS MILLET

Date	1814–75	Influences	French Academic painter Paul Delaroche (1797–1856), Barbizon painter Théodore Rousseau (1812–67), The Barbizon School (see p. 273)
Cities	Cherbourg, Paris, Fontainebleau		
Movement	Realism		
Themes	The French landscape, French peasants, portraiture	Style	Naturalistic, realistic

Millet was the son of a peasant farm labourer and was a firm socialist. He was one of the founders of the Barbizon School, and was a portrait painter until he met Théodore Rousseau, who shared his passion for the countryside and rural life. Although the Realists were originally criticised for their choice of subject matter, Millet's work became popular in his later years and he achieved considerable financial success.

The Gleaners, 1857

This painting celebrates the importance and nobility of the working classes. Here, Millet portrays three women collecting the remaining scraps of grain after the harvest (a practice known as 'gleaning'). The painting was considered controversial when first seen, as Millet imbued what was thought of as the ordinary, trivial tasks and those who undertook them with a solemn stateliness.

- The figures of the women are poorly dressed and sturdy bodied, showing Millet's preoccupation with realistic detail rather than idealising his subject matter.

- The artist shows us how physically demanding this labour is, in the way the figure on the left's hand rests on the small of her back as she continuously bends to pick up the grain.

- The women have weather-beaten brown skin, devoid of the delicate beauty previously admired by the preceding generations of artists, with scarves around their heads to protect them from the heat of the sun. However, the scale of the monumental figures in the immediate foreground lends them an importance and their diligence gives them a sense of dignity and grandeur.

- The women in the foreground are the focus of the painting, and Millet easily achieves this by their scale against the distant background.

- The scene behind them, bathed in golden sunlight, is a beautiful pastoral image, which serves to contrast with the laborious toil of the gleaners.

▲ *'The Gleaners,' Musée d'Orsay, Paris, Millet*

- There is a great sense of realism in this work, largely due to the colour palette used by the artist. The landscape is saturated with light, from the pale blues and gentle pinks in the sky, to the gold and russet tones of the cornfield.

- The only dark tones seen in the picture are on the figures in the foreground, helping them to stand out from the background and giving them a heavy, earthy, three-dimensional volume.

Realism Revision Questions

1 Discuss how Gustave Courbet appears to elevate a simple country funeral to the level of a history painting in 'A Burial at Ornans.'

2 Describe how Jean-François Millet created a sense of realism in his painting 'The Gleaners.'

Academic Art and the Salons

The French *Academie des Beaux Arts*

The *Academie Royale de Peinture et de Sculpture* (The Royal Academy of Painting and Sculpture in France) was based on the *Accademia dell'Arte del Designo* (Academy of the Art of Drawing) in Florence which was founded in 1562 by Giorgio Vasari (1511–74) a prominent painter, architect and art theorist. Founded in 1648, the Academy trained students in the traditional style, showing them how to portray anatomy and perspective as well as instructing them in Greek and Roman history. In 1683 Charles Le Brun (1619–90), a painter and aesthetic theorist, became the director and set out a list of rigid guidelines for the education of students and also created a hierarchy of Academy members. After the French Revolution (see p. 250) the 'Royal' was dropped from the name of the Academy. In 1816 the name of the Academy changed again to the *Academie* (or *École*) *des Beaux Arts* when it was merged with the *Academie de Musique* (founded in 1669) and the *Academie d'Architecture* (founded in 1671). The Academy was sponsored by the government and held yearly exhibitions called 'Salons.' It was extremely difficult to become a member of the Academy and to take part in these exhibitions as places were much sought after.

▲ *Charles Le Brun, first director of the Royal Academy of Painting and Sculpture*

Education of Artists

Students attending the Academy had to follow rigid steps. First, the student had to draw the nude form from prints is of classical sculpture, mastering the artistic principles of light and shade and contour lines. They had to submit these pictures to the Academy for evaluation. If they passed this first test, they then proceeded to draw the nude again, but this time from plaster casts of classical statues and also from a life model. If the student proved he was good enough at these he was then able to learn how to paint in the academic style by an academian, who was a member of the Academy. To assess the progress and skill of the students, there were regular competitions staged by the Academy, the most famous and prestigious of these being the *Prix de Rome* which enabled the winner to live and study in Rome for five years and also ensured him considerable fame and success. To be eligible for this prize the entrant had to be a single male less than 30 years of age.

The Salons

The famous salon exhibitions began in 1725 with an official art exhibition organised by the *Academie des Beaux Arts* in Paris. These exhibitions became even more important and influential between the years 1748 and 1890 when the *Société des Artistes Français* took over the running of them. The *Société* consisted of artists who had received awards from the Academy and they formed a jury to consider who was eligible to submit paintings to the Salon. Artists had to have one painting approved by the jury before they were able to exhibit their work. Although the Paris Salon was the most famous and influential, there were also other salons in Bordeaux, Toulouse and Lille.

Subject Matter

Academic artists painted mainly classical and mythological subjects, using a traditional and highly finished technique with no trace of brushstrokes. History painting was seen as the most noble of subject matters and was usually produced on large-scale canvases. Portraiture was the second most popular type of painting and was thought to be a much superior theme than *genre* painting which portrayed the lives of middle or working-class people. The lowest forms of art were considered to be landscape and still life painting.

Artists were expected to have knowledge of the mythology of ancient Greece and Rome and were not considered sufficiently intellectual if they did not. They were aware of the classical principles of harmonious balance within a composition and the glorification of beauty. Nudes appeared frequently in the work of academic artists, but only represented mythological beings such as gods or nymphs.

The Role of Academic Art

The French academies held full control over what they considered to be appropriate subject matter and acceptable painting techniques. Paintings were created to be adornments in stately homes and to embellish public buildings. The academies prized highly finished works with references to classical subjects and did not appreciate attempts to break the traditional conventions of painting.

THE CHANGING DEPICTION OF THE NUDE

The portrayal of the female nude is a subject that has recurred constantly throughout art history, but the way it was depicted changed in the 1800s. To illustrate the development of the nude throughout the centuries we will examine three paintings that demonstrate these advances:

1 'The Venus of Urbino,' 1538, by Titian, the Uffizi Gallery, Florence
2 *'La Grande Odalisque,'* 1814, by Jean Auguste Dominique Ingres, Musée du Louvre, Paris
3 'Olympia,' 1863, by Édouard Manet, Musée d'Orsay, Paris.

The Venus of Urbino, 1538

In this painting Italian artist Titian (see p. 219) depicted a naked Venus, the goddess of love, reclining on a daybed in a luxurious Renaissance palace. Rich furnishings surround her and two servants can be seen in the background.

- We are aware that she is Venus because of the roses she holds in her hand which traditionally symbolise the goddess.

- Her skin is modelled in subtle flesh tones, and her eyes are gently inviting.

- The dog on the bed is a symbol of faithfulness while the pot of myrtle on the window represents constancy in love.

- Although this is intended to be a sensual painting of a beautiful woman, the symbols of marriage and fidelity coupled with the elements likening her to the goddess of love make this picture publicly acceptable.

▼ *'The Venus of Urbino,' Uffizi Gallery, Florence, Titian*

La Grande Odalisque, 1814

Jean Auguste Dominique Ingres (see p. 257) painted *'La Grande Odalisque'* in the classical style, with smooth, almost indefinable brushstrokes and detailed textures, seen in the cloth, feathers and the softness of the skin. Although Ingres painted in the approved classical style, this painting still drew criticism when it was first exhibited. This was due to the length of the sitter's spine which appears too long to be anatomically accurate. It is now thought that this was a deliberate error on the part of the artist as he may have wished to create a long, smooth curve of the body to create a sensual effect and also because it has similarities to the elongated figures seen in the art of Renaissance Venice which Ingres greatly admired. The woman depicted is an *Odalisque*, meaning a female slave or harem girl.

▼ *'La Grande Odalisque,' Musée du Louvre, Paris, Ingres*

- Even though she is looking out at the viewer, she appears modest by turning her body the other way.

- Her features are the height of idealised beauty, making us think of ancient Greek and Roman statues.

- As with the previous picture, the artist's celebration of feminine beauty and classical references combine to ensure the success of the painting.

Olympia, 1863

When Édouard Manet (see p. 282) painted 'Olympia,' it caused a public outcry. Although Manet based his picture on Titian's 'The Venus of Urbino,' there is a huge difference between how the two paintings were executed. This was mostly because the woman in the picture was not portrayed as either a goddess or a modest beauty.

- She is realistic and worldly, looking candidly out at the viewer without shyness or seductiveness in her gaze. The white stark light flooding the picture does not serve to flatter her but instead causes her to look pale and unhealthy. This is in severe contrast to the gentle modelling of light and shade in the previous paintings.

- Olympia is shown wearing only a bracelet, a flower in her hair and a string around her neck. She shows no interest in the bouquet proffered to her by her servant, indicating that she is used to receiving gifts from men.

- Another element of the painting which was shocking to the viewers was that the woman was most likely a woman of questionable morals placed in a contemporary setting.

- The real reason for the uproar was the harsh realism of the work; Manet had painted the subject as he saw her and not as an idealised and virtuous beauty.

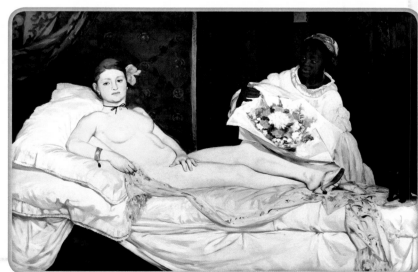

▶ *'Olympia,' Musée d'Orsay, Paris, Manet*

WILLIAM-ADOLPHE BOUGUEREAU			
Date	1825–1905	**Themes**	Religious, mythological, *genre*
Cities	Paris, La Rochelle		
Movement	Academic	**Style**	Dreamlike, detailed, classical
Influences	Classical art, Renaissance masters (especially Raphael, see pp. 209–13)		

William-Adolphe Bouguereau, born in La Rochelle, France, was one of France's most successful and prolific painters. He received his artistic education in the *École des Beaux Arts* in Paris and his work was much admired by the public and critics alike. He contributed to more than 50 exhibitions at the Paris salons and worked hard to create beautifully composed paintings with delicate paint strokes and peopled with technically perfected figures. After his death his popularity suffered as his whimsical subject matters were considered to be superficial and old-fashioned in comparison to the more modern styles of painting evolving at the time. In the later twentieth century his work was rediscovered and appreciated once more.

▲ *'Nymphs and Satyr,' Clark Art Institute, Williamstown, Bouguereau*

Nymphs and Satyr, 1873

This work is based on classical mythological creatures: a satyr (a man with the hindquarters of a goat, and the ears and tail of a horse), and wood nymphs, who are spiritually connected to trees. This was a typical theme for academic artists. Here, the satyr has been caught intruding on the nymphs as they bathe.

- Some nymphs, seen in the background on the right, have been frightened into running away to hide. The four in the foreground, however, are trying to punish the satyr by pulling him into the water, knowing he cannot swim.

- Although there are realistic elements in the execution of the painting, which can be seen in the foliage of the trees and the proportions of the figures, there is also a sense of illusion: a graceful dreamlike quality pervades the piece.

- The smooth brushstrokes and **chiaroscuro** technique are both indicative of an Academic education and tradition.

- The idealised beauty and playful stances of the nymphs echo classical poses.

dic·tion·ar·y

Chiaroscuro is the use of contrasting light and dark colour to create the illusion of depth and volume in a painting.

Rest, 1879

This painting focuses on a small family group resting in the countryside.

- Although this appears to be a straightforward family portrait it is a highly idealised image of a mother and her two children.

- The characters are dressed in costumes from another era and possess classically beautiful features.

- The meticulous rendering of light and dark tones model their bodies in convincing three-dimensional volume.

- The background is not typical of a French landscape but is more reminiscent of the Italian countryside.

The *Salon des Refusés*

As the style of art preferred by the Academy was so conservative, a lot of artists' work was rejected. In 1863, Emperor Napoleon III (1808–73) opened another salon in

▲ *'Rest,' Cleveland Museum of Art, Bouguereau*

Paris to display more than 4,000 pieces turned down by the Academy. This exhibition was named the *Salon des Refusés* (The Salon of the Rejected). Although many visited the exhibition, a lot of the work on show was critically derided including Manet's *'Le Déjeuner sur l'Herbe'* (see p. 283). However, it was an extremely influential landmark in the history of painting and art dealership, as it provided a platform for more radical and independent styles of art. It also inspired artists to host their own independent exhibitions, such as the many Impressionist exhibitions and the Society of Independent Artists who held annual shows of their work.

Academic Art and the Salons Revision Questions

1 Describe the education of artists in the French *Academie des Beaux Arts* and discuss a painting by an artist who exemplified the academic style, with particular reference to style and subject matter.

2 Compare and contrast two paintings by Bouguereau, referring to their subject matter and composition.

Modernity

During the 1800s major changes took place which were to affect the entire future of art. These occurred for a number of reasons:

- The traditional subjects and themes, such as religion and history, lost the relevance they had in previous times.

- Realistic painting was challenged by the invention of the camera, making the need for exact duplication of people and places in paint almost redundant.

- Religious and royal patrons no longer commissioned vast quantities of art.

Artists began to look inward instead of outward. Instead of concentrating solely on naturalistic images of people, places and objects, they explored more abstract themes, breaking with traditional methods and relying more on their imaginations. The introduction of independent art dealers and exhibitions gave artists freedom to paint subjects they enjoyed, instead of having to rely exclusively on commissions from wealthy patrons or work within the boundaries of Academic art. In some cases artists no longer painted alone, but worked in groups to experiment with techniques and concepts.

> **Did you know?**
> Although the first photograph was made by Joseph Nicephore Niepce (1765–1833) in 1826, the first working photographic technique was created by Niepce's partner Louis Jacques Daguerre ▾ (1787–1851) after Joseph's death.

ÉDOUARD MANET

Date	1832–83	**Themes**	Café scenes, scenes of leisure, portraits
City	Paris		
Movement	Impressionism	**Style**	Loose brushstrokes, flat colour, sharp outlines
Influences	Francisco Goya (1746–1828), Diego Velázquez (1599–1660) – two Spanish painters; Frans Hals (c. 1580–1666), a Dutch painter		

Édouard Manet is often referred to as the 'Father of Impressionism,' as his work was extremely influential to a new generation of French artists and indeed modern art as we know it today. He was born in Paris to a wealthy family, and after several false career starts, settled down to study art under academic painter Thomas Couture (1815–79). Manet's subject matter was considered shocking and controversial in its day and he was criticised for his crude painting techniques, which were very different to the established painting styles seen in the Academic Salons. Despite the notoriety of his art, Manet himself was not a rebellious or revolutionary man, but was instead a wealthy, polite and restrained gentleman, who was surprised at the effect his work had on the public. His flat colours, strongly lit scenes and thick, unrefined brushstrokes had a huge impact on artists to follow.

Le Déjeuner sur l'Herbe, 1863

Manet borrowed this subject matter (meaning 'luncheon on the grass') from a print of a painting by Italian artist Raphael (see p. 209). The themes of picnics and relaxation in woodland settings were not new ones and had often been portrayed by artists such as Giorgione (see p. 217) and French painter Watteau (1684–1721). However, it is Manet's approach to the subject that sets it apart from paintings of a similar theme. The painting of the female nude was always a popular subject matter usually depicting a goddess, nymph, or other mythical character. Here, we are presented with the unidealised figure of a naked woman, seated in the midst of two fully dressed contemporary gentlemen in a parkland scene.

- The people in the painting are realistically portrayed and seem perfectly at ease, the woman gazing calmly and confidently out at the viewer.

- The female figure was **Victorine Meurent**, a favourite model of Manet's, and the gentlemen were **Ferdinand Leenhof**; a sculptor, and Manet's brother **Eugene** (seen on the right).

- The painting was hung in the *Salon des Refusés* and caused an outrage when first seen, as it appeared to celebrate shameless promiscuity and a scandalous disregard for the traditional Academic style.

- Perhaps what the critics of the time found so shocking about Manet's art was the way he stripped away the fantasy and romanticism of his subjects to reveal a truthful and inelegant realism. He created this effect by his brushwork and use of light.

▲ *'Le Déjeuner sur l'Herbe,' Musée d'Orsay, Paris, Manet*

Brushwork

- The background, including the figure of the second female, are loosely painted and appear to be less in focus than the figures in the foreground.

- The artist also uses thick, *impasto* brushstrokes which can be seen in the hair and beard of Eugene Manet on the right.

Light and Dark

- The scene is harshly lit; a strong, bright light hitting the figures in the foreground. There is very little gradation of tone on the skin of the female model. This is possibly as a result of the influence of the recently developed flash photography which had a similar flattening effect on tonal values, but Manet was also influenced by the work of Velázquez and Frans Hals (see p. 282) who used very broad tones in their portrait work.

- Manet does not lend importance to the 'middle tones,' instead filling his painting with strong contrasts between light and dark. The pale skin tone of the female helps her to stand out in the composition, and focuses our attention against the dark tones surrounding her.

> **dic·tion·ar·y**
>
> *Impasto* is a method of painting in which the artist applies paint so thickly that it stands out from the surface.

A Bar at the *Folies-Bergère*, 1882

This is one of the last paintings Manet ever produced and is often regarded as his masterpiece. The *Folies-Bergère* was a very popular Parisian music hall which had a variety of shows, ranging from **burlesques** to trapeze artists. In the top-left corner of the picture, reflected in the mirror, we can see the legs (clad in green boots) of a trapeze artist. Although the subject matter could be simply the depiction of a moment in time at a bar, Monet's depiction of the artificial lighting and its reflection in the mirror raise it to another level.

> **dic·tion·ar·y**
>
> A **burlesque** is a theatrical show featuring comedy acts and scantily clad women dancers.

- Manet loved depicting the modern, fashionable Parisian lifestyle, using models who were his friends and associates. The young barmaid was a girl named **Suzon**, portrayed as a stylish beauty who appears a little preoccupied or even sad. At the time of painting this picture Manet was terminally ill and the expression of the barmaid may possibly be a reflection of the artist's state of mind.

- Also reflected in the mirror, in the left background, the artist has placed two more friends, **Méry Laurent** and **Jeanne Demarsy.** One wears a yellow gown, while the other has long yellow gloves and a black hat.

- The figure of Suzon is placed centrally in the foreground of the painting, taking up the full height of the picture space. It is an unusual composition as it is somewhat puzzling. It is, in fact, a shallow space, which appears to have great depth as a result of the reflection of the bar in the large mirror behind Suzon.

- At the time, critics criticised Manet's use of perspective, as in the reflection we can see a man facing Suzon whereas he does not appear in the front of the composition. This was because Manet was using a device to introduce the viewer into the picture space, by letting us take the place of the customer.

- The beers on the left and right on the bar with the red triangles on the labels are Bass Pale Ale, an English beer. The fact that the bar served imported beer tells us that this was an expensive establishment catering for tourists.

▲ *'A Bar at the Folies-Bergère,' Courtauld Institute of Art, London, Manet*

The Function of the Painted Surface

- Artists who preceded Manet had looked upon the picture's painted surface as a window to an illusion of space and reality. Manet was not concerned about creating the illusion of reality, but instead concentrated on the effects of light on objects and their surroundings, reducing shades of colour and creating strong contrasts between light and dark.

- This technique forces us to recognise that the painting is exactly what it is: a collection of colours and brushstrokes on a two-dimensional surface.

The Effects of Light

- Manet's depiction of artificial light is one of the main reasons why this painting achieved such fame and acclaim. The reflection of the bright gas globes in the background bounce off the seated figures, creating dark shadows and vividly bright colours.

- The huge chandelier, shown behind the barmaid's head, is roughly painted, a mixture of gold, blues, and brilliant white giving the impression of dazzling light.

- Hazy purplish-blue patches of paint are applied to the surface of the mirror, demonstrating the two-dimensional surface, while also helping to create the smoky atmosphere of a bar.

Modernity Revision Questions

1. Manet was one of the most influential painters in the history of art. Discuss this statement including in your answer a detailed description and sketch of one of his paintings.

2. Describe Manet's *'Le Déjeuner sur l'Herbe'* and explain why the painting caused such controversy when it was first shown.

Impressionism

The movement of painting known as Impressionism began in the 1860s, influenced by Realism and in particular by the work of Manet. The Impressionist artists included Pierre-Auguste Renoir (see p. 297), Claude Monet (see p. 288), Edgar Degas (see p. 301) and Camille Pissarro (see p. 294), all fashionable, middle-class Parisians who were well educated and cultivated. They regularly met up to discuss art and other matters in the popular *Café Guerbois*. The term 'Impressionism' was originally meant in a derogatory sense, when the critic Louis Leroy used it to describe Monet's painting 'Impression: Sunrise' at the *Salon des Refusés* in 1874. However, the group adopted it and used it as a title for their independent exhibitions. Although the artists associated with Impressionism are seen as a group, their styles varied greatly, particularly later in their careers, though they did adhere to the main aims of the genre.

▲ *Édouard Manet influenced the Impressionist movement.*

The Impressionist Group

The first meeting of what was to become the Impressionist group of painters occurred in 1859 when Monet and Pissarro met while attending the *Académie Suisse*, an art school in Paris. In 1862, four of the future leading Impressionists, Monet, Renoir, Alfred Sisley (see p. 296) and Frédéric Bazille (1841–70), met at a fine arts studio run by Swiss painter Charles Gleyre (1808–74). Bazille died eight years later at the young age of 29. Degas also encountered one of the Impressionists in 1862 after meeting Manet, but only became fully involved four years later when he met Monet and Renoir four years later at the *Café Guerbois*. After Gustave Caillebotte (1848–94), a wealthy painter, met Degas, Renoir and Monet in 1873, they set up the first Impressionist exhibition. It took place on 15 April, 1874, at 35 Boulevard des Capucines, Paris. Monet did not take part in this exhibition. Although the Impressionists worked as a group drawn together by their common interests and aims, they frequently argued and fell out with each other, due to professional jealousy and disagreements about techniques. Only Pissarro contributed to all of the Impressionist exhibitions. Eventually the Impressionists parted ways and continued their work as individuals, but the progress they had made in art was to pave the way for artists to follow.

Aims of the Impressionists

1. To use tones of colour to create the illusion of form and volume.
2. To explore the effects of light on colour. They realised that the actual colour of an object is subject to the quality of light shining on it.
3. To paint directly from nature to obtain the truest depiction and colours of a scene.
4. To paint pure pigment colours directly onto the canvas, instead of painting over a worked drawing. This was done for two reasons, the first for practical purposes, as paint had to be applied quickly to capture the transient light and atmosphere. The second reason was because Impressionist artists felt that by placing contrasting colours directly beside each other instead of mixing them a greater intensity of colour was achieved.
5. To use loose, thick brushstrokes when applying the paint onto the canvas. This was not only to save time capturing the image – artists also sought to create an *impression*, rather than an exact replica of the scene.

Subject Matter

One of the most popular themes for painting during the Impressionist era was that of recreation. With the onset of industrialisation (see p. 250), working hours for the rich middle classes became fixed, allowing people the freedom to make time for meeting friends, go to the theatre, music halls, the ballet, dances and cafés. Impressionist painters such as Renoir and Degas were interested in the here and now and the hustle and bustle of everyday life, wishing to capture fleeting moments of pleasure and enjoyment. Landscape continued to be one of the most common subject matters chosen by artists. Impressionist painters such as Monet explored the effects of light and atmosphere on the countryside, working *en plein air* to capture a moment in time.

Influences on the Impressionists

Several factors occurring around the mid nineteenth century combined to have an influence on the Impressionists and how they painted.

Japanese Prints

Japanese art had a huge impact on French artists during the nineteenth century. After 1854, Japanese cultural objects became more accessible as a result of the trading privileges obtained by the American Naval forces. In 1867, the Japanese pavilion erected for the **Universal Exposition** attracted the attention of the wealthy Parisians. They were fascinated by the exotic prints, screens, kimonos, fans, cabinets and jewellery on display, as nothing like this had been seen before. The exquisite detail, delicate craftsmanship, and two-dimensional feel of the work particularly intrigued artists. **Woodblock printing** was the most common artwork available, and the simplicity of line and flat colour interested the Impressionists and other artists, particularly Manet, Degas, Vincent Van Gogh and Toulouse-Lautrec (see p. 304).

> **dic·tion·ar·y**
>
> The **Universal Exposition** was organised by Emperor Napoleon III (1808—73). It took place in the Champ de Mars in Paris, and had 50,226 exhibitors.

> **dic·tion·ar·y**
>
> **Woodblock printing** is a method of creating numerous prints by applying ink onto an engraved block of wood and pressing it on paper.

Realism and *Plein-Air* Painting

The Impressionist artists were heavily influenced by the Realist artists such as Millet (see p. 275) and Courbet (see p. 274). Contemporary life was considered the most valid subject matter, although unlike Realist painters, Impressionist painters were not interested in socialist propaganda (such as equal rights for the working classes), preferring to paint lively scenes of middle-class leisure activities. The practice of *plein-air* painting was also adopted by the Impressionists, as they valued the first-hand experience of the effects of life on a scene.

Scientific Discoveries

At this time scientists discovered that light, which consists of energy particles, travels in straight lines and also that vision is caused by light rays hitting the eye. This discovery heightened the artists' interest in the effects of light on colour. New pigments were invented such as cobalt violet, viridian green and cerulean blue, giving paint a greater brilliance. The Impressionists often used a white painted base on their canvases to create brighter tones in their paintings. Previously artists had used browns, greens and ochres (a type of yellow).

Photography

The invention of the camera had a great effect on the art of the nineteenth century. It was no longer necessary for art to imitate life precisely, as the camera could now record images with great clarity. Artists became more interested in colour and light, which photography had not yet explored. They were also interested in the 'accidental compositions' captured by the camera, with objects and figures cut off by the boundaries of the picture space.

Impressionist Exhibitions

As a result of the rejection of their works by the Salon, the Impressionists decided to form their own society of art in 1873. They also held their own independent exhibitions, giving them the freedom to practise their own style and choose whatever subject matter pleased them. This broke the control the Salons had over art, ushering in a new era, with the control placed firmly in the hands of the artists themselves. The Impressionist Exhibitions took place every year or every two years between the years 1874 and 1886. The individual exhibitions were held at a later stage.

CLAUDE MONET				
Date	1840–1926	Themes	Landscape	
Cities	Paris, Le Havre, Giverny, London	Style	Loose brushstrokes, fragmented brilliant colour	
Movement	Impressionism			
Influences	Frédérick Bazille, Alfred Sisley, Pierre-Auguste Renoir, Édouard Manet, Camille Pissarro, English painters J.M.W. Turner, John Constable			

Claude Monet was the first artist to paint in what was to become known as the Impressionist style. He was immensely prolific throughout his long career and was most renowned for his three great series of paintings, 'The Haystacks,' 'Rouen Cathedral' and the 'The Water Lily Pond'. He was born in Paris but grew up in Le Havre, only returning to Paris to pursue a career in art, where he met the other Impressionist artists. His painting 'Impression: Sunrise,' which was based on the countryside around Le Havre, gave rise to the term 'Impressionism.' He worked in London for a time, where he was influenced by the work of Turner and Constable. In 1883 Monet moved to Giverny in the northwest of France, where he lived for the remainder of his days. Here, he could paint directly from nature, in surroundings created for this particular reason.

Theory of Painting

Monet was the ultimate Impressionist artist, taking the science of light and colour to new territories. He promoted the idea of naivety in observing nature in order to paint it the way he saw it. He said that the artist should try to forget what the objects were in the landscape, and look merely at the blocks and streaks of colours that made up the shapes. His brushstrokes were short, thick and choppy, giving his paintings a sense of immediacy.

Monet's Painting Series

While other Impressionist artists were interested in painting transient (temporary) social scenes, such as scenes in cafés or parks, Monet radically chose to depict the same subject matter repeatedly under varying weather conditions, times of day and months of the year. His three most notable series of paintings were:

- ⬥ 'The Haystacks series,' 1890–91
- ⬥ 'The Rouen Cathedral series,' 1892–94
- ⬥ 'The Water Lily series,' 1894–1920

The Haystacks Series, 1890–91

This was the first of Monet's painting series, and focused on capturing haystacks in a field at different times of day. Monet chose this theme for his work as, after the harvest, the stacks of grain were left in the fields for a few months. Because of this, he could observe and record not only the different times of day but also the different types of light to be seen as the days and weeks progressed. He also saw haystacks as synonymous with nourishment and abundance.

Stacks of Wheat (End of Summer), 1890–91

It is very probable that this painting is one of the first in the series as it depicts a day during the latter end of the summer, with a golden sun set low in a blue sky.

➤ Monet skilfully contrasts the golden, orange hues of the hayfield with the vivid blues in the shadows to create the impression of an evening sunset.

➤ The loosely painted sky combines the misty blue of a summer day with a golden glow appearing over the receding hills in the background.

➤ The composition of the painting is quite straightforward with a large haystack in the right foreground, a smaller one in the left middleground with deep greens, blues and purples merging to form the hedges bordering the field, thus separating foreground from the background of indistinct hills.

▲ 'Stacks of Wheat (End of Summer),' the Art Institute of Chicago, Monet

Stacks of Wheat (Snow Effect, Overcast Day), 1890–91

This painting, painted months later than the previous picture, shows the artist's development in style.

▲ *'Stacks of Wheat (Snow Effect, Overcast Day),' the Art Institute of Chicago, Monet*

Photography © The Art Institute of Chicago

- His brushwork has become freer and there are even less outlines defining the shapes within the composition.
- The background is simply suggested by loose strokes of blue, purple and white with almost indefinable shapes of farm buildings in the right middleground.
- A large haystack painted in warm russet oranges and yellows with shadows of contrasting blues and purples dominates the entire picture as the cold blues of the background recede in contrast.
- The composition is cleverly balanced by the placing of warm colours in the shadows of the farm buildings and the hazy trees in the middleground.

The Rouen Cathedral Series

Monet painted a series of around 31 views of Rouen Cathedral in northwestern France. The paintings are particularly outstanding, demonstrating Monet's fascination with light and atmosphere and his extraordinary ability to convey the optical illusions created by light. These pictures were always intended to be seen together for maximum effect and some of them can be viewed in the Musée d'Orsay in Paris. Monet concentrated on the western façade of Rouen Cathedral, with its three entrance portals, rose window and twin spires.

- Monet used quick, sketchy brushstrokes to apply paint to the canvas. Thick, *impasto* layers of paint gradually built up the form of the church façade and suggest the rough stonework of the cathedral.

- There is a sense of movement in the fluid, hasty paintwork which gives us an impression of the volatility of the weather and light conditions under which the artist worked. He was often working on several paintings simultaneously, one for each time of day.

- His blurred edges and rough surface texture are at an extreme variance to the smooth, finished Academic Salon art, and he was criticised for his lack of understanding of form. However, Monet was exploring the effects of light and shade on form, by recording how variations in daylight visibility can affect the appearance of form and shape.

Colour and Light

- Many of the Rouen Cathedral paintings were painted from exactly the same viewpoint, making the composition of the pictures practically identical to each other. The only dissimilarities were in the light conditions under which they were created.

- Through the repetition of the same subject matter, Monet's almost scientific investigations into the effects of light on colour and form are instantly apparent. Previously, artists had created shadow by adding black and grey to their palettes. Monet and other Impressionist painters realised that shadows are largely made up of reflected colours, often including the complementary colour of the object depicted. This can be observed in 'Rouen Cathedral, Harmony in Blue and Gold,' 1894, which is mostly created through the use of radiant white, yellows and golden orange hues, contrasting with the blue of the sky and the violet tones in the shadows.

▼ *'Rouen Cathedral, Harmony in Blue and Gold,' Musée D'Orsay, Paris, Monet*

▼ *'Rouen Cathedral, Blue Morning Harmony, Morning Sunlight,' Musée D'Orsay, Paris, Monet*

'Rouen Cathedral, Blue Morning Harmony, Morning Sunlight,' 1894, has almost exactly the same composition as the previous painting but here Monet has used a paler palette of hazy blues and purples with golden hues to create the impression of a sunny morning.

The painting 'Rouen Cathedral, Main Door and Saint Romain Tower, Full Sun, Harmony of Blue and Gold,' 1893 also uses the same viewpoint but suggests mid-afternoon sunshine through the golden glow which saturates the front of the cathedral and deeper, darker shadows.

Compare these portrayals with 'Rouen Cathedral, The Portal, Morning Effect,' 1894 to see the difference the time of day makes to the appearance of form and colour. Instead of the sun-drenched hazy vision in yellows, whites and cobalt blues, we see a cathedral moulded in purplish shades, semi-silhouetted against the blinding morning sun flooding over the roof.

▼ *'Rouen Cathedral, Main Door and Saint Romain Tower, Full Sun, Harmony of Blue and Gold,' Musée D'Orsay, Paris, Monet*

▼ *'Rouen Cathedral, The Portal, Morning Effect,' The Beyeler Gallery, Basle, Switzerland, Monet*

▼ *'Rouen Cathedral, Portal in Front View, Harmony in Brown,' Musée D'Orsay, Paris, Monet*

◈ 'Rouen Cathedral, Portal in Front View, Harmony in Brown,' 1892 looks very different from the other paintings even though it is portraying the same subject. We see the cathedral from a more frontal position in much more sober colours of browns and blues against a stark white background, giving the sense of a bleak cold day. There is greater clarity of form, as there is more contrast in tone, but there is still the sense of the changeability of the weather and the fleeting moments which make up the day.

The Water Lily Series, 1894–1920

The design of the Monet's garden at his house in Giverny was influenced by Japanese prints he had seen, including a curved bridge over a water lily pond which he added in 1893. He painted 18 huge canvases in total of the lily pond, exploring the effects of light on the shimmering water, and the abstraction of shape and form.

The Water Lily Pond, 1899

In this painting, Monet has left out any hint of sky, enveloping the viewer in the beauty of the sunlit garden. Monet let each layer of paint dry before he painted the next one. His brushstrokes were thick and heavy, gradually building up a three-dimensional, rough texture. This can be seen particularly on the depiction of the bridge, making it appear to stand out from the background.

▼ *'The Water Lily Pond,' National Gallery, London, Monet*

Vertical and Horizontal Brushwork

- Monet used his brushstrokes to emphasise the directional lines in the scenery he observed. The foliage in the trees in the upper left of the painting and their reflection in the water are created by strong vertical strokes of the paintbrush.

- These are in striking contrast to the horizontal lines representing the water lilies on the surface of the pond. The horizontal strokes are applied heavily over the vertical reflections, creating an aesthetic contradiction.

- It creates the illusion of a three-dimensional reality with the water lilies overlying the calm water while at the same time the rough texture of the paint draws our notice to the surface of the canvas, making us aware of the two-dimensional reality of painting.

Colour and Light

- The dominant colours on the canvas are luminous greens, lush yellows, shady purples and blues and delicate pinks.

- The light-infused scene is hazy; the edges of objects and vegetation blurred and indistinct.

- Complementary colours are placed side by side to heighten the vibrancy of the colours – even the artist's signature is painted in reds to contrast with the green of the water lily pads and to unite it with the pinks and reds of the flowers.

CAMILLE PISSARRO			
Date	1830–1903	**Themes**	Country life, landscapes, city views
Cities	Paris, London		
Movement	Impressionism, Pointillism (see p. 306)	**Style**	Atmospheric, use of light, varied brushstrokes
Influences	Gustave Courbet, Georges Seurat, J.M.W. Turner, John Constable		

Pissarro was the oldest member of the Impressionist circle and was well liked. He produced many paintings and displayed pictures in all eight Impressionist exhibitions. He went to London during the **Franco-Prussian War** where he saw the work of Romantic artists John Constable and J.M.W. Turner (see p. 271). Pissarro was a fervent supporter of new and fresh ideas and techniques, which affected his style throughout his career, ranging from a Realist approach, through Impressionism and experimenting with Pointillism later in life. He is well known for his portrayal of simple country life and his landscapes, and as his health began to deteriorate, views of Paris from his window.

dic·tion·ar·y

The **Franco-Prussian War (1870–71)** was a war between France and the powerful German state, Prussia. With the support of the northern German states, Prussia won the war, which resulted in the unification of Germany under the rule of King William I (1797–88) of Prussia. France lost the territories of Alsace and Lorraine, situated in the northwest of present-day France, until the end of World War 1 (1918).

The Boulevard Montmartre on a Cloudy Morning, 1879

Pissarro became increasingly interested in cityscapes as he got older, often painting the same subject repeatedly under differing weather conditions or seasonal changes. He enjoyed living at a time of industrial growth, and relished painting the modern buildings, throngs of working-class citizens on their way to and from work in the boulevards, and the smoggy atmosphere of Paris. He felt that all of these factors gave the city streets character, which he believed was equal to beauty.

- The artist's viewpoint is high, giving us an overview of the busy street. Pissarro painted his subjects in dabs of colour, the edges blurred and indistinct. This helps to create a sense of movement and the hustle and bustle of daily life as well as establishing the impression of observing a view from a distance.

- Pissarro created great depth in this work through a number of techniques. He draws our gaze into the painting by constructing a triangular composition, the vanishing point disappearing into the hazy fog in the background. The vertical lines of the buildings, lampposts and the tall trees lining the street create a sense of towering height, dwarfing the figures and carriages.

- The light in the picture is typical of the atmosphere Pissarro enjoyed painting most in his cityscapes: dull and wintry with a misty light brightening the end of the street, creating atmospheric perspective.

▼ *'The Boulevard Montmartre on a Cloudy Morning,' National Gallery of Victoria, Melbourne, Pissarro*

ALFRED SISLEY			
Date	1839–99	Influences	Monet
Cities	Paris, Fontainebleau, Port Marly, Louveciennes	Themes	Landscapes
Movement	Impressionism	Style	Colourful, expressive

Sisley was of English descent but was brought up in Paris. Although he belonged to a wealthy family, he died of cancer in a state of poverty. He met Renoir and Monet in 1862 while attending Charles Gleyre's studio (see p. 286). He was chiefly a landscape artist, interested in contrasting colour and the depiction of views from a distance.

Port Marly – White Frost, 1872

This is one of the many landscapes painted in Barbizon (see p. 273) by Sisley, depicting a sunrise over a frosty landscape. The location of the scene is Port Marly, a town on the River Seine.

- The colours in the picture enhance the effect of the composition, with the frosty foreground lying in shade, while the tops of the trees catch the light of the sun.
- There is a vast expanse of sky, taking up almost half of the pictorial space, moving gradually from pale blue to orange and yellow hues as it reaches the horizon.
- The background is left indistinct as if out of focus in the morning mist, the shadows and mountains painted in purple tones beside the flame red trees.

▼ *'Port Marly – White Frost,' Musée des Beaux Arts, Lille, Sisley*

Brushwork

- Sisley believed that an artist should vary his brushstrokes in order to portray correctly the textures of the objects within a composition. He used long vertical brushstrokes to create the effect of sunlit trees on the far side of the lake, and short dabs of colour in the foliage of the trees in the left.

- He applied thick curved strokes to suggest the frost covering the foreground and clouds in the sky, and fine, white, horizontal lines to represent the shine on the water.

- The colours used in the painting are beautifully accurate, giving the viewer a glimpse of the dawn breaking on a cold Autumn morning.

PIERRE-AUGUSTE RENOIR

Date	1841–1919	**Themes**	Portraits, open-air group scenes, the female nude
Cities	Limoges, Paris, Florence, Rome, Madrid		
Movement	Impressionism	**Style**	Vibrantly lit, saturated colours
Influences	Monet		

Renoir started his career as an artist as a porcelain painter. He was one of the original members of the Impressionist movement and one of the most popular. He worked in the village of Barbizon with the group and participated in the first three Impressionist exhibitions (see p. 288). After this, he showed his work in his own independent exhibitions and sometimes at the Paris Salon, taking part in only one more of the Impressionist exhibitions. His favourite subject matter was that of the idle pursuits of wealthy middle-class Parisians. Later in his career, his style changed, becoming softer and more indistinct. His subject matter also varied, from mythology to nudes and bathers.

The Luncheon of The Boating Party, 1881

In this painting, also know as *'Le Déjeuner des Canotiers,'* Renoir depicts a group of his friends relaxing on the terrace of the *Maison Fournaise* in Chatou. This is a small village on the Seine, popular with fashionable Parisians taking excursions down the river during the summer months. A number of the characters Renoir has included in his painting are wearing straw hats, known as boaters, which were popular when river boating. Renoir loved painting social scenes, peopled with characters and momentary scenes of pleasure. Renoir often used his friends and family as models for his paintings and this one is no exception. A number of people can be identified, including:

1 **Aline Charigot**, who was later to become Renoir's wife, is seated on the left holding a dog.

2 **Monsieur Fournaise**, son of the restaurant's owner, is portrayed standing behind her.

3 Renoir's friend and fellow artist, **Gustave Caillebotte**, is sitting on the back-to-front chair in the right foreground.

4 **Angele**, a flower seller and singer, is shown wearing a blue dress.

5 **Antonio Maggiolo**, an Italian journalist is portrayed in the light-coloured striped jacket leaning over Caillebotte and Angele.

6 **Jeanne Samary**, an actress at the *Comédie Française* (a Parisian theatre) is wearing a black hat in the right background.

7 **Paul Lhote,** a journalist and writer, is portrayed wearing a straw hat with a red band.

8 **Pierre Lestringuez,** wearing a bowler hat, worked in the Ministry of the Interior.

9 **Charles Ephrussi,** shown with a top hat and dark coat in the background, was the editor of the *Gazette des Beaux Arts,* an Impressionist French paper.

10 **Jules Laforgue,** shown in the middle background wearing a cap, was a symbolist poet.

11 **Ellen Andrée,** a mime at the *Folies-Bergère,* is shown in the centre drinking from a glass.

12 **Alphonsine Fournaise,** the sister of Alphonse, wears a straw boater hat and leans on the railing.

13 **Baron Raoul Barbier,** wearing a bowler hat and shown talking to Alphonsine, was a celebrated cavalry soldier and the former mayor of Saigon (present-day Vietnam).

- The strong diagonal of the terrace rail in the left draws the eye into the background, creating a sense of depth in the painting. This is further enhanced by the figures in the foreground facing inwards, particularly the figure of Monsieur Fournaise who seems to be lost in a daydream as he stares idly into the distance.

- Within Renoir's busy composition, our eye is led from person to person, following the line of their gaze and their interactions with the other characters. We can tell a little about the people from this moment captured in time. The man standing behind the girl in blue at the foreground table, is leaning over the back of her chair, his hands placed on either side of her, signifying a close relationship between the characters.

- Alphonsine, leaning on the rail, appears to be enjoying a conversation with Baron Barbier, while Aline in the foreground is completely engrossed in admiration of her little dog.

Le Moulin de la Galette, 1876

This painting is another example of Renoir's favourite subject and is one of his most accomplished works. He depicts a mixture of Parisian upper, middle and working classes who are attending a fashionable Sunday afternoon music-hall dance. The *Moulin de la Galette* was one of the few places where it was acceptable for the social classes to mingle on the same level. The painting is also known as *Bal au Moulin de la Galette* (Dance at the Moulin de la Galette).

- The composition of the picture is lively and energetic, suggesting constant movement. The figures of the two girls in the foreground, while in fact chatting to the men on the right, face outwards, inviting the viewer to participate in the scene.

- Renoir's painting technique helps to create a sense of depth in the painting, concentrating on depicting detail in the foreground characters clearly, while reducing the background figures to daubs of colour. This makes them appear out of focus, giving the impression of the throngs of people at the dance without necessarily showing each individual.

- The placement of the figures within the picture seems casual and unplanned, as do the carefree, smiling faces of the characters, lending the work the feeling of a snapshot depiction of life as it was at the time.

> **Did you know?**
>
> The *Moulin de la Galette* is a windmill near the top of the Montmartre district in Paris. It consists of two mills, *Blute-fin* and *Radet*. The name 'galette' comes from the fare that was served in the place, which was a type of crepe. *The Moulin de la Galette* is now a restaurant and can be visited to this day.

Light and Colour

- The beautiful depiction of light falling through the branches of the acacia trees overhead onto the ground and the figures give the impression of transient light and shifting movement.

- Most of the people are wearing dark colours, blending into the shade, and highlighted by the dapples of sunlight. There is a uniformity of colour which unites the painting, as the artist repeats the pink and red tones in the ladies' dresses, contrasting with the greens of the foliage and background buildings and the golden hues of the straw boater hats. The dapples of light on the ground are echoed in the globes of light in the top of the picture.

▲ *'Le Moulin de la Galette,' Musée d'Orsay, Paris, Renoir*

Impressionism Revision Questions

1. Give an account of the artistic aims of the Impressionists and discuss how they were applied to any Impressionist painting of your choice. Include sketches in your answer.

2. Leisure activities and social gatherings were popular subjects of Impressionist paintings. Name and describe an Impressionist painting which portrays either of these subjects including a diagram in your answer.

3. Describe and discuss any series by Monet, referring to his painting techniques and use of colour in your answer.

Urban Art

The Industrial Revolution in France was a large factor in the emergence of Urban Art. Although the Industrial Revolution affected all of Europe, Parisian artists were the first to embrace the ever-changing city and its inhabitants as worthy subjects for painting. The rapid growth of Paris and its environs and the ever-changing skyline gave the city a sense of being constantly in a state of transition. This manifested itself in the fleeting, transitory images created by the Impressionist painters at this time. The urban developments brought about a new social atmosphere, which crept into the artists' work. For example, they started painting modern subjects, such as streets, cafés, and commercial districts with their high, new buildings and train stations. Artists also explored a broader range of art techniques, instead of focusing solely on paintings: they worked on prints, graphic posters and illustrations. In summary, Urban Art was a celebration of city life, featuring paintings of the exteriors and interiors of buildings, streets and city dwellers both working and partaking of leisure activities.

EDGAR DEGAS			
Date	1834–1917	**Themes**	Dancers, music halls, race horses
Cities	Paris		
Movement	Impressionism	**Style**	Spontaneous, full of movement
Influences	Jean Auguste Dominique Ingres, Gustave Courbet, realism		

Degas was the son of wealthy parents and had a classical training as a history painter. He had a great interest in movement, which led him to observe contemporary culture, and he began to paint racehorses, and figures in motion, particularly ballet and opera dancers. He was part of the Impressionist movement, participating in all of the exhibitions except one, but his work is slightly more independent in feel to the rest of the group. His 'snapshot' composition technique and work in **mixed media** along with his fascination with the effects of artificial light established his painting as truly unique. Degas's snapshot compositions were inspired by photography.

He was interested in how spontaneous a scene appeared when the composition was cropped to create a close-up view, often abruptly cutting off the edges of the composition or even parts of the focal point of the picture. He introduced this to his work, creating a sense of impulsiveness, action and intimacy in his paintings. Later in his career, Degas made wax models of ballet dancers and horses which were cast in bronze after his death.

dic·tion·ar·y

Mixed media paintings combine two or more art mediums, such as pastels and oil paint or pencil and watercolours.

The Dancing Class, c. 1873–75

This is one of the many pictures Degas created of ballet dancers. Unlike many other artists' work on the same theme, Degas focuses on the informal scene of a training session of the chorus instead of a homage to the stars of the stage. Most of the dancers are shown taking a break from their rigorous training schedule, while the dancing master Jules Perrot teaches one dancer her steps. The setting of the painting is the opera in the Rue le Peletier in Paris which Degas visited regularly to sketch the dancers.

▲ *'The Dancing Class,' Musée d'Orsay, Paris, Degas*

- Degas's composition is a wonderful exploration of spatial depth. The format of the painting changed over the space of two years.

- Originally, there were two dancers in the foreground facing outwards towards the viewer, while the figure of the dance teacher was facing the back wall of the studio. In 1875, Degas changed the stance of Perrot and one of the girls, who now faces inwards, also adding the figure of the girl seated on the piano on the left.

- The other girl who was originally portrayed looking out is now semi-covered by the girl on the piano. Degas enhances the sense of depth in this large space by use of the floorboards to create natural perspective lines and by the carefully constructed perspective lines of the ceiling and doorway.

- This is further strengthened by the uses of aerial perspective as the smaller figures in the background show much less detail than the ones in the foreground.

- Even his use of the colour red running through the picture, from the red bow in the girl in the foreground's hair, to the fan in her hand and further back to a hat worn by a figure at the back wall serves to unify the painting and draw our eye deep into the work.

- The snapshot technique he was famous for is also visible here, cutting off part of the figure of the dancer on the right to create a sense of spontaneity.

- Degas often re-used his favourite dance poses over and over in his paintings and sketches, the figure of the dancer practising her steps appearing again in 'Ballet Rehearsal on Stage,' c. 1874. The informality of this work has a fresh appeal to the viewer, as each character portrayed conveys different attitudes through their postures.

- The girl on the piano scratches her back, another adjusts an earring, while the seated figures in the background chat.

- Somewhat incongruously a small dog appears at the feet of the girl in the foreground looking out at the spectator.

L'Absinthe, 1876

This painting portrays two figures seated in a Parisian café, and provoked a storm of controversy when first shown in London in 1893. The setting for the picture was the *Café Nouvelles Athènes* in Paris, and the models were Degas's fellow artist Marcellin Desboutin, and actress Ellen Andrée. The woman, dressed in dreary tones of brown and beige, sits with a dull, glazed expression, while in front of her is a glass of the absinthe (a highly alcoholic herbal drink) mentioned in the title. Beside her the man, pipe clenched between his teeth, stares fixedly out of the window. Degas was often criticised for his unfeeling portrayal of the people in his paintings, and this was probably the most infamous of these. There is no idealisation of these characters, who slouch in their seats, unspeaking, giving the impression of disillusionment and boredom. This was seen as an unfit subject for an artist: the patrons of the arts had no wish to be presented with such a depressing image of working-class life.

- The composition of the painting is perhaps the most revolutionary aspect of the work. The figures are shown in the top-right of the picture, while the rest of the space is broken up by the large flat shapes of the tabletops. The picture has the spontaneous immediacy of a quickly taken photograph, capturing a moment in time.

- The edges of the painting dramatically cut off the end of the man's pipe, his arm and the ends of the tables.

- A large triangular tabletop protrudes into the space from the bottom left, making the viewer feel as if they are seated on the other side of it, watching the scene from within the space of the café.

- Degas's painting is fluid and loose, blurring the features and dress of the characters. There are some darker outlining of the forms however, seen on the shoulder of the woman and the edge of the table in front of her, distinguishing his work from that of the other Impressionists.

▲ *L'Absinthe,' Musée d'Orsay, Paris, Degas*

Posters

One of the effects of the industrial development of cities was the huge growth of social entertainment centred around the cafés and dance halls. These establishments commissioned posters to advertise the acts and **revues** that regularly took place in them. The function of these posters was to deliver a simple clear message to the public about the venue, acts, and dates of the shows. Many of the poster designers were painters, who enjoyed the freedom from the conventional modes of painting poster-making allowed them. The most famous and influential of these poster artists was Henri de Toulouse-Lautrec.

dic·tion·ar·y

A **revue** is a variety show featuring music, topical comedy and dancing.

HENRI DE TOULOUSE-LAUTREC			
Date	1864–1901	Themes	Parisian nightlife, portraits, life drawings
Cities	Albi, Paris		
Movement	Post-Impressionism	Style	Linear, strong contours, exaggerated forms
Influences	Degas, The Impressionists, Hokusai (1760–1849) and Hiroshige (1797–1858), two Japanese painters and printmakers, Van Gogh, Gauguin		

Henri de Toulouse–Lautrec was born into an aristocratic family from the Tarn region in southern France. During his life he experienced numerous health problems which are now considered to be due to generations of in-breeding in his family. When he was in his early teens he broke both of his thighbones which never fully healed. This stunted his growth and he only grew to 1.4 m in height. As he was unable to participate in a lot of physical activities he devoted himself to art, creating numerous illustrations, posters, drawings and watercolour paintings. He was drawn to Montmartre, the bohemian quarter of Paris where artists mingled with stage performers and writers. He used the medium of poster design to express his opinion of the social scene in Paris and created a new art form out of graphic design. His work was often satirical, creating unflattering caricatures of his subjects. In bold contrast to the Impressionist style, which placed the utmost importance in the exploration of light and shade, he used broad areas of flat colour and strong outlines in his posters, simplifying and exaggerating the forms and creating patterns of colour and shape. He made 31 posters in his career, and his style influenced many artists' work to follow, including the posters of Pablo Picasso (see p. 349). He died at the age of 37 as a result of his heavy drinking.

Moulin Rouge – La Goulue, 1891

This is the first poster designed by Lautrec, commissioned by the *Moulin Rouge*, which was the most notorious nightlife burlesque hall in Montmartre in Paris. The nightclub boasted a hall for dancing, another for music and cabaret, and a **pleasure garden** for the customers. Lautrec was a regular visitor from the opening of the club in 1889, and created many posters and paintings of the performers and clientele over the years. This poster portrays the most celebrated dancer in the Moulin Rouge, Louise Weber (1866–1929), who was also known as *La Goulue* (the Glutton). The other prominent figure in the poster is Jacques Renaudin (1843–1907), a dancer, who was known as Valentin *le Désossé* (the Boneless).

dic·tion·ar·y

A **pleasure garden** is a park open to the public which provides entertainment such as a zoo or concerts.

- We can note the growing influence of Japanese prints (see p. 287) in the pictorial construction of the poster. Like Degas, Lautrec admired the snapshot technique, which sliced off parts of the figures, objects and background to create a fresh, spontaneous look.

- The artist's love of Japanese imagery is easily seen in his style with the bold, dark outlining and two-dimensional aspect. He omits any unnecessary details from the costumes and features of the people and their surroundings. The clientele in the background are simply and effectively reduced to a cohesive black silhouette, throwing the main characters into sharp focus.

- The central character, *La Goulue*, appears half-turned, frozen in the act of dancing, the white of her underskirt and bloomers standing out from the yellows, blacks and reds, making her the primary focus of the poster.

- The shadowy figure of Valentin occupies the right-foreground, seen from close range and cut off from the waist down.

- Colour plays a large part in unifying the poster. The yellow of the floorboards is echoed in the light fixtures in the background and in the dancer's hair, the red of her blouse reflects the poster's lettering, and the black lettering in turn picks out the black figures of the customers seen behind *La Goulue*. This simple palette in vivid colours helps to create a strong dynamic image.

- Lautrec's posters were **lithographic** prints. There is a very effective use of broad areas of flat colour contrasting with the more gradated areas of tone (seen in Valentin's figure and the background).

▲ *'Moulin Rouge – La Goulue,'* San Diego Museum of Art, Toulouse-Lautrec

Reine de Joie, 1892

The poster was produced for a book written by Polish author Victor Joze, named *Reine de Joie*, (Queen of Joy). The subtitle was *Mœurs du Demi-Monde* (Morals of the Half-World) and was about wealthy, elderly Parisian men and their younger, dashing mistresses.
The poster depicts one of these men being embraced by his lover, while seated at table.

- The composition is divided by the strong diagonal line of the edge of the dining table, separating the figures from the title of the poster. The people portrayed are also arranged at a diagonal angle. This was a device often used by Lautrec to create an energetic, powerful image.

- Again, the striking use of colour is expertly applied for pictorial structure. The minimal range highlights the main characters and the lettering, while unifying the poster as a whole. The red dress the girl is wearing symbolises her career as a courtesan, while linking it with the red of her lover's chair, the crest on the plate and the red-orange tone of the man in the background's hair. Similarly, the orange liquid in the decanter on the table reflects the background colour, while the olive green lettering also appears in the hair of the old man.

- Lautrec's paintings and posters were never intended to flatter the people he painted. This work exemplifies this, contrasting the youthful glamour of the young woman with the over-indulged, balding elderly man.

- He uses strong, fluid lines to outline the figures and objects, this time using red for the female figure and olive green for the man and the tableware.

▲ 'Reine de Joie,' San Diego Museum of Art, Toulouse-Lautrec

Urban Art Revision Questions

1 Describe the work of Edgar Degas and discuss the reasons for its controversial reception in France at the time.

2 Compare and contrast two works by Henri de Toulouse-Lautrec, discussing his subject matter, composition and style in your answer.

Neo-Impressionism

The Neo-Impressionist style of painting developed from Impressionism in the 1880s and continued until the early years of the 1900s. The style used by the Neo-Impressionists was called the 'Divisionist' technique at first but is now more commonly known as **'Pointillism.'** In this method, the artist places small dots of vivid colour close together so that they mix in the viewer's eye instead of on the palette, creating a luminous effect. French artists Georges Seurat and Paul Signac, who were heavily influenced by the work of the Impressionists and the advances made in colour theory, were the main Pointillist artists. There are a number of similarities between Impressionism and Neo-Impressionism:

- Artists chose similar subject matters such as scenes of recreation and landscapes.
- Artists used glowing colours to achieve the effect of light, volume and shade.

Colour Theory

During the nineteenth century, great advances were made in the understanding of colour and how it is produced and affected by light. Scientists began to look at why certain colour combinations are more appealing to the eye than others. Michel Eugène Chevreul (1786–1889), a French chemist, and Ogden Rood (1831–1902), an American physicist, conducted tests, asking people to determine which colour combinations worked best together. They found that the majority people thought that complementary colour combinations were the most stimulating and that one colour helped to balance the other out. Complementary colours are colours which are contrasting, found at the opposite end of the colour wheel from each other, for example; blue and orange, red and green and yellow and purple. They also discovered that these colours were most effective when they were placed close side-by-side without blending, as the colours remained vibrant, almost appearing to vibrate against each other. Rood also concluded that many small dots rather than large patches of contrasting colour had a more pleasing effect. He discovered that small dots of colour painted closely together would appear to achieve grades of tone and shade, as the eye of the viewer would automatically blend them.

> **Did you know?**
>
> The term 'Pointillism' was first coined by critics of the Neo-Impressionist style to ridicule the work of artists such as Seurat and Signac, but it has since lost its derogatory meaning and is now used as a real name for the style.

GEORGES SEURAT

Date	1859–91	Influences	The Impressionists, Jean Auguste Dominique Ingres, Rembrandt and the Renaissance masters (see pp. 189–213)
Cities	Paris, Grandcamp	Themes	Social scenes, landscapes
Movement	Neo-Impressionism	Style	Pointillism

Georges Seurat is most famous as the founder of the Pointillist painting technique and his masterpiece 'Sunday Afternoon on the Island of *La Grande Jatte*.' Seurat was brought up in a wealthy Parisian family and studied at the *École des Beaux-Arts* in Paris between 1878 and 1879. In 1883 his drawing of friend and fellow painter Aman-Jean (1860–1936) was accepted and exhibited in the Paris Salon, but the next year his Pointillist painting 'Bathers at Asnières' was refused. He began to exhibit with the Impressionists' independent exhibitions. During his career he spent his winters in Paris and his summers in Grandcamp, a town on the coast in Normandy.

Sunday Afternoon on the Island of *La Grande Jatte*, 1884–86

This was the first of Seurat's pointillist paintings and was exhibited in the final Impressionist exhibition in 1886. He began working on it in 1884, creating 28 preparatory sketches, 28 small paintings and three large canvases. He combined elements from a number of these works to form the final composition of this large-scale painting. He was due to show the painting in an Impressionist exhibition in 1885 which was cancelled. As he had to wait until the next year to exhibit he began working on it again, adding more curved outlines to the shapes, thus creating a more harmonious effect.

▲ *'Sunday Afternoon on the Island of La Grande Jatte,' the Art Institute of Chicago, Seurat*

- This is the most well known of Seurat's paintings and exemplifies his Divisionist style.

- Seurat has portrayed a typical Sunday afternoon in a popular Parisian park. The *Grande Jatte* is an island in the River Seine, a very fashionable place for city dwellers to relax and socialise. The artist chose to depict the green parkland on the island instead of the other part which was composed of dance halls, cafés and drinking establishments.

- Seurat's composition is very busy, incorporating many elements and characters including 48 people, three dogs and eight boats.

- There is a real mixture of social classes relaxing in the sun, such as the soldiers depicted just left of the middle background and fashionably dressed couples such as the pair in the right foreground, the man in a top hat and the woman wearing a bustle (a frame which expanded the back of a skirt) and carrying a parasol.

- Children and more casually dressed people are also part of the scene, such as the man in the vest leaning back on his elbows and smoking a pipe.

PAUL SIGNAC

Date	1836–1935	Influences	Georges Seurat, the Impressionists
Cities	Paris, Collioure, Saint Tropez	Themes	Landscapes, seascapes
Movement	Neo-Impressionism	Style	Pointillism

Paul Signac began his career studying to be an architect before turning to painting. He was initially influenced by the Impressionists and worked in their style. In 1884 he met Georges Seurat and became intrigued by his experiments with colour and his pointillist technique. The two artists worked closely together and became recognised leaders of the Neo-Impressionists. Seurat derived a lot of his inspiration from the coastlines of France, combining his love of painting outdoors with his love of sailing. He sailed his yacht, which was based in the southern port of Saint Tropez, all around the Mediterranean, creating many quick watercolour sketches to record the coastal scenery. In his studio in Paris he painted large-scale paintings from these sketches. Signac published a book on the principles of Pointillism in 1889 called *From Eugène Delacroix to Neo-Impressionism* and was appointed President of the **Société des Artistes Indépendants** in 1908, a role he held until his death. Through his influence and encouragement, artists working in modern-art movements, such as Expressionism (see p. 339) and Cubism (see p. 348), became recognised and successful. Signac's later work varied from Seurat's dots of colour compositions, enlarging the dots to form square shapes of colour, in a mosaic-like style. The painting 'Chateau des Papes, Avignon' is executed in this style.

dic·tion·ar·y

The *Société des Artistes Indépendants* was founded in Paris in 1884 as a forum for artists to show their work to the public without any official restrictions. Its motto was 'no jury, nor awards.' It still exists to this day, renamed the Salon des Artistes Indépendants, and promotes the same freedom of expression for artists as was its founding aim. It is based in the Espace Champerret in Paris.

Chateau des Papes, Avignon, 1900

Signac's painting is based on a view of the coast of southern France. The building depicted is the Pope's palace, a massive fortress-like castle which was begun in 1309 after the French pope Clement V (c. 1264–1314) moved the papal court from Rome to Avignon because of the growing trouble between aristocratic Roman families. The building was expanded and developed by subsequent popes until their return to Rome in 1408.

▼ 'Chateau des Papes, Avignon,' Musée d'Orsay, Paris, Signac

- This is a beautiful example of Signac's later style. His use of vivid colour and **daubing technique** creates a glowing, vibrant painting.

- Instead of the small dots he used in his previous early work, his paint strokes are longer and wider, resembling small mosaic tiles.

- The colour combinations shimmer and vibrate against each other, giving the impression of a glowing sunset.

- The sun reflects off the sandstone castle in the background in hues of pink, orange, red and yellow making it the main focus of the composition.

- These warm colours stand out against the blues and purples of the sky and water, and are picked up again in the reflection of the palace in the water and the clouds overhead, giving the composition balance and cohesion.

dic·tion·ar·y

The **daubing technique** involves applying paint to a surface with hasty, often crude strokes.

Neo-Impressionism Revision Questions

1 Discuss what you know of 'Sunday afternoon on the Island of *La Grande Jatte*' by Seurat under the following headings: a) setting, b) composition, c) colour, d) techniques used.

2 Compare and contrast Seurat's 'Sunday afternoon on the Island of *La Grande Jatte*' with Renoir's 'The Luncheon of the Boating Party' with reference to subject matter, composition and style.

3 Explain colour theory and how it affected the work of the Neo-Impressionists, referring to a painting of your choice in your answer.

French Painting in the Irish Collections

The two main galleries housing collections of French Impressionist art in Ireland are the Hugh Lane Municipal Gallery and the National Gallery of Ireland.

HUGH LANE

Hugh Lane (1875–1915) founded the Dublin City Gallery The Hugh Lane in 1908, which now stands in Parnell Square in Dublin. He was instrumental in bringing international, world-renowned art to Ireland, in particular the work of the Impressionists. He was born in Co. Cork in November 1875, and moved to England, where he was brought up in Cornwall. He often visited his playwright aunt, Lady Gregory (1852–1932) in Co. Galway, and retained his Irish connections. He was originally apprenticed as a restorer of paintings and later became an art dealer in London. On one of his trips to Ireland he became acquainted with the work of Irish artists, Nathaniel Hone (1831–1957) and Jack B. Yeats (1871–1957). Much impressed with their paintings, he set up the first exhibition of Irish artists' work abroad, in London's **Guildhall**, which was a great success. Lane's great ambition was to establish a gallery of modern international and national art in Ireland. He set about collecting paintings for this purpose, buying many Impressionist works such as:

- *'La Musique aux Tuileries'* (The Music of the Tuilerie Gardens), 1862, by Manet

- *'Sur la Plage'* (On the Beach), c. 1876, by Degas

- *'Les Parapluies'* (The Umbrellas), 1881–86, by Renoir

- *'La Cheminée'* (The Mantlepiece), 1905 by French painter Édouard Vuillard (1868–1940).

He also asked famous contemporary artists to donate a painting for his public gallery where it would be housed permanently in its collection. By 1908 he had accumulated enough paintings to set up a temporary gallery in Harcourt Street in Dublin, which became the first public gallery of modern art in the world. Hugh Lane died seven years later in the sinking of the **Lusitania** off the coast of Cork. After his death, the gallery found a permanent home in Parnell Square, North Dublin. A disagreement between the National Gallery in London and his Dublin Gallery broke out after he died, involving the bequest of the international paintings to England's National Gallery. This was because Hugh Lane had added a **codicil** to his will stating that he wished to leave the 39 international paintings to the Dublin Gallery. However as this codicil didn't have witnesses' signatures, it was strongly contested by the National Gallery of London. After a prolonged dispute, an agreement was reached in 1959 to share the paintings. The gallery currently has almost 2,000 pieces of modern art in its collection and is funded by Dublin Corporation.

dic·tion·ar·y

Built in the 1100s, the **Guildhall** in London was used as a town hall for hundreds of years and is now the home of a museum, library and art gallery.

A **codicil** is a legal amendment to a will, giving information on how the deceased wished to dispose of his/her property after death.

Did you know?

The **LUSITANIA** was a luxury ocean liner built in Liverpool in 1903. On 1 May 1915, the Lusitania left New York for Liverpool but never reached its destination. On 7 May as the ship approached the Irish coast, eight miles from Kinsale in Co. Cork, it was targeted by a German U-boat (submarine) which fired a torpedo. After the torpedo hit, it set off a number of explosions, resulting in the ship sinking rapidly in less than 18 minutes, killing most of its passengers.

The Lusitania arriving in New York on her maiden voyage, September 13, 1907

The Dublin City Gallery The Hugh Lane – French Collection

As well as many Irish and international paintings, the gallery has one of the largest collections of French Impressionist art in Ireland. This includes paintings by Manet, Monet, Pissarro, Renoir, Degas, Vuillard, and Berthe Morisot (1841–95), a female Impressionist.

Les Parapluies, 1881–86, Pierre-Auguste Renoir

This beautiful painting is a depiction of a bustling Parisian street on a rainy day. Renoir (see p. 297) completed a number of paintings of street scenes, and this is one of his later works.

- The painting appears at first glance to be quite shallow in depth due to the dominance of the large full-length figures in the foreground and the canopy of umbrellas obscuring most of the background.

- There is however, a real sense of depth and space, seen in the smaller figures in the background and in the trees depicted in the top of the composition.

- The picture was painted in Renoir's later style which was beginning to break away from the principles of his earlier Impressionist works. There is more order to the composition of the characters and there is a strong pattern emerging in the shapes of the over-lapping umbrellas.

- The outlines of the figures and forms are also much more clearly delineated.

- There are still many elements of Renoir's Impressionist technique visible in the painting. His beloved blues and purples feature largely in this somewhat dark painting, while the effects of the dull, drizzly weather can be seen in the misty blues and greys overhead and in the orange-gold highlights of the milliner's (hat-maker's) basket and stems of the umbrellas.

- The viewer is invited into the scene by two of the characters in the scene; the lady on the left and the little girl, shown with a hula hoop. They glance out of the frame, connecting with the viewer and involving them in the picture. The little girl is very typical of the Renoir's portraits of children with her soft innocent expression. Her mother appears to be trying to engage her attention which seems to be riveted on something or someone outside the picture.

◀ 'Les Parapluies,' Dublin City Gallery
The Hugh Lane, Renoir

La Musique aux Tuileries, 1862, Édouard Manet

The setting of this painting is in the grounds of the imperial palace at Tuileries, where groups of fashionable Parisians went to socialise and listen to music played by military bands. Impressionist artists often visited the Tuileries gardens to sketch the passers-by and capture the light effects through the trees.

- This was not regarded as one of Manet's best works partly due to the fact that it is not considered to be fully finished, and also because the composition is not resolved in a traditional manner.

- One of the considered flaws is that there is no central focus for the viewer, with the same colours echoing each other throughout to create a sense of movement and activity. The trunks of the trees intersect the groups with strong dark lines.

- Many of Manet's friends and associates feature in the painting. The man standing wearing cream-coloured trousers is his brother **Eugene**, with the composer **Jacques Offenbach** seated behind him against a tree. Between the figures of the ladies dressed in yellow another group of associates appear, featuring portraits of French poets **Charles Baudelaire** (1821–67) and **Théophile Gautier** (1811–72), and Belgian commissioner of the *Théâtre Français* **Baron Isidore Taylor** (1789–1879). In the extreme left of the picture, **Manet** himself appears, cropped in half by the edge of the painting. Beside him is his good friend **Albert de Balleroy**.

- The style of the artist is quite difficult to determine fully, given its unfinished state, particularly in the right of the painting, where the figures seem to be suggested rather than completed.

- The canopy of foliage overhead is painted in a vigorous style with thick fluid brushstrokes. The cropping of the image gives the painting a feeling of spontaneity, as if the artist has captured a fleeting moment in time.

▼ *'La Musique aux Tuileries,' Dublin City Gallery The Hugh Lane, Manet/Renoir*

The National Gallery of Ireland – French Collection

The National Gallery, situated on Merrion Square West with another entrance on Clare Street in Dublin 2 boasts a large collection of both Irish and European Fine Art. The gallery was founded in 1854 as a result of an act of Parliament and opened in 1864. Some of the gallery's paintings were donated by wealthy patrons but most were purchased by the gallery, including the Impressionist works in the collection. These works include paintings by Monet, Sisley, Pissarro and Degas, the most recent being Renoir's 'Young Woman in White Reading,' 1873, which was acquired in an auction at Sotheby's, New York in 2007.

Bord du Canal du Loing a Saint Mammes, 1888, Alfred Sisley

This is a landscape featuring the village of Saint Mammes (near Fontainebleau) which Sisley (see p. 296) painted more than 60 times in his career. It translates as 'The Banks of the Loing Canal, Saint Mammes.' The painting also shows a canal upon which a boating party are about to set sail. Images of boating parties were a popular theme in Impressionist paintings of middle-class leisure pursuits.

- The grassy shore of the canal is painted in the foreground of the painting, with a large stretch of sky taking up more than half of the picture's composition. This vast expanse of sky was a recurring feature of Sisley's work.

- A red-roofed building occupies a near-central position in the piece, with two boats and figures situated in the left of the picture space.

- This is a fine example of Sisley's style, with his various methods of applying paint obvious in different areas of the painting.

▼ *'Bord du Canal du Loing a Saint Mammes,' National Gallery of Ireland, Sisley*

- He uses scratchy diagonal strokes to create the movement of the small white clouds overhead, with thick swirling layers creating the rough grass in the foreground.

- The blue water, echoing the colour of the sky, is created using short horizontal strokes of colour.

Un Bouquet de Fleurs dans un Vase Chinois, 1872, Camille Pissarro

Although Pissarro was more well known for his landscapes and cityscapes such as 'The Boulevard Montmartre on a Cloudy Morning' (see p. 294), he painted a number of still-life paintings. This simple still-life painting, which translates as 'Bouquet of flowers in a Chinese Vase,' shows a centrally placed arrangement of flowers and foliage in a decorative Chinese vase placed on a polished table dominating the composition. A casually placed pile of books occupies the left of the table. Still-life painting was often a subject matter for the Impressionist painters, as there was a ready market for such works, giving them the funding to pursue their *plein-air* work (see p. 287).

▲ *'Un Bouquet de Fleurs dans un Vase Chinois,'*
National Gallery of Ireland, Pissarro

- Pissarro uses layers of thick paint to create an almost three-dimensional quality to the chrysanthemums pictured in the painting. These are in strong contrast to the indistinct design of the artificial floral decoration on the blue and white vase.

- The floral theme of the painting is picked out again in the wallpaper in the background, which creates a lively sense of movement in the piece.

- Deep shadows lie to the right of the books on the table, while daubs of paint in purple tones make up the dappled shadows of the flowers in the left of the painting.

French Painting in the Irish Collections Revision Questions

1. Give an account of the French Impressionist collection in the Dublin City Gallery The Hugh Lane, with particular reference to two paintings.

2. Compare two French Impressionist paintings in the National Gallery of Ireland with reference to subject matter, composition and colour.

Bibliography

1. Beckett, Sister Wendy, *The Story of Painting*, Dorling Kindersley Ltd, 2001

2. Bohm-Duchen, Monica, & Cook, Janet, *Understanding Modern Art*, Usborne Publishing, 1991

3. Bourke, Marie, *Exploring Art at The National Gallery*, The National Gallery of Ireland, 1997

4. Cunningham, Payne & Hawksley, Bradbury, *Essential History of Art*, Parragon, 2000

5. Feist, Peter H, *Impressionism*, Benedikt Taschen, 1996

6. Kleiner, Fred S., Mamiya, Christin J & Tansey, Richard G., *Gardner's Art Through The Ages: The Western Perspective,* Wadsworth, a division of Thomson Learning, 2003

7. Langmuir, Erika, *The National Gallery Companion Guide*, National Gallery Publications Ltd, 1994

8. *The Great Artists: Ingres*, Marshall Cavendish Partworks Ltd, 1985

9. *The Great Artists: Monet*, Marshall Cavendish Partworks Ltd, 1985

10. *The Great Artists: Renoir*, Marshall Cavendish Partworks Ltd, 1985

unit 5

Modernism

Introduction

Modernism began in the nineteenth century with movements such as Realism, Impressionism and Post-Impressionism. Artists from these movements broke with the conventional rules and traditions of painting to create their own individual styles, transcending limits on aesthetic principles in art. In the beginning their work was only acceptable to their fellow artists, who alone seemed to appreciate and understand the necessity to question the long-established painting conventions. Modernist artists began to use the art elements of line, shape and colour to express emotions and the inner workings of the human mind, creating an abstract vision instead of simply mirroring nature. Changes in the political and social atmosphere in Europe also inspired artists to use their art to communicate their own beliefs and dissatisfaction, causing them to be seen as **avant-garde anarchists**. There were some artists who led the field in breaking down boundaries in art:

- ⟡ Spanish painter **Pablo Picasso** (see p. 349) used a Cubist style, which challenged long-established traditions of perspective.
- ⟡ Russian artist **Wassily Kandinsky** (see p. 356) broke with realistic representation to develop a more cerebral approach to painting.
- ⟡ French artist **Marcel Duchamp** (see p. 368) questioned the true meaning of art itself.

> **dic·tion·ar·y**
>
> **Avant-garde anarchists** used new and innovative concepts and techniques and were unafraid to express radical views and opinions.

Primitivism

Twentieth-century art was largely influenced by non-European art and culture. Many of the wealthy European countries, such as Holland, France, Britain and Portugal, had widespread colonies in Africa, Asia and America dating back to the previous century. The colonists regarded these lands and their inhabitants as 'primitive' and in need of a western civilising influence and missionary work to counteract the 'paganism' they encountered. As with Impressionism, early twentieth-century art was also greatly influenced by oriental art, particularly the linear graphic style of Japanese prints and the decorative patterns featured in Chinese ceramic craftwork.

Ethnographic Museums

Native objects from the colonised countries were sent back to Europe as artefacts of exotic and primitive culture. As a result of public interest, large exhibitions and museums of these artefacts grew in abundance. Amongst the objects on display were carved figures , masks, idols, weaponry, beadwork, headdresses, and other native crafts. In Paris several major museums opened, including:

- ⟡ The *Musée d'Ethnographie* in 1882
- ⟡ The *Musée Permanent des Colonies* in 1931.

▶ *African mask*

There were similar museums in Vienna, Copenhagen, London, Liverpool, Glasgow, Edinburgh, Stuttgart, Berlin, Chicago, Munich and Leiden.

The *Expositions Universelles*, a French industrial and scientific exhibition also began to display craftwork from the colonies from 1851. The exhibitions ran from 1855 to 1937 and were held every 13 years.

Influence of Primitivism on Art

The influence of 'primitive' art was, and still is, a major contributor to the revolutionary changes in Western art. Modernist artists sought to break away from the boundaries of traditional European art conventions and saw the cultural objects in the ethnographic museums as fresh and natural. They admired the simple honesty of the craftsmanship and the directness with which the non-European cultures expressed themselves. It became a source and building block for twentieth-century artists to create innovative, dynamic art forms. Many artists had their own ethnic collections which they used as inspiration for their work.

Post-Impressionism

As Impressionism (see pp. 286–300) became more accepted and admired, a new generation of artists, although initially influenced by the work of the Impressionists, gradually became dissatisfied with their single-minded desire to capture the fleeting moments of changing light conditions. They wanted to re-establish some of the art elements and compositional structure in their paintings, which the Impressionists had considered unimportant. Although they worked these traditional elements into their paintings, they didn't always use them in conventional ways. Backgrounds were sometimes painted in an abstract manner with colour, line and pattern used to create an atmosphere in the picture instead of simply representing the actual reality of the scene. Different viewpoints were also used to create interesting and innovative compositions. The Post-Impressionists were never a formal group or movement, even though some worked in close proximity with each other. Each artist was very individual in style and technique, their outlooks on life and in their subject matter, even though they were all united in their desire to explore colour, line, pattern and form in their work. The most influential and significant of these artists were Vincent van Gogh, Paul Gauguin, Paul Cézanne, and Georges Seurat.

▼ *Vincent van Gogh,
 'Self-Portrait,' 1887*

▼ *Paul Cézanne, 'Self-Portrait
 with Beret,' 1898–1900*

PAUL GAUGUIN			
Date	1848–1903	Influences	Primitive art, Impressionism, Symbolism, Camille Pissarro
Cities	Paris, Peru, Panama, Martinique, Brittany, Tahiti, The Marquesas	Themes	France and Tahiti, peasant life in Brittany
Movement	Post-Impressionism	Style	Vibrant colours and strong outlines

Gauguin was born in Paris in 1848, but moved to Peru with his family at the age of three, remaining there for four years. He began his career in the French merchant marines at the age of 17. On his return to Paris after five years he took a job as a stockbroker and met and married Mette Sophie Gad, a Danish girl.

Career as an Artist

Although he built a successful career as a stockbroker, Gauguin's real love was for painting, taking lessons from Pissarro (see p. 294), and exhibiting with the Impressionists. When he was 35 Gauguin gave up his job and became a professional painter. This was not a successful venture and he was soon reduced to poverty, leading to the breakdown of his marriage. His wife returned to Denmark with their five children. In 1887, he travelled to Panama and Martinique for inspiration, coming back with vivid and exciting work. He continued his quest for a more simplistic and natural way of life in trips to Brittany in Northern France, where he painted the local people and the landscape in bold bright colours with heavily delineated outlines. He was joined on a trip to Arles in southern France by Vincent van Gogh (see p. 323). Although Gauguin had become recognised in Parisian circles as an inspirational painter, he was still impoverished.

Move to Tahiti

In 1891, he moved to Tahiti in French Polynesia to immerse himself in a 'primitive' society, unmarred by western civilisation. There, he produced some of his best and most famous works, although he had frequent problems with the colonial authorities and the Catholic Church. This was because he frequently took the side of the native Tahitians against the rule of the colonial government and the rigid doctrines of the Church. He returned to Paris for two years in 1893 to exhibit his work. Dreaming of fame and success, his hopes were dashed and he again departed Paris for Tahiti. His health had begun to deteriorate, making it difficult to paint regularly.

Final Years

In 1901, Gauguin settled in the Marquesas islands in French Polynesia. His life quickly became complicated, again through altercations with the local authorities. While appealing against a libel charge he suffered a stroke and died.

The Vision After the Sermon, 1888

This painting is also known as 'Jacob Wrestling with the Angel' and was painted during one of Gauguin's trips to Brittany. The women of the village are returning from church, where they have listened to a sermon on the above subject. Gauguin portrays a spiritual vision of the story, witnessed by the peasant women.

▲ *'The Vision After the Sermon,' National Gallery of Scotland, Edinburgh, Gauguin*

- The congregation appear large at the forefront of the picture space looking on the scene in devout prayer, creating the illusion that we are part of the group witnessing the vision over the heads of the figures in front.

- The women are depicted in the traditional costume of the Bretons, with white, starched caps and sombre, black dresses.

- Gauguin does not adopt the realistic approach to composition, preferring to distort the scene to reflect the impact such an apparition would have. He had no interest in creating realistic three-dimensional perspective, filling the background instead with broad flat patterns and striking colours.

- The figures of Jacob and his opponent are scaled down in contrast with the large figures of the spectators. The wrestling figures were inspired by the Japanese artist Katsushika Hokusai (1760–1849), whose work influenced many Impressionist and Post-Impressionist painters.

- Although Gauguin began his career under the wing of the Impressionist movement, this works bears little resemblance to the undelineated Impressionist style. He developed a style with another artist, Emile Bernard, which became known as the synthetist style. This involved painting from the imagination and memory instead of life to create more primitive and spiritual work, where everything that was not essential to the painting was left out.

- There is some naturalism to be seen in the faces of the women in the foreground of the painting, particularly when compared with Jacob and the angel. His reasoning behind this was to show the contrast between the supernatural and the natural.

- The struggle is shown against a vibrant red background, symbolising the red of battlefields. He painted with strong, pure colour, outlining the shapes with thick dark lines. This portrays his interest in stained glass and Japanese prints, which were very popular and influential at the time (see p. 287)

Arearea, 1892

This is a simple scene of rural Tahitian natives, painted in the year before Gauguin's return to Paris. The title of the painting means 'joyousness' in Tahitian. On viewing the painting in Paris a year later, critics derided the artist's choice of unrealistic and unnatural colours. Gauguin defended his work by affirming that he deliberately chose these hues to create a harmonious balance of colour and tone to recreate an image drawn from nature and life.

▼ *'Arearea,' Musée d'Orsay, Paris, Gauguin*

- The two girls in the foreground of the painting are seated in the shade of a tree beside a lake, the girl in blue shown playing a lute.

- The indistinct figures in the background are worshipping a large Polynesian idol. This is an example of Gauguin's desire to portray the primitive rituals of the Tahitians, even though such practices had long since been abandoned by the people of the island.

- Gauguin used broad areas of flat colour and strong horizontal, vertical and diagonal lines in creating this scene. The repetition of the contrasting colours of red and green serve to unify the painting.

- The warm orange-red of the dog in the left of the picture is echoed in the water behind the girls.

- The work is framed at the top and bottom by the rich green of the grass.

- Gauguin's use of white, from the flower in the foreground, to the girl's dress, draws our eye back to the figure praying in the left background.

- He uses thick solid brushstrokes to establish areas of tone on the skin and clothing of the figures.

VINCENT VAN GOGH

Date	1853–90	Influences	Paul Gaugin (see p. 320), Camille Pissarro (see p. 294), Henri de Toulouse-Lautrec (see p. 304)
Cities	The Hague, London, Paris, Borinage, Arles	Themes	Self-portraits, landscapes, still lifes
Movement	Post-Impressionism	Style	Thick *impasto* brushstrokes, vibrant colour, dramatic swirling lines

Vincent van Gogh was born in Groot–Zundert, a small village in Holland, to Theodorus van Gogh, a Methodist preacher, and his wife, Cornelia. Exactly one year previously, their first son, also called Vincent, was delivered stillborn. He had one other brother, Theo, who was destined to help support Vincent in his career throughout his life. Van Gogh had many careers before becoming an artist.

> dic·tion·ar·y
>
> *Impasto* is a method of painting in which the artist applies paint so thickly that it stands out from the surface.

Art Dealer

At the age of 16, van Gogh began work for his uncle, who owned a prosperous art dealership in the Hague. After four years, he was transferred to the London branch, where he met and fell in love with his landlady's daughter. The relationship failed and this affected van Gogh to such a degree that his work suffered, resulting in his dismissal from the dealership. In 1876 he took a post as a voluntary teacher in a private school in London. Part of his job consisted of the collection of school fees and this often brought him in contact with the extreme poverty of the London slums. He was outraged and horrified at what he saw and refused to take money from people in impoverished conditions, bringing about his second job dismissal.

Minister and Missionary

After this, van Gogh, who had always been religious, decided to become a Methodist minister, determined to help the poor and assisting in a Methodist church. He returned to Holland to train but only remained there for a year, leaving for the Borinage district in Belgium to work as a missionary evangelist in 1868. This was a coal-mining region which was infamous for its urban poverty. Van Gogh became totally immersed in his work, devoting himself tirelessly and fervently to the poor of the area. He even gave away his own clothes and food, causing his co-workers to question his zeal. They were also shocked by his gaunt and unkempt appearance. Once again van Gogh was dismissed.

Artist

After this rejection van Gogh went through a traumatic two years, finally returning home with the decision to become an artist. While at home he fell in (unrequited) love with his widowed cousin Kee Vos, and had a disagreement with his father, which forced him to leave home for The Hague, where he was supported by a small allowance given to him by his brother. He returned home briefly in 1884, where he stayed until the death of his father in 1885. Van Gogh attended one year of formal training in the academy of Antwerp in Belgium. After failing this he joined his brother Theo in Montmartre, Paris, where he continued his tuition under French historical painter Fernand Cormon (1845–1924). Here he met and was influenced by Paul Gauguin, Camille Pissarro, Toulouse-Lautrec and Émile Bertrand. Although his work improved, he soon made enemies in Paris, due to his uncontrollable temper and bouts of heavy drinking.

Colony in Arles

He left to begin afresh in Arles in the south of France. Filled with artistic fervour, he persuaded Gauguin to join him to set up an artists' colony there. This did not work out, culminating in a serious disagreement when van Gogh threatened to stab Gauguin with a razor, then cut his own ear off, and delivered it to a prostitute. After his release from hospital, where he suffered hallucinations, he spent only one more year in Arles.

Final Years

Worried about his state of mind, the artist entered a mental asylum in Saint-Rémy-de-Provence in 1889, where he continued to work steadily even though he regularly suffered from hallucinations and convulsive fits. He spent one year there and then moved to Auvers, an artists' village north of Paris. Initially happy, van Gogh suffered a setback upon realising that his brother was struggling to support his wife and son, also named Vincent, and was finding it difficult to pay his brother's allowance. On 27 July 1890, van Gogh shot himself in the chest and died with his brother at his bedside the following day. Throughout his prolific career he had only sold one painting.

Self-Portrait, 1889

Van Gogh produced many self-portraits during his lifetime. This one in particular was painted in the first month of his stay in the asylum at Saint Rémy. Although the artist was tortured by the fear of hallucinations and convulsions, the face in the portrait shows composure, as if he is steadfastly holding his emotions under control. There is a sense of realism in his portrayal of his countenance. He makes no attempt to idealise his bony features, severe expression and the vivid red of his hair and beard.

- The predominant colours used in the artist's palette are a range of blues and greens, clashing vibrantly with oranges and reds. Van Gogh was passionately interested in colours and their effect in a picture, and used them to reflect mood and atmosphere. He was aware of the dramatic effect **complementary colours** had when placed side by side. In his self-portrait he uses this knowledge, dispensing with realistic or natural colours and replacing them with clashing colours which emphasise the turmoil in his mind.

* The red and orange in the beard and hair throw his face into sharp relief against the cool blues and greens in the background, while the green tones underneath the eyes focus our attention on them.

* Van Gogh's style, although originally influenced by the Impressionist movement was highly unique. Instead of blending his brushstrokes together, he laid them down in a thick, *impasto* technique. This is clearly visible in this painting.

* The background and the clothing are painted loosely in swirling lines of colour in contrast to the more detailed and precise painting of the face. It is probable that he saw the face as showing his real identity, while the twisted strokes around him echoed the chaos of his personal life.

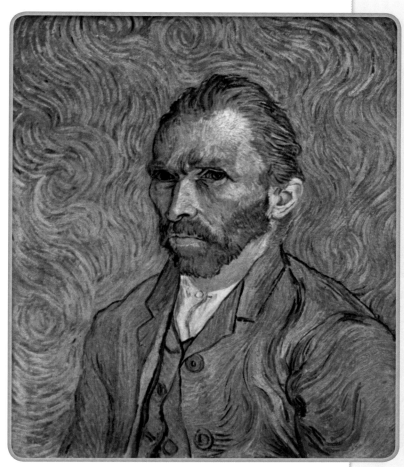

▲ *'Self-Portrait,' 1889, Musée d'Orsay, Paris, van Gogh*

dic·tion·ar·y

Complementary colours are colours placed directly opposite to each other on the colour wheel and contrast vividly with each other. Examples of these are red and green, blue and orange and yellow and purple.

Sunflowers, 1888

Van Gogh painted a series of sunflower pictures during his stay at Arles. He chose two of them to hang in the room he prepared for Gauguin to stay in as he had previously shown appreciation of his sunflower paintings. The arrangement in the vase consists of newly-budding, mature and dying plants, symbolising the life cycle of humanity. The artist also painted nature to reflect a range of mood and emotions.

* This is a great example of 'light on light' paintings perfected by van Gogh. Here, he was influenced by the French artist Louis Anquetin (1861–1932) who experimented with monochrome compositions, which are paintings created in varying shades of a single colour. The painting is almost entirely composed of tones of yellow. Van Gogh had a particular love for the colour; to him it symbolised joy and happiness. Indeed, one of the reasons why he chose his house in Arles was because it was painted yellow.

▲ *'Sunflowers,' the National Gallery, London, van Gogh*

- Even the background of the painting consists of flat areas of yellow tones. The pale luminosity of the wall behind the vase, being the brightest part of the picture, creates a struggle between the **positive** and **negative shapes.**

- The table on which the vase stands echoes the colour of the flowers and the upper part of the vase.

- The only other colours to be seen are the greens of the stems and leaves and the dark blue outline of the table, vase and the artist's signature.

- There is a definite lifelike quality to the sunflowers; his stippled impasto technique to depict the seed-heads of the young plants and the flowing brushstrokes indicating the leaves and petals bring the painting to life. The flowers are in sharp contrast to the vase holding them and the background which are painted flat and two-dimensionally. Van Gogh has placed more importance on his portrayal of the sunflowers; it is also possible that he was influenced by Japanese prints.

dic·tion·ar·y

In a painting the **positive shapes** are created by the objects in the picture space while the **negative shapes** make up the areas not occupied by any shapes or forms.

Starry Night, 1889

This is another painting completed by van Gogh during his stay at the asylum at Arles and is one of his many landscapes. 'Starry Night' is one of his most famous and emotive works and is dominated by a vivid deep blue sky filled with huge luminous stars with a towering cypress tree situated in the left foreground. In the distance, nestled below the rolling hills on the horizon, lies the town with a church spire in the centre reaching towards the swirling night sky.

- The vibrant, deep blues and purples of the sky are reflected in the undulating landscape and provide a rich contrast to the brilliant yellows and glowing white of the stars and twisting clouds. Hints of orange gleam out of the town, representing the warm light which shines from the windows of the buildings. It is very likely that van Gogh used these yellow and orange hues to represent warmth and happiness which can survive even amidst turbulence and depression, possibly itself symbolised by the surging blues and purples in the landscape and sky. Daubs of red appear on the dark tree in the left, which could be a symbol of danger or blood.

➤ The style of the work is similar in many ways to the other paintings van Gogh created at this time. The thick *impasto* brushstrokes, the whirling shapes and lines and rich contrasting colours all indicate his inner turmoil and individual technique.

▼ *'Starry Night', Museum of Modern Art, New York*

PAUL CÉZANNE

Date	1839–1906	**Influences**	Impressionism
Cities	Aix-en-Provence, Paris	**Themes**	Landscapes, still lifes, peasants
Movement	Post-Impressionism	**Style**	Forms modelled in light and colour, complex compositions

Paul Cézanne was one of the most influential artists of his time, inspiring generations of artists to follow including Picasso and the Cubist movement. Born in Aix-en-Provence, southern France, to a wealthy banking family, he attended the *College Bourbon* there to study law where he met and befriended the French Realist writer Émile Zola (see p. 274). He dropped out of university to pursue his ambitions as a painter in Paris in 1861. There, he became friendly with the Impressionist painter Pissarro and through him became involved in the Impressionist movement, exhibiting in its first independent exhibition in 1874. 'The Modern Olympia' was one of his exhibited works which caused controversy similar to Manet's painting on the same theme (see p. 279).

Cézanne began by painting landscapes according to Impressionist techniques, but gradually developed an interest in capturing the essence of a scene or still life through the use of colour and tone. He used these to model objects, giving his painting a more solid and structured appearance than Impressionist paintings. He also had an interest in depicting the peasants from his hometown of Aix-en-Provence. In 1886 his father died leaving Cézanne a wealthy man and in possession of a house near Aix-en-Provence, where he continued to paint and gain recognition and success for his work. Cézanne's studio there is preserved as a shrine for devotees of his style to see the environment in which he produced his works. Some of the items he painted are still there.

The Card players, c. 1890–1905

This is one of five pictures Cézanne painted of card-playing peasants and is the most well known. It is thought that he was inspired by seventeenth-century paintings of the same subject. Here, he depicts two local men seated on either side of a wooden table with a bottle situated between them.

- Cézanne's painting has a symmetrical composition, with the bottle in the middle serving as the centre. A dark panel runs behind the card players, providing a contrast to the two men and the rich chestnut brown of the table. The players themselves are directly facing each other, situated at right angles to the viewer.

▼ *'The Card Players', Musée d'Orsay, Paris, Cézanne*

- Cézanne was not merely interested in perfect symmetry however, and this can be seen in the very different poses of the men and the tilt to the left of the table in the centre. The men appear to have their own individual personalities, despite their similar absorption in the game they are playing. The man on the right of the composition is slouched over his cards, concentrating hard on the choice he is making. He also seems to have a stronger, thick-set body than his slimmer opponent, who sits back in his chair, giving the impression that he is less intensely concerned with the outcome of the game. The vertical lines of the structure behind the figure on the right also draw attention to the diagonal line of the player, emphasising the difference between the two men.

- The tilted table in the centre echoes the composition in 'Apples and Oranges'; the subtle shifts in perspective give the picture a sense of unreality in spite of the solidity of the figures within it.

- Cézanne has chosen his colour palette carefully to create contrast and harmony within his composition. Both men are wearing the same contrasting purplish hue and pale yellows. The man on the left wears a purplish grey jacket with yellow toned trousers; the figure on the right has a yellow jacket with purple trousers. The rich red-brown of the table is echoed in the wooden structure behind the players, tying the composition together.

Le Chateau Noir, 1900–04

The castle depicted in this painting belonged to a rich industrialist from Marseilles. The name of the chateau comes from the occupation of the owner, who made his fortune from manufacturing lamp-black paint from soot, decorating some of the rooms with it. The locals associated his love for the colour with black magic; hence the legend of the *Chateau Noir* which was known locally as the *'Chateau du Diable'* (The Devil's Castle).

- Cézanne's composition is organised through diagonal, horizontal and vertical lines, creating a strong sense of balance. Every part of his picture is treated with equal importance; he was as concerned with the negative spaces in his compositions as with the positive. This is demonstrated in the use of the vivid blue of the sky which has as great an impact as the trees and castle in the foreground.

- It is clear in this work how Cézanne created form and structure through tone and colour, applied with thick brushstrokes of even length. He called this process modulation.

- The forms of the branches in the painting's foreground are fragmented, letting the colour of the sky pierce through.

Apples and Oranges, 1895–1900

This painting is one of the many still lifes painted by Cézanne during his career and possibly the greatest. It consists of a selection of apples and oranges arranged on a cloth-covered table with a jug and dishes.

- Pictorial organisation played a huge role in the artist's still lives. Cézanne was not trying to achieve an exact replica of what he saw in front of him. He looked at the objects and table from a few different angles, creating the impression that some of the objects are tilted while others are observed from an entirely different viewpoint.

▲ 'Apples and Oranges,' Musée d'Orsay, Paris, Cézanne

- The dish closest to the foreground is viewed almost from above while the jug appears to be painted from a lower viewpoint.

- The table itself seems to be tilted forward towards the viewer, lending the painting a feeling of unreality and distortion.

- Despite these complexities, there is a certain geometry underlining the structure of the picture, in the triangular form of the table and the circular oval of the dish of fruit and the shapes of the apples and oranges.

- Cézanne's use of colour to determine volume and form is beautifully demonstrated in this painting. Instead of looking to shadow and light to help create this effect, he applies graduated hues of colour. This can be seen in his portrayal of the fruit. The outer circumference is dark, the colours getting brighter as they reach the centre (browns and deep reds giving way to reds and oranges and then to yellow). This vividly shows the artist's preoccupation with not trying to fool viewers into believing this is reality, but to make them aware of the surface of the two-dimensional canvas it is painted on.

- The white tablecloth is treated in a similar way, the edges of the folds painted in pinks and yellows, while the deep folds are painted in blues, purples and greens. Cézanne deliberately used the warm and cool colours to convey depth, knowing that cool colours recede when placed in close proximity to warm tones.

> dic·tion·ar·y
>
> **Colour optics** defines the hue, saturation and lightness of colour.

Colour Theory

With the increasing growth of scientific research in all areas in the nineteenth century, new theories on **colour optics** flourished. Michel-Eugene Chevreul (1786–1889), a chemist, discovered that varied hues of colour could appear intensified when placed directly side by side. For example, a deep blue when painted beside a pale blue would seem darker, while the lighter tone would appear paler. He also noted the effect of successive contrasts. This means that if a person gazed intently at a patch of colour and then transferred their gaze to a white page, they would glimpse the complementary colour of the original for an instant. Art expert Charles Blanc (1813–82) developed the theory that in a small area of undiluted complementary colours, the eye of the beholder would try to mix them involuntarily to create a neutral colour. This theory was further studied by the physicist Ogden Rood (1831–1902), who noted that small dots of colour painted closely together would achieve gradation of tone, as the eye would automatically blend them.

GEORGES SEURAT			
Date	1859–91	**Influences**	Charles Blanc and Eugène Chevreul
Cities	Paris	**Themes**	Social scenes, landscapes
Movement	Pointillism	**Style**	Pointillism – small dots of colour applied close together

Georges Seurat, born in Paris, was a very intellectual artist who was greatly interested in, and influenced by, the work of the colour theorists, using the knowledge he gained from them to create a new form of painting. His style is very refined and dignified in contrast to the loose, free paintings of the Impressionists. Like these artists he completed sketches and studies *en plein air*, but always executed his paintings in his studio. His artistic influences also varied from the tastes of the

Impressionists, as he admired the work of Ingres (see pp. 257–60; 264–5) and the classical elegance of the Renaissance artists. His paintings often invoke a sense of mystery.

Bathers at Asnières, 1884

This large-scale painting depicts a typical afternoon scene of recreation. The location was on the banks of the Seine, northwest of Paris, which is also the setting of another of his most famous paintings 'Sunday Afternoon on the Island of *La Grande Jatte*'. The figures portrayed in the painting are lower-class Parisians, who worked in the nearby factories, seen in the background. This was an obvious social statement, as the Salon did not approve of the aggrandisement of the lower levels of society. Traditionally, large figural paintings were peopled with highborn or prominent political figures. Here, by contrast, Seurat has created a monumental image of everyday people enjoying a relaxing day in the sunshine. The artist has imbued the characters with nobility and dignity, even elevating his models to godlike status; the figure of the boy with the red hat in the water is portrayed in the typical pose of Triton, the mythological water god.

▲ *'Bathers at Asnières,' the National Gallery, London, Seurat*

➥ Seurat had a classical approach to pictorial organisation and planned the layout of his work carefully. He made more than 20 preparatory drawings before attempting this painting. The strong diagonal of the riverbank cuts the composition in half, ending in the bottom-right corner of the picture, giving the viewer the impression of being an onlooker of the scene.

- This is a good example of Seurat's changing techniques from the Impressionist style to his own pointillist technique (see p. 306). Some of the painting is executed using loose, thick brushstrokes (areas of the river), while other parts demonstrate linear cross-hatching stripes of colour (the grass on the riverbank).

- The figure of the slouching boy seated at the water's edge shows the development of Seurat's pointillist style; his form consists entirely of small dots of colour placed closely together.

- Parts of the composition show evidence of pointillist re-working (dots of colour added later to create a different effect). These include the boy in the water's red hat, which has dots of blue and yellow added, and sections of the river.

Post-Impressionism Revision Questions

1 Compare and contrast two paintings by Paul Gauguin. In your answer include a discussion of his composition designs, style and subject matters.

2 Give an account of van Gogh's painting 'Sunflowers' and discuss the main characteristics of his style.

3 Describe Cézanne's use of colour and approach to pictorial composition by referring to two of his paintings. Include diagrams to illustrate your answer.

4 Describe and discuss Seurat's 'Bathers at Asnières' under the following headings:
a) subject matter, b) composition, c) style, d) colour.

Irish Art at the Turn of the Century

The artistic revolution taking place in France was by no means restricted to the main European continent. Irish artists were quick to recognise and gain inspiration from the ideas and techniques developed by artists such as Gauguin and Cézanne. Many Irish painters sought to improve their skills by travelling abroad to the continental centres of art such as France and Italy. They studied at the foremost art schools such as the **Slade School of Fine Art** in London and the *Académie Julian* in Paris, alongside the most influential artists of the time. Their work shows how they adapted to new ideas in art and developed their own work by combining natural ability with contemporary methods and concepts.

dic·tion·ar·y

The **Slade School of Fine Art** was founded in London in 1871 as a result of a bequest by Felix Slade (1788–1868), a wealthy art collector.

The *Académie Julian* was a private art studio opened in Paris in 1868 by Rodolphe Julian (1839–1917). At the time of its opening, it was the only art school not only to accept female students, but to allow them to draw from nude models. As, unlike the national establishment, the *École des Beaux Arts,* it had no entrance requirements, it attracted many foreign artists and also served as a stepping-stone into that national school. The *Academie Julian* is now part of the *École Supérieure d'Arts Graphiques-Penninghen* in Paris.

RODERIC O'CONOR

Date	1860–1940	Influences	The Impressionists, Gauguin, van Gogh
Cities	Dublin, Antwerp, Paris	Themes	Landscape, portraiture
Movement	Post-Impressionism	Style	Vivid colours, *impasto* technique

Roderic O'Conor was born in Castleplunkett, Co. Roscommon in 1860. He studied art in the **Dublin Metropolitan School of Art** before attending the *Académie Royale des Beaux-Arts* in Antwerp, Belgium. He moved to Paris to study under the tutelage of French portrait painter Carolus Duran (1837–1917), where he became aware of the Impressionist style and also the styles of the Post-Impressionists, becoming friendly with Gauguin (see p. 320). As a result of these influences, O'Conor's work throughout his career displays a range of techniques, from painting in a pointillist style which echoes van Gogh, to using vivid, unnatural colours similar to the Fauves (see p. 339). However, as a successful artist in his own right, this versatile painter never fully adopted any one style, merely using some of their techniques to explore his own ideas. He lived in Paris from 1904, marrying French painter Renée Honta in 1933, the same year his solo exhibition showed in Paris.

> dic·tion·ar·y
>
> The **Dublin Metropolitan School of Art** was founded in 1746. It is now known as the National College of Art and Design and is in Thomas Street, Dublin.

A Breton Girl, 1903

The painting portrays a French peasant girl in the traditional clothing and headgear of the women of Brittany. We have seen similar clothing in Paul Gauguin's painting, 'The Vision after the Sermon.' Unlike Gauguin however, O'Conor did not revel in painting the lower classes as symbols of simplicity and unmaterialistic innocence, but as he really saw them. Here, he wished to create a straightforward portrait of a peasant girl. She appears to be wearing the black garb of a mourner, as the white collar is hidden by a shawl, and the ribbons of her headdress are limp, instead of rigidly starched.

> ⟜ The pictorial layout of the picture is based around the simple triangular composition formed by the body of the sitter.

> ▶ *'A Breton Girl,' Dublin City Gallery The Hugh Lane, O'Conor*

- The background is reduced to a tonal backdrop behind her, ensuring her position as the focal point of the painting, by using similar tints to those he uses to paint her face.

- The harmonious colours create an intimate atmosphere within the picture.

- The influence of the Impressionist movement can be seen in this painting to some degree. There are no sharp, clear outlines – the only detail shown in great focus are the eyes.

- Although this is quite a restrained portrait, the grief the girl is feeling is eloquently expressed in the slumped posture of her figure, the hands tightly clasped together and in the sombre expression of her dark eyes.

- A little of O'Conor's **Pont-Aven** pointillist style can be seen in the flowing stripes of tone in the background.

> **dic·tion·ar·y**
>
> **Pont-Aven** is a coastal town in Brittany, northern France, which was popular among artists who wished to paint the surrounding countryside.

WILLIAM JOHN LEECH

Date	1881–1968	**Influences**	The Impressionists, Henri Matisse, van Gogh
Cities	Dublin, Paris, Concarneau, London	**Themes**	Landscapes, interiors, portraits
		Style	Bright, rich colours, the portrayal of sunlight and shadow
Movement	Post-Impressionism		

> **dic·tion·ar·y**
>
> The **Royal Hibernian Academy** (RHA) is an Irish art institution set up to foster the patronage and development of Irish artists. It was founded in 1823 and by the end of the nineteenth century was the main art institution in Ireland. Initially its headquarters were in Academy house in Abbey Street, Dublin, until that building was burnt down during the 1916 uprising. Its next headquarters were in Ely Place, Dublin, where it remained. In the 1940s the RHA was criticised for hindering the development of modernism, but changes were made to this approach and its reputation was redeemed. In 1970 a new building housing four different galleries was built in Ely Place. The RHA holds an annual exhibition which showcases both Irish and international art in many forms.

William Leech was born in Dublin in 1881, the son of a professor of law in Trinity College, and began his art education in the Dublin Metropolitan School of Art. He also attended the **Royal Hibernian Academy** (RHA) and the *Académie Julian* in Paris. Although the influence of Impressionism is obvious in his work, his abiding stylistic influence was Walter Osbourne, an Irish artist who tutored him in the RHA. Leech became an extremely successful painter, exhibiting regularly in the RHA gallery in Dublin and winning the Taylor Prize (awarded by the Royal Dublin Society) more than once. In 1910 he moved to London, and travelled from there to Italy.

▲ *'The Tinsel Scarf,' one of Leech's most famous paintings, Dublin City Gallery The Hugh Lane*

He married Elizabeth Saurine in 1912. She was an American-born French painter who he met in Concarneau, Brittany, in 1909 and served as a model for some of his most famous works, such as 'The Tinsel Scarf,' (c. 1911), 'The Goose Girl,'(c. 1910–14) 'The Sunshade,' (1913) and 'A Convent Garden, Brittany,' (c. 1911). Leech spent a time in Brittany where he painted the local countryside and its inhabitants, leaving at the outbreak of war and returning to visit afterwards. He settled beside London towards the end of his life.

A Convent Garden, Brittany, c. 1911

▼ *'A Convent Garden, Brittany,' National Gallery of Ireland, Dublin, Leech*

The painting is set in the garden of a Breton convent. The nuns, dressed in white, are depicted walking among the sun-drenched trees deep in contemplation of the divine. The nun featured in the foreground is modelled on Leech's wife Elizabeth Saurine.

- The way the picture is organised is similar to that of the Impressionist painters' works. The main focus, the nun in the foreground, is shown off-centre, situated in the right of the painting, while the nuns' figures in the background are cut off at the top. This shows the use of the snapshot technique favoured by artists such as Degas (see p. 301).

- Leech uses thick daubs of colour to create a sun-filled, pastoral paradise. The long flowers and foliage in the foreground along with the deep shadows under the trees in the background frame the scene.

- In the middle of the composition, the lawn is painted in bright, vivid tones of green, to convey the effect of light on grass.

- Leech used different tones of pale purple and blue hues contrasting with the yellows and greens in the background to enhance the brilliance of the white garments worn by the nuns.

SIR JOHN LAVERY

Date	1856–1941	Influences	The Impressionists, Henri Matisse, van Gogh
Cities	Dublin, Paris, Concarneau, London	Themes	Landscapes, interiors, portraits
		Style	Bright, rich colours, the portrayal of sunlight and shadow
Movement	Post-Impressionism		

John Lavery was born in Belfast. He moved to Glasgow with his family, where he began a career as a photographer's apprentice. His art education consisted of classes at Glasgow's Haldane Academy and later the *Académie Julian* in Paris, which he entered in 1881. His teacher there was the popular Salon painter Bougereau (see p. 280). In 1884 he joined fellow artists in Grez, a village on the Seine, and studied *plein-air* art (see p. 271), painting typically Impressionist subjects such as boating parties and other fashionable pursuits of the wealthy upper and middle classes. His style, however, differed from their techniques, having a more classical approach to technique and composition. Lavery is probably most famous for his portraits, his popularity extending to include Queen Victoria (1819–1901), who commissioned a portrait from him. His success as a portrait artist enabled him to enjoy a fashionable lifestyle. He bought a house in Tangiers, painted in Ireland, England and France and married socialite Hazel Trudeau in 1910. He also received a knighthood for his services as Official War Artist in 1918. This work involved travelling around Europe during World War I and painting pictures of the Royal Navy fleet. After the death of his wife, he moved back to Ireland, where he spent his remaining years.

Hazel, Lady Lavery in an Evening Cloak

The subject of the portrait is Hazel Trudeau, who was later to become the wife of Lavery. In 1904, while working in Brittany, Lavery met Hazel, a wealthy woman from a rich, American, industrialist family. She became the inspiration for many of his paintings, including 'The Artist's Studio,' and was his model for his portrayal of Cathleen Ní Houlihan who featured on the Irish pound note.

- The portrait is simple and uncomplicated, with the central figure of Hazel set against a dark background.

- It appears to be an outdoor, night-time scene, with a hint of grass in the green at her feet, and a moonlit tree to the left.

- The lady is presented half-turned, looking over her shoulder with an archly flirtatious expression which is mixed with dignity.

- Lavery's brushstrokes are loose and flowing, the background reduced to a mere suggestion by his use of colours.

- The treatment of the figure is more refined, with the rich texture of the furs around her shoulders and the heavy folds of her cloak captured in detail.

- Lavery limits his palette to create a striking portrait, letting the vibrant red of the cloak and the pale tints of Hazel's features contrast with the deep tones of the background.

◄ *'Hazel, Lady Lavery in an Evening Cloak,'*
National Gallery of Ireland, Lavery

SIR WILLIAM ORPEN

Date	1878–1931	Influences	Spanish painter Diego Velázquez (1599–1660), Édouard Manet (see p. 282)
Cities	Dublin, London	Themes	Portraits, still lives, war paintings
Movement	Post-Impressionism	Style	Realistic, detailed

William Orpen was born in Stillorgan, Co. Dublin, and had a very early start to his career as an artist – at the young age of 11 he took his first classes in the Dublin Metropolitan School of Art. He continued his education in London's Slade School. Orpen exhibited his work in the **New English Art Club** and the RHA gallery in Dublin, and started his teaching career in the Dublin Metropolitan School in 1902, also setting up a school with Welsh painter Augustus John (1878–1961) in London in the same year. He was also an Associate of the Royal Hibernian Academy,

dic·tion·ar·y

The **New English Art Club** was set up by a group of English artists in 1886 to provide an alternative to the exhibitions held annually by the Royal Academy, which had a conservative taste in painting.

becoming an Academian (member) within five years. Through his friendship with Hugh Lane (see p. 310), Orpen became interested in the rise of the **Irish Literary Movement** and painted many pictures relating to Irish life, countryside and customs. Like John Lavery, he was appointed Official War Artist and became a knight.

(see p. 310)

> ## dic·tion·ar·y
>
> The **Irish Literary Movement** was led by writers and poets such as William Butler Yeats and playwright Lady Gregory (1852–1932), who became interested in re-establishing a national identity for Ireland by deriving inspiration for their work from ancient Irish myths and legends.

Reflections: China and Japan, 1902

The painting is a basic still life, the objects chosen to display the artist's great gift for detail and precision. The objects portrayed include a peacock feather, a Chinese doll, a hand-painted china bowl and a Japanese porcelain statuette. It was painted by the artist when he was just 24.

- Orpen arranged the still life on a polished dark wooden table, with a pale background wall behind it to maximize the reflection of the objects.
- The foreshortened diagonal of the fallen china doll is continued in the curved peacock feather reaching to the upper-right of the painting.
- Although Orpen was aware of the Impressionist movement and the art which followed, he was more interested in the realism and naturalism of earlier artists from Holland and also by the work of American painter James Whistler (1834–1903).

▼ *'Reflections: China and Japan,' Dublin City Gallery The Hugh Lane, Orpen*

- He aspired to the Dutch still-life tradition of creating accurate depictions of the textural qualities of objects and their surroundings. This can be seen in his treatment of the plush silk of the doll, the brittle shine of the china, the natural, organic texture of the feather and the hard, glossy surface of the table top.
- The painting shows how Orpen lavished the utmost attention on minute details and the effect of light on surfaces.

Irish Art at the Turn of the Century Revision Questions

1. Roderic O'Conor's painting 'A Breton Girl' and William John Leech's painting 'Convent Garden in Brittany' are both inspired by the customs and traditions of northern France although they are portrayed in different ways. Explore the similiarities and differences of these two works, using sketches to illustrate your answer.

2. Discuss the painting 'Hazel, Lady Lavery in an Evening Cloak' by Sir John Lavery including in your answer a description of the model, her relationship to the artist and the style of the painting.

3. Discuss William Orpen's arrangement of his composition and his portrayal of detail and light in his painting 'Reflections: China and Japan.'

Expressionism

The term 'Expressionism' covers a broad range of art created in the twentieth century and is largely associated with two groups of painters:

- 'Les Fauves,' who were French
- 'Die Brücke,' who were German.

Expressionists were particularly influenced by Post-Impressionist artists such as Paul Gauguin and Vincent van Gogh, who challenged the traditional approach to painting in favour of a more personal and individual response to the world around them. Artists were aware of the psychoanalytical research of **Sigmund Freud**, who maintained that the unconscious and subconscious mind was the main driving force behind human behaviour. They were increasingly interested in expressing emotion in their painting through the intense use of colour and strong, bold brushwork, and replaced naturalistic painting with a more stylised approach. The Expressionist painters wished to evoke empathy from their viewers and to express their own feelings through their art.

biography

SIGMUND FREUD (1856–1939) was a famous Austrian neurologist who established regular meetings between a client and a psychologist to correct behavioural problems. He also believed that dreams could be interpreted as symbolic of unconscious desires.

Les Fauves

The first Expressionist movement began in France, with an exhibition of work in the **Salon d'Automne** in 1905. Critics were so shocked by the artists' vivid, intense colours and simplified compositions that they were named 'Les Fauves'; which translates as 'the wild beasts.' The leading painter in the movement was Henri Matisse. Other artists included André Derain (see p. 342), Albert Marquet (1875–1947), Georges Rouault (see p. 344), and Maurice de Vlaminck (1876–1958). These artists, although working towards a similar goal, had very different means of painting and were never a tightly knit unit; instead they branched off to find their own individual styles. Fauvism was only a short-lived movement, lasting over a span of five years, but its freedom of expression and abstraction of form and composition was to influence twentieth-century art heavily.

dic·tion·ar·y

The **Salon d'Automne** (autumn salon) was founded in Paris on 31 October 1903 as an alternative to the official Paris Salon exhibitions. The quality of the work exhibited varied as there was no specific jury or requirements needed to exhibit but it was an extremely significant development in the growth of independence of the artist.

HENRI MATISSE

Date	1869–1954	Influences	Cézanne, van Gogh, Gauguin, Gustave Moreau (1826–98)
Cities	Paris	Themes	Interiors, still lifes, female figures
Movement	Fauvism	Style	Vibrantly coloured, carefully constructed compositions

Henri Matisse was born into a wealthy middle-class family in the northeast of France. He initially trained as a lawyer and only began painting when he was 20 years old as a hobby when recovering from appendicitis. He attended the *Académie Julian* in Paris (see p. 332), where he learned how to paint in the traditional French style under the tutelage of William Bouguereau (see p. 380).

Use of Colour

After a visit to the studio of the Australian Impressionist painter John Peter Russell (1858–1930) off the coast of Brittany, he became inspired by the work of both the Impressionists and the Post-Impressionists and began collecting their work. He introduced vibrant expressive colour into his art which was badly received by both critics and the public alike. Gradually, however, mostly due to the recognition of expressive style by his peers, his work became appreciated and valued. In 1907, his friends set up the *Académie Matisse* which ran until 1911, where Matisse himself taught many students. In 1917 he moved to Cimiez, a suburb of Nice in the south of France, where he continued to work and receive commissions.

Later Years

In his later years he began to create cut-out paper collages. Two years before his death in 1954 the Matisse Museum which houses an extensive collection of his work, opened in Nice.

The Conversation, 1909

This painting portrays a domestic interior, showing a husband and wife in a blue room.

- Matisse's composition is simple and effective. He organises the figures facing each other on either side of a window.
- The attitudes of the characters convey a sense of antagonism between the pair: the husband is standing straight, hands in his pyjama pockets, looking down on the seated figure of his wife, who is shown in a defensive pose.

▼ *'The Conversation,' Hermitage Museum, St Petersburg, Russia, Matisse*

- Although their forms are stylised and composed of simple shapes, Matisse eloquently portrays their emotions through his use of line. The rigid blue and white stripes of the husband's pyjamas show his dominance and stern manner, while the backward thrust of the wife's neck reveal her tension. The artist has created a scene of disharmony through his use of colour and line, which is heightened by the sense of unreality due to the flat perspective.

- The colour of the interior is purely painted in blue, conveying sadness and oppression. Even the chair in which the wife is seated is the exact hue of the walls around her. This is echoed in the blue stripe in the man's clothing.

- Through the window, new colours are introduced into the painting. Vivid greens and oranges give us the idea that the outside world is a happier and more exciting place to be. The green is reflected in the collar of the woman's black dress, perhaps to suggest that she yearns to go outside and escape.

- The contrast between inside and outside is further emphasised by the starkly delineated railings separating the grim interior from the lively exterior.

Red Room (Harmony in Red), 1908–09

The artist depicts a simple, everyday domestic scene. A maidservant is shown setting a table in an opulent, luxurious dining room.

▼ *'Red Room (Harmony in Red),' Hermitage Museum, St Petersburg, Matisse*

- This painting demonstrates Matisse's preoccupation with pattern and colour. The red walls and tablecloth patterned with bold, **organic shapes** blend together to create a harmonious rhythmical composition.

- He deliberately flattens the volume and perspective using only a thin line to separate the table from the background while the maid, the chairs, and the objects on the table, are painted as a series of flat outlined shapes.

- The window in the left of the picture shows a stylised landscape outside in harmonious tones of blue and green, uniting it with the colours in the patterns on the walls and table.

- Matisse used colour to express atmosphere and emotion in his painting. He often painted over his work until he found the right colour combinations to convey these in the best possible way. In this particular picture, he had originally decided on an overall colour scheme of green, then blue, and finally this predominantly red composition. This rich and vibrant colour gives us the impression of warmth, comfort and elegance.

- He uses colour to unify his composition, echoing the same hues over and over to create this effect of pattern and balance; for example, the amber hues in the maid's hair are reflected in the house outside in the top-left of the painting, in the chair in the left-foreground, the window frame and the bread rolls on the right of the table.

dic·tion·ar·y

Organic shapes are natural-looking forms with curved and flowing outlines. They are often contrasted with geometric shapes which are rigid with sharp corners and straight lines.

ANDRÉ DERAIN

Date	1880–1954	Influences	Matisse, the Impressionists
Cities	Paris, London	Themes	Landscapes
Movement	Fauvism	Style	Richly coloured, loose brushwork

André Derain was born near Paris and began his student life training to be an engineer. Although he had done some painting previously, it was only after 1904 that he began his painting career in earnest, when he enrolled in the *Académie Julian* in Paris. Derain met and befriended Matisse and they worked together, exhibiting their works in the *Salon d'Automne*. In 1907 the art dealer and collector Ambroise Vollard (1866–1939) commissioned Derain to do a series of paintings in London which are now among his most popular works. On his return to Paris he moved to the Montmartre district, where he became friendly with Pablo Picasso (see p. 349). Towards the end of his life, Derain's style changed, becoming steadily more influenced by classical and Renaissance art which brought him renewed success. In 1928 he won the Carnegie Prize awarded by the Carnegie Museum of Art in Pittsburgh. Pennsylvania. He died in the Ile de France, Paris, in 1954 after being run down by a car.

London Bridge, 1906

This is a landscape painting which shows a view of London Bridge over the River Thames.

- The subject is seen from a distance above, with the bridge creating a strong diagonal from the bottom-right corner of the painting and receding in size towards the upper left.

- The background is sketched in loose brushstrokes in a continuous horizontal line across the top of the picture. Although there is a certain element of traditional painting in the structure of the work, the way in which it is painted defies these traditions.

▶ *'London Bridge,' Museur Modern Art, New York, L*

- The perspective is warped and flattened, which can be seen in Derain's treatment of the bridge as it appears to bend in the middle and is portrayed in shapes of flat colour.
- The water of the Thames is painted not with tones of colour, but with various blocks of contrasting colours to suggest the effects of light and dark.

GEORGES ROUAULT			
Date	1871–1958	Influences	Matisse, Gustave Moreau, van Gogh
Cities	Paris	Themes	Religious, moralistic
Movement	Fauvism	Style	Thick dark outlines, rich colour

Georges Rouault came from a Parisian working-class family. He began his artistic career as a glass painter, which appears to have influenced his painting style, which features elements reminiscent of coloured glass such as thick dark outlines and deep rich colour. He enrolled in the *École des Beaux Arts* in Paris in 1891. His teacher there was Gustave Moreau who was to become a great influence on his work and a lifelong friend. On meeting Matisse, he became inspired by the Fauves' expressive techniques and fluid use of brilliant colour. The themes of his paintings are mostly religious with particular emphasis on the Passion of Jesus Christ (Christ's arrest, trial and crucifixion).

Portrait Work

Rouault differed from most of the Fauve artists in that he was not solely involved in expressing or conveying emotion through his work. He was also concerned with expressing social and political statements. He painted mostly portraits, depicting a broad range of characters; from clowns to prostitutes to kings. These portraits gave a powerful insight into the social struggle of the people they portrayed. Rouault used the darkest and grainiest palette of the artists associated with the Fauve movement. He was a deeply religious man who felt strongly about social injustices and was absorbed in expressing the inner turmoil of his characters. To achieve this, he used heavy blacks and dark tones of blue.

Head of Christ, c. 1939

This portrait depicts the upper body of Christ, which dominates the painting. The heavy lines around the figure imbue him with strength and power. Yet there is an element of sadness or reverie in this painting: Christ's eyes are downcast and he appears lost in thought.

▼ *'Head of Christ,' Hermitage Museum, St Petersburg, Rouault*

- Rouault's painting technique is rough and uncompromising, using thick daubs of colour. The dark outlines of the figure call to mind the leaded panes of stained glass.
- The blues dominating the portrait create a more introspective mood of a man weighed down by troubles and despair.

Die Brücke

In 1905, a group of German artists came together in Dresden to form a movement named 'Die Brücke.' The term Die Brücke means 'the bridge,' which explains the group's aim to bridge the gap between the art which had gone before to the art of the future. The painters lived and worked in a colony environment, believing that by doing this, they would help nurture each others' gifts and ideas. They were heavily influenced by the colourful, exciting images painted by the French Expressionists, but they were much more concerned with making social and political statements than the Fauve artists. One of the most influential members of the group, Ludwig Kirchner, railed against the German capitalist government and the hypocrisy of those in power in the build up to World War I (1914–18). His paintings convey his anxiety about the detached, remote society brought about by the rapid growth of industrialisation.

ERNST LUDWIG KIRCHNER			
Date	1880–1938	**Influences**	German medieval art, *Les Fauves*
Cities	Dresden, Berlin	**Themes**	Street scenes, the female nude, mountain landscapes
Movement	*Die Brücke*	**Style**	Spontaneous, vigorous brushstrokes, strong colours

Born in Bavaria in Germany, Ernst Ludwig Kirchner began his art education studying architecture in the *Königliche Technische Hochschule*, a technical college in Dresden. He became more interested in painting and formed the art group known as *Die Brücke* with two of his fellow architecture students; Karl Schmidt-Rottluff (1884–1976) and Erich Heckel (1883–1970). Members of the group strove to create a link between the past, particularly Dutch Renaissance artists such as Albrecht Dürer (see p. 235) and Matthias Grünewald (see p. 238), and contemporary art. Their interest in Dutch Renaissance masters led them to use the medium of woodcut printing which had been popular at that time. Kirchner painted very quick sketches of life models, believing this method encouraged spontaneity. His paintings mostly featured the female nude or street scenes. He had a nervous breakdown in 1915 as a result of his involvement in World War I and moved to Switzerland to recover. He remained in Switzerland for most of the rest of his life, painting landscapes in the mountains. His work was very successful until the outbreak of World War II in 1939. The Nazi authorities renounced his art as '**degenerate**' in 1937 and ordered more than 600 of his paintings to be confiscated or burned. In 1938 Kirchner committed suicide, profoundly depressed over the destruction of his work and the effects of the war.

dic·tion·ar·y

The Nazi regime described most modern art as being **degenerate**. They claimed it was un-German in what it represented, and degenerate artists were banned from exhibiting their work.

Street, Dresden, 1908

This is a busy city street scene, a popular subject for artists since the birth of Impressionism (see p. 286). However this differs greatly from the pleasant urban scenes of frivolity and leisure painted by artists such as Renoir (see p. 297). Here, Kirchner's aim was to portray the ugliness of the modern city and the alienation of its residents.

- The picture is organised within a shallow composition, the roughly painted figures in the right foreground appearing large and facing directly towards the viewer, creating an antagonistic atmosphere.

- This effect is further enhanced by the perspective seeming to be flattened and warped, tilting the characters forward. Kirchner uses the broad, bold brushstrokes favoured by Matisse (see p. 339) to create large flat expanses of colour.

▲ *'Street, Dresden,' Museum of Modern Art, New York, Kirchner*

- The faces of the characters are mask-like and expressionless, adding to the mood of impersonal alienation.

- The gaudy, clashing colours combined with deep, moody blues and greens used in the painting heighten the uncomfortable atmosphere.

- The artist is not interested in recreating an image from reality, but is seeking to convey his thoughts on city living and modern society through the expressive use of colour. The faces of the women in the foreground are painted in bright green and orange, making them look hideous and artificial, while the pavement they are walking on is over-painted in vivid clashing hues of pink and orange. The background from which the characters are emerging is a menacing gloomy mixture of dark blue, purple and green.

EMIL NOLDE			
Date	1867–1956	Influences	van Gogh
Cities	Nolde, Berlin	Themes	Still lives, seascapes, landscapes, religious
Movement	*Die Brücke,* Expressionism	Style	Instinctive, clashing colours, loose brushstrokes

This artist was named Emil Hansen at birth, but later took the name of Nolde, his home town in northern Germany. He originally trained as a woodcarver and only began his art education at the age of 22 in the School of Applied Arts in Karlsruhe. He worked as an art teacher until he was 31 and then moved to Berlin in 1902 where he joined *Die Brücke* in 1906. Nolde was a member of *Die Brücke* for only a year, never fully conforming to their style and ideas. He moved to the north of Germany where he worked in seclusion, painting mostly religious paintings, still lifes, seascapes and landscapes. He developed his own style which became known as '*Blut und Boden*' (blood and soil), which described his earthy imagery and rough, violent brushstrokes. Like Kirchner, he was condemned as a degenerate artist and his work was removed from museums and galleries. After the end of the World War II (1945), this was revoked and he was awarded the German Order of Merit, which was a state decoration rewarding outstanding achievements in many areas including art.

Entry into Jerusalem, 1915

This is one of Nolde's many religious paintings. It depicts a scene from the New Testament, showing Christ entering the city of Jerusalem on a donkey, surrounded by rejoicing crowds of people waving branches of palm trees which were symbols of victory. The people of Jerusalem had heard of Christ's miracles and welcomed him into the city, hailing him as the King of the Jews.

- The scene is painted from a close viewpoint, giving the figures total dominance within the confines of the composition. Nolde deliberately pushes the characters close together to heighten the intense atmosphere, and to emphasise the drama of this subject.

- Entry into Jerusalem is a good example of Nolde's technique, with its vivid, brilliant colours against a dark sombre background. His brushwork is thick and heavy, creating striking contrasts of colour and tone.

- The people and animals depicted in his work are not the usual idealised figures generally seen in Biblical paintings, but appear rough and uncouth, their features large and unrefined.

▶ *'Entry into Jerusalem,' private collection, Nolde*

Cubism

In early twentieth-century Paris, a radical new art movement was formed by two young artists living the Montmartre district of the city. The artists were a Spaniard, Pablo Picasso, and native Frenchman Georges Braque. The Cubist style, as it was known, was probably the most significant and influential development in the history of twentieth-century art. Cubism was seen to be fighting against convention and this led to the idea that Cubist painters were revolutionary and radical minded. Some critics viewed it as subversive and disrespectful to artists' work from previous centuries. Although it was initially shocking and incomprehensible to viewers, Cubism's break from traditional styles and its intellectual rethinking of how the world should be portrayed was to be a stepping stone for many art movements to follow.

▲ *Pablo Picasso was one of the founders of the Cubist movement.*

Three-Dimensional Interpretation of Form

Cubist artists derived a large amount of their ideas from the work of Cézanne (see p. 327) and also from non-European primitive sources (see p. 318). Cézanne had composed his paintings by using simple forms such as cylinders and rectangles to represent nature. The cubists took this a step further by looking at an object from many different angles to comprehend every visual aspect fully. By looking at the object from every angle of its three-dimensional form they were then able to compose a new representation of it by combining all of these viewpoints. For example; if they wished to depict a cup, they could include both the top and bottom of the cup, the handle and the front of the cup all in the one image.

Analytical Period

This era of Cubism, between 1909 and 1912, saw Picasso and Braque dissecting the objects they painted into fragments of shape, analysing and studying the objects from every conceivable angle and then re-forming them on the page. Sometimes they broke an object apart in their art, painting sections of it interspersed with the background and within other objects. The paintings were most often monochromatic – using hues and tints of a single colour. They reduced the colour palette so that the emphasis of the paintings, form and shape, would not have any interference. It also helped to unify their work as the eye of the viewer was not distracted by a variety of colours contrasting with each other.

Synthetic Period

The art of Braque and Picasso took a new turn in 1912 when they began to introduce **collage** into their work. Instead of merely continuing with the fragmentation and realigning of shapes within forms, they expanded this by including 'ready-made' elements in their paintings to emphasise the idea that we understand what these mean without the artist having to resort to tricks of perspective and visual painted representation to portray them. Examples of the ready-made items used were pieces of newspaper, fragments of chair caning and wallpaper, used in most cases to represent themselves in actuality within the picture space. They also used these items, shaped to represent completely different objects, to make us see the objects in a very different way.

dic·tion·ar·y

The term 'collage' is derived from the French verb meaning 'to glue.' A collage is a work of art created by sticking a variety of materials on to a two-dimensional surface. A collage can include pieces of artwork, newspaper, clippings from magazines or any found materials.

PABLO PICASSO			
Date	1881–1973	Influences	Cézanne, African art, **Iberian sculpture**
Cities	Malaga, Barcelona, Paris	Themes	Bulls, women, acrobats, war
Movement	Cubism	Style	Dislocated forms, many-angled viewpoints, powerful

Picasso is probably the most well-documented artist of the twentieth century, famed not only for his precocious talent and revolutionary style of painting and sculpting, but also for his flamboyant lifestyle and notorious womanising. Pablo Picasso was born in Malaga, Spain in 1881, the only son of an artist-curator father who nurtured his son's gift in art early. When Picasso was 14, the family moved to live in Barcelona, where he joined the *La Lonja* Academy, a prestigious art school where his father taught. Picasso soon became a part of the bohemian, artistic society, participating in philosophical and aesthetic discussions in the city's cafés.

dic·tion·ar·y

Iberian sculpture, dating from the Bronze Age to the Roman invasion in 17 B.C., comes from the Iberian Peninsula (present-day Spain and Portugal) and was influenced by classical Greek sculpture.

Move to Paris

In 1900 he moved to Paris, where he visited the Louvre and contemporary exhibitions, absorbing the avant-garde culture that prevailed. There he met Max Jacob, a poet, and shared a house with him. Picasso was not an immediate success – he lived in terrible poverty, which became a recurring theme in his work for a time. This work became known collectively as Picasso's 'Blue Period.' In 1905 he met Fernande Oliver, his first real love, and gradually became more successful, entering the 'Rose Period' of his career. He painted many self-portraits in the guise of dancers, harlequins (clowns) and circus performers.

Cubist Style

It was in 1907 that Picasso's Cubist style emerged with the painting of *'Les Demoiselles d'Avignon,'* influenced by the work of Cézanne, ancient Iberian sculpture and 'primitive' African art. At this time he had met the new woman in his life; Marcelle Humbert, and had formed an artistic partnership with Georges Braque. In 1915 Marcelle died of tuberculosis, leaving Picasso depressed and alone.

Relationships With Women

In 1917 he went to Rome to design a production of the ballet 'Parade,' where he admired the work of the Renaissance masters and met Olga Koklova, a ballet dancer. He married her in 1918, returning to Paris where his son Paolo was born in 1921. As his marriage began to deteriorate, he found love briefly again with Marie-Thérèse Walter who gave birth to his daughter Maia. By that time he had met another woman, Dora Maar, a photographer with whom he had a tempestuous relationship, which was later to become symbolised in his many paintings of weeping women.

In 1937 Picasso painted 'Guernica' in a personal response to the **Spanish Civil War**. He met and fell in love with 21-year-old Françoise Gilot, moving to Vallauris on the Cote d'Azur where he experimented with pottery and ceramic sculpture. The couple had two children, Claude and Paloma, and stayed together until 1953.

Final Years

Picasso's last relationship was with Jacqueline Roque, a saleswoman in the pottery workshop where Picasso completed his ceramic pieces. He married her in 1961 and they remained happily together until his death. In the last two decades of his long and eventful life, Picasso continued to work, becoming increasingly more inspired by past masters such as Delacroix and Manet until his eyesight began to fail. He died in *Notre Dame de Vie*, a mansion on the French Riviera, on 8 April 1973.

Les Demoiselles d'Avignon, 1907

The painting was originally intended to depict the salon in a brothel where prostitutes met their prospective customers, and the first studies for the picture included male as well as female figures. The title at this stage was 'Philosophical Bordello.' As Picasso worked on the piece, however, he gradually lost interest in the inclusion of men and changed the title to *'Les Demoiselles d'Avignon,'* which referred not to the southern French city, but to the red-light district in Barcelona at the time. The title translates as 'The young ladies of Avignon.' The bowl of fruit depicted in the bottom of the painting was used as a symbol of life and death. For a time before it was unveiled to the public, Picasso only showed the painting to his fellow artists. The reaction was mixed although it certainly created a huge impression. Painters such as Braque were very excited, as the painting challenged them to explore this new-found Cubist art form to create their own style.

- Picasso's painting here is a blend of the different sources which influenced him heavily, the combination of which created the innovative technique which was to make him famous. The ideas of Cézanne added to his growing interest in African and Indian art and Iberian sculpture helped to create his first major Cubist work.
- This is a very large-scale work, approximately 2.4 m square. The picture-space is shallow, the five figures of the women filling the composition, framed by the drapery.
- The integration of the background cloth with the sharp, angular shapes of the women was a new compositional departure for art, as Picasso did not discriminate between his treatment of the human form and the way he painted inanimate objects.
- Picasso wished to interpret the five female figures in an absolute way, contorting their bodies to display varying aspects of their figures and fracturing the shapes within and

around them, instead of the traditional continuous portrayal of form which had been previously explored. Picasso had no desire to fool the eye of the beholder into believing that what they viewed was a three-dimensional figure. Instead, he presented a pure study of three dimensions on a flat two-dimensional surface. He was bringing to life his observations that an object cannot be represented simply by the one facet which is presented from one angle, but must be seen from multiple viewpoints to comprehend fully its totality.

- The two figures on our right of the painting best demonstrate this reasoning. The seated figure shows the face from the front, a three-quarter view facing to our left in the lower body, and also a three-quarter view to the right in the upper body. The drapery which surrounds the women is also treated in a similar technique, appearing to be dissected into jagged shapes, often blending with the figures.

- The faces of the women are directly influenced by Picasso's preoccupation with primitive art – the women on the right with their terrifying mask-like features in bold unnatural colours were inspired by African imagery, while the more serene, stylised faces of the three women on the left derive their inspiration from ancient Iberian sculpture.

▼ *'Les Demoiselles d'Avignon,' Museum of Modern Art, New York, Picasso*

Guernica, 1937

This, perhaps the most famous of Picasso's paintings, was painted in response to the atrocities of the Spanish Civil War. Picasso was living in Paris when he saw photographs of the town of Guernica after it had been bombed by Nationalists, and was so appalled by them that he painted this work to express his outrage at what was happening in his native country. The artist had no intention of displaying the painting in Spain until Franco's reign had ended, but the painting toured Europe to promote the Republican cause. After the death of Franco, the painting eventually arrived in Spain in 1981, eight years after Picasso himself had died.

▲ *Guernica, a town in northern Spain, was almost completely destroyed by the bombing in April 1937.*

- This is a huge painting (3.49 m x 7.76 m) which was produced in under a month by Picasso for the **Spanish Pavilion** in the **Paris World Fair**. Picasso filled every space with line and shape, creating a sense of movement and drama. Strong diagonal lines lead the eye towards the centre and then propel it around the canvas, via line and shape.

- The chaotic mix of figures overlapping and battling with each other for space in the composition expresses vividly the terror and commotion of the bombing. In the middle a 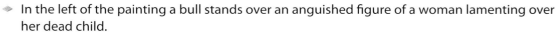 wounded horse throws its head back in agony under a sun with a light bulb at its centre.

- In the left of the painting a bull stands over an anguished figure of a woman lamenting over her dead child.

- At her feet, a dead soldier lies, gripping a broken Roman sword and a flower. The broken sword symbolises the Spanish peoples' resignation to the atrocities of the war, and their lack of resistance.

- In the right, a woman screams, trapped in a house which has caught fire, while another female figure emerges through a window holding aloft a lamp.

- A fifth human figure below them stretches into the painting diagonally, holding her arms apart in a gesture of despair.

- The painting is entirely executed in stark tones of black, grey and white, adding to the sombre atmosphere of the work. Picasso's style of painting is simplified into clear, delineated shapes and forms, but is not subject to traditional perspective or realistic portrayal of the characters and background.

- He deftly conveys the horror of the characters through the contortion of their bodies. The Cubist painting technique is visible in the faces, some having two eyes placed on one side of the head, which was a feature of his work at the time such as the 'Weeping Woman,' 1937.

Symbolism

Picasso includes some of the symbols he had used previously in other works, some now appearing in a new context, while others are new to his work.

- **The bull** was sometimes used as a symbol of Picasso himself, but here it represents war and brutality. Picasso was fascinated by bullfights in his native Spain because of their savage cruelty.

- **The horse** appeared in some of Picasso's bullfight paintings and usually symbolized the female. In this picture it represents the innocent civilians caught up in violence and destruction.

- In previous paintings, **the weeping woman** image was a symbol of his tempestuous relationship with Dora Maar, his mistress at the time. In this context, she appears to reflect the grief and pain inflicted by war.

- **The lamp** shown in the centre, held in a woman's hand, could symbolise the lamp of truth, showing the viewer the full extent of the atrocity.

- **The flower** seen clutched in the fist of the dead soldier could appear as a promise of hope.

- **The light bulb** is placed within an abstract sun, perhaps symbolising the Fascist regime's desire to become all-powerful.

◄ *'Guernica,' Museo Reina Sofia, Madrid, Picasso*

The She-Goat, 1950

This work is one of many of Picasso's sculptures. These tended to have a spontaneous feel to them, creating art out of what was perceived by others to be useless pieces of bric-a-brac. In this piece, Picasso created an image of a goat. He was fascinated by animals and kept many in and around his home, often serving as inspiration for his work.

- The sculpture was constructed by means of different materials moulded together to form the semblance of a goat.

- Picasso used metal tubing for the shoulders, flower pots for the udders, pieces of china, palm leaves for the ribs and spine, a wicker basket for the stomach and plaster to bind the sculpture together.

- Although Picasso used materials found at random to construct this piece, he still managed the make his depiction of the she-goat look realistic and natural.

- His innate inventiveness saw how each material could be used to form a goat-like structure, giving it a humorous quality.

▶ 'The She-Goat,' *Museum of Modern Art, New York, Picasso*

GEORGES BRAQUE				
Date	1882–1963	**Influences**	Fauvism, Cézanne, Picasso
Cities	Le Havre, Paris	**Themes**	Still lifes, landscapes
Movement	Cubism	**Style**	Monochromatic, fragmented shapes

Georges Braque originally began his artistic career as a decorator but abandoned this to concentrate on fine art. He started by attending the *École des Beaux-Arts* in the French harbour city of Le Havre followed by studying in the *Académie Humbert*, Paris, which was founded in 1878 by King Humbert of Italy (1844–1900). He became friendly with the Fauves (see p. 339) and worked with them for a time until meeting Picasso. Together they developed Cubism and collaborated closely until 1914. Like Picasso, Braque's work was not confined to painting only, but included graphic art, sculpture, woodcuts, etchings and plaster reliefs and plaques.

Fruit Dish and Cards, 1913

The subject of this painting is a still life of playing cards, plates and fruit arranged on a table. This paint and collage picture was produced during the Synthetic Period of Cubism.

- ➤ The painting is mostly monochromatic, composed of tints of grey and blue. The brown-hued paper collage is treated like wood grain and contrasts with the rest of the work.

- ➤ The depth in the picture leaves viewers bemused, as in some parts elements appear to push themselves forward for our attention, but then are paradoxically overlapped by what appears to be an object in the background.

- ➤ Although the wood-grained paper collage is placed above the drawing, we can often see through it to the pencil lines beneath. This was a deliberate device used by the artist to force viewers to engage their minds while contemplating his work.

- ➤ Braque used a mixture of media to create this work, including oil paint, charcoal, paper collage, and pencil on canvas. He wished to make the viewer aware that he was deliberately manipulating form and structure to analyse the objects fully, but he was also trying to explore the idea that the media itself described the objects.

- ➤ The wood-grained paper represented the texture of the table on which the objects were placed. The objects themselves are seen from multiple viewpoints, scattered throughout the composition, through his use of line and tone and through pencil and charcoal sketching.

▲ *'Fruit Dish and Cards,' Centre Georges Pompidou, Paris, Braque*

Cubism Revision Questions

1 Cubism was perceived as a revolutionary and unconventional movement. Discuss this statement with reference to one Cubist painting, including in your answer a description of its subject matter and style.

2 Discuss how Pablo Picasso's 'Guernica' reflected his opinion of the Spanish Civil War through his use of symbolism, colour and style. Include a labelled diagram to illustrate your answer.

3 Describe a painting produced during the Synthetic Period of Cubism and explain how the artist used collage to explore texture and depth.

Abstract Art

Abstract art is a broad term which incorporates many forms and styles. All of these are united by the fact that they do not depict realistic or even recognisable objects or scenes. Instead they use colour, line and shape to express an emotion or simply to create an aesthetically pleasing picture. Abstract artists used simplified forms or invented shapes to create a new visual language, which did not require the viewer to have a prior knowledge of art to understand. Some art, created to express emotion, used vigorous brushstrokes and expressive lines to convey its meaning, while other artworks employed the use of simplified geometric shapes within their compositions to create purely aesthetic, non-objective (not representing an object) art. Abstract art is largely based around intellectual concepts, forcing the viewer to think about the art on display to discover the true meaning of the work, instead of being merely a passive observer.

WASSILY KANDINSKY			
Date	1866–1944	Influences	Fauvism, *Die Brücke*
Cities	Moscow, Odessa, Munich	Themes	Music, spirituality
Movement	*Der Blaue Reiter*	Style	Expressive, spontaneous, colourful

Wassily Kandinsky was born in Moscow in 1866 and moved to Odessa where he spent his childhood. He returned to Moscow to study economics and law in 1886. He began his painting career after he moved to Berlin when he was 30 years old. He became one of the two leading members of the German Expressionist group named '*Der Blaue Reiter*,' meaning 'the blue rider.' The other artist involved in the forming of the group in 1911 was German artist Franz Marc (1880–1916). They chose their group name because they both loved horses and the colour blue. Like their fellow group of German Expressionists, *Die Brücke*, Kandinsky and Marc sought to evoke an emotional response to their work through intense use of colour and line.

Link with Music

Kandinsky was an extremely well-read man, who studied various religions, music, history, philosophy and science. He was particularly captivated by the idea that musical harmonies and colour were intrinsically linked, and claimed that in theory they were very similar; likening the shade or tone of a painting to the **timbre** of an instrument, the intensity of colour to volume and the hue of a colour to the **pitch**.

dic·tion·ar·y

Timbre is the characteristic sound quality of an instrument or voice. Pitch is the frequency of vibration of a tone from high to low. The slower the sound waves, the lower the pitch.

First Abstract Artist

As his career progressed, Kandinsky began to replace figural representation in his paintings by carefully placed lines and colours to express emotion and ideas. Kandinsky became the first Abstract artist, creating the equivalent of musical symphonies in his painting through the use of line and colour to express form and space. He wrote a book on his theories on art abstraction in 1912 called *Concerning the Spiritual in Art*.

Did you know?

'DER BLAUE REITER' is also the title of a painting done by Kandinsky in 1903. It shows a figure wearing a blue cloak riding a horse across a field.

Improvisation 31, (1913)

This is an example of Kandinsky's earlier works, which were bold, colourful, gestural pictures, with a great sense of energy and vibrancy.

- There is still an almost intangible element of figurative painting in this piece, which is also titled 'Sea Battle,' with its vigorous, animated brushstrokes and exciting colours.

- The two ships are indicated merely by the suggestions of sails in the middleground and the violence of the sea battle is hinted at by the dashes of crimson red symbolising blood.

▼ *'Improvisation 31,' National Gallery of Art, Washington D.C., Kandinsky*

Accent in Pink, (1926)

In his later career, Kandinsky's work became more difficult to interpret in a representational way. He created large paintings filled with abstract patterns and carefully placed colours, requiring viewers to reflect on the artist's intentions and develop their own ideas on what emotions the picture evoked in them in an individual way. 'Accent in Pink' is a great example of this later style, with a restrained well-planned composition and clearly defined geometric shapes.

▼ *'Accent in Pink,' Musée National d'Art Moderne, Paris, Kandinsky*

PIET MONDRIAN

Date	1872–1944	Influences	Cubism, Theosophy
Cities	Amersfoort, The Hague, Amsterdam, Paris	Themes	Positive and negative shapes, abstraction of form and colour
Movement	*De Stijl*	Style	Geometric, linear, primary colours

Piet Mondrian, born in Amersfoort, the Netherlands, was brought up in a middle-class family. His father, who was an art teacher, introduced him to art at an early age, leading to Mondrian's enrolment in the Academy of Fine Arts in Amsterdam. He began his career as a primary school teacher, although he continued to paint, experimenting in various styles from Pointillism (see p. 306) to Fauvism (see p. 339). He moved to Paris in 1912 to pursue a painting career where he became briefly influenced by Picasso and Cubism. He returned home to the Netherlands in 1914 where he met another painter named Theo van Doesberg (1883–1931). In 1917 they both established an art group and magazine named *'De Stijl'* (the style) to promote their views on the place of art in society in the aftermath of World War I. The two artists developed the style of art known as Neoplasticism which reduced artwork to simple geometric shapes and line to express the inner meaning of ideas and objects rather than reproduce the surface exterior. His interest in theosophy (teachings from various religions), combined to create art which was at the same time both simple and complex.

Composition in Red, Blue and Yellow, 1930

Mondrian was expressing two main aims in his work. The first was to create a work of beauty for all to admire, the second to express his own aesthetic sensibilities.

- Mondrian's compositions, as seen in this painting, were structured around grids filled with flat colour. The lines of the grid are thick black lines. In all of the artist's works of this nature, the lines always ran vertically and horizontally, creating square and rectangular shapes between them.

- He deliberately reduced his colour palette to the three primary colours of red, blue and yellow, with the addition of black, grey and white. He picked these colours because of their purity and simplicity.

- The grids in his paintings always differed in design – in this work a large red square dominates the picture, with two white rectangles running vertically down the left side. In the bottom left-hand corner is a square of blue, while in the bottom-right corner a panel is bisected into two equal halves of white and yellow.

▲ *'Composition in Red, Blue and Yellow,' 1930, Piet Mondrian*

KASIMIR MALEVICH			
Date	1878–1935	**Influences**	Two Russian avant-garde painters: Mikhail Larionov (1881–1964) and Aristarkh Lentuluv (1882–1943); Cubism
Cities	Kiev, Moscow	**Themes**	Emotions, aerial views
Movement	Suprematism	**Style**	Geometric, abstract

Kasimir Malevich was born into a large middle-class family beside Kiev in present-day Ukraine, which was then part of the Russian Empire. In 1904 he moved to Moscow where he attended the Moscow School of Painting, Sculpture and Architecture (founded in 1865). Malevich believed that painting should not imitate life in a representational way, an approach he considered artificial. Instead of constructing the visual image of objects, people or places on canvas, he wished to create an entirely novel form of art through the organisation of lines and geometrical shapes in his work. He called this 'Non-Objective Painting.'

Malevich tried many different styles of avant-garde art in painting and sculpture before creating his own niche in the art world. He called his style of art 'Suprematism.' He believed that the ultimate reality was not to be found in the observation of things that could be touched but in intangible emotions, feelings and ideas. His abstract art reflects these ideas. He chose shapes and colours which could not be equated with real objects to convey the abstract nature of emotion.

Aeroplane Flying, 1915

In this painting the artist was endeavouring to capture the emotions associated with flight rather than a straightforward image of an aeroplane.

➤ The painting consists of a number of geometric shapes (rectangles), placed against a flat white background.

▶ *'Aeroplane Flying,' Museum of Modern Art, New York, Malevich*

- The colours chosen are vivid primary colours of canary yellow, red, and blue with black. These have a very direct and fresh appeal.

- Malevich placed the shapes at varying angles to one another to enhance the dynamic effect of the work. He wished to communicate to the viewer the sensations experienced by flight through his art, using simple shapes and forms to be more accessible to everyone.

Abstract Art Revision Questions

1 Compare and contrast two works by Kandinsky and explain his link between music and painting.

2 Explain Suprematism and describe and discuss one work by a Suprematist artist.

Surrealism

Surrealism was a movement which originated in Paris early in the twentieth century and encompassed the arts of writing, painting and sculpture.

Exploration of the Subconscious

In 1924, a French writer called André Breton founded the Surrealist movement in literature. Breton believed that the aim of the arts should be to express the intuitive, creative inner mind. In order to do this, writers should abandon all moral, logical and aesthetic reasoning instilled in them to explore fully the deep-seated imagination. The Surrealist painting movement grew directly from this literary movement: Surrealist artists allowed their fantasies to come to life by following their random processes of thought and dreams without the control of the conscious mind. There was no conclusive style followed by the surrealist artists; some, such as Joan Miró used stylised symbolic imagery, while others such as Salvador Dalí painted pictures in a very realistic way combining with this imaginative unnatural fantasy elements.

▶ André Breton (1896–1966) founded the literary surrealist movement.

Influence of Psychoanalysis

Dr Sigmund Freud's theories on psychoanalysis (see p. 339) were an extremely important influence on the Surrealists. Freud believed that through hypnosis, patients could unlock disturbing events from their past that they had purposely forgotten. He also believed that in their acceptance of their memories, they could bring about a healing of their problems. The Surrealists were fascinated with Freud's ideas on the importance and intrinsic meaning of dreams and the workings of the subconscious mind expressed in his book, *Interpretations of Dreams*. Through their art, they wished to set free the subconscious mind, with all of its desires and fears.

JOAN MIRÓ			
Date	1893–1983	**Influences**	André Breton, Surrealism, Dutch seventeenth-century art, medieval Catalan art
Cities	Barcelona, Paris, New York	**Themes**	The Spanish Civil War, day and night, the female body
Movement	Surrealism	**Style**	Radiant colour, simple shapes, childlike

Miró was born into a family of craftsmen in Barcelona and began his art education at *La Lonja*, the school of fine arts in the city. Due to pressure from his family, Miró was forced to accept a job as a book-keeper, which did not last long as he suffered a nervous breakdown. On his recovery he decided to pursue his dream of painting and began his career in Barcelona.

Move to Paris

In 1920 he moved to Paris where he met Picasso (see p. 349) and became involved with the Surrealist movement. He was intrigued by the Surrealists' experiments in exploring the subconscious by using hallucinogenic drugs although he never took the drugs himself. In the 1920s Miró was so poverty stricken he could barely afford to survive, and painted many paintings under the influence of hallucinations brought on by extreme hunger and deprivation. He visited Holland in 1928 where he admired the work of seventeenth-century Dutch artists such as H. M. Sorgh (c. 1610–70), often reproducing them with humour in a Surrealist style. The Spanish Civil War of 1936 (see p. 350) and both World Wars (1914–18; 1939–45) influenced Miró to paint pictures and posters depicting and the horrors of war.

Move to Escape Wars

He moved to Majorca to escape from World War II and then to New York in 1947, where he was inspired by the energy and freshness of the art he saw there. On his return to Paris in 1948, his work was a huge success and he produced a great amount of art until his death in 1983, working with a broad range of media including paint, print, sculpture, collage and ceramics.

Harlequin's Carnival, 1924–25

This is one of Miró's most famous works, painted during the era when he was living in a deprived state in Paris. It depicts the bare furnishings of his living room peopled with the results of his imagination, brought on by hallucinations from hunger.

- Some of the items in the painting vaguely resemble animals and insects and are shown in the act of playing (the two creatures in the bottom right are playing with a piece of string); and playing music (the yellow-headed creature in the upper-centre is depicted with a violin from which musical notes issue).

- A window can be seen in the top right-hand corner of the painting, with a table placed beneath it. The floor and walls of the room are also visible. The rest of the pictorial space is busy with fantastical creatures from Miró's imagination.

- An element of childlike innocence can be noticed in this painting, with its vivid colours and flatly painted shapes appearing almost at random throughout. However, the artist intentionally created a fantasy world by allowing his characters to assume distorted and unrealistic shapes and forms. He often painted the same objects repeatedly during his career, imbuing them with his own meaning; for example ladders were used to imply a bridge between the heavens and the earth.

▶ 'Harlequin's Carnival,' Albright-Kn◦
Art Gallery, Buffalo, New York, Mir

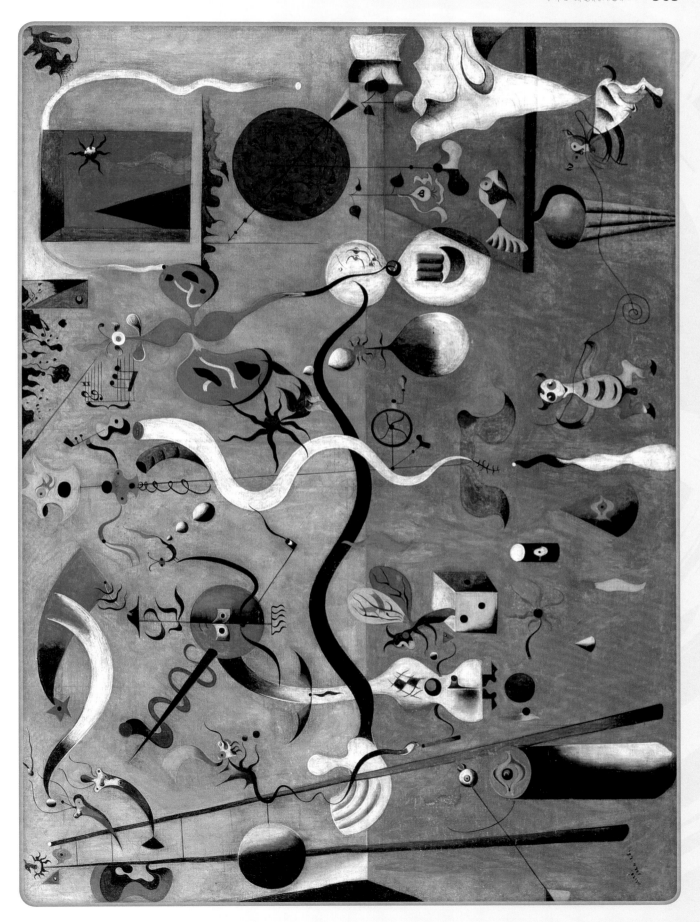

MAX ERNST			
Date	1891–1976	Influences	Paul Klee, Joan Miró, André Breton
Cities	Brühl, Bonn, Cologne, Paris, New York	Themes	Birds, forests, the Spanish Civil War
Movement	Surrealism	Style	Dreamlike, mysterious

Ernst was born in Germany and enrolled to study philosophy in Bonn university in 1901. However, he never finished the course, but instead decided to pursue a career as an artist. He was a founder member of the artistic Dada group based in Cologne (see p. 368). After serving as a soldier in World War I, he felt that his experience of the atrocities of war had affected him so deeply that he had gone through a rebirth both in his thinking and in his way of life. He moved to Paris in 1922, where he explored the processes of the mind in his work. Here, he was introduced to the Surrealists by André Breton. Ernst invented a new kind of collage called 'frottage,' which involved taking rubbings from objects and pasting them to his paintings, thereby creating random textures within his work to represent various ideas or objects.

The Entire City, 1934

We can see Ernst's frottage technique in his picture 'The Entire City,' where he created a gloomy cityscape from floorboard rubbings overlapping each other to give the piece an ominous atmosphere. It is probable that in creating this depressing and dark ruined cityscape Ernst was portraying how he felt about the state of Germany as a result of the War.

▼ *'The Entire City,' Tate Gallery, London, Ernst*

Two Children Are Threatened by a Nightingale, 1924

This work is painted in the Surrealist tradition of superimposing dreamlike fantasy over a realistically painted picture.

➤ In the background we see the buildings of a city, with the nightingale flying in from the left.

➤ A girl rushes into the left corner, hair streaming out behind her, while another lies on the ground. Ernst introduced actual three-dimensional wooden objects into his work (the gate, bell push and house) to add a further dimension of mystery to the scene.

➤ The figure of a man clutching an infant appears on top of the building, about to press the button.

➤ Ernst uses conventional perspective drawing as the base of his painting, overlaying it with three-dimensional construction. The background is painted in bright, vivid colours which are almost realistic, yet have a strange unearthly brilliance to them.

➤ Ernst placed the grey figures over this, giving the painting a nightmarish quality. The title of the piece is also included in the frame, a line taken from a poem written by the artist.

▲ 'Two Children Are Threatened by a Nightingale,' Museum of Modern Art, New York, Ernst

SALVADOR DALÍ

Date	1904–89	Influences	Sigmund Freud, classical art, Surrealism
Cities	Figueres, Barcelona, Paris	Themes	Dreams, religion, mythology
Movement	Surrealism, Classicism	Style	Fantastical, dreamlike, smooth brushstrokes

Dalí was born in Figueres in Catalonia, northeastern Spain nine months after the death of his older brother (also named Salvador). His mother was a very devout Catholic; his father an atheist with strong Republican beliefs. Dalí's talent became clear at an early age – he began producing artwork from the age of six. In 1921 he attended the School of Fine Arts in Madrid. Here he encountered Sigmund Freud's book *The Interpretation of Dreams*, which was to influence his future work to a great extent. His rebellious and outrageous personality did not sit well with the school's authorities and he was expelled for bad behaviour.

Move to Paris

After he left school he continued to paint, trying out various styles, until he moved to Paris in 1929, where he met André Breton, the founder of Surrealism. He began to draw inspiration from his dreams and imagination, becoming almost delirious with the intensity of his feelings. The surrealist poet Paul Éluard and his wife Gala visited him, leading to the romance between Dalí and Gala. This relationship became the mainstay of his life, Dalí seeing her as his saviour and often using her as a model in his paintings, sometimes portraying her as a Madonna. They married in 1934.

Painting, Writing, and Film

Although Dalí's work stemmed from a fantasy dream world, his style was smoothly realistic, reflecting his love of Renaissance painting. He also admired the Renaissance painters' mastery over many different areas of art and literature. As well as painting, Dalí wrote essays, poems and books including *The Secret Life of Salvador Dalí* and produced Surrealist films with filmmaker Luis Buñuel (1900–83) such as *Un Chien Andalou* (An Andalusian Dog).

Later Years in Spain

He returned to Spain in 1949 and spent the rest of his life there. Fellow artists disapproved of his choice to live in Franco-led Spain (see p. 350) but Dalí refused to get involved in their battle against Fascism (see p. 373). He was also a devout Catholic and a monarchist which conflicted with the Surrealist manifesto. Around 1958 Dali became increasingly more influenced by Renaissance art, his own becoming more classical in its approach. Dalí was a showman, his bizarre behaviour and strange imagery making him the most celebrated of the Surrealists. He died in Catalonia at the age of 84.

The Metamorphosis of Narcissus, 1937

The inspiration for the painting was from Greek mythology, in particular the story of Narcissus. Narcissus was a handsome boy, who on seeing his own reflection in a pond, fell in love. He refused to leave his image and consequently starved to death. After his death the gods, mourning the passing of his beauty, immortalised him as a flower: the narcissus.

- In the foreground of the painting are two monumental sculptural shapes, which echo each other in form. The one in the right of the composition resembles a giant hand holding an egg, out of which sprouts the narcissus flower. Large ants crawl up the surface of the sculpted hand.

- The form on the left takes the shape of a boy's body, with the forehead resting on the knee in a gesture of despair. This represents the Greek boy Narcissus, crouching to look at his reflected image in the pool depicted in the foreground. The narcissus flower is echoed in the ponytail of hair flowing over his shoulder on the right.

- In the right foreground a dog is shown devouring meat, symbolic of death, while behind him is a Greek figure on a pedestal above a chessboard, perhaps suggesting that mortals are the pawns of the gods.

- In the centre, naked figures are shown admiring their youthful and elegant bodies to continue the theme of vanity. The scene is all set within a brooding fantasy landscape, with high, rugged rocky edifices and deep shadows.

- Dalí's beautiful smooth brushwork is evident in this dramatic painting. The still waters of the lake and the soft visual texture of the clouds demonstrate his technique.

◈ There are also elements of a rougher, grainier style, in his depiction of the dog, the rocks in the left background and the crude track leading from the pool into the background.

◈ Dalí's use of strong colour helps to heighten the drama of the scene and unify the picture, with vivid reddish tones in the ground on the left and in the mountain in the background contrasting with the vibrant turquoise blue of the sky and its reflection on the left.

◈ The deep, dark shadows create an atmosphere of unease and nightmarish unreality.

▼ *'The Metamorphosis of Narcissus,' Tate Gallery, London, Dalí*

Surrealism Revision Questions

<u>1</u> Discuss the influences on the Surrealist movement and how these affected a Surrealist painting of your choice.

<u>2</u> Compare and contrast two paintings by Max Ernst under the following headings:
a) subject matter, b) composition, c) style.

<u>3</u> Give an account of the life of Salvador Dalí and describe one of his paintings in detail.

The Dada Movement

The Dada movement was formed as a direct result of World War I (1914–18). Artists escaping from war-torn countries, ravaged by death, disease and collapsing economies expressed their outrage and horror by delving into the subconscious for inspiration. They deliberately broke with previous traditional artistic and figurative styles which they saw as symbolic of the decadent and corrupt Western culture which brought about the war. Artists such as Max Ernst (see p. 364) and Marcel Duchamp (see below) wished to provoke strong reactions by their works which were created with random found objects or designed to jolt the bourgeois art world into thinking about subjects beyond the merely visual and representational.

MARCEL DUCHAMP			
Date	1887–1968	**Influences**	Cubism, Fauvism, French Symbolist painter Odile Redon (1840–1916)
Cities	New York, Paris	**Themes**	Movement, change, visual puns
Movement	Dadaism	**Style**	Ready-made sculptures, combining found objects, humorous

Marcel Duchamp was born in Blainville, near Rouen, into a well-to-do culture-loving family. He began painting in 1908, but after a time abandoned this art to pioneer the 'ready-made' school of sculpture. Duchamp lived in Paris until 1915, when he moved to New York to avoid World War I. Some of his earlier paintings had been displayed there previously and he was already a popular and controversial figure in the art world. He became a highly influential artist, making close friends with prominent patrons of the arts such as Peggy Guggenheim (1898–1979), a prolific art collector, and the Museum of Modern Art directors Alfred Barr (1902–81) and James Johnson Sweeney (1900–86). He advised them on their exhibitions and purchases and became a dealer and collector himself.

Ready-made Sculptures

These sculptures were deliberate acts of provocation to an art world Duchamp regarded as aesthetically destitute. He wished to create a new kind of art form through his work, by breaking the fundamental traditions of art, and replacing them with sculptures which encouraged the viewer to engage with the object instead of merely being a passive observer. For centuries critics had hailed art which was imbued with aesthetic beauty and exquisite craftsmanship. Duchamp stripped his work of these qualities, substituting mass-produced or custom-made articles in place of skilled craftwork, and creating sculptures from random combinations of objects instead of pre-conceived artistic ideas. He was not interested in recreating an object artificially; he wished instead to make viewers see everyday objects in a new and stimulating way. Duchamp completed 21 ready-made sculptures between the years 1915 and 1923. He believed that art, like life, was based on a series of random events and chance. He was convinced that every person viewing his work would derive a different meaning from it. This conviction that artists should be freed from the constraints of tradition and deliberately set out to challenge the public forms the basis of most modern art today. It made Duchamp one of the most important artists of all time.

Bicycle Wheel, 1913

This was the first ready-made sculpture created by Duchamp, and features a bicycle wheel placed upside-down on a pedestal. The original was lost and Duchamp created a replica in 1951.

- Although at first glance it appears to be an aimless creation, Duchamp chose the wheel for a number of reasons. He had a great love of the ridiculous, the up-turned bicycle wheel, devoid of its function, gave the piece comedic value. Duchamp was also responsible for painting a moustache on the face of a reproduced Mona Lisa, which was regarded as a wildly irreverent statement.

- The notion of a wheel which by its nature was produced to move, being held immobile by the plinth, appealed to the artist as a fundamental impasse between stasis and movement.

- In a very basic sense, Duchamp simply enjoyed spinning the wheel and watching it rotating, stating that it was similar to relaxing in front of a fireplace watching the flicker of flames in the hearth.

- The resemblance of the sculpture to an old-fashioned spinning wheel strengthened this idea, being the focus of a popular fireside activity in the past.

▲ *'Bicycle Wheel,' Museum of Modern Art, New York, Duchamp*

Hidden Noise, 1916

This is probably the most mysterious of Duchamp's ready-mades.

- He commissioned two engraved copperplates and four bolts from skilled craft workers to enclose a rolled ball of twine.

- Inside this ball of twine resides an unseen object which rattles when the sculpture is shaken.

- The most surprising element of this piece is that even the artist was not aware of what this object is. He asked a friend to place something inside and it is still unknown to this day what it is.

▶ *'Hidden Noise,' Philadelphia Museum of Modern Art, Duchamp*

The Fountain, 1917

Of all the sculptures Duchamp created, this is the one which gained him his notorious reputation. It consisted of a urinal placed upside down and renamed 'The Fountain.' He produced this ready-made for an avant-garde art show (*Société des Artistes Indépendants*, Paris), as there would be no panel of judges to withhhold it from being viewed. However, this deliberate attack on modern art, equating it with a toilet, was deemed too shocking for public display and was withdrawn, and reportedly lost. A second version of the sculpture was recreated by the artist in 1950, and many replicas were made subsequently. The signature scrawled on the side of the urinal was R. Mutt, chosen by Duchamp as a witty reference to the toilet manufacturers Mott Plumbing and the cartoon characters **Mutt and Jeff**. Although it might appear that the artist was merely interested at poking fun at his contemporary art world, he did write an article about it in his magazine *The Blind Man*. Here, he explained that the reason he chose the urinal was to place it in a different way, and create a new meaning for it, so its old function was defunct.

▲ *'The Fountain,' (replica made 1964) The Israel Museum, Jerusalem, Duchamp*

dic·tion·ar·y

Mutt and Jeff were characters in a popular newspaper cartoon strip published in the *San Francisco Chronicle*. Cartoonist Bud Fisher created Mutt, a tall, lanky horse-racing fanatic, and his short sidekick Jeff, also a horse-racing enthusiast, in 1907.

The Dada Movement Revision Questions

1 Discuss what inspired the Dada movement and write about one work in particular which provoked a strong reaction.

2 Marcel Duchamp created a series of ready-made sculptures. Compare and contrast three of these, explaining his motives for creating them.

Images of War

The two great world wars of the twentieth century, World War I and World War II, had a huge effect on the art produced during and after the wartime periods. The Russian Revolution, which took place in the early twentieth century, also heavily influenced the work of Russian artists during this time. The death and destruction caused by war left artists looking for a way to express their horror visually, and also provided a vehicle for promoting causes and political views.

World War I

World War I began in the summer of 1914 when Austria-Hungary invaded Serbia. The powerful countries in Europe were divided into two alliances:

- The **Triple Entente** included Russia, Great Britain and France.
- The **Triple Alliance** included Italy, Austria-Hungary and Germany, although Italy switched sides in 1915.

In 1917 the United States entered the war. Although the war ended in 1919, the five years of fighting had destroyed economies, cities and countless lives, bringing about a world-wide depression (economic downturn). The First World War had a profound effect on art in Europe, particularly art produced in Germany. A group of German artists who came to be known as *Neue Sachlichkeit* (New Objectivity) expressed their feelings and opinions about the war in their work. They wished to depict the horrors of war and its devastating effect in an honest manner.

OTTO DIX			
Date	1891–1959	**Influences**	*Die Brücke*
Cities	Dresden, Berlin	**Themes**	War, religion, portraits
Movement	Expressionism	**Style**	Powerful, dramatic, satirical

Otto Dix, one of the founders of *Neue Sachlichkeit,* served as a machine gunner in the German army in the First World War. He was initially intrigued by the devastation he witnessed, believing that man should be exposed to the extreme highs and lows of life to understand fully the true nature of mankind. The extent of the damage done to the countries and people involved however soon turned him away from this opinion, and his work began to reflect his outrage at the suffering and despair he witnessed.

Der Krieg (The War), 1929–32

Dix painted these images in a triptych format, with a square-shaped central panel, two narrower side panels and a lower panel running along the bottom of the main part. The painting mixes realism with fantasy, creating a disturbing and harrowing vision of war at its ugliest.

- The figures and background in the painting are depicted in a realistic way, heightening the impact of the visual effect on the viewer.
- Dix does not flinch from portraying the dreadful wounds inflicted on the bodies, graphically depicting the gory lacerations and bullet holes.

He further enhances the drama of his work through his use of colour. The bone-white figures in the upper panels appear ghostly, while the figures in the bunker are painted in hues of grey, giving them the appearance of cold statues.

The churning red skies on the side panels, along with the grey dawn in the main panel give the viewer the impression of an apocalyptic vision.

Main Panel

In the middle of the triptych we see the hideous devastation wreaked by war. Against a backdrop of a destroyed city lie mutilated corpses of soldiers and civilians. A skeletal figure skewered by a girder overhangs the scene pointing down to the pile of bodies. A man in a gas mask is shown in the left, looking alien and strangely impersonal.

Left Panel

On the left we are presented with the back views of soldiers about to go into battle. To the left of them a stream of soldiers marches to join them. They are partly obscured by a low-lying mist under an ominous red sunset.

Right Panel

The pale figure dragging a stricken soldier away from the debris is a self-portrait of the artist himself, showing his own personal involvement in the war. Black clouds of smoke gather over a fiery background while dead bodies of soldiers pile up at the foot of the panel.

Bottom Panel

In a bunker-like space lie the dead bodies of soldiers.

▼ *'Der Krieg,' Gemäldegalerie Neue Meister, Dresden, Dix*

World War II

The economic depression and the dissatisfaction with the treaties imposed on countries after World War I led to a build up in tension in Europe which culminated in the second Great War of the century. Three **fascist regimes** heightened the atmosphere of unease:

- Joseph Stalin (1878–1953) in Russia
- Adolf Hitler (1889–1945) in Germany
- Benito Mussolini (1883–1945) in Italy.

dic·tion·ar·y

Fascist regimes were led by a supreme dictator who had total control of a single party state, was in command of the state's economy and army and advocated strong right-wing nationalism and the supremacy of a single ethnic race.

War broke out in 1939 when Hitler invaded of Poland. Britain and France came to the aid of Poland, declaring war on Germany. The fighting spread worldwide, involving the Asian countries of China and Japan, as well as the United States. The opposing sides in the Second World War were named the Allies and the Axis:

- The **Allies** were made up of a large number of countries led by the Big Three: Great Britain, the United States of America and the Union of Soviet Socialist Republics.
- Germany was the dominant force of the **Axis** alliance, aided by Italy and Japan along with countries colonised by these empires.

The war finally ended in 1945 with the defeat of Germany by the Allied Nations. When the Second World War ended, it left an even bigger scar in Europe than the first, resulting in the deaths of 45 million people and the destruction of cities all across Europe. This left artists bitter and disillusioned, expressing the pessimism they felt about the state of Europe and the brutal, horrific nature of war in their paintings.

FRANCIS BACON

Date	1909–92	**Influences**	Picasso, Surrealism, the film *The Battleship Potemkin (1925)* by the Russian film director Sergei Eisenstein (1898–1948)
Cities	Dublin, London		
Movement	Bacon was not a member of any structured movement although his style has been linked with Expressionism.	**Themes**	The Crucifixion of Christ, portraits, politics, screaming figures
		Style	Grotesque, haunting, dramatic

Francis Bacon is one of Ireland's best known painters, although he spent most of his life in London. He was born in Dublin into a wealthy family, his father an English captain born in Australia and his mother an Irish-born English heiress. Bacon was a self-taught artist, beginning his career as an interior designer in London in 1928. He only became a successful artist in his thirties after he attracted both controversy and admiration in equal measures for his triptych 'Three Studies for Figures at the Base of a Crucifixion' in 1944. Bacon's work, focusing largely on tortured-looking men isolated in cage-like structures against bleak, uncompromising backgrounds gives us an insight into his own inner turmoil and views on mortality, although in life he was a well-known sociable character with tendencies for gambling, drinking and high living. He died in Madrid at the age of 82, and bequeathed the contents of his studio to the Hugh Lane Gallery in Dublin, where it was reconstructed exactly as it been when he was alive.

Painting, 1946

Francis Bacon painted this picture a
year after the end of World War II. In
the background a carcass split in two
hangs behind the figure seated before a
revolving rail of meat. His work shows his
disgust at the brutality of war, likening it
to the slaughter and butchery of animals.
He has possibly used images of wartime
leaders to inspire his image of the central
character. He may represent the British
Prime Minister, Neville Chamberlain
(1869–1940) who was often pictured
with an umbrella. The man has flecks of
blood on his mouth, suggesting that he is
eating the raw meat. This is powerful and
haunting statement about war.

- Francis Bacon had a very unique
  style of painting which was
  extremely effective in portraying
  disturbing and grisly imagery.
  The thick brushstrokes suggest
  form rather than depict it in a
  realistic manner.

- His choice of colours; reds, pinks,
  white and greys, help to echo the
  theme of slaughter, reminding us
  of skin, flesh and bone.

▲ 'Painting,' Museum of Modern Art, New York, Francis Bacon

War Photography

Although photography had previously been used to document war footage in both the Crimean
and American Civil War, developments in photographic equipment meant that cameras became
much more manageable and portable, with the introduction of the 35 mm roll-film in 1925 and
the twin lens Rolleiflex in 1930. Photography became more accessible; the subjects less poised
and more spontaneous. Photographers were seeking out reality instead of idealistic images,
capturing disturbing images of war or victims of political situations: works which were celebrated
for their authenticity. Magazines such as *Life* became the new exhibition space for new and
exciting photography.

ROBERT CAPA			
Date	1913–54	**Cities**	Budapest, Berlin, New York

Capa was an American-based photographer, who was originally from Hungary. He was a firm
believer in being close to the action on the battlefield, considering it was the only way to record the
actuality of the experience. He himself was killed during conflict in Indo-China in 1954.

Death of a Loyalist, 1936

This famous photograph shows a man being shot, capturing the moment of the bullet's impact. The photograph elicits an immediate emotional and shocked response from the viewer. It was taken in Cordoba, Spain, during the Spanish Civil War (see p. 350).

© Cornell Capa

◀ *'Death of a Loyalist,' Capa*

LEE MILLER

Date	1907–77	Cities	New York, London

Lee Miller was born in Poughkeepsie, New York in 1907 and began her career as a successful photographic model in New York City. In 1927 she moved to Paris to pursue a career in fine-art photography, where she worked as an assistant to **Man Ray**, later setting up her own studio. She became increasingly interested in taking pictures of the effects of the Second World War. During the 1940s she produced her own photographs of the **London Blitz** and later became an American war correspondent.

dic·tion·ar·y

Man Ray (1890-1976) was an American Dada and Surrealist painter and photographer who spent a lot of his career working in Paris.

The **London Blitz** began on 7 September 1940 when the German air force, the *Luftwaffe*, began a period of intense bombing on London targets that was to last for 57 consecutive nights. It caused devastation to the city, leaving many homeless. The photograph below (not by Lee Miller) gives an idea of the destruction caused by the bombing.

▼ *London Blitz*

Concentration Camp Guards, 1945

Some of Miller's most famous photographs are taken after the closure of the German concentration camps in Dachau and Buchenwald, where she captured images of the guards who had previously worked in the prison and were brutally beaten and imprisoned by the former inmates. This photograph was taken in Buchenwald after the prisoners had been granted their freedom by U.S. troops at the end of the war. The sight of the two men, hopeless and forced to their knees in supplication, is a hauntingly powerful image. Harrowing images of the concentration camps were recorded by other photographers, but her images added a further dimension to the savage and horrific ordeals endured by all participants in the war.

▲ 'Concentration Camp Guards' (Buchenwald), Lee Miller

JOHN HEARTFIELD			
Date	1891–1968	**Cities**	Berlin, London

John Heartfield, born Helmut Herzfelde, was an influential member of the Berlin Dada group, who brought political photography to a new level by introducing **montage** into the medium. This instilled his work with real subjectivity. He did not depend on recording a chance moment to express the horrors of war; instead he manipulated his images to voice his opinions, often in a satirical fashion. His left-wing political stance induced him to create derisive photo-montages of Hitler and other leaders of the Nazi party.

> dic·tion·ar·y
>
> A **montage** consists of a number of different photographs cut up and joined together to create a new image.

Adolf the Superman: Swallows Gold and Spouts Junk, 1932

Throughout history one of the main aims of alchemy was to alter the substance of base metals such as iron (here, 'junk') into precious metals such as gold and silver. The title of this work cleverly turns this around to suggest that Hitler's regime consumed and destroyed a lot of the good things in life to create instead terrible atrocities. This photo-montage portrayed Hitler in an authoritarian pose, with a see-through torso. A **swastika** is superimposed on the right of his chest (Hitler's left, over his heart), with curved ribs protecting the coins flowing down his throat into his stomach. The stack of coins also resembles a spine, indicating that capitalist money from wealthy German industrialists were the 'backbone' of the Fascist regime in the country.

> dic·tion·ar·y

A **swastika** is an ancient religious symbol in the shape of a Greek cross, with the ends of the arms bent at right angles. It was later used as the emblem of Nazi Germany (1933–45).

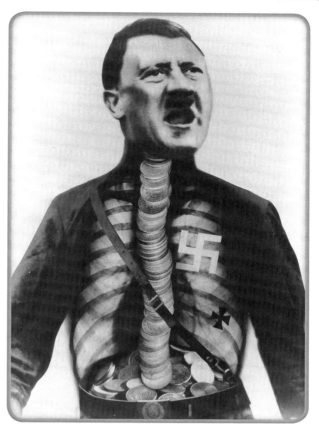

▶ *'Adolf the Superman: Swallows Gold and Spouts Junk,' Academie der Kunst, Berlin, Heartfield*

The Russian Revolution

The Russian Revolution began in 1917. The Tsar (Russian ruler) Nicholas II was forced to abdicate (give up) his throne by the workers, who took over the ruling of the country. Later in the year the **Bolsheviks** led by revolutionary Vladimir Lenin (1870–1924) took control of the government and began a **Communist** state. The wealth and lands of the former Russian aristocracy were redistributed among the workers. In 1923 Russia became known as the Soviet Union.

This revolution and upheaval of government came at a heavy price. The civil war which followed in 1918 between the Bolshevik Red Army and the opposing White Army, consisting of supporters of the Tsar and those who resisted the extreme Communist principles, also contributed to widespread deaths, war atrocities and food shortages. It is thought that the death toll of all of these factors combined is in excess of eight million.

> dic·tion·ar·y

The **Bolsheviks**, led by Lenin, formed the majority of the Marxist Communists. They split from the main group and took control of the government, creating a Communist state.

Communism is a political system of government based on the writings of the German philosopher and political revolutionary Karl Marx. It advocates the abolition of private ownership, replacing this with communal and equal ownership of all property, economic wealth and work.

Art as Propaganda

Many artists in Russia were staunch supporters of the Russian Revolution and Communism and created posters to promote the cause and influence others to become Communists. One of the most popular styles was Soviet Socialist Realism which combined realistic images with heroic gestures and dramatic flat colour. These posters portrayed the leaders of the Revolution as well as peasants, soldiers, and factory workers shown in heroic poses.

DMITRY MOOR			
Date	1883–1946	Themes	The depiction and glorification of Russian workers and Communism
Cities	Moscow		
Movement	Soviet Socialist Realism	Style	Dramatic, limited colour palette, block colours
Influences	Socialist literature		

Dmitry Moor began his career in 1910 studying art in the studio of the Russian artist Kelin (1874–1946). He worked as an illustrator for many Russian magazines during his lifetime including *Krasnoarmeyets* (Red Army Soldier) and national newspapers such as *Pravda*. He was a highly successful and respected artist, becoming art director of magazines such as *Bezbozhnik* (Atheist), devising and planning political festivals and teaching in Moscow's High State Technical Institute.

Have You Volunteered?, 1920

This **lithograph** poster shows a soldier in a red uniform directly looking out, and pointing at the viewer. He is a symbol of the red Russian Army demanding volunteers to join them in overthrowing the rule of the Tsar. The smoking chimneys in the background are representative of the working-class people and the power of industry.

The urgent, challenging stare and pointing finger immediately involve the viewer. The simplicity of the colour palette (black, red and beige) and the clean, linear style also heighten the drama of the image. There were 45,000 copies of this particular poster in circulation in Russia.

dic·tion·ar·y

Lithographic printing is a style of printing created by drawing the design in greasy crayon on a flat stone or metal plate. This is then rinsed with water and ink is applied which sticks to the crayon marks. Paper is then pressed onto the stone or metal to create the print.

◀ *'Have You Volunteered?,' Moscow, Literature Edition RSVR (Department of Political Management), Moor*

VLADIMIR TATLIN

Date	1885–1953	Influences	Poetry, sailing
Cities	Kharkiv (Ukraine), Moscow	Themes	Movement, flight
Movement	Productivism	Style	Symmetrical, sculptural

The Russian artist Vladimir Tatlin was the foremost member of the 'Productivist' movement. His art was created in reaction to the devastation caused by the Russian Revolution, creating large sculptures in an effort to re-introduce beauty into the new Soviet Union. He used many different materials in the construction of his models and sculptures, including metal, glass, wood and plaster.

Monument to the Third International, 1919–20

In 1919 a design for a building to be erected in the centre of Moscow was commissioned by the Department of Artistic Work of the **People's Commissariat for Enlightenment**. The building was to be used as the Russian news centre.

▲ *Model of 'Monument to the Third International,' Museum of Modern Art, Stockholm, Tatlin*

- Tatlin's design was for a spectacular slanted, revolving building. The main axis (slanted line around which it revolved) was tilted with a spiral cone form. He had planned that each chamber would revolve at different speeds: the large bottom floor every year, the first floor every month and the top room every day.
- The highest floor was to be used as a radio tower with a large outdoor screen to broadcast news.
- The conical shape, tapering at the top, was symbolic of the power structure in the Soviet Union, with the bottom representing the workers and the smaller top symbolising the small group of people who led the government.
- The building was designed to be constructed on a massive scale, but was never built due to lack of funding in the post-war years. The artist's model was eventually lost, but a new model was made to the specifications outlined in Tatlin's sketches in 1968.

dic·tion·ar·y

The **Third International**, formed by Lenin in Moscow in 1919, was a communist organisation which operated internationally. It was the third attempt to create an international communist organisation: the previous two had been dissolved due to political conflicts within the administration.

The **People's Commissariat for Enlightenment**, founded in 1918, was the new government administrative body formed after the Russian Revolution. It had a number of divisions which included music, theatre and fine art. The Department of Artistic work within the Commissariat commissioned paintings and sculptures from Soviet artists.

The Portrayal of Capitalism

The Mexican revolution (1910–1920) began as a protest against the corrupt and oppressive government under the president Porfirio Diaz (1830–1915). It escalated into a bloody and violent civil war which resulted in an estimated two million deaths and a complete breakdown in the stability and economy of the country. After the war ended, the new president Alvaro Obregon (1880–1928) encouraged a strong sense of national identity and pride in Mexican culture and heritage. He also instilled a socialist ethos in the country, criticising the capitalist culture of North America.

Mexican Muralism

Mexican muralism was an art movement that began in the 1920s with a rediscovery amongst Mexican artists of their history and artistic heritage. All over Mexico, muralists portrayed their views on capitalism, Mexican culture and the Mexican Revolution by painting large-scale murals on schools, public buildings, churches and museums. Their aim was to expose the oppression suffered by the working classes in capitalist societies and to influence and educate a broad range of people through their work. Like the **Socialist Realists**, they embraced the Socialist ethos, although instead of portraying the Socialist way of life in a positive way, they chose to represent a negative image of Capitalism.

> dic·tion·ar·y
>
> **Socialist Realism,** originating in Moscow, was a movement which depicted socialist and communist ideals in a realistic manner.

CREATING MEXICAN MURALS

Mexican artists painted their murals in the same way that the Italian Renaissance masters painted their frescoes (see p. 155). Creating a mural involved a series of steps:

1. Artists began by plastering their wall panel in thin layers of sand and lime plaster.

2. They then traced original drawings on fine tissue paper and punctured small holes along the lines.

3. Smearing a charcoal powder called pounce over these lines transferred the picture onto the panel.

4. Artists laid the last layer of plaster in sections bounded by these lines then painted over them with natural colour pigments. Rivera, in the example opposite, began by painting the darker outlines and shading and then applied the lighter colours.

DIEGO RIVERA			
Date	1886–1957	Influences	Picasso, Cézanne, Italian Renaissance frescoes
Cities	Guanajuato City, Mexico City, Madrid, Paris, New York, Detroit	Themes	Mexican society and culture, the Mexican Revolution
Movement	The Mexican Muralist Movement	Style	Vividly coloured, simplistic

Diego Rivera was the most famous and controversial artists involved with the Mexican Muralists. His career began in Guanajuato City, about 370 km northwest of Mexico City, where he was a member of the Communist Party. He received invitations from clients in the United States to paint murals which he accepted, earning him criticism from his fellow Mexican who believed he was selling out to become rich from Capitalist money. Although he left the Communist Party, his communist ideals remained and were portrayed in his work.

Detroit Industry (Man and Machine), 1932–33

Diego was commissioned to paint four walls of a courtyard in the Detroit Institute of Arts, USA. He studied the poor working conditions of the factory workers at the **Ford Motors** industrial plant and portrayed his vision of both the positive and negative aspects of their jobs along with his admiration for man's achievements in creating such advanced machinery.

The murals depict the history of Detroit's people and the industries in the area, particularly the Ford car manufacturing plant. This series of murals transformed the previously considered mundane subjects of factory work and machinery into vibrant and exciting compositions. The walls on the north and south sides portray the ethnic races which made up the American people, the car industry and other Detroit industries. The bottom panels show the daily work undertaken by the Ford plant workers.

South Wall

This mural has a number of panels featuring different aspects of Detroit life, work and raw materials used in industry.

Top

Two large figures on the top of the mural represent the Caucasian and Asian races. The white figure on the left holds limestone in his hand while the Asian figure holds sand. Underneath these figures is a long panel depicting these stone materials in their natural geological strata (layers). In the top-left corner is a scene from a pharmaceutical company, while in the top-right corner is one from a chemical industry. There are two smaller panels underneath these, the one on the left portraying a surgical operation and the right one showing potash and crystallised sulphur.

> **dic·tion·ar·y**
>
> The **Ford Motor Company** is a multinational car manufacturing company founded by Henry Ford (1863–1947) in Detroit in 1903. It was the first factory to use assembly lines to create mass-produced inexpensive cars.

▼ *'Detroit Industry' or 'Man and Machine,' South Wall, Detroit Institute of the Arts, Rivera*

Middle

In the middle layer are frescoes of the production of the exterior of the Ford cars. On the right is a large stamping press which was used to create the fenders.

Bottom

In the bottom right is a double portrait. The men featured are Dr William Valentiner (1880–1958), the director of the Detroit Institute of Arts who commissioned the murals, and Edsel B. Ford (1894–1943) who was the president of the Detroit Arts Commission and also the Ford Motor Company.

North Wall

The upper panels show Native American and African figures holding iron ore and coal. The middle panels depict the process of manufacturing the engine and transmission of the Ford car.

East Wall

The East wall features several panels showing the origins of humanity and technology and industry.

West Wall

This wall portrays the technologies of aviation and shipping. It shows both the positive and negative aspects of these inventions, with representations of passenger aeroplanes and war planes. This idea is reinforced by the symbolic use of birds: the dove represents peace while a hawk symbolises cruelty and destruction.

Images of War Revision Questions

1 The beginning of the twentieth century was a time of great political upheaval and war. Describe how two artists portrayed their opinions on war by discussing in detail a painting or photograph by each artist.

2 Discuss how Soviet artists used the medium of art and sculpture to promote their political beliefs referring to two artworks to explain your answer.

3 Discuss the Mexican muralist movement, describing in your answer the aims of the muralists, the techniques they used and a detailed description of one mural in particular.

Irish Modernism

Irish Modern artists (working between c. 1910 –1950) were inspired by two major sources:

- They studied abroad and became aware of the modern trends in painting such as Expressionism, Cubism and Abstract art. Artists in this movement differed from those on pages 332–38, as they were not so influenced by the Post-Impressionists.

- They experienced a growing sense of national identity in Ireland, with the Irish Literary movement (see p. 338). Writers such as William Butler Yeats (1865–1939), George Russell (1867–1935) and John Millington Synge (1867–1935) were producing fresh new literature which celebrated Irish culture, which in turn inspired a national pride in Irish scholars and painters.

SEÁN KEATING

Date	1889–1977	**Influences**	William Orpen
Cities	Limerick, Dublin, London, Aran Islands	**Themes**	Irish nationalism, politics, industrial growth
Movement	Romantic Realism	**Style**	Realistic, naturalistic

Seán Keating's work is largely dominated by the two subjects which interested him most: Irish nationalist values and the growth of industrialisation in Ireland. When the **Irish Free State** came into being in 1921, he became the foremost political Irish painter, imbuing his images with cultural references, some of which he gleaned from the traditions he witnessed in the Aran Islands (off Galway Bay) in 1913. He was vigorously opposed to the new Modernist painting styles, having studied under William Orpen (see p. 337) and later taught his realistic approach to painting in the Dublin Metropolitan School and The National College of Art, then situated in Kildare Street, Dublin. A brief stint as the president of The Royal Hibernian Academy ended in 1962, as he felt that the techniques being taught there were inclining towards Modernism.

dic·tion·ar·y

Following the Anglo-Irish Treaty in 1921, the 26 southern counties in Ireland were named the **Irish Free State**. The remaining northern six counties made up the state of Northern Ireland.

The Men of the West, 1917

The painting depicts three Irishmen waiting to go into battle during the 1916 Easter Rising. The men are portrayed as staunchly heroic, grimly anticipating the fight with unflinching courage. The artist used real-life models – even himself. The character looking out at the viewer on the left is modelled on Keating, while the other two figures are those of his brother and a friend.

▼ *'The Men of the West,' Dublin City Gallery The Hugh Lane, Keating*

- The effectiveness of the painting is largely due to the simplicity of its composition. The three figures are seen from a close viewpoint, taking up most of the pictorial space.

- We are shown the figures from various angles, the figure on the left at a three-quarter view, looking out from the canvas, the middle in direct profile to the viewer and the third from the back.

- The background is reduced to a minimum, painted in neutral tones, with the flag of green, white and gold contrasting brightly against this to the left.

- Keating's style, while traditional and realistic in its approach, is not strictly conventional. The close viewpoint, the gritty realism and strong political message create a fresh look for Irish art.

PAUL HENRY			
Date	1876–1958	Movement	Post-Impressionism
Cities	Belfast, Paris, London, Achill Island, Dublin	Influences	Whistler, Post-Impressionism

Henry was born in Belfast and received formal art training in the Belfast School of Art and later the *Académie Julian* in Paris. There, he was inspired by the bohemian lifestyle and by the works of art he saw in the galleries. The art of French painter van Gogh (see p. 323) and American-born James Whistler (1837–1903) were his personal favourites – he briefly attended Whistler's classes while in Paris. He moved to London in 1900, where he married the painter Grace Mitchell (1868–1953), whose work is as well-renowned as her husband's. During his stay in London, he worked as an illustrator, completing many charcoal drawings, and co-founded the **Allied Artists' Association**. In 1912, he left London for Achill Island off the west coast of Ireland, to pursue his dream of painting the rural landscape and the everyday lives of the farmers and fishermen who lived and worked there.

> dic·tion·ar·y
>
> The **Allied Artists' Association** was founded in London in 1908 to challenge the conservative choices and attitude of the New English Art Club and the Royal Academy.

Lakeside Cottages, c. 1929

Henry's painting is a simple landscape, devoid of human presence. The main focus is on the small, white, thatched cottages surrounding the lake. This work demonstrates a common feature of Henry's artworks: the large expanse of sky which takes up most of the picture space.

- The painting is organised along a horizontal format, from the lines in the path in the foreground, to the lake in the middleground and the mountains in the horizon in the background. This conveys a mood of serenity and peace to the viewer.

- This serenity is further enhanced by the lack of movement in the painting. There are no people represented in the picture, the water of the lake is still and tranquil and the solid form of the distant mountain gives the painting a timeless quality. Even the clouds appear unmoving with their sculptured tones and dark outlines.

- The artist uses realistic, natural hues to interpret the scene, simplifying the features of the landscape to create an uncomplicated calm painting of rural Ireland.

- He shows his admiration of the work of van Gogh in his handling of the paint, using thick brushstrokes to lay down patches of tone and colour.

▲ *'Lakeside Cottages,' Dublin City Gallery The Hugh Lane, Henry*

MAINIE JELLETT

Date	1897–44	**Influences**	Cubism, Albert Gleizes
Cities	Dublin, Paris, London	**Themes**	Religion
Movement	Modernism	**Style**	Abstract, rhythmic organic lines and shapes

Mainie Jellett was born in Dublin and began her art education in the Dublin Metropolitan School of Art, followed by the Westminster School of Art in London. She won a scholarship to work under the tutelage of French sculptor and painter André Lhote (1885–1962) in Paris in 1921, where she learned about the Cubist technique. This was further strengthened by French Cubist painter Albert Gleizes (1881–1953) who was to become a great influence on her work, teaching her more about this and other abstract modern styles. When Jellett returned to Dublin to teach and exhibit her work, she encountered derision from the Irish critics who did not place any value on her style as a valid painting technique. Jellett continued to battle for the recognition and appreciation during her lifetime, creating her own unique style of Cubism.

The Ninth Hour, 1941

Mainie Jellett's earlier work was mostly based around simple shapes, with no recognisable figures or objects. In the later stages of her career, her paintings became more figurative, while retaining their Cubist style. This picture is one of the latter and portrays a crucifixion scene, with a central figure of Christ on the cross, with the two crosses of the thieves on either side. The Virgin Mary, Saint Mary Magdalene, Mary the mother of James and the apostle John are shown at the foot of the cross. This is one of many of Jellet's later pictures to be inspired by her deep religious faith.

▲ 'The Ninth Hour,' Dublin City Gallery The Hugh Lane, Jellett

- Although she painted this in a modern style, the basic structure of the picture is quite traditional as a composition. Christ is shown in the centre of the piece, conforming to tradition, with his mourners portrayed lamenting at the foot of the cross.

- The colours used tell us who the figures are, blue being the conventional colour associated with Mary, while Saint Mary Magdalene wears red, reminding us of her sinful past and redemption.

- The figure on the cross in the left is that of the good thief who repents of his crimes to join Jesus in heaven. He is shown gazing at Christ whose radiant glow illuminates the face of the thief.

- The unrepentant thief is depicted in shadow to accentuate his despair.

- This painting is a good example of Jellett's later style, combining her love of harmonious colours and abstract shapes with a bold figurative approach to Cubism.

JACK B. YEATS

Date	1871–1957	Influences	The Expressionists
Cities	London, Sligo, Dublin	Themes	Rural scenes, Irish nationalism, religion
Movement	Resembles Expressionism	Style	Thick *impasto* brushstrokes, vibrant colours, atmospheric

Jack B. Yeats was the son of the famous Irish painter John Butler Yeats (1839–1922) and the brother of poet William Butler Yeats. He lived in Sligo with his family and attended art school in South Kensington in London. He did not have the same extensive art education as the other Irish artists mentioned previously, but drew upon his own experiences and the Irish landscape and culture as inspiration for his work, painting many rural scenes depicting fishermen, horsemen and market traders to name but a few. The rise of nationalism sweeping across the country was also an influence on his art, seen clearly in his painting 'Going to **Wolfe Tone's** Grave,' 1929. Artistic influences were the Expressionist painters who worked largely from memory instead of observation to express themselves (see p. 339). Jack B. Yeats was famous for his use and application of colour, using thick daubs of brilliant colour, applied by brushes, palette knives and often his fingers. He sometimes used paint straight from the tube which gave more intensity to his

biography

THEOBALD WOLFE TONE, the 'Father of Irish Republicanism,' was born in Dublin in 1763. Although a well-to-do Protestant, he championed the cause of downtrodden Irish Catholics, and wanted to achieve an Ireland independent from Britain. He brought troops over from France to help fight for this cause in the 1798 rebellion but it was unsuccessful. He killed himself in prison in 1798 rather than die an ignoble death by execution.

work. His later paintings from the 1930s onwards became increasingly more abstracted and difficult to comprehend easily, as a result of the indistinct shapes formed by the palette knife. This helped to create more atmospheric pieces, his art appearing more expressive and intriguing.

There is No Night, 1949

The title of the painting is taken from the Book of Revelations in the Bible. Yeats often chose titles from literary sources and used them to inspire his work, but did not strictly adhere to the subject in the context of the books they were taken from. In the Book of Revelations Saint John awakes to see a rider on a white horse. In the foreground of this painting we see the figure of a man waking to see a white horse galloping towards him. The theme of horses was often present in Yeats's work, as were solitary figures alone in a landscape.

▼ *'There is no Night,' Dublin City Gallery The Hugh Lane, Yeats*

- This painting, one of Yeats's later and more Expressionist works, is not a conventional landscape, although it does have a foreground (the man), a middleground (the horse), and a background (the horizon and the sea in the right).

- The details of the scenery are vaguely suggested, the purples and blues of the heather on which the man sits and the blues in the sky and sea are also indicative of the nature of the scene.

- Yeats also uses colour to unify. The blue in the sea and sky appear in the clothes of the man and in the coat of the horse. The reds, yellows and blacks seen in the sky are repeated on the ground and the white of the horse can also be seen in the face of the man and on the horizon underneath the black brushstrokes in the moody sky. This all combines to create an energetic, turbulent atmosphere within the work.

- The stormy blue sky dominates the composition, executed in swirls of thick blue paint, with daubs of yellow, red and white to echo the colours of the earth below, and long, energetic strokes of black blended on the horizon. The figures of the horse and man are suggested rather than absolutely rendered, giving them a dream-like unsubstantial feel.

The Irish Exhibition of Living Art

This was an annual exhibition set up by young Irish artists as a reaction against the conventional tastes of institutions such as the Royal Hibernian Academy. These young artists had received artistic education in Paris and were aware of the changing nature of art styles. They were frustrated on their return to Ireland by the lack of interest and understanding of modern art in the academies. The first exhibition was set up in 1943, and the first chairperson was Mainie Jellett. The name of the exhibition reflected the message of the exhibitors, as only art from living artists was accepted for display. Artists who exhibited their work in the Irish Exhibitions of Living Art included:

- Painter and stained-glass artist Evie Hone (see p. 141)
- Mainie Jellett (see p. 385)
- Mary Swanzy (1882–1980), considered to be the first Irish Cubist
- Painter and tapestry designer Louis Le Brocquy (born 1916)
- Painter and illustrator Norah McGuinness (1901–80)
- Painter, architect, and designer Patrick Scott (born 1921).

Irish Modernism Revision Questions

1 Describe the impact of the growth of Irish nationalism on Irish art by discussing one artist's work in particular.

2 Describe 'The Ninth Hour' by Mainie Jellett in terms of theme, colour and style.

3 Jack B. Yeats is one of Ireland's most recognised and famous artists. Discuss the reasons for this, referring to his style, themes and techniques in your answer.

American Avant-Garde

The centre of the Modern art world shifted from Europe to New York during the 1940s. This was partly due to the devastation wreaked upon European countries during wartime (see p. 371). Artists escaped to the more stable environment of the United States to pursue their artistic careers.

> **Did you know?**
> The expression *avant-garde* comes from the French language and means 'advance guard.' It refers to something, previously unthought-of, which is experimental and innovative.

Abstract Expressionism

The influence of Cubist and Dada principles quickly affected the work of the American painters, culminating in a new form of art called Abstract Expressionism. These artists believed that art should express the inner workings of the mind, while unfettered by reason or conventional methods of painting. They also thought that art should evoke an emotional response from the viewer. The New York School, as the group was known, broke into two sets of artists, working in two different ways.

- One group focused on **Gestural Abstraction**. This is often called 'Action Painting,' and is characterised by repeated variations of lines and shapes applied by dripping, splashing and throwing paint quickly and spontaneously across a large canvas using gestures rather than a careful touch.

- The other group focused on **Chromatic Abstraction**. These artists were more concerned with how the colour in the picture reflected its meaning and the emotions of the painter.

JACKSON POLLOCK			
Date	1912–56	**Influences**	Mexican Muralism, Picasso, Kandinsky, Jung
Cities	Cody, Los Angeles, New York	**Themes**	Psychology, mathematics
Movement	Abstract Expressionism	**Style**	Energetic, spontaneous

Jackson Pollock was born in Cody, a town in Wyoming, the son of a farmer. He began his art career as a student of Thomas Hart Benton (1889–1975), an American muralist, in New York. He started working for the Federal Art Project in 1938 which was a government agency that commissioned murals and artworks to decorate public buildings such as courthouses and libraries. He worked for the Project for four years. In 1945 he married another Abstract Expressionist artist Lee Krasner (1908–84). Pollock began to develop his famous gestural painting technique in his work during the 1940s, but it was not until 1950 onwards that his style had fully matured. He was also influenced by the work and ideas of Kandinsky, developing his theories on abstraction and vigorous, dynamic painting to express emotion and the workings of the subconscious mind. Although Pollock's work was popular, his paintings were derisively named 'drip paintings' by some critics. He died in a car accident when he was 44 years old.

Technique

Pollock created his paintings on a large scale, and began by laying a large uncut canvas on the floor of his studio. He then threw, dripped and splattered paint onto the canvas, developing his ideas as the work took shape. He used a variety of materials from standard oil paint to enamels and aluminium paint and worked from every angle of the piece. Pollock was passionate about his work, painting with great energy and dedication.

Number 1 (Lavender Mist), 1950

It is difficult to determine the exact meaning or subject matter of the painting, although we do know that Pollock drew his inspiration from the theories of the psychologist **Carl Jung** and from his own imagination.

biography

CARL JUNG (1875–1961), was a Swiss psychologist and theoris who explored dreams, religion and sociology in order to understand and interpret the human mir

- At 3 m x 2.2 m, this is a characteristically large-scale painting.

- Although named 'Lavender Mist,' there is actually no lavender colour present in the composition. The palette for the painting consists of blues, yellows, greys, pinks, browns along with black and white, which together form an impression of a base colour of lavender.

- Pollock used commercial enamel house paint to create this painting as it was thicker and more viscous, allowing him to create more organic curved lines. These lines form a multi-stranded net covering the entire canvas in a rhythmic manner, appearing to have no beginning or end.

- The artist left his personal physical mark on the painting by applying his own handprints on the top-right of the composition.

▼ *'Number 1 (Lavender Mist),' National Gallery of Art, Washington D.C., Pollock*

MARK ROTHKO

Date	1903–70	Influences	Surrealism, Cubism, Paul Klee
Cities	Daugavpils (Latvia, formerly part of Russia), Portland, New York	Themes	Mythology, spiritualism
Movement	Chromatic Abstraction	Style	Large areas of colour, translucent layers of paint

Mark Rothko was born in Russia and moved to the United States in 1913. The work he painted in the 1940s was originally influenced by Surrealism and Cubism. He grew to believe that painting should reflect the supernatural and the deepest emotions of human experience, such as despair, ecstasy and anxiety. He was one of the founders of Chromatic Abstraction – large-scale abstract paintings featuring blocks of solid colour.

Untitled, 1961

This glowing painting is a good example of Rothko's technique. He applied thin layers of paint in a wash method, overlapping the edges of the shapes to create the effect of objects suspended in space. The iridescent (luminous) warm palette of reds in this work shimmers on the surface of the canvas. The painting is divided by two darker red horizontal parallel lines, with a panel of crimson on the top with lighter, scarlet reds below. There is a beautiful simplicity and symmetry in the soft geometrical design of the painting.

▲ 'Untitled,' National Gallery of Art, Berlin, Rothko

WILLEM DE KOONING

Date	1904–97	Influences	Arshile Gorky (1904–48), an Armenian Abstract Expressionist painter
Cities	Rotterdam, New York	Themes	The female figure, landscape
Movement	Abstract Expressionism	Style	Energetic, overlapping lines and shapes, thick *impasto* brushstrokes

Willem de Kooning was born in Holland where he was chiefly known as a portrait painter and commercial artist. In 1926 he moved to New York, adopting Gestural Abstract Expressionism (see p. 389) and developing it to his own style as a figure painter. He is most famous for his large-scale series of paintings of women.

Woman 1, 1950–52

▼ *'Woman 1,' Museum of Modern Art, New York, de Kooning*

De Kooning's inspiration for his paintings was sourced from his earlier career as a commercial artist. The women in this series of paintings were largely influenced by the billboard advertisements depicting glamorous women – Kooning claimed that the toothy smile on the face was derived from a Camel cigarette advertisement. His painting seems to parody the sensual idealised feminine beauty popular at the time and incorporate the image of a sturdy 'earth-mother' symbolising fertility and nature. The painting consists of a huge female figure dominating the canvas with an abstracted energetically painted background.

- De Kooning's style is most notable for its fluidity of brushstroke and powerful imagery.

- He uses thick, dark, linear strokes to outline roughly the form of the woman, while simultaneously combining subtle changes in hue with vibrant flat colour within and surrounding the figure.

- The result is a picture which appears to be halfway between a finished painting and a quick sketch, giving it an ever-changing dynamic appeal.

American Avant-Garde Revision Questions

1 Explain Abstract Expressionism and compare the work of two artists working in New York at this time.

2 Describe Woman 1 by Willem de Kooning under the following headings: a) theme, b) style, c) composition.

Pop Art

During the last few centuries art was considered as a product designed for the enjoyment of the wealthy upper and middle classes and the well educated. The working classes had little leisure time to allow pastimes to interfere with their busy work schedules. During the twentieth century, however, all this changed. The onset of mass production and industrialisation, combined with more reasonable working hours, gave the people of a lower social order the means and the time to enjoy cultural pursuits such as reading, cinema, television and music. Despite this, art was still thought of as belonging to an elitist culture, and inaccessible to most. Pop artists were so-called because they derived their inspiration from popular culture. Following the Dada ideals of creating understandable art for the masses (see p. 368), they sought to break down these barriers. They did this by using contemporary references that everyone would be familiar with. These included images from advertising, television, magazines and comic books, as well as everyday household items. Pop artists often imbued their paintings of everyday things with irony and humour.

ANDY WARHOL			
Date	1928–87	**Influences**	Popular culture
Cities	Pittsburgh, New York	**Themes**	Consumer products, film stars, musicians
Movement	Pop Art	**Style**	Graphic, bright colours, strong black outlines

Andy Warhol was born Andrew Warhola in Pittsburgh in 1928, to parents who had emigrated from present day Slovakia. Due to an early illness called Saint Vitus's Dance, a disease of the nervous system, he spent a lot of time alone drawing and becoming fascinated with popular culture, music and movies. He studied commercial art and advertising at the School of Fine Arts in Pittsburgh.

Move to New York

After moving to New York in 1949 he pursued a successful career as an illustrator for magazines and advertising companies, which led to his interest in the huge impact mass production and the growth in TV and advertising media had on modern society. He chose well-known images from popular culture as the subject matter for his work, using silk-screen printing to reproduce his images repeatedly within large compositions. This echoed his conflicting opinions on mass production and over-exposure of products and famous people in the media, being fascinated by them and repelled by them at the same time.

▲ *Andy Warhol, 1977*

First Exhibition

He first exhibited his art in 1962 in the Ferus Gallery in Los Angeles. This exhibition included his now-iconic images of Marilyn Monroe and the Campbell's soup cans, themes he continued to work with throughout the 1960s.

The Factory

Warhol worked in collaboration with other artists to produce his work, reflecting the mass-production techniques which influenced his work. He would begin a project and then hand it over to be finished according to his design. The studio in which he worked was named 'The Factory.' This also produced films and sculptures. In 1968, one of the Factory collaborators Valerie Solanas (1936–88) shot Warhol, claiming that he was too controlling. Although he survived the shooting, Warhol was deeply disturbed by the incident and asserted a more rigid control over his collaborators at the Factory. During the 1970s he became more interested in portraiture, and created famous prints of many famous singers and film stars, including John Lennon (1940–80) and the French actress Brigitte Bardot (born 1934).

Music Interest and Later Years

He also became involved in music, becoming a patron of the New York experimental rock group The Velvet Underground (1965–73) and designing the famous cover of their album *The Velvet Underground and Nico* which featured a yellow and black banana against a plain white background. Warhol himself became as well known as his work, achieving celebrity status in his lifetime. He died in New York aged 58, following a routine gallbladder operation.

Campbell's Soup Cans, 1962

This art work consists of 32 canvases of equal size (0.5 m x 0.4 m) in four rows of eight. Warhol chose Campbell's soup cans as his subject matter as they were very recognisable consumer items which were popular and mass produced. When they were first exhibited they were placed in a single horizontal line as if they were on display on a supermarket shelf.

▼ *'Campbell's Soup Cans,' Museum of Modern Art, New York, Warhol*

- Although initially they all look identical, these canvases are subtly different, showing the 32 varieties of soup available at the time. They range from Clam Chowder through to Beef Noodle.
- As well as the change in lettering, giving the different names of the soups, there are also other small variations on some of the cans, some showing extra labels and changes in the font size and colour.

SILK-SCREEN PRINTING TECHNIQUE

Each one of these canvases was created in the same way using the silk-screen printing technique. Silk screening is a printing process which uses pre-cut stencils to transfer an image gradually onto a surface in a number of steps. It was first used for creating commercial products and packaging and then adopted by the Pop Artists to give the impression of mass production.

1 The first stencil is placed on the screen, which is made of silk or other fine-mesh fabric.

2 The silk screen is painted with a single colour. The surfaces covered by the stencil remain unpainted. The design can then be transferred to the printing surface (such as canvas or paper).

3 To create more colours multiple stencils can be used, and the process repeated.

CLAES OLDENBURG

Date	Born 1929	Influences	Allen Kaprow, (1927–2006), an American painter and performance artist, Paul Wieghardt (1897–1969), an American artist and art professor
Cities	Stockholm, New York, Chicago		
		Themes	Everyday objects
Movement	Pop Art	Style	Large-scale sculptures, representational, humorous

Claes Oldenburg was a Pop-Art sculptor who made large versions of food and clothes. He was born in Stockholm, Sweden in 1929 and moved first to New York with his family in 1936 and then to Chicago. He began painting at the Art Institute of Chicago under the tutelage of Paul Wieghardt who was to become a life-long influence on his work. In 1956 he returned to New York where he met Allen Kaprow and other artists who were interested in creating **installations** and sculptures and were also involved in **performance art**.

Oldenburg was most famous for his oversized sculptures. He used a base of chicken wire, over which he moulded plaster. His later works were made to a very large scale, stuffing vinyl or canvas to create the desired effect. He deliberately chose everyday items to sculpt to emphasise the effect of mass production in a greedy consumer society. He also worked in partnership with his wife Coosje van Bruggen (1942–2009) to create huge sculptures which were placed outdoors. These consisted of representations of mundane objects such as snooker balls and clothes pegs.

dic·tion·ar·y

An art **installation** is a form of art incorporating three-dimensional sculptures. It can also involve video and audio equipment to transform the environment of a gallery space.

Performance art consists of a live performance by an artist using the body and props to express an opinion, theme or emotion.

Floor Cake, 1962

Oldenburg created this large-scale soft sculpture from canvas filled with foam rubber and cardboard boxes and painted it with synthetic polymer paint. It measures 1.5 m x 2.9 m x 1.5 m. The sculpture resembles a cartoon-like giant-sized slice of chocolate cake, complete with chocolate frosting. In creating this soft sculpture, Oldenburg was aware that when it was moved it would slightly change shape, making it constantly interesting. He made the Floor Cake as part of a one-man show called 'The Store,' which took place in a real shop outlet in New York for added authenticity. Other items in the exhibitions included a giant ice-cream cone made in the same way as the Floor Cake and plaster casts of clothing and food as well as a cash register.

▶ *'Floor Cake,' Museum of Modern Art, New York, Oldenburg*

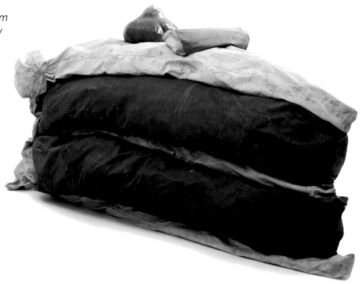

ROY LICHTENSTEIN			
Date	1923–97	**Influences**	American artist and teacher Hoyt L. Sherman (1903–81), Allen Kapro
Cities	New York	**Themes**	Comic-book imagery
Movement	Pop Art	**Style**	Dark heavy outlines, primary colours, Benday dots

Roy Lichtenstein was born in New York in 1923. He studied art in Ohio State University where he completed both a master's degree in art and a teaching diploma. He taught art along with Allen Kaprow at Douglass College in New Jersey. He was briefly interested in Abstract Expressionism but soon turned to comic-book art for inspiration. His enlarged comic-strip panels reflected the Pop artists' interest in images taken from popular culture.

Lichtenstein's colouring system also echoed comic-book imagery. Illustrator and printer Benjamin Day (1810–89) had invented a colour printing technique which came to be known as the 'Benday' system. This technique involved placing dots of colour on the page to create tones of colour. To create pale colours, for example skin tones, tiny dots of colour were arranged against the white background of the page, where the colour was mixed optically by the viewer. The larger the dots, the deeper and more intense the hue became. Lichtenstein adopted this technique and the scale of his work made it very obvious in his paintings, which was the effect he wanted to achieve.

Whaam!, 1963

The large painting (1.7 m x 4 m) depicts an air battle, with an American jet-fighter gunning down an enemy plane. Lichtenstein chose to depict the most exciting moment in the battle: the impact of the rocket and the explosion of the plane.

- The painting was inspired by a panel from the comic *All American Men of War*, 1962, D.C. Comics.

- This is a very dynamic image, with the **foreshortened** jet fighter shooting diagonally across the pictorial space. The large organic lines of the explosion are filled with red and yellow as is the expressive lettering. These colours are echoed in the rapid lines in the bottom left-hand corner and the in the upper right behind the comic book style script. This creates an acute triangular visual, drawing the eye towards the action.

- In this image, the artist recreates the feel of the contemporary comic strip with thick black lines contouring the shapes of flat colour.

> ### dic·tion·ar·y
>
> **Foreshortening** is the technique artists use to create the illusion that an object is extending backwards into space. It is achieved by making the nearest part of the object larger in comparison to the rest of the object, which reduces in size as it recedes.

▲ *'Whaam!,' Tate Modern Gallery, London, Lichenstein*

Pop Art Revision Questions

1 Describe the inspiration behind Pop Art and discuss how Andy Warhol used popular culture to create iconic art.

2 Describe a 'soft sculpture' by Claes Oldenburg, explaining his reasons for creating it and how it was made.

3 Discuss the influence of comic-book art on the work of Roy Lichtenstein by describing one of his paintings in detail.

Gallery Visit

Over the years art galleries and museums have made understanding and appreciating modern art more accessible to the viewer through their production of audio and printed guides, catalogues and guided tours. They also provide a valuable service for new and upcoming artists as well as established contemporary artists in allowing the public to view their work. It is important to understand the role that the modern art gallery plays in the world of art as well as the work that is carried out in them.

The Irish Museum of Modern Art

The Irish Museum of Modern Art, known as IMMA, is situated in the old Royal Hospital of Kilmainham in Dublin. The building was constructed between 1680 and 1684. Originally it was a home for elderly or infirm soldiers, and was founded by **James Butler** and designed by **William Robinson.**

During the years the building passed through a number of hands:

- It became the property of the Irish Free State in 1922 (see p. 383).
- It became the home of the Commander-in-Chief of the army in 1927.
- It became the main Garda Headquarters in 1930.

In 1991, the Irish Museum of Modern Art took over the premises, filling the rooms with permanent and temporary exhibitions of twentieth-century art from Ireland and abroad.

biography

JAMES BUTLER (1610–88) was the Duke of Ormonde and an Anglo-Irish general who was a staunch supporter and viceroy to Charles II of England (1630–87).

WILLIAM ROBINSON (1645–1712) was an English architect and the surveyor general in Ireland from 1670. A surveyor general is responsible for establishing land boundaries and maps of a country.

Exhibitions of Contemporary Art

The participants in the exhibitions are varied and include:

- Established Irish and international artists
- Historical (early twentieth-century) artists
- Contemporary up-and-coming painters and sculptors.

For an artist, the value of having their artworks exhibited in the museum is immense as curators from other galleries get to see the work, as do the public. This can establish the artist, giving their work distinction.

Exhibition Forms

There are a number of exhibition forms which take place in the Irish Museum of Modern Art:

1 **Retrospective** exhibitions look back on the career of an individual artist or movement.

2 **Solo** exhibitions display the work of a single artist.

3 **Group** exhibitions feature a number of artists' work. These artists generally share something in common, such as theme or style.

4 **Project-based** exhibitions involve work from a group of artists who work in collaboration with each other on a chosen theme or subject.

5 The **temporary** exhibitions usually last around three months and there can be up to five separate exhibitions on display at any given time, giving the collection a dynamic diversity of content.

Along with the collection owned by the gallery, numerous temporary exhibitions occur within the year, most of which are curated (see below) by the gallery itself, while others are curated in partnership with the museums which have loaned the works.

Collecting Policy and Practice

The collection of twentieth-century artworks is the result of donations, purchase and loans. The museum has also added to its collection by commissioning works by contemporary artists. IMMA primarily buys works of living twentieth-century artists but also accepts loans or donations of older artefacts or works which have a particular relevance to the work displayed.

The Role of the Curator

The curator of a gallery has many different functions, primarily in ensuring the care of the gallery's artwork and exhibitions. Curators must also have a thorough knowledge of the gallery's collection and about art in general. Some of the work undertaken by the curator includes:

- **Looking after the collection**. As some paintings in the gallery might be very old or in bad condition the curator may employ a conservator or restorer to repair the piece. The job of a conservator or restorer is to examine objects or paintings in a gallery or museum and assess if there has been any physical or chemical damage. If there has been they then use treatments to restore the object or painting back to its original condition as best they can.

- **Having extensive knowledge of art**. The curator must be able to give information about the work in the gallery. This involves researching the artists' lives, their work and their inspirations. This information is catalogued and housed in the gallery.

- **Arranging displays.** The way paintings and other artwork in the gallery are positioned and shown is part of the curator's job. They organise the work in a way that will maximise the effect of the art on the viewer.

- **Choosing what to display.** Public galleries often have a large amount of artwork. The curator decides which works to display and where they should be situated. Works not on display are kept in storage or can be sent out on loan to another gallery.

- **Organising temporary exhibitions.** Visiting exhibitions are planned by the curator, which includes designing the layout, researching the work to be shown and positioning of each piece.

- **Compiling photographs and catalogues and labelling the work on show.** This provides visitors to the gallery with extra information on the pieces on display as well as a memento of the exhibition.

- **Liaising with curators from other galleries.** This is an important way to gain art information and to organise loaning of work.

- **Overseeing the care of paintings on loan to other galleries.** This includes arranging the packing of the artwork and its security.

Bibliography

<u>1</u> Barnicoat, John, *Posters, a Concise History*, Thames & Hudson, 1972

<u>2</u> Beckett, Sister Wendy, *The Story of Painting*, Dorling Kindersley Ltd, 2001

<u>3</u> Bourke, Marie, *Exploring Art at The National Gallery*, The National Gallery of Ireland, 1997

<u>4</u> Bohm-Duchen, Monica & Cook, Janet, *Understanding Modern Art*, Usborne Publishing Co., 1991

<u>5</u> Duane, O.B., *Picasso, Discovering Art*, Brockhampton Press, 1996

<u>6</u> Kleiner, Fred S., Mamiya, Christin J & Tansey, Richard G., *Gardner's Art Through The Ages: The Western Perspective,* Wadsworth, a division of Thomson Learning, 2003

<u>7</u> Langmuir, Erika, *The National Gallery Companion Guide*, National Gallery Publications Ltd, 1994

<u>8</u> Leslie, Richard, *Pablo Picasso*, Tiger Books International, 1996

<u>9</u> Lucie-Smith, Edward, *Visual Arts in the 20th Century*, Laurence King Publishing, 1996

<u>10</u> Mannering, Douglas, *Gauguin*, Parragon, 1994

<u>11</u> Sheehy, Jeanne, *The Rediscovery of Ireland's Past: The Celtic Revival*, Thames & Hudson, 1980

<u>12</u> Turner, Jane, *From Expressionism to Post-Modernism,* Macmillan Reference Ltd, 2000

<u>13</u> Wiggins, Colin, *Post-Impressionism*, Dorling Kindersley Ltd, 1993

<u>14</u> *The Great Artists: Lautrec*, Marshall Cavendish Partworks Ltd, 1985

<u>15</u> *The Great Artists: van Gogh*, Marshall Cavendish Partworks Ltd, 1983

unit 6

Art Appreciation

> 'It's on the strength of observation and reflection that one finds a way. So we must dig and delve unceasingly'
>
> Claude Monet (1840–1926)

This chapter focuses on section three of the art history exam paper – appreciation of art and design. This part of the exam asks the student to observe and reflect, asking whether they like or dislike a particular piece of art and design. These pieces come from a wide variety of areas:

- **Gallery/Museum visit**
- **Film (including animation)**
- **Architecture**
- **Sculpture**
- **Product design**
- **Graphic design (posters, packaging)**
- **Interior design**
- Fashion design
- Garden design and so on

For the purposes of this book we have studied the areas in **bold** in the chapter.

Gallery/Museum Visit

There is a wealth of galleries and museums to visit in Ireland. Most are free of charge and give regular tours to the public. They have education departments with knowledgeable and helpful staff. Here is a sample of these:

1 The National Gallery of Ireland, Merrion Square, Dublin 2. *www.nationalgallery.ie*

2 The National Museum – Decorative Arts and History, Collins Barracks, Dublin. *www.museum.ie*

3 The National Museum – Natural History, Kildare Street, Dublin 2. *www.museum.ie*

4 The National Museum – Archaeology, Kildare Street, Dublin 2. *www.museum.ie*

5 The National Museum – Country Life, Castlebar, Co Mayo. *www.museum.ie*

6 The Chester Beatty Library, Dublin Castle. *www.cbl.ie*

7 Dublin City Gallery The Hugh Lane, Parnell Square West, Dublin 1. *www.hughlane.ie*

8 The Galway City Museum, Spanish Parade, Galway. *www.galwaycitymuseum.ie*

9 The Crawford Art Gallery, Emmet Place, Cork. *www.crawfordartgallery.ie*

10 The Hunt Museum, Rutland Street, Limerick. *www.huntmuseum.com*

11 The Ulster Folk and Transport Museum, Cultra, Co. Down. *www.nmni.com/uftm*

12 Sligo Art Gallery, Hyde Bridge, Sligo. *www.sligoartgallery.com*

▲ *The Francis Bacon Studio, Dublin City Gallery The Hugh Lane*

ABOUT THE QUESTION

The gallery/museum visit question is a great opportunity for the student, as they have the chance to visit an exhibition and write about their experience. They get to see the artwork first-hand, which brings it to life. After studying art and design for five years it is very important for a student to be able to go to an art gallery/museum and discuss the exhibition and give an opinion on it, and to use proper terminology when answering the question.

It is perhaps the most answered and popular question on the appreciation section of the art history paper. While the gallery visit question varies from year to year, the key components to be answered are as follows:

1 Name the gallery; give location and description of gallery building.

2 Name the artist and exhibition and give information on their background and style of art/movement.

3 Describe an artwork (this may be a painting/sculpture/installation/print, etc.).

4 Describe a second artwork.

5 Explain why you liked/disliked the artwork.

6 Illustrate your answer.

The following information table and the **'Ask Yourself'** questions that follow will give guidance for responding to an artwork and for the gallery visit generally.

FACTORS TO CONSIDER	DESCRIPTION	EXAMPLES
Before you go	You should look up the artists you are going to see to find out as much information as you can on their work, style and background.	Go to the gallery/museum website and read up on the current exhibitions.
Accessibility	Museums and galleries are required to be accessible on every level to wheelchair users by installing ramps and lifts. Is there a cloakroom in which to hang up your jacket/bag?	The Hunt Museum in Limerick has lift access to all floors of the museum.
Architecture	The architecture of the gallery/museum can add to the overall visit. Is the building modern or from a different century?	The National Gallery of Ireland has two entrances – the original one on Merrion Square and the new, more modern one on Clare Street.
Colour scheme	Modern art galleries tend to use white as a neutral clean backdrop for the paintings, whereas more long-established galleries tend to use deeper tones to create a more traditional environment for the works displayed.	Some galleries such as the Crawford Gallery in Cork use varying colour schemes depending on what is being displayed in the rooms. Most of the gallery is painted a stark white except for the sculpture room which is painted a rich red to provide a contrast to the white sculpture casts.
Information	The education department in a gallery or museum generally provides guided tours. Information on current and upcoming exhibitions is given on their websites. Usually galleries and museums provide catalogues and information about key artists in the permanent collections and these are often available in the bookshop.	The National Gallery in Dublin provides guided tours, catalogues of visiting exhibitions, information labels and audio guides. Listen carefully to your tour guide and ask questions – they will be delighted to give answers.
Interactive facilities	Many galleries now have online facilities which allow you to take a virtual tour of exhibitions. Some museums and galleries also have touch screen interactive information or activities that you can do to help you immerse yourself in the experience.	The Barracks Life Room in the National Museum – Decorative Arts and History, Collins Barracks, has interactive capabilities: here students can try on uniforms and use computer-driven interactive resources to help them appreciate what a soldier's life was like in the nineteenth and twentieth centuries.

FACTORS TO CONSIDER	DESCRIPTION	EXAMPLES
Layout	The layout of a museum or gallery depends on the size of the building and rooms and also what type of art is being exhibited. In general, the more room the exhibit has around it, the more it can be seen at its best as an individual piece of art.	The Irish Museum of Modern Art (IMMA), Kilmainham, which exhibits modern art and sculpture, is a large building with many rooms designed around a courtyard. This allows it to hold several exhibitions simultaneously.
Lighting	Lighting is a very significant element to be considered in a gallery. Is it natural or artificial?	The Chester Beatty Library, Dublin Castle is mainly dimly lit throughout to preserve the rare manuscripts and prints displayed.
Location	The name and location of the gallery or museum.	The Hunt Museum, Limerick; Dublin City Gallery The Hugh Lane, Dublin.
Paintings	What height are the paintings hung at? How many paintings are on each wall? What size are the paintings? Is the labelling easy to read? What information does it carry?	Most galleries hang paintings at eye level to make them easier to access. The information on the labels generally includes the name of the artist, the title of the work, the date, the medium used, when the painting was acquired and from whom. In Dublin City Gallery The Hugh Lane, three Impressionist paintings hang side by side at eye level, to show the development of this movement.
Recording information	One of the most important factors for students is to record as much information as they can while they are there. Some galleries provide their own worksheets.	On your worksheet make a note of each of the artworks you see. It is good to write your opinions straight away before you forget. See the '**Ask Yourself**' questions below for help on how to do this.
Type of exhibition	There are many different types of exhibition which would necessarily have different layouts and be approached in various ways: print, painting, photography, craft, etc.	The National Craft Gallery, Kilkenny Castle showcases contemporary crafts. The Irish Museum of Modern Art (IMMA), Kilmainham exhibits modern art and sculpture.
At the end of your visit	Draw a labelled sketch of one/two paintings you really liked. At the end of the tour, make a note of your overall opinion of the exhibition. Do this straight away when it's fresh in your mind.	See the '**Ask Yourself**' questions on the next page for help on this.

You need to use proper vocabulary when describing the artwork (history/ subject matter, colour/ composition/ texture/ perspective/ pattern/ light/ form and structure/ materials, etc.). See below for help with this.

Ask Yourself

History

- Does the artwork have an interesting history (did it travel far, is it unique, etc.)?
- Is the artist important in this area?
- What style of art is it?

Subject Matter

- What story is the artist trying to tell? (Is it a religious, historical, modern, etc.?)
- Can I describe what's happening?

> **SUBJECT MATTER** is what something is about. In artwork, the subject matter is what the artist has chosen to paint, draw or sculpt.

Colour

- What colours are in the artwork? Is it multicoloured, all different tones of blue, monochrome (black and white), etc.?
- Are the colours in the distance faded in relation to the colours in the foreground?
- What colour is the main character? How does it contrast with the rest of the artwork?
- Was colour important to the artist?

- Did they mix their own colours and make new tones or were they restricted to the colours on offer?
- If it's a painting did the artist use oil paint, acrylic paint or fresco paint? What is the quality of colour?
- Is there a strong contrast between light and dark colours?
- How does this add drama to the painting, e.g. 'The Taking of Christ' by Caravaggio?

Composition

- Is the format of this artwork portrait (vertical) or landscape (horizontal)?
- Is it an abstract composition?
- Is it a realistic composition?
- Is there a background, middle-ground, foreground?
- Does the composition have a mathematical layout, e.g. Michelangelo's Sistine Chapel ceiling (see pp. 202–7) or his 'Pieta' sculpture (see p. 196)?

> **COMPOSITION** is the deliberate arrangement of objects, forms, shapes in a painting/sculpture.
>
> An **ABSTRACT** painting/sculpture does not portray recognisable objects, shapes, people, etc. The colours, lines and patterns are the subject matter of the artwork.
>
> In a **REALISTIC** composition we can clearly understand the subject matter of the artwork.

Texture

- Does the artwork have texture? Can I list off the different textures on the artwork?
- Is it visual texture, or tactile texture?
- Am I allowed to touch the artwork?
- Can I walk around the artwork?

Perspective

- Does the painting have perspective; does it have a vanishing point?
- Where in the painting is the vanishing point?

Pattern

- Does the artwork have a pattern? Can I describe the pattern?
- Has the pattern added to the piece? The Book of Kells, for example, has beautiful pattern work (see p. 37).
- What would it be like without the pattern?

Light

- How is light used in the artwork (is it bright, dark, etc.?

Form and Structure

- What size is the artwork?
- What shape is it?

Materials

- What materials have been used to make this artwork (stone, clay, metal, etc.)?
- Why were these materials chosen?
- What is the media (oil/ woodblock print) of the image?

Like/Dislike

- Did I like/dislike the artwork (was it the subject matter, colours, textures, etc., or a combination of many art elements)?
- Did I like the way it was displayed?
- Did the guide explain it well to the class?
- Was it more impressive in reality than in the books?
- Could I bring anything that I've learned from this artwork and incorporate it into my own work?
- Was there music playing at the exhibition? Did this add to the experience?

Sketch

- What sketch would best illustrate the exhibition?
- How much detail can I put into this sketch (as much as possible)?
- How do I label this sketch (make it clear as possible)?

TEXTURE is the surface quality of an object. Texture can be **TACTILE** (where you can touch it and the surface can feel rough or smooth, e.g. a stone is rough and a silk dress is smooth) or **VISUAL** (where you can see a texture painted, e.g. the furs and velvets on the clothes in *'The Arnolfini Wedding'* by Jan Van Eyck; see p. 231).

PERSPECTIVE is the illusion of distance in a painting.

VANISHING POINT is where all the receding lines meet, thus creating the illusion of distance, e.g. in *'The Last Supper'*, by Leonardo da Vinci, the vanishing point is behind the head of Christ (see p. 192).

A **PATTERN** occurs when an image repeats itself. **PLAIN PATTERN** is a simple image repeating itself one after the other. **HALF DROP PATTERN** is where the motif (design) is dropped at the halfway point and repeated over and over, e.g. a redbrick wall. **ABSTRACT PATTERN** is created by mixing a motif up at random, e.g. if you threw a bunch of leaves up in the air, the pattern they make when they land would be an abstract pattern.

Descriptions of Artworks

'The Taking of Christ,' c. 1602, at The National Gallery of Ireland, Dublin

This oil on canvas painting is on indefinite loan to the National Gallery of Ireland from the Irish Jesuit Fathers. Caravaggio (1571–1619) was one of the most famous, influential and original Italian painters of the seventeenth century. His paintings of religious themes were new, radical, naturalistic and bold. They created some controversy at the time. 'The Taking of Christ' was commissioned by the Roman Marquis Ciriaco Mattei.

▲ *'The Taking of Christ', National Gallery of Ireland, Dublin, Caravaggio*

- The **subject matter** of this painting, which shows Judas arriving with the soldiers at the moment he is going to betray Christ with a kiss, has been depicted by many artists throughout history. However, no other artist's depiction of this topic was as dramatic or bold as Caravaggio's. He painted dirt under Christ's fingernails, which was not considered respectful by the Church at this time, but Caravaggio felt this was a true portrayal of Christ and society. Christ is placed left of centre in the composition, waiting to be arrested. He is composed, ready for his fate, with his hands joined. Judas stands at the right of Christ leaning over him, with his left hand clutching Christ's shoulder. Beside Judas are two soldiers ready to arrest Christ. The lantern-bearer to the very right of the painting is a self-portrait of Caravaggio, acting as a spectator in this terrible event. Notice the way he holds the lantern – it's similar to the way a painter holds his paintbrush. On the very left behind Christ is Saint John the Evangelist.

- Caravaggio uses **light** in a very skilful way to add even more drama and tension to an already emotional scene. Notice the strong contrast between light and shade. We can use the light to guide us through the painting, to follow the light from the lantern, down the helmet and across the shine on the soldier's armour to Christ's face and then out of the painting with Saint John the Evangelist. Notice that the only light colours in the painting are on Christ's and Saint John's garments and the soldier's trousers.

- There is very little **pattern** in the painting, apart from a little on the bottom half of the soldier's uniform.

- **Texture** has been richly employed onto Christ's garments. Those soft smooth textures are a direct contrast to the cold hard textures of the soldiers' uniforms.

- *Pentimenti* is a term used to describe a mistake made by the artist which he then paints over. In this painting you will notice a mistake over Judas's ear: originally Caravaggio placed the ear higher up and did not like it, so he painted over it.

'The Bibendum Chair', (1921), at The National Museum – Decorative Arts and History, Dublin

Eileen Gray (1878–1976), was one of the most influential designers and architects of the twentieth century. Her exhibition is on permanent display at the National Museum – Decorative Arts and History. The exhibition includes the adjustable chrome table, the non-conformist chair, the Bibendum chair, her lacquering tools and miscellaneous personal items.

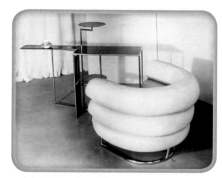

▲ *'The Bibendum Chair', National Museum – Decorative Arts and History, Dublin*

- The **artist** was born in Ireland then studied painting at the Slade school of fine Art, London. In 1900 her father died and her mother took her to Paris where she studied at the *Académie Julian* and the *Académie Colarossi*. She was very interested in lacquer work, and later opened a shop in Paris to sell her work. In the 1930s she built and designed a new home for herself – 'Tempe à Pailla.'

- The Bibendum chair is one of the most recognisable pieces of furniture of the twentieth century, and was named after the character from the Michelin tyre advertisements.

- The backrest **material** consisted of two stuffed u-shaped pieces and the legs were made from polished, chrome-plated stainless tubes. The actual frame was made from beechwood.

- The chair is very **comfortable** and has a lovely soft leather finish.

'Time of the Hare', c. 1801, at The Chester Beatty Library Museum, Dublin

▼ *'Time of the Hare', Chester Beatty Library Museum, Dublin, Utamaro*

The Chester Beatty Library Museum has the largest collection of Japanese art in Europe outside of Japan. Sir Alfred Chester Beatty (1875–1968) assembled a great collection of drawings, rare books, miniature paintings, manuscripts and decorative arts. All are on display in the art museum and library. Visiting this gallery, you get a flavour of different cultures from around the world including China, Japan, North Africa, the Middle East and Europe.

- The **artist,** Kitigawa Utamaro (1753–1806), is considered one of the greatest artists of *Ukiyo-e*, or woodblock prints. The term literally means 'pictures of the floating world.' This **style** of art was produced for the new trendy population of Japan's capital Edo (modern-day Tokyo). The newly introduced and very popular woodprints were available to the poor as well as the rich. Utamaro is known for elegant depictions of women, known as *Bijinga*.

- In this print the **subject matter** is two women leaning over a well, using the water as a mirror. The 'time of the hare' was between five and seven o'clock in the morning.

Film

As a society, we love to watch films. There are many different genres in this art form, including horror, romance, western, historical, animation, science fiction and fantasy.

Study the following table of information and '**Ask Yourself**' questions that follow for guidance on responding to and answering a question on film.

FACTORS TO CONSIDER	DESCRIPTION	EXAMPLES
Camera work	Varied camera work is essential in making a film exciting and entertaining. There are many techniques used such as **panning** (showing a panoramic view), **close-ups, low-lying shots, zoom shots, different angle shots, fade in/fade out shots** and **tracking shots**, which follow a character around a scene. **Stop motion** is a technique in which physical objects are photographed, moved slightly then photographed again. This gives the impression the objects are moving themselves when the pictures are viewed sequentially.	*The Matrix* (1999) was the first film to use '**bullet time**' effects. This was achieved by placing numerous cameras around a character which recorded movements simultaneously. Still frames from each were then shown in sequence to make it appear as if the viewer was in orbit around a frozen character. The popular animation films about Wallace and Gromit (Nick Park) were produced using stop motion.
Cinematography	Cinematography encompasses many different aspects of film making. The cinematographer works closely with the director and oversees the choice of cameras, lenses, camera angles, lighting of scenes, and inclusion of special effects.	*Crouching Tiger, Hidden Dragon* (2000) won an Oscar for its cinematography. This was largely due to the seamless visuals achieved by blending stunning matte-painted scenery with breathtaking action sequences and panoramic camera shots.
Costume	Costumes play an important role in establishing the period of the film and also what sort of character is being portrayed.	*Gladiator* (2000) is a film in which costumes play a vital part in setting the story in ancient Roman times and making the characters believable in their environment.
Editing	The editing of a film is an essential process in telling the story. It involves cutting scenes, selecting camera shots and arranging them in sequence.	The **montage** is a very effective way of telling a story in a concise and exciting way. The boxing film *Rocky* (1976) shows a montage of short scenes of the character training in different locations.
Genre	The genre of a film determines what type of film it is – horror, action, fantasy, period drama, animation, comedy, thriller or science fiction (sci-fi). Thrillers can be a mix of two genres, e.g. sci-fi/thriller.	**Horror:** *A Nightmare on Elm Street* (1984). **Action:** *Terminator 2* (1991). **Fantasy:** *Harry Potter and the Philosopher's Stone* (2001). **Period drama:** *Pride and Prejudice* (2005). **Animation:** *Toy Story* (1995). **Comedy:** *Anchorman* (2004). **Thriller:** *Psycho* (1960). **Science Fiction:** *Avatar* (2009). **Sci-fi/Thriller:** *Aliens* (1979).
Lighting	Lighting in a film contributes heavily to the atmosphere; flash lighting, spotlights, explosions of light all generate different feelings from the audience. Bright sunny light denotes happiness, whereas deep shadows create a scary atmosphere.	Alfred Hitchcock's black-and-white thrillers such as *Psycho* (1960) made great use of dramatic lighting, creating long dark shadows to build up an atmosphere of suspense and unease.

FACTORS TO CONSIDER	DESCRIPTION	EXAMPLES
Make-up	Make-up in films serves to develop our idea of the characters on screen. Make-up can tie characters to an era or turn them into fantasy creatures through the use of prosthetics.	The character of Freddie Krueger in *A Nightmare on Elm Street* (1984) is one of the most enduring icons of horror movies due to the terrifying prosthetic makeup applied to create the burn tissue on his face.
Scenery/sets	The scenery and sets are integral to the story of a film, creating a believable world for the characters and plot.	The *Lord of the Rings* trilogy exploited beautiful rural locations in New Zealand to represent the fantasy landscape of Middle Earth.
Sound	Sound in films is a key element in creating a realistic atmosphere. It also helps to give the viewer the sense of being involved in the film.	In *WALL-E* (2008) the sound was innovative and exciting as the robot's speech was entirely made up from sound instead of speech.
Soundtrack and sound effects	The soundtrack of a movie is created by a composer to accompany and enhance scenes in a film. Themes associated with a character can often be repeated throughout the film. Sound in a film is very important in creating a sense of reality, fantasy, etc.	The theme from *Jaws* (1975), with its simple but effective two-note melody, has become part of popular culture used to signify oncoming danger. In the opening scene of *Saving Private Ryan* (1998) the sounds made by the bullets were extremely realistic.
Special effects	Special effects is an area in film which is constantly developing. **Computer-generated imagery (CGI)** is the use of computer-aided design to create a three-dimensional reality and has, in a lot of cases, replaced the use of models and matte painted backgrounds. Other techniques involve characters acting out scenes in front of bluescreens which will later be replaced by actual or virtual backgrounds. Films produced in 3D require the viewer to wear 3D glasses to get the full effect. Each lens in these glasses has different filters, which removes different parts of the image as it enters each eye. This gives the brain the illusion that it is seeing the picture from two different angles, creating the 3D effect.	In *Jurassic Park* (1992) the special effects combined large-scale models with CGI to stunningly realistic effect. This is most spectacularly seen in the scene where the Tyrannosaurus rex approaches the stranded jeep through the dark rainy night. *Avatar* (2009) is a great example of a 3D film where the beautiful and unusual scenery and characters of Pandora come to life on the screen.
Typography	The typography used to advertise a film can often send messages to the reader about the kind of film it is. The credits are usually in keeping with the overall design of the film.	The typography for *The Godfather* is a great example of how this can be used to clarify the meaning or message of a film. The contrast of the white lettering against the black background is stark and striking, while the puppet strings attached to the letters reflect the hierarchy of the mafia, with the 'don' pulling the strings.

Ask yourself the following questions when looking at a film.

Ask Yourself

- What genre is the film?

- What is the style of the film?

- Who are the audience?

- Can I name the director, producer and leading actors?

- Does it have a good story?

- Who are the central characters in the film? Are they well chosen? Is their acting believable? Do I care what happens to the characters? Who was my favourite character and why? Who was my least favourite character and why?

- Who delivered the best performance in the film, and why?

- Was there any character who delivered a bad performance?

- What techniques did the director use to make me connect with the characters?

- How was drama delivered to the audience in the film?

- Are there special effects? If so, what are they? How were they produced?

- Was the camera work good? What type of shots were used and to what effect?

- What sounds do I remember and why?

- Was lighting important in the making of this film? Why? How did it make me feel?

- What was my favourite scene and why? Would this be the best scene to write about or was there a better one in the film?

- Where was it filmed? In what way was location important for this film?

- How important was the make-up department in this film? Did they do a good job?

- Do the costumes play an important role in this film?

- What was the cinematography like?

- Was the film well edited? Did the story flow well from beginning to end?

- What impact did the film have on me? Does it convey a strong message?

- Was the music appropriate to the theme of the film?

- Did I like this movie? Why?

Descriptions of Films

Avatar (2009)

Genre

This fantasy film was directed by Canadian James Cameron (b.1954). In it, he invented new technology, a new language, and even created a new world – 'Pandora'. Although it cost $237 million to produce, *Avatar* turned out to be one of the highest grossing films of all time. Cameron is renowned for his classic blockbusting films such as *Terminator* (1984), *Aliens* (1986) and *Titanic* (1997).

The Story

Avatar tells the story of a future battle between Earth and alien moon, Pandora. Pandora is a rainforest-covered moon with amazing humanoid beings known as the Na'vi. The Na'vi beings are blue-skinned native creatures, wrongly considered primitive by humans. Pandora is full of interesting beasts and is rich in minerals.

The plot focuses on a former marine, Jake, who is confined to a wheelchair following a war on Earth. He is chosen to take part in the avatar program and travel on a mission to take over Pandora. In this avatar world his mind will control a healthy body. Jake has a dilemma – where do his loyalties lie in the war? The war will, in the end, decide the fate of the two planets. We, the viewers, are challenged to decide which is the good side and which is the bad side.

One Scene

This film is packed with great scenes from beginning to end. An example of a powerful scene occurs near the beginning. Jake enters 'The Link' (a machine which connects his real body with his avatar body) and he is transported to the Pandora world. Suddenly, as an avatar, he can walk and run again. We share in his elation as he runs, feeling the sand under his feet. He feels alive again.

Special Effects and Camerawork

For Cameron the special effects are as important as the story. In *Avatar*, he combined computer-generated images (CGI) with live action using a process called **motion capture.** In filmmaking it refers to recording the actions of human actors, and using that information to animate digital character models in 2D or 3D.

During filming, Cameron made use of his **virtual camera system,** a new way of directing motion-capture filmmaking. The system shows the director the actors' virtual counterparts in their digital surroundings in real time, allowing them to adjust and direct scenes just as if shooting live action.

Cameron had a clear image in his head of what the Na'vis in *Avatar* should look like. Bringing the image to life took a dedicated team led by 3D designer Ben Procter and head sculptor Jordu Schell. Cameron gave them a pencil sketch of the face of one of the Na'vis – the heroine, Neytiri. Schell translated Cameron's sketch of Neytiri into a **3D maquette** (scale model) bringing the image to life. This set the style for the rest of the Na'vi creatures.

> ### *Did you know?*
>
> An Irish artist, Richard Baneham, was part of the *Avatar* team. He and his colleagues Andrew R. Jones, Joe Letteri and Stephen Rosenbaum won Oscars for the film's visual effects.

Costume

Like everything else in *Avatar*, the costumes were designed with enormous attention to detail. The Na'vi clothing was developed by Weta Workshop. Cameron and his art team all felt that real clothing, jewellery and weapons should be produced so that the director, the art department and the digital-effects team could see how they work and handle them. They needed to understand how the fabric would blow in the wind, or how much the weapons would weigh in order for them to translate it onto the big screen.

Actual costumes were made and information on how fabrics would move, for example, were sent to Weta. The information was combined on to fully synthetic mobile characters within CGI software. The attention to detail in the costumes was incredible, down to the colour of the thread and the size of buttons.

Scenery and Location

From his imagination, James Cameron developed a beautiful, never before seen, dangerous alternative world in the 3D landscape of Pandora. It had vast lush rainforests, sweeping panoramic views, cascading waterfalls, floating mountains and a huge variety of wildlife.

Pandora had its own ecosystem and precious, wealthy minerals in the ground. Cameron's attention to detail was immense, down to the leaves on the trees and the small insects crawling on the leaves. *Avatar* moved in and out of the real world, Earth, and the world of Pandora. In this world Cameron created many wild creatures including the hammerhead (like a Rhino) and the viperwolf (like a large wild dog). He also created new machines with names such as the amp suit (a power suit) and the dragon (a fantasy vehicle).

Make-up

Samantha Lyttle and special make-up effects artist Malcolm Aitchison were responsible for the make-up in *Avatar*. They stuck to Cameron's vision of the Na'vi people being a blue-coloured race. It took hours of work to prepare each actor for their scenes, and the results are amazing.

Typography

The typography used in the start of the film, along with that used in the promotional posters and credits, reflected its subject matter. In *Avatar* the lettering is a light blue colour with a simple naturalistic shape to reflect the beautiful world of Pandora. It gives the audience an idea of what to expect from the film. In *Avatar* image and lettering are combined very well, one complementing the other. The large close-up image of the eye and the lettering under it echo the theme of the Pandora world.

▼ *A poster for Avatar*

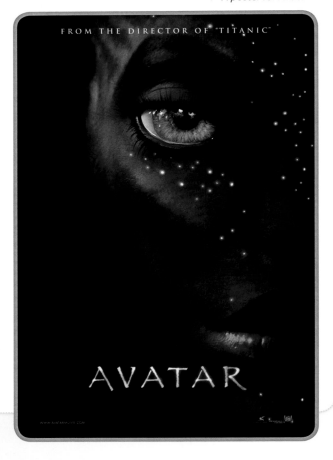

Shrek (2001)

The history of animation can be traced back as far as 1917 with Argentinian Quirino Cristiani's first-ever animated film *The Apostle*. Since then animators such as Walt Disney, the teams at Pixar, DreamWorks and more have created some amazing films that the whole family can enjoy. At the core of all these films is a creative team of hardworking and dedicated artists, writers, technicians and special effects people who combine their talents to produce classics such as *Shrek* (DreamWorks, 2001), *Sleeping Beauty* (Disney, 1959) and *Bambi* (Disney, 1942).

Animation is a unique film genre because what cannot be created in real life is possible in the animated world. Technology has progressed greatly from the old animation classics such as Mickey Mouse and there are various techniques such as **stop motion** (see p. 410) and **CGI animation** (see p. 411) that have made a huge difference.

The focus in the future will be to perfect the animation of humans. It is proving difficult to perfect the movement of hair and clothing on animated characters, but studios are getting closer by the day. Films such as *Avatar* managed successfully to combine animation with live action to create humanoid creatures.

Shrek, made by DreamWorks and directed by Andrew Adamson and Vicky Jenson, is one of the best-loved animations of all time. The film is loosely based on William Steig's 1990 fairytale picture book of the same name. Shrek has his own star on the Hollywood walk of fame. The first *Shrek* film had a budget of $60 million and made $484,409,218 worldwide in 2001. The same year it was part of the Cannes Film Festival. *Shrek* won the first-ever Academy Award for Best Animated Feature, and won a BAFTA Award for Best Adapted Screenplay. From the original there followed three sequels:

- *Shrek 2* (2004)
- *Shrek the Third* (2007)
- *Shrek Forever After 3D* (2010).

The Story

The main character in the film is a big, ugly, loud and intimidating green ogre called Shrek, voiced by Mike Myers. He befriends a talking donkey, voiced by Eddie Murphy. When Shrek's swamp is invaded by fairytale creatures dumped there by villain Lord Faraquaad (voiced by John Lithgow), the pair go to visit him. He sends them to find the feisty Princess Fiona, voiced by Cameron Diaz, as Farquaad cannot become king unless he marries her. The princess is a beautiful girl by day, but an ogre by night, as the result of a wicked spell. She becomes the love of Shrek's life. In the end Fiona becomes an ogre forever and she and Shrek outwit the evil Lord Farquaad, to live happily ever after.

The following three *Shrek* films continue to explore the ups and downs and many adventures of Shrek and Fiona's life together.

Special Effects

Shrek is an example the new trend in animation at the time. Computer graphics have become the norm in cartooning with more movies of this type now being produced, than the traditional 2-D.

Shrek took the Oscar for Best Animated Feature Film from its only real competition, Pixar's *Monsters Inc.*, and placed DreamWorks Animation as a close second to Pixar in the CGI animated game. The film also would introduce the notion of the CGI animated film as blockbuster.

▲ *The poster from the 2001 film, showing the main characters*

Architecture

Architecture forms an important part of our lives, from the houses we live in to the local shopping centre, church or theatre.

FACTORS TO CONSIDER	DESCRIPTION	EXAMPLES
Form	The form or shape of a building is often defined by the period in which it is built, the space it occupies and its function.	The Sydney Opera House is one of the most famous modern buildings in the world because of its distinctive arched shell shapes.
Function	The function of a building is essential to the design of its structure.	Castletown House in Kildare is the largest Georgian stately home in Ireland that has been restored to its former glory. It is the headquarters of the Irish Georgian Society, and is open to public as a stately home.
Impact on the environment	Architects must take into account the surrounding environment when designing a building in order to ensure it is in keeping with its environs.	If designing a shop front in a small rural village, it would be important to avoid bright colours and plastic signs, and instead utilise traditional materials such as wood or locally sourced stone.
Materials	Materials are one of the first considerations for architects as they decide on the look and texture of a building. These can include stone, bricks, wood, metal or glass.	Glass is the most prominent material used in modern commercial or public buildings, often to utilise the light from outside. A fine example of this is the Convention Centre in Dublin.
Proportion/balance	Proportion and balance have always been considerations in architecture throughout history. It refers to the mathematical relationship between different features in a building to create a harmonious appearance.	The Villa Rotunda by Andrea Palladio (see p. 225) is a perfect example of precise symmetry and balance: each side of the building is constructed to be identical to the other.
Style	The style of a building is most often defined by the period in which it was built, for example the Georgian period or the Gothic period. It can also reflect the purpose of the building.	The Custom House in Dublin, with its arcades and columns, is a fine example of Georgian architecture and was the first public building in the city.
Sustainability	Sustainable design is a growing concern in modern architecture. It involves using ecological and energy-saving devices to prevent future environmental problems.	Sustainable design features include recycled materials such as reclaimed wood, solar panels, waste management systems and insulation with recycled materials.

Ask yourself the following questions when looking at a piece of architecture.

Ask Yourself

- What is the function of this building? Is the scale related to this function?
- What style is the building?
- What materials have been used to make this building?
- What impact is this building having on the environment?
- What are the social aspects of the building?
- Is the design of the façade (outside) beautiful? Does it have any classical features?
- Is its design appropriate to the local surroundings?
- Do I like this architecture?
- Has this piece of architecture responded to the social and environmental needs of the surrounding area?

Descriptions of Architecture

The Dublin Docklands Project

Function

The Dublin Development Authority (DDA) was established in 1997. The idea behind it was to develop the east side of Dublin, along both banks of the River Liffey. In a programme of **urban regeneration**, it aimed to bring physical, social and economic changes to this area.

> **dic·tion·ar·y**
>
> **Urban regeneration** involves an attempt to renew or refresh a run-down area in a town or city.

This project is a strong example of how architecture responds to the social and environmental concerns of an area, such as affordable housing, schools, entertainment, waste management and transport issues. When designing the Docklands, great thought was put into public transport in and out of the area, for example the Luas line was extended into it.

Social regeneration was a major part of this development – 11,000 new houses were built, as well as shops, restaurants and schools.

Scale

This project has cost a total of €7 billion from both public and private sources. The Dublin Docklands Authority will continue working on this development until 2012. The economic downturn has affected the completion of some of the project's work.

Some of the Buildings

Regeneration work included the restoration of some of the Dockland buildings. One example is **The chq Building** (Custom House Quay). The original structure was built in 1820 by a famous engineer, John Rennie (1761–1821), as a wine and tobacco warehouse, and it is the last surviving warehouse of the Docklands.

This grade-one listed building is situated in the heart of the busy Irish Financial Services Centre (IFSC) in the Docklands and overlooks the River Liffey and George's Dock. It has undergone a €40 million refurbishment funded by the Docklands Authority. Designed by Michael Collins Associates, it shows how developers can harmonise old with new. It was opened to the public in November 2007 offering an array of restaurants, bars and retail shops, such as Louis Copeland and Sons, Meadows & Byrne, Fran & Jane, and many more. Materials used in this restoration project include glass and stainless steel.

▼ *The chq building, Dublin*

New buildings were also constructed. **The Convention Centre,** located next to the Royal Canal, between North Wall Quay and Mayor Street, was designed by Irish architect **Kevin Roche** (b.1922), and cost €380 million to build.

biography

KEVIN ROCHE studied architecture at University College Dublin and graduated in 1945. He left for America in 1948 where he studied with celebrated German architect Ludwig Mies Van der Rohe (1886–1969). From 1951 to 1961 he worked with Eero Saarinen (1910–61), a Finnish modernist architect and designer. Saarinen died in 1961 and Kevin Roche and John Dinkeloo (1918–81) continued the practice, finishing several projects including The Gateway Arch at St Louis Missouri and the TWA Terminal at JFK Airport, New York. Their first new commission together was the Oakland Museum of California, which features terraces, roof gardens, ponds, patios and sculpture gardens. In 1982 Roche achieved the highest honour any architect could get when he won the Pritzker Architecture prize.

The centre is designed to attract international conferences to Dublin. It is versatile – it can function as one space or as many spaces, so can accommodate a variety of events, from big concerts, conferences and exhibitions to small meetings. The building is 45,921 sq m in size. The entrance hall on the main level can be subdivided into two areas. The second exhibition hall can also be divided into two areas. On the second floor of the building is a space that can hold 2,000 people.

The building's most striking feature is the stunning glass-fronted atrium running the full height of the building, giving panoramic views of the river Liffey and the Wicklow Mountains beyond. This tilted glass cylinder, 54 m high and 39 m in diameter, intersects the granite wall of the south façade.

The Grand Canal Theatre, located on Grand Canal Square, opened in March 2010. Polish-born architect **Daniel Libeskind** (b.1946) designed the building. The theatre can hold 2,100 people. It presents the best national and international performances in opera, theatre, musicals and Broadway productions.

The façade of the Grand Canal Theatre is diamond shaped, with a glass front from floor to ceiling. The building is a mix of steel, concrete and glass walling which produces a modern contemporary effect, optimising the use of light.

▼ *The Convention Centre, Dublin*

biography

DANIEL LIBESKIND is one of the world's most significant and sought-after architects today. His work includes the Denver Art Museum in Colorado, the Memorial War Museum in Manchester, the Jewish Museum in Berlin and 'Memory Foundation', his design study plan for the rebuilding of the World Trade Centre Site in New York. His work ranges from museums, convention centres, theatres and hotels to landscape and urban projects and installations.

▼ *The Grand Canal Theatre, Dublin*

Sculpture

Whether it's public and outdoors, or in a private collection, sculpture makes us stop, look and think. We have many examples of sculpture throughout Ireland, both traditional and modern.

Irish sculpture has a rich history which is part of our unique heritage. It dates back to the Middle Stone Age when the megalithic tomb at Newgrange, Co Meath (see p. 4), was created (c. 3300–2900 B.C.). Examples followed with the Turoe Stone in Bullaun, Co Galway, c. 50 B.C. (see p. 17); the Celtic High Crosses, such as the Cross of Moone, Co. Kildare, ninth century (see p. 46), right up to the stark modern-day sculpture of 'The Spire' on O'Connell Street, Dublin (see p. 424).

FACTORS TO CONSIDER	DESCRIPTION	EXAMPLES
Balance	The sculptor must consider every aspect of the sculpture in relation to the rest of it to create a balanced composition.	'The Pieta' (see p. 196) by Michelangelo is formed around a classic triangular composition with the flowing robes of the Virgin tying the figures together.
Form	The form of a sculpture is the overall three-dimensional shape of the object. It can be realistic or abstract in shape.	Michelangelo's statue of 'David' (see p. 195) is based on an idealised and classic version of the human form.
Light	Light is an important element to consider in designing a sculpture as it creates shadows and shapes on the piece. Some metallic sculptures also reflect light, changing their appearance.	Indoor sculptures such as 'David' by Donatello (see p. 188) depend on the light within the room to create shapes and shadows, whereas outdoor reflective sculptures such as 'The Spire' on O'Connell Street in Dublin, (see p. 424) constantly transform according to the changing weather.
Mass/volume	The mass of the sculpture is determined by the shape, width, height and depth of the piece. In general, this is something that is rigid and unchanging.	'Floor Cake' by Claes Oldenburg (see p. 396) is a large-scale soft sculpture which can change shape when moved. The artist was playing with the concepts of mass and volume.
Materials and texture	There are many different materials and textures used in the creation of sculpture, depending on what method of sculpting is used: subtractive (carving), manipulation (moulding) or additive (combining materials).	Picasso's 'The She-Goat' (see p. 354) combines numerous materials to create an individual and unusual sculpture.
Scale	The scale of the sculpture can be largely determined by the size of the space it is intended for. As a result, monumental outdoor sculptures are generally larger.	'The Spire' dominates the entire street with its impressive size, which stands out even amongst the tall buildings on either side of the street.
Space	The relationship of the sculpture with the space it occupies is very significant. Because it exists in three dimensions, our view of the sculpture changes as we walk around it.	'Famine' by Rowan Gillespie (see p. 423) shows very clearly how the sculpture affects the space around it. As the life-size sculptures are separated by space we are free to walk among them and interact with them.

Ask yourself the following questions when looking at a sculpture.

Ask Yourself

- Where is it located? Is its location important?
- What does it symbolise?
- What colour is it? Does its colour change?
- What textures and patterns can I see on it?
- Can I touch it, walk around it, through it?
- What size is it? Does its size suit its location?
- What materials were used in its production? How was it made?
- Do I like this sculpture?
- Can I understand what the artist was trying to express here?

Descriptions of Sculptures

Statue of Daniel O'Connell (1882)

Sculpture of the nineteenth century and the first half of the twentieth century was mainly used to commemorate deceased politicians, soldiers, bishops and rebels. An example of this is the **Daniel O'Connell** bronze statue on Dublin's O'Connell Street, by **John Henry Foley**. Daniel O'Connell (1775–1847) was an Irish political leader who campaigned for Catholic Emancipation (the right for Catholics to become members of parliament) and for the repeal of the Act of Union, which joined Britain and Ireland.

▼ *Daniel O'Connell statue, O'Connell Street, Dublin, Foley*

biography

JOHN HENRY FOLEY was the first major Irish sculptor. He studied at the Royal Dublin Society art school, then moved to London where he became one of the youngest exhibitors at the Royal Academy of Arts. In 1840 he was chosen along with other sculptors to decorate the new Houses of Parliament in Westminster. Here he created statues of statesman John Hampden and jurist John Selden. He also sculpted a statue of Prince Albert – at the Albert Memorial in Hyde Park. Examples of his work in Ireland are the bronze sculptures of statesman Edmund Burke and writer Oliver Goldsmith outside Trinity College, Dublin and the Daniel O'Connell statue.

Famine (1997)

It was not until the latter half of the twentieth century that the subject matter for sculptures expanded to show individual artistic expression in artists' work.

Rowan Gillespie created 'Famine', at the Custom House Quay in Dublin to focus on the hardships endured by the Irish people during the Great Famine of 1845–49. However, it can also relate to hardships in other cultures around the world. It's impossible to walk past this sculpture without feeling sorrow for the Irish people during the Famine. Gillespie's work can be found all around the world, for example 'The Cycle of Life' and 'The Minstrels' are on display in Colorado, USA.

▼ *'Famine', Custom House Quay, Dublin, Gillespie*

biography

ROWAN GILLESPIE (b.1953) is one of the most movingly expressive contemporary Irish sculptural artists. He was born in Dublin, but soon after he and his parents moved to Cyprus where his father worked as a doctor. He went to boarding school in England and his family stayed on in Cyprus until he was ten. In 1969 he went to the York School of Art where Sally Arnup, a leading sculptor of bronze animals, introduced him to the **lost wax casting process**. This is a method of casting in which a wax form is encased in a heat-resistant material, such as clay. When that material is hardened it is then heated to melt the wax inside, which is then drained away to leave a mould. Material can be poured into this mould for various purposes. In 1970 Gillespie attended Kingston College of art where he studied wood carving under John Robson and through him met celebrated sculptor Henry Moore (1898–1986). Gillespie is famous for his bronze sculptures which express emotional themes and tell a story.

'The Spire' (2003)

This striking piece of sculpture, which cost €4 million to build, was erected on the site of the former Nelson's Pillar on Dublin's O'Connell Street. The monument was commissioned as part of a redesigned street layout in 1999. It was designed by British firm Ian Ritchie Architects and built by Radley Engineering of Dungarvan, Co. Waterford. The spire is an elongated cone 121.2 m high, measuring 3 m at the base, then narrowing to 15 cm at the top. It is made up of eight hollow tubes of stainless steel and has a device called a tuned mass damper to counteract swaying. The steel was treated with a system known as shot penning in order to subtly reflect the light falling on it. The metal changes colour due to the reflections of the weather on it. The base has been specially treated in order to stop graffiti, so writing won't stick.

▶ *'The Spire', O'Connell Street, Dublin, also called 'The Monument of Light'*

Product Design

Product design surrounds us every minute of our lives. From the moment we wake up we encounter design – from the cereal box, the breakfast table, our clothes, to the phones we use every day. There are several elements to consider when we talk about product design.

Product Design

FACTORS TO CONSIDER	DESCRIPTION	EXAMPLES
Advertising	How are the public attracted to the product? The producers and sellers rely on advertising companies, where creative teams come up with new ideas to sell products to the public.	Nike, the global sportswear company, has spent vast sums of money on advertising to ensure the brand is seen as the most popular among the most elite sportspeople.
Colour	Colour plays a big part in the design and success of a product.	Coca-Cola has always used a bright primary red with white lettering on their products, which have now become linked with the product itself.
Ergonomic design	Ergonomic design explores how products and devices can be developed to improve the relationship between the human body and the product.	Sony PlayStation's placement of the buttons, analogue sticks and shoulder buttons on its games console controller all facilitate easy gameplay. A further introduction of dualshock controllers that vibrate according to the action, helped to further involve the player in the world of the game.
Form	The form (shape, scale and volume) of an item is one of the first major concerns of the designer.	The Volkswagen Beetle is one of the most enduring icons in the car industry due to its quirky form.
Function	Product design must facilitate the function of the object. It must be easy to use for its purpose.	The Dyson 'Airblade' hand driers are a good example of a simple modern design that came about specifically to promote the product's function, with two arcs ideal for placing your hands in to be dried.
Mass production	This is the manufacture of goods in large quantities by standardising parts, techniques and machinery.	Eli Whitney (1765–1825) introduced mass production in 1798 to produce weapons.
Materials	The use of appropriate materials and textures is an important element in product design.	Levi 501s are the most popular item of clothing in history. This is largely due to the denim material along with the metal rivets and zip, which are hardwearing and timeless in style.
Style	The overall look of an object is vital to ensure its success, particularly in a market that may be saturated with similar products.	The iPod is a modern design classic because of the sheer simplicity of its shape, its slimline form, vivid colours and instantly recognisable logo.

Ask Yourself

Ask yourself the following questions when looking at any product design.

- What are the striking features of the product?
- What is the colour of the product?
- What is the texture and pattern of the product?
- What is the function of the product?
- Who is this product aimed at? What age group?
- Where would you find this product?
- What is the style of this product?
- What materials were used in its production?
- Is this product stationary or portable?
- What size is the product?

- Is it powered by electricity, gas, battery, or solar? Maybe it needs no power?
- Is it a one-off piece or mass produced?
- What is the price point of the product?
- Is there a celebrity advertising this product? Do you think this makes it more appealing?
- Is this product easy to use?
- Is this product environmentally friendly?
- Has this product been designed to facilitate the busy lifestyles we live today?
- Is this product multifunctional?
- Do I like this product?

Descriptions of Product Designs

Telephone Design

Alexander Graham Bell invented the telephone in 1876. He invented the **prototype** by using soft iron that vibrated to sound waves. These vibrations caused disturbances in the magnetic field of a bar magnet, which caused an electric current of intensity. The current could then be transmitted through wire to a distant identical device that reversed the process to produce sound.

dic·tion·ar·y

A **prototype** is an original form of something that serves as a standard for later stages.

Early Telephone Designs

- **The Skeleton, 1900:** This telephone was decorated with gold transfers and finished in high-quality lacquer. L M Ericsson was the first to produce this phone. The design exposes the working parts, including the bell.

- **The Candlestick, 1910:** This was a hugely successful design that lasted for several years. It was the standard table telephone with a separate bell-set, consisting of a ringer capacitor and induction coil. The only disadvantage to this design was that the mouthpiece was fixed into the stand or base which the user had to talk into. They listened with the other moveable piece held to the ear.

- **The Neophone, 1929:** This was the first moulded plastic phone. The Siemens Neophone was originally made of black bakelite.

- **The Desk Telephone, 1937:** New Yorker Henry Dreyfuss (1904–72) created this first self-contained metal model for American Telephone and Telegraph.

- **The Ericofon or Single-Element Telephone, 1949:** This was designed for Swedish company Ericsson by a team including Ralf Lysell (1907–87). The unusual design involves the ear piece and the mouthpiece harmonized into one plastic body, with the dial at the base.

- **The BT Videophone, 1990s:** Brilliant technological advances took place in the 1980s and 1990s, from the appearance of cordless telephones to videophones. Regular calls are also possible on this videophone.

Modern Telephone Designs

Mobile phone

Modern phones have changed a lot from the days when you had to stay in one place to talk on the phone. Now many people have mobile phones that can be carried everywhere. Mobiles were originally clunky designs but that changed quickly.

- The 2000 Nokia 9210 communicator is a smartphone – a phone with more advanced computing ability. It's one of the few mobile phones able to send and receive faxes.

- In the mid-2000s, designs of mobile phones with multipurpose ability, such as the Blackberry Quark 6210 evolved. This brought instant email to the business user.

- In 2007 the first iPhone appeared from Apple. They abandoned the keyboard in favour of a large screen that was perfect for viewing web pages, images, video and other mulitmedia content.

▼ *The Candlestick*

▼ *The Ericofon*

▼ *The BT Videophone*

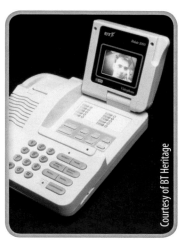

Courtesy of BT Heritage

▼ *The Nokia 9210 Communicator*

▼ *The Blackberry Quark 6210*

▼ *The iPhone*

Graphic Design (Posters, Packaging)

A poster is a printed image designed to be eye-catching and to communicate a message. They are used in many fields and can be any size, colour, language or topic. Poster design can be traced back as far as the 1870s when mass production became available and the printing world developed **colour lithography**.

Key names in the development of the poster were French artists Henri de Toulouse-Lautrec (1864–1901) and Jules Cheret (1836–1932) and Czech painter Alphonse Mucha (1860–1939). Modern-day poster artists include Americans Peter Max (b.1937), Milton Glaser (b.1929) and Robert Indiana (b.1928).

The art of the poster developed into a real art form, thanks mainly to some of the artists mentioned above. Later, however, in the twentieth century, the art poster reached a new high with the **Pop Art** movement and it has continued to grow to this day, with artists like Peter Max and Milton Glaser.

Because of the growth of the art poster, art was brought into the bedroom for the first time. It was now possible to have a replica poster of Vincent van Gogh's 'Sunflowers', Leonardo da Vinci's 'The Last Supper' or an original Peter Max or Milton Glaser poster. Posters were the new form of decoration in the bedroom. They made your room unique and could transport you to an exciting place.

dic·tion·ar·y

A **coloured lithograph** is an authorised reproduction of an artist's work, using a special printing process. The process of lithography uses a smooth surface to transfer the image. Lithography was used a lot in the nineteenth century by artists such as Goya, Delacroix and Toulouse-Lautrec.

dic·tion·ar·y

Pop Art is a twentieth-century art movement that emerged in the mid-1950s in Britian and in the late 1950s in America. Pop Art stands for popular art. Pop artists such as Andy Warhol used images of people and objects which were popular in society (see p. 393).

FACTORS TO CONSIDER	DESCRIPTION	EXAMPLES
Colour	Colour is a vital element in graphic design. To grab the attention of the viewer, strong contrasting colours can be used. Harmonious colours can be used to create a more restful effect.	Peter Max's 'Expo '74' stamp fully exploits the most vivid and brilliant of colours to capture the eye of the viewer. In some cases a minimal colour palette is used to unify the composition.
Composition	The composition of a poster is usually decided after all the poster elements have been chosen. The lettering, image and text must be organised tastefully and dynamically within the layout of the design.	'Folies Bergeres, La Loïe Fuller' by Jules Cheret shows how an effective poster design can be achieved by using a dynamic focal image and unifying the colours of the font with the main image.
Font	The style of lettering in the poster should reflect its message. Some posters rely on lettering alone to convey the message; in this case the lettering must be particularly expressive. The size, style and colour of the font are important.	Most modern posters use computer fonts that have been designed to express a particular style or mood. However, to create a more vintage art or craft poster, handcrafted styles are still used.

Image	The image is usually the main focus of a poster. It can be a photograph, painting or print or any other art form that visually expresses the subject of the poster.	Toulouse-Lautrec's poster 'Les Ambassadeurs' shows the power of a strong visual image to convey a sense of drama.
Logo	A logo is a unique symbol or emblem that can incorporate either an image and lettering or both in a simple graphic way to attain instant recognition of a brand.	Milton Glaser's 'I ❤ NY' logo is a perfect example of how iconic a logo can be. The simplicity of the lettering and colours make it a timeless and lasting design.
Purpose	Posters are designed for many reasons: to advertise an upcoming event, to raise awareness of an issue, to advertise a product or to be used as propaganda for political reasons. Art posters were also produced to create an artistic image for cultural icons.	An example of a propaganda poster is the very famous American recruitment poster, 'Uncle Sam Wants You for U.S. Army' which personifies the United States as a kindly but stern figure who expects loyalty and obedience.
Slogan	In some cases there is an accompanying message or tagline to reinforce the subject of the poster.	Slogans are mostly used to draw attention to a brand or company and are reused throughout an advertising campaign, e.g. Nike's slogan 'Just do it'.
Text/copy	The text or copy of a poster gives added information about the event, cause, or subject matter it is promoting.	Some art posters don't include text in their design. Posters advertising a product or event generally use a simpler version of the larger main font.

Ask yourself the following questions when looking at graphic design.

Ask Yourself

- What is the purpose of the poster/ packaging?
- Who created it?
- Who is it aimed at? What age is the audience it's trying to appeal to?
- Is it trying to convey a message (propaganda/ information)?
- Is it being used to good effect?
- What is the composition of the poster/ package and how does it work?
- What is the effect of the placement of image, lettering, etc.?
- Does it have pattern or texture?
- What materials were used to produce it?
- How is colour used and to what effect?
- What size is it and why?
- Do I like it and why?

Descriptions of Graphic Designs

'Folies Bergère, La Loïe Fuller' 1897 (Poster)

- Folies-Begère is a music hall in Paris, France and Loïe Fuller was an American dancer who appeared there in the early 1890s. Jules Cheret's exuberant image of the dancer captures the spirit of sensuality and excitement in the cabaret culture at the end of the nineteenth century in Paris.

- There is a strong **contrast** between the brightly coloured lady in the foreground and the dark background. This image is of one dancer in motion, head tilted and dress moving.

- The **lettering** in the top half of the poster is red against a light background; that in the bottom half is red against a black background, which makes it stand out strongly.

- All these elements combine to give a very strong visual impact to the viewer.

biography

JULES CHERET was a French painter, lithographer and poster designer. He studied lithography in London from 1859 to 1866. When he came back to France he produced posters for everything from the Moulin Rouge and Folies Bergère to bicycle shops and wine. He was influenced by the Rococo artists such as Jean-Honore Fragonard (1732–1806) and Antoine Watteau (1684–1721). He is famous for his large posters depicting women in happy and carefree attitudes. Cheret inspired a new generation of artists, including Henri de Toulouse-Lautrec, to try poster design.

◄ *'Folies-Bergère, La Loïe Fuller', Cheret*

'Les Ambassadeurs: Aristide Bruant', 1892 (Poster)

➤ The model for this poster by **Toulouse-Lautrec** was Aristide Bruant (1851–1925), a singer and the owner of the Montmartre nightclub *Le Mirliton*. Its visual effect is very striking as the **image** takes up most of the composition.

➤ The **colour** is very flat and the red scarf really stands out against the flat black coat/cape. Bruant's face is pale, with dark black outlined eyebrows. He has light brown hair and wears a large black hat which jumps out at us because it is set against a yellow/beige background.

➤ The **lettering** at the top of the poster appears handwritten – it is brown/beige with a black outline. Further down the poster is more lettering, cream against a black background. At the bottom of the poster brown/beige lettering is set against a black background.

biography

HENRI DE TOULOUSE-LAUTREC (1864–1901) was a French artist who vividly captured the nineteenth century's Parisian nightlife in paintings and posters. Toulouse-Lautrec began his artistic career when, as a teenager, he injured both of his legs and immersed himself in art during his long recovery. In adulthood, he joined the culture of Paris's bohemian Montmartre area, and painted its spectacle of circuses, dance halls, nightclubs and racetracks, as well as the artists, streetwalkers, writers, aristocrats and dancers he befriended. It was while in London to gain experience in poster design that he became friends with the poet Oscar Wilde (1854–1900). He was a great support to Wilde while he was on trial for homosexuality. Toulouse-Lautrec produced a huge range of work in his lifetime, from canvasses, drawings, prints and ceramic work to stained glass and posters.

▲ *'Les Ambassadeurs: Aristide Bruant', Toulouse-Lautrec*

Postage Stamp – Expo'74

Expo'74 was a world fair about the environment. **Peter Max** was commissioned to design a 10c 'Preserve the Environment' postage stamp to commemorate the event. The stamp portrays the image of a happy, healthy environment.

- This is **colourful image** and in the centre of the stamp a man glides across a hilltop. He is wearing a blue jumpsuit with a yellow star on his back. His jumpsuit has red flared bellbottoms – which was fashionable at the time. His hair and shoes are orange. He wears a yellow top hat with a pink pattern. His face and hands are white. In the background is a blue sea with a pink sailing boat set against a white cloud and a yellow and orange wide striped sunset. There are two birds flying above the clouds: one is pink, one is purple. There is a blue side-profile of a smiling face at the very right of the image.

- In the foreground we have simple white block **lettering** on a dark green curved hill.

biography

PETER MAX (b.1937) and his parents fled Nazi Germany when he was just one, travelling extensively to visit China, France, Israel, Tibet and South Africa, before settling in New York. He drew inspiration from the art in each of these countries. During the 1960s a young Peter Max set the art world on fire with his dynamic Pop Art work. He produced colourful, bold, linear paintings and posters using a variety of media, from oils to charcoal. Themes included the preservation of the environment and American patriotism. Max painted for five American presidents: Ford, Carter, Reagan, Bush and Clinton.

He was commissioned to design the postage stamp for the world Expo '74, which took place in Spokane, Washington, USA in 1974. He was also the official artist for the World Cup '94; and in 1995 was artist for the Super Bowl and the Grammy Awards.

◀ *Postage stamp, Expo'74, Peter Max*

Interior Design

Interior design involves planning and arranging the layout of an interior architectural space as well as designing the decoration of the space and choosing furniture and fittings. There are many considerations that have to be worked out before deciding on a finished scheme or plan.

The function of the space is the most important concern to be considered before the interior designer can decide on a scheme to suit the space. Interior design applies to domestic and commercial spaces and serves an important function in creating a suitable environment for both.

Interior designers create a mood board when beginning any design for an interior. This links in with the concept of the room, where ideas on colour, ambience and fabrics are developed to suit the purpose of the space.

◀ *A child's room needs to be colourful and safe.*

▶ *An office needs to be bright with appropriate furniture.*

FACTORS TO CONSIDER	DESCRIPTION	EXAMPLES
Colour scheme	Deciding on a colour scheme is a key factor in determining the atmosphere the designer wishes to achieve for an interior space and is very dependent on the function of the room.	A children's crèche would typically be painted in very bright vibrant primary colours to stimulate young minds. In contrast to this, rich, deep colours are more suitable in a bedroom of a luxury hotel. A more neutral palette of creams or greys would be more appropriate in an open-plan office space as it caters for many instead of reflecting individual taste.
Compatible furniture	When choosing furniture for a space, consideration of the function of the room is vital. It must also be compatible with the design of the room.	In an office, a swivelling, height-adjustable, soft chair on wheels is fit for its purpose. This allows for multiple users to have movement and comfort over extended periods. In contrast, a deeply-cushioned recliner chair would be more suited to a living room where relaxation and leisure are more valued. A dining room chair often has a straight back and washable surfaces in order to facilitate eating and allow for spills.
Concept	This is the overall scheme or idea behind the room. It again will be partly decided by the function of the space but also by the taste of the client.	In designing a fast-food restaurant, the function is to serve quick, inexpensive food with a rapid turnover of customers. This is often reflected in the concept of the space, which regularly features plastic furnishings, bright lighting and primary colours. A more expensive restaurant expects their clientele to linger over their food and order more than one course. Therefore the concept in this case is often designed around comfort and luxury, with darker colours, luxurious fabrics and dim lighting to create a mellow, relaxing ambience.
Focal point	In most domestic spaces a focal point is a key factor in design. This is the area in a room that first attracts the eye.	This can often be the mantelpiece/fireplace, or a painting or large mirror emphasised by a feature wall. A feature wall is generally wallpapered in a distinctive pattern or painted in a deeper colour than the rest of the space.
Function	Function is the most important factor to be addressed. The design must be suitable for the intended purpose.	A kitchen with a carpet would simply not work as it would be soon ruined by spills and dropped food, whereas a tiled floor would make perfect sense as organic mess can be cleaned away easily.

FACTORS TO CONSIDER	DESCRIPTION	EXAMPLES
Lighting	Lighting can be an essential element in design as it helps to create a mood or serve an important function.	In an office space or classroom, bright fluorescent lighting is regularly used, as it aids alertness and productivity, whereas dim, adjustable lighting and lamps are more suitable in a bedroom to create an atmosphere of relaxation and rest.
Repetition and unity	Repeating colours, patterns and similar shapes within a space can help to unify a room. To create a harmonious atmosphere in a room there should be some repetition of these elements.	In a living room, an interior designer could pick out a colour in the wallpaper and repeat tones of this colour in the furniture or carpet. Harmony in design can also be achieved by choosing similar shapes within the scheme; a circular mirror can be echoed by a round coffee table or a circular rug on the floor.
Safety	Architects and engineers must adhere to strict building regulations and health and safety guidelines to ensure that the buildings are safe to use by the occupants and workers.	When designing a building to be used by children such as a crèche, safety regulations are very important. Environmental health and fire safety regulations must be observed as well as ensuring that the furniture and fittings within it are suitable for small children.
Scale and proportion	It is vital to work out the relationships between the objects to be placed in an interior and the space itself. The scale of the object must be compatible with the size of the space it is placed in to fit in with the scheme.	A very large coffee table in the centre of a small living room would not work as it would impede the function of the room, whereas it would be perfect for a large living space.
Soft furnishings	Soft furnishings are often the finishing touches on any design.	These include any elements within the room that are made from fabric such as cushions, curtains and rugs.
Symmetry and balance	In order to create an interior that works, the space as a whole must be considered. The placement of the objects within a room should be well thought-out as well as should the size, texture and colour of the objects themselves.	In a conference room a formal, symmetrical balance is generally adhered to, with seating mirroring itself across a table to create a businesslike atmosphere. In contrast to this a child's playroom would have much more informal balance, using repetitive colours and shapes to create a more relaxed mood.

Art Appreciation Revision Questions

1 'An art gallery is an environment designed to display artwork and help us to a greater understanding and appreciation of art.' Discuss this statement in relation to a recent visit to a named museum or art gallery.

2 Choose one fantasy film and describe and discuss it under the following headings: a) one scene, b) special effects and camerawork, c) scenery and location, d) costume, e) make-up, f) how the typography used in the title and credits reflect the subject matter of the film. Illustrate your answer.

3 'Architecture responds to social and environmental concerns.' Discuss this in relation to any building development. Mention a) function, b) scale, c) materials, d) impact on the environment, e) social aspect, f) outline your own ideas for the landscaping of a development in your locality. Illustrate your answer.

4 Describe how public sculpture has changed in Ireland from the Celtic high crosses to the modern-day Spire. Discuss this in relation to two sculptures, one old and one modern. Discuss: a) themes – what does it symbolise? b) form and function, c) scale, d) its location, e) materials used. Illustrate your answer.

5 'Product design involves a balance between appearance and function.' Discuss this in relation to one of the following products: a) mobile phone, b) electric kettle, c) handbag or sports bag. Discuss its form/function/materials/decorative qualities/the influence fashion has had on your chosen product over time. Illustrate your answer.

6 Outline the artists who were instrumental in the developments of poster design. Describe how poster design has changed over the years and describe what art elements make up a good poster. Illustrate your answer.

7 What factors does an interior designer consider when designing? Discuss in relation to the design of: a) a child's playroom, b) the foyer of a 5-star hotel. Illustrate your answer.

Bibliography

1 Arnason, H.H. & Prather, Marla F., *A History of Modern Art, 4th edition*, Thames & Hudson, 1998

2 *Avatar 3D*, Titan Books, 2010

3 Becker, Annette, Olley, John & Wang, Wilfried, *20th Century Architecture Ireland,* Prestel Verlag, 1997

4 Beckerman, Howard, *Animation,* Allworth Press, 2003

5 Horton, Charles, Pollard, Clare, Ryan, Michael, & Wright, Elaine, *The Chester Beatty Library, Dublin Castle,* Scala, 2001

6 Glancy, Jonathan, *The Story of Architecture,* Dorling Kindersley Ltd, 2000

7 Hay, John, *Masterpieces of Chinese Art,* Phaidon Press Ltd, 1974

8 Jlajln, Zhu, *Treasures of the Forbidden City,* Viking, 1996

9 Lorin, Philippe, *5 Giants of Advertising,* Assouline Publishing Inc., 2001

10 McDermott, Catherine, *Twentieth Century Design,* Carlton Books Ltd, 1997

11 Tambini, Michael, *The Look of the Century,* Dorling Kindersley Ltd, 1997

12 Thompson, Kristin, & Bordwell, David, *Film Art: An Introduction,* McGraw-Hill Education Europe, 2009

13 Vince, John, *3-D Computer Animation,* Addison-Wesley Publishers, 1992

Index

The authors and Publisher gratefully acknowledge the following for permission to reproduce photographs:

Alamy Images; AKG Images; Bridgeman; Corbis; DK Images; JupiterImages; iStockphoto; Getty Images; Wikimedia Commons; Photocall Ireland; Thinkstock; Photoshot; Department of the Environment, Heritage and Local Government, Ireland; National Museum of Ireland; The Board of Trinity College, Dublin; Dublin City Gallery The Hugh Lane; George Walsh; Tara Fahey; Siobhán Geoghegan-Treacy; Liz White; Maria Murphy; John Reynolds; Declan Corrigan; Steve Ford Elliott; Manresa Jesuit Centre of Spirituality, Dublin; Kristin Thompson; Lauri Koski; Paul Kemp; Tim Bekaert; St Saviour's Church, Glendalough, reproduced by permission of the Royal Society of Antiquaries of Ireland ©; John Armagh; Jim Fitzpatrick; Frederick Hollyer; Mirko Battisti; Kirsten Rühl; Theresa Dower; Liam Heffernan; José Manuel Álvaro Sanz; Church of Saint-Pierre, Aulnay de Saintonge, and Church of Saint Sernin, Toulouse, by Jacques Mossot, Nicolas Janbert's Structurae (http://en.structurae.de); Annaghdown Cathedral by John Smyth © www.johnsmyth.ie; Robert Linder; stained glass windows in Chartres Cathedral by MathKnight, Hebrew Wikipedia & WikiCommons; Ed Sanders; Jon Sullivan, PD Photo.org; Jennifer Gernon; Don Bullens; Aschwin Prein; Jean-Marc Labbe; 'Stacks of Wheat (End of Summer)' by Claude Monet, 1890–91, oil on canvas, 60 × 100 cm, gift of Arthur M. Wood, Sr in memory of Pauline Palmer Wood, 1985.1103, The Art Institute of Chicago. Photography © The Art Institute of Chicago; 'Stack of Wheat (Snow Effect, Overcast Day)' by Claude Monet, 1890–91, oil on canvas, 66 × 93 cm, Mr and Mrs Martin A. Ryerson Collection, 1933.1155 The Art Institute of Chicago. Photography © The Art Institute of Chicago; 'Young Breton Girl' by Roderic O'Conor, Dublin City Gallery The Hugh Lane, reproduced by permission of Gráinne Rigney; 'Girl with a Tinsel Scarf' by William John Leech, Dublin City Gallery The Hugh Lane © The Estate of William John Leech; 'A Convent Garden, Brittany' by William John Leech, c. 1913, oil on canvas, 132 × 106 cm. Collection, the National Gallery of Ireland. © The Estate of William John Leech. Photo © The National Gallery of Ireland; 'Lady Lavery in an Evening Cloak' by Sir John Lavery, oil on canvas, 46 × 36 cm. Collection, The National Gallery of Ireland. © By Courtesy of Felix Rosenstiel's Widow and Son Ltd, London, on behalf of the Estate of Sir John Lavery. Photo © The National Gallery of Ireland; 'Reflections: China and Japan' by William Orpen, Dublin City Gallery The Hugh Lane; 'London Bridge' by André Derain, 1906, oil on canvas, 66 × 99.1 cm. Museum of Modern Art, New York. Gift of Mr and Mrs Charles Zadok. © ADAGP, Paris and DACS, London 2009. Digital image © 2009 The Museum of Modern Art/Scala, Florence; 'Conversation', 1909–1912, by Henri Matisse. Hermitage, St Petersburg. © Succession H Matisse/DACS 2009. Photo © Archives Matisse; 'Harmony in Red', 1908, by Henri Matisse. Hermitage, St Petersburg. © Succession H Matisse/DACS 2009. Photo © Archives Matisse; 'Head of Christ' by Georges Rouault, 1939, oil on canvas. Hermitage, St Petersburg/Bridgeman. © ADAGP, Paris and DACS, London 2009; 'Street, Dresden' by Ernst Ludwig Kirchner, 1908 (reworked 1919; dated on painting 1907), oil on canvas, 47½" × 35⅞". Museum of Modern Art, New York. Digital image © 2009 The Museum of Modern Art/Scala, Florence; 'Entry into Jerusalem' by Emil Nolde, 1915, oil on canvas. Private Collection/Bridgeman. © Nolde Stiftung Seebüll; 'Les demoiselles d'Avignon' by Pablo Picasso, 1907. M. Flynn/Alamy. © Succession Picasso/DACS 2009; 'Guernica' by Pablo Picasso, 1937. The Print Collector/Alamy. © Succession Picasso/DACS 2009; 'The Goat' by Pablo Picasso, 1950. Musée Picasso, Paris/Bridgeman. © Succession Picasso/DACS 2009; 'Fruit Dish and Cards' by Georges Braque, 1913. Musée National d'Art Moderne, Centre Pompidou, Paris/Bridgeman. © ADAGP, Paris and DACS, London 2009; 'Improvisation XXXI', 1913, and 'Accent en Rose', 1926, both by Wassily Kandinsky. Musée National d'Art Moderne, Centre Pompidou, Paris/Bridgeman. © ADAGP, Paris and DACS, London 2009; 'Composition with Red, Blue and Yellow' by Piet Mondrian, 1930. Private Collection, Lauros/Bridgeman. © 2009 Mondrian/Holtzman Trust c/o HCR International Warrenton, VA; 'Suprematist Composition: Airplane Flying' by Kasimir Malevich, 1914–15, oil on canvas, 22⅞ × 19". Museum of Modern Art, New York. 1935 acquisition confirmed in 1999 by agreement with the Estate of Kasimir Malevich and made possible with funds from the Mrs John Hay Whitney Bequest (by exchange). Digital image © 2009 The Museum of Modern Art/Scala, Florence; 'Harlequin's Carnival' by Joan Miro, 1924–25, p.359; detail, p.315. Albright Knox Art Gallery, Buffalo, New York/Bridgeman. © Succession Miro/ADAGP, Paris and DACS, London 2009; 'The Entire City' by Max Ernst, 1934. Kunsthaus, Zurich/Bridgeman. © ADAGP, Paris and DACS, London 2009; 'Two Children Are Threatened by a Nightingale' by Max Ernst, 1924, oil on wood with painted wood elements and frame, 27½ × 22½ × 4½". Museum of Modern Art, New York. © ADAGP, Paris and DACS, London 2009. Digital image © 2009 The Museum of Modern Art/Scala, Florence; 'The Metamorphosis of Narcissus' by Salvador Dalí, 1937, oil on canvas, 511 × 781 mm. Tate, London. © Salvador Dali, Gala-Salvador Dali Foundation, DACS, London. Digital image © Tate, London 2009; 'Bicycle Wheel' by Marcel Duchamp, 1913/64. The Israel Museum, Jerusalem. © DACS/Vera & Arturo Schwarz Collection of Dada and Surrealist Art/Bridgeman. © Succession Marcel Duchamp/ADAGP, Paris and DACS, London 2009; 'With Hidden Noise', 1916/64, and 'Fountain', 1917/64, both by Marcel Duchamp. The Israel Museum, Jerusalem/Bridgeman. © Succession Marcel Duchamp/ADAGP, Paris and DACS, London 2009; 'War' by Otto Dix, 1932. Galerie Neue Meister, Dresden/Bridgeman. © DACS 2009; 'Painting' by Francis Bacon, 1946. By kind permission of DACS and the trustees of the Estate of Francis Bacon; 'Death of a Loyalist Soldier', 1936. Robert Capa/Magnumphotos; Concentration Camp Guards' by Lee Miller, Lee Miller Archives, England 2009. All rights reserved. www.leemiller.co.uk; 'Adolf the Superman Swallows Gold and Spouts Junk' by John Heartfield, before 28 August 1932, printed before 1942. National Gallery of Canada, Ottawa. © The Heartfield Community of Heirs/VG Bild-Kunst, Bonn and DACS, London 2009. Photo © National Gallery of Canada; 'Migrant Mother' by Dorothea Lange, 1936, Farm Security Administration Collection, US Library of Congress; 'You – Are You a Volunteer Yet?' by Dmitri Stahievic Moor (Orlov), 1920. Museum of the Revolution, Moscow/Bridgeman; Model of the Monument to the Third International ('Tatlin's Tower'). Private Collection/Bridgeman; Diego Rivera mural south wall, Detroit Institute of Arts. Dwight Cendrowski/Alamy; 'Men of the West' by Seán Keating, 1915, oil on canvas, 97 × 125 cm. Presented by the artist in memory of Hugh Lane. Collection Dublin City Gallery The Hugh Lane; 'Lakeside cottages' by Paul Henry, oil on canvas. Collection Dublin City Gallery The Hugh Lane; 'The Ninth Hour' by Mainie Jellett, 1941, oil on canvas, 86.3 × 64.2 cm. Presented by Miss Mary Rynne, 1963. Collection Dublin City Gallery The Hugh Lane. Reproduced by permission of Dr Michael Purser; 'There Is No Night' by Jack B. Yeats. Dublin City Gallery The Hugh Lane. © Estate of Jack B Yeats. All rights reserved, DACS 2009; 'Lavender Mist: Number 1', by Jackson Pollock, 1950. National Gallery of Art, Washington DC/Bridgeman. © The Pollock-Krasner Foundation ARS, NY and DACS, London 2009; 'Red Number 5' by Mark Rothko, 1961, oil on canvas, 177.8 × 160 cm. Nationalgalerie, Staatliche Museen zu Berlin. Digital image © bpk/Nationalgalerie, SMB/Jörg P. Anders. © 1998 Kate Rothko Prizel & Christopher Rothko/ARS, NY and DACS, London 2009; 'Woman I' by Willem de Kooning, 1950–52. Museum of Modern Art, New York/Bridgeman. © The Willem de Kooning Foundation, New York/ARS, NY and DACS, London 2009; 'Campbell's Soup Cans' by Andy Warhol, 1962. Museum of Modern Art, New York. Synthetic polymer paint on 32 canvases, each 20 × 16". © 2009 Andy Warhol Foundation/ARS, NY and DACS, London/TM Licensed by Campbell's Soup Co. All rights reserved. Digital image © 2009 The Museum of Modern Art/Scala, Florence; 'Whaam!' by Roy Lichtenstein, 1963, acrylic and oil on canvas, 1727 × 4064 mm. Tate, London. © The Estate of Roy Lichtenstein/DACS 2009. Digital image © Tate, London 2009; 'Floor Cake' by Claes Oldenburg, 1962. Museum of Modern Art, New York. Synthetic polymer paint and latex on canvas filled with foam rubber and cardboard boxes (148.2 × 290.2 × 148.2 cm). Digital image © 2009 The Museum of Modern Art/Scala, Florence. The following photos were sourced from Wikimedia Commons under the Creative Commons Attribution 2.0 licence: Apóstoles del Pórtico de la Gloria by Pedronchi; Basilique Saint-Andoche, Saulieu by Damouns/Damien Boilley. The following photos were sourced from Wikimedia Commons under the Creative Commons Attribution 2.5 licence: Gallarus Oratory by Jibi44; the 'Pietà' by Stanislav Traykov; Cathedral of Santiago de Compostela; St Patrick's Cathedral, Dublin; St Finbarr's Cathedral, Cork. The following photos were sourced from Wikimedia Commons under the Creative Commons Attribution 3.0 licence: Jerpoint Abbey, Thomastown, Co. Kilkenny, and St Flannan's Cathedral, Killaloe, Co. Clare, by Andreas F. Borchert; nave of Church of Sainte-Foi by Bernard Leprêtre; doorway carving, Church of Sainte-Foi at Conques, by Peter Campbell; Reims Cathedral by Alwin Nagel; Christ Church Cathedral, Dublin, by Mike Peel; Church of Santa Maria Novella, Florence, by Georges Jansoone; interior of Pazzi Chapel by Ricardo André Frantz; Spedale degli Innocenti, Florence, by Francesco Bini.